UNDERSTANDING CRIMINAL LAW

SEVENTH EDITION

UNDERSTANDING CRIMINAL LAW

SEVENTH EDITION

Joshua Dressler
Distinguished University Professor
Frank R. Strong Chair in Law
Michael E. Moritz College of Law
The Ohio State University

ISBN: 978-1-6328-3864-3 (Print)

Library of Congress Cataloging-in-Publication Data

Dressler, Joshua, author.

   Understanding criminal law / Joshua Dressler, Distinguished University Professor, Frank R. Strong Chair in Law, Michael E. Moritz College of Law, The Ohio State University. — Seventh edition.

   pages cm

   Includes index.

   ISBN 978-1-63283-864-3 (softbound)

   1. Criminal law—United States. I. Title.

KF9219.D74 2015

345.73—dc23

2015033311

NOTE TO USERS

To ensure that you are using the latest materials available in this area, please be sure to periodically check the LexisNexis Law School web site for downloadable updates and supplements at www.lexisnexis.com/lawschool.

Editorial Offices

630 Central Ave., New Providence, NJ 07974 (908) 464-6800

201 Mission St., San Francisco, CA 94105-1831 (415) 908-3200

www.lexisnexis.com

MATTHEW◆BENDER

To Dottie, David, Jessica, Lucy Belle, Maya Shoshana, and Gideon Jacob:
You give my life meaning and pleasure.

Preface to the Seventh Edition

This text is primarily designed for use by law students enrolled in a course in Criminal Law. It also has served successfully in undergraduate courses covering substantive criminal law. As well, based on comments I have received from practicing attorneys, judges, and scholars (and citations to this text in judicial opinions and scholarly works), this text should be helpful to *anyone* looking for a survey of American criminal law substance and theory. The text considers common law doctrine, statutory reform (with particular emphasis on the Model Penal Code), and constitutional law affecting the substantive criminal law.

This edition has undergone the most substantial revisions and updating since the original publication.

I am gratified by the extremely favorable response UNDERSTANDING CRIMINAL LAW has received over the years. Therefore, I have avoided the temptation to unnecessarily tinker. As before, I have included citations to new scholarship in the field in the hope that users will look to some of these sources for additional insights into the various topics. I believe each chapter has been improved overall.

Gender policy of the text. For most of Anglo-American legal history men monopolized the critical roles in the system of criminal justice. With only a few exceptions, lawyers, judges, legislators, jurors, and criminals were men. The only place for a woman in the system was as a crime victim. Such inequality, of course, is changing. As an author of a book that will be read and used by readers of both sexes I wanted to make sure that the text recognized the increasing importance of women in the law. Therefore, when discussing hypothetical defendants and victims, and when writing in general terms about other parties in the legal system — e.g., lawyers, judges, and legislators — I have balanced the account between male and female parties. In odd-numbered chapters the parties are female; in the even-numbered chapters males get equal time. I diverge from this approach only when the gender policy would distort history (e.g., there were no female property-holders in 16th century England), prove inaccurate as a principle of law, or confuse the reader. Although I received some criticism of this style with the first edition, I am gratified that this approach is no longer viewed as particularly noteworthy.

Acknowledgments

A book of this length is not possible without help from many people. I wrote the first edition while I was on the faculty at Wayne State University. My colleague there, LeRoy Lamborn, read the first, and often the second, draft of every chapter of the first edition. He provided remarkably helpful editorial and substantive suggestions and encouragement.

Many readers have assisted me over the years in improving the text. I have been blessed with many e-mail messages, letters (remember those?), and telephone calls from professors (here and in Europe, Australia, and New Zealand!), judges, practitioners, and law students, all providing advice, corrections, and citations to lesser-known sources of knowledge. I thank all of you.

I thank Dean Alan C. Michaels for the support he has provided over the years. And that "support" goes well beyond the ordinary scholarly assistance that any fine law school, such as ours, offers its faculty.

I received help on this edition from past and present Research Assistants at my law school. They include Sierra Cooper, Gregory Djordjevic, and Allison Meena. Very special thanks goes to graduated Moritz student, Lisa Herman, who provided incredibly thoughtful research on a number of topics, which were incorporated into this edition.

Finally, I thank my extended family — my wife Dottie; my son, David; my daughter-in-law Jessica; my granddaughters Lisa Belle and Maya Shoshana; and my brand new grandson Gideon Jacob — for being there for me.

Joshua Dressler
May 2015
Columbus, Ohio

This text frequently cites to the MODEL PENAL CODE COMMENTARIES, found in two volumes:

American Law Institute, MODEL PENAL CODE AND COMMENTARIES (OFFICIAL DRAFT AND REVISED COMMENTS) (PART I: GENERAL PROVISIONS) (1985); and

American Law Institute, MODEL PENAL CODE AND COMMENTARIES (OFFICIAL DRAFT AND REVISED COMMENT) (PART II: DEFINITION OF SPECIFIC CRIMES) (1980).

* * *

These sources are cited in footnotes of this text by use of the shorthand "American Law Institute."

Table of Contents

Table of Contents

Table of Contents

Table of Contents

Table of Contents

Table of Contents

Table of Contents

Table of Contents

Table of Contents

Table of Contents

Table of Contents

Table of Contents

Table of Contents

Table of Contents

Table of Contents

Table of Contents

Table of Contents

Table of Contents

Table of Contents

Table of Contents

Table of Contents

Table of Contents

Table of Contents

Table of Contents

Table of Contents

Table of Contents

Table of Contents

Table of Contents

Chapter 1

CRIMINAL LAW: AN OVERVIEW

§ 1.01 NATURE OF "CRIMINAL LAW"[1]

The study of the criminal law is the study of crimes and the principles of criminal responsibility for those crimes.

[A] Crimes

[1] Comparison to Civil Wrongs

What is a crime? If we are to believe some judicial opinions and treatises, the answer is simple, circular, and largely useless: A "crime" is anything that lawmakers say is a crime. That could make "being left-handed" or "having the flu" a crime if a legislature chose to do so. We need to look deeper for an answer to this question and, thus, to understand how a crime differs from a civil wrong, such as a tort or breach of contract.

First, unlike torts and contracts, the criminal law involves *public* law. That is, although the direct and immediate victim of a crime typically is a private party (*e.g.*, the person who is robbed, assaulted, or kidnapped), and other individuals are indirectly harmed (*e.g.*, the family members of the direct victim), a crime involves more than a private injury. A crime causes "social harm,"[2] in that the injury suffered involves "a breach and violation of the public rights and duties, due to the whole community, considered as a community, in its social aggregate capacity."[3] For this reason, crimes in the United States are prosecuted by public attorneys representing the community as a whole, and not by privately retained counsel.

There is more, however, that *should* distinguish a criminal wrong from its civil counterpart. A person convicted of a crime is punished. The technical definition of "punishment" awaits consideration in the next chapter,[4] but what is significant here

---

[1] *See generally* John C. Coffee, Jr., *Paradigms Lost: The Blurring of the Criminal and Civil Law Models — And What Can Be Done About It*, 101 Yale L.J. 1875 (1992); Claire Finkelstein, *Positivism and the Notion of an Offense*, 88 Cal. L. Rev. 335 (2000); Henry M. Hart, Jr., *The Aims of the Criminal Law*, 23 Law & Contemp. Probs. 401 (1958); Sanford H. Kadish, *Why Substantive Criminal Law — A Dialogue*, 29 Clev. St. L. Rev. 1 (1980).

[2] For a definition of this term, see § 9.10[B], *infra*.

[3] 4 William Blackstone, Commentaries on the Laws of England *5 (1769).

[4] *See* § 2.02, *infra*.

is that the "the essence of punishment . . . lies in the criminal conviction itself,"[5] rather than in the specific hardship imposed as a result of the conviction. The hardship suffered as a result of the criminal conviction may be no greater or even less than that which results from a civil judgment. For example, a person who lacks substantial financial resources might prefer to spend a few days in jail as punishment for an offense than to pay a civil judgment of $10,000 — the latter is likely to feel like a much more severe hardship. And, it is *not* the case that a civil proceeding can *never* result in loss of liberty: A mentally ill person who has committed no crime may, in a civil proceeding, be committed involuntarily to a mental institution, and so-called "sexual predators" may be confined "civilly" due to their perceived dangerousness to the community.[6] What, then, essentially distinguishes the criminal law from its civil counterpart, *or at least should be*, is the societal condemnation and stigma that accompanies the conviction.[7]

When the fact finder (ordinarily, a jury) determines that a person is guilty of a criminal offense, the resulting conviction is an expression of the community's moral outrage, directed at the criminal actor, for her act. It follows, therefore, that a crime might properly be defined as "an act or omission and its accompanying state of mind which, if duly shown to have taken place, will incur a formal and solemn pronouncement of the moral condemnation of the community."[8] To the extent that conduct that does *not* justify moral condemnation is treated as criminal,[9] as is

---

[5] George K. Gardner, *Bailey v. Richardson and the Constitution of the United States*, 33 B.U. L. Rev. 176, 193 (1953).

[6] *E.g.*, Kan. Stat. Ann. § 59-29a02 (2015) (in the state probate code, defining a "sexually violent predator" as "any person who has been convicted of or charged with a sexually violent offense and who suffers from a mental abnormality or personality disorder which makes the person likely to engage in repeat acts of sexual violence"; and making such a person eligible for indefinite, even life-long, civil commitment). Approximately 20 states and the federal government have laws authorizing civil commitment of so-called "sexual predators." Eric S. Janus & Robert A. Prentky, *Sexual Predator Laws: A Two-Decade Retrospective*, 21 Fed. Sent. R. 90 (2008). By mid-2008, more than 3,450 persons were confined under such laws. Tamara Rice Lave, *Controlling Sexually Violent Predators: Continued Incarceration at What Cost?*, 14 New Crim. L. Rev. 213, 215 (2011). These laws are controversial: individuals lose their liberty as the result of a science not yet proven to predict future dangerousness accurately, *id.*; and they blur the line, perhaps to the point of extinction, between criminal commitment (loss of liberty for *past* wrongful conduct) and civil commitment (loss of liberty based on predicted future dangerous conduct). *See generally* Eric S. Janus & Brad Bolin, *An End-Game for Sexually Violent Predator Laws: As-Applied Invalidation*, 6 Ohio St. J. Crim. L. 25 (2008); Stephen J. Schulhofer, *Two Systems of Social Protection: Comments on the Civil-Criminal Distinction, With Particular Reference to Sexually Violent Predator Laws*, 7 J. Contemp. Legal Issues 69 (1996); William J. Stuntz, *Substance, Process, and the Civil-Criminal Line*, 7 J. Contemp. Legal Issues 1 (1996).

[7] Hart, Note 1, *supra*, at 404; *see also* Leo Katz, Bad Acts and Guilty Minds: Conundrums of the Criminal Law 28 (1987) ("[P]unishment condemns, the [civil] penalty does not.").

[8] Hart, Note 1, *supra*, at 405.

[9] Even if all criminal conduct arguably should involve morally wrongful behavior (a not universally accepted assumption) it does not follow that all morally wrongful conduct is, or should be, criminal. In a society that values individual liberty, the criminal law serves a *minimalist* role — it only seeks to identify and regulate wrongful conduct that results in significant social harm. The purpose of the criminal law, in other words, is not "to purify thoughts and perfect character," United States v. Hollingsworth, 27 F.3d 1196, 1203 (7th Cir. 1994). That is the responsibility of family, religion, and other private institutions. Thus, telling lies may be a character flaw and, in many contexts, morally wrongful, but the criminal law

sometimes the case,[10] the line between the civil and the criminal processes is unfortunately blurred.[11]

[2] Classification of Crimes

The English common law[12] divided crimes into two general categories: felonies and misdemeanors.[13] A felony "comprise[d] every species of crime which occasioned at common law the forfeiture of lands and goods."[14] All common law felonies were punishable by death. The list of felonies was short: felonious homicide (later divided by statute into murder and manslaughter), arson, mayhem, rape, robbery, larceny, burglary, prison escape, and (perhaps) sodomy.[15] All other criminal offenses were misdemeanors.

In modern penal codes, the line distinguishing felonies from misdemeanors is drawn differently than in the past. Typically, an offense punishable by death or imprisonment in a state prison is a felony; an offense for which the maximum punishment is a monetary fine, incarceration in a local jail, or both, is a misdemeanor. For sentencing purposes, the Model Penal Code,[16] and the statutory schemes of various jurisdictions, divide felonies (and, sometimes, misdemeanors) into degrees.[17] Some states, as well, have added an additional classification of crime, *e.g.*, "violations"[18] or "infractions." These offenses encompass misconduct so minor that incarceration is prohibited.

[B] Principles of Criminal Responsibility

As one scholar has observed, "[i]t is deeply rooted in our moral sense of fitness that punishment entails blame and that, therefore, punishment may not justly be imposed where the person is not blameworthy."[19]

The study of the criminal law is, therefore, much more than the study of crimes. It is also the investigation of the doctrines that have developed over the centuries for determining when a person may justly be held criminally responsible for the

---

only punishes the most harmful lies, *e.g.*, material misstatements made under oath in judicial proceedings (perjury).

[10] *See* Chapter 11, *infra.*

[11] The civil/criminal line has significant *procedural* implications. Many of the rights accorded to defendants in criminal proceedings, such as the presumption of innocence, the requirement that guilt be proven beyond a reasonable doubt, and the bar on double jeopardy, do not apply in civil proceedings.

[12] The "common law" is judge-made law. *See* § 3.01[A], *infra.*

[13] Because of its special heinousness, treason was categorized separately, but strictly speaking it was a felony. 4 Blackstone, Note 3, *supra*, at *95.

[14] *Id.* at *94.

[15] Rollin M. Perkins & Ronald N. Boyce, Criminal Law 14 (3d ed. 1982). Sodomy originally was punished as an ecclesiastical offense, and later made a felony by statute, but it is "old enough to be recognized as common law in this country." *Id.* at 15.

[16] For an explanation of the Model Penal Code, see § 3.03, *infra.*

[17] *E.g.*, Model Penal Code § 6.01; N.Y. Penal Law § 55.05 (2015).

[18] Model Penal Code § 1.04(5).

[19] Kadish, Note 1, *supra*, at 10.

harm that she has caused. Put another way, the principles of criminal responsibility, which are at the core of the criminal law, identify the point at which it is believed fair to go from the factual premise, "*D* caused or assisted in causing X (a social harm) to occur," to the normative judgment, "*D should* be punished for having caused or assisted in causing X to occur." The rules of criminal responsibility are considered in Chapters 9–30, *infra.*

§ 1.02 PROVING GUILT AT THE TRIAL

[A] Right to Trial by Jury

[1] In General

The Sixth Amendment to the United States Constitution provides that "in all criminal prosecutions, the accused shall enjoy the right to a speedy and public trial, by an impartial jury." The right to trial by jury is "fundamental to the American scheme of justice," and therefore applies in all criminal proceedings, both state and federal.[20] The Supreme Court has stated that the constitutional guarantee reflects a "profound judgment about the way in which law should be enforced and justice administered." The right is granted "in order to prevent oppression by the Government. . . . If the defendant prefer[s] the common-sense judgment of a jury to the more tutored but perhaps less sympathetic reaction of the single judge, he [is] to have it."[21]

Notwithstanding the Sixth Amendment phrase, "in all criminal prosecutions," the jury-trial right only applies to "non-petty" offenses. According to the Supreme Court, "no offense can be deemed 'petty' for purposes of the right to trial by jury where imprisonment for more than six months is authorized."[22] An offense is also non-petty, even if the maximum authorized period of confinement is six months or less, if any additional statutory penalties (including fines) "are so severe that they clearly reflect a legislative determination that the offense in question is a 'serious' one."[23] As a practical matter, this means that a criminal defendant has a constitutional right to trial by jury in all felony and many misdemeanor prosecutions.

[2] Scope of the Right

In the federal courts[24] and in nearly all states, a jury in a felony criminal trial is composed of 12 persons who must reach a unanimous verdict to convict or acquit. Juries as small as six, however, are constitutional.[25] State laws permitting non-

---

[20] Duncan v. Louisiana, 391 U.S. 145, 149 (1968).

[21] *Id.* at 155–56.

[22] Baldwin v. New York, 399 U.S. 66, 69 (1970).

[23] Blanton v. City of North Las Vegas, 489 U.S. 538, 543 (1989).

[24] Fed. R. Crim. P. 23(b)(1) (setting the size of the jury at 12); 31(a) (unanimity requirement).

[25] Williams v. Florida, 399 U.S. 78 (1970) (a jury of six is permissible); Ballew v. Georgia, 435 U.S. 223 (1978) (a jury of five is too small).

unanimous verdicts are also allowed, as long as the vote to convict represents a "substantial majority" of the jurors.[26]

Because the jury system is meant to protect an accused from governmental oppression and to provide her with the common-sense judgment of the community, a defendant is entitled to a jury drawn from a pool of persons constituting a fair cross-section of the community.[27] This Sixth Amendment right is violated, therefore, if large, distinctive groups of persons, such as women, racial minorities, or adherents of a specific major religion, are systematically and unjustifiably excluded from the jury pool.

[B] Burden of Proof

The Due Process Clauses of the United States Constitution[28] require the prosecutor in a criminal trial to persuade the fact finder "beyond a reasonable doubt of every fact necessary to constitute the crime . . . charged."[29] The meaning of this language, and the effect of failing to meet this burden of proof, are matters considered in detail in Chapter 7.

[C] Jury Nullification[30]

[1] The Issue

Are there circumstances in which a jury should acquit an individual, even if the prosecutor proves beyond a reasonable doubt that the accused committed the offense charged? For example, should jurors acquit a defendant if they believe that the criminal law she violated is immoral or unwise, or because they feel that she has been "punished enough" already (perhaps because the defendant has lost her job as the result of her arrest), or because of perceived police or prosecutorial misconduct? Should jurors, in short, "nullify" the law if they feel there are justifications for doing so?

One matter is clear: jurors have the raw power to nullify the law. Two interrelated factors make this possible. First, a jury ordinarily returns a "general"

---

[26] Johnson v. Louisiana, 406 U.S. 356 (1972) (a 9-3 guilty verdict is constitutional).

[27] Taylor v. Louisiana, 419 U.S. 522 (1975).

[28] The Fifth and Fourteenth Amendments each contain a Due Process Clause. The Fifth Amendment applies in the federal system, whereas the Fourteenth Amendment pertains to the states.

[29] *In re* Winship, 397 U.S. 358, 364 (1970).

[30] *See generally* Thomas Andrew Green, Verdict According to Conscience (1985); Kenneth Duvall, *The Contradictory Stance on Jury Nullification*, 88 N. Dak. L. Rev. 409 (2012); Erick J. Haynie, Comment, *Populism, Free Speech, and the Rule of Law: The "Fully Informed" Jury Movement and Its Implications*, 88 J. Crim. L. & Criminology 343 (1997); Alan Scheflin & Jon Van Dyke, *Jury Nullification: The Contours of a Controversy*, 43 Law & Contemp. Probs. 51 (1980); Irwin A. Horowitz, *Jury Nullification: An Empirical Perspective*, 28 N. Ill. U. L. Rev. 425 (2008); Thomas Regnier, *Restoring the Founders' Ideal of the Independent Jury in Criminal Cases*, 51 Santa Clara L. Rev. 775 (2011); Phillip B. Scott, *Jury Nullification: An Historical Perspective on a Modern Debate*, 91 W. Va. L. Rev. 389 (1989).

verdict — "guilty" or "not guilty" — in criminal proceedings.[31] A jury is not required to explain or defend its verdict. It does not have to say, for example, "we believe the defendant committed the offense, but we acquit her because . . . ." Second, the Fifth Amendment of the United States Constitution provides that "[n]o person shall . . . be subject for the same offense to be twice put in jeopardy." Because the government may not reprosecute a defendant for the same crime after a "not guilty" verdict, jurors have the ability to acquit a defendant they are convinced committed an offense, fail to state their reason for acquittal, and then leave the government powerless to reprosecute.

Is such jury *power* of nullification, however, a good thing? Should we conclude that jurors not only have the *power* to nullify, but also the *right*? We turn to the debate.

[2] The Debate

"Jury nullification" has been the subject of rich and sometimes eloquent debate over the centuries. Advocates of jury nullification point out that the trial-by-jury constitutional right is recognized in order to protect against governmental oppression, and to provide the accused with the common sense judgment of lay people.[32] As Judge Learned Hand put it, the institution of the jury "introduces a slack into the enforcement of the law, tempering its rigor by the mollifying influence of current ethical conventions."[33] This "slack" makes sense, advocates of nullification claim: A finding of guilt is not simply a determination that the accused did the acts charged; it also represents a judgment by the jury — the "conscience of the community"[34] and "the oracle of the citizenry"[35] — that the defendant *should* be subjected to the condemnation and formal punishment that results from a conviction.

The jury-nullification power, therefore, serves as the community's safeguard against what jurors believe are morally unjust or socially undesirable (albeit legally proper) criminal convictions — convictions that law-trained judges might impose.[36] For example, a colonial jury in 1735 acquitted Peter Zenger, the confessed printer of a journal that published articles critical of British authorities, of seditious libel. And, in the 19th century, Northern juries acquitted individuals who assisted slaves to escape their "owners," who were prosecuted under then-existing federal fugitive slave laws.

---

[31] One common exception exists: In many states a jury that acquits a defendant on the basis of insanity will return a specific verdict of "not guilty by reason of insanity." *See* § 25.02[C], *infra.*

[32] *See* § 1.02[A][1], *supra.*

[33] United States *ex rel.* McCann v. Adams, 126 F.2d 774, 776 (2d Cir.), *rev'd on other grounds*, 317 U.S. 269 (1942).

[34] Witherspoon v. Illinois, 391 U.S. 510, 519, 519 n.15 (1968).

[35] United States v. Gilliam, 994 F.2d 97, 101 (2d Cir. 1993).

[36] There is little discussion in the literature of *judicial* nullification, although it doubtlessly occurs on occasion. The Model Penal Code provides for judicial authority to dismiss a prosecution in specified circumstances, notwithstanding the defendant's possible factual guilt. The Code does not characterize this as judicial nullification, but rather as the implementation of a "de minimis" defense. Model Penal Code § 2.12.

Critics of jury nullification respond that juries should not exercise their raw power to nullify the law. For every benevolent example of jury nullification to which its advocates point, there are "numerous and notorious examples" of malignant nullification, such as when Southern juries in the 1950s refused to convict white men for lynchings and other murders of civil rights workers, despite overwhelming evidence of guilt.[37] Moreover, to the extent that a jury acts on the basis of its conclusion that a particular law is unjust, the jury-nullification power "[c]ast[s] aside . . . our basic belief that only our elected representatives . . . determine what is a crime and what is not, and only they may revise that law if it is found to be unfair."[38] Critics also point out that jurors take an oath before they are empaneled to obey the judge's instructions on the law. If jurors ignore the law out of sympathy for the defendant, lack of compassion for the victim, or dislike for the governing law, the jurors have violated their sworn oath. To require jurors to take such an oath and yet recognize jury nullification "would confuse any conscientious citizen serving on a jury."[39]

[3] The Law

The issue of jury nullification arises in various legal contexts. First, the judge might instruct the jury that, if it finds beyond a reasonable doubt that the defendant committed the crime charged, it "must" find her guilty, which by implication suggests that they are barred from nullifying the law. Or, the judge might expressly inform the jury that it has a duty to follow her legal instructions, even if it disagrees with them. Although the rule seems to have been otherwise in the 18th century,[40] the general rule today is that, although questions of fact are in the exclusive province of the jury, matters of law are within the judge's sole jurisdiction. Therefore, instructions that expressly or by implication preclude juries from nullifying the law are permissible.[41] Today, although juries have the *power* to nullify laws, they have no *right* to do so.

Second, the defense may be bold enough to request the judge to instruct the jury that it is entitled to act upon its conscientious feelings to acquit the defendant, or the issue may arise in the context of a defense counsel's unilateral call to the jury during closing arguments to exercise its power to nullify the law and acquit. Although an occasional court has allowed the defense to make nullification arguments to the jury,[42] and one state by statute permits the defense to inform the

---

[37] *See* United States v. Thomas, 116 F.3d 606, 616 (2d Cir. 1997).

[38] State v. Ragland, 519 A.2d 1361, 1369 (N.J. 1986).

[39] *Id.* at 1371.

[40] Chief Justice John Jay instructed a jury in 1794, that "the good old rule [is] that on questions of fact, it is the province of the jury, on questions of law, it is the province of the court to decide." He went on, however, to state that "it must be observed, that by the same law, which recognizes this reasonable distribution of jurisdiction, you have nevertheless a right to take upon yourselves to judge of both, and to determine the law as well as the fact in controversy." Georgia v. Brailsford, 3 U.S. (3 Dall.) 1, 4 (1794).

[41] *E.g.*, Watts v. United States, 362 A.2d 706 (D.C. 1976) (*en banc*) (approving use of "must" in an instruction); State v. Ragland, 519 A.2d 1361 (N.J. 1986) (same).

[42] *E.g.*, United States v. Datcher, 830 F. Supp. 411 (M.D. Tenn. 1993) (permitting the defense to argue to the jury that it should acquit because of a "draconian sentence" hanging over the defendant; but

jury of its nullification power,[43] the overwhelming rule is that such arguments and pro-nullification jury instructions are impermissible.[44]

Third, a prosecutor may seek to have a juror discharged before or during deliberations if she believes the juror intends to nullify the law. Trial courts, however, are exceedingly hesitant to grant such motions. Jury deliberations occur in secret in order that jurors may talk freely amongst themselves; a discharge motion cannot realistically be granted without intruding into the deliberative process. Moreover, it is often difficult to distinguish between a juror who plans to ignore the judge's legal instructions, on the one hand, and one who simply believes that the government has failed to satisfy its burden of proof, on the other hand. Although there is little case law on point, the better rule seems to be that judges "may not delve too deeply into a juror's motivations," and that "if the record evidence discloses any possibility that the request to discharge stems from the juror's view of the sufficiency of the government's evidence, the court must deny the request."[45] Nonetheless, if a trial judge determines that a juror *is* "unable or unwilling" to discharge her legal duty "to determine the facts and render a verdict in accordance with the court's instruction on the law," the juror may be discharged.[46]

[4]   Race-Based Nullification[47]

Professor Paul Butler, a former prosecutor, has written: "[F]or pragmatic and political reasons, the black community is better off when some nonviolent lawbreakers remain in the community rather than go to prison."[48] Therefore, he has called on African-American jurors to acquit African-American defendants charged with victimless and nonviolent offenses, even if they are guilty, except in unusual circumstances. For example, Butler suggests, a jury should acquit a black thief who steals goods from an expensive department store, but perhaps should not acquit if the victim is a neighbor.

---

stating in dictum that it would not have permitted an instruction on jury nullification if it had been requested).

[43] N.H. Rev. Stat. § 519:23-a (2015) ("In all criminal proceedings the court shall permit the defense to inform jury of its right to judge the facts and the application of the law in relation to the facts in controversy.").

[44] *E.g.*, United States v. Chesney, 86 F.3d 564, 574 (6th Cir. 1996) (observing that *Datcher, supra,* "is contrary to Supreme Court pronouncements on this issue"); State v. Hatori, 990 P.2d 115 (Haw. Ct. App. 1999); Holden v. State, 788 N.E.2d 1253 (Ind. 2003); State v. Ragland, 519 A.2d 1361 (N.J. 1986); State v. Bjerkaas, 472 N.W.2d 615 (Wis. Ct. App. 1991).

[45] United States v. Brown, 823 F.2d 591, 596 (D.C. Cir. 1987).

[46] People v. Williams, 21 P.3d 1209, 1223 (Cal. 2001).

[47] *See generally* Paul D. Butler, *Race-Based Jury Nullification: Case-In-Chief,* 30 J. Marshall L. Rev. 911 (1997); Paul Butler, *Racially Based Jury Nullification: Black Power in the Criminal Justice System,* 105 Yale L.J. 677 (1995); Andrew D. Leipold, *Race-Based Jury Nullification: Rebuttal (Part A),* 30 J. Marshall L. Rev. 923 (1997); Andrew D. Leipold, *The Dangers of Race-Based Jury Nullification: A Response to Professor Butler,* 44 UCLA L. Rev. 109 (1996).

[48] Butler, Yale Law Journal, Note 47, *supra,* at 679.

Butler states that his "goal is the subversion of American criminal justice, at least as it now exists."[49] He advocates "black self-help" outside the courtroom (through community-building activities, such as mentoring, tutoring, providing medical and legal care for the poor) and inside the courtroom (though jury nullification).[50] He defends his proposal on the ground that African-Americans are imprisoned disproportionately as a result of malignant factors (*e.g.*, racial discrimination in the criminal justice system and society as a whole), and on the ground that imprisonment of nonviolent offenders causes more harm than good in the African-American community. Butler states that black jurors should send a message of their disapproval of, and lack of faith in, the justice system by acquitting nonviolent and victimless offenders.

Professor Andrew Leipold, while sympathetic to many of Butler's criticisms of the justice system, has argued forcefully against race-based jury nullification. First, he provides a narrow, technical argument: Given ordinary rules of evidence, the typical jury will not have the information it needs (for example, information relating to the defendant's degree of dangerousness) to make an informed decision whether to nullify the law. Second, he fears that "[o]nce we have agreed that jurors can legitimately decide the outcome of cases by a cost-benefit analysis rather than by applying the law as written to the evidence presented, we have started down a dangerous road."[51] Leipold's fear is that if black jurors begin nullifying the law, other groups will do the same, and the result would be legal anarchy. For example, a jury might acquit a guilty wife beater because the victim nagged him: "We might be repelled by this reasoning, but we [would] not have any standing to complain about the process by which the outcome was reached."[52] Finally, Leipold rejects the Butler proposal because "whether you go to jail or get set free should not depend on the color of your skin."[53] He argues that race-based judgments are bad on principle, and bad because they encourage precisely the type of stereotyping that has unfairly led to the evils that inspired Butler's plan.

---

[49] *Id.* at 680.

[50] Butler, John Marshall Law Review, Note 47, *supra*, at 912–13.

[51] Leipold, John Marshall Law Review, Note 47, *supra*, at 925.

[52] *Id.* at 926.

[53] *Id.*

Chapter 2

PRINCIPLES OF CRIMINAL PUNISHMENT

§ 2.01 "PUNISHMENT" AND CRIMINAL LAW THEORY

The subject of this chapter is punishment, and more specifically the moral theories used to justify it.[1] Why should we care about these theories? First, the criminal law is a blunt instrument, *used in our name*. The criminal justice system, which enforces our criminal laws, intentionally inflicts pain on persons convicted of criminal conduct by taking their life, liberty, and/or property. Any system that purposely causes such suffering certainly requires a justification. The principles discussed in this chapter provide some potential bases for legitimizing our criminal justice system.

Second, lawmakers must ascertain not only what conduct is wrongful, but must also determine *who* may properly be held accountable for the wrongful conduct. And, when punishment *is* deemed appropriate, legislators must decide *what* and *how much* punishment fits the offense and the offender. The principles discussed here provide different means for making these determinations.

Third, criminal laws ought to be fair and, to the extent possible, deal coherently with persons charged with crime. The penal theories considered below provide intellectual foundations for evaluating the fairness and coherence of our criminal laws.

---

[1] Professor Guyora Binder has questioned whether "the justification of punishment [is] a moral question." Guyora Binder, *Punishment Theory: Moral or Political?*, 5 Buff. Crim. L. Rev. 321, 321 (2002). Although, as he observes, most modern writers on the subject of punishment answer his question in the affirmative, Binder contends that debate regarding the various justifications for punishment "will become more productive once [the debate] is redefined as a political debate about institutions" — a discussion, if you will, of political theory — "rather than a moral debate about the conduct of criminals and officials." *Id.* at 371. He suggests that the competing moral theories of punishment are necessarily bound up with questions regarding the legitimacy "of the institutions promulgating the norm[s]." *Id.* at 322.

Binder is right. The moral justifications of punishment considered in this chapter should be considered within the context of political theory. The ultimate issue is how we justify punishment — and principles of criminal responsibility predicated on penal theory — in a liberal democratic legal system. Besides Professor Binder's article, an excellent source for discussion of punishment in a liberal political community is R.A. Duff, Punishment, Communication, and Community (2001).

§ 2.02 "PUNISHMENT": DEFINED[2]

[A] In General

What does it mean to "punish" someone? The issue is a critical one. For example, the Constitution provides that a person may not be *punished* twice for the same criminal offense, may not be *punished* retroactively, and may not be subjected to cruel and unusual *punishment*. These constitutional protections do not apply in non-penal circumstances. State laws, as well, typically provide greater procedural protections to persons subject to *punishment* than to those who may suffer "mere" civil penalties.

Clearly, sending a convicted criminal to prison for his offense is punishment. Suppose, however, that a very wealthy person is required by a court to pay a very small fine — a "drop in the bucket" — for violating a criminal statute. Is this punishment? Is a physician "punished" when he is compelled by a criminal court to perform public service in a hospital? What if a convicted criminal must undergo outpatient psychiatric care in lieu of a prison sentence? Is an alleged or convicted wrongdoer "punished" if a mob lynches him? May we say that a lawyer has been punished if he is disbarred for embezzlement of a client's funds?

There is no universally accepted non-arbitrary definition of the term "punishment." Criminal law scholars have generally concluded, however, that *D* may be said to suffer "punishment" when, *but only when*, an agent of the government, pursuant to authority granted to the agent by virtue of *D*'s criminal conviction, intentionally inflicts pain on *D* or otherwise causes *D* to suffer some consequence that is ordinarily considered to be unpleasant.[3] Pursuant to this definition, payment of a fine by a wealthy individual for a criminal violation constitutes punishment, albeit perhaps inadequate punishment, because the monetary fine is a consequence that ordinarily is considered unpleasant. For the same reason, post-conviction court-compelled public service[4] and outpatient psychiatric care of a convicted actor constitute punishment. On the other hand, penalties imposed outside the criminal justice system, such as disbarment of a lawyer by the licensing authority or the actions of a lynch mob, although painful and unpleasant, do not constitute "punishment."

---

[2] *See generally* Kent Greenawalt, *Punishment*, *in* 3 Encyclopedia of Crime and Justice 1282 (Joshua Dressler ed., 2d ed. 2002).

[3] *E.g.*, H.L.A. Hart, Punishment and Responsibility 4–5 (1968); Greenawalt, Note 2, *supra*, at 1282–83.

[4] In United States v. Bergman, 416 F. Supp. 496 (S.D.N.Y. 1976), *B*, a rabbi and nursing home operator, pleaded guilty to two counts of Medicaid and tax fraud, relating to operation of his nursing homes. *B* proposed to the trial judge that he be required to create and run a program of Jewish vocational and religious high school training or a "Committee on Holocaust Studies." The judge expressed doubt that this would constitute punishment, because the proposed work was "honorific" in nature and "not unlike that done [by *B*] in other projects." *Id.* at 500–01. According to the definition in the text, however, the proposed community service *is* punishment.

[B]   Constitutional Law Analysis

The constitutional line between "punishment" and civil remedies is exceptionally difficult to draw and may, in fact, be illusory. For example, various states have enacted "sexual predator" laws that authorize a "civil" process that can result in involuntary confinement of a person who, as a result of a sexual disorder, is determined to be dangerous to the community. The commitment proceeding may be initiated if the person has been convicted of (or simply charged with) a specified sexual offense. And, a person declared to be a sexual predator may remain "civilly" confined until he no longer is dangerous, which may never occur. During the period of confinement, the sexual predator may be, but is not always, offered treatment for his mental condition.

Is confinement of such a person, who has already been punished for the original sexual offense, a violation of the individual's right not to be punished twice for the same offense? Or, does it constitute cruel and unusual punishment to restrict an individual's liberty, perhaps for the duration of his life, simply on the speculative ground that he may cause harm in the future, rather than on the basis of proof of prior criminal wrongdoing? The answer to these constitutional questions initially depends on whether the confinement is characterized as "punishment."

The United States Supreme Court has held that the categorization of a proceeding as "civil" — and, therefore, that the restriction on a person's liberty imposed at such a proceeding is not "punishment" — "is first of all a question of statutory construction."[5] That is, if the legislature apparently intended to treat a proceeding as civil — for example, by placing the questioned law in the civil code, rather than in the jurisdiction's penal code — it presumptively will be treated as such.

The label the legislature attaches to a law, however, is not dispositive.[6] If there is clear proof that "[a] civil sanction . . . cannot fairly be said to serve a remedial purpose, but rather can only be explained as also serving either retributive or deterrent purposes," then the sanction will be deemed "punishment," thereby triggering the protections accorded to persons charged with crimes.[7] But, there is no bright-line basis for determining when the sanctions cross the line to punitiveness.[8]

---

[5] Smith v. Doe, 538 U.S. 84, 92 (2003) (quoting Kansas v. Hendricks, 521 U.S. 346, 361 (1997)).

[6] See id. at 94 (in which placement of a sexual predator provision in the state's criminal procedure code was not considered dispositive of its "criminal" nature: "[t]he location and labels of a statutory provision do not by themselves transform a civil remedy into a criminal one").

[7] United States v. Halper, 490 U.S. 435, 448 (1989).

[8] For a thoughtful discussion of the criminal/civil divide, in particular in the "sexual predator" context, see David Ball, The Civil Case at the Heart of Criminal Procedure: In re Winship, Stigma, and the Civil-Criminal Distinction, 38 Am. J. Crim. L. 117 (2011).

§ 2.03 THEORIES OF PUNISHMENT[9]

[A] Utilitarianism[10]

[1] Basic Principles

Utilitarianism is a form of "consequentialism," which in its pure form "holds that the justification of a practice depends *only* on its consequences."[11] Specifically, according to classical utilitarianism, formulated by Jeremy Bentham,[12] the purpose of all laws is to maximize the net happiness of society. Laws should be used to exclude, as far as possible, all painful or unpleasant events. To a utilitarian, both crime and punishment are unpleasant and, therefore, normally undesirable occurrences. In a perfect world, neither would exist.

As we do not live in a perfect world — some persons are disposed to commit crimes — utilitarians believe that the pain inflicted by punishment is justifiable if, but only if, it is expected to result in a reduction in the pain of crime that otherwise would occur. For example, the imposition of five units of pain (however the "units" are measured) on *D* is only justifiable if it will prevent more than five units of pain (in the form of crime or other undesirable consequences) that would have occurred but for *D*'s punishment.

Classical utilitarianism is founded on the belief that the threat or imposition of punishment can reduce crime because, in Bentham's words, "[p]ain and pleasure are the great springs of human action," and "[i]n matters of importance every one calculates."[13] Put slightly differently, utilitarians believe that human beings generally act hedonistically and rationally: A person will act according to his immediate desires to the extent that he believes that his conduct will augment his overall happiness. As a rational calculator, however, a person contemplating criminal activity (to augment his happiness) will balance the expected benefits of the proposed conduct against its risks, taking into account such factors as the risk of detection and conviction, and the severity of the likely punishment. He will avoid criminal activity if the perceived potential pain (punishment) outweighs the expected potential pleasure (criminal rewards).[14] All of this assumes, of course, that

---

[9] For an overview of the competing theories of punishment, see generally Duff, Note 1, *supra*; Hart, Note 3, *supra*, at 1–27; Herbert L. Packer, The Limits of the Criminal Sanction 9–70 (1968); Albert W. Alschuler, *The Changing Purposes of Criminal Punishment: A Retrospective on the Past Century and Some Thoughts About the Next*, 70 U. Chi. L. Rev. 1 (2003); Greenawalt, Note 2, *supra*; Mark A. Michael, *Utilitarianism and Retributivism: What's the Difference?*, 29 Am. Phil. Q. 173 (1992).

[10] *See generally* Johannes Andenaes, Punishment and Deterrence (1974); Contemporary Utilitarianism (Michael D. Bayles ed., 1968); Jeremy Bentham, An Introduction to the Principles of Morals and Legislation (J. Bowring ed., 1843); John Stuart Mill, Utilitarianism (1863); Daniel S. Nagin, *Deterrence in the Twenty-First Century, in* Crime and Justice in America, 1975–2025 (Michael Tonry ed., 2013; J.J.C. Smart, *Utilitarianism and Punishment*, 25 Israel L. Rev. 361 (1991).

[11] Duff, Note 1, *supra*, at 3.

[12] Bentham, Note 10, *supra*.

[13] Jeremy Bentham, *Principles of Penal Law, in* J. Bentham's Works 396, 402 (J. Bowring ed., 1843).

[14] Theoretically, if *D* believes that there is a 50% chance of being caught, prosecuted, convicted, and subjected to 10 units of punishment, he will commit the crime if his expected gain from the offense is

the would-be offender has the information necessary to make the cost-benefit calculations and is a *rational* calculator, often a dubious assumption.[15]

[2] Forms of Utilitarianism

Utilitarianism as applied to the criminal law takes different forms. Most commonly, utilitarians stress *general deterrence*. That is, D is punished in order to convince the *general* community — more particularly, potential criminal offenders — to forego criminal conduct in the future. In this model, D's punishment serves as an object lesson to others; D is used as a means to the desired end of a net reduction in crime. D's punishment teaches us what conduct is impermissible; it instills fear of punishment in would-be violators of the law; and, at least to some extent, it habituates us to act lawfully, even in the absence of fear of punishment.

Individual deterrence (sometimes characterized as *specific deterrence*) is a second utilitarian goal. Here, D's punishment is meant to deter, specifically, D's future misconduct by intimidation. By punishing D — by inflicting pain and suffering upon him for his criminal actions — we provide a clear reminder to him of the risks of future offending. We "scare him straight."

A third form of utilitarianism is *incapacitation*. Quite simply, D's imprisonment prevents him from committing crimes in the outside society during the period of segregation.[16]

A non-classical variety of utilitarianism is *rehabilitation* (or *reform*). Although the goal is the same — to reduce future crime — advocates of this model prefer to use the correctional system to reform the wrongdoer rather than to secure compliance through the fear or "bad taste" of punishment. The methods of reformation will vary from case to case, but could consist of, for example, psychiatric care, therapy for drug addiction, or academic or vocational training.[17]

---

more than five units of pleasure (10 units of pain-by-punishment ×.50 chance of its infliction = 5 units of expected pain). On the other hand, if D thinks that the risk of detection, conviction, and punishment is 90%, he will not commit the crime unless he believes that the likely benefits are much greater (more than nine units of pleasure). Notice that if an actor believes that there is virtually no chance of detection and punishment, virtually no threat of punishment will deter him. In general, therefore, an increase in the *likelihood* of punishment will deter more effectively than an increase in the *severity* of punishment. *See* Steven Klepper and Daniel Nagin, *The Deterrent Effect of Perceived Certainty and Severity of Punishment Revisited*, 27 Criminology 721 (1989).

[15] Paul H. Robinson, *The Ongoing Revolution in Punishment Theory: Doing Justice as Controlling Crime*, 42 Ariz. St. L.J. 1089, 1093 (2011) ("the people most likely to be offenders are the people who are most likely to be bad calculators, or be indifferent to future consequences").

[16] This theory does not justify the simplistic notion that society should put all convicts in prison and "throw away the key" (or, for that matter, impose the death penalty). It must be remembered that, to a utilitarian, punishment-by-incapacitation will be unjustifiable unless D's likely future anti-social behavior is expected to result in more pain to society than the pain inflicted on D and others (*e.g.*, harm to D's family by bis continued incarceration; costs to society of incarceration; and the loss of the offender's potential productivity in the community) by his lifetime imprisonment. *See generally* Linda S. Beres & Thomas D. Griffith, *Do Three Strikes Laws Make Sense? Habitual Offender Statutes and Criminal Incapacitation*, 87 Geo. L.J. 103 (1998); Michael Vitiello, *Three Strikes: Can We Return to Rationality?*, 87 J. Crim. L. & Criminology 395 (1997).

[17] Adherents of rehabilitation prefer to call the reformative process "treatment," rather than "punishment." However, because the process does not require the person's consent and is the result of

[B] Retributivism[18]

[1] Basic Principles

Retributivists believe that punishment is justified when it is deserved. It is deserved when the wrongdoer freely chooses to violate society's rules. To an uncompromising retributivist,[19] the wrongdoer should be punished, whether or not it will result in a reduction in crime. As Immanuel Kant made the latter point, "[e]ven if a civil society resolved to dissolve itself, . . . the last murderer lying in the prison ought to be executed." This suggested act of punishment, which can provide no utilitarian benefit, is required because of the "desert of [the murderer's] deeds."[20] According to a retributivist, "[i]t is morally fitting that an offender should suffer in proportion to [his] desert or culpable wrongdoing."[21]

Notice two basic differences between retributivism and utilitarianism. First, retributivism looks backward in time and justifies punishment solely on the basis of the previous, voluntary commission of a crime. In contrast, utilitarians look forward in time. They care about the past only to the extent that it helps predict the future: No matter how egregious the wrongdoing, utilitarians do not advocate punishment unless they believe it will provide an overall social benefit. Second, whereas the premise of utilitarianism is that people are generally hedonistic and rational calculators, retributivists focus on their view that humans generally possess free will or free choice[22] and, therefore, may justly be blamed when they choose to violate society's mores.[23]

---

a criminal conviction, reformative procedures constitute "punishment." *See* § 2.02[A], *supra*. For more on rehabilitation, see generally Mark W. Lipsey & Francis T. Cullen, *The Effectiveness of Correctional Rehabilitation: A Review of Systematic Reviews*, 3 Ann. Rev. L. & Soc. Sci. 297, 315 (2007); and Michael Vitiello, *Reconsidering Rehabilitation*, 65 Tul. L. Rev. 1011 (1991).

[18] *See generally* Immanuel Kant, The Metaphysical Elements of Justice (J. Ladd trans., 1965); Immanuel Kant, The Philosophy of Law (W. Hastie translation 1887); Michael S. Moore, Placing Blame (1997); Jeffrie G. Murphy, Getting Even (2003); Jeffrie G. Murphy & Jean Hampton, Forgiveness and Mercy (1988); Mitchell N. Berman, *Two Kinds of Retributivism*, *in* Philosophical Foundations of Criminal Law 433 (RA Duff & Stuart P. Green eds., 2011); Joshua Dressler, *Hating Criminals: How Can Something That Feels So Good Be Wrong?*, 88 Mich. L. Rev. 1448 (1990); Chad Flanders, *Can Retributivism Be Saved?*, 2014 B.Y.U.L. Rev. 309; Jean Hampton, *Correcting Harms Versus Righting Wrongs: The Goal of Retribution*, 39 UCLA L. Rev. 1659 (1992); Herbert Morris, *Persons and Punishment*, 52 Monist 475 (1968).

[19] Some people support a mixture of retributivism and utilitarianism; others favor a weaker version of retributivism than is set out here. *See* § 2.05, *infra*.

[20] Kant, The Philosophy of Law, Note 18, *supra*, at 197–98. Many retributivists reject the proposition that the death penalty must inevitably (or, even, at all) be imposed for the offense of murder.

[21] Russell L. Christopher, *Deterring Retributivism: The Injustice of "Just" Punishment*, 96 Nw. U.L. Rev. 843, 860 (2002).

[22] This is not to say that retributivists reject the idea that humans generally are capable of rational calculation, but they emphasize that the actor ordinarily has the capacity to choose whether to act in conformity with their calculation.

[23] Do people *really* have free will? Some philosophers, termed "hard determinists," deny its existence. The thesis of determinism is that every event has a cause. According to hard determinists, humans are little more than marionettes whose strings are pulled by genetic and environmental forces beyond their control. They are "merely another cog in the wheel of nature." Luis E. Chiesa, *Punishing*

[2] Forms of Retributivism

Although retribution is based on the dual premises that humans possess free will and that punishment is justified when it is deserved, retributivists differ among themselves regarding the best way to defend their "just deserts" philosophy. Retributivists must answer why wrongdoers deserve punishment, and they must explain why society should purposely inflict pain upon a person even if it will do no good in the future, in the form of reduced crime.

According to one form of retribution, variously described as *assaultive retribution*,[24] *public vengeance*, or *societal retaliation*, "it is morally right to hate criminals."[25] Because the criminal has harmed society, it is right for society to "hurt him back." This version of retribution is apt to "regard[] criminals rather like noxious insects to be ground under the heel of society."[26] Some advocates of this view argue that retributive punishment gratifies the passion for revenge that would otherwise be satisfied through private vengeance. However, so understood, this justification turns out to be a disguised form of utilitarianism, since it defends punishment in order to deter private revenge. On the other hand, Professor Jeffrie Murphy once defended what he characterized as "retributive hatred" this way: When a person is the victim of a crime, he justifiably resents the criminal for violating his rights; such resentment takes the form of righteous anger or hatred, in which the resenter wants to see the wrongdoer suffer; these passions are morally desirable because they demonstrate that the crime victim respects himself, *i.e.*, that he believes that he should be treated with dignity.[27]

A second, quite different, version of retribution may be called *protective retribution*. For adherents of this form of retribution, punishment is not inflicted because society wants to hurt wrongdoers, as with assaultive retribution, but because punishment is a means of securing a moral balance in the society. As Herbert Morris has explained, society is composed of rules that forbid various forms of harmful conduct; compliance with these rules burdens each member of the community who exercises self-restraint. These same rules provide a benefit in the form of "noninterference by others with what each person values, such . . . as

---

Without Free Will, 2011 Utah L. Rev. 1403, 1403. Under this view, because free will is a fiction, there is no basis for praising good conduct or — most pertinently — blaming wrongdoers. According to this view, a criminal is "more a victim of misfortune than a villain on the cosmic stage." Greenawalt, Note 2, *supra*, at 1284. Hard determinism, therefore, is incompatible with retributivism.

By contrast, "soft determinists" or "compatibilists" reason that although human actions are caused, they are not necessarily compelled. A person is free, and therefore properly the recipient of praise or blame, if he is able to act according to the determinations of his own will, *i.e.*, if his actions spring from his own rationally based motives. A person is unfree when he must do something against his own will — the result of external constraints — or when he lacks the capacity to reason. Soft determinism, therefore, is compatible with retributivism.

[24] Margaret Jane Radin, *Cruel Punishment and Respect for Persons: Super Due Process for Death*, 53 S. Cal. L. Rev. 1143, 1168 (1980). Professor Radin also coined the term "protective retribution" discussed in the text, *infra*.

[25] 2 James Fitzjames Stephen, A History of the Criminal Law of England 81 (1883).

[26] Murphy & Hampton, Note 18, *supra*, at 3 (describing the attitude of James Fitzjames Stephen).

[27] *Id.* at 88–110.

continuance of life and bodily security."[28] As long as everyone follows the rules, an equilibrium exists — everyone is similarly benefitted and burdened. If a person fails to exercise self-restraint when he could have — when he voluntarily renounces a burden that others have assumed — he destroys the balance. He becomes a free rider: He has the benefits of the system of rules, without accepting the same burdens. Thus, a criminal owes a debt to society. It is fair, therefore, to require payment of the debt, *i.e.*, punishment equal or proportional to the debt owed (*i.e.*, the crime committed). Advocates of this form of retribution emphasize that by punishing the wrongdoer, society demonstrates its respect for him: By stating that the criminal deserves punishment and is morally blameworthy, society treats him as a responsible moral agent. Indeed, according to this school of thought, the wrongdoer has a *right* to be punished. Punishment permits the offender to pay his debt to society, and to return to it free of moral guilt and stigma.

A third form of retribution might be termed *victim vindication.*[29] According to Jean Hampton, punishment is a way to "right a wrong." By committing an offense, a criminal implicitly sends a message to the victim and society that his (the criminal's) rights and desires are more important than those of the victim. Thus, by committing a crime, the offender elevates himself with respect to others. By doing so, the criminal makes a false moral claim as to his relative worth; in reality the criminal and the victim have equal moral worth as human beings. Retributive punishment corrects this false claim. It reaffirms the victim's worth as a human being in the face of the criminal's challenge.[30] Retributive punishment, therefore, represents a "defeat of the wrongdoer"; he is mastered in much the way that he mastered the victim. Once the criminal receives punishment proportional to the offense, the "score" is made even.

[C] Denunciation (Expressive Theory)[31]

Most efforts to justify punishment are based on utilitarianism or retributivism. *Denunciation* or, alternatively, the *expressive* view of punishment, is probably the most frequently suggested alternative basis of punishment. According to this view, punishment is justified as a means of expressing society's condemnation, and the relative seriousness, of a crime. Upon a closer look, denunciation turns out to be a hybrid of sophisticated aspects of utilitarianism and the victim vindication form of retribution. According to one commentator, however, "[i]t might be the case that any plausible conception of the expressive view can be fit into the framework of deterrence or retributivism, but it would be fallacious to conclude that the expressive theory can therefore be ignored."[32] The view here is that any sensible

---

[28] Morris, Note 18, *supra*, at 477.

[29] Hampton, Note 18, *supra*, at 1686 ("retribution is a response to a wrong that is intended to vindicate the value of the victim"); and Murphy & Hampton, Note 18, *supra*, at 111–61.

[30] *See also* Duff, Note 1, *supra*, at 28 (explaining the concept, in part, on the ground that "censure of conduct declared to be wrong is owed to its victims, as manifesting that concern for them and their wronged condition that the declaration itself expressed").

[31] *See generally* Duff, Note 1, *supra*, at 27–30; Dan M. Kahan, *What Do Alternative Sanctions Mean?*, 63 U. Chi. L. Rev. 591, 594–605 (1996).

[32] Kahan, Note 31, *supra*, at 601.

version of utilitarianism or retribution must include the ideas found in the denunciatory theory.

Why is denunciation desirable? First, it is educative. We inform individuals that the community considers specific conduct improper and that we value the victim's worth. Second, public denunciation through the criminal justice system channels community anger away from personal vengeance. The collective expression of condemnation also serves to maintain social cohesion.[33] In all of these ways denunciation is utilitarian in nature, in that it affects future conduct.

Denunciation is also retributive, in that it is a form of moral condemnation: Denunciation serves to stigmatize the offender for his offense. It vindicates the victim. By denunciation, society announces that the wrongdoer deserves punishment, precisely because he has "engage[d] in behavior that conveys disrespect for important values."[34] As Professor Samuel Pillsbury has explained, "[t]hose persons who rationally resolve to hurt others in certain fundamental respects should be punished in order that they, and others, can see the moral significance of their actions."[35] These expressive feelings are consistent with retributivism.

§ 2.04   THE DEBATE BETWEEN THE COMPETING THEORIES[36]

[A]   Criticisms of Utilitarianism

[1]   Deterrence

Retributivists criticize deterrence theory on the ground that it justifies using persons solely as a means to an end. To the utilitarian, the punished individual is an instrument for the improvement of society. This system ignores the dignity and human rights of the wrongdoer. Utilitarians respond that humans possess no immutable rights for utilitarians to ignore.[37] The right each member of society possesses is the right to have the law used for the benefit of the whole community. Also, utilitarians argue, because the wrongdoer is a member of society, he benefits from his own punishment. Therefore, he is not used *solely* as a means to an end.

A second criticism of utilitarianism, closely allied to the first charge, is that utilitarianism can justify the punishment of a person known to be innocent of

---

[33] Emile Durkheim, The Division of Labor in Society 108–09 (G. Simpson trans., 1933).

[34] Kahan, Note 31, *supra*, at 602.

[35] Samuel H. Pillsbury, Judging Evil 35 (1998).

[36] *See generally* Contemporary Utilitarianism, Note 10, *supra*; Christopher, Note 21, *supra*; David Dolinko, *Three Mistakes of Retributivism*, 39 UCLA L. Rev. 1623 (1992); David Dolinko, *Some Thoughts About Retributivism*, 101 Ethics 537 (1991); Paul H. Robinson & John M. Darley, *The Role of Deterrence in the Formulation of Criminal Law Rules: At Its Worst When Doing Its Best*, 91 Geo. L.J. 949 (2003).

[37] Bentham wrote that "*[n]atural rights* is simple nonsense; natural and imprescriptible rights, rhetorical nonsense, — nonsense upon stilts." Jeremy Bentham, *Anarchical Fallacies, in* 2 The Works of Jeremy Bentham 501 (J. Bowring ed., 1843).

wrongdoing.[38] The following hypothetical illustrates the issue:[39] A white woman, living in a racially divided community, is brutally raped by an unidentified black male. A mob of white racists respond by surging into an area of town with a predominantly African-American population, intending to indiscriminately kill many innocent persons and burn their houses. The town's sheriff lacks the personnel to stop the mob. According to retributivist critics, a utilitarian sheriff could justify immediately arresting and framing an innocent African-American for the crime in order to placate the mob. Retributivism flatly rejects this outcome: An innocent person never deserves punishment because he has no debt to repay society; therefore, punishment of an innocent person is unalterably wrong.

Some utilitarians do not deny the *theoretical* possibility that punishment of an innocent person could be justified, but they insist that the real-world circumstances supporting such a result would never come into play. In the hypothetical above, for example, the sheriff could have arrested the innocent man, and then released him after the mob dispersed. Furthermore, utilitarians argue, the sheriff ignored the wider consequences of his actions. By framing an innocent person, a guilty individual remains free to kill and rape again. Moreover, a sensible utilitarian would consider the possibility that the public would eventually learn that the sheriff has framed an innocent person. The loss of the public's respect for the criminal justice system, anger at the sheriff, and fear of similar treatment of other innocents, will cause greater harm over time than the mob would have committed.

Indeed, the latter defense of utilitarianism raises a more fundamental claim of some utilitarians: The accusation that framing the innocent could be justifiable "rests on a misunderstanding of utilitarian penology as an application of an 'act-utilitarian' ethic governing individual behavior."[40] That is, the hypothetical only makes sense if one applies (improperly, the argument is made) *act-utilitarianism* — a calculation of whether a particular act, on this immediate occasion, is justified on utilitarian grounds. In contrast is *rule-utilitarianism* — the determination of whether a particular act, publicly announced as a rule of law that applies to an entire community, would be justified. A *rule* that an innocent person should be punished whenever it would do more good than harm would conflict with a theory of law and legal process that intends to create not only happiness in general, but which also favors the formulation and publication of rules, legal decision-making, and a sense of security among the public.

---

[38] This accusation has been the subject of considerable literature. *See generally* Guyora Binder & Nicholas J. Smith, *Framed: Utilitarianism and Punishment of the Innocent*, 32 Rutgers L.J. 115 (2000); H.J. McCloskey, *A Non-Utilitarian Approach to Punishment*, *in* Contemporary Utilitarianism, Note 10, *supra*, at 239; James McCloskey, *Convicting the Innocent*, Crim. Just. Ethics, Winter/Spring 1989, at 2; T.L.S. Sprigge, *A Utilitarian Reply to Dr. McCloskey*, *in* Contemporary Utilitarianism, Note 10, *supra*, at 261.

[39] The hypothetical is based on H.J. McCloskey, Note 38, *supra*, at 248.

[40] Binder & Smith, Note 38, *supra*, at 118–19.

[2] Rehabilitation

Some critics of rehabilitation doubt that criminals can be reformed. They ask, in essence: "If family, school, and religion have failed, why should we think that prisons, psychiatric care, or any other involuntarily imposed treatment will succeed?" Opponents of rehabilitation point to some studies that suggest that reform efforts have failed.[41]

Proponents contend that empirical studies demonstrate "that opponents . . . [have] grossly overstated the case against rehabilitation."[42] Rehabilitative efforts *have* reduced recidivism.[43] Although reformation may not be possible in all circumstances, advocates argue that it will often work if society is prepared to commit the necessary resources to the process. And, in the long run, the costs of rehabilitation would result in long-term cost savings.[44]

Retributivists criticize rehabilitation on the ground that, in the name of humanitarianism, the "theory removes from Punishment the concept of Desert. . . . [W]hen we cease to consider what the criminal deserves and consider only what will cure him . . . , we have tacitly removed him from the sphere of justice altogether."[45] Critics state that proponents of rehabilitation demean offenders by treating them as sick, childlike, or otherwise unable to act as moral agents. Moreover, a system based on rehabilitation can potentially justify "cures" (*e.g.*, a lobotomy) that violate the offender's personhood.

Advocates of rehabilitation believe that reformation is preferable to punishment based on fear (classical utilitarian theory) or the "hurt the criminal, he deserves it" attitude of assaultive retribution. They point out that the rehabilitative model preserves the concept of redemption evident in most religions' teachings. When such a transformation occurs, "it is difficult to find a continued justification for imposing suffering on that offender."[46]

---

[41] *E.g.*, Robert Martinson, *What Works? Questions and Answers About Prison Reform*, 35 Pub. Int. 22 (1974).

[42] Vitiello, Note 17, *supra*, at 1032. One early critic of rehabilitation (*see* Note 41, *supra*) changed his mind and pointed to successes in the field. Robert Martinson, *New Findings, New Views: A Note of Caution Regarding Sentencing Reform*, 7 Hofstra L. Rev. 243 (1979).

[43] Francis T. Cullen & Shannon A. Santana, *Rehabilitation, in* 3 Encyclopedia of Crime and Justice 1314, 1324 (Joshua Dressler, editor-in-chief, 2d ed. 2002) (based on hundreds of studies, "rehabilitation programs reduce recidivism about 10 percentage points").

[44] *E.g.*, Christopher S. Wren, *Arizona Finds Cost Savings in Treating Drug Offenders*, N.Y. Times, Apr. 21, 1999, at A16 (reporting on an Arizona Supreme Court finding that the state's new policy of treating, rather than jailing, addicts had saved an estimated $2.5 million in its first year and would reap greater long-term savings; and reporting the view that such early intervention may be more beneficial to the addict than incarceration).

[45] C.S. Lewis, *The Humanitarian Theory of Punishment, in* Contemporary Punishment: Views, Explanations, and Justifications 194 (Gerber & P. McAnany eds., 1972).

[46] Vitiello, Note 17, *supra*, at 1051.

[B] Criticisms of Retributivism

Utilitarians state that the intentional infliction of pain through punishment is senseless and even cruel if it does no good, and yet retributivists favor precisely that — the infliction of pain that need not result in future benefit. Society's goal should be to reduce overall human suffering, not purposely cause more of it. In contrast, retributivists believe that there are moral imperatives, *i.e.*, acts that are unalterably right or wrong, regardless of their consequences. To a retributivist, once it is determined that a wrong has been committed and that the wrongdoer is morally responsible for committing it, a measured response in the form of punishment proportional to the crime is unalterably right. That it results in a reduction of future crime (if it does) is good, but to the retributivist it is a collateral, not required, benefit of punishment.

Second, some utilitarians criticize retributivism because, they say, it glorifies anger and legitimizes hatred.[47] The reality of retribution, therefore, conflicts with its purported respect for the rights of all persons, including criminals. A retributivist response is that this observation, if valid at all, applies only to the assaultive form of retribution,[48] which most modern retributivists reject.

Third, and closely related to the preceding argument, is the claim that retributivism is irrational, because it is founded on emotions, such as anger, rather than on reason. Retributivists believe, however, that emotion can have a moral content.[49] Just as most people believe that an emotion such as compassion is morally good — it says something good about the character of the person possessing that emotion — anger, when directed at a wrongdoer for his wrongdoing, is also a morally proper emotion. Our anger demonstrates our awareness that the criminal has violated our rights, has acted unjustly and, therefore, deserves punishment. That anger — including the retributive urge to punish — is morally good when it demonstrates that we value ourselves and the rights of other crime victims.

§ 2.05 MIXED THEORIES OF PUNISHMENT[50]

Utilitarianism and retributivism often conflict with each other. Although adherents of both theories may agree on results in particular cases, a criminal justice system that seeks *exclusively* to prevent future crime is apt to look different from one that seeks *exclusively* to impose punishment based on a just-deserts philosophy. The difficulty is that, although some people are thoroughgoing utilitarians and others are uncompromising retributivists, most people find aspects of each theory

---

[47] Dolinko, *Three Mistakes of Retributivism*, Note 36, *supra*, at 1650.

[48] *See* § 2.03[B][2], *supra*.

[49] *See generally* Samuel H. Pillsbury, *Emotional Justice: Moralizing the Passions of Criminal Punishment*, 74 Cornell L. Rev. 655 (1989).

[50] *See generally* Michael T. Cahill, *Retributive Justice in the Real World*, 85 Wash. U. L. Rev. 815 (2007); Stephen P. Garvey, *Lifting the Veil on Punishment*, 7 Buff. Crim. L. Rev. 443 (2004); Paul H. Robinson, *Hybrid Principles for the Distribution of Criminal Sanctions*, 82 Nw. U. L. Rev. 19 (1987); Andrew von Hirsch, *Hybrid Principles in Allocating Sanctions: A Response to Professor Robinson*, 82 Nw. U. L. Rev. 64 (1987).

attractive (and unattractive). It is not too surprising, therefore, that the criminal law that has, in fact, developed in the United States is not philosophically consistent. As will be seen in subsequent chapters of this text, some rules of criminal responsibility are primarily retributive in nature, whereas others are more utilitarian in character.

It is also true that many scholars advocate a mixed theoretical system. For example, as Professor H.L.A. Hart has shown,[51] we may want to ask two different questions in the criminal law. The first question is: Why have we set up a criminal justice system, *i.e.*, devised criminal laws prohibiting certain conduct, created a police force to arrest law violators, set up courts to adjudicate guilt and innocence, and imposed penalties for violations of those laws? Is the general justifying aim of the criminal law to punish murderers, rapists, and robbers (retribution) or is it to prevent those crimes in the first place (utilitarianism)? A separate question is: Given the existence of our justice system — created for whichever reason — *who* should be held responsible for their actions, and *how much* punishment is appropriate for those who are held responsible?

According to Hart, a person may coherently argue that the general aim of the criminal law is to deter unwanted behavior, but that retributive concepts of just deserts should be applied in determining *whether* and *how much* to punish a particular person. For example, suppose that *D*, suffering from a severe mental illness, kills *V*. An advocate of this hybrid penal system might say that the criminal homicide statutes were, of course, enacted to deter unjustified killings, but that *D* should only be punished if he is morally blameworthy, which he might not be in light of his mental illness. And, even if he *is* blameworthy, his punishment should be in proportion to his moral desert (retribution) and not to his future dangerousness (utilitarianism).

Especially when one shifts from the general justifying aim of the criminal, and even the question of *who* deserves punishment, to the question of *how much* punishment should be imposed, there are mixed theories of punishment. For example, the section of the Model Penal Code setting out "the general purposes of the provisions governing the sentencing and treatment of offenders,"[52] as originally drafted, provided a "laundry list" of penal theories. However, this provision has recently undergone redrafting. It now promotes a version of so-called "limiting retributivism."[53] The idea here is that, pursuant to retributivist thought, punishment should be proportional to the crime and the criminal's blameworthiness. Retributivists, however, cannot realistically identify the precise amount of punishment deserved in any particular case. They can only provide a "range of severity" of proportional punishment: punishment below a certain amount would be retributively too little, and punishment above a certain amount would be too much. Punishment must be within the retributively proportional range. Within that defined range, however, non-retributive factors may properly be applied in sentenc-

---

[51] Hart, Note 3, *supra*, at 8–13.

[52] Model Penal Code § 1.02 (Official Draft, 1962).

[53] American Law Institute, Model Penal Code Sentencing, (Preliminary Draft No. 3, May 28, 2004), at 8.

ing.[54]

Other mixed theorists would go further and say that, although punishment should never exceed that which is retributively justifiable (even if there are utilitarian reasons for exceeding it), it is permissible to inflict *less* punishment than is deserved (below the proportional range), if there is no good utilitarian justification for the punishment.[55]

§ 2.06 SENTENCING

Traditionally, criminal codes have provided that a defendant convicted of a noncapital felony receive a sentence consisting of a term of years of imprisonment in a state prison, a monetary fine, or a combination thereof. Alternative non-incarcerative sanctions — for example, compelled community service or shaming[56] — are less common, but permitted in some circumstances. In some sentencing systems, the trial judge also has the option of sentencing a defendant to a term of years in prison, for example, five years, but then suspending the sentence and placing the individual on probation for that term.[57] In the latter case, the offender remains free, subject to conditions set by the judge (*e.g.*, that he undergo random drug testing, avoid contact with known ex-felons, not possess a firearm, and/or report to a probation officer on regularly scheduled dates). If the probationer violates a condition of release, the judge may order the offender to serve the suspended sentence or part thereof.

The sentencing provisions of the Model Penal Code, as originally adopted by the American Law Institute in 1962, were consistent with the rehabilitative goals dominant in legal thought in the 1960s. Consistent with rehabilitation, many states by 1960 utilized some form of "indeterminate sentencing." In such a system, judges had considerable sentencing discretion. They were encouraged to individualize a defendant's maximum sentence based on information obtained in a post-conviction

---

[54] Model Penal Code § 1.02(2)(a)(ii), as amended, and currently under consideration by the Council of the ALI, provides that, within the retributive range, "when reasonably feasible," the Code's sentencing provisions are intended to "achieve offender rehabilitation, restitution to crime victims, and reintegration of offenders into the law-abiding community."

[55] Garvey, Note 50, *supra*, at 450.

[56] *E.g.*, United States v. Gementera, 379 F.3d 596 (9th Cir. 2004) (judge sentenced a mail thief to up to eight hours of community service during which time the offender was required to wear a sandwich-board sign stating "I stole mail; this is my punishment" in front of a San Francisco postal facility; held: the judge had statutory authority to impose the sentence, and that it reasonably related to the statutory objective of rehabilitation); *see also* People v. Letterlough, 655 N.E.2d 146 (N.Y. 1995) (*L*, convicted of driving under the influence of alcohol, was required to attach a sign to his car identifying himself as a convicted drunk driver). Notwithstanding *Gementera*, *supra*, some shaming sentences have been struck down by appellate courts on the ground that the judge lacked statutory authority to impose the sentence. *See generally* Stephen P. Garvey, *Can Shaming Punishments Educate?* 65 U. Chi. L. Rev. 733 (1998); Kahan, Note 31, *supra*; Toni M. Massaro, *Shame, Culture, and American Criminal Law*, 89 Mich. L. Rev. 1880 (1991).

[57] In recent years, some legislatures have enacted statutes providing for mandatory minimum sentences for specific crimes. Under these statutes, the judge lacks authority to place a defendant on probation or to impose a sentence below the mandatory minimum figure, even if the judge believes that a lesser sentence is justified in the individual case.

sentencing hearing that considered the defendant's character and the circumstances of the offense. However, what made a sentencing system "indeterminate" was that the judge only defined the outer reaches of the sentence. Correctional officers (primarily parole boards) had the authority to release the prisoner *before* completion of the sentence imposed by the judge if the prisoner satisfied rehabilitative goals during confinement.

Nearly all states have abandoned indeterminate sentencing systems in favor of a determinate one. This trend is the result of many factors and social forces, including disillusionment with the rehabilitative model, pressure from the public during high-crime periods for longer prison sentences, increased interest in retributive goals, and a widespread desire to cut back on judicial sentencing discretion because of perceived unjustifiable disparity in sentences meted out by different judges for similar offenses.[58]

Determinate sentencing systems vary, but they have one feature in common: The offender's sentence is determined, *once and for all*, at the time of sentencing. Corrections officers lack authority to reduce the sentence based on evidence of rehabilitation in prison. In a determinate system, either the legislature or a sentencing commission sets a specific punishment for a defined offense (*e.g.*, armed robbery receives 10 years' imprisonment, no more and no less) or, more often, it sets a range of incarcerative penalties for that offense and the judge (or jury) imposes a specific sentence within that range.

---

[58] Sanford H. Kadish, *Fifty Years of Criminal Law: An Opinionated Review*, 87 Cal. L. Rev. 943, 979–80 (1999).

Chapter 3

SOURCES OF THE CRIMINAL LAW

§ 3.01 ORIGINS OF THE CRIMINAL LAW[1]

[A] Common Law

American criminal law is primarily English in its heritage and judicial in its origin. In large measure, the original 13 American states and most later states adopted English law as their own.[2]

Originally, English criminal law was "common law" in nature. That is, it was judge-made law: The definitions of crimes and the rules of criminal responsibility were promulgated by courts rather than by the Parliament. When American courts and criminal lawyers use the term "common law," therefore, they are describing the law developed over the centuries by English judges and imported to this country. However, the common law of England was reworked by American courts to meet local needs and morés, so that by the turn of the 20th century this country's common law diverged in some significant respects from its British progenitor.

[B] Criminal Statutes

Inspired by the Enlightenment, there was a movement in 18th and 19th century Europe and United States to shift the locus of lawmaking from the courts to legislative bodies. In part, this effort was based on the belief that crimes should be defined by an institution more representative of those being governed than the judiciary.[3] The "romance with reason" also inspired reformers of different philosophical stripes (both utilitarians and believers in natural law) to try to codify the criminal law in order to produce "a legislated body of reordered, reformed, and reconceived law" in accordance with their respective principles.[4]

---

[1] *See generally* Markus Dirk Dubber, *Reforming American Penal Law*, 90 J. Crim. L. & Criminology 49 (1999); Ford W. Hall, *The Common Law: An Account of Its Reception in the United States*, 4 Vand. L. Rev. 791 (1951); Sanford H. Kadish, *The Model Penal Code's Historical Antecedents*, 19 Rutgers L.J. 521 (1988); Sanford H. Kadish, *Codifiers of the Criminal Law: Wechsler's Predecessors*, 78 Colum. L. Rev. 1098 (1978).

[2] *See* Hall, Note 1, *supra*, at 798–805.

[3] *See* John Calvin Jeffries, Jr., *Legality, Vagueness, and the Construction of Penal Statutes*, 71 Va. L. Rev. 189, 190 (1985).

[4] Kadish, *The Model Penal Code's Historical Antecedents*, Note 1, *supra*, at 521–22.

In general, early codification efforts failed. Over time, however, legislatures asserted themselves and enacted penal statutes, initially to supplement, but ultimately to replace, the common law. Today, the changeover is virtually complete. The legislature is the pre-eminent lawmaking body in the realm of criminal law in the United States and England.

§ 3.02 MODERN ROLE OF THE COMMON LAW

Although the legislative branch of government now has primary lawmaking authority, the common law of crimes remains important to modern lawyers.

[A] "Reception" Statutes

Most states, often by statute, have abolished common law crimes.[5] In these jurisdictions, a person may only be convicted and punished for conduct defined as criminal by statute or other legislative enactment.

A very few states, however, expressly recognize common law offenses. These states have enacted "reception" statutes, which essentially provide that "[e]very act and omission which is an offense at common law and for which no punishment is prescribed by the [state penal code] may be prosecuted and punished as an offense at common law."[6] In effect, such a statute "receives" the common law offenses in place at the time of the reception statute's enactment: to the extent that the written criminal code has not dealt with the subject, these crimes become an unwritten part of the state's criminal law, and are defined as they existed at the time of the reception statute's enactment.

As a practical matter, prosecutions of common law offenses in jurisdictions that retain the common law are very rare. Common law crimes, although not abolished in such states, are superseded by statutes prohibiting similar conduct.[7] A common law prosecution is not possible, therefore, unless there is a true gap in the statutory system, and today there are few lacunae. Nearly all legislatures have enacted statutes encompassing all of the common law felonies and most of the misdemeanors.

A lingering issue in the few states recognizing common law offenses is whether a court may assert its traditional authority to devise *new* crimes. The authors of early 20th century treatises assumed that this judicial power remained intact, and

---

[5] *E.g.*, Cal. Penal Code § 6 (Deering 2015) ("No act or omission . . . is criminal or punishable, except as prescribed or authorized by this code."); Model Penal Code § 1.05(1) ("No conduct constitutes an offense unless it is a crime or violation under this Code or another statute of the State.").

[6] R.I. Gen. Laws § 11-1-1 (2015); *see also*, *e.g.*, Ala. Code § 1-3-1 (2015) ("The common law of England, so far as it is not inconsistent with the Constitution, laws and institutions of this state, shall, together with such . . . laws, . . . continue in force . . . ."); Mich. Comp. Laws § 750.505 (2011) ("Any person who shall commit any indictable offense at common law for the punishment of which no provision is expressly made by any statute of this state, shall be guilty of a felony.").

[7] *E.g.*, State v. Palendrano, 293 A.2d 747 (N.J. Super. Ct. Law Div. 1972) (holding that the common law offense of "being a common scold" — a woman who habitually acts in a quarrelsome manner — was no longer a crime, in part because the non-gender-biased elements of the offense were encompassed by New Jersey's Disorderly Persons Act).

a few courts have exercised such authority,[8] but it is now commonly accepted that "[j]udicial crime creation [in the United States] is a thing of the past."[9] In contrast, a few modern courts believe that they are empowered by reception statutes to *abolish* common law offenses that they consider no longer "compatible with . . . local circumstances and situation."[10]

[B] Statutory Interpretation

Even in states without reception statutes, the common law retains significance. Almost without exception, states have codified the common law felonies and most common law misdemeanors. These statutory offenses are usually defined, at least in part, in common law terms.[11] A familiar maxim of statutory interpretation is that when a statute contains a common law term, the presumption is that this term retains its common law meaning, absent a statutory definition to the contrary.[12] Therefore, lawyers (and law students) need to be familiar with the common law.

For example, in *Keeler v. Superior Court*,[13] *K* learned that his ex-wife was pregnant by another man. He intentionally struck her in the abdomen in order to kill the fetus. The fetus was delivered stillborn. *K* was prosecuted for murder, which was defined by statute, as at common law, as the "unlawful killing of a human being, with malice aforethought."

K sought to bar his prosecution. He claimed that a fetus born dead was not a "human being" within the meaning of the state's murder statute. Because the statute did not define this critical term, the state supreme court sought to identify legislative intent; it did so by looking to the common law of 1850, the year the murder statute was enacted and the same year the state legislature abolished common law offenses. In short, absent evidence to the contrary, the court assumed that the 1850 legislature intended that the term "human being" be defined as it was

---

[8] *E.g.*, Commonwealth v. Donoghue, 63 S.W.2d 3 (Ky. 1933) (upholding an indictment for participation in "a nefarious plan for the habitual exaction of gross usury," although no such offense had previously existed). An example of judicial crime-creation in England is Shaw v. Director of Public Prosecutions, [1962] A.C. 220, in which the House of Lords affirmed a conviction for conspiracy to corrupt public morals, for the publication of a telephone directory of prostitutes. Viscount Simonds stated that he "entertain[ed] no doubt that there remains in the courts of law a residual power to enforce the supreme and fundamental purpose of the law, to conserve . . . the moral welfare of the State" against "novel and unprepared for" attacks. *Id.* at 268.

[9] Jeffries, Note 3, *supra*, at 195. However, some courts have maintained that they have authority to expand the definition of *existing* crimes, including statutory offenses. *See* Note 14, *infra.*

[10] Pope v. State, 396 A.2d 1054, 1078 (Md. 1979) (concluding that the common law offense of "misprision of felony" should be abolished because "its origin, the impractical and indiscriminate width of its scope, its other obvious deficiencies, and its long non-use" rendered it incompatible with that state's "general code of laws and jurisprudence"); *see also* State v. Palendrano, 293 A.2d 747 (N.J. Super. Ct. Law. Div. 1972) (holding that the common law offense of "being a common scold" was no longer an offense, in part because the crime had been ignored by the state legislature and had been mentioned only twice in the reports of judicial proceedings during almost two centuries of statehood).

[11] At times, a state will enact a common law offense but not define it, in which case the common law definition applies. *E.g.*, Mich. Comp. Laws § 750.321 (2011) (prohibiting, but not defining, manslaughter).

[12] Morissette v. United States, 342 U.S. 246 (1952).

[13] 470 P.2d 617 (Cal. 1970).

in 1850 common law. The court ruled that a fetus born dead was not a "human being" for purposes of homicide law under the common law and, therefore, could not be the basis for a modern-day prosecution, in the absence of legislative action to the contrary.[14]

The common law may also be used to fill in gaps in a penal code. For example, a common law principle is that a person may not be charged with murder if the victim did not die within a year and a day of the assault.[15] Federal law defines murder in common law terms,[16] but is silent regarding the year-and-a-day rule. In the absence of legislative history suggesting that Congress intended to eliminate the rule's requirements, a court may interpret this silence as evidence that the common law rule still applies.[17]

§ 3.03　MODEL PENAL CODE[18]

Although criminal code drafting by legislatures was a major project in the United States through the first half of the 19th century, subsequent codification and reform efforts stalled. One result of this long neglect of penal reform was "a substantive criminal law that was often archaic, inconsistent, unfair, and unprincipled."[19] Therefore, in 1952 the American Law Institute (ALI), an organization composed of prominent judges, lawyers, and law professors, began to draft a penal code intended to inspire a new reformative spirit among state legislatures. In 1962, after completion of 13 tentative drafts and accompanying explanatory commentaries, the ALI approved and published its Proposed Official Draft of the Model Penal Code, a carefully drafted code containing general principles of criminal responsibility, definitions of specific offenses, and sentencing provisions.

---

[14] *See also* Vo v. Superior Court, 836 P.2d 408 (Ariz. Ct. App. 1992) ("Although there are no common law crimes in Arizona, when a crime such as murder is enacted by its common law name, we assume the legislature was aware of the common law meanings of the words in that statute and intended their use.").

In jurisdictions in which the judiciary asserts that it retains residual common law authority, a few courts have *expanded* the definition of "human being" to include viable fetuses born dead. Commonwealth v. Cass, 467 N.E.2d 1324 (Mass. 1984); Hughes v. State, 868 P.2d 730 (Okla. Crim. App. 1994); State v. Horne, 319 S.E.2d 703 (S.C. 1984). Such changes, however, can only apply prospectively. *See* § 5.01, *infra*.

[15] *See* § 31.01[C], *infra*.

[16] 18 U.S.C. § 1111(a) (2015).

[17] *E.g.*, United States v. Chase, 18 F.3d 1166 (4th Cir. 1994); Ex parte Key, 890 So. 2d 1056 (Ala. 2003) (in the absence of express evidence, the state legislature's enactment of a new criminal code did not abolish the common law year-and-a-day rule); *but see* State v. Rogers, 992 S.W.2d 393 (Tenn. 1999), *aff'd*, 532 U.S. 451 (2001) (finding that the common law year-and-a-day rule was inconsistent with modern public policy, and judicially abolishing it).

[18] *See generally* Commentary Symposium, *Model Penal Code Second: Good or Bad Idea?*, 1 Ohio St. J. Crim. L. 157–244 (2003); Symposium, *The 25th Anniversary of the Model Penal Code*, 19 Rutgers L.J. 519–954 (1988); Paul H. Robinson & Markus D. Dubber, *The American Model Penal Code: A Brief Overview*, 10 New Crim. L. Rev. 319 (2007).

[19] Sanford H. Kadish, *Fifty Years of Criminal Law: An Opinionated Review*, 87 Cal. L. Rev. 943, 947 (1999).

In 1999, the ALI determined that its sentencing provisions, which were inspired by the rehabilitative goals of the 1950s and 1960s,[20] were outdated, so it approved a project to reformulate its sentencing provisions. The sentencing project is nearing its conclusion. And, in 2012, the Institute approved another project, this one to revise the Code's sexual offense provisions, which although progressive at the time of their adoption in the 1960s, has become woefully outdated in view of changing societal mores.[21] This project is underway as this text is going to press.

The impact of the Model Penal Code on American criminal law has been "stunning."[22] Although the Code is not the law, in whole, in any jurisdiction — it is, after all, a *model* penal code — it heavily influenced adoption of revised penal codes in 34 states.[23] And, "[t]housands of court opinions have cited the Model Penal Code as persuasive authority for the interpretation of an existing [non-MPC] statute or in the exercise of a court's occasional power to formulate a criminal law doctrine."[24] As Professor Sanford Kadish has aptly put it, the Model Penal Code "has become a standard part of the furniture of the criminal law."[25]

Many criminal law professors treat the Model Penal Code as "the principal text in criminal law teaching,"[26] because its influence on the law has been so dramatic. As a consequence, this text considers in detail both the common law and Model Penal Code, the primary sources of modern statutory law.

---

[20] *See* § 2.06, *supra.*

[21] Deborah W. Denno, *Why the Model Penal Code's Sexual Offense Provisions Should Be Pulled and Replaced*, 1 Ohio St. J. Crim. L. 207 (2003).

[22] Kadish, *The Model Penal Code's Historical Antecedents*, Note 1, *supra*, at 538.

[23] Robinson & Dubber, Note 18, *supra*, at 326.

[24] *Id.* at 327.

[25] Kadish, *The Model Penal Code's Historical Antecedents*, Note 1, *supra*, at 521.

[26] *Id.*

Chapter 4

CONSTITUTIONAL LIMITS ON THE CRIMINAL LAW

§ 4.01 THE CONSTITUTION: OVERVIEW

Are there limits to a legislature's lawmaking authority? For example, may a state legislature or Congress make it an offense to desecrate an American flag, or prohibit consensual sexual conduct among adults in their home? May it make it a crime to be a drug addict, to suffer from cancer, or to be infected with the HIV virus? What if it wants to make it an offense to drive gasoline-powered automobiles? May a state legislature abolish common law defenses, such as self-defense and insanity, and thereby punish persons who kill in self-defense or who act due to an insane delusion?

As explained in Chapter 3, modern legislatures, rather than judges, ordinarily determine what conduct is criminal and define the circumstances under which a person may be held accountable for his actions. Their considerable authority, however, is not unlimited: Various provisions of the United States Constitution, as interpreted by the judiciary, limit legislative action. A state legislature is also limited by its own state constitution, which may place greater restrictions on the legislature than does the Federal Constitution.

This chapter provides a brief overview of some of the federal constitutional provisions that limit legislative authority in the realm of criminal law, and which are considered throughout this text. These provisions, however, are not interpreted by judges in a policy vacuum. Various overarching policy considerations, which may motivate a court to interpret the Constitution either narrowly or broadly, are also considered here.

§ 4.02 RELEVANT CONSTITUTIONAL PROVISIONS[1]

[A] Bill of Rights

The first 10 amendments to the United States Constitution, the so-called "Bill of Rights," restrict the power of the federal government in its relationship to individuals. Various provisions of the Bill of Rights are relevant in the study and practice of the substantive criminal law. The First Amendment provides, in part, that "Congress shall make no law . . . abridging the freedom of speech." Criminal laws that prohibit speech or chill expression, such as some laws prohibiting the

---

[1] *See also* § 5.01[C][1], *infra* (Bill of Attainder and *Ex Post Facto* Clauses considered).

defacing or burning of the American flag, are subject to constitutional attack under this amendment.[2]

The Second Amendment provides, in full, that "[a] well regulated Militia, being necessary to the security of a free State, the right of the people to keep and bear arms shall not be infringed." Although this amendment was once thought by many to deal merely with the right of a militia to be armed, the Supreme Court recently held that the "right to bear arms" is a personal right, although this right is subject to regulatory and criminal laws imposing reasonable conditions on the sale and possession of weapons.[3]

The Fourth Amendment provides in pertinent part that "[t]he right of the people to be secure in their persons, houses, papers, and effects against unreasonable searches and seizures, shall not be violated." Evidence obtained by the police in violation of this amendment may be excluded at a defendant's criminal trial.[4] This amendment also limits the degree of force that a police officer may use in arresting a suspect or preventing an arrestee from escaping. This limitation can affect the scope of criminal law defenses that would otherwise apply to law enforcement officers.[5]

The Eighth Amendment states that "cruel and unusual punishment [shall not be] inflicted." This amendment restricts legislative action in two ways: (1) it imposes limitations on what legislators may define as criminal;[6] and (2) it prohibits punishment that is barbarous in its infliction[7] or grossly disproportional to the offense committed.[8]

[B]   Fourteenth Amendment

Whereas the Bill of Rights limits the *federal* government in its relations with individuals, the Fourteenth Amendment to the United States Constitution imposes limits on *state* and local government. The amendment reads in full:

> No State shall make or enforce any law which shall abridge the privileges or immunities of citizens of the United States; nor shall any State deprive any person of life, liberty, or property, without due process of law; nor deny to any person within its jurisdiction the equal protection of the laws.

The most significant portion of the Fourteenth Amendment as it pertains to the criminal law is the Due Process Clause.[9] Although the meaning of this clause has

---

[2] *See* § 9.11, *infra.*

[3] District of Columbia v. Heller, 554 U.S. 570 (2008).

[4] *See* generally 1 Joshua Dressler & Alan C. Michaels, Understanding Criminal Procedure Ch. 4–20 (6th ed. 2013).

[5] *See* § 21.04, *infra.*

[6] *See* § 9.04, *infra.*

[7] Weems v. United States, 217 U.S. 349, 368 (1910).

[8] *See* § 6.05, *infra.*

[9] The Fifth Amendment, which applies to the federal government, includes a Due Process Clause. In

been the source of great controversy, it is now settled that it requires states not only to guarantee procedural fairness to criminal defendants, but also to respect substantive principles of justice "so rooted in the traditions and conscience of our people as to be ranked as fundamental."[10] The "fundamental rights" that states must respect are virtually the same as those that the federal government must honor, *i.e.*, nearly all of the provisions of the Bill of Rights have been "incorporated" to the states through the Fourteenth Amendment Due Process Clause.

Citizens also possess certain unenumerated fundamental rights (rights not expressly specified in the Constitution) that are protected within the constitutional term "liberty" found in the Fourteenth Amendment. The Supreme Court has held that among the implicit constitutional rights of Americans is a right of privacy.[11] However, the precise contours of this right remain highly controversial.[12]

The Fourteenth Amendment also prohibits states from denying citizens "the equal protection of the laws."[13] A criminal law that distinguishes on its face between two classes of persons (*e.g.*, females and males, felons and misdemeanants, wealthy and poor people),[14] or which is discriminatory in the manner in which it is applied, may be subject to constitutional attack.[15]

§ 4.03 POLICY FACTORS IN ENFORCING THE CONSTITUTION[16]

[A] In General

Courts are often called upon to determine whether a criminal statute, or the punishment of an offender pursuant to statute, violates one or more of the constitutional principles summarized in Section 4.02. In determining whether a violation has occurred, various competing principles come into play.

---

most respects, the scope of the two Due Process Clauses are the same. *See* West Coast Hotel Co. v. Parrish, 300 U.S. 379, 391 (1937).

[10] Snyder v. Massachusetts, 291 U.S. 97, 105 (1934).

[11] Griswold v. Connecticut, 381 U.S. 479 (1965).

[12] *See* § 9.11, *infra.*

[13] By judicial interpretation this provision applies to the federal government through the Fifth Amendment Due Process Clause. Bolling v. Sharpe, 347 U.S. 497, 499 (1954).

[14] For example, the common law offense of "being a common scold" expressly applies to women, but not to men. As there is no valid justification for this sex-based distinction, the offense violates the Equal Protection Clause. State v. Palendrano, 293 A.2d 747, 752 (N.J. Super. Ct. Law Div. 1972).

[15] This equality right is not absolute. The legislature may lawfully distinguish between groups if there is rational basis for the distinction. Classifications such as race and religion, however, are inherently suspect and subject to much closer judicial scrutiny. *See In re* Griffiths, 413 U.S. 717 (1973).

[16] *See generally* Louis D. Bilionis, *Process, the Constitution, and Substantive Criminal Law*, 96 Mich. L. Rev. 1269 (1998); Joshua Dressler, *Kent Greenawalt, Criminal Responsibility, and the Supreme Court: How a Moderate Scholar Can Appear Immoderate Thirty Years Later*, 74 Notre Dame L. Rev. 1507 (1999); Kent Greenawalt, *"Uncontrollable" Actions and the Eighth Amendment: Implications of Powell v. Texas*, 69 Colum. L. Rev. 927 (1969).

In some sense, the Constitution is divided against itself.[17] On the one hand, the document embodies the principles of separation-of-powers and federalism, which are doctrines that suggest that courts should hesitate to intervene in constitutional disputes; on the other hand, the Constitution guarantees persons certain fundamental rights, which means that the judiciary will sometimes need to act forthrightly to ensure those rights against legislative encroachment. These competing policies are briefly explained below.

[B]   Separation of Powers

Many judges are reluctant to intrude on the lawmaking domain of the legislature because members of the latter branch of government are elected, whereas federal judges are appointed and hold office for life. Although judges in many states are elected, legislators are viewed as more immediately subject to the will of the public.

Because criminal laws intimately affect the lives of citizens and are intended to represent the moral values of the community, judges generally believe that, whenever possible, they should defer to the wishes of the public as represented by legislative action. As a consequence, courts presume the constitutionality of criminal statutes, *i.e.*, the party attacking a statute must demonstrate its constitutional invalidity.[18]

[C]   Federalism

State governments have primary authority for defining and enforcing the criminal laws of their respective jurisdictions. The Constitution does not give the federal government the right to compel statutory uniformity among the states. In fact, legislative experimentation and interstate diversity is welcomed in our federal system.

Left to their own devices, state legislatures are apt to generate criminal codes that differ from each other in key respects. For example, State X might consider sexual relations among adults of the same sex, although consensual, a serious moral offense and prohibit and punish it as a felony, whereas the people of State Y might consider such conduct morally acceptable and, therefore, lawful. At the same time, State Y, with an agriculturally-based economy, might believe that it needs to punish theft of crops more severely than urban neighbor State X does. And each of the 50 states might choose to deal with the burgeoning problem of crime on the Internet, but they might do so in a myriad of ways, as each jurisdiction experiments in search of a viable solution.

---

[17] *See* Akhil Reed Amar, *Of Sovereignty and Federalism*, 96 Yale L.J. 1425, 1426 (1987).

[18] United States v. Watson, 423 U.S. 411, 416 (1976).

[D] Protecting Individual Rights

Although the principles discussed above support caution by the judiciary in dealing with statutes, the Constitution "explicitly compels the States [and federal government] to follow . . . constitutional commands."[19] Among the most important constitutional commands are those found within the Bill of Rights and Fourteenth Amendment. These provisions guarantee that the fundamental rights of individuals will *not* be trampled upon by the majority. In short, these provisions are intended to serve as a "minority rights' charter," in the sense that the Constitutional framers intended to place limits on the extent to which majority will may prevail over the interests of the less powerful.

The legislative branch of government represents the public, as a whole. Some branch of government must protect the constitutional rights of individuals. That branch is the judiciary.[20] Therefore, a court that defers to legislative judgment out of respect for the doctrines of separation-of-powers and federalism may be guilty of abdicating its institutional duty to enforce constitutional edicts. Judges concerned about potential governmental overreaching are apt to de-emphasize the doctrines of separation-of-powers and federalism. Judges concerned about the vitality of the latter principles are likely to de-emphasize the principle that the judiciary should serve as a watchdog against governmental overreaching.

---

[19] Rummel v. Estelle, 445 U.S. 263, 303 (1980) (Powell, J., dissenting).

[20] *See* Marbury v. Madison, 5 U.S. (1 Cranch) 137 (1803).

Chapter 5

LEGALITY

§ 5.01 PRINCIPLE OF LEGALITY[1]

[A] "Legality": Definition

Some conduct is immoral, harmful, or both. Some conduct is criminal and punishable. The fact that conduct is immoral or harmful does not necessarily mean that it is criminal and punishable. The American legal system espouses the principle, *nullum crimen sine lege, nulla poena sine lege*, or "no crime without law, no punishment without law." That is, a person may not be punished unless her conduct was defined as criminal — today, in the United States, by legislation, rather than the result of judicial crime-creation[2] — *before* she acted.[3] This prohibition on retroactive criminal lawmaking constitutes the essence of the principle of legality.

The doctrine of legality, which has been characterized as reflective of the "central values of liberal societies,"[4] is considered the first principle of American criminal law jurisprudence.[5] That is, the legality principle should override *all* other criminal law doctrines; it should apply even though its exercise might result in dangerous and/or morally culpable peoples escaping punishment.[6] As one court stated when it reversed the conviction of a defendant on the basis of the principle of legality:

---

[1] *See generally* Herbert L. Packer, The Limits of the Criminal Sanction 79–102 (1968); Francis A. Allen, The Habits of Legality: Criminal Justice and the Rule of Law (1996); Timothy Endicott, *Law Is Necessarily Vague*, 7 Legal Theory 379 (2001); Douglas N. Husak & Craig A. Callender, *Wilful Ignorance, Knowledge, and the "Equal Culpability" Thesis: A Study of the Deeper Significance of the Principle of Legality*, 1994 Wis. L. Rev. 29; John Calvin Jeffries, Jr., *Legality, Vagueness, and the Construction of Penal Statutes*, 71 Va. L. Rev. 189 (1985); Dan M. Kahan, *Some Realism About Retroactive Criminal Lawmaking*, 3 Roger Williams U. L. Rev. 95 (1997); Paul H. Robinson, *Fair Notice and Fair Adjudication: Two Kinds of Legality*, 154 U. Pa. L. Rev. 335 (2005); Peter Westen, *Two Rules of Legality in Criminal Law*, 26 Law & Phil. 229 (2007).

[2] *See* § 3.02[A], *supra*.

[3] *E.g.*, Model Penal Code § 1.01(2).

[4] Allen, Note 1, *supra*, at 15.

[5] Packer, Note 1, *supra*, at 79–80.

[6] Donald A. Dripps, *The Constitutional Status of the Reasonable Doubt Rule*, 75 Cal. L. Rev. 1665, 1685 (1987) ("[T]he legality principle enjoys nearly complete priority over the public interest in punishing wrongdoers.").

That [the defendant] will go largely unpunished . . . is frustrating. There are, however, basic principles upon which this country is founded which compel the result we reach. . . . [Legality] is one of them. The retroactive application of criminal law . . . is so abhorrent that we must occasionally endure some frustration in order to preserve and protect the foundation of our system of law.[7]

There are three interrelated corollaries to the legality principle: (1) criminal statutes should be understandable to reasonable, law-abiding persons; (2) criminal statutes should be crafted so as not to "delegate[] basic policy matters to policemen, judges, and juries for resolution on an *ad hoc* and subjective basis";[8] and (3) judicial interpretation of ambiguous statutes should "be biased in favor of the accused" (the lenity doctrine).[9]

The legality principle is explained in this chapter section. Its corollaries are considered in subsequent sections of this chapter. As will be seen, the corollaries (especially, the first and third ones) have frequently been enforced less than rigorously in recent years, despite the eloquent language quoted above.

[B] Rationale

The legality doctrine is defended on various grounds. First, the principle that a person may not be punished unless her conduct was defined as criminal before she acted is designed to serve fundamental justice by preventing the "arbitrary and vindictive use of the laws."[10] In countries that reject this principle, it is possible for powerful agents of the government to use the criminal law to punish their political enemies. Second, the legality principle enhances individual autonomy by "maximiz[ing] the opportunity of individuals to pursue their own . . . ends,"[11] by negating the risk that one's lawful conduct will be punished retroactively.

Third, the legality principle is justified on fair notice grounds. Specifically, the pre-existence of "legislative enactments 'give[s] fair warning of their effect and permit[s] individuals to rely on their meaning until explicitly changed.' "[12] If a person can be punished for conduct that was lawful at the time that she acted, she lacks a fair opportunity to conform her conduct to the law. In the absence of such an opportunity, the retributive basis for punishment of the actor is lacking — the person has not chosen to violate the law. Also, the requirement of fair notice arguably enhances general deterrence principles: A person cannot be deterred from committing what is subsequently determined to be a socially unacceptable act

---

[7] Hughes v. State, 868 P.2d 730, 736 (Okla. Crim. App. 1994); *see also* Dripps, Note 6, *supra*, at 1685 ("punishment unauthorized by law is, in civilized communities, simply beyond the pale").

[8] Grayned v. City of Rockford, 408 U.S. 104, 108–09 (1972).

[9] Jeffries, Note 1, *supra*, at 189.

[10] Rogers v. Tennessee, 532 U.S. 451, 460 (2001).

[11] Kahan, Note 1, *supra*, at 100 (but rejecting this rationale).

[12] Miller v. Florida, 482 U.S. 423, 430 (1987) (quoting Weaver v. Graham, 450 U.S. 24, 28–29 (1981)); *see also* Model Penal Code § 1.02(1)(d) (stating that one purpose of the Code is to "give fair warning of the nature of the conduct declared to constitute an offense").

unless she has notice at the time of her conduct of the line separating proper from improper behavior.

As some commentators have demonstrated,[13] however, the fair notice argument is not entirely persuasive. It assumes that individuals always, or even commonly, consult criminal codes before acting and, thus, can legitimately claim surprise if the legislature acts retroactively to criminalize their conduct. Moreover, in some cases, those who investigate the law in advance do so for the purpose of looking for loopholes in the law, rather than to enhance obedience to the law. In short, "rule-of-law benefits . . . always come at a price."[14] But, this reality is consistent with the point made earlier, namely, that the legality principle is so fundamental that it trumps other concerns; rigorous enforcement of this doctrine may sometimes bar government from punishing dangerous persons.

Although courts often reject claims that a particular criminal statute is unduly vague,[15] the basic rule of legality — that, in order to prosecute and punish a person, there must be an applicable criminal law in existence at the time of the defendant's conduct — *is* strictly enforced, and retroactive lawmaking is barred.

[C] Constitutional Law

The legality principle has constitutional foundations.

[1] Bill of Attainder and *Ex Post Facto* Clauses

According to the Supreme Court, the "presumption against the retroactive application of new laws is an essential thread in the mantle of protection that the law affords the individual citizen."[16] As the Supreme Court has observed, "[t]he Framers considered *ex post facto* laws to be 'contrary to the first principles of the social compact and to every principle of sound legislation.' "[17] Indeed, the presumption against retroactivity is not only "deeply rooted in our jurisprudence," but it is "centuries older than our Republic."[18] It is meant to place "limits on the sovereign's ability to use its law making power to modify bargains it has made with its subjects."[19]

Specifically, Article I, Sections 9 and 10 of the United States Constitution prohibit federal and state legislatures from enacting bills of attainder and *ex post facto* (after the fact) legislation.[20] A *bill of attainder* is special legislation that declares a specific person to be guilty of a crime and subject to punishment without

---

[13] Kahan, Note 1, *supra*, at 99–101.

[14] Endicott, Note 1, *supra*, at 380.

[15] *See* § 5.02, *infra.*

[16] Lynce v. Mathis, 519 U.S. 433, 439 (1997).

[17] Peugh v. United States, 133 S. Ct. 2072, 2084 (2013) (plurality opinion) (quoting The Federalist).

[18] Landgraf v. USI Film Products, 511 U.S. 244, 265 (1994).

[19] Lynce v. Mathis, 519 U.S. at 440.

[20] "No Bill of Attainder or ex post facto Law shall be passed." U.S. Const. art. I, § 9, cl. 3. "No State shall . . . pass any Bill of Attainder [or] ex post facto Law." U.S. Const. Art. I, § 10, cl. 1.

either a trial or conviction.[21] The *Ex Post Facto* Clause prohibits:

> 1st. Every law that makes an action done before the passing of the law, and which was innocent when done, criminal; and punishes such action. 2d. Every law that aggravates a crime, or makes it greater than it was, when committed. 3d. Every law that changes the punishment, and inflicts a greater punishment, than the law annexed to the crime, when committed. 4th. Every law that alters the legal rules of evidence, and receives less, or different testimony, than the law required at the time of the commission of the offense, in order to convict the offender.[22]

Under the first category of protection noted in the above quotation, if *D* performs lawful act X on December 31, 2015, she cannot be convicted of a criminal offense prohibiting X, enacted by the legislature on January 1, 2016. Similarly, if *D* kills *V* in self-defense on December 31, 2015, *D* may not be convicted of murder if the legislature subsequently abolishes the statutory defense of self-defense — yes, murder was an offense on December 31, but the legislature may not retroactively criminalize what was an innocent act (a killing in self-defense) at the time of the conduct. Under the third category above, it is impermissible to disadvantage a defendant by applying stricter sentencing guidelines, adopted after the crime was committed;[23] and, pursuant to the fourth category, a legislature may not enact a new statute of limitations permitting prosecutions of offenses for which the prior limitations period has expired.[24]

[2] Due Process Clause

The *Ex Post Facto* and Bill of Attainder Clauses discussed in subsection [1] apply to state and federal *legislatures*, but not to the judiciary.[25] Nonetheless, the legality principle — more specifically, the requirement of fair notice that specific conduct constitutes an offense — applies as well to the judicial branch of government through the Fifth and Fourteenth Amendment Due Process Clauses. However, the Supreme Court in *Rogers v. Tennessee* warned that the Due Process Clause does *not* "incorporate jot-for-jot"[26] the specific categories of *Ex Post Facto* Clause protections set out in subsection [1] above, in regard to the retroactive application of *judicial* decisions. That is, in the legality context, the *Ex Post Facto Clause* provides somewhat broader constitutional protections to citizens than does the Due Process Clause.

According to *Rogers*, a court (as distinguished from a legislative body) *may* give its interpretation of a common law doctrine or statute retroactive effect unless such a reading of the doctrine or statute is "unexpected and indefensible," when interpreted in light of judicial opinions expressed before the conduct in question.

---

[21] Cummings v. Missouri, 71 U.S. (4 Wall.) 277, 325 (1867).

[22] Calder v. Bull, 3 U.S. (3 Dall.) 386, 390 (1798) (emphasis omitted).

[23] Miller v. Florida, 482 U.S. 423 (1987).

[24] Stogner v. California, 539 U.S. 607 (2003).

[25] Rogers v. Tennessee, 532 U.S. 451, 456 (2001).

[26] *Id.* at 459.

Notwithstanding this limitation, the Due Process Clause provides significant protection. For example, "it is clear the courts cannot go so far as to create an offense by enlarging a statute, by inserting or deleting words, or by giving the terms used false or unusual meanings."[27] Thus, a criminal trespass statute that prohibits *"entry* upon the lands of another . . . after notice from the owner . . . prohibiting such entry" cannot be expanded unforeseeably by judicial interpretation and then applied retroactively to prohibit the act of *remaining* on land lawfully entered after being told to leave.[28] However, such an interpretation of the statute may be applied *prospectively*, because future actors are put on constructive notice by the court's decision of the broader reading of the statute.

§ 5.02 STATUTORY CLARITY[29]

A corollary of the common law legality principle — one that is constitutionally enforceable through the Due Process Clause — is that a criminal statute must "provide a person of ordinary intelligence fair notice of what is prohibited."[30] The statute must give "sufficient warning that men may conduct themselves so as to avoid that which is forbidden."[31] Vague statutes are unacceptable not just because they deny a law-abiding person fair notice, but also because they "may authorize and even encourage arbitrary and discriminatory enforcement" by police and prosecutors.[32]

The requirement of reasonable statutory clarity is easy to state but difficult to apply. Supreme Court Justice Felix Frankfurter has stated that the doctrine "is itself an indefinite concept. There is no such thing as 'indefiniteness' in the abstract. . . . [W]hether notice is or is not 'fair' depends on the subject matter to which it relates."[33] As a practical matter, in an effort to determine how much clarity is required, courts look at three factors: the purpose of the statute (*i.e.*, the societal interest at stake by the legislation); the extent to which the statutory ambiguity was necessary to further the legislative goal; and the impact of the statute on the protected rights of the individual.[34]

---

[27] Keeler v. Superior Court, 470 P.2d 617, 625 (Cal. 1970).

[28] Bouie v. City of Columbia, 378 U.S. 347 (1964).

[29] *See generally* Robert Batey, *Vagueness and the Construction of Criminal Statutes — Balancing Acts*, 5 Va. J. Soc. Pol'y & L. 1 (1997); Endicott, Note 1, *supra*; Jeffries, Note 1, *supra.*

[30] United States v. Williams, 553 U.S. 285, 304 (2008).

[31] Rose v. Locke, 423 U.S. 48, 50 (1975) (footnote omitted); Desertrain v. City of Los Angeles, 754 F.3d 1147, 1155 (9th Cir. 2014) ("A penal statute cannot require the public to speculate as to its meaning while risking life, liberty, and property in the process.").

[32] City of Chicago v. Morales, 527 U.S. 41, 56 (1999). The issue of arbitrariness is considered in § 5.03, *infra.*

[33] Winters v. New York, 333 U.S. 507, 524 (1948) (dissenting opinion); *see also* Jeffries, Note 1, *supra*, at 196 ("The difficulty is that there is no yardstick of impermissible indeterminacy.").

[34] Batey, Note 29, *supra*, at 4–39. In regard to the third factor, the Supreme Court has stated that "when a statute 'interferes with the right of free speech or of association, a more stringent vagueness test should apply.'" Holder v. Humanitarian Law Project, 561 U.S. 1, 19 (2010) (quoting Hoffman Estates v. Flipside, Hoffman Estates, Inc., 455 U.S. 489, 495 (1982)).

Courts are generally reluctant to rule that a criminal statute is unconstitutionally vague. Judges do not want to reward unreasonable misunderstandings of law, and they are cognizant of the "practical difficulties in drawing criminal statutes both general enough to take into account a variety of human conduct and sufficiently specific to provide fair warning that certain kinds of conduct are prohibited."[35]

The "root of the vagueness doctrine is a rough idea of fairness."[36] "[P]erfect clarity" is not required.[37] Fairness requires only "that there is sufficient warning to one bent on obedience that he comes *near* the proscribed area."[38] As England's House of Lords has put it, "[t]hose who skate on thin ice can hardly expect to find a sign which will denote the precise spot where they may fall in."[39] Thus, a statute is not invalid "simply because it requires conformity to an imprecise normative standard,"[40] such as the requirement that a person not act "negligently."[41] As Justice Holmes has observed, "the law is full of instances where a man's fate depends on his estimating rightly, that is, as the jury subsequently estimates it, some matter of degree."[42]

Furthermore, "[e]ven trained lawyers may find it necessary to consult legal dictionaries, treatises, and judicial opinions before they may say with any certainty what some statutes may compel or forbid."[43] Therefore, the Due Process Clause is *not* violated unless a law-abiding person would still have to guess as to the meaning of a statute after she or her attorney conducts research into the meaning of the law. For example, consider a statute that provides that "[w]hoever commits the abominable and detestable crime against nature, either with mankind or beast, shall be guilty of a felony." On its face, the statute is quite arguably vague. Ordinary persons might have to guess as to the meaning of the critical phrase "crime against nature."[44] Nonetheless, the statute is not unconstitutional if its meaning can be ascertained by reading prior state court opinions construing the law.[45] And, if these prior opinions indicate that judicial interpretations of a statute in *another* state are relevant in ascertaining the first statute's meaning, a person may be held respon-

---

[35] Colten v. Kentucky, 407 U.S. 104, 110 (1972); *see also* Endicott, Note 1, *supra*, at 382 ("Laws can be precise, but a legal system with no vague laws is impossible. The reason is that any legal system needs to regulate a *variety* of human activity in a *general* way.").

[36] Colten v. Kentucky, 407 U.S. at 110.

[37] Ward v. Rock Against Racism, 491 U.S. 781, 794 (1989).

[38] Winters v. New York, 333 U.S. at 539 (Frankfurter, J., dissenting) (emphasis added); *see also* State v. Downey, 476 N.E.2d 121, 122 (Ind. 1985) (A statute "need only inform the individual of the generally proscribed conduct, [and] need not list with itemized exactitude each item of conduct prohibited.").

[39] Regina v. Knuller, [1973] A.C. 435, 463.

[40] Eanes v. State, 569 A.2d 604, 615 (Md. 1990).

[41] Nash v. United States, 229 U.S. 373 (1913).

[42] *Id.* at 377.

[43] Rose v. Locke, 423 U.S. 48, 50 (1975).

[44] In case *you* wondered, in its broadest meaning, the crime consists of consensual or nonconsensual oral or anal sexual relations between persons of the same or opposite sex, or sexual relations between a human being and a "brute beast."

[45] Wainwright v. Stone, 414 U.S. 21 (1973) (*per curiam*); *see also In re* Banks, 244 S.E.2d 386 (N.C. 1978) (holding that a statute prohibiting "peep[ing] secretly into any room occupied by a female" was not vague in light of prior judicial interpretations of the statute).

sible for learning the applicable law of the other jurisdiction.[46] Furthermore, if a statute uses, but does not define, a common law term, a law-abiding person may be assumed to have read the treatises of Blackstone, Coke, or other common law sources in order to learn the term's common law meaning.[47] In short, an "ordinary, law-abiding person" unrealistically is one who is willing and able to do significant legal research (or has sufficient funds to hire a lawyer to do it for her) before acting![48]

§ 5.03   AVOIDING UNDUE DISCRETION IN LAW ENFORCEMENT

A statute that lacks clarity not only provides insufficient notice to law-abiding persons, but is also susceptible to arbitrary or discriminatory enforcement. The Supreme Court observed in *Kolender v. Lawson* that a statute or ordinance must "establish minimal guidelines to govern law enforcement."[49] In the absence of such guidelines, the *Kolender* Court warned, "a criminal statute may permit a standardless sweep [that] allows policemen, prosecutors, and juries to pursue their personal predilections." The Due Process Clause forbids the enforcement of any statute that, due to vagueness in language, "vests virtually complete discretion in the hands of the police to determine whether the suspect has satisfied [its requirements]."[50]

So-called vagrancy statutes are prime examples of such impermissible legislation. For example, in *Papachristou v. City of Jacksonville*,[51] a city ordinance prohibited a person from being a "vagrant." Under the ordinance, "[r]ogues and vagabonds," "common drunkards," "persons wandering or strolling around from place to place without any lawful purpose," "habitual loafers," and others, were "vagrants."

On its face, of course, this language is vague. What is a "common" drunkard? What makes a person a "habitual loafer"? Worse than its imprecision, however, is that the ordinance gives the police virtually unfettered discretion to determine who is a vagrant. According to *Papachristou*, such laws, "though long common in Russia, are not compatible with our constitutional system." A primary concern is that a prosecution "may be merely the cloak for a conviction which could not be obtained on the real but undisclosed grounds for the arrest,"[52] for example, that the "vagrant" was an African-American person "strolling" in a white community,[53] a poorly dressed person found in a wealthy business district, or a person whose lawful

---

[46] *See* Rose v. Locke, 423 U.S. at 52–53.

[47] *See* Keeler v. Superior Court, 470 P.2d 617, 620, 633 (Cal. 1970).

[48] Batey, Note 29, *supra*, at 5 (the no-vagueness doctrine "focuses on a sort of 'lawyer's notice' that seems far removed from ordinary life").

[49] 461 U.S. 352, 358 (1983) (internal quotation marks omitted).

[50] *Id.*

[51] 405 U.S. 156 (1972).

[52] *Id.* at 169.

[53] In *Papachristou*, two black males and two white females driving together to a nightclub were arrested for "prowling by auto."

conduct, *e.g.*, males holding hands or kissing, offended the sensibilities of the arresting officer.

The Supreme Court invalidated another ordinance on similar grounds in *City of Chicago v. Morales*.[54] In an effort to reduce criminal street gang activity, the Chicago City Council enacted an ordinance that provided that "[w]henever a police officer observes a person whom he reasonably believes to be a criminal street gang member loitering in any public place with one or more other persons, he shall order all such persons to disperse and remove themselves from the area." The ordinance defined "loitering" as "remain[ing] in any one place with no apparent purpose." Any person who did not "promptly" obey the dispersal order was subject to a fine or jail sentence.

Three members of the Supreme Court stated that the ordinance was unconstitutionally vague. For example, these justices pointed out, it is unclear how far loiterers, once ordered to disperse, must move apart from each other, and how long they must remain separate before they can meet again. The more significant problem according to six members of the Court, however, was that the ordinance provided absolute discretion to police officers to determine what activities constituted loitering. Based on the language of the ordinance, "[i]t matters not whether the reason that a gang member and his father, for example, might loiter near Wrigley Field is to rob an unsuspecting fan or just to get a glimpse of Sammy Sosa leaving the ballpark." The Court worried that "in either event, if their purpose is not apparent to a nearby police officer, she may . . . order them to disperse." Thus, the ordinance could be applied by the police to attack entirely innocent activity.

The ordinance's triggering mechanism — making the decision that the street gang member and another are in one place "with no apparent purpose" — "is inherently subjective because its application depends on whether some purpose is 'apparent' to the officer on the scene." The ordinance permits an officer to treat some purposes, "perhaps a purpose to engage in idle conversation or simply to enjoy a cool breeze on a warm evening . . . as too frivolous to be apparent if he suspected a different ulterior [criminal] motive."[55]

Or, consider a Los Angeles ordinance that provided that "[n]o person shall use a vehicle parked or standing upon any City street . . . as living quarters either

---

[54] 527 U.S. 41 (1999).

[55] Model Penal Code Section 250.6 ("Loitering or Prowling"), drafted prior to *Papachristou* and *Morales*, provides in part that a person commits a violation if she "loiters or prowls in a place, at a time, or in a manner not usual for law-abiding individuals, under circumstances that warrant alarm for the safety of persons or property in the vicinity." Except when it is impracticable (*e.g.*, the suspect flees), the Code requires a police officer, prior to arrest, to "afford the actor an opportunity to dispel any alarm which would otherwise be warranted." The Code provision further provides that a person may not be convicted if the officer failed to comply with this requirement or if the explanation given by the actor was true and, if believed, would have dispelled the alarm. Courts that have considered statutes patterned on Section 250.6 have reached conflicting conclusions as to their constitutionality under the Due Process Clause. *Compare* Fields v. City of Omaha, 810 F.2d 830 (8th Cir. 1987), City of Portland v. White, 495 P.2d 778 (Or. Ct. App. 1972), *and* City of Bellevue v. Miller, 536 P.2d 603 (Wash. 1975), *abrogated on other grounds*, State v. Smith, 759 P.2d 372 (Wash. 1988) (all cases invalidating ordinances based on the Model Penal Code provision), *with* State v. Ecker, 311 So. 2d 104 (Fla. 1975), *and* City of Milwaukee v. Nelson, 439 N.W.2d 562 (Wis. 1989) (upholding MPC-based ordinances).

overnight, day-by-day, or otherwise." In *Desertrain v. City of Los Angeles*,[56] a federal court declared this language to be unconstitutionally vague and to promote arbitrary enforcement of the rights of the homeless. What is wrong with this ordinance? The ordinance "does not define 'living quarters,' or specify how long — and when — is 'otherwise.' " Does this ordinance make it unlawful to eat in the vehicle, to keep a sleeping bag in the trunk, or stay in the car for hours because it is raining? The provision, the court held, "raise[d] the same concerns of discriminatory enforcement as the ordinance in *Papachristou*."

§ 5.04   STRICT CONSTRUCTION OF STATUTES (RULE OF LENITY)[57]

When the language of a statute is clear and unambiguous, "there is no room for judicial construction and the courts must give the statute its plain and definite meaning."[58] When a statute in unclear or ambiguous, however, a court's primary function is to ascertain the intent of the legislature that enacted the law.[59] To do this, a court may seek assistance by all "appropriate means and *indicia*, such as the purposes appearing from the statute taken as a whole, the phraseology, the words ordinary or technical, the law as it prevailed before the statute, the mischief to be remedied, . . . statutes *in pari materia*, the preamble, the title, and other like means."[60] In the effort to divine the legislative intent, courts will often turn to dictionaries, to legislative debates, and to careful parsing of the language, and even punctuation, used in the statute.

What does a court do, however, if, after such careful analysis, the meaning of a statute remains uncertain? In response to a "vast and irrational" expansion in the number of capital offenses in 18th century England, British courts developed the rule, carried over to the United States, that when a criminal statute is subject to conflicting reasonable interpretations, the statute (including sentencing provisions thereto) should be interpreted in favor of the defendant.[61] This so-called rule of lenity (the "junior version of the vagueness doctrine"[62]) is *not* constitutionally compelled, but is said to support the principle of legality by preventing a court from inadvertently enlarging the scope of a criminal statute through its interpretive powers.

---

[56] 754 F.3d 1147 (9th Cir. 2014).

[57] *See generally* Batey, Note 29, *supra*; Jeffries, Note 1, *supra*; Dan M. Kahan, *Lenity and Federal Common Law Crimes*, 1994 Sup. Ct. Rev. 345; Lawrence M. Solan, *Law, Language, and Lenity*, 40 Wm. & Mary L. Rev. 57 (1998).

[58] *In re* Banks, 244 S.E.2d 386, 388 (N.C. 1978). Put differently, "[t]he language of the statute is the starting point for interpretation, and it should also be the ending point if the plain meaning of that language is clear." United States v. Choice, 201 F.3d 837, 840 (6th Cir. 2000).

[59] Whitner v. State, 492 S.E.2d 777, 779 (S.C. 1997).

[60] *In re Banks*, 244 S.E.2d at 389 (quoting State v. Partlow, 91 N.C. 550 (1884)).

[61] Jeffries, Note 1, *supra*, at 198; *see* Fowler v. United States, 131 S. Ct. 2045, 2055 (2011) (Scalia, J., concurring) ("In light of the rule of lenity . . . we must construe ambiguous criminal statutes in favor of the defendant.").

[62] Packer, Note 1, *supra*, at 95.

Although the lenity doctrine requires strict construction of statutes, it should be observed that many modern courts, sometimes including the United States Supreme Court in its interpretation of federal statutes, strictly construe *the lenity doctrine itself*. The lenity doctrine, the high court said recently, "only applies if, after considering text, structure, history, and purpose, there remains a grievous ambiguity . . . , such that the Court must simply guess as to what Congress intended."[63] In essence, the lenity doctrine serves as a tie breaker;[64] but it only comes into play if there *truly* is a "tie" — two or more *equally* reasonable interpretations of a statute.

Even the most well-drafted criminal statutes are often susceptible to multiple, reasonable interpretations. Overuse of the lenity doctrine, therefore, may result in the application of a statute contrary to legislative intent. As a result, some American states have abolished the rule of lenity outright.[65]

The Model Penal Code does not recognize the lenity principle. It requires instead that criminal statutes be construed according to their "fair import," and that ambiguities be resolved in a manner that furthers "the general purposes [of the Code] and the special purposes of the particular provision involved."[66] That is, although one general purpose of the Code is to provide fair warning regarding the nature of the conduct that is deemed to be criminal,[67] a statute should be interpreted to further, not frustrate, the legislative policies behind the specific law in question.

---

[63] Barber v. Thomas, 560 U.S. 474, 488 (2010) (internal quotation marks omitted).

[64] People v. Manzo, 270 P.3d 711, 717 (Cal. 2012).

[65] Jeffries, Note 1, *supra*, at 198.

[66] Model Penal Code § 1.02(3).

[67] Model Penal Code § 1.02(1)(d).

Chapter 6

PROPORTIONALITY

§ 6.01 "PROPORTIONALITY" IN THE CRIMINAL LAW: OVERVIEW[1]

"Proportionality" is an important and recurring concept in the criminal law. For example, all justification defenses, *e.g.*, self-defense, defense-of-others, defense-of-property, contain a proportionality requirement: A person is not justified in using force against another unless it is "proportional or reasonable in relation to the harm threatened or the interest to be furthered."[2] Thus, a person may not justifiably kill another in order to prevent a minor battery to himself or another, or to prevent a theft of personal property.

The doctrine of proportionality is also asserted in the context of sentencing, to ensure that an offender receives punishment appropriate to the crime he has committed. Both utilitarians and retributivists recognize proportionality in their theoretical structures, although the doctrine is more closely linked to retribution.[3] Modern penal codes, as well, acknowledge that one purpose of a criminal code is "to render punishment within a range of severity proportionate to the gravity of offenses, the harms done to crime victims, and the blameworthiness of offenders."[4] And, according to Supreme Court case law, the Constitution, through the Eighth Amendment, prohibits grossly disproportional punishment.

This chapter considers two questions relating to proportionality of punishment. First, how much (or what) punishment is excessive or disproportionate to a particular crime? Utilitarians and retributivists go about answering this question differently. Punishment that is proportional according to utilitarian principles might be retributively disproportional, or vice-versa. Second, under what circumstances is disproportional punishment not only unwise or unfair, but also unconstitutional?

---

[1] *See generally* Paul Robinson, Distributive Principles of Criminal Law: Who Should Be Punished How Much? (2008); Michael Tonry, Why Punish? How Much?: A Reader on Punishment (2011); Paul H. Robinson & John M. Darley, Justice, Liability and Blame: Community Views and the Criminal Law (1995); Andrew von Hirsch & Andrew Ashworth, Proportionate Sentencing: Exploring the Principles (2005); Paul H. Robinson & Robert Kurzban, Concordance and Conflict in Intuitions of Justice, 91 Minn. L. Rev. 1829 (2007); Christopher Slobogin & Lauren Brinkley-Rubinstein, *Putting Desert in Its Place*, 65 Stan. L. Rev. 77 (2013); Andrew von Hirsch, *Proportionality in the Philosophy of Punishment: From "Why Punish?" to "How Much?,"* 1 Crim. L.F. 259 (1990); Jeremy Waldron, *Lex Talionis*, 34 Ariz. L. Rev. 25 (1992). *See also* § 2.03, *supra.*

[2] 1 Paul H. Robinson, Criminal Law Defenses 87 (1984).

[3] Harmelin v. Michigan, 501 U.S. 957, 989 (1991) (opinion of Scalia, J. & Rehnquist, C.J.) ("[p]roportionality is inherently a retributive concept").

[4] Model Penal Code § 1.02(2)(a)(i)(2007).

Few criminal law issues have more sharply divided the United States Supreme Court than this one.

§ 6.02 UTILITARIANISM AND PROPORTIONALITY

[A] General Principles

Utilitarian philosophy directs that punishment be neither too little nor too much, but rather that it be proportional, *i.e.*, that punishment be inflicted in the amount required — but no more than is required — to satisfy utilitarian crime prevention goals. In his classic account on utilitarianism, Jeremy Bentham announced five rules intended to ensure proportional punishment.[5]

In order to deter crime, the first rule is that punishment must not be less than is required to outweigh the potential profit to the criminal of committing the offense. If too little punishment is imposed, criminal conduct will remain profitable and, as a consequence, the threat of punishment will be ineffective. It follows from this, according to the second rule, that "[t]he greater the mischief of the offense, the greater is the expense, which it may be worth while to be at, in the way of punishment."

Utilitarian analysis also directs lawmakers (Rule 3) to grade offenses in a manner that will induce a person "to choose always the least mischievous of two offenses," by making sure that "[w]here two offenses come into competition, the punishment for the greater offense must be sufficient to induce a man to prefer the less." For example, a criminal battery should be punished less severely than a murder, in order to induce a wrongdoer (if not otherwise deterred) to commit the less harmful act. Punishment should also be set in a manner to induce the criminal "to do no more mischief than what is necessary for his purpose" (Rule 4).

The final rule of proportionality is that "punishment ought in no case to be more than what is necessary to bring it into conformity with the [previous] rules." In other words, because punishment is itself a mischief that should be avoided to the extent possible, punishment is disproportional if more pain is inflicted than is required to satisfy the previous goals.

[B] Application of the Principles

[1] General Deterrence

Very dangerous crimes should be punished more severely than less dangerous ones. To a utilitarian legislator concerned with general deterrence, however, the degree of dangerousness of an offense is not measured by calculating the injury likely to be caused in a single incident by a particular offender, but rather by predicting the overall mischief that is likely to result from commission of this type of offense in the future by this and other offenders. This means that the appropriate

---

[5] *See generally* Jeremy Bentham, An Introduction to the Principles of Morals and Legislation ch. 14 (1789).

punishment for a crime may differ over time and among jurisdictions. For example, in a rural community in which theft of cattle occurs frequently and is apt to cause serious economic hardship to its inhabitants, it would be appropriate to punish this conduct more severely than in an urban community where the crime rarely occurs and does not threaten the economic well-being of its people.

In setting the punishment for an offense, a utilitarian lawmaker will also consider the degree to which the conduct in question is deterrable. Consider, for example, how a utilitarian might treat the offense of driving an automobile under the influence of alcohol. Little or no injury may occur in a specific case of intoxicated driving. In terms of future mischief, however, the offense is a serious one because drunk driving is common and frequently results in loss of life or injury to persons and property. Moreover, some criminologists claim that drunk driving is especially difficult to deter by threat of punishment.[6] If this is so, it may be appropriate to impose penalties much greater than would be set for equally dangerous, but more easily deterred, behavior. Conversely, if drunk driving can only be deterred by directing substantial law enforcement efforts away from violent crimes, thereby increasing the frequency of the latter offenses, or only by application of such draconian punitive measures that the community would lose respect for the justice system, a utilitarian might favor attacking the problem in a non-penal manner.

[2] Individual Deterrence or Incapacitation

When deterrence of a specific offender is desired, punishment is proportional to the extent, *but only to the extent*, that it is necessary to prevent the individual offender from committing future criminal acts more painful to society than the punishment that will be inflicted on the wrongdoer.

Evidence may exist that a specific criminal is less susceptible to deterrence than the ordinary offender. As a result, he may be more likely than the usual wrongdoer to commit future crimes. Consistent with concepts of individual deterrence or incapacitative goals, therefore, a more dangerous offender may be punished more severely than an ordinary offender who commits the same crime. For example, the offense of criminal battery may merit "x" units of punishment pursuant to general deterrence principles. D, however, may be more dangerous and less easily deterred than the usual batterer, as evidenced by his previous convictions for violent offenses. Enhanced punishment of D, *e.g.*, "x + 5" units of punishment, might be appropriate. Under these hypothesized circumstances, recidivist D's punishment would be significantly greater than that imposed for battery under general deterrence principles, and D's punishment would result in more pain than the harm suffered by the victim of the specific battery.

---

[6] Dale E. Berger, et al., *Deterrence and Prevention of Alcohol-Impaired Driving in Australia, the United States, and Norway*, 7 Just. Q. 453 (1990) (finding general deterrence relatively weak in the United States).

[3] Rehabilitation

Proportionality of punishment has little meaning in a rehabilitative system of treatment. C.S. Lewis has written that it is possible to speak of "just punishment," but not of "just cure," where "just" means "proportional."[7] Although compelled rehabilitation constitutes "punishment" for purposes of the criminal law,[8] Lewis's observation is still pertinent, because the duration of such treatment and the potential harshness of some rehabilitative techniques are logically unrelated to the severity of the offense committed and to the degree to which the treatment/ punishment will deter others from committing the offense. Indeed, unless limited by other doctrines (such as the constitutional bar on grossly disproportional punishment), rehabilitative "procedures"/punishment logically may be exercised until they succeed, which in some cases might never occur.

§ 6.03 RETRIBUTIVISM AND PROPORTIONALITY

[A] General Principles

The concept of proportional punishment is closely allied with retributivism. Retributivists justify punishment on the ground that a crime has been committed. The offender owes a debt to society; punishment is the mode of repayment. The payment due varies with the crime committed: Punishment must be proportional to the offense committed, taking into consideration both the harm caused by the offender *and* the wrongdoer's degree of moral desert for having caused it.

Modern retributivists reject the concept of *lex talionis* — the infliction upon the wrongdoer of precisely the same injury he has caused the victim — except, perhaps, in the case of murder. For example, to punish a rapist by raping him, whatever that would mean in practice, would violate modern schools of retributive thought, which require that the offender be treated with dignity and as a person possessing moral worth.[9] Moreover, with the exception of the death penalty for murder, punishment equivalent in kind to the offense committed is impractical. Therefore, retributivists only require that the wrongdoer symbolically repay the debt he owes, by undergoing punishment reasonably proportionate to the gravity of the offense, as measured by the harm done and the moral blameworthiness of the offender in causing the harm.

[B] Application of the Principles

[1] In General

As discussed more fully in subsequent chapters of this text, a crime has two basic components: the external part, involving the harm inflicted by the actor; and an internal portion, involving the actor's moral blameworthiness, as represented by the

---

[7] C.S. Lewis, *The Humanitarian Theory of Punishment*, 6 Res. Judicatae 224, 225 (1953).

[8] *See* § 2.02, *supra.*

[9] *See* § 2.03[B][2], *supra* (the protective retribution and victim vindication models).

offender's mental state in causing the harm inflicted. Both components must be considered in calculating the actor's retributive-based just deserts.

Regarding the harm component, a legislature seeking to impose retributively fair punishment looks backward at the crime committed and determines how much harm — physical, psychological, moral, economic, etc., to the immediate victim, the victim's family, and the broader community — generally results from the commission of the offense in question. To the extent that a trial judge has sentencing discretion, the judge may consider, as well, the actual harm inflicted (which might be more or less than ordinary) in the case before him.

Regarding the blameworthiness component, retributivists consider a person more deserving of punishment if he intentionally, rather than, for example, negligently, causes the particular harm. Thus, a retributivist would punish an automobile driver who negligently kills a pedestrian less severely than an assassin who purposely takes a human life. The retributivist would also take into consideration other factors, relating to an offender's moral blameworthiness. For example, if A intentionally kills $V1$ as the result of an insane delusion, he is less blameworthy (if he is blameworthy at all) than B, a contract killer who intentionally, but rationally, kills $V2$.

[2] Devising a Proportional Retributive System

Just as it is difficult to determine with precision what punishment is appropriate according to utilitarianism — the calculation of costs and benefits can be no more than approximate and, often, hit-and-miss — retributivism provides no real-world non-arbitrary way to determine what punishment is precisely proportional to a crime. In the absence of *lex talionis* punishment — "an eye for an eye" — penalties can only roughly approximate the retributively just outcome.

One way to scale deserts in a sentencing system based exclusively on retribution is to proportion punishment *between* offenses, rather than *to* offenses. Imagine for a moment a society in which there are only three statutory offenses: criminal homicide, rape, and theft. The first step for the legislator would be to rank these crimes in the order of their seriousness. The lawmaker would determine the overall harmfulness of each offense. People generally consider crimes of violence more serious than non-violent offenses; and, among violent crimes, the unjustifiable taking of human life (criminal homicide) is ordinarily viewed as the most heinous offense. Therefore, the legislature might rank an intentional killing as the most serious offense, rape as less serious, and theft as the least severe.

The next step would be to impose punishment commensurate to the relative gravity of the offenses. One way to do this is to begin with the least serious offense — here, theft — and to set its punishment at the low end of the continuum of acceptable forms and degrees of punishment. For example, theft would receive "x" units of punishment, such as two years' imprisonment. Then, each successively more serious crime would be compared to the last one in terms of increased degree of seriousness, with penalties set in rough proportion to the last crime. If rape is considered approximately 10 times more serious than the ordinary theft (based on the comparative harm of the two offenses), then rape would receive "10x" units of punishment (20 years' imprisonment). If an intentional homicide is two times as serious as rape, then the homicide would merit "20x" units of punishment (40 years', or perhaps life, imprisonment). Alternatively, the grading system could start at the top (setting the maximum punishment for murder at death, if the jurisdictions permit this, or life imprisonment) and the legislature could work its way down through the lesser offenses.[10]

The preceding analysis considered only the harm component of criminal offenses. As previously indicated, however, the personal blameworthiness of an actor in causing the harm is also a critical factor. Therefore, a legislature would subdivide criminal homicide and other serious offenses into sub-offenses based on the actor's degree of culpability. For example, an intentional killing would be graded as a more serious offense than a negligent homicide.

This approach to retributive proportionality is very difficult to calibrate.[11] Thus, for many legislators inclined toward retributivist-based punishment, the most realistic approach is, simply, to concede that, taking into consideration both the harm and blameworthiness components, one can do no more than set upper and lower parameters to specific offenses. Thus, lawmakers might determine that, for Crime A, more than "x" units of punishment would be too severe, and fewer than "y" units of punishment would be too little punishment, and thus any punishment between these parameters is roughly proportional to the offense.

§ 6.04 COMPARING THE TWO THEORIES OF PROPORTIONALITY

For purposes of determining the appropriate punishment for an offense, retribution and utilitarianism differ in two key respects. First, utilitarian punishment is linked to predictions of future harm and the extent to which the undesired conduct is deterrable. In contrast, retributivists seek to proportion punishment to the offense already committed, without consideration of future harm. Second, retributivists believe that punishment for wrongdoing is morally right, perhaps obligatory. Utilitarians contend that punishment is undesirable unless it will result in a net benefit to society. Because of these differences in outlook, utilitarian and retributive versions of proportionality may differ substantially in specific cases.

For example, for some retributivists the death penalty for the most serious forms of murder is justifiable,[12] but disproportional for offenses in which no life is taken. In contrast, utilitarians favor capital punishment for murder and/or other offenses

---

[10] Of course, in a real system, involving many offenses, the differences in seriousness between crimes will be relatively small and, in some cases, non-existent. Once the ranking is done, and the upper and lower limits of punishment are set, penalties can be graduated in a relatively simple manner.

[11] What is especially difficult to determine is how to interrelate the harm and blameworthiness components. For example, is the *intentional* commission of rape more, equally, or less serious than the *negligent* taking of a human life?

[12] Some retributivists reject capital punishment on the ground that humans lack the knowledge required to determine with sufficient reliability a wrongdoer's degree of depravity, a necessary component of retributive analysis. *See* Jeffrie G. Murphy, *Moral Epistemology, The Retributive Emotions, and the "Clumsy Moral Philosophy" of Jesus Christ, in* The Passions of Law 149 (Susan Bandes ed., 1999). Other retributivists, while not opposed philosophically to capital punishment, oppose it because of increasing evidence (particularly in light of the DNA revolution) that innocent persons have

if, but only if, its deterrent benefits are proven to outweigh its human and economic costs.

The two theories may also lead in very different directions if the offense in question involves dangerous conduct that does not result in significant harm on a specific occasion. For example, as discussed earlier,[13] under one scenario, general deterrence theorists might justify substantial punishment of persons who drive under the influence of intoxicants because such conduct is a major social problem, resulting in great harm on many occasions, and is especially difficult to deter, thereby requiring greater penal "disincentives." The retributivist, however, would not consider the difficulty-of-deterrence or likely-future-harm factors in calibrating the proper punishment. Instead, the penalty would be based on the harm of drunk driving *per se*, which is apt to be fairly minor,[14] and on the actor's culpability in causing the minor harm. Under such circumstances, the penalty is likely to be relatively light.[15]

Retributivists and specific-deterrence utilitarians may also differ, for example, in their approach to recidivists. As noted before,[16] utilitarians can justify enhanced punishment of repeat offenders, assuming there are reliable grounds for determining such actors' future dangerousness. For a retributivist, however, heightened punishment cannot be approved on the basis of the offender's predicted future conduct. Also, assuming that the repeat offender has been punished for his prior crimes — he has paid his debt to society — a retributivist cannot justify punishing the offender more for the present offense merely because of the prior wrongs.[17]

§ 6.05   CONSTITUTIONAL REQUIREMENT OF PROPORTIONALITY

[A]   General Principles

The Eighth Amendment to the United States Constitution prohibits the infliction of "cruel and unusual punishment" by agents of the federal government on persons convicted of criminal conduct. Freedom from such punishment is a fundamental right that state governments must also respect.[18]

---

been sentenced to death, Lawrence C. Marshall, *The Innocence Revolution and the Death Penalty*, 1 Ohio St. J. Crim. L. 573 (2004), or because of proven racial discrimination in sentencing.

[13] *See* § 6.02[B][1], *supra*.

[14] If a drunk driver kills another, of course, he may be prosecuted for criminal homicide.

[15] *See* Douglas N. Husak, *Is Drunk Driving a Serious Offense?*, 23 Phil. & Pub. Aff. 52 (1994) (concluding that the offense is not a serious one, and that drunk drivers should not be imprisoned).

[16] *See* § 6.02[B][2], *supra*.

[17] Although many retributivists reject laws that authorize enhanced punishment of repeat offenders, see, for example, George Fletcher, Rethinking Criminal Law 459–66 (1978), some retributivists have sought to justify some habitual offender laws. *E.g.*, Andrew von Hirsch, *Desert and Previous Convictions in Sentencing*, 65 Minn. L. Rev. 591 (1981).

[18] *See* Robinson v. California, 370 U.S. 660 (1962).

The Supreme Court ruled in 1910 that an implicit requirement of the Eighth Amendment is that "punishment for crime . . . be graduated and proportioned to [the] offense."[19] This interpretation of the Eighth Amendment is controversial. Although the Supreme Court has stated that the proportionality doctrine is "deeply rooted" in common law jurisprudence,[20] two members of the Court (one of whom is still sitting on the high bench) have stated that, based on their historical study, "the Eighth Amendment contains no proportionality guarantee."[21] Nonetheless, the Supreme Court is presently wedded to the principle in some form. Accordingly, courts are occasionally called upon to determine whether punishment imposed for violation of a criminal statute was grossly disproportional to the offense.

[B] Death Penalty

The death penalty for intentional murder — death for death — presents no significant proportionality problems. More difficult is whether death is ever appropriate for a crime in which life is *not* taken. In this regard, the Supreme Court has ruled twice on the constitutionality of the death penalty for rape.

The first case, *Coker v. Georgia*,[22] involved what the Court characterized as the rape of an "adult woman," namely, a 16-year-old married female.[23] In the case, Ehrlich Coker raped a woman and stabbed her to death. Still free eight months later, he kidnapped and twice raped a second woman. Finally caught, Coker was sentenced to three life terms in prison for his offenses. A year and a half later, however, he escaped from prison and robbed and raped the present 16-year-old victim in front of her husband, threatening to kill her. Ultimately caught and convicted for the latest rape and robbery, Coker was sentenced to death by a Georgia jury.

Based on these facts, an extremely compelling utilitarian argument for Coker's execution was possible. He was an exceedingly dangerous man for whom incapacitation had proven to be an insufficient remedy. The community, as represented by the jury that sentenced him to death, had reason to fear that if he were not executed, Coker might escape prison again and commit additional rapes and murders. On such principles, therefore, death was quite arguably proportional punishment for Coker's deed. Nonetheless, the Supreme Court ruled that death is grossly disproportional punishment for the crime of rape of an adult woman.

Writing for the Court, Justice Byron White utilized two methods of constitutional analysis in reaching its conclusion. First, pursuant to an approach followed in death penalty opinions generally, he considered objective indicia of the

---

[19] Weems v. United States, 217 U.S. 349, 367 (1910).

[20] Solem v. Helm, 463 U.S. 277, 284–85 (1983).

[21] Harmelin v. Michigan, 501 U.S. 957, 965 (1991) (opinion of Scalia, J. & Rehnquist, C.J.).

[22] 433 U.S. 584 (1977).

[23] As the Supreme Court subsequently observed, "[t]he [*Coker*] Court did not explain why the 16-year-old victim qualified as an adult, but it may be of some significance that she was married, had a home of her own, and had given birth to a son three weeks prior to the rape." Kennedy v. Louisiana, 554 U.S. 407, 427 (2008).

public's attitude regarding the death penalty for adult rape. At that time, only a few states authorized capital punishment for adult rape and, even in Georgia, juries rarely sentenced rapists to death. Justice White determined, therefore, that death was now a societally unacceptable punishment for rape.[24]

The jury statistics, however, only proved that Georgia juries did not want to sentence *all* rapists to death. The numbers did not demonstrate that Georgians viewed the penalty as excessive in *all* "adult woman" cases, as the Court ultimately concluded. Also, if the doctrine of federalism[25] is highly valued, the fact that Georgia was among a small minority of states permitting execution of rapists should not have served as grounds for overturning the legislature's judgment.

Perhaps because of these difficulties with his analysis, Justice White stated that the foregoing evidence did not resolve the issue, "for the Constitution contemplates that in the end our own judgment will be brought to bear on the question of the acceptability of the death penalty under the Eighth Amendment." As a consequence, the Court proceeded to determine whether in *its* judgment death was an excessive penalty for Coker's crime.

Although he did not say so, Justice White applied a strictly retributive conception of proportionality to the Georgia law. Coker's dangerousness was ignored. Nor did the Court seriously consider whether death was a suitable penalty according to principles of general deterrence.[26] Instead, as a retributivist would do, Justice White compared the harm caused by rape with the penalty of death. He described rape as "highly reprehensible" and "[s]hort of homicide . . . the 'ultimate violation of self.'" Nonetheless, applying what the dissenters described as the "primitive simplicity" of *lex talionis*, Justice White concluded that rape "does not compare with murder, which . . . involve[s] the unjustified taking of human life. . . . The murderer kills; the rapist, if no more than that, does not." Therefore, the Court overturned Coker's sentence of death on constitutional proportionality grounds.

Coker's holding technically was limited to the constitutionality of the death penalty for rape of adult women,[27] but its retributive reasoning ("[t]he murderer kills; the rapist, if no more than that, does not") would support the claim that capital punishment is unconstitutional in *all* rape cases — indeed, for *all* crimes in which human life is not taken. Nonetheless, after *Coker* was decided, the Louisiana legislature introduced the death penalty for the rape of children under the age of 12, and five other states (Georgia, Montana, Oklahoma, South Carolina, and Texas) followed suit. As well, at least eight additional states authorized the death penalty for other non-homicide crimes.

---

[24] Unstated by the Court, but perhaps critical, was the fact that capital punishment historically was "reserved overwhelmingly for black defendants, especially those convicted of raping white women." James R. Acker, *Social Science in Supreme Court Death Penalty Cases: Citation Practices and Their Implications*, 8 Just. Q. 421, 431 (1991). Thus, concern regarding racism silently affected the justices.

[25] *See* § 4.03[C], *supra*.

[26] The issue received one sentence of attention in a footnote. *Coker*, 433 U.S. at 592–93 n.4.

[27] The phrase "adult woman" or "adult female" was used eight times in the *Coker* Court's main opinion. *Kennedy v. Louisiana*, 554 U.S. at 428.

Are such statutes constitutional? The answer, at least in child rape and most non-homicide cases, came in *Kennedy v. Louisiana*,[28] a case involving a stepfather's horrific rape of his 8-year-old stepdaughter. The Court, by a 5-4 vote,[29] held that the death penalty for rape of a child, where death of the rape victim does not result, and was not intended to result, is unconstitutional.[30]

As in *Coker*, the Court reviewed objective indicia of contemporary attitudes regarding the death penalty for the crime of child rape. It found insufficient evidence of a consensus in favor of the penalty, nor did it observe any defined trend in that direction. Again, however, as in *Coker*, it brought to bear its own judgment of the matter. And, here again, the Court principally (although not exclusively[31]) emphasized the retributive-based *lex talionis* concept. Yes, the Court majority conceded, the harm to a child rape victim is horrendous:

> Here the victim's fright, the sense of betrayal, and the nature of her injuries caused more prolonged physical and mental suffering than, say, a sudden killing by an unseen assassin. The attack was not just on her but on her childhood. . . . Rape has a permanent psychological, emotional, and sometimes physical impact on the child. . . . We cannot dismiss the years of long anguish that must be endured by the victim of child rape.[32]

Nonetheless, the Court stated, "[i]t does not follow . . . that capital punishment is a proportionate penalty for the crime." But, why not? It went on: "Evolving standards of decency . . . counsel us to be most hesitant before interpreting the Eighth Amendment to allow the extension of the death penalty, a hesitation that has special force where no life was taken in the commission of the crime." The majority opinion went on:

> [W]e conclude that, in determining whether the death penalty is excessive, there is a distinction between intentional . . . murder on the one

---

[28] 554 U.S. 407 (2008); *see generally* Heidi M. Hurd, *Death to Rapists: A Comment on* Kennedy v. Louisiana, 6 Ohio St. J. Crim. L. 351 (2008).

[29] It is worth noting, given the close vote, that (as of the time this text goes to press) two justices (Stevens and Souter) who voted with the majority, but none of the dissenters, have since retired from the Court.

[30] As Professor Hurd powerfully put the significance of *Kennedy*:

> No matter how much life-long physical damage a man inflicts while raping a three-year-old little girl, no matter how ritualistically he tortures her over hours or days, no matter how delicious he finds her sobbing agony . . . , no matter whether he has stolen her away from all she knows and kept her naked, starved, and terrorized in a pitch dark hole in the ground . . . so long as she survives the torment, he has a constitutional right to live out his natural life free of the threat that death will be visited upon him in punishment.

Hurd, *supra*, Note 28, at 351.

[31] The Court *did* apply utilitarian considerations more than in *Coker*. Among its utilitarian observations were that the "death penalty adds to the risk of nonreporting, that . . . diminishes the penalty's objectives," 554 U.S. at 444; and by "making the punishment for child rape and murder equivalent, a State that punishes child rape by death may remove a strong incentive for the rapist not to kill the victim." *Id.* at 445. The latter concern is consistent with Bentham's third rule of proportionality, namely, that offenses be graded to induce a criminal "to choose always the least mischievous of two offenses." *See* § 6.02[A], *supra*.

[32] *Kennedy*, 554 U.S. at 435.

hand and nonhomicide crimes against individual persons, including child rape, on the other. The latter crimes may be devastating in their harm, as here, but [quoting *Coker*] "in terms of moral depravity and of the injury to the person and to the public," they cannot be compared to murder in their [again quoting *Coker*] "severity and irrevocability."[33]

Inexplicably, the Supreme Court left open one possible role for the death penalty in non-homicide cases: "Our concern here is limited to crimes against individual persons. We do not address, for example, crimes defining and punishing treason, espionage, terrorism, and drug kingpin activity, which are offenses against the State." This remark, which will need further explication from the Court, motivated a comment by the *Kennedy* dissenters:

> The Court takes pain to limit its holding to "crimes against individual persons" and to exclude "offenses against the State," a category that the Court stretches — without explanation — to include "drug kingpin activity." But the Court makes no effort to explain why the harm caused by such crimes is necessarily greater than the harm caused by the rape of young children.[34]

[C]   Terms of Imprisonment

The Supreme Court's Eighth Amendment proportionality jurisprudence relating to non-death penalty sentences has not been a model of clarity or consistency. It is helpful, therefore, to follow the Court's struggle on a case-by-case basis.

[1]   *Rummel v. Estelle*[35]

William Rummel was convicted in Texas of the felony of obtaining a check for $120.75 by false pretenses, and then cashing it. The offense carried a two-to-ten year prison term. However, Rummel had previously been convicted twice of theft (in which two offenses he fraudulently amassed property or cash valued at $108.36), so he was sentenced under the state's habitual offender law to life imprisonment. Rummel was eligible for parole consideration after approximately 12 years in prison.

Rummel argued that his life sentence constituted grossly disproportional punishment. If the Supreme Court had applied its retributive-based *Coker-Kennedy*[36] analysis, Rummel's argument almost certainly would have been persuasive. Texas did not, nor could it seriously, claim that pursuant to retributive theory, life imprisonment fit the offense of obtaining $120.75 by false pretenses. Nonethe-

---

[33] *Id.* at 438.

[34] *Id.* at 467 (Alito, J., dissenting).

[35] 445 U.S. 263 (1980); *see generally* Joshua Dressler, *Substantive Criminal Law Through the Looking Glass of* Rummel v. Estelle: *Proportionality and Justice as Endangered Doctrines*, 34 Sw. L.J. 1063 (1981); Charles Walter Schwartz, *Eighth Amendment Proportionality Analysis and the Compelling Case of William Rummel*, 71 J. Crim. L. & Criminology 378 (1980).

[36] *See* § 6.05[B], *supra*.

less, by a vote of 5 to 4, the Supreme Court upheld Rummel's sentence.

Rummel and the four dissenting justices asserted that the disproportionality of his life sentence could be established by weighing three objective factors: (1) the gravity of the offense compared to the severity of the penalty; (2) penalties imposed within Texas for similar offenses ("*intra*-jurisdictional" analysis); and (3) penalties imposed in other jurisdictions for the same offense ("*inter*-jurisdictional" analysis). Speaking for the majority, however, Justice William Rehnquist rejected the proposition that the excessiveness of Rummel's sentence could be determined by use of this three-pronged test.

Regarding the first factor, Rummel reasoned that his offense was a petty, nonviolent crime, which did not justify the severe sentence he received. The Court rejected his characterization of the offenses as petty. It stated that the state legislature was entitled to draw the line between felony theft and petty larceny as it wished, "subject only to those strictures of the Eighth Amendment that can be informed by objective factors." As for the fact that Rummel's offenses were nonviolent in nature, Justice Rehnquist made the utilitarian observation that the fact of violence "does not always affect the strength of society's interest in deterring a particular crime or in punishing a particular criminal."

As for the *intra*-jurisdictional factor, persons convicted of what Rummel considered to be far more serious offenses in Texas, *e.g.*, first-time rapists, were not subject to the mandatory sentence of life imprisonment. The Court disapproved of this test, however, because identification of some offenses as more serious than others was "inherently speculative."

As for *inter*-jurisdictional analysis (the third prong), the Texas recidivist statute was among the three most severe in the country in Rummel's circumstances. Again, the five-justice majority was unimpressed. First, it observed that Rummel was eligible for parole consideration after 12 years, which meant that it could not know with certainty how long Rummel would actually be imprisoned. Furthermore, even if it could be shown that Texas's recidivist law was the harshest in the nation, this would not render Rummel's sentence excessive: "Absent a constitutionally imposed uniformity inimical to traditional notions of federalism, some State will always bear the distinction of treating particular offenders more severely than any other State." Justice Rehnquist also made the following utilitarian observation about recidivist laws:

> [T]he interest of the State of Texas here is not simply that of making criminal the unlawful acquisition of another person's property; it is in addition the interest . . . in dealing in a harsher manner with those who by repeated criminal acts have shown that they are simply incapable of conforming to the norms of the society . . . [T]he State of Texas, or any other State, has a valid interest in so dealing with that class of persons.

The implicit message of *Rummel* was that, although states are prohibited from inflicting grossly disproportional punishment, the Supreme Court will almost always defer to a state legislature's judgment in a non-capital case. On a more theoretical level, *Rummel* stands for the proposition that legislatures may consti-tutionally apply utilitarian factors in setting criminal penalties, even if this process results in *retributively* disproportional sentencing.

[2]   *Solem v. Helm*[37]

Jerry Helm was sentenced to life imprisonment without possibility of parole pursuant to South Dakota's habitual offender law, upon conviction of fraudulently passing a "no account" check for $100.00. This was Helm's seventh conviction. Although the Court described Helm's prior felonies as nonviolent in nature, his crimes included three burglaries, and driving an automobile while intoxicated.

Helm asserted that his sentence constituted grossly disproportional punishment. Based on *Rummel*, his legal claim seemed exceptionally weak. Nonetheless, by a 5-4 vote, the Court invalidated Helm's sentence. In an opinion written by Justice Lewis Powell, author of the dissent in *Rummel*, the Court stated that although reviewing courts should grant substantial deference to legislatures in setting punishments for crimes, "no penalty is *per se* constitutional."

The Court applied the same three-pronged test the dissent (but not the majority) invoked in *Rummel*, and concluded that the sentence was excessive on the basis of each prong: Helm received a severe sentence for "relatively minor" conduct; he was treated more harshly than other criminals in South Dakota who committed more serious crimes; and the recidivist statute was one of the two toughest in the country in these circumstances. The Court distinguished *Rummel* on the ground that Texas had a relatively liberal parole policy, whereas Helm's life sentence was without possibility of parole: absent executive pardon or commutation, life imprisonment meant life imprisonment.

[3]   *Harmelin v. Michigan*[38]

By 1991, when the Supreme Court again tackled the proportionality issue in *Harmelin v. Michigan*, Justice Powell, the author of *Solem v. Helm* and a dissenter in *Rummel v. Estelle*, had retired from the Court, as had two other members of the *Solem* Court. These personnel changes resulted in a different constitutional picture.

In *Harmelin*, the defendant was convicted of possessing 672 grams of cocaine. Although this was his first offense, he received the statutory mandatory term of life imprisonment without possibility of parole. Because there was no death penalty in Michigan, this was the harshest penalty available for *any* offense in the state, and was reserved for only two other crimes: first-degree murder; and manufacture, distribution, or possession with intent to manufacture or distribute 650 grams or more of narcotics. Moreover, the Michigan drug possession statute was by far the harshest in the nation. Based on the three-pronged test of *Solem*, therefore, a very strong case of unconstitutionality could be made.

Justice Antonin Scalia announced the judgment of the Court, which was that Harmelin's sentence did *not* violate the Eighth Amendment.[39] However, only Chief Justice Rehnquist joined his opinion. Based on an examination of the background of

---

[37]   463 U.S. 277 (1983).

[38]   501 U.S. 957 (1991).

[39]   Subsequently, the Michigan Supreme Court invalidated the statute pursuant to that state's own

the Eighth Amendment, Justices Scalia and Rehnquist concluded that the framers of the Constitution did not include within the Eighth Amendment a guarantee against disproportionate sentences. Therefore, they would have overruled *Solem*.[40]

As the *Rummel* Court did a decade earlier, the two justices rejected as unduly subjective the first two prongs of the test applied in *Solem*. As for the first prong (seriousness of the offense), Justice Scalia said that although violent crimes are serious, "that is only half the equation. The issue is *what else* should be regarded to be *as serious* as these offenses." On this matter, the justices deferred to the state legislature: "The members of the Michigan Legislature, and not we, know the situation on the streets of Detroit."[41] Nor were Justices Scalia and Rehnquist willing to compare penalties for offenses *within* Michigan: "[S]ince deterrent effect depends not only upon the amount of the penalty but upon its certainty, crimes that are less grave but significantly more difficult to detect may warrant substantially higher penalties."

Justice Scalia conceded that the *inter*-jurisdictional test "can be applied with clarity and ease. The only difficulty is that it has no conceivable relevance to the Eighth Amendment." Just as one state may punish conduct that another state permits, it follows that one state may "treat with stern disapproval an act that other States punish with the mildest of sanctions."

Justices Anthony Kennedy, Sandra O'Connor, and David Souter concurred in the judgment against Harmelin, but refused to overrule *Solem*. Justice Kennedy conceded that the Court's "proportionality decisions have not been clear or consistent in all respects, [but] they can be reconciled." According to the concurring justices, the previous cases yielded the following four principles: (1) the fixing of prison terms "involves a substantive penological judgment that, as a general matter, is 'properly within the province of legislatures, not courts'"; (2) "the Eighth Amendment does not mandate adoption of any one penological theory"; (3) substantial divergences in penological theories and in prison sentences are the "inevitable, often beneficial" result of living in a federal system; and (4) proportionality analysis should be informed by objective factors whenever possible.

In light of these principles, Justice Kennedy announced a new way to apply the three-pronged test in imprisonment cases: "[I]ntrajurisdictional and interjurisdictional analyses are appropriate only in the rare case in which a threshold comparison of the crime committed and the sentence imposed leads to an inference of gross disproportionality." That is, a court should apply the first prong of *Solem*, and if it determines that the offense was a serious one, any penalty short of death

---

constitutional bar on excessive punishment. People v. Bullock, 485 N.W.2d 866 (Mich. 1992).

[40] However, they would not have overruled *Coker v. Georgia*, considered in subsection [B], *supra*, because the holding in that case was "an aspect of our death penalty jurisprudence, rather than a generalizable aspect of Eighth Amendment law."

[41] In response to the dissent's argument that by this reasoning a legislature could properly make overtime parking a felony punishable by life imprisonment, Justice Scalia responded that it was unlikely "that the horrible example imagined would ever in fact occur, unless, of course, overtime parking should one day become an arguably major threat to the common good, and the need to deter it arguably critical." Thus, Justice Scalia was unwilling to state in dictum that, in such a "horrible example," life imprisonment would be unconstitutionally excessive.

is proportional. The other prongs of the test only come into play if a court determines that the offense at issue is petty and the sentence imposed severe. In the present case, the three-justice plurality determined that the offense for which Harmelin was convicted was a serious one. Further analysis was unnecessary.

The four dissenters would have applied the standards announced in *Solem* without variation. Although Justice White, the author of the primary dissent, agreed that "[d]rugs are . . . a serious societal problem," he did not believe that mere possession of drugs justified a mandatory life sentence. In view of the severity of the penalty in comparison to other laws within the state, and in comparison to similar laws elsewhere, the dissenters would have held that the Michigan law "fail[ed] constitutional muster."

[4] *Ewing v. California*[42]

In 2003, the justices again confronted the proportionality issue. Three years earlier, Gary Ewing entered a pro shop and stole three golf clubs, each worth $399. He was convicted of one count of felony grand theft. Because Ewing had previously been convicted of robbery and three counts of burglary, Ewing was sentenced to a term of imprisonment of "twenty-five years to life" pursuant to California's "three strikes" recidivist law.

By the time Ewing's case reached the high court, three of the four dissenters in *Harmelin* (Justices White, Blackmun, and Marshall) had retired from the Supreme Court. Nonetheless, the Court's division in *Harmelin* repeated itself in *Ewing*: two justices held that the Eighth Amendment contains no proportionality guarantee; three justices defended a limited proportionality doctrine; and four justices would have upheld a broad, *Solem v. Helm* approach to the Eighth Amendment. As in each earlier case discussed in this chapter section, as well, the Court split 5-4. This time, as in *Rummel* and *Harmelin*, it found no Eighth Amendment violation.

Justice O'Connor, writing for Chief Justice Rehnquist and Justice Kennedy, asserted that the Eighth Amendment contains a "narrow proportionality principle" in non-capital cases. Rather than redefine this narrow principle, the plurality adopted Justice Kennedy's four principles from *Harmelin*. And, in view of the additional factor raised in *Ewing* — the defendant's recidivism — Justice O'Connor observed:

> Throughout the States, legislatures enacting three strikes laws [have] made a deliberate policy choice that individuals who have repeatedly engaged in serious or violent criminal behavior, and whose conduct has not been deterred by more conventional approaches to punishment, must be isolated from society in order to protect the public safety. Though three strikes laws may be relatively new, our tradition of deferring to state legislatures in making and implementing such important policy decisions is longstanding.

---

[42] 538 U.S. 11 (2003); *see also* Lockyer v. Andrade, 538 U.S. 63 (2003) (companion case); *see generally* James J. Brennan, *The Supreme Court's Excessive Deference to Legislative Bodies Under Eighth Amendment Sentencing Review*, 94 J. Crim. L. & Criminology 551 (2004); Erwin Chemerinsky, *Cruel and Unusual: The Story of Leandro Andrade*, 52 Drake L. Rev. 1 (2003).

Echoing Justice Kennedy's observation in *Harmelin*, the plurality stated that the Constitution does not require the adoption of any particular penological theory, and that incapacitation, as here, "may play a role in a State's sentencing scheme."

The plurality then turned to the specifics of Ewing's punishment. It first "address[ed] the gravity of the offense compared to the harshness of the penalty." Justice O'Connor, however, stated that the case did not involve "merely 'shoplifting three golf clubs.' Rather, Ewing was convicted of felony grand theft for stealing nearly $1,200 worth of merchandise after previously having been convicted of at least two 'violent' or 'serious' felonies." According to the plurality, "[i]n weighing the gravity of Ewing's offense, we must place on the scales not only his current felony, but also his long history of felony recidivism."

In short, these justices controversially were not determining that the punishment (25 years to life) fit the crime (grand theft), but whether the punishment fit the crime *plus* "his long history of felony recidivism." To avoid the impression that this meant that California improperly was punishing Ewing *again* for his *prior* crimes, Justice O'Connor stated that "Ewing's sentence is justified by the State's public-safety interest in incapacitating and deterring recidivist felons" from committing future crimes, which was "amply supported by [Ewing's] own long, serious criminal record."

Justice Scalia (now joined by Justice Thomas) concurred in the judgment. He reasserted his *Harmelin* claim that there is no proportionality principle, narrow or otherwise, contained in the Eighth Amendment. He also criticized the plurality for the proportionality analysis set out above. He pointed out that proportionality, "inherently a concept tied to the penological goal of retribution," has always meant that punishment must fit a crime, but that the plurality had "not convincingly establish[ed] that 25-years-to-life is a 'proportionate' punishment for stealing three golf clubs." The plurality had to "*add* an analysis" — the utilitarian consideration of protecting society from future crime. Scalia stated that legislatures have every right to consider public safety, "though why that has anything to do with the principle of proportionality is a mystery."

Justice Breyer, joined by Justices Stevens, Souter, and Ginsburg, dissented. For them, the three-pronged test of *Solem v. Helm* controlled, and the facts of that case and the present one were similar enough to suggest that Ewing's sentence violated the Eighth Amendment. The dissenters also believed that, even applying Justice Kennedy's *Harmelin* approach, the sentence here was grossly disproportional.

[5] Summary

At the time of *Ewing*, seven justices were on record for the belief that the Eighth Amendment prohibits grossly disproportional sentences of imprisonment, but they were divided on whether the relatively broad *Solem v. Helm* three-pronged test, or Justice Kennedy's narrow formulation from *Harmelin v. Michigan*, should control.

As time passes, so may interpretations of the Constitution. Chief Justice Rehnquist and Justice O'Connor, both of whom voted in *Ewing* for the narrow approach to proportionality analysis, have left the bench, replaced by Chief Justice John Roberts and Justice Samuel Alito, respectively. And, two of the four justices who favored the broad *Solem* approach have also retired: Justices Souter and Stevens have been replaced by Justices Sonia Sotomayor and Elena Kagan. So, as this book goes to press, there are two members of the Court (Scalia and Thomas) who question whether the Eighth Amendment contains any proportionality principle; one sitting justice (Kennedy) favors the narrow proportionality test set out in *Harmelin* and used again in *Ewing*; and two justices (Ginsburg and Breyer) prefer the broader *Solem* approach. This leaves resolution of the issue in the hands of the justices who have joined the Court since *Ewing*.

Chapter 7

BURDENS OF PROOF

§ 7.01 PUTTING THE ISSUES IN PROCEDURAL CONTEXT

During a criminal trial, the prosecutor, representing the state, will introduce evidence pertaining to the crime or crimes charged. Usually, although not always, the defendant will dispute many of the relevant facts. She may assert an alibi defense ("I wasn't there"), or she may attack the prosecutor's version of the facts more narrowly, *e.g.*, by claiming that she did not intend to cause the harm charged, or by pleading a defense, such as self-defense. At the conclusion of the trial, the factfinder, usually a jury, determines whose version of the evidence was more persuasive.

The jury is not wholly free in its deliberative process. Rules exist to ensure that the jury considers only those legal issues about which sufficient factual evidence was presented at trial, such that it can reach a rational, rather than speculative, verdict. Moreover, assuming that an issue is properly before it, the jury will be instructed as to "how to decide close cases, and when to regard a case as close."[1]

Among the rules that guide the fact-finding process are those establishing two types of burdens of proof: (1) the burden of production (also called the "burden of going forward (with evidence)"; and (2) the burden of persuasion. As to any particular issue raised at a criminal trial, both burdens of proof may fall on a single party, or one party may have the burden of production while the other has the burden of persuasion. Although states have wide discretion in determining on whom the burdens should be allocated, and how substantial the burdens should be, their discretion is not unlimited: the Due Process Clause of the United States Constitution sets some limits on legislative authority.

§ 7.02 BURDEN OF PRODUCTION

[A] Nature of the Burden

Prior to trial the prosecution must file a document with the court that indicates the crime or crimes it believes that the defendant has committed. This document provides the accused with notice of the essential elements of the offense(s) charged, and the basic facts that the prosecutor intends to prove at trial to support her

---

[1] Barbara D. Underwood, *The Thumb on the Scales of Justice: Burdens of Persuasion in Criminal Cases*, 86 Yale L.J. 1299, 1299 (1977).

allegation that the defendant committed the crime(s).[2] In turn, the defendant is sometimes required to provide advance notice to the prosecution of defenses she intends to assert at trial.

At trial, the parties are expected to introduce evidence supporting their pre-trial claims. The rule establishing the "burden of production" identifies the party on whom the initial obligation is placed to introduce evidence at trial to support the particular legal claim in question.

[B]   Who Has the Burden?

The prosecutor has the burden of production regarding all of the elements of the crime charged.[3] Almost always, however, the defendant has the burden of producing evidence pertaining to any affirmative defense she wishes to raise. For example, assume that murder is defined by statute as "the killing of a human being by another human being with malice aforethought." For current purposes, this definition may be divided into four elements: (1) a killing; (2) of a human being; (3) by another human being; (4) with malice aforethought. The prosecutor has the burden of producing evidence at trial regarding each of these elements. That is, she must introduce evidence that a life was taken, that the victim was a human being,[4] that the killer was the defendant, and that the killing occurred with the mental state described by the law as "malice aforethought." Unless the prosecutor introduces sufficient evidence (as discussed below) regarding each of these four elements, she has not met her burden of production.

In the preceding example, if the defendant intends to have the jury consider a defense to the murder charge, for example, that she killed in self-defense or that she was insane at the time of the crime, she — not the prosecutor — is obligated to introduce evidence at trial supporting this claim.

[C]   How Great Is the Burden?

The prosecutor must produce sufficient evidence that a rational trier of fact — typically, a jury — may reasonably determine, rather than speculate, that the elements of the crime have been proved beyond a reasonable doubt.[5] Thus, in the hypothetical murder prosecution discussed immediately above, the prosecutor has not met her burden of production unless she puts on enough evidence that a rational juror could believe beyond a reasonable doubt that the defendant (1) killed

---

[2] "In all criminal prosecutions, the accused shall enjoy the right . . . to be informed of the nature and cause of the accusation." U.S. Const. amend. VI. The document that charges the defendant with a crime (called an "indictment" if prepared by a grand jury, or called an "information" if a grand jury is not involved) must "be a plain, concise, and definite written statement of the essential facts constituting the offense charged." Fed. R. Crim. P. 7(c)(1).

[3] See Jackson v. Virginia, 443 U.S. 307 (1979); 1 Paul H. Robinson, Criminal Law Defenses § 4(a)(2) (1984).

[4] This would be a serious issue if the victim were a fetus that arguably was born dead. See § 31.01[B][1], infra.

[5] See Jackson v. Virginia, 443 U.S. at 319. For a definition of the phrase "beyond a reasonable doubt," see § 7.03[C][1], infra.

(2) another (3) human being (4) with malice aforethought.

Regarding affirmative defenses to crimes for which the defendant has the burden of production, jurisdictions differ in the language used to characterize the amount of evidence that the defendant must introduce in order to have the jury instructed on the defense. For example, some jurisdictions state that the defendant has met her burden of production if there is "any foundation in the evidence" to support the defense, which means that a defendant is entitled to a jury instruction on her defense "so long as there is evidence to support it, regardless of whether the evidence is weak, inconsistent, believable, or incredible."[6] A different and more onerous version of the standard is that the evidence introduced by the defendant should be "sufficient for [a] reasonable jur[or] to find in [her] favor" regarding the defense.[7]

[D]   Effect of Failing to Meet the Burden

The trial judge — and not the jury — decides whether the parties have met their respective burdens of production. If the judge concludes that the prosecutor failed to satisfy her burden of production regarding *any* element of the offense charged, the defendant is entitled to a directed verdict of acquittal at the conclusion of the prosecutor's case-in-chief or at the end of the trial. This result follows from the fact that, as discussed in the next section, the prosecutor must *persuade* a jury beyond a reasonable doubt that the defendant committed the crime. If the prosecutor failed to introduce enough evidence for a jury to so find, there is no reason for it to deliberate on the matter: the defendant is entitled to acquittal.

If the defendant fails to meet her burden of production regarding an affirmative defense, the judge will not instruct the jury on the law pertaining to the defense, and the defendant is not entitled to have that issue considered by the jury in its deliberations.

§ 7.03   BURDEN OF PERSUASION[8]

[A]   Nature of the Burden

Once a party satisfies her burden of production pertaining to an issue, that matter is properly before the jury as factfinder, *i.e.*, it will decide whose factual claims are more persuasive. How is the jury supposed to make this determination?

---

[6] Hoagland v. State, 240 P.3d 1043, 1047 (Nev. 2010).

[7] Government of Virgin Islands v. Lewis, 620 F.3d 359, 364 (3d Cir. 2010).

[8] *See generally* Larry Alexander, *The Supreme Court, Dr. Jekyll, and the Due Process of Proof*, 1996 Sup. Ct. Rev. 191; Ronald J. Allen, Montana v. Egelhoff — *Reflections on the Limits of Legislative Imagination and Judicial Authority*, 87 J. Crim. L. & Criminology 633 (1997); Ronald J. Allen, *The Restoration of* In re Winship: *A Comment on Burdens of Persuasion in Criminal Cases After* Patterson v. New York, 76 Mich. L. Rev. 30 (1977); Luis E. Chiesa, *When an Offense Is Not an Offense: Rethinking the Supreme Court's Reasonable Doubt Jurisprudence*, 44 Creighton L. Rev. 647 (2011); Donald A. Dripps, *The Constitutional Status of the Reasonable Doubt Rule*, 75 Cal. L. Rev. 1665 (1987); John

Rules are needed to instruct it on how to weigh the conflicting evidence.

The rules establishing the "burden of persuasion" determine who is obligated to convince the jury of the accuracy of the particular factual claim in question. That is, the party who has the burden of persuasion bears the risk of failing to convince the jury that her factual claim is true.

[B]   Who Has the Burden?

[1]   The Presumption of Innocence: The *Winship* Doctrine (In General)

The Fifth and Fourteenth Amendments to the United States Constitution provide that a person may not be deprived of her life, liberty, or property without due process of law. Pursuant to the Due Process Clause, a person charged with a crime is presumed innocent and, to enforce this presumption, the Supreme Court held in *In re Winship*[9] that the prosecution must persuade the factfinder "beyond a reasonable doubt" — a concept developed more fully later in this chapter section — of "every fact necessary to constitute the crime charged." This rule has come to be known as "the *Winship* doctrine."

According to *Winship*, the presumption of innocence "lies at the foundation of the administration of our criminal law." Although this presumption increases the risk that a guilty person will go free, the *Winship* Court determined that "a society that values the good name and freedom of every individual" does "not view the social disutility of convicting an innocent man as equivalent to the disutility of acquitting someone who is guilty." Indeed, the law's commitment to protecting the innocent is so great that, according to Blackstone, "the law holds that it is better that ten guilty persons escape, than that one innocent suffer."[10]

Winship teaches that the prosecutor must prove (beyond a reasonable doubt) every fact necessary to constitute the crime charged, but what precisely *are* the "facts" for which the government must constitutionally carry the burden of persuasion? The Supreme Court had difficulty answering this question.

Calvin Jeffries, Jr. & Paul B. Stephan III, *Defenses, Presumptions, and Burden of Proof in the Criminal Law*, 88 Yale L.J. 1325 (1979); Irene Merker Rosenberg, *Winship Redux: 1970 to 1990*, 69 Tex. L. Rev. 109 (1990); Louis B. Schwartz, *"Innocence" — A Dialogue with Professor Sundby*, 41 Hastings L.J. 153 (1989); Scott E. Sundby, *The Reasonable Doubt Rule and the Meaning of Innocence*, 40 Hastings L.J. 457 (1989); Peter Westen, *Egelhoff Again*, 36 Am. Crim. L. Rev. 1203 (1999).

[9] 397 U.S. 358 (1970).

[10] 4 Blackstone, Commentaries on the Laws of England *352 (1769). This deep protection of the accused person "has deep Judeo-Christian roots . . . . It is . . . a reminder that in judging our fellow human beings we are dealing with something unique: a being with dignity and extraordinary worth . . . ." Miller W. Shealy, Jr., *A Reasonable Doubt About "Reasonable Doubt,"* 65 Okla. L. Rev. 225 (2013). Not everyone agrees with Blackstone. For a thoughtful dialogue on this matter, see Jeffrey Reiman & Ernest van den Haag, *On the Common Saying That It Is Better That Ten Guilty Persons Escape than That One Innocent Suffer: Pro and Con*, 7 Soc. Phil. & Pol'y 226 (Spring 1990); *see also* Daniel Epps, *The Consequences of Error in Criminal Justice*, 128 Harv. L. Rev. 1065 (2015); Vidar Halvorsen, *Is It Better That Ten Guilty Persons Go Free than That One Innocent Person Be Convicted?*, 23 Crim. Justice Ethics, Summer/Fall 2004, at 3.

[2] *Mullaney v. Wilbur*[11]

W was charged with murder by a Maine prosecutor. Evidence presented at his trial tended to show that *W* intentionally killed the victim, but that he may have done so "in the heat of passion on sudden provocation." The trial court instructed the jury that Maine recognized two forms of criminal homicide, murder and manslaughter, and that the common elements of both offenses are that the homicide: (1) was "unlawful — *i.e.*, neither justifiable nor excusable"; and (2) it was committed intentionally. The jury was further instructed that the prosecution was required to prove both of these elements (beyond a reasonable doubt), and only if it met this burden was the jury to consider the distinction between murder and manslaughter.

On the distinction between murder and manslaughter, the trial court further informed the jury that if the prosecution proved that *W* killed the victim unlawfully and intentionally, then the killing was murder, unless *W* persuaded the jury by a preponderance of the evidence that the killing was "in the heat of passion on sudden provocation," in which case it constituted the lesser offense of manslaughter. That is, the prosecution had the burden of persuading the jury beyond a reasonable doubt that *W* unlawfully and intentionally killed the victim; if it did, the burden of persuasion shifted to *W* to prove that he was provoked into killing the victim in heat of passion. If *W* failed in *this* proof, he was guilty of murder; if he succeeded, he was guilty of manslaughter.

W appealed his conviction on the ground that the preceding jury instructions, which placed on him the burden of persuasion that the killing occurred "in the heat of passion on sudden provocation," violated the *Winship* doctrine. The State of Maine responded, however, that the instructions were constitutional — the prosecution only had the responsibility to prove (beyond a reasonable doubt) that *W* was guilty of some form of criminal homicide. Under the instructions given, the State of Maine did not require *W* to prove his innocence; he only had the burden of persuasion regarding his level of guilt (murder versus manslaughter). In such circumstances, the State argued, "the defendant's critical interests in liberty and reputation are no longer of paramount concern since, irrespective of . . . the heat of passion on sudden provocation, he is likely to lose his liberty and certain to be stigmatized."

The Supreme Court disagreed. In an opinion written by Justice Lewis Powell, the Court summarized the historical roots of homicide law, and concluded that the presence or absence of heat of passion was "the single most important factor in determining the degree of culpability attaching to an unlawful homicide." It observed that "the clear trend has been toward requiring the prosecution to bear the ultimate burden of proving this fact."

The Court criticized Maine's argument as unduly formalistic. It pointed out:

> [If the *Winship* doctrine] were limited to those facts that constitute a crime as defined by state law, a State could undermine many of the interests that [the Due Process Clause] sought to protect without effecting any substan-

---

[11] 421 U.S. 684 (1975).

tive change in its law. It would only be necessary to redefine the elements that constitute different crimes, characterizing them as factors that bear solely on the extent of punishment.

In contrast to such formalism, the Supreme Court held that the Due Process Clause required the prosecution not only to prove that *W* was guilty of criminal homicide, but also to persuade the jury regarding the facts relating to *W*'s "degree of criminal culpability."

Although the precise contours of the *Mullaney* decision were disputed by scholars, one highly plausible interpretation of the opinion was that, once a defendant satisfies her burden of *production* regarding an affirmative defense, the prosecution is constitutionally required to disprove the defense. This potential reading of *Mullaney*, however, proved short-lived.

[3] *Patterson v. New York*[12]

Patterson narrowed the import of *Mullaney*. Indeed, without saying so expressly, *Patterson* "signal[ed] that it [believed it] had erred in *Mullaney*."[13]

In *Patterson*, *P* was charged with murder. He believed that he was guilty of the lesser offense of manslaughter because he suffered from what New York law described as an "extreme emotional disturbance." This provision, based on the Model Penal Code,[14] was a broader version of the "heat of passion on sudden provocation" doctrine considered in *Mullaney*.

Under New York law, murder required proof of three facts: (1) a human death; (2) that the accused caused it; and (3) that the accused intended the result. The homicide statute expressly provided that "extreme emotional disturbance" was an affirmative defense to murder which, *if proved by the defendant*, reduced the criminal homicide to manslaughter. The jury was instructed consistently with these statutory provisions.

P argued that *Mullaney* invalidated the statute because the homicide law improperly permitted the State of New York to shift to him the burden of proving his lesser level of culpability due to extreme emotional disturbance. Nonetheless, in an opinion written by Justice Byron White, the Supreme Court upheld the statute. The Court conceded that there was "language in *Mullaney* that has been understood as perhaps construing the Due Process Clause to require the prosecution to prove . . . any fact affecting 'the [defendant's] degree of criminal culpability.'" It rejected this reading of *Mullaney* as unduly restrictive of legislative authority to allocate burdens of proof. The *Patterson* Court reasoned that if such a broad reading of *Mullaney* were correct, legislatures might be inclined to repeal defenses altogether or, at least, not broaden them as New York had done here. Justice White suggested that such a response would serve only to prejudice defendants' interests and undermine legislative reform. The Supreme Court stated that it did not intend *Mullaney* to have such a far-reaching effect.

---

[12] 432 U.S. 197 (1977).

[13] Allen, Montana v. Egelhoff, Note 8, *supra*, at 645.

[14] Model Penal Code § 210.3(1)(b). *See* § 31.10[C][3], *infra*.

According to *Patterson*, the prosecution is constitutionally required to prove "every *ingredient* of an offense." As used in this opinion, however, *Winship*'s "facts" and *Patterson*'s "ingredients" are synonyms for the word "elements." That is, a state is required by the Due Process Clause to prove every element in the definition of an offense, but the legislature may, *if it chooses to do so*, ordinarily allocate to the defendant the burden of persuasion regarding defenses to crimes.

The Court claimed that this interpretation of *Winship* was consistent with *Mullaney*. It pointed out that one element of the crime of murder in Maine was that the killing be "unlawful." In turn, "unlawful" meant "neither justifiable nor excusable." "Heat of passion," however, is an excuse defense. Therefore, to be guilty of murder in Maine, there had to be an *absence* of heat of passion (or any other justification or excuse). This *absence* of a defense, therefore, was an element of murder, as defined by Maine law. To require the prosecutor in *Mullaney* to prove the *absence* of heat of passion was consistent, therefore, with the proposition stated in *Patterson* that the government should prove every element of the crime charged.

In contrast, absence of "extreme emotional disturbance" was not an element of the New York murder statute. Instead, existence of such a disturbance was, expressly, an affirmative defense to murder that mitigated the offense to manslaughter. As a non-element of murder, *Patterson* stated, New York could properly place the burden of proving its existence on the defendant.

Justice Powell, author of *Mullaney*, sharply dissented in *Patterson*. He understandably complained that the majority's explanation of the *Mullaney* holding bore "little resemblance to the basic rationale of that decision." In Justice Powell's mind, and in the view of many scholarly critics of *Patterson*,[15] the holding elevated form over substance: It permitted legislatures to (in Powell's words) "shift, virtually at will, the burden of persuasion with respect to any factor in a criminal case, so long as it is careful not to mention the nonexistence of that factor in the statutory language that defines the crime." Indeed, Powell worried, a legislature could now constitutionally redefine murder as, for example, "mere physical contact causing death," and then set up an affirmative defense requiring the defendant to prove that she killed the victim blamelessly. This was exactly the formalism rejected in *Mullaney*.

[4] Post-*Patterson* Case Law

[a]   In General

A prosecutor must prove every element of an offense beyond a reasonable doubt, and, except in certain limited circumstances, a legislature may allocate to the defendant the burden of persuasion regarding "facts not formally identified as elements of the offense charged."[16] Thus, generally speaking, a legislature may

---

[15] *See* Alexander, Note 8, *supra*, at 193.

[16] McMillan v. Pennsylvania, 477 U.S. 79, 86 (1986); Smith v. United States, 133 S. Ct. 714, 719 (2013) (where a defense " 'does not controvert any of the elements of the offense itself,' the Government has no constitutional duty to overcome the defense beyond a reasonable doubt"). A "limited circumstance" in which the prosecutor *is* required by the Due Process Clause to prove a fact, beyond a reasonable doubt,

allocate to the defendant the burden of persuasion regarding facts that relate to an affirmative defense. The challenge is to determine, as a matter of legislative intent, whether a particular "fact" relates to an "element" of an offense or, instead, a "defense."

[b]　　　　Element of an Offense Versus a Defense

In *Martin v. Ohio*,[17] *M* was prosecuted for aggravated murder, defined in Ohio as "purposely, and with prior calculation and design, caus[ing] the death of another." *M* claimed he acted in self-defense, the elements of which defense were that he: (1) was not at fault in creating the situation giving rise to the argument; (2) had an honest belief that he was in imminent danger of death or great bodily harm; and (3) did not violate any duty to retreat. The jury was instructed that to convict *M*, it had to find, in light of all of the evidence, that each of the elements of aggravated murder had been proved by the State of Ohio beyond a reasonable doubt. However, the jury was told that *M* had the burden of proving self-defense, by a preponderance of the evidence.

M argued that these instructions violated the *Winship* doctrine as interpreted by *Patterson*. He reasoned that one element of self-defense — the presence of an "imminent" deadly threat — negates one element of the crime of aggravated murder, "prior calculation and design." (That is, if a person is confronted with an imminent threat, she does not have time for "prior calculation and design," *i.e.*, to premeditate.) In effect, *M* argued that the *absence* of the right to kill in self-defense was an implicit ingredient of the offense charged; therefore, it was wrong to allocate to *M* the burden of persuasion on self-defense.

By a 5-4 vote, the Supreme Court rejected *M*'s plausible argument. It emphasized the fact that the trial court did *not* instruct the jury "that self-defense evidence could not be considered in determining whether there was a reasonable doubt about the State's case . . . . Such an instruction would . . . plainly run afoul of *Winship*'s mandate." That is, the jury *was* permitted by the judge's instructions to consider self-defense evidence, along with all the other evidence introduced by either side, in order to determine whether Ohio proved the elements of the offense beyond a reasonable doubt. The Court warned that it "would be quite different if the jury had been instructed that . . . self-defense evidence must be put aside for all purposes unless it satisfied the preponderance standard."

The Court agreed with *M* "that the elements of aggravated murder and self-defense overlap in the sense that evidence to prove the latter will often tend to negate the former." However, a state may allocate to a defendant the burden of persuasion regarding an affirmative defense, as long as the jury may *also* consider the evidence relating to that defense as a basis for negating an element of a crime.

---

that is *not* an element of an offense, involves some sentencing factors (an issue not ordinarily relevant in a Criminal Law class). Basically, the prosecutor has the burden to prove, beyond a reasonable doubt, any fact (other than the defendant's prior criminal history) that will have the effect of increasing the penalty for the crime beyond the prescribed statutory maximum. Apprendi v. New Jersey, 530 U.S. 466 (2000). For an explanation of this exception, see 2 Joshua Dressler & Alan C. Michaels, Understanding Criminal Procedure § 15.04 (4th ed. 2006).

[17] 480 U.S. 228 (1987).

The dissenters, with good reason, feared that the confusing instructions approved by the Supreme Court could cause a jury to wrongly believe "that by raising the defense, the accused has assumed the ultimate burden of proving that particular element."

Martin was a controversial opinion, but nowhere near as much (or as confusing) as the Supreme Court's ruling in *Montana v. Egelhoff*.[18] The State of Montana defined the offense of "Deliberate Homicide" (murder) as "purposely" or "knowingly" causing the death of another human being. This murder statute was supplemented, however, by another statute that provided that a voluntarily-induced "intoxicated condition is not a defense to any offense and *may not be taken into consideration in determining the existence of a mental state which is an element of the offense.*"[19] According to the defendant, this latter statute impermissibly allowed the government to satisfy its burden of persuasion by denying the defendant the opportunity to introduce evidence (here, his intoxication) that might cast doubt on the prosecutor's claim that he killed "purposely" or "knowingly."

The Court, again 5-4, approved the Montana statutory system. *Egelhoff*'s long-term meaning is unclear, however, because the Court was badly split. Justice Antonin Scalia announced the judgment of the Court, but delivered an opinion for only four justices; a fifth justice (Ruth Bader Ginsburg) only concurred in the judgment. The four dissenters, in turn, wrote three opinions amongst themselves.

There are two ways to read the Montana statutory system.[20] One reading of Montana law is that the murder definition supplemented by the intoxication statute stands for the proposition that a person is guilty of Deliberate Homicide if she kills purposely or knowingly or, *in the case of a voluntarily intoxicated person, if she simply kills another person, even if the killing was not purposeful or knowing.* According to *this* reading, which approximates concurring Justice Ginsburg's understanding of Montana law, *Winship* and *Patterson* are not violated because, in essence, the legislature has defined murder two ways, one way to deal with sober killers (they are not guilty of murder unless they purposely or knowingly — intentionally — took a human life), and another way to deal with intoxicated killers (they are guilty of murder if they took a human life, even accidentally). According to *this* reading of Montana law, in regard to voluntarily intoxicated defendants, there is no mental state element in the murder statute for the State to prove beyond a reasonable doubt. This is very arguably a highly objectionable way to define murder, but it would not offend the *Winship* doctrine, because all elements of the crime, so understood, must be proved beyond a reasonable doubt.

There is another way to read the Montana homicide law, however, which conforms with the understanding of Justice Scalia's plurality opinion. According to *this* version, the Montana legislature intended to retain the ordinary culpability requirement for murder (proof that the homicide was purposeful or knowing) *in all*

---

[18] 518 U.S. 37 (1996).

[19] Mont. Code Ann. § 45-2-203 (1995) (emphasis added).

[20] *See* Allen, Montana v. Egelhoff, Note 8, *supra*, at 636.

cases, but then with "a certain Alice-in-Wonderland quality,"[21] it bars a voluntarily intoxicated defendant from introducing evidence relating to her intoxication that might cause a jury to possess a reasonable doubt that she acted with the statutorily required purpose or knowledge (for example, that she was so intoxicated that she did not know what she was doing). According to Justice Scalia, however, as long as an evidentiary rule such as the present one does not offend fundamental principles of justice, it does not violate the Due Process Clause for a state to make "changes in their criminal law that have the effect of making it easier for the prosecution to obtain convictions."[22] This is reasoning that the Supreme Court in *Winship* might very well have rejected.

[C]　How Great Is the Burden?

[1]　Elements of Crimes: Proof Beyond a Reasonable Doubt[23]

The Due Process Clause requires the prosecutor to prove every element of a crime "beyond a reasonable doubt."[24] This burden of proof "defies easy explication."[25] In terms of probability, it is the highest burden recognized in the law. Guilt is not proven on the basis of the traditional civil standard of "preponderance of the evidence" (just over 50%), or even on the heightened basis of "clear and convincing evidence." Instead, a "very high level of probability [is] required."[26] Jurors must "reach a subjective state of near certitude of . . . guilt."[27] However, courts hesitate to quantify the "inherently qualitative" reasonable-doubt standard.[28]

Chief Justice Shaw of the Massachusetts Supreme Judicial Court crafted the traditional definition of "beyond a reasonable doubt," which served for more than a century as the basis for many reasonable-doubt jury instructions. In *Commonwealth v. Webster,*[29] he explained that "reasonable doubt" is "not merely possible doubt; because every thing relating to human affairs, and depending on moral evidence, is open to some possible or imaginary doubt." Instead, reasonable doubt

---

[21]　Sanford H. Kadish, *Fifty Years of Criminal Law: An Opinionated Review,* 87 Cal. L. Rev. 943, 955 (1999).

[22]　*Egelhoff,* 518 U.S. at 55 (quoting McMillan v. Pennsylvania, 477 U.S. 79, 89 (1986)).

[23]　*See generally* Barbara J. Shapiro, "Beyond a Reasonable Doubt" and "Probable Cause": Historical Perspectives on the Anglo-American Law of Evidence (1991); Ronald J. Allen, *On the Significance of Batting Averages and Strikeout Totals: A Clarification of the "Naked Statistical Evidence" Debate, the Meaning of "Evidence," and the Requirement of Proof Beyond a Reasonable Doubt,* 65 Tul. L. Rev. 1093 (1991); Irwin A. Horowitz & Laird C. Kirkpatrick, *A Concept in Search of a Definition: The Effects of Reasonable Doubt Instructions on Certainty of Guilt Standards and Jury Verdicts,* 20 Law & Hum. Behav. 655 (1996); William S. Laufer, *The Rhetoric of Innocence,* 70 Wash. L. Rev. 329 (1995). Also consider the citations in footnotes 8 and 10, *supra.*

[24]　*See* § 7.03[B], *supra.*

[25]　Victor v. Nebraska, 511 U.S. 1, 5 (1994).

[26]　*Id.* at 14.

[27]　Jackson v. Virginia, 443 U.S. 307, 315 (1979).

[28]　McCullough v. State, 657 P.2d 1157, 1159 (Nev. 1983).

[29]　59 Mass. (5 Cush.) 295, 320 (1850).

exists when the "state of the case . . . leaves the minds of jurors in that condition that they cannot say they feel an abiding conviction, to a moral certainty, of the truth of the charge."

In *Victor v. Nebraska*,[30] the Supreme Court warned trial courts that the term "moral certainty" may have "lost its historical meaning, and that a modern jury [might] understand it to allow conviction on proof that does not meet the beyond a reasonable doubt standard." The critical language in *Webster*, the Court said, is that the jurors must have "an abiding conviction" — a "settled and fixed" conviction — of the defendant's guilt.

[2] Defenses

At common law, the burden of persuasion regarding affirmative defenses rested on the defendant.[31] Today, jurisdictions differ in their allocation of the burden of persuasion regarding affirmative defenses. Some states require the government to disprove beyond a reasonable doubt some or all defenses, once the defendant has met her burden of production. In states that allocate to the defendant the burden of persuasion regarding defenses, it is typical to require her to prove the validity of the claim by the less strict preponderance-of-the-evidence standard.

[D] Effect of Failing to Meet the Burden

[1] Elements of Crimes

If the prosecutor fails to prove each element of the crime charged beyond a reasonable doubt, the defendant must be acquitted of the offense charged. The acquittal may occur in either of two procedural contexts. First, after the prosecution completes its presentation of evidence or immediately before the case is due to be submitted to the jury, upon motion of the defendant, the trial court must direct a verdict of acquittal if the evidence, viewed in the manner most favorable to the prosecution,[32] can support no reasonable verdict other than acquittal.[33] Alternatively, if the judge believes that reasonable minds can differ and, therefore, permits the case to go to the jury, the jury must acquit if *it* possesses a reasonable doubt regarding one or more elements of the offense charged.

---

[30] 511 U.S. 1 (1994).

[31] Dixon v. United States, 548 U.S. 1, 7 (2006) (citing Patterson v. New York, 432 U.S. 197, 202 (1977)).

[32] Because the factfinder may rationally decide to believe the prosecutor's version of disputed facts, on a motion to direct a verdict in favor of the defendant, the judge must consider the evidence in the manner most favorable to the opposing side. The same test is applied in any appeal of a conviction. *See* Jackson v. Virginia, 443 U.S. 307, 319 (1979).

[33] United States v. Temple, 447 F.3d 130, 137 (2d Cir. 2006). No matter how overwhelming the evidence of guilt, the prosecution is never entitled to a directed verdict of conviction. Sullivan v. Louisiana, 508 U.S. 275, 277 (1993). The grant of such a motion would deny the accused her constitutional right to trial by jury. *See* § 1.02[A], *supra.*

[2] Defenses

If a defendant presents sufficient evidence to meet her burden of *production* regarding a defense to the crime charged, the jury must be permitted to evaluate the defense claimed. When the defendant also has the burden of *persuasion* regarding the defense, a jury should reject the claimed defense if she fails to satisfy the stated burden. Assuming that the state has proven the elements of the crime beyond a reasonable doubt, and that no other defenses have been proven, the defendant may properly be convicted.

If the prosecution has the burden of *disproving* a defense, the jury must acquit the defendant if the prosecution fails to persuade the jury beyond a reasonable doubt of the defense's non-existence.

§ 7.04 MODEL PENAL CODE

The Model Penal Code provides that the prosecutor has the burden of *production* regarding each element of an offense. Regarding affirmative defenses, the prosecutor is not required to disprove an affirmative defense "unless there is evidence supporting such defense."[34] The Code does not specify the strength of the evidence required to satisfy the defendant's burden of production regarding affirmative defenses, choosing instead to leave the matter to the courts.[35]

Regarding the burden of *persuasion*, the general rule is that the prosecution must prove every "element" of an offense beyond a reasonable doubt.[36] The term "element" as used in the Code, however, includes conduct that "negatives an excuse or justification" for the action.[37] That is, the Model Penal Code allocates to the prosecution the duty to disprove defenses, assuming that the defendant has satisfied her burden of production. However, this rule does not apply to defenses that the Code expressly requires the defendant to prove by a preponderance of the evidence.[38]

---

[34] Model Penal Code § 1.12(2)(a).

[35] American Law Institute, Comment to § 1.12, at 193.

[36] Model Penal Code § 1.12(1).

[37] Model Penal Code § 1.13(9)(c).

[38] *E.g.*, Model Penal Code § 2.13 (the defense of entrapment).

Chapter 8

PRESUMPTIONS

§ 8.01 THE NATURE OF A PRESUMPTION[1]

Assume that murder is defined by statute as the "unlawful and intentional killing of a human being by another human being." The prosecutor must prove beyond a reasonable doubt that: (1) a human being was killed; (2) the defendant was the killer; (3) the defendant intended to take a human life; and (4) the killing was unlawful.

Sometimes, a prosecutor will find it difficult to prove an element of an offense. For example, it might be hard to prove the third element — the defendant's subjective intent to kill — in a prosecution based on the hypothetical murder statute. Assume, therefore, that in order to prove that D intended to kill V, the prosecutor introduces evidence that D picked up a loaded gun, pointed it in V's direction, and fired it. Has the prosecutor proved the requisite intent beyond a reasonable doubt? Perhaps so, but perhaps not: depending on the context, it may appear, for example, that D intended only to frighten or wound V.

Suppose, however, that a legislature or court establishes the following rule: "Whenever it is proved in a criminal trial that a person fired a loaded gun at another person, the factfinder must [or, perhaps, "may"] presume that the actor intended to kill the other person."

This rule establishes a presumption. Presumptions operate in the following manner: Upon proof of Fact (or set of facts) A, a factfinder must (or "may," depending on the language of the instruction) presume Fact B. In the nomenclature of presumptions, Fact A is the *basic* fact, and Fact B is the *presumed* fact. Usually, although not always, the presumed fact in a criminal prosecution is an element of the crime charged. In our hypothetical, the presumption requires (or permits) the jury to presume intent to kill (Fact B) upon proof that D fired a loaded gun at V (Fact A).[2]

If a jury is instructed that it *must* presume Fact B upon proof of basic Fact A, the presumption is a "mandatory presumption." If the jury is told that it *may*, but need not, presume Fact B, the instruction is called a "permissive presumption."

---

[1] *See generally* Ronald J. Allen, *Structuring Jury Decisionmaking in Criminal Cases: A Unified Constitutional Approach to Evidentiary Devices*, 94 Harv. L. Rev. 321 (1980); Charles R. Nesson, *Reasonable Doubt and Permissive Inferences: The Value of Complexity*, 92 Harv. L. Rev. 1187 (1979).

[2] Of course, the basic fact here is actually a set of facts: (1) that the weapon used was a gun (rather than some other weapon); (2) that it was loaded; (3) that D aimed it at V; and (4) that D fired it. If one of these facts is not proved, the presumption does not apply.

The practical effect of presumptions, especially those of a mandatory nature, is to make it easier for the party with the burden of proof — typically, the prosecutor — to persuade the factfinder regarding the issue in question. It is not necessarily improper for the legislature or a court to make the prosecutor's job easier in this manner. At times, however, a presumption runs counter to constitutional protections of the defendant.

§ 8.02 MANDATORY PRESUMPTIONS

[A] Rebuttable Presumptions

A mandatory rebuttable presumption requires a finding of the presumed fact upon proof of the basic fact, unless that finding is rebutted by the opposing party. Essentially, in a criminal trial, the jury is instructed regarding a presumption that "if the State proves Fact A, then you must find Fact B, unless the defendant disproves Fact B by a preponderance [or some other quantum] of the evidence."

The procedural effect of a mandatory rebuttable presumption is to shift to the defendant the burden of persuasion regarding the presumed fact, upon proof by the prosecution of the basic fact. Applying this presumption to the example described in Section 8.01, the jury would be required to find that D intended to kill V [Fact B] if the prosecution proved that D fired a loaded gun at V [Fact A], unless D disproved his intent to kill by a preponderance of the evidence.

Rebuttable mandatory presumptions are unconstitutional when the presumed fact is an element of the crime charged. For example, in *Sandstrom v. Montana*,[3] S was charged with "deliberate homicide," that is, that S "purposely or knowingly caused the death" of V. At trial, S admitted that he killed V, but he denied that he did so purposely or knowingly. At the conclusion of the trial, the judge instructed the jury that "the law presumes that a person intends the natural and probable consequences of his voluntary acts." As the Supreme Court explained the effect of this presumption, "upon proof by the State of the slaying, and of additional facts not themselves establishing the element of intent, the burden was shifted to the defendant to prove that he lacked the requisite mental state." The Court held that the presumption was unconstitutional. By shifting to S the burden of proof regarding his mental state, the presumption "conflict[ed] with the overriding presumption of innocence with which the law endows the accused and which extends to every element of the crime."

Similarly, in a prosecution for theft of a rented car, it is unconstitutional to charge the jury that "intent to commit theft by fraud is presumed if one who has leased or rented the personal property of another pursuant to a written contract fails to return the . . . property . . . within 20 days." By shifting the burden of proof regarding intent, this instruction "subvert[s] the presumption of innocence accorded to accused persons."[4]

---

[3] 442 U.S. 510 (1979).

[4] Carella v. California, 491 U.S. 263, 265 (1989) (*per curiam*).

A mandatory rebuttable presumption is not saved by the requirement that the prosecution prove the basic fact beyond a reasonable doubt. In the hypothetical case described in Section 8.01, even if *D* undoubtedly fired a loaded gun at *V*, this does not necessarily prove beyond a reasonable doubt that he intended to kill *V*. *D* may have believed that the gun was unloaded, or he may have intended to fire in the direction of, but purposely miss, *V*, in order to frighten him. Yet, pursuant to the presumption, the jury would be required to find the element of the offense, unless *D* disproved his intent to kill. The Constitution does not permit this, because the presumption "invade[s] the truth-finding task assigned solely to juries in criminal cases."[5]

[B]   Irrebuttable ("Conclusive") Presumptions

An irrebuttable or conclusive presumption requires the jury to find the presumed fact upon proof of the basic fact, even if the opposing party introduces rebutting evidence. For example, a jury might be charged that "upon proof that *D* fired a loaded gun at *V*, you *must* find that *D* intended to kill *V*."

True irrebuttable presumptions are hard to find in the criminal law. However, occasionally a judge will instruct the jury regarding a *rebuttable* presumption in language that could cause a reasonable juror to believe that it is irrebuttable, in which case an appellate court will treat it as such. A mandatory irrebuttable presumption pertaining to an element of an offense is unconstitutional for the same reasons that mandatory rebuttable ones are impermissible.[6]

§ 8.03   PERMISSIVE PRESUMPTIONS ("INFERENCES")

A permissive presumption is one in which the fact finder may, but need not, find the existence of the presumed fact upon proof of the basic fact.

A permissive presumption is not a true presumption. It is more accurately described as an "inference." An inference is not a rule that *formally* shifts the burden of proof from one party to another, as a true presumption does. Rather, an inference is a (hopefully) logical bridge between one fact believed to be true and a second fact, the truth of which is at issue. For example, a New Jersey homicide statute provides that, in prosecution of a driver for recklessly causing a death in his automobile, "[p]roof that the defendant was operating a hand-held wireless telephone while driving a motor vehicle . . . may give rise to an inference that the defendant was driving recklessly."[7] Here, a jury "may" infer Fact B (recklessness) from proof of Fact A (operating a cell phone while driving), if the jury chooses to cross the inferential bridge from Fact A to Fact B, but it need not do so.

Because permissive presumptions, or inferences, do not formally affect the prosecution's constitutional obligation to prove every element of an offense beyond

---

[5] *Id.*

[6] *Sandstrom v. Montana*, 442 U.S. at 521–24.

[7] N.J. § 2C:11-5 (2015) ("Death by Vehicular Homicide").

a reasonable doubt, they are not unconstitutional per se.[8] Nonetheless, an inference is constitutionally impermissible if there is no rational connection between the basic fact and the presumed (inferred) fact. As the Court explained in *Tot v. United States*,[9] "where the inference [created] is so strained as not to have a reasonable relation to the circumstances of life as we know them," the fact-finding process is rendered unreliable, and the defendant is denied due process of law.

An inference is rational if, but only if, the presumed fact more likely than not flows from the basic fact.[10] For example, an appellate court held that a trial judge should not have instructed the jury that it could infer criminal recklessness upon proof that the defendant drove slightly in excess of the maximum lawful speed limit.[11] In these circumstances, the inferred fact did not more likely than not flow from the basic fact. On the other hand, it is rational, and therefore permissible, for a jury to infer that "any person who enters or remains unlawfully in a building . . . [has the] intent to commit a crime . . . therein."[12]

The constitutionality of a permissive presumption often depends on the particular facts of the case. For example, in *County Court of Ulster County v. Allen*,[13] the Supreme Court upheld an instruction to the jury that permitted it to infer from presence of two firearms in an automobile that all four car occupants were in illegal possession of the weapons. In the case, two very heavy, large-caliber handguns were positioned crosswise in the open handbag belonging to a 16-year-old female occupant. The bag was either on the front seat or front floor of the car that contained her and three adult males.

The Supreme Court held that, as applied to the facts of this case, the inference of constructive possession by the four defendants was rationally based. As the weapons were heavy, large, and in full view, the Court reasoned that it was more likely than not true that the youth was not solely responsible for their presence in her purse. More likely that not, the Court said, each of the adult male occupants could exercise control over the weapons, and therefore were also in constructive possession of them. If the evidence at trial had been different — for example, if one of the occupants had been a hitchhiker — the inference of possession by this casual occupant might not have withstood analysis. Or, if the weapons in this case had been small and concealed in the girl's purse, the inference of possession by the adult males might not have satisfied the more-likely-than-not test.

---

[8] County Court of Ulster County v. Allen, 442 U.S. 140, 157 (1979).

[9] 319 U.S. 463 (1943).

[10] *Ulster County*, 442 U.S. at 165.

[11] Hanna v. Riveland, 87 F.3d 1034 (9th Cir. 1996); *see also* McDowell v. State, 885 N.E.2d 1260 (Ind. 2008) (*D* stabbed *V* in neck; *V* died six days later of asphyxiation; judge instructed jury that it could infer intent to kill from "evidence that a mortal wound was inflicted upon an unarmed person with a deadly weapon"; held: based on the facts of this case, the instruction violated *D*'s rights by improperly shifting the burden of proof on intent).

[12] State v. Brunson, 905 P.2d 346 (Wash. 1995).

[13] 442 U.S. 140 (1979).

§ 8.04   MODEL PENAL CODE

The Model Penal Code does not recognize mandatory presumptions. The drafters of the Code took the position that when a legislature wishes to allocate to the defendant the burden of persuasion regarding a particular issue, it should do so directly by recognizing an affirmative defense, and expressly requiring the defendant to establish the facts pertaining to the defense by the preponderance of the evidence.[14]

The Code permits *permissive* presumptions (inferences) regarding elements of criminal offenses. Such presumptions, when established by the legislature, affect a criminal trial in two procedural ways. First, if any evidence of the basic fact is presented at trial, the issue of the existence of the presumed fact — *i.e.*, the element of the crime — must be submitted to the jury unless, in the language of the Code, the trial judge is "satisfied that the evidence as a whole clearly negatives the presumed fact."[15] In essence, the permissive presumption is triggered unless the presumption is so lacking in foundation that the defendant is entitled to a directed verdict on the matter.

Second, assuming that the permissive presumption is not irrational, the Model Code requires the judge to instruct the jury that the element at issue must still be proved by the prosecutor beyond a reasonable doubt, but that the law permits it to regard the basic facts as sufficient evidence of the presumed fact.[16] Thus, with the hypothetical considered in Section 8.01, if the prosecutor introduced evidence that D fired a loaded gun at V, the jury would be instructed (assuming that the inference has a rational foundation) that the prosecutor must prove beyond a reasonable doubt that D intended to kill V, but that the law allows the jury, if it chooses, to treat proof of the fact that D fired the loaded gun at V as adequate evidence to meet the prosecutor's burden of persuasion on the matter of D's mental state.

---

[14] American Law Institute, Comment to § 1.12 at 203. *See* § 7.04, *supra.*

[15] Model Penal Code § 1.12(5)(a).

[16] Model Penal Code § 1.12(5)(b).

Chapter 9

ACTUS REUS

§ 9.01 *ACTUS REUS*: GENERAL PRINCIPLES[1]

[A] Definition

Generally speaking, crimes have two components: the *"actus reus,"* the physical or external portion of the crime; and the *"mens rea,"* the mental or internal feature.[2] The concept of *"actus reus"* is the focus of this chapter.

The term *"actus reus"* reportedly was not generally used by scholars in criminal law treatises prior to the 20th century,[3] but it has found currency in modern Anglo-American jurisprudence. Unfortunately, there is no single accepted definition.

As used in this text, the term *"actus reus"* generally includes three ingredients of a crime, which can be encapsulated in a single sentence: The *actus reus* of an offense generally consists of (1) a voluntary act;[4] (2) that causes; (3) social harm.[5] For example, if *A* picks up a knife and stabs *B*, killing *B*, the *actus reus* of a criminal homicide has occurred: *A* has performed a *voluntary act* (stabbing *B*) that *caused B*'s death (the *social harm*). As is developed in this chapter, "voluntary act" and "social harm" are legal terms of art that require special attention. The element of causation, which links the defendant's voluntary act to the social harm, is discussed in Chapter 14.[6]

---

[1] *See generally* Michael S. Moore, Act and Crime: The Philosophy of Action and Its Implications for Criminal Law (1993); Paul H. Robinson, *Should the Criminal Law Abandon the Actus Reus-Mens Rea Distinction?, in* Action and Value in Criminal Law 187 (Stephen Shute, et al., eds., 1993); Albin Eser, *The Principle of "Harm" in the Concept of Crime: A Comparative Analysis of the Criminally Protected Legal Interests,* 4 Duq. L. Rev. 345 (1965).

[2] People v. Likine, 823 N.W.2d 50, 65 (Mich. 2012); Ramirez-Memije, 444 S.W.3d 624, 627 (Tex. Crim. App. 2014).

[3] Jerome Hall, General Principles of Criminal Law 222 (2d ed. 1960).

[4] In exceptional circumstances, failure to perform an act — an omission — will serve as the basis for criminal responsibility, *i.e.,* as a substitute for a voluntary act. *See* §§ 9.06–9.08, *infra.*

[5] Eser, Note 1, *supra,* at 386.

[6] Warning: Because *"actus reus"* has no universally accepted meaning, some courts and commentators use the term more narrowly than is suggested in this text, simply to describe the defendant's conduct (in the example given, the voluntary acts of picking up the knife and stabbing *B*) or the result of that conduct (the social harm of *B*'s death), rather than a combination thereof.

[B] Punishing Thoughts: Why Not?

Suppose that three people separately would like the President of the United States to die: *A* fantasizes killing the President; *B*, intending to kill the President, devises a mental plan to commit the offense, but goes no further; and *C* actually kills the President. A society might plausibly punish all three persons. *A* would be punished for her morally objectionable fantasy; *B* would be punished for mentally devising her wrongful plan; and *C* would be punished for acting out her intentions. In Anglo-American criminal law, however, only *C* is punishable, as "[t]he reach of the criminal law has long been limited by the principle that no one is punishable for his thoughts."[7]

Reasons of pragmatism and principle justify the non-criminalization of mere thoughts. On a pragmatic level, the requirement of conduct is "[r]ooted in skepticism about the ability . . . to know what passes through the minds of men."[8] We often have difficulty accurately reconstructing our own thoughts, much less "reading" another person's mind.

But, suppose that we *could* read another person's mind? Suppose that the government implanted an electrode in every infant's brain at birth or used "precogs"[9] to read our thoughts or see the future with perfect clarity. Even if this were possible, punishment for thoughts alone would be objectionable to persons living in a free society. Virtually all people, most of whom are entirely law-abiding, occasionally hope harm will befall another or (like *A*) even fantasize personally causing harm to others. A society that would invade mental privacy in this manner to punish for idle thoughts would be an intolerable place to live.[10]

But, what about *B*? Many people have momentary antisocial thoughts or fantasies, but very few actually devise a plan of criminal action. On its face, a rule that allows *B* to escape punishment seems counter-utilitarian. For various reasons, however, *B*'s punishment would be unacceptable. First, precogs aside, there is no reliable way to distinguish "between desires of the day-dream variety and fixed intentions that may pose a real threat to society."[11]

Second, in a society such as ours that values individual freedom, use of the criminal law should be limited to situations in which harm is seriously threatened,

---

[7] United States v. Muzii, 676 F.2d 919, 920 (2d Cir. 1982); *see* Proctor v. State, 176 P. 771, 773 (Okla. Crim. App. 1918) ("Guilty intention, unexecuted or unconnected with an overt act . . . [is not] the subject of punishment.") (quoting Ex Parte Smith, 36 S.W. 628 (Mo. 1896)). The English Statute of 1351 punished "compassing [devising] the death of the King," but even this statute was interpreted to require an overt act. George Fletcher, Rethinking Criminal Law 207–13 (1978).

[8] Abraham S. Goldstein, *Conspiracy to Defraud the United States*, 68 Yale L.J. 405, 405 (1959).

[9] *See* Philip K. Dick, *The Minority Report, in* The Minority Report and Other Classic Stories (2002) (in which psychics — "precogs" — could see future acts, specifically, crimes not yet committed); Minority Report (Dream Works 2002) (movie directed by Steven Spielberg based on the short story). For more on the criminal law implications of the world described by Dick, see Robert Batey, *Minority Report and the Law of Attempts*, 1 Ohio St. J. Crim. L. 689 (2004).

[10] 2 James Fitzjames Stephen, A History of the Criminal Law in England 78 (1883) ("If [the law] were not so restricted it would be utterly intolerable; all mankind would be criminals, and most of their lives would be passed in trying and punishing each other.").

[11] Powell v. Texas, 392 U.S. 514, 543 (1968) (Black & Harlan, JJ., concurring).

and not simply "to purify thoughts and perfect character."[12] We should leave character perfection to parents, religious institutions, and/or schools. Respect for individual liberties, therefore, requires that the criminal law be enforced only in response to conduct.

Finally, and perhaps most basically, the *actus reus* requirement — the refusal to punish for thoughts alone — is premised on the retributive belief that it is morally wrong to punish people for unacted-upon intentions. Retributive theory justifies punishment of those who freely choose to harm others; the corollary of this is that society must give each person some breathing space, *i.e.*, the opportunity to choose to desist from planned wrongful activity. To a retributivist, voluntary conduct serves as a minimum precondition for the infliction of punishment.

§ 9.02 VOLUNTARY ACT: GENERAL PRINCIPLES[13]

[A] General Rule

Subject to a few limited and controversial exceptions,[14] a person is not guilty of a crime unless her conduct includes a voluntary act. Few statutes defining criminal offenses expressly provide for this requirement. Nonetheless, the voluntary act requirement has common law support, modern courts usually treat it as an essential, albeit implicit, element of criminal statutes,[15] and an increasing number of states now include a general statutory provision, cast in terms similar to the Model Penal Code, that sets out this requirement.[16]

For analytical purposes the voluntary act rule may be separated into two components, the "act" and its "voluntary" nature.

---

[12] United States v. Hollingsworth, 27 F.3d 1196, 1203 (7th Cir. 1994) (en banc).

[13] *See generally* Larry Alexander, *Reconsidering the Relationship Among Voluntary Acts, Strict Liability, and Negligence in Criminal Law*, Soc. Phil. & Pol'y, Spring 1990, at 84; Deborah W. Denno, *Crime and Consciousness: Science and Involuntary Acts*, 87 Minn. L. Rev. 269 (2002); Ian P. Farrell & Justin F. Marceau, *Taking Voluntariness Seriously*, 54 B.C. L. Rev. 1545 (2013); Douglas Husak, *Rethinking the Act Requirement*, 28 Cardozo L. Rev. 2437 (2007); Michael S. Moore, *Responsibility and the Unconscious*, 53 S. Cal. L. Rev. 1563 (1980); Kevin W. Saunders, *Voluntary Acts and the Criminal Law: Justifying Culpability Based on the Existence of Volition*, 49 U. Pitt. L. Rev. 443 (1988); A.P. Simester, *On the So-Called Requirement for Voluntary Action*, 1 Buff. Crim. L. Rev. 403 (1998).

[14] *See* §§ 9.06–9.07, *infra*.

[15] This is true even when an offense seemingly does not require a voluntary act. *E.g.*, Martin v. State, 17 So. 2d 427 (Ala. Ct. App. 1944) (*M* was charged with violation of an offense that provided that "[a]ny person who, while intoxicated or drunk, appears in any public place . . . and manifests a drunken condition [shall be convicted of an offense]"; the court interpreted the word "appears" to presuppose a voluntary appearance in public, which was not proven at *M*'s trial); United States v. Macias, 740 F.3d 96 (2d Cir. 2014) (federal statute makes it a crime to be "found" in the U.S. without permission; *M*, a Honduras citizen, was in the U.S. unlawfully, voluntarily left the U.S. and entered Canada, and was then deported back to the U.S., where he was "found"; held: the term "found" requires proof that *M* voluntarily entered the country); *see also* Farrell & Marceau, Note 13, *supra*, at 1558 ("a voluntary act is an essential implied element of every crime").

[16] Model Penal Code § 2.01. *See* § 9.05, *infra*.

[B] The "Act"

For purposes of the *actus reus* requirement, an "act" is, simply, a bodily movement, a muscular contraction.[17] A person "acts" when she pulls the trigger of a gun, raises her arm, blinks her eyes, turns the ignition key in an automobile, or simply puts one leg in the front of the other to walk. Understood this way, an act involves *physical*, although not necessarily *visible*, behavior. For example, the muscular contractions involved in talking — the movements of the vocal chords and tongue — constitute "acts" for present purposes. However, the term "act" *excludes* the internal mental processes of thinking about, or of developing an intention to do, a physical act (*e.g.*, "mental acts").

Three aspects of the term "act" should be noted here. First, sometimes there can be bodily movement, but really no "act" at all by the person whose body has moved. For example, if *A* grabs *B*'s arm and swings it into *C*'s body, *B* has not acted (voluntarily or involuntarily), although her arm has moved. In this case, *B*'s arm was simply propelled, like a leaf blown by the wind, as the result of *A*'s act of grabbing her arm.

Second, the term "act" does *not* apply to the *results* of a person's bodily movements. For example, suppose that *D*, intending to kill *V*, places dynamite around *V*'s house, where *V* is asleep, and then activates a detonator that causes an explosion, killing *V*. In a criminal homicide prosecution, the pertinent acts by *D* are the positioning of the dynamite around *V*'s house and her activation of the detonator. The term "act," however, does *not* include the result of *D*'s acts, *i.e.*, *V*'s death. The latter constitutes the "social harm" element of the *actus reus*.[18]

Third, some courts and many scholars contend that, to be an "act" — or, more specifically, a human act — the muscular contraction must itself be voluntarily performed (as defined below). As one court put it, "[a]n [involuntary] 'act'. . . is in reality no act at all. It is merely a physical event . . . ."[19] Most modern lawyers and the Model Penal Code,[20] however, use the term "act" as it is defined in this subsection, as a bodily movement that is voluntarily *or* involuntarily performed, as these terms are discussed immediately below.

[C] "Voluntary"

Unfortunately, the word "voluntary" is used by criminal lawyers in two different senses. The two usages of the term are often confused. It is important to be able to distinguish between these two usages.

---

[17] Oliver Wendell Holmes, The Common Law 54 (1881).

[18] *See* § 9.10, *infra.*

[19] State v. Utter, 479 P.2d 946, 950 (Wash. Ct. App. 1971).

[20] *See* § 9.05, *infra.*

[1]   Broad Meaning: In the Context of Defenses

The terms "voluntary" and "involuntary" are often used by lawyers and courts in discussing criminal law defenses to express the general conclusion that the defendant possessed or lacked sufficient free choice to be blamed for her conduct.[21] Thus, it is sometimes said that a person who acted under duress (*e.g.*, commits a crime because a loaded gun is pointed at her child's head) or as the result of a mental disorder acted "involuntarily." This simply means that because the actor faced an extremely hard choice (duress) or was irrational (insane), she does not deserve to be punished for her actions. This is *not* how the term "involuntary" is used in the context of the *actus reus* requirement, the topic of this chapter.

[2]   Narrow Meaning: In the Context of the *Actus Reus*

The term "voluntary" has a much narrower meaning when used to determine whether the *actus reus* of an offense has occurred. Nineteenth century scholar John Austin defined a "voluntary act" in this sense as a "movement of the body which follows our volition."[22] Similarly, Holmes described it as a "willed" contraction of a muscle.[23]

What did Austin mean by "volition," or Holmes by a "willed" act? Austin posited a view of human behavior, in which a person consciously decides to move a part of the body, and then that part of the body "invariably and immediately [follows] our wishes or desires for those same movements."[24] Applying this definition, nearly all human acts are voluntary,[25] and thus it may be more useful to give examples of *involuntary* acts. Examples of these include reflexive actions, spasms, seizures and convulsions, and bodily movements while the actor is unconscious[26] or asleep.[27]

Austin's explanation of volition is too simplistic. Today, we realize that bodily movements occur as the result of complicated physiological and psychological mechanisms, many of which are not fully understood even now. However, no human act occurs simply as the result of wishing it to take place.[28] A person receives stimuli

---

[21]   Fletcher, Note 7, *supra*, at 803.

[22]   1 John Austin, Lectures on Jurisprudence 426 (3d ed. 1869).

[23]   Holmes, Note 17, *supra*, at 54.

[24]   Austin, Note 22, *supra*, at 426 (emphasis omitted).

[25]   Notice that if *X* points a gun at *D* and threatens to kill her unless she shoots *V*, *D*'s coerced act of pulling the trigger of a gun to shoot *V* is "voluntary" in the Austinian sense, although it is arguably "involuntary" in the broader sense described in subsection [1], *supra*.

[26]   The claim of unconsciousness is sometimes described as "automatism."

[27]   People v. Likine, 823 N.W.2d 50, 65–66 (Mich. 2012); *e.g.*, State v. Jones, 527 S.E.2d 700 (N.C. Ct. App. 2000) (*J* suffered from REM sleep disorder; while asleep on various occasions he kicked a wall, kicked a bedpost, and in this case, picked up a gun and shot his wife; these facts, if proven, demonstrated a lack of a voluntary act); State v. Newman, 302 P.3d 435 (Or. 2013) ("sleep driving" — driving an automobile while in an unconscious state — is involuntary conduct); People v. Nelson, 2 N.E.3d 613 (Ill. App. Ct. 2013) (*N* was charged with telephone harassment; *N* suffered from Tourette's Syndrome; according to unrebutted expert testimony, *N*'s harassing calls were the result of a "complex tic" over which he had no bodily control; held: conviction reversed).

[28]   Denno, Note 13, *supra*, at 326 ("Some of the most powerful research in neuroscience suggests that the unconscious may be in charge of how human beings make decisions about willed movements, such as

from outside and from within herself, which themselves act as further stimuli, some of which ultimately produce electrical impulses from the brain that result in bodily movements.[29]

So, what does it *really* mean to say that a person may not be punished unless her conduct includes a voluntary — "willed" — act? The concept of volition is tied to the notion that criminal law responsibility should only attach to those who are accountable for their actions in a very personal way. As Professor Sanford Kadish has explained, the criminal law distinguishes

> between genuine human actions, which are susceptible of praise and blame, and mere events brought about by physical causes which happen to involve a human body. . . . When a person claims the involuntary-act defense he is conceding that his own body made the motion but denies responsibility for it.[30]

Professor Kadish's point can be seen if one considers the difference in meaning of the following two sentences: (1) "I raised my arm"; and (2) "My arm came up."[31] Both statements suggest that bodily movement has occurred. Yet, the difference in language expresses our understanding of the difference between a voluntary act (sentence (1)) and an involuntary one (sentence (2)). In both cases, the arm movement was the result of impulses from the actor's brain. But, in the first sentence, the implication is that the act was the result of something more than mere physiological brain activity. That extra "something" was the more sophisticated thought process that goes into the decision — the choice — to raise one's arm. Put slightly differently, a voluntary act involves the use of the human *mind*; an involuntary act involves the use of the human *brain*, without the aid of the mind.[32] With a voluntary act, a human being — a person — and not simply an organ of a human being, causes the bodily action.

Thus, when *D*'s arm strikes *V* as the result of an epileptic seizure, we sense that *D*'s *body*, but not *D* the person, has caused the impact. In the context of the criminal law, the movement of *D*'s arm is conceptually the same as a tree branch bending in the wind and striking *V*. When *D* "wills" her arm to move, however, we feel that *D*, and not simply her arm, is responsible for *V*'s injury. Her "acting self" is implicated. A personal, human agency is involved in causing the bodily contact.[33] Another way of making this point is to say, as H.L.A. Hart has put it, that involuntary acts are "inappropriate" actions, *i.e.*, they are bodily movements not "required for any action . . . which the agent believed himself to be doing." They are "wild" acts, "not 'governed by the will' in the sense that they are not subordinated to the agent's

---

choosing when to flex a wrist, bend a figure, or . . . even to fire a gun.").

[29] D. O'Connor, *The Voluntary Act*, 15 Med. Sci. L. 31, 32 (1975).

[30] Sanford H. Kadish, *Excusing Crime*, 75 Cal. L. Rev. 257, 259 (1987).

[31] Ludwig Wittgenstein, Philosophical Investigations 161 (G. Anscombe trans., 3d ed. 1958) ("[W]hat is left over if I subtract the fact that my arm goes up from the fact that I raise my arm?").

[32] *See* Bratty v. Attorney-General, [1963] A.C. 386, 409 (House of Lords) (an involuntary act is one "which is done by the muscles without any control by the mind").

[33] Moore, Note 13, *supra*, at 1576.

conscious plans of action."[34]

One should be careful not to assume that an act is, legally speaking, involuntary simply because the actor is unaware of what she is doing while she is doing it. For example, people act habitually: A chain-smoker may light up a cigarette "without thinking"; a driver coming home from work may change lanes on the freeway at precisely the same place each day, without even noticing that she is doing this. Although, at our best, we are aware of both our external and internal (mental) surroundings, sometimes we "don't notice that [we] notice. . . . [We are] aware of everything except [ourselves]."[35] In this sense, consciousness is a matter of degree,[36] and the law treats habitual acts as falling on the voluntary side of the continuum.

[3] "Voluntariness": At the Controversial Edges

[a] Hypnotism

Suppose that X hypnotizes D to immediately shoot and kill V, or suppose that X uses post-hypnotic suggestion to cause D to kill V. When D shoots V, is she acting "voluntarily" in the narrow (*actus reus*) sense of the term?

Depending on our ultimate understanding of how hypnotism works upon the human mind, D's acts might be classified as involuntary. The thought to kill V was planted in D's mind by X. If D lacked the ability to disregard X's "suggestions" — a matter of considerable dispute[37] — one may view D as little more than a marionette whose strings were pulled by X. The hypnotized subject might be equated to a sleepwalker, whose acts *are* considered legally involuntary.

A very plausible case, however, can be developed for the proposition that acts under hypnosis or as the result of hypnotic suggestion are voluntary. After all, in the hypnosis example, D *did* "will" her finger to pull the trigger of the gun. Although this "willed" act was in response to hypnotist X's suggestion, it is difficult to draw a principled line between this situation and that of a "weak-willed" person *not* under hypnosis who submits "blindly" to the suggestions of a far more dominant personality. It may be better — and more consistent with our assumptions about human free will — to recognize the acts of the hypnotized subject as voluntary (in the narrow sense under discussion), and deal with her culpability, if any, as a potential excusing defense.[38]

---

[34] H.L.A. Hart, Punishment and Responsibility 105 (1968).

[35] Leo Katz, Bad Acts and Guilty Minds 120 (1987).

[36] Denno, Note 13, *supra* (controversially arguing that the law should recognize voluntary, involuntary, and "semi-voluntary" acts).

[37] Early and conflicting scientific evidence in this regard is summarized in Ernest R. Hilgard, *Hypnosis*, 26 Ann. Rev. Psychol. 19 (1975); *see also* Renzo Carlo Lanfranco et al., *Hypnotic Suggestion: A Test for the Voluntary Action Problem*, 5 Cognitive Neuroscience 209 (2014).

[38] In the textual discussion, the hypnotist has introduced the suggestion in D that she commit an *act* — kill X. A related issue occurs when a person implants a *belief* in another person (*e.g.*, that X deserves to be killed), who thereafter acts on the basis of that implanted belief. This is sometimes discussed in terms of "brainwashing." *See* Richard Delgado, *Ascription of Criminal States of Mind: Toward a*

[b]   Multiple Personality (or Dissociative Identity) Disorder[39]

As explained in subsection [2], a voluntary act involves the use of the mind, and not simply of the brain. But, is it possible for more than one mind to inhabit a single brain?[40] William James reported[41] that in 1811 a melancholy Pennsylvania woman fell into a profound sleep from which she could not be awakened, and woke up 18 hours later as a "different person," with an exuberant personality and no memory of her past. Five weeks later, after another deep sleep, her old personality returned. This woman may have suffered from what has been described as "multiple personality disorder" (MPD), and is now called "dissociative identity disorder" (DID), a recognized mental disease.[42]

A person suffering from DID may be insane, but the condition, in a strange way, arguably implicates the voluntary act requirement. For example, in *State v. Grimsley*,[43] G (Robin Grimsley), who suffered from this disorder, drove an automobile under the influence of alcohol while she was dissociated from her primary personality. G introduced psychiatric evidence that she had a secondary personality, "Jennifer," who had a drinking problem, which personality was in control when G was in the automobile. As a consequence, she argued that *she*, Robin, was unconscious while "Jennifer" was acting. The court flatly rejected G's reasoning. It stated:

> There was only one person driving the car and only one person accused of drunken driving. It is immaterial whether she was in one state of consciousness or another, so long as in the personality then controlling her behavior, she was conscious and her actions were a product of her own volition.

However, who is the "her" in the phrase "product of her own volition"? Robin and Jennifer had separate identities; Jennifer did not think of herself as Robin, or vice-versa. With separate memories, separate feelings, and separate characters, can we genuinely treat G as a single volitional agent? Although extremely few courts have confronted this question, *Grimsley*'s approach is typical. As another court that has confronted the issue has put the matter, "we will not begin to parcel criminal accountability out among the various inhabitants of the mind."[44]

Defense Theory for the Coercively Persuaded ("Brainwashed") Defendant, 63 Minn. L. Rev. 1 (1978) (favoring a criminal law defense); and Joshua Dressler, *Professor Delgado's "Brainwashing" Defense: Courting a Determinist Legal System*, 63 Minn. L. Rev. 335 (1979) (critiquing Delgado's analysis).

[39] *See generally* Elyn R. Saks, Jekyll on Trial: Multiple Personality Disorder and Criminal Law (1997).

[40] *See* Katz, Note 35, *supra*, at 104.

[41] William James, The Principles of Psychology 359–63 (1981).

[42] American Psychiatric Association, Diagnostic and Statistical Manual of Mental Disorders 292 (V 2013).

[43] 444 N.E.2d 1071 (Ohio Ct. App. 1982).

[44] Kirkland v. State, 304 S.E.2d 561, 564 (Ga. Ct. App. 1983).

[D]   Voluntary Act Requirement: Rationale

Why should a person whose involuntary act causes harm to another escape punishment? One frequent explanation is that the law cannot deter involuntary movement.[45]

This utilitarian explanation is insufficient. Although the *threat* of punishment cannot deter a person while she is acting involuntarily (*e.g.*, during a seizure), it can motivate her to adjust her behavior in the first place (*e.g.*, if she is prone to seizures, she can be motivated to take medication or not use dangerous instrumentalities), so as to reduce the risk to others from her involuntary conduct. Moreover, even if the *threat* of the criminal sanction cannot deter, its *use* is one rational way to segregate (or in some other manner render less dangerous) those prone to repeated involuntary acts. To a utilitarian lawmaker, whose overall goal is to protect society from dangerous people, the criminal justice system is "simply another method of social control."[46] That is, the line between civil commitment and criminal punishment is blurry, at best, in a purely utilitarian system of laws,[47] so there is no reason categorically to exclude liability for involuntary actions.

The voluntary act requirement is far more closely linked to the retributivist's respect for human autonomy. Retributive theory is premised on the view that "the critical distinction between criminal law and other systems of confinement . . . is that the criminal sanction carries with it something more — the stigmatization of moral blameworthiness."[48] Criminal punishment, with its attendant pain, stigma, and formal condemnation of the offender, should only be imposed on those who deserve it, *i.e.*, on those who act as the result of free choice. In the absence of a voluntary act, there is no basis for social censure and loss of liberty.

[E]   Burden of Proof

There is serious dispute regarding whether "involuntariness" — claims of seizure, acts during unconsciousness, and the like — should be characterized as a "defense." Courts frequently describe it as a defense, "much like claims of . . . insanity."[49] To the extent that the word "involuntariness" is used in the broad sense of the term,[50] this characterization is perfectly appropriate. However, omissions aside,[51] a "voluntary act" (in the narrow, *actus reus*, sense of the term) *should be understood to be an essential element of every criminal offense.*[52] Involuntariness

---

[45] American Law Institute, Comment to § 2.01, at 214–15.

[46] Richard Singer, *The Resurgence of Mens Rea: II — Honest but Unreasonable Mistake of Fact in Self Defense*, 28 B.C. L. Rev. 459, 512 n.285 (1987).

[47] Herbert L. Packer, The Limits of the Criminal Sanction 77–78 (1968).

[48] Singer, Note 46, *supra*, at 512 n.285.

[49] State v. Deer, 287 P.3d 539, 542 (Wash. 2012); *see also*, People v. Newton, 8 Cal. App. 3d 359, 376 (Ct. App. 1970); People v. Grant, 377 N.E.2d 4, 7 (Ill. 1978); Fulcher v. State, 633 P.2d 142, 145 (Wyo. 1981) (all describing claims of involuntariness as a "defense").

[50] *See* § 9.02[C][1], *supra*.

[51] *See* § 9.07, *infra*.

[52] Farrell & Marceau, Note 13, *supra*, at 1558.

— the other side of the coin of voluntariness — should *not* be considered an affirmative defense.

This distinction — that a voluntary act is an element of a criminal offense, rather than that involuntariness is a defense — is procedurally significant. Under the Due Process Clause, the government must prove beyond a reasonable doubt every element of an offense, but it is not constitutionally required to carry the burden of persuasion regarding affirmative defenses, such as insanity.[53] Jurisdictions that treat claims of involuntariness as an affirmative defense, therefore, improperly require the defendant who asserts such a claim (*e.g.*, a seizure), to carry the burden of persuasion regarding this fact. As long as one understands, however, that a voluntary act is an essential element of every offense, it follows that the prosecution is required to prove beyond a reasonable doubt that the defendant's conduct was *not* involuntary — *i.e.*, that her conduct included a voluntary act.[54] Put simply, properly understood, the rule ought to be that "involuntariness" is *not* like a claim of insanity.[55]

[F] The Issue of "Time-Framing"[56]

As explained in this chapter section, a person is not ordinarily guilty of an offense in the absence of a voluntary act. The prosecution does not need to show, however, that *every* act, or even that the defendant's *last* act, was voluntary in order to establish criminal liability.[57] It is sufficient that the defendant's conduct *included* a voluntary act.[58]

However, what does it mean to say that the defendant's "conduct" must "include" a voluntary act? What is at issue here is how one "time-frames" an event. That is, at what point in time do we start looking at a defendant's conduct to see if

---

[53] *See* § 7.03[B], *supra.*

[54] Among states that place the burden of persuasion regarding voluntariness on the prosecutor are People v. Nelson, 2 N.E.3d 613, (Ill. App. Ct. 2013); Baird v. State, 604 N.E.2d 1170 (Ind. 1992); Fain v. Commonwealth, 1879 Ky. LEXIS 84 (Nov. 18, 1879); United States v. Tinoco, 304 F.3d 1088 (11th Cir. 2002). As a practical matter, however, this is not a significant burden. Nearly all human actions involve a willed muscular contraction. Unless evidence of involuntary conduct arises in the prosecutor's case-in-chief or is raised by the defense, a jury is likely to be persuaded beyond any reasonable doubt that the defendant's conduct included a voluntary act.

[55] There is another important reason, beyond the question of the allocation of the burden of persuasion, to care about the distinction under discussion. For example, in Smith v. State, 663 S.E.2d 155 (Ga. 2008), a trial court required a defendant, who claimed to be sleepwalking when he killed his wife, to assert his claim as a form of insanity. The state supreme court found this to be reversible error. Had the trial court's ruling been affirmed, and if the defendant had succeeded in persuading the jury that he was "insane," he would have been subject to commitment to a mental hospital. That would not follow from a finding that the prosecutor failed to prove an essential element of the offense of murder.

[56] *See generally* Moore, Note 1, *supra* at 35–37; Alexander, Note 13, *supra*; Douglas Husak & Brian P. McLaughlin, *Time-Frames, Voluntary Acts, and Strict Liability*, 12 L. & Phil. 95 (1993); Mark Kelman, *Interpretive Construction in the Substantive Criminal Law*, 33 Stan. L. Rev. 591 (1981).

[57] State v. Burrell, 609 A.2d 751, 753 (N.H. 1992).

[58] Rogers v. State, 105 S.W.3d 630, 638 (Tex. Crim. App. 2003) ("The operative word . . . is 'include' "; and "the 'voluntary act' requirement does not necessarily go to the ultimate act (*e.g.*, pulling the trigger), but only that criminal responsibility for harm must 'include an act' that is voluntary.").

it included a voluntary act? If one identifies the defendant's conduct broadly enough — for example, if we look for a voluntary act well before the ultimate act — there will *always* be a voluntary act. After all, even if *D*, a killer, was unconscious at the time of the homicide, she was surely conscious and acting voluntarily some time prior to the moment of the victim's death, if only when she woke up in the morning, dressed, and drove to the scene of the crime. On the other hand, if we look only at *D*'s conduct at the precise moment of the shooting — very narrowly time-frame — then we would necessarily conclude that the *D*'s conduct did not include a voluntary act.

Professor Mark Kelman has suggested that courts can choose between narrow and broad "time-frames" in identifying the conduct that must include a voluntary act.[59] He contends that the time-framing choice is "arational"; that is, the decision to frame the actor's conduct broadly — or narrowly — is based (if only subconsciously) on a court's desired outcome. If a court wants to convict a defendant who acted involuntarily at some point during the commission of an offense, it will construct a time-frame broad enough to include some remote, but voluntary, act; if it wants the defendant to escape responsibility, it will construct a narrower time-frame, which excludes the prior or subsequent voluntary movements. If Kelman is right in this regard, of course, the voluntary act requirement is "vacuous."[60]

Manipulation of the voluntary act requirement can be avoided if a court applies the fully stated rule of criminal responsibility: *A person is not guilty of an offense unless her conduct, which must include a voluntary act, and which must be accompanied*[61] *by a culpable state of mind (the mens rea of the offense), is the actual and proximate cause of the social harm, as proscribed by the offense.* That is, in time-framing, a court may not properly choose *any* conduct it wishes, no matter how tenuously related;[62] it must focus on the *relevant* conduct, *i.e.*, the conduct (performed with the requisite *mens rea*) that actually and proximately caused the social harm of the offense charged. Once it identifies *this* conduct, the court can fairly determine whether it includes a voluntary act.

To see how a court should construct the proper time-frame, consider, first, a simple example. *D* decides to kill *V*. She builds a bomb and mails it to *V* in a package. The bomb reaches its destination three days later. Coincidentally, at precisely the moment *V* opens the package and is killed in the ensuing explosion, *D* is asleep 3000 miles away. *D* is prosecuted for murder, which for current purposes will be defined as the "intentional killing of another human being." At the murder trial, it will do no good for *D* to point out that she was asleep at the moment of *V*'s death. The relevant conduct — the "killing" acts that were the actual and proximate cause of *V*'s death, and which were accompanied by the requisite intent to kill — occurred three days earlier, when *D* acted voluntarily.

---

[59] Kelman, Note 56, *supra*, at 593–94, 603–05.

[60] Alexander, Note 13, *supra*, at 91.

[61] *See* Chapter 15 (Concurrence of Elements), *infra*.

[62] State v. Newman, 302 P.3d 435, 442 (Or. 2013).

Now, consider a far more difficult case. In *People v. Decina*,[63] D was an epileptic who killed four children when the car he was driving went out of control during a seizure. The prosecutor alleged that D knew that he was highly susceptible to seizures and failed to take proper precautions. As a result, D was prosecuted for "criminal negligence in the operation of a vehicle, resulting in death."

Was such a prosecution appropriate in view of the fact an epileptic seizure constitutes an uncontroversial example of an involuntary act? The answer depends on time-framing. If one constructs an extremely narrow time-frame — specifically, the conduct at the instant the car struck the victims — D's conduct did not include a voluntary act. A broader time-frame, however, would include the voluntary acts of entering the car, turning the ignition key, and driving.

On the matter at issue here, the appellate court determined that a conviction could stand (although the conviction was overturned on unrelated grounds). After all, D was charged with the *operation of a vehicle* resulting in death. It was perfectly appropriate, therefore, for the prosecution to include in its focus the voluntary acts immediately preceding the epileptic seizure, which constituted the arguably negligent "operation" of the car.[64]

§ 9.03 VOLUNTARY ACT: SUPPOSED (BUT NOT REAL) EXCEPTIONS TO THE REQUIREMENT

[A] Poorly Drafted Statutes

Some statutes appear to dispense with the requirement of a voluntary act. For example, a Vermont statute once prohibited persons not married to one another "to be *found* in bed together."[65] Read literally, this statute would unfairly and implausibly allow the conviction of a person who, while unconscious, was placed in a bed with someone to whom she was not married. Although a court could conceivably apply such a statute literally,[66] it is likely (and to be hoped) that it would interpret the law to require a voluntary act.

---

[63] 138 N.E.2d 799 (N.Y. 1956).

[64] *See also* State v. Burrell, 609 A.2d 751 (N.H. 1992); Rogers v. State, 105 S.W.3d 630 (Tex. Crim. App. 2003) (both cases stating that the last act of the defendant, pulling the trigger of a gun, need not be voluntary, as long as the homicidal conduct, as a whole, included a voluntary act).

[65] *See* State v. Woods, 179 A. 1 (Vt. 1935) (applying Vt. Pub. L. No. § 8602 (1933), repealed in 1979) (emphasis added).

[66] *E.g.*, Regina v. Larsonneur, (1933) 24 Cr. App. R. 74 (upholding the conviction of L, a French citizen, for being an alien "found" in the United Kingdom without permission, based on the following facts: she entered England with permission; when English authorities learned she was committing acts of prostitution there, she left for Ireland; Irish officials arrested her and handed her back to English police, whereupon L was charged with the offense). For an example of a court sensibly finding that "found" requires a voluntary act, see Note 15, *supra*.

[B]   Status Offenses

In the past, many legislatures enacted so-called status offenses. For example, vagrancy laws made it an offense to "be a vagrant." Likewise, a California statute prohibited one "to be addicted to the use of narcotics." These offenses required proof of a status (vagrancy or addiction), rather than conduct. These type of statutes punish being, rather than doing.[67]

The Supreme Court has not looked kindly upon such offenses. It invalidated a typical vagrancy law on the ground that it was unduly vague and could result in arbitrary police enforcement;[68] and it held that a California statute that criminalized being an addict violated the Eighth Amendment bar on cruel and unusual punishment.[69] Very likely any statute that punishes a person for a mere propensity to act will run afoul of constitutional principles.[70]

[C]   Crimes of Possession

Virtually all states prohibit possession of contraband (e.g., cocaine) or criminal instrumentalities. On their face, these penal provisions do not require the defendant to act, only that she passively possess the prohibited objects.

Crimes of possession are "inchoate," or incomplete, offenses. That is, their real purpose is to provide the police with a basis for arresting those whom they suspect will later commit a socially injurious act (e.g., sell narcotics, or use the tools to commit a crime).

Possession crimes do not necessarily dispense with the voluntary act requirement. Courts typically interpret possession statutes to require proof that the defendant knowingly procured or received the property possessed (thus, a voluntary act must be proven), or that she failed to dispossess herself of the object after she became aware of its presence.[71] In the latter case, "possession" is equivalent to an omission, in which the defendant has a statutory duty to dispossess herself of the property.[72] She is not guilty if the contraband was "planted" on her, and she did not have sufficient time to terminate her possession after she learned of its presence.

---

[67] Jones v. City of Los Angeles, 444 F.3d 1118, 1133 (9th Cir. 2006), *vacated on other grounds*, 505 F.3d 1006 (9th Cir. 2007).

[68] Papachristou v. City of Jacksonville, 405 U.S. 156 (1972). *See generally* § 5.03, *supra*.

[69] Robinson v. California, 370 U.S. 660 (1962).

[70] *See* § 9.04, *infra*.

[71] *See, e.g.*, People v. Ackerman, 274 N.E.2d 125, 126 (Ill. App. Ct. 1971); State v. Flaherty, 400 A.2d 363, 366 (Me. 1979); Ramirez-Memije v. State, 444 S.W.3d 624, 628 (Tex. Crim. App. 2014).

[72] *See* § 9.07, *infra*.

§ 9.04   VOLUNTARY ACT: CONSTITUTIONAL LAW[73]

The United States Supreme Court has twice considered the question of whether voluntary conduct is a constitutional prerequisite to criminal punishment.

[A]   *Robinson v. California*[74]

The California legislature enacted a law making it an offense, punishable by incarceration from 90 days to 1 year, for a person to "be addicted to the use of narcotics." No act by the defendant — just his present addiction — was required for conviction. The Supreme Court ruled that the statute violated the "cruel and unusual punishment" prohibitions in the Eighth and Fourteenth Amendments to the United States Constitution.

The Court focused on the fact that the statute made the illness of drug addiction (a status that it pointed out could be contracted innocently or involuntarily) a criminal offense. The justices analogized drug addiction to other illnesses — mental illness, leprosy, venereal disease, and the common cold: If a state were to punish persons for suffering from *these* ailments, it would "doubtless be universally thought to be an infliction of cruel and unusual punishment." The Court believed that the same discernment should be shown the status of drug addiction.

The constitutional infirmity in this case was not that a drug addict might receive a 90-day or longer jail sentence, but rather that he could be punished at all. "Even one day in prison," the justices said, would have rendered Robinson's fate impermissible. Essentially, the Court held that, although a legislature may use criminal sanctions against the unauthorized manufacture, sale, purchase, or possession of narcotics, and may attack the social problems arising from drug addiction through health education, civil commitment, and other non-penal programs, California lacked constitutional authority to treat Robinson as a criminal solely because of his addiction.

The *Robinson* Court's approach to the Eighth Amendment is intriguing. Perhaps unwittingly, it invoked retributive, rather than utilitarian, values of punishment. That is, retributivism is based on the principle that punishment should not be inflicted unless a person voluntarily chooses to commit a socially harmful act; the condemnatory feature of criminal punishment should not be used against one whose only "crime" is her illness. In contrast, arguably a utilitarian would not categorically rule out the use of the criminal justice system, among other methods, to deal with drug addiction. To utilitarians, there is no wall absolutely separating

---

[73] *See generally* Joshua Dressler, *Kent Greenawalt, Criminal Responsibility, and the Supreme Court: How a Moderate Scholar Can Appear Immoderate Thirty Years Later,* 74 Notre Dame L. Rev. 1507 (1999); Martin R. Gardner, *Rethinking* Robinson v. California *in the Wake of* Jones v. City of Los Angeles: *Avoiding the "Demise of the Criminal Law" by Attending to "Punishment,"* 98 J. Crim. L. & Criminology 429 (2008); Kent Greenawalt, *"Uncontrollable" Actions and the Eighth Amendment: Implications of* Powell v. Texas, 69 Colum. L. Rev. 927 (1969); David Robinson, Jr., Powell v. Texas: *The Case of the Intoxicated Shoeshine Man Some Reflections a Generation Later by a Participant,* 26 Am. J. Crim. L. 401 (1999).

[74] 370 U.S. 660 (1962).

civil from criminal commitment; the law should be permitted to use every weapon available to it to reduce net social pain.

Essentially, the retributive message of *Robinson* seemed to be the following: Although drug addicts constitute a danger to society and, therefore, it may be *rational* to incarcerate some of them, it is *unjust* to punish them simply because they are sick.

[B]   *Powell v. Texas*[75]

Leroy Powell was charged with violation of a Texas statute that prohibited "get[ting] drunk or be[ing] found in a state of intoxication in any public place." Powell attempted to prove at trial that he suffered from the disease of chronic alcoholism and that, therefore, he was unable to avoid appearing in public in a drunken condition. His punishment, he argued, violated the underlying principles enunciated in *Robinson*. After all, Powell was a sick person. To the extent that he represented a social problem, Texas should be required to deal with him in a non-criminal manner.

Speaking for only four justices, Justice Thurgood Marshall upheld Powell's conviction and $20 fine. He distinguished *Robinson* on the ground that Powell "was convicted, not for being a chronic alcoholic, but for being in public while drunk on a particular occasion." As such, Texas was punishing conduct, not an illness. The plurality explained the import of *Robinson* as follows:

> The entire thrust of *Robinson*'s interpretation of the Cruel and Unusual Punishment Clause is that criminal penalties may be inflicted only if the accused has committed some act, has engaged in some behavior, which society has an interest in preventing, or perhaps in historical common law terms, has committed some *actus reus*.

Although this statement of *Robinson* is correct in terms of its holding, *Powell*'s underlying reasoning runs counter to *Robinson*'s retributivist thrust. In *Powell*, Justice Marshall said that the Court was "unable to assert that the use of the criminal process as a means of dealing with the public aspects of problem drinking can never be defined as rational." He said it would be "tragic to return large numbers of helpless, sometimes dangerous and frequently unsanitary inebriates to the streets of our cities without even the opportunity to sober up adequately which a brief jail term provides." Thus, the plurality blurred the rather bright line drawn in *Robinson* between the civil and criminal processes.

If Justice Marshall's test of rationality had been applied in *Robinson* to drug addicts, the Court might have determined that the use of the criminal sanction was one rational way to deal with the addiction problem. To the *Robinson* Court, however, it was wrong to punish an addict for her disease, even if housing her in a prison until she could "get clean" was one sensible approach to her rehabilitation.

Why did the Court back off from the possible implications of *Robinson*? The answer lies in Justice Marshall's observation that a broad reading of *Robinson*

---

[75] 392 U.S. 514 (1968).

would have made the Supreme Court, "under the aegis of the Cruel and Unusual Punishment Clause, the ultimate arbiter of the [states'] standards of criminal responsibility."[76] That is, if the Eighth Amendment prevents a state from punishing an alcoholic for the act of becoming drunk in public, it might also bar punishing a drug addict for possessing drugs[77] or even for committing a robbery in order to secure the money necessary to feed her habit. It would then be just a small step to the proposition that the Eighth Amendment requires states to draft specific criminal law defenses (*e.g.*, insanity and duress) that would exculpate persons whose conduct was "involuntary" in some sense of that term.[78] The Court plurality was unwilling to intrude that far into the state penal systems.

It must be kept in mind, however, that Justice Marshall only spoke for three other members of the Court. His four-justice plurality was answered by a four-justice dissent. To the dissenters, the issue in the case was "a narrow one," namely: "[W]hether a criminal penalty may be imposed upon a person suffering the disease of 'chronic alcoholism' for a condition — being 'in a state of intoxication' in public — which is a characteristic part of the pattern of his disease." According to the dissent, "[c]riminal penalties may not be inflicted upon a person for being in a condition he is powerless to change." As the dissenters felt there was sufficient evidence that Powell's alcoholism caused him to appear in public involuntarily, they would have held his punishment unconstitutional.

With this 4-4 deadlock, Justice White cast the critical fifth vote. Although he concurred in the judgment, affirming Powell's conviction, he agreed with much of the dissent, stating that

> [i]f it cannot be a crime to have an irresistible compulsion to use narcotics, I do not see how it can constitutionally be a crime to yield to such a compulsion. . . . Unless *Robinson* is to be abandoned . . . the chronic alcoholic with an irresistible urge to consume alcohol should not be punishable for drinking or being drunk.

[C] Current Law: *Powell* in Light of *Robinson*

As seen, the Supreme Court was splintered in *Powell*. Nonetheless, this much is clear: (1) *Powell* did not overrule *Robinson*; and (2) omissions aside, these two cases stand at least for the proposition that a state may not constitutionally punish a person for non-conduct, *i.e.*, punish a person for her thoughts or her status, even if the person's thoughts or status are dangerous. Some conduct by the defendant is constitutionally required in order to punish a person.

The two cases might stand for more than this, however, in light of Justice White's critical fifth vote. The thrust of his opinion is that as long as *Robinson* is

---

[76] In concurrence, too, Justices Black and Harlan observed that a broad reading of *Robinson* "would have [had] a revolutionary impact on the criminal law."

[77] *See* United States v. Moore, 486 F.2d 1139 (D.C. Cir. 1973) (rejecting the petitioner's claim that he could not be convicted of possession of heroin because of his overpowering addiction to drugs).

[78] Sanford H. Kadish, *Fifty Years of Criminal Law: An Opinionated Review*, 87 Cal. L. Rev. 943, 965 (1999) ("The *Robinson* decision could plausibly have been seen as a vital opening toward establishing lack of self-control as a constitutional bar to punishment.").

the law, there should be recognized a constitutional defense to involuntary conduct that is an inevitable symptom of the status or disease syndrome from which the person suffers. Thus, if Powell had been homeless and, thus, could not have avoided being in public when drunk, Justice White apparently would have voted with the four dissenters.

Recently, a few lower courts have followed Justice White's approach. One federal court has ruled that a city ordinance that criminalized the conduct of "sitting, lying, or sleeping" in public streets or sidewalks, although the ordinance expressly punished conduct and not a mere status, violated the Constitution when enforced against homeless persons,[79] and one state court has held that a criminal registration statute requiring sex offenders to provide the address at which they reside was unconstitutional when applied to homeless sex offenders.[80] In such circumstances, the state court ruled, a person is being punished for the status of being homeless.

§ 9.05 VOLUNTARY ACT: MODEL PENAL CODE

[A] General Principles

The Model Penal Code provides that no person may be convicted of a crime in the absence of conduct that "includes a voluntary act or the omission to perform an act of which he is physically capable."[81] The Code allocates to the prosecution the responsibility to persuade the factfinder beyond a reasonable doubt of the existence of a voluntary act.[82]

The Code defines the term "act" as a "bodily movement whether voluntary or involuntary."[83] It does not define the term "voluntary," except "partially and indirectly,"[84] by listing bodily movements that are involuntary: reflexes; convulsions; conduct during unconsciousness, sleep, or due to hypnosis;[85] and, generally, any conduct that "is not a product of the effort or determination of the actor, either conscious or habitual."[86] The Model Code also provides that, for purposes of the voluntary act rule, "possession" is an "act" if the possessor either knowingly obtained the object possessed or knew she was in control of it "for a

---

[79] Jones v. City of Los Angeles, 444 F.3d 1118, 1133 (9th Cir. 2006), *vacated*, 505 F.3d 1006 (9th Cir. 2007).

[80] State v. Adams, 91 So. 3d 724 (Ala. 2010).

[81] Model Penal Code § 2.01(1).

[82] Model Penal Code § 1.12(1).

[83] Model Penal Code § 1.13(2).

[84] American Law Institute, Comment to § 2.01, at 219.

[85] The drafters of the Code justified this controversial inclusion on the ground that conduct during hypnosis or resulting from hypnotic suggestion is "characterized by the subject's dependence on the hypnotist, [so] it does not seem politic to treat conduct [in such circumstances] as voluntary, despite the state of consciousness involved." *Id.* at 221 (footnote deleted). The Commentary acknowledged, however, that the general view is that a hypnotized subject will not follow suggestions contrary to her moral views. For more on hypnosis, including arguments against the Code's position, see § 9.02[C][3][a], *supra*.

[86] Model Penal Code § 2.01(2)(d).

sufficient period to have been able to terminate . . . possession."[87]

[B]   Exception to the Rule

The "voluntary act" rule stated in Section 2.01 of the Model Penal Code applies to liability for "crimes," *i.e.*, felonies, misdemeanors, and petty misdemeanors.[88] However, Section 2.05(1) of the Code provides that the requirements set out in Section 2.01 do not apply to offenses that constitute "violations," unless a court determines that application of Section 2.01 is "consistent with effective enforcement of the law defining the offense." A "violation" is an offense for which the maximum penalty is a fine or civil penalty.[89]

Accordingly, under Section 2.05, a driver who suffers an unforeseeable blackout and, as a consequence, fails to halt at a stop sign, may be convicted of a motor vehicle violation in the absence of proof of any voluntary act. The Commentary to Section 2.05 concedes that the fairness of this outcome is "debatable";[90] but with extremely minor offenses, the drafters of the Code determined that litigation of involuntary-act claims should not be permitted to undermine effective law enforcement.

§ 9.06   OMISSIONS: GENERAL PRINCIPLES[91]

[A]   General Rule

Consider the following two incidents. First, in *People v. Beardsley*,[92] a married man failed to come to the aid of the woman with whom he was having a sexual relationship after she took a lethal dose of poison in his presence. She died. Second, in a heavily reported after-midnight 1964 assault in Queens, New York, a young woman, Kitty Genovese, purportedly cried out for help for approximately 30 minutes as she was attacked and ultimately killed outside her apartment building. It was later suggested that 38 of her neighbors heard her cries and saw the attack in progress from their apartment windows, but did nothing.[93]

---

[87]   Model Penal Code § 2.01(4).

[88]   Model Penal Code § 1.04(1) (classifying crimes).

[89]   Model Penal Code § 1.04(5).

[90]   American Law Institute, Comment to § 2.05, at 292.

[91]   *See generally* Larry Alexander, *Criminal Liability for Omissions: An Inventory of Issues in Criminal Law Theory, in* Criminal Law Theory: Doctrines of the General Part 121 (2002); Joshua Dressler, *Some Brief Thoughts (Mostly Negative) About "Bad Samaritan" Laws*, 40 Santa Clara L. Rev. 971 (2000); George P. Fletcher, *On the Moral Irrelevance of Bodily Movements*, 142 U. Pa. L. Rev. 1443 (1994); Graham Hughes, *Criminal Omissions*, 67 Yale L.J. 590 (1958); F.M. Kamm, *Action, Omission, and the Stringency of Duties*, 142 U. Pa. L. Rev. 1493 (1994); Arthur Leavens, *A Causation Approach to Criminal Omissions*, 76 Cal. L. Rev. 547 (1988); A.P. Simester, *Why Omissions Are Special*, 1 Legal Theory 311 (1995); A.D. Woozley, *A Duty to Rescue: Some Thoughts on Criminal Liability*, 69 Va. L. Rev. 1273 (1983).

[92]   113 N.W. 1128 (Mich. 1907).

[93]   *See generally* Abraham M. Rosenthal, Thirty-Eight Witnesses (1964). There is increasing reason to believe that Rosenthal's report is factually false. *See* Nicholas Lemann, *A Call for Help, The New*

In both situations, a human being died. In both situations, one or more persons knew that a life was in jeopardy. In both situations, the harm that occurred might have been prevented or mitigated at no apparent physical risk of harm to those aware of the victim's plight. Nonetheless, adulterer Beardsley was not held criminally responsible for his omission; and none of Genovese's neighbors were prosecuted in relation to her death.

The lesson to be learned from these two incidents is that not every moral obligation to act creates a concomitant legal duty.[94] *Subject to a few limited exceptions, a person has no criminal law duty to act to prevent harm to another, even if she can do so at no risk to herself, and even if the person imperiled may lose her life in the absence of assistance.* In essence, the criminal law distinguishes between an act that affirmatively *causes* harm, on the one hand, and the failure of a bystander to take measures to *prevent* harm, on the other hand. As Professor Woozley has described the principle: "[T]he law should see to it that we do not do harm, but not see to it that, in the absence of a specific statutory duty, we do things to prevent harm."[95] As a matter of criminal law doctrine, we are not our brothers' and sisters' keepers.

[B] Criticisms of the General Rule

Many critics of the omission rule, as set out in italics in the preceding paragraph, consider it morally repugnant. As one scholar stated in relation to *Beardsley*, "[i]n a civilized society, a man who finds himself with a helplessly ill person who has no other source of aid should be under a duty to summon help, whether the person is his wife, his mistress, a prostitute or a Chief Justice."[96] The implication is that there is no meaningful moral difference between an act and an omission — there is no meaningful difference between slamming shut one's open door to bar entry of a child trying to escape a wild animal, and failing to open a closed door for the same child.[97] It is all one and the same.

The effect of the omission rule is to exonerate people, such as Beardsley-the-adulterer and Kitty Genovese's neighbors in Queens, who are guilty of moral indifference. The rule may even absolve one who is guilty of an extremely culpable state of mind. For example, imagine *S*, an Olympic-level swimmer, who stands by and watches an infant (not her own) drown in a wading pool. According to the general no-liability rule, *S* is not criminally responsible for the death, although she could have saved the child at no risk to herself, even if she failed to act because she experienced sadistic pleasure watching the infant struggle to survive and finally drown.

From a utilitarian perspective, the callousness of the omission rule may breed contempt for society's system of criminal justice. In contrast, a rule that requires

---

Yorker, Mar. 10, 2014, at 73. However, for current purposes, assume that the Rosenthal's version of the story is true.

[94] State v. Sherman, 266 S.W.3d 395, 404 (Tenn. 2008).

[95] Woozley, Note 91, *supra*, at 1273.

[96] Hughes, Note 91, *supra*, at 624.

[97] Katz, Note 35, *supra*, at 140.

people to assist others in peril might promote social cohesion; and some wrongdoers might desist from planned criminal activity if they knew that others were likely to intervene.

[C] Defense of the General Rule

Arguments vary in defense of the general no-liability-for-omissions rule. There are both pragmatic and principled arguments offered. First, if people were as legally responsible for their "not-doings"[98] as they are for their harmful "doings," criminal prosecutions would burgeon (38 additional prosecutions in the Genovese story), adding to the expense of litigation and creating huge backlogs of cases.

A second practical problem is one of line-drawing. For example, in the Genovese case, should all 38 persons who heard her cries for help be held responsible, or only those who heard her in the early moments and, therefore, had the maximum time to help? Either the police and prosecutors would have nearly unbridled discretion in determining whom to prosecute, thereby raising legality concerns,[99] or a legislature would need to devise difficult-to-apply standards, which might result in similar vagueness problems.

Third, liability for non-actions would create serious problems of proof of *mens rea*. For example, if Beardsley had poisoned his mistress, a jury could easily have inferred that he intended to kill her. Or, if a person puts a loaded gun to another person's head and pulls the trigger, it is sensible to infer an intent to kill. Omissions, however, are more ambiguous. In the Genovese tragedy, it is possible that some of the apartment residents assumed that someone else had called the police;[100] and one who stands by as a murder occurs may plausibly do so out of fear or shock, rather than malice.

How, too, does one go about proving causation in omission cases? As developed in Chapter 14, a person is not responsible for an offense unless she caused the harm in question. Some philosophers argue that a non-act is *never* the cause of a consequence — how can nothing be the cause of something? — but even if this philosophical claim is rejected,[101] more line-drawing problems arise. It is easy to determine that the victim in *Beardsley* "caused" her own death by ingesting poison; it is far more difficult to say that Beardsley's failure to secure medical care for his paramour caused her death. She might have died from the poison despite his best efforts. Similarly, even if one of Genovese's neighbors had called the police, how can we know whether help would have come in time? For that matter, if they

---

[98] Simester, Note 91, *supra*, at 320.

[99] *See* § 5.03, *supra*.

[100] *See* Bibb Latané & John Darley, *Group Inhibition of Bystander Intervention in Emergencies*, 10 J. Personality & Soc. Psychol. 215, 215 (1968) ("We have found that the mere perception that other people are also witnessing the event will markedly decrease the likelihood that an individual will intervene in an emergency."); Katz, Note 35 *supra*, at 150 ("For Kitty Genovese, then, there was no safety in numbers.").

[101] There is rich debate on the subject of causation-for-omissions. For example, see Eric Mack, *Bad Samaritanism and the Causation of Harm*, 9 Phil. & Pub. Aff. 230 (1980); H.L.A. Hart & Tony Honoré, Causation in the Law 48 (2d ed. 1985) (concluding that some non-actions are causes because they represent an unexpected "deviation from a system or routine").

were a cause of her death, isn't *everyone* in the world a cause, since *nobody* helped her?

The line-drawing problems raise more than purely pragmatic concerns. If it is difficult to determine a non-actor's mental state or degree of contribution to resulting harm, there is an enhanced risk that a jury will *incorrectly* resolve these issues. That is, they might find an intention to cause harm when none was present, or they may attach causal responsibility where none exists. Thus, the risk of punishing a legally innocent person is substantially enhanced in omission cases.

A general rule that persons are criminally responsible for their omissions could also have an unintended counter-utilitarian effect. People sometimes misconstrue what they observe: an apparent wrongdoer might really be an undercover police officer performing her lawful duties; the Good Samaritan intervenor may end up frustrating a lawful arrest. Additionally, intervenors often cause injury to themselves or others by their intervention. A bystander, helping out of fear of criminal responsibility if she stands by, might provide poor medical assistance or fire a weapon unsafely, causing more harm than if she had done nothing.

Defenders of the general rule also reject the moral claim that omissions and acts are morally symmetrical. They contend that causing harm, on the hand, and allowing it to occur, on the other, are not morally similar: "[A] doctrine of general liability for not-doings would result in a system that is largely insensitive to ideas of individual responsibility and authorship."[102] The man who stabbed Kitty Genovese is the person who harmed her. Those who figuratively stood by and did nothing did not hurt her. "[W]ithout an act/omissions doctrine like the one our legal system presently recognizes, this truth would be valueless."[103]

Or, consider the drowning child hypothetical involving S, the Olympic swimmer. Suppose that we learned that X pushed the child into the pool. Even assuming that S obtained sadistic pleasure from watching the child die, would we say that X's act and S's omission are morally equivalent? X *caused* the child to die; S merely *permitted* it. X changed the state of affairs by putting the child in jeopardy; S merely failed to put things right. X killed the child; S withheld a benefit. Advocates of the no-liability-for-omissions rule contend that the positive duty not to make the world worse is, morally speaking, more stringent than the duty to make it better.[104]

The latter point leads to a final justification for the general no-liability rule, which is that the omission doctrine is consistent with the principle of autonomy. In a society such as ours, which values individual freedom and limited governmental power over its citizens, the criminal justice system should be used discriminately. Even if a person is *morally* obligated to come to the aid of others, not every violation of a moral duty should result in criminal punishment. It is the role of religion and other moral institutions to perfect human character; the purpose of the criminal law is limited to deterring or punishing persons for causing harm. If it

---

[102] Simester, Note 91, *supra*, at 329.

[103] *Id.*

[104] Kamm, Note 91, *supra*, at 1493.

were otherwise, the criminal justice system would intrude too deeply into peoples' lives.

§ 9.07 OMISSIONS: EXCEPTIONS TO THE NO-LIABILITY RULE

[A] Common Law Duty to Act: "Commission by Omission"

[1] Overview

In the limited circumstances set out in subsection [2] below, common law liability for a criminal offense may be predicated on an omission, rather than on a voluntary act. Such cases involve what may be termed "commission by omission"[105] liability. When a common law duty to act exists, and *assuming that she was physically capable of performing the act*, a defendant's omission of the duty to act serves as a legal substitute for a voluntary act. Therefore, if the remaining elements of the charged offense are proven (that is, the omitter caused[106] the social harm of the offense with the requisite *mens rea*), the defendant may be convicted of the specified crime. For example, courts have upheld criminal homicide convictions based on omissions. A person with a legal duty to act who negligently fails to provide or summon needed care to someone in great medical distress may be guilty of manslaughter if the person dies as a result of the omission.[107] A person who has a legal duty to report a fire may be convicted of some form of criminal homicide if her failure to report the fire recklessly or negligently results in death.[108] A parent who has a duty to act may be convicted of child or sexual abuse if she fails to prevent such harm from being committed by another person.[109]

Punishment for "commission by omission," even if otherwise defensible, has been criticized by a few scholars[110] as violative of the legality principle. That is, the definitions of most criminal offenses contain verbs such as "kill," "burn," or "break and enter." It is questionable whether, for example, a person who stands by passively while another dies, even if she has a duty to intervene, can be said to have "killed" the other person, as distinguished from "permitting" such a death to occur. Nonetheless, courts rarely bar omission-based convictions on legality or statutory construction grounds.

We turn now to those uncommon circumstances in which a person *does* have a common law duty to act.

---

[105] Fletcher, Note 91, *supra*, at 1447.

[106] *But see* the text to Note 101, *supra*.

[107] *E.g.*, Commonwealth v. Twitchell, 617 N.E.2d 609 (Mass. 1993); People v. Oliver, 210 Cal. App. 3d 138 (Ct. App. 1989).

[108] Commonwealth v. Levesque, 766 N.E.2d 50 (Mass. 2002).

[109] Degren v. State, 722 A.2d 887 (Md. 1999) (sexual abuse); State v. Williquette, 385 N.W.2d 145 (Wis. 1986) (child abuse); Pope v. State, 396 A.2d 1054 (Md. 1975) (child abuse).

[110] *E.g.*, Fletcher, Note 91, *supra*, at 1448–49.

[2]   When There Is a Duty to Act

[a]   Status Relationship

A person may have a common law duty to act to prevent harm to another if she stands in a special status relationship to the person in peril. Such a relationship is usually founded on the dependence of one party on the other, or on their interdependence. Such status relationships include: parents to their minor children;[111] married couples to one another;[112] employers to their employees;[113] and invitors to their invitees.[114] Thus, a mother who allows her children to remain with their father, whom she knows is abusing them, is herself guilty of child abuse by her omission;[115] and, a parent's failure to seek medical attention for her seriously ill child, which omission results in the child's death, will support a conviction for criminal homicide, assuming that the parent acted with the requisite *mens rea.*[116]

[b]   Contractual Obligation

A duty to act may be created by implied or express contract. For example, one who breaches an agreement to house, feed, and provide medical care to an infirm stranger,[117] or to care for one's mentally and physically disabled parent,[118] may be held criminally responsible for an ensuing death. Similarly, a babysitter owes an implied contractual duty to protect her ward, and a doctor has a duty to provide ordinary medical care for her patient.

[c]   Omissions Following an Act

In some circumstances an act, followed by an omission, will result in criminal responsibility for the omission, even when there is no liability for the original act.

[i]   Creation of a Risk

A person who wrongfully harms another or another's property, or who wrongfully places a person or her property in jeopardy of harm, has a common law duty to aid the injured or endangered party. If she breaches her duty in this

---

[111] Jones v. United States, 308 F.2d 307 (D.C. Cir. 1962); *see also* State v. Sherman, 266 S.W.3d 395 (Tenn. 2008) (*S*, who conducted religious services at his home, permitted a mother and her young daughter to live in his home, and he held himself out as her father and caretaker; held: a duty to act may be created, even if one is not a parent, if the person establishes an *in loco parentis* relationship with a child, as here).

[112] State v. Smith, 65 Me. 257 (1876); *see also* State *ex. rel.* Kuntz v. Thirteenth Judicial District, 995 P.2d 951 (Mont. 2000) (unmarried couple who lived together for approximately six years owed each other the same protective duty as exists between spouses).

[113] Rex v. Smith, 2 Car. & P. 449, 172 Eng. Rep. 203 (1826).

[114] State v. Brown, 631 P.2d 129, 132 (Ariz. Ct. App. 1981).

[115] State v. Williquette, 385 N.W.2d 145 (Wis. 1986).

[116] State v. Williams, 484 P.2d 1167 (Wash. Ct. App. 1971).

[117] Commonwealth v. Pestinikas, 617 A.2d 1339 (Pa. Super. Ct. 1992).

[118] Davis v. Commonwealth, 335 S.E.2d 375 (Va. 1985).

regard, she may be held criminally responsible for the harm arising from the omission. For example, if *D* negligently injures *V*, *D* has a common law duty to render aid to *V*. If *D* fails to do so, and *V* dies as the result of the omission, *D* may be held criminally responsible for *V*'s death.[119]

Although there is considerably less case law in this regard, a duty to act arguably arises from *non*-culpable risk-creation, as well. For example, a few courts have held that one who *accidentally* starts a house fire, and who, therefore, is free of liability for the initial blaze, may be convicted of arson if (with the requisite wrongful state of mind) she fails to act to extinguish the fire or prevent damage to property therein.[120] There is also some authority for the proposition that even one who *justifiably* shoots an aggressor in self-defense, seriously wounding the latter, may have a subsequent duty to obtain medical aid for the wounded aggressor once the aggressor no longer represents a threat.[121]

[ii]   Voluntary Assistance

One who voluntarily commences assistance to another in jeopardy has a duty to continue to provide aid, at least if a subsequent omission would put the victim in a worse position than if the actor had not initiated help. This rule applies even if the omitter had no initial responsibility to rescue the victim.

For example, a well-meaning individual who takes a sick person into her home, but then fails to provide critical care, may be held responsible for a death arising from this failure. By letting the victim rely on her for care, and by secluding the victim so that others are unaware of her deteriorating condition, the defendant has made matters worse than if she had never become involved.[122]

[B]   Statutory Duty (Including "Bad Samaritan" Laws)[123]

Independent of any existing common law duty to act, a duty to act may statutorily be imposed. Examples of such statutes are those that require: a person to pay taxes on earned income;[124] a driver of a motor vehicle involved in an accident

---

[119] *See also* Jones v. State, 43 N.E.2d 1017 (Ind. 1942) (*D* raped *V*; emotionally distraught, *V* jumped or fell into a creek; *D* did not attempt to rescue *V*, although he was aware of her peril; *D* was convicted of murder for *V*'s death resulting from his omission).

[120] Regina v. Miller, [1983] 1 All ER 978 (House of Lords); *see* Commonwealth v. Cali, 141 N.E. 510 (Mass. 1923).

[121] State ex rel. Kuntz v. Thirteenth Judicial District, 995 P.2d 951 (Mont. 2000).

[122] *See, e.g.*, People v. Oliver, 210 Cal. App. 3d 138 (Ct. App. 1989) (*O* permitted *V*, who was extremely intoxicated, to come to her home, and then allowed *V* to use her bathroom, where *V* injected himself with narcotics; when *V* collapsed, *O* did not summon aid; held: *O* was guilty of manslaughter because "she took [*V*] from a public place where others might have taken care to prevent him from injuring himself, to a private place — her home — where she alone could provide such care"); Regina v. Instan, 17 Cox Crim. Cas. 602 (1893) (*I*, who lived alone with *V*, her elderly and sick aunt, in *V*'s house, failed to obtain needed food and medical care for *V*, who died as a result; held: *I* was properly convicted of manslaughter).

[123] *See generally* Dressler, Note 91, *supra*; Alison McIntyre, *Guilty Bystanders? On the Legitimacy of Duty to Rescue Statutes*, 23 Phil. & Pub. Aff. 157 (1994); Sandra Guerra Thompson, *The White-Collar Police Force: "Duty to Report" Statutes in Criminal Law Theory*, 11 Wm. & Mary Bill Rts. J. 3 (2002); Woozley, Note 91, *supra*; Daniel B. Yeager, *A Radical Community of Aid: A Rejoinder to Opponents of*

to stop her car at the scene;[125] and parents to provide food and shelter for their minor children.[126] Failure to satisfy a statutory duty (assuming, again, that the actor had the capacity to perform the duty and failed to do so with the requisite *mens rea*) constitutes a violation of a statutory "duty to act" offense.

Controversial in this regard are "Good Samaritan Laws," which might more appropriately be characterized as "Bad Samaritan" laws, which have been adopted in just a few states. These statutes make it an offense, typically a misdemeanor, for a person not to come to the aid of a stranger in peril under specified circumstances. For example, a Vermont statute provides that it is an offense for a bystander to fail to give "reasonable assistance" to another person whom she "knows . . . is exposed to grave physical harm," if such aid "can be rendered without danger or peril" to the bystander, "unless that assistance or care is being provided by others."[127]

Even if such offenses are otherwise desirable, they are difficult to enforce fairly. It is unclear, for example, who (if anyone) would have been guilty of such an offense in a case in which multiple persons observe a crisis and fail to act, as supposedly existed in the Kitty Genovese case.[128] Critics of Bad Samaritan laws assert that either nobody can fairly be prosecuted under them (thus rendering them of no practical benefit) or a prosecutor might arbitrarily single out one among multiple persons for prosecution as an object lesson, even though that individual was no more culpable than the other bystanders not prosecuted. There is also the risk that juries, inflamed by the facts, will convict a bystander even though her guilt is legally doubtful.

§ 9.08   OMISSIONS: MODEL PENAL CODE

The Model Penal Code does not differ significantly from the common law regarding omissions. A person is not guilty of any offense unless his conduct "includes a voluntary act or the omission to perform an act of which he is physically capable."[129]

Liability based on an omission is permitted in two circumstances: (1) if the law defining the offense provides for it;[130] or (2) if the duty to act is "otherwise imposed by law."[131] The latter category incorporates duties arising under civil law, such as torts or contract law.[132]

Affirmative Duties to Help Strangers, 71 Wash. U. L.Q. 1 (1993).

[124]   26 U.S.C. § 7203 (2011).

[125]   *E.g.*, Cal. Veh. Code § 20001 (Deering 2015).

[126]   *E.g.*, N.Y. Penal Law § 260.06 (2015).

[127]   Vt. Stat. Ann. tit. 12, § 519(a) (2015).

[128]   *See* § 9.06[A], *supra.*

[129]   Model Penal Code § 2.01(1).

[130]   *E.g.*, Model Penal Code § 220.1(3) (failure to control or report a dangerous fire).

[131]   Model Penal Code § 2.01(3)(b).

[132]   American Law Institute, Comment to § 2.01, at 222–23.

§ 9.09   MEDICAL "OMISSIONS": A DEFINITIONAL PROBLEM[133]

Consider this problem. Patient, *P*, is in an irreversible coma, kept alive by use of a respirator. *D*, *P*'s doctor, concludes that future medical treatment would be useless, so she turns off the respirator, aware that the effect will be to cause *P*'s imminent death, which occurs.

[A]   Act or Omission?

One way to analyze the scenario set out above is as follows: *D* committed a voluntary act by turning off the respirator; this conduct caused *P*'s death, which is the social harm of murder; *D* caused *P*'s death knowingly, the *mens rea* of murder; therefore, the elements of common law (and, doubtlessly, statutory) murder have been proven. As there is no recognized legal defense of euthanasia, *D* is guilty of murder.

Is it self-evident, however, that *D* is performing an act, rather than omitting conduct, when she turns off a respirator on a comatose patient? Literally, of course, *D*'s conduct *does* include the voluntary act of pulling the plug or turning off the switch on the respirator. But, does this scenario differ significantly from one in which *D fails* to turn the respirator *on* in the first place, a clear-cut omission? From a semantic point of view, the act/omission distinction seems to fail us here. One can as reasonably describe what occurred by saying "*D* failed to provide medical treatment to *P*" as by saying, "*D* voluntarily turned off the machine, causing *P*'s death."

To some it seems morally obtuse for the line in such cases to be drawn on the basis of the fortuity of whether a doctor initially turned on a respirator (and, thus, must turn it off, a voluntary act) or simply refused to initiate medical treatment in the first place. What troubles us about *D*'s behavior (if anything does) is that a doctor, trained to heal others, has chosen — initially or later — to deny future treatment to her patient. The voluntary act of turning off the machine is merely the means of omitting future medical care. Arguably (but not inevitably), therefore, we ought to analyze *D*'s behavior as an omission.

[B]   Analysis as an Omission

Even if the act of turning off a respirator or discontinuing other medical treatment is analyzed as an omission, this does not necessarily resolve all the legal issues. A physician ordinarily has a duty to provide medical treatment for her patients; therefore, she could theoretically be held criminally responsible for an omission of her duty of care.

---

[133] *See generally* Luis E. Chiesa, *Actmissions*, 116 W. Va. L. Rev. 583 (2013); George P. Fletcher, *Prolonging Life*, 42 Wash. L. Rev. 999 (1967); Sanford H. Kadish, *Letting Patients Die: Legal and Moral Reflections*, 80 Cal. L. Rev. 857 (1992); Arthur Leavens, Note 91, *supra*; H. M. Malm, *Killing, Letting Die, and Simple Conflicts*, 18 Phil. & Pub. Aff. 238 (1989); Judith Jarvis Thomson, *Physician-Assisted Suicide: Two Moral Arguments*, 109 Ethics 497 (1999).

But, what is the scope of a doctor's duty to her patient? Modern technology has required courts (and legislatures) to more deeply consider this question. The traditional approach to the issue is to state that a physician owes a duty to provide "ordinary," but not "extraordinary," care to her patient.[134] This distinction, however, arguably raises more questions than it answers, for what *is* "extraordinary" care? Organ transplants once seemed extraordinary; today they are commonplace. Would the physician who fails to perform a needed transplant operation be violating a duty of ordinary care to her patient? Some new approach to the problem may be needed.

[C] The *Barber* Approach

In *Barber v. Superior Court*,[135] the defendants were physicians charged with murder and conspiracy to commit murder, of Clarence Herbert, their patient. Herbert had been in a deep coma from which he was unlikely to recover. After they received permission from the patient's family, the doctors caused life-sustaining equipment to be turned off and, when Herbert continued to live, they removed intravenous tubes that provided needed hydration and nourishment to their patient. Herbert eventually died from the loss of fluids and nourishment.

The court stated that the physicians' conduct of removing the tubing actually amounted to a withdrawal, or omission, of further treatment, rather than an affirmative act. It reasoned that although the life-support devices were "self-propelled," each drop of fluid introduced into the patient's body by intravenous feeding was "comparable to a manually administered injection or item of medication." Therefore, it concluded, the disconnection of the mechanical devices that fed and hydrated the patient was tantamount to withholding medical treatment.

The court framed the resulting omission issue in terms of what "duties [are] owed by a physician to a patient who has been reliably diagnosed as in a comatose state from which any meaningful recovery of cognitive brain function is exceedingly unlikely." In resolving this issue, the court expressed the view that the ordinary/extraordinary care distinction begged the real question. In its place, the court asked "whether the proposed treatment [was] proportionate . . . in terms of the benefits to be gained versus the burdens caused." The court reasoned that medical treatment that is even minimally painful or intrusive is apt to constitute disproportionate treatment when the patient has no meaningful chance of medical improvement. In such circumstances, a physician owes no duty to provide further medical treatment to her patient.

Who determines whether the proposed medical treatment is disproportionate? The court's answer was that "the patient's interests and desires are the key ingredients of the decision making process." When the patient is unable to indicate her wishes, the immediate family is the proper "surrogate" for the patient. In the absence of legislation to the contrary, the court held that medical personnel, along

---

[134] *See* Superintendent of Belchertown State Sch. v. Saikewicz, 370 N.E.2d 417, 424 (Mass. 1977); *In re* Quinlan, 355 A.2d 647, 667–68 (N.J. 1976).

[135] 147 Cal. App. 3d 1006 (Ct. App. 1983).

with the family, may decide whether to withdraw treatment without prior judicial authorization.

[D]   Reflections Regarding *Barber*

The act/omission distinction is based, at least in part, on the premise that the law should prevent people from actively causing harm, but that it should not compel persons to benefit others.[136] Based on this reasoning, did the doctors here withhold a benefit from their patient, or did they actively cause his death (*i.e.*, kill him)?

Before the respirator was turned off, Herbert was medically and legally alive. Even after the physicians shut off the machinery, he was not in imminent danger of death. Only after the doctors stopped providing nourishment and fluids to Herbert did he finally die. Therefore, "it is difficult to avoid concluding that the doctors caused [Herbert's] death."[137] From this perspective, the situation was no different than if Herbert's wife had starved her comatose husband to death at home, in order to speed his death. Whether family members or health professionals should be allowed to cut off food and fluids to a chronically comatose person in order to hasten death has been a matter of considerable moral controversy. Arguably, the matter ought to be resolved directly — through debate regarding whether euthanasia (and, with competent patients, suicide assistance) should be permitted — rather than indirectly through the act/omission, duty/no-duty analysis.[138]

§ 9.10   SOCIAL HARM: GENERAL PRINCIPLES

[A]   Overview

Holmes has written that the "aim of the law is not to punish sins, but is to prevent certain external results."[139] Joel Feinberg has stated that "[a]cts of *harming* . . . are the direct objects of the criminal law.[140] These statements remind us that, to be guilty of an offense, a person must do more than think bad thoughts; she must be guilty of wrongdoing. The voluntary act is the "doing"; the

---

[136] *See* § 9.06[C], *supra.*

[137] Leavens, Note 91, *supra*, at 586; *see also* Thomson, Note 133, *supra*, at 501 (in such a circumstance, the act "seems to be most plausibly seen as not merely letting nature take its course but rather causing it to").

[138] Constitutional issues are raised in some medical omission cases. A competent patient has a "liberty" interest encompassed by the Due Process Clause of the Constitution to refuse medical treatment. This interest must be weighed against the state's legitimate interest in preserving life. In the case of an incompetent patient, as in *Barber*, a state has the right to refuse to accept the substituted judgment of a close family member, and it may refuse to permit the cessation of medical care in the absence of clear and convincing evidence of the person's pre-incompetency expressed desire for withdrawal of medical care in such circumstances. Cruzan v. Dir., Mo. Dep't. of Health, 497 U.S. 261 (1990). Even though a person has a liberty interest in refusing medical treatment, she has no constitutional right to medical assistance in causing her own death by way of suicide. Washington v. Glucksberg, 521 U.S. 702 (1997).

[139] Commonwealth v. Kennedy, 48 N.E. 770, 770 (Mass. 1897).

[140] Joel Feinberg, Harm to Others 31 (1984).

harm caused by the voluntary act is the "wrong" in "wrongdoing."[141] The harm is the body — the linchpin — of the crime. Because crimes are public wrongs, however, we may describe the harm caused in a criminal case as "social harm."

Some scholars state that "social harm" is an essential element of every crime.[142] This is only true, however, if the term "social harm" is very broadly defined. Some conduct that is criminal may cause no "injury" at all, in the usual sense of that term. What is the "social harm," for example, in driving while intoxicated, if nobody is hurt and no property is damaged? Or, if *D*, intending to kill *V*, who is asleep, pulls the trigger of what turns out to be an unloaded gun, *D* may be charged with attempted murder, but where is the harm in *D*'s conduct? If all crimes require "social harm," must such conduct go unpunished?

To a utilitarian, there is no reason why resulting harm should be considered a prerequisite to criminal liability, as long as the actor's conduct demonstrates her propensity to cause *future* harm, or if punishment of the person will deter future harm by others. In contrast, many retributivists believe that punishment of an actor is unjustified in the absence of social harm. Only then has the actor taken something from society. Only then is a debt owed. Only then is it right for society to take something from the actor by means of punishment.

In most circumstances the views of both schools of thought converge. Murder needs to be deterred and, in any case, causes harm that justifies punishment as repayment; so both utilitarians and retributivists typically can justify punishing murderers. Moreover, even in the case of an intoxicated driver who causes no immediate tangible harm, but who threatens future harm, a retributivist may be able to justify punishment: A drunk driver weaving on the highway, for example, endangers others by her conduct, which endangerment frequently causes apprehension of harm in other drivers who observe the dangerous conduct. Disturbing the public repose is a form of intangible, but entirely real, injury that may justify penal sanction.

Frequently, however, it is hard to conclude that dangerous conduct has hurt anyone, even intangibly. If nobody is on the highway to see the intoxicated driver weaving, there is no public alarm. If *V*, asleep, is alone when *D* pulls the trigger of an unloaded gun, nobody is put in fear by *D*'s conduct. In these situations, however, the intoxicated driver and attempted murderer *are* subject to criminal punishment. For us to say, therefore, that "social harm" is an essential element of all offenses, the term "social harm" must be carefully — and broadly — defined.

[B] A Definition of "Social Harm"

Society values and has an interest in protecting people and things. The "things" that society values and has an interest in protecting may be tangible (*e.g.*, an automobile or an animal) or intangible (*e.g.*, emotional security, reputation, personal autonomy). Society is wronged when an actor invades *any* socially

---

[141] In the unusual case in which a person may be punished for an omission, "wrong *non*-doing" would be a more apt characterization of the situation.

[142] *E.g.*, Eser, Note 1, *supra*, at 346.

recognized interest and diminishes its value.[143] Specifically, "social harm" may be defined as the "negation, endangering, or destruction of an individual, group or state interest which was deemed socially valuable."[144] Thus, the drunk driver and the attempted murderer of the sleeping party have endangered the interests of others, and have caused "social harm" under this definition.

[C] Finding the "Social Harm" Element in a Criminal Statute

Every crime contains an *actus reus* and, as discussed in the next chapter, nearly all crimes require proof of a culpable state of mind (*mens rea*). The definition of an offense will set out the *actus reus* component of the crime. More accurately, the definition of the offense will identify the proscribed *social harm*. The *actus* in *actus reus* — the voluntary act (or, rarely, omission) — is typically unstated but implied.

For example, the common law definition of murder is "**the killing of a human being by another human being** *with malice aforethought*." The italicized words constitute the *mens rea* of the offense, *i.e.*, the culpable state of mind required to be guilty of the crime. The words in bold tell us what society does not want to occur (the social harm) — here, the taking of a human life by another human being. The voluntary act/omission component of the *actus reus* is implicit in this definition: the "killing" of a human being must be the result of conduct that includes a voluntary act or an omission (when there is a duty to act).[145]

[D] Dividing "Social Harm" into Sub-Elements

The social harm of an offense, as defined by statute or at common law, may consist of wrongful conduct, wrongful results, or both. Moreover, the offense will *always* contain "attendant circumstance" (or, simply, "circumstance") elements. Frequently, it is necessary for a lawyer or court to distinguish between "conduct," "result," and "attendant circumstance" elements in the definition of the crime.

[1] "Conduct" Elements (or "Conduct" Crimes)

Some crimes are defined, at least in part, in terms of harmful conduct. Harmful *results* are not required. An example of a so-called "conduct" crime would be the offense of "intentionally **driving under the influence of alcohol**." The words in

---

[143] *See* Hall, Note 3, *supra*, at 217.

[144] Eser, Note 1, *supra*, at 413.

[145] Of course, the social harm of murder is not simply the loss of one human life. This is the *definitional* social harm, *i.e.*, the social harm as explicitly defined by the common law or statute in question. The *underlying* social harm — the *full* reason why society prohibits murder — is broader and deeper: When a human life is taken by another person, there are deep psychological injuries to loved ones and friends; there are apt to be financial losses suffered by family members and by those with whom the victim worked; there is harm to strangers who, upon learning of the homicide, become fearful for their own safety and, consequently, restrict their public activities; there may be economic injury to the community by the loss of an able-bodied worker; and, of course, there is the tear in the fabric of society that results when one of its members unjustifiably takes the life of another. The focus in the text, however, is on the definitional social harm of criminal offenses.

bold state the *actus reus* of the offense. More specifically, they state the social harm of the crime — the wrongful conduct of driving a car in an intoxicated condition (which conduct implicitly must include a voluntary act). This is a so-called "conduct" crime because no harmful result is required to be guilty of the offense. That is, the offense is complete whether or not anyone or any property is tangibly injured because of the intoxicated driving. It is enough that socially valuable interests have been endangered by the actor's conduct.

[2] "Result" Elements (or "Result" Crimes)

An offense may be defined in terms of a prohibited result. Common law murder is a "result" crime, because the social harm of the offense, as defined, involves "the death of another human being." Although the killing of another — the result — obviously occurs because of some conduct, the *nature* of the actor's conduct *definitionally* is irrelevant. That is, it does not matter *how* the result occurs (*e.g.*, whether the actor kills by gun or knife or poison), just that it does result.

On the other hand, some offenses contain both "conduct" and "result" elements. For example, a statute may define first-degree murder as the killing of another human being, "by means of a destructive device or explosive, . . . poison, . . . [or] torture."[146] The social harm of this hypothetical statute includes a result (another person's death) brought about by a specified type of conduct (use of explosives, poison, or torture).

[3] Attendant Circumstances

In order for *any* offense to occur, certain facts or conditions — "attendant circumstances" — must be present when the actor performs the prohibited conduct and/or causes the prohibited result that constitutes the social harm of the offense.

"Attendant circumstance" elements are found in the definition of the crime. *The "social harm" of the offense, definitionally speaking, has not occurred unless the specified attendant circumstances are present.* For example, the social harm of common law burglary is the "breaking and entering of the dwelling house of another at nighttime." This means that for the defendant to be guilty of criminal offense of burglary, the breaking and entering by the actor *must* be of a "dwelling house" (not, for example, of a commercial structure or chicken coop); the dwelling *must* belong to someone other than the actor; and the events *must* occur at night. These elements of the offense — "dwelling house," "of another," and "at night" — are the "attendant circumstance" elements of burglary, as defined above. In the absence of these facts or conditions, the *social harm* of burglary has not occurred (although the social harm of a different offense, *e.g.*, trespass, may have occurred), and thus the *crime* of burglary cannot be proven.

---

[146] *See, e.g.*, Cal. Penal Code § 189 (Deering 2011).

§ 9.11 SOCIAL HARM: CONSTITUTIONAL LIMITS

May a legislature punish anything it chooses? May it say that "X" is a social harm and, therefore, it is a crime to "intentionally do X"? What if "X" is, for example, driving one's automobile? Or, reading the *New York Times*? Or watching Fox News?

Various constitutional provisions limit the extent to which a legislature may properly prohibit socially harmful conduct. For example, the Supreme Court has held that the First Amendment bars a legislature from making it a crime for a person to place on property a Nazi swastika, burning cross, or other symbol that the actor should know "arouses anger, alarm or resentment in others on the basis of race, color, creed, religion, or gender"[147]; similarly, the First Amendment bars the criminalization of possession of videos depicting animal cruelty.[148] The Court is *not* suggesting by this that there is no social harm in such circumstances, but rather is asserting that constitutional rights — here, freedom of speech — outweigh the society's interest in preventing this social harm in the manner chosen by the legislature.

The Supreme Court has also stated that constitutionally protected liberty "presumes an autonomy of self that includes . . . certain intimate conduct."[149] As a consequence, the high court has invalidated laws that prohibit physicians from dispensing contraceptive information to married and unmarried persons,[150] and adults from possessing obscene literature in their homes[151] or engaging in intimate consensual sexual conduct.[152]

---

[147] R. A. V. v. City of St. Paul, 505 U.S. 377 (1992).

[148] United States v. Stevens, 130 S. Ct. 1577 (2010) (limited to statutes that *depict* cruelty, as distinguished from statutes that prohibit the cruelty itself).

[149] Lawrence v. Texas, 539 U.S. 558, 562 (2003).

[150] Griswold v. Connecticut, 381 U.S. 479 (1965); Eisenstadt v. Baird, 405 U.S. 438 (1972).

[151] Stanley v. Georgia, 394 U.S. 557 (1969).

[152] Lawrence v. Texas, 539 U.S. 558 (2003) (constitutionally protecting consensual same-sex adult sexual conduct).

Chapter 10

MENS REA

§ 10.01 GENERAL PRINCIPLE[1]

Actus non facit reum nisi mens sit rea, or "an act does not make [a person] guilty, unless the mind be guilty," expresses the principle that, except in relatively rare circumstances,[2] a person is not guilty of a criminal offense unless the government not only proves the *actus reus* of the crime (discussed in the last chapter), but also the defendant's *mens rea* (literally, a "guilty mind"). As the Supreme Court has put it, criminal liability requires proof of "an evil-meaning mind with an evil-doing hand."[3]

This has not always been the case. In ancient English law, criminal responsibility was based solely on proof of commission of an *actus reus*. The actor's state of mind was irrelevant. By as early as the 13th century, however, English courts had begun to require proof that the person charged with a criminal offense had a culpable state of mind.[4]

By the 20th century, the concept of *mens rea* had become so deeply entrenched in American law that the Supreme Court could state that "[t]he contention that an injury can amount to a crime only when inflicted by [*mens rea*] is no provincial or transient notion. It is . . . universal and persistent in mature systems of law."[5] As one scholar has put it, "the requirement of mens rea contributes to the meaning and value of our lives as moral beings,"[6] Today, *mens rea* is "the criminal law's mantra."[7]

---

[1] *See generally* Jerome Hall, General Principles of the Criminal Law 70–104 (2d ed. 1960); Rollin M. Perkins, *A Rationale of Mens Rea*, 52 Harv. L. Rev. 905 (1939); Stephen J. Morse, *Inevitable Mens Rea*, 27 Harv. J.L. & Pub. Pol'y 51 (2003); Paul H. Robinson, *A Brief History of Distinctions in Criminal Culpability*, 31 Hastings L.J. 815 (1980); Francis Bowes Sayre, *Mens Rea*, 45 Harv. L. Rev. 974 (1932).

[2] *See* Chapter 11, *infra*.

[3] Morissette v. United States, 342 U.S. 246, 251 (1952).

[4] Robinson, Note 1, *supra*, at 821–46; Sayre, Note 1, *supra*, at 975–94.

[5] *Morissette v. United States*, 342 U.S. at 250.

[6] Morse, Note 1 *supra*, at 61.

[7] United States v. Cordoba-Hincapie, 825 F. Supp. 485, 490 (E.D.N.Y. 1993).

§ 10.02   DEFINITION OF *"MENS REA"*

[A]   Ambiguity of the Term

Professor George Fletcher has observed that "there is no term fraught with greater ambiguity than that venerable Latin phrase that haunts the Anglo-American criminal law: *mens rea.*"[8] Holmes, too, has noted "that most of the difficulty as to the *mens rea* was due to having no precise understanding what the *mens rea* is."[9] *"Mens rea"* has been described as "chameleon-like, [because it] takes on different colors in different surroundings."[10] Professor Sanford Kadish has ruefully observed that "the term '*mens rea*' is rivaled [by few legal terms] for the varieties of senses in which it has been used and for the quantity of obfuscation it has created."[11]

Generally speaking, *"mens rea"* has two meanings. Particularly during the early development of the doctrine, the term had a broad meaning, described below in subsection [B]. Over time, however, "the law [has] embarked upon the long journey of refinement and development"[12] of the doctrine, resulting in a narrower, more precise meaning, considered in subsection [C]. Although the latter meaning has gained prominence, both usages of the term *"mens rea"* persist today.

[B]   Broad Meaning: The "Culpability" Meaning of *"Mens Rea"*

Broadly speaking, *"mens rea"* is defined as "a general immorality of motive,"[13] "vicious will,"[14] or an "evil-meaning mind."[15] Although each of these phrases has a slightly different connotation, *"mens rea"* as used here suggests a general notion of moral blameworthiness, *i.e.*, that the defendant committed the social harm of an offense with a morally blameworthy state of mind. For current purposes, this may be termed the "culpability" meaning of *"mens rea."*

According to this definition of *"mens rea,"* guilt for an offense is not dependent on proof that the actor caused the proscribed harm with any specific mental state, *i.e.*, it is not necessary to show that he committed the offense "intentionally," "knowingly," or with any other particular frame of mind. Indeed, common law definitions of some offenses failed to specify any particular *mens rea* term.[16] It was

---

[8] George Fletcher, Rethinking Criminal Law 398 (1978).

[9] Letter from Oliver Wendell Holmes to Harold J. Laski (Jul. 14, 1916), *in* Holmes-Laski Letters 4 (Mark DeWolfe Howe ed., 1953).

[10] Francis Bowes Sayre, *The Present Signification of Mens Rea in the Criminal Law, in* Harvard Legal Essays, 399, 402 (1934) (italics omitted).

[11] Sanford H. Kadish, *The Decline of Innocence*, 26 Cambridge L.J. 273, 273 (1968).

[12] United States v. Cordoba-Hincapie, 825 F. Supp. 485, 491 (E.D.N.Y. 1993).

[13] Sayre, Note 10, *supra*, at 411–12.

[14] 4 William Blackstone, Commentaries on the Laws of England *21 (1769).

[15] Morissette v. United States, 342 U.S. 246, 251 (1952).

[16] Early on, some offenses did specify a particular mental state in their definition. These offenses came to be known as "specific intent" crimes. *See* § 10.06, *infra*.

sufficient that the defendant committed the social harm in a manner that demonstrated his bad character, malevolence, or immorality.

For example, in *Regina v. Cunningham*,[17] *C* entered the cellar of a building, where he tore the gas meter from the gas pipes and stole the coins deposited in the meter. As a consequence, gas escaped from the pipes, seeped through the cellar wall, and nearly asphyxiated *V*. Although *C* had not intended to endanger anyone's life by his actions, he was charged with an offense that provided, in part, that "[w]hosoever shall . . . maliciously . . . cause to be administered to or taken by any other person any poison . . . or noxious thing, so as thereby to endanger the life of such person, . . . shall be guilty of a felony."

The evidence presented at trial demonstrated that the *actus reus* of the offense occurred: as a result of conduct that included a voluntary act, *C* "caused to be administered" to *V* a "noxious thing" that endangered *V*'s life. The primary issue was whether *C* had the requisite *mens rea*. The trial judge instructed the jury that the statutory term "maliciously" meant only that the prosecution had to show that the defendant acted "wickedly." Thus, the court invited the jury to convict *C* if it found that he caused the social harm of the offense (basically, administering a noxious thing that endangered the life of another) with a morally culpable state of mind. Since *C* caused the harm, albeit unintentionally, while attempting to steal money from the meter, the jury found the requisite wickedness.[18]

[C] Narrow Meaning: The "Elemental" Meaning of "*Mens Rea*"

"*Mens rea*" may also be defined, simply, as "the particular mental state provided for in the definition of an offense." This is the "elemental" meaning of "*mens rea.*" A person may possess "*mens rea*" in the *culpability* sense of the term, and yet lack the requisite *elemental* "*mens rea.*"

For example, assume that murder is defined by statute as "the intentional killing of a human being by another human being." The *actus reus* of the offense is "the killing of a human being by another human being." The "*mens rea*" — the particular mental state provided for in the definition of the offense — is "intentional." Applying the elemental meaning of "*mens rea*," *D* is guilty of murder if he intentionally kills another human being. However, if he kills *un*intentionally, albeit with a morally blameworthy state of mind (for example, if he takes another's life accidentally while trying to perpetrate a robbery), he would *not* be guilty of murder as defined, because he lacked the particular mental state required in the definition of the offense.

---

[17] 41 Crim. App. 155, 2 Q.B. 396, 2 All E.R. 412 (1957) (Court of Criminal Appeal).

[18] However, the Court of Criminal Appeal in *Cunningham* allowed *C*'s appeal on the ground that the trial judge's *mens rea* instruction was erroneous. *See* § 10.04[E], *infra*.

§ 10.03 RATIONALE OF THE *MENS REA* REQUIREMENT[19]

[A] Utilitarian Arguments

The *mens rea* requirement is sometimes explained on grounds of deterrence. A person cannot be deterred from criminal activity, it is argued, unless he "appreciate[s] that punishment lies in store" if he persists in his actions.[20] Therefore, punishment of one who lacks a culpable state of mind will be ineffective and, consequently, wasteful. It may also be reasoned that one who causes harm accidentally, rather than intentionally or with an "evil-meaning mind," is harmless and not in need of reformation.

These claims are only partly persuasive. Even if one acting without a culpable state of mind cannot be deterred on the present occasion, his punishment may serve as a useful warning to others to be more careful in their activities, thereby potentially reducing the number of accidentally inflicted injuries.[21] Furthermore, although it may be agreed that one who acts with a *mens rea* is apt to be dangerous and in need of reformation, the accidental harmdoer may also need incapacitation or some other corrective influence. Some people are accident-prone; the criminal sanction may be a rational way to protect society from them. At a minimum, their punishment may influence them to change their lifestyle and to avoid activities that may result in injury to others.

The *mens rea* requirement may be counter-productive for another reason. The prosecution is constitutionally required to prove beyond a reasonable doubt every element of a criminal offense, including the defendant's *mens rea*.[22] This is sometimes a difficult burden to satisfy; consequently, some persons who are culpable are able to avoid conviction. Their acquittals send the potential counter-utilitarian message to would-be wrongdoers — those who are looking for a legal loophole — that they might also be able to escape the criminal sanction.

[B] Retributive Arguments

The Supreme Court once observed that "[a] relation between some mental element and punishment for a harmful act is almost as instinctive as the child's familiar exculpatory [statement], 'But I didn't mean to'."[23] Oliver Wendell Holmes has made the same point with animals rather than children when he suggested that "even a dog distinguishes between being stumbled over and being kicked."[24]

Whether Holmes's observation about dogs is right or wrong, the preceding observations assist in making the vital point that the principle of *mens rea* has its roots far deeper in retributive than in utilitarian soil. Although a society

---

[19] See generally the sources in Note 1, *supra*.

[20] Glanville Williams, Criminal Law: The General Part 30 (2d ed. 1961).

[21] Richard A. Wasserstrom, *Strict Liability in the Criminal Law*, 12 Stan. L. Rev. 731, 736–37 (1960).

[22] *See* § 7.03[B], *supra*.

[23] Morissette v. United States, 342 U.S. 246, 250–51 (1952).

[24] Oliver Wendell Holmes, The Common Law 3 (1881).

presumably wants to deter harmful conduct, the *mens rea* requirement "flows from our society's commitment to individual choice";[25] the principle is founded on the belief that it is morally unjust to punish those who innocently, rather than culpably, cause social injury.

Crimes are public wrongs. The implication of a guilty verdict is that the convicted party wronged the community as a whole. By convicting a criminal defendant, society denounces the actor; it condemns and stigmatizes him as a wrongdoer.[26] Respect for human dignity suggests, if it does not dictate, that such stigma should not attach, and liberty should not be denied, to one who has acted without a culpable state of mind.

§ 10.04 FREQUENTLY USED *MENS REA* TERMS[27]

[A] "Intentionally"

[1] Definition

Many common law and statutory offenses are defined in terms of "intent," that is, the prosecution must prove that the defendant intentionally committed the social harm that constitutes the *actus reus* of the offense. On occasion, the "intent" to cause a particular result (*e.g.*, to kill another) or to engage in specified conduct (*e.g.*, drive an automobile) is defined narrowly in a statute to mean that it was the actor's purpose, desire, or conscious objective to cause the result or to engage in the specified conduct.[28]

The more typical common law definition of "intent," however, is somewhat broader. At common law, a person "intentionally" causes the social harm of an offense if: (1) it is his desire (*i.e.*, his conscious object) to cause the social harm; *or* (2) he acts with knowledge that the social harm is virtually certain to occur as a result of his conduct.[29] For example,[30] suppose that bomb expert *D* wants to kill *V*, his wife, in order to obtain the proceeds from her life insurance policy. *D* constructs a bomb and places it on an airplane on which *V* is a passenger. He sets the bomb to

---

[25] United States v. Cordoba-Hincapie, 825 F. Supp. 485, 495 (E.D.N.Y. 1993).

[26] *See* § 1.01[A][1], *supra*.

[27] *See generally* Larry Alexander & Kimberly Kessler Ferzan, Crime and Culpability 23–168 (2009); Larry Alexander, *Insufficient Concern: A Unified Conception of Criminal Culpability*, 88 Cal. L. Rev. 931 (2000); Joshua Dressler, *Does One Mens Rea Fit All?: Thoughts on Alexander's Unified Conception of Criminal Culpability*, 88 Cal. L. Rev. 955 (2000); Douglas N. Husak, *The Sequential Principle of Relative Culpability*, 1 Legal Theory 493 (1995); Kenneth W. Simons, *Rethinking Mental States*, 72 B.U.L. Rev. 463 (1992).

[28] People v. Conley, 543 N.E.2d 138 (Ill. App. Ct. 1989) (applying an Illinois statute defining "intent").

[29] United States v. Tobin, 552 F.3d 29, 32–33 (1st Cir. 2009); Thornton v. State, 919 A.2d 678, 691 (Md. 2007).

[30] As explained in § 9.10, *supra*, the prohibited "social harm" may be an unwanted result or wrongful conduct. The "intent" definition encompasses both types of offenses. However, because most "intent" issues arise in the context of results, rather than conduct, the examples here focus on "result" offenses, such as murder or manslaughter.

explode while the plane is in air. Although D does not want anyone on the plane other than V to die — indeed, he prays that the others will survive — he knows that the bomb will destroy the airplane. The bomb goes off as planned, killing V and the other 100 persons on board.

According to the ordinary common law definition, how many people did D "intentionally" kill? Clearly, D "intentionally" killed V. This follows from the simple fact that D wanted V to die; it was his conscious object — his purpose — to take her life. Under the first prong of the definition of "intent" set out above, it does not matter how likely it was that the result would occur; it is enough that D desired his wife's death.

D's mental state as to the other victims must be analyzed differently. He did not desire their deaths; in fact, he prayed that they would live. Nonetheless, assuming that D was not mentally incapacitated in some manner, a jury could readily determine that he "intended" their deaths as well. According to the second meaning of "intent" set out above, he *knew* that the social harm of their deaths was *virtually certain* to occur when his bomb exploded. This second prong may be termed the "known certainties" prong, for it is not satisfied if the outcome was merely highly probable; the actor must realize, in essence, that short of a divine intervention or a secular "miracle," the undesired event will occur "for sure."[31]

Both versions of "intent" are said to involve *subjective* fault. An actor's fault is "subjective" if he actually — internally, if you will — possesses a wrongful state of mind: in this case, the conscious desire to cause the social harm, or the actual awareness that the harm will almost certainly result from his conduct.[32]

The significance of the subjective nature of "intent" is seen by a minor change in the bombing hypothetical. Suppose that D belonged to a religious sect that espoused the belief that members of the faith always have their wishes fulfilled by God. Therefore, as a member of the sect, D genuinely believed that his fervent prayers would save everyone on the airplane except his wife, for whom he did not pray for divine protection. Based on these revised facts, D (as before) intentionally killed his wife, because he desired her death. However, assuming that a jury believes his testimony about his religious beliefs, D did not "intentionally" kill the other passengers — he was not subjectively aware that their deaths were a near certainty. "Intent" requires such awareness; a prosecutor has not proved "intent" by merely showing that D *should have been aware*, as a reasonable person, that the passengers would be killed.

---

[31] Glanville Williams, *Oblique Intention*, 46 Cambridge L.J. 417, 418 (1987).

[32] Arguably, a person who *desires* a certain outcome (the first prong of the "intent" definition) is more culpable than one who does not want it to occur but proceeds with *knowledge* that it will result (the alternative second prong). The common law definition, however, merges these two types of culpability. In contrast, the Model Penal Code distinguishes between these two states of mind. *See* § 10.07[B], *infra*.

[2] "Motive" Distinguished[33]

Some legal scholars state that motive is irrelevant in the substantive criminal law.[34] This statement is only correct if they mean that the "intention" to cause social harm is no less "intentional" simply because the actor's motive was not evil in character. For example, a doctor who kills his terminally ill patient to "put him out of his misery" arguably has a benevolent motive, but the killing is still "intentional."[35]

A defendant's motive, however, *is* often relevant in the criminal law. First, some offenses (so-called "specific intent" crimes[36]) *by definition* require proof of a specific motive in order to convict the actor. For example, common law larceny is the trespassory taking and carrying away of the personal property of another *with the intent to steal, i.e., with the intent to permanently deprive the other of the property.* Although this definition includes the term "intent" — English scholars sometimes call it an "ulterior intention" — the italicized language denotes the actor's motive for committing the social harm of the offense. In the absence of this motive — for example, if *D*, without your consent, intentionally takes and carries away your laptop computer with the intention of returning it in an hour ("I just borrowed it!") — no larceny has occurred. Yes, *D* has committed the social harm of larceny (he wrongfully took and carried away your personal property) and, yes, he did *this* intentionally, but he is not guilty of the offense because he lacked the specific intent — the specified motive — of *permanently* depriving you of your property.

Second, motive is relevant to claims of defense. That is, if the defendant's motive for his intentional conduct is legally justifiable (*e.g.*, he intentionally kills an aggressor in order to protect his own life), he will be acquitted. As this example demonstrates, the existence of a justifiable motive does not render the defendant's conduct or the consequences of it any less intentional, but it may affect his ultimate criminal liability.

Third, motive is often highly relevant at the sentencing phase of a criminal proceeding. For example, if it wishes to do so, a state may impose enhanced punishment for an offense if the actor selected his victim on account of an unlawful factor, such as race, religion, disability, or sexual orientation.[37] Likewise, in jurisdictions permitting sentencing discretion, a defendant's good motive for wrongful conduct may be considered in mitigation.

---

[33] *See generally* Martin R. Gardner, *The Mens Rea Enigma: Observations on the Role of Motive in the Criminal Law Past and Present*, 1993 Utah L. Rev. 635; Douglas N. Husak, *Motive and Criminal Liability*, Crim. Just. Ethics, Winter/Spring 1989, at 3.

[34] *E.g.*, Hall, Note 1, *supra*, at 88 ("[H]ardly any part of penal law is more definitely settled than that motive is irrelevant.").

[35] Even here, however, the doctor's motive is relevant to the criminal law, in the sense that proof of his motive *reinforces* the prosecution's claim that the doctor acted with the requisite intent.

[36] *See* § 10.06, *infra*.

[37] *E.g.*, Wis. Stat. § 939.645(1)(a) (2015).

[3]   "Transferred Intent"[38]

[a]   General Doctrine

Suppose *A* wrongfully fires a gun at *B*, intending to kill him, but the bullet instead strikes and kills unintended victim *C*, a bystander. Is *A* guilty of intent-to-kill murder of *C*? Or, suppose *A* attempts to strike *B*, *B* ducks, and *A*'s fist strikes *C* instead. May *A* be convicted of battery of *C* (for current purposes, hypothetically defined as "intentional touching or striking of another")?

In both hypotheticals, the answer is "yes." Courts typically reach this outcome by applying the legal fiction of "transferred intent."[39] According to this doctrine, which originated in the 16th century,[40] we attribute liability to a "bad aim" defendant who, intending to kill (or injure) one person, accidentally kills (or injures) another person instead.[41] The law "transfers" the actor's state of mind regarding the intended victim to the unintended one. Some judges instruct juries in these cases that "the intent follows the bullet."[42]

The transferred intent doctrine is justified on grounds of necessity and proportionality. The necessity argument is that the bad aimer should not avoid conviction for intent-to-kill homicide simply because he killed the "wrong person," *i.e.*, someone he did not intend to kill. The proportionality argument is that the doctrine is meant "to ensure that prosecution and punishment accord with culpability."[43] That is, one who intends to cause a particular harm to one individual, and instead causes precisely the same harm but to a different person, is "as culpable . . . as if the defendant had accomplished what he had initially intended."[44]

Unfortunately, as uncontroversial and simple as transferred intent seems on quick inspection, it is neither. Some scholars have argued against the moral soundness of the transferred intent doctrine,[45] which has been characterized as a "name attached to an unexplained mystery."[46] This "mystery" is not only a legal

---

[38] *See generally* Anthony M. Dillof, *Transferred Intent: An Inquiry into the Nature of Criminal Culpability*, 1 Buff. Crim. L. Rev. 501 (1998); Shachar Eldar, *The Limits of Transferred Malice*, 32 Oxford J. Leg. Studies 633 (2012); Douglas N. Husak, *Transferred Intent*, 10 Notre Dame J.L. Ethics & Pub. Pol'y 65 (1996); Peter Westen, *The Significance of Transferred Intent*, 7 Crim. L. & Phil. 321 (2013).

[39] People v. Bland, 48 P.3d 1107, 1110 (Cal. 2002) (characterizing this "artificial doctrine" as "universally accepted" in such circumstances).

[40] Regina v. Saunders, 2 Plowd. 473, 75 Eng. Rep. 706 (1576).

[41] Poe v. State, 652 A.2d 1164, 1169 (Md. Ct. Spec. App. 1995), *aff'd*, 671 A.2d 501 (Md. 1996).

[42] *Poe*, 652 A.2d at 1168.

[43] People v. Czahara, 203 Cal. App. 3d 1468, 1474 (Ct. App. 1988).

[44] People v. Scott, 927 P.2d 288, 291 (Cal. 1996); *see* People v. Birreuta, 162 Cal. App. 3d 454, 460 (Ct. App. 1984), *overruled on other grounds*, People v. Bland, 48 P.3d 1107 (Cal. 2002) ("The transferred intent doctrine is borne of the sound judicial intuition that [a bad-aim] defendant is no less culpable than a murderer whose aim is good.").

[45] *E.g.*, Dillof, Note 38, *supra*.

[46] Husak, Note 38, *supra*, at 67.

fiction — states of mind hardly follow bullets to unintended victims[47] — but it is a potentially misleading and, therefore, mischievous doctrine.[48] Moreover, as suggested immediately below, the doctrine is unnecessary to ensure a proper outcome in ordinary bad-aim cases.

[b]   An Unnecessary and Potentially Misleading Doctrine

It is submitted here that the transferred intent doctrine is unnecessary and, if invoked without great care, misleading. Consider the typical "bad aim" case: *A* intends to kill *B*, but instead kills *C*, and is prosecuted for intent-to-kill murder of *C*. In this case, there is no need to transfer *A*'s intention to kill *B* to unintended victim *C*; *A* has the requisite intent *without* the doctrine. There is no need to think in terms of *A*'s *mens rea* following a bullet to its eventual victim. One need only look at the definition of criminal homicide to see this: The social harm of murder is the "killing of a human being by another human being." The requisite intent, therefore, is the intent to kill *a*, not a specific, human being.[49] In the present case, *A* intended to kill *a* human being (*B*), so the *mens rea* is satisfied; and he did in fact kill *a* human being (*C*), so the social harm is proven. Thus, the elements of murder are proved without invoking the legal fiction of transferred intent.[50]

The correctness of this assertion — and the danger of applying the transferred intent doctrine mindlessly — is demonstrated if one looks at offenses that *do* require proof of a specific victim. For example, in *Ford v. State*,[51] *F* threw rocks at a moving vehicle, with the intention of disabling the driver. He was charged according to an assault statute that made it an offense to "assault or beat any person, with intent to maim, disfigure, or disable *such person*." The trial judge instructed the jury that *F*'s intent could be transferred to an injured passenger, although *F* rock was meant for the driver. Essentially, the judge believed that the intent to disable followed the rock, but it does not. The appellate court correctly ruled that the transferred intent doctrine does not apply to "statutory offenses which require that the defendant's criminal intent be directed towards the actual victim."

There is another subtle error that can occur if a court thoughtlessly applies the transferred intent doctrine. By its terms, the doctrine serves to transfer the intent from the intended victim to the unintended one, but it does *not* transfer the intent to cause one type of social harm to another. For example, if *A* intends to kill a dog, but the bullet strikes and unintentionally kills a human, it would be impermissible

---

[47] "By thinking of the *mens rea* in such finite terms — as some discrete unit that must be either here or there — we have created a linguistic problem for ourselves where no real-life problem existed. . . . It neither follows nor fails to follow the bullet. . . . It remains in the brain of the criminal actor and never moves." Harvey v. State, 681 A.2d 628, 637 (Md. Ct. Spec. App. 1996).

[48] People v. Scott, 927 P.2d at 294 (Mosk, J., concurring) ("a peculiarly mischievous legal fiction").

[49] People v. Stone, 205 P.3d 272, 277 (Cal. 2009) (quoting People v. Scott, 927 P.2d 288 (Cal. 1996), which quoted this text).

[50] Ramsey v. State, 56 P.3d 675, 681 (Alaska Ct. App. 2002); Millen v. State, 988 S.W.2d 164, 165 (Tenn. 1999).

[51] 625 A.2d 984 (Md. 1993).

to charge *A* with intent-to-kill murder and transfer the intent from the dog to the human, because the social harm of murder involves the death of humans and not canines. Similarly, if *A* throws a rock at *B*, intending to injure him, but the rock instead breaks a window in a building behind *B*,[52] *A*'s intent to batter a person — one type of social harm — should not be used to prove that *A* intended to cause property damage, the social harm of the offense charged.[53]

Overall, confusion could be avoided if courts rejected the transferred intent doctrine outright, and simply sought to determine whether the actor had the intent to cause the particular social harm required in the definition of the charged offense.

[c]   Looking Past the Easy Cases

The paradigmatic transferred intent case has these characteristics: (1) *A* intends to cause a specific harm to one — *just one*[54] — specific individual, *B*; (2) *B* escapes unscathed; and (3) an unintended victim, *C*, suffers the precise harm meant for *B*.

Many supposed transferred intent cases are not so simple.[55] Reconsider the classic case, where *A*, with intent to kill, fires at *B*, misses him entirely, and accidentally kills bystander *C* instead. *A* is guilty of intent-to-kill murder of *C* according to the transferred intent doctrine. But may *A* also be charged with *attempted* murder of *B*, an offense that also requires the intent to kill? Or, suppose that the bullet meant for *B*, and only *B*,[56] *does kill B*, but *also* kills bystander *C*. Can *two* counts of intent-to-kill murder be permitted here? It is submitted that the answer in such circumstances normally should be "no," yet courts are divided on facts of this sort. Most courts apply the transferred intent doctrine in these and related examples, and permit use of *A*'s intent to kill one person to convict him of multiple "intent" crimes,[57] while a smaller number of courts properly (it is

---

[52]   Regina v. Pembliton, 12 Cox C.C. 607 (1874) (Court of Criminal Appeal).

[53]   *See* Mordica v. State, 618 So. 2d 301 (Fla. Dist. Ct. App. 1993) (*M*, a prison inmate, attempted to kick fellow inmate *X*; *M*'s foot hit *V*, a prison guard; held: the transferred intent doctrine does not apply in a prosecution for "battery upon a law enforcement officer"; *M* intended to commit a battery, but not battery of a police officer, a different and more serious type of social harm).

[54]   This is an important, and sometimes forgotten, characteristic. There is no need to transfer intent to a second victim if the actor intended the harm to both victims. For example, so-called "kill zone" or "concurrent intent" cases do not involve "transferred intent" issues, although courts sometimes incorrectly ignore this fact. Assume that *A*, intending to kill *B*, who is holding her baby *C* in her arms, fires a single bullet at *B*, knowing that the bullet will have to go through *C* in order to kill *B*. In short, although *A* only desires to kill *B*, he knows that he will concurrently kill *C*, who is in the line of fire. Therefore, on these facts, *A* has the "intent" to kill *two* people (*B* purposely, *C* knowingly). *See* People v. Smith, 124 P.3d 730 (Cal. 2005).

[55]   Harvey v. State, 681 A.2d 628, 634 (Md. Ct. Spec. App. 1996) (there is "a matrix of no less than nine combinations of criminal harms" that plausibly fall under the "transferred intent" umbrella).

[56]   This is an important qualification. *See* Note 54, *supra*.

[57]   *E.g.*, People v. Scott, 927 P.2d 288 (Cal. 1996) (*A* may be convicted of attempted murder of intended victim *B*, who was not hit, and intentional murder of unintended victim *C*); Henry v. State, 19 A.3d 944 (Md. 2011) (conceding that courts are divided on the subject, this court holds that the death of the defendant's intended victim does not preclude application of the transferred intent doctrine to a second, unintended homicide victim); Poe v. State, 671 A.2d 501 (Md. 1996) (*A* may be convicted of attempted

submitted) reject use of the doctrine in such circumstances.[58]

To see why the transferred intent doctrine should not apply in such circumstances, it is important to remember that the purpose of the doctrine is to put the "bad aim" wrongdoer in the same position he would have found himself if his aim had been good. The doctrine is meant to result in punishment proportional to the wrongdoer's culpability. Improper invocation of the transferred intent doctrine can result in disproportional punishment.

This can be seen by the following hypothetical, with two scenarios: Assume *A* observes *B* hugging his wife, *C*. *A*, therefore, intends to kill *B* but leave wife *C* unscathed. *A* believes that he can shoot and kill *B* from a distance without harming *C*. In Scenario 1, *A* does exactly what he intended — he kills *B* and does not kill or wound *C*. *A* is guilty of intent-to-kill murder of *B*. And, in many modern penal codes, *A* would also be guilty of reckless endangerment of *C*.[59] In short, the single act of firing one bullet may justifiably result in conviction of *A* for two offenses, one for each victim, *because A had two culpable states of mind*, the intent to kill *B*, and recklessness as to *C*.[60]

In Scenario 2, assume that *A*'s aim is bad, and not good, and the bullet kills *C*, his wife, rather than intended victim, *B*. Although the identities of the homicide victim and the person endangered have been switched, *A*'s moral culpability for the incident seemingly remains the same — he intended to kill one person, and he recklessly endangered another. Therefore, it would be reasonable to convict *A* here either of attempted murder of *B*, and *reckless* murder of *C*, or one count of intent-to-kill murder (of *C*) and one count of reckless endangerment (of *B*). However, if a court thoughtlessly applies the transferred intent doctrine in this scenario — thereby convicting *A* of two intent-to-kill offenses, namely, murder of *C* (by transferred intent) and attempted murder of *B* — *A* improperly will be convicted in Scenario 2 more severely than if his aim had been good (Scenario 1)!

---

murder of intended victim *B*, who was wounded, and intentional murder of unintended victim *C*); Lloyd v. United States, 806 A.2d 1243 (D.C. 2002) (answering affirmatively the question of "whether the transferred intent doctrine . . . permits a first-degree murder conviction for the shooting death of an unintended victim when the intended victim has also been shot dead").

[58] *E.g.*, Roberts v. State, 273 S.W.3d 322 (Tex. Crim. App. 2008) (*D* intentionally shot to death *V*, unaware that *V* was in the early stages of pregnancy; although the fetus is considered a "human being" under Texas law for these purposes, the court held that "transferred intent" may not be used to prove the intentional killing of the fetus); People v. Czahara, 203 Cal. App. 3d 1468 (Ct. App. 1988) (if *A* shoots to kill *B*, wounding *B* and *C*, *A* may be charged with attempted murder of *B*, but not attempted murder of *C*); State v. Brady, 903 A.2d 870 (Md. 2006) (same); Bell v. State, 768 So. 2d 22 (Fla. Dist. Ct. App. 2000) (same).

[59] *E.g.*, Model Penal Code § 211.2 ("recklessly engages in conduct which places or may place another person in danger of death or serious bodily injury").

[60] *See also* Note 54, *supra*.

[B] "Knowingly" or "With Knowledge"[61]

As explained in subsection [A][1] above, a person who knowingly causes a particular result or knowingly engages in specified conduct is commonly said to have "intended" the harmful result or conduct. Sometimes, however, knowledge of a material fact — an "attendant circumstance"[62] — is also a required element of an offense. For example, it is a federal crime for a person knowingly to import any controlled substance into the country.[63] Under this statute, a person, D, who drives an automobile containing marijuana into the United States, is not guilty unless he "knows" of the presence of the contraband — an attendant circumstance — when he crosses the border.

A person has "knowledge" of a material fact if he: (1) is aware of the fact; or (2) correctly believes that the fact exists. Thus, in the marijuana importation hypothetical, D "knows" of the presence of the marijuana if he concealed it in the vehicle himself or personally observed its presence ("actual knowledge"); alternatively, he "knows" of the marijuana's existence if he smells it and, as a consequence, believes that it is present ("correct belief" form of "knowledge").

Most jurisdictions also permit a finding of knowledge of an attendant circumstance in a third, more controversial, circumstance, namely, when the actor is guilty of so-called "willful blindness" or "deliberate ignorance."[64] Although courts and scholars do not agree entirely on the definition of this concept, it often is stated that "willful blindness" exists if the actor: (1) believes that there is a high probability that the fact (attendance circumstance) exists; and (2a) takes deliberate action to avoid confirming the fact, or (2b) purposely fails to investigate in order to avoid confirmation of the fact.[65] A "willful blindness" instruction to the jury is often called an "ostrich instruction." Judge Richard Posner has explained the ostrich analogy this way:

> [Supposedly, real ostriches] do not just fail to follow through on their suspicions of bad things. They are not merely *careless* birds. They bury their heads in the sand so that they will not see or hear bad things. They

---

[61] *See generally* Robin Charlow, *Wilful Ignorance and Criminal Culpability*, 70 Tex. L. Rev. 1351 (1992); Deborah Hellman, *Willfully Blind for Good Reason*, 3 Crim. Law & Philos. 301 (2009); Douglas N. Husak & Craig A. Callender, *Wilful Ignorance, Knowledge, and the "Equal Culpability" Thesis: A Study of the Deeper Significance of the Principle of Legality*, 1994 Wis. L. Rev. 29; David Luban, *Contrived Ignorance*, 87 Geo. L.J. 957 (1999); Alan C. Michaels, *Acceptance: The Missing Mental State*, 71 S. Cal. L. Rev. 953 (1998); Ira P. Robbins, *The Ostrich Instruction: Deliberate Ignorance as a Criminal Mens Rea*, 81 J. Crim. L. & Criminology 191 (1990); Kenneth W. Simons, *Does Punishment for "Culpable Indifference" Simply Punish for "Bad Character"? Examining the Requisite Connection Between Mens Rea and Actus Reus*, 6 Buff. Crim. L. Rev. 219 (2002).

[62] *See* § 9.10[D][3], *supra*.

[63] 21 U.S.C. § 952(a) (2015).

[64] *See* Global-Tech Appliances, Inc. v. SEB S.A., 131 S. Ct. 2060, n.4 (2011) (citing cases in all federal circuit courts, recognizing the "willful blindness" doctrine); *see also* State v. LaFreniere, 481 N.W.2d 412 (Neb. 1992); *contra* State v. Nations, 676 S.W.2d 282 (Mo. Ct. App. 1984) (interpreting state law, rejecting the "willful blindness" concept, and requiring proof of actual knowledge).

[65] Global-Tech Appliances, Inc. v. Seb S.A., 131 S. Ct. at 2070 (summarizing the doctrine under federal law). For a slightly different version of the doctrine, under the Model Penal Code, see subsection 10.07[B][2], *infra*.

deliberately avoid acquiring unpleasant knowledge. The ostrich instruction is designed for cases in which there is evidence that the defendant, knowing or strongly suspecting that he is involved in shady dealings, takes steps to make sure that he does not acquire full or exact knowledge.[66]

Thus, in the importation hypothetical, *D* would be guilty of "willful blindness" if, for example, he agreed to drive *X*'s car into the country although he was highly suspicious that drugs had been concealed in it (he believes there is a high probability that drugs are in the car), and he purposely avoided looking in the trunk or elsewhere because he was afraid that it would confirm his suspicions.[67]

The "willful blindness" form of "knowledge" is controversial. First, notwithstanding the ostrich analogy, the actor need not take steps of an active nature, equivalent to putting his head in the sand, to be found guilty of willful blindness; as a practical matter, his culpability may ultimately be based on little or nothing more than his *failure* to take obvious and simple steps to confirm or dispel his suspicions. The risk in giving an ostrich instruction, therefore, is that a jury might convict a defendant for merely being a careless bird, *i.e.*, for being negligent, which is a far less culpable state of mind than knowledge.[68] Second, critics maintain that a person who is "guilty" of willful blindness (*e.g.*, someone who smells something in a car, believes that there is a substantial risk that what he is smelling is an illegal drug, and yet fails to further check out the situation) should be characterized as *reckless* for proceeding notwithstanding his suspicion, but recklessness is a lesser form of culpability than actual knowledge.[69]

Advocates of the willful blindness doctrine respond that "willful blindness" *does* constitute a higher level of culpability than recklessness. The reckless actor is merely aware of the risk that a fact exists, whereas the defendant-as-ostrich, with such awareness, *purposely* blinds himself to direct proof of the fact in question, in order to avoid criminal liability. Without this doctrine, it is suggested, people who behave in this manner could avoid conviction.

Critics disagree with these arguments. First, all the legislature needs to do to ensure conviction of such actors is redraft the statute to require recklessness, rather than knowledge, of the attendant circumstance. Second, even if one believes that a willfully blind person is as culpable as one who is actually aware of a fact, that only proves that "willful blindness" is *morally equivalent* to "knowledge"; it is not the same as saying that "willful blindness" *is* "knowledge." As long as an offense is expressly defined in terms of "knowledge," the principle of legality teaches that an equivalent — but different — state of mind should be insufficient for conviction.[70]

---

[66] United States v. Giovannetti, 919 F.2d 1223, 1228 (7th Cir. 1990). For what it is worth, according to Judge Posner, this description of ostriches is "pure legend and a canard on a very distinguished bird." United States v. Black, 530 F.3d 596, 604 (7th Cir. 2008), *vacated*, 130 S. Ct. 2963 (2010).

[67] *See* United States v. Jewell, 532 F.2d 697 (9th Cir. 1976).

[68] United States v. Alvarado, 838 F.2d 311, 314 (9th Cir. 1987).

[69] Robbins, Note 61, *supra*, at 220–27. "Recklessness" is defined in subsection [D][3], *infra*.

[70] *See generally* Husak & Callender, Note 61, *supra*.

[C] "Willfully"[71]

"Willful" (or, alternatively, "wilful") is a "word of many meanings."[72] It is sometimes used as a synonym for "intentional."[73] Sometimes, however, the term means "an act done with a bad purpose"[74] or with "an evil motive."[75] "Willful" may also connote an "intentional violation of a known legal duty,"[76] or "a purpose to disobey the law."[77] The meaning of the term often cannot be determined except in the context of the legislative history of the offense itself.

In most circumstances, an intentional wrongdoer acts with a bad purpose or evil motive, and with knowledge that he is violating the law, so it does not matter which meaning of "willful" is applied. Sometimes, however, the difference is significant. For example, in one federal case,[78] D asserted what he believed to be his constitutional privilege not to incriminate himself, by refusing to answer questions propounded to him by the Internal Revenue Service. As it turned out, the constitutional provision did not apply in his circumstances. Therefore, he was prosecuted for "willfully" refusing to answer the questions.

If "willful" means "intentional," D was guilty because he intentionally refused to answer the questions. D's conviction was overturned, however, because his refusal, although intentional, was based on an erroneous belief that he had a lawful right to refuse to answer. Therefore, he lacked an evil motive for the violation, and did not act with the purpose of disobeying the law. It should be noted that when the latter meaning of "willful" is applied, the presence of this term in the definition of an offense results in an exception to the usual rule that a mistake of law is not a basis for exculpation of an actor.[79]

---

[71] *See generally* Sharon L. Davies, *The Jurisprudence of Willfulness: An Evolving Theory of Excusable Ignorance*, 48 Duke L.J. 341 (1998); Michael E. Tigar, *"Willfulness" and "Ignorance" in Federal Criminal Law*, 37 Cleve. St. L. Rev. 525 (1989).

[72] Ratzlaf v. United States, 510 U.S. 135, 141 (1994) (quoting Spies v. United States, 317 U.S. 492, 497 (1943)).

[73] *E.g.*, Commonwealth v. Welansky, 55 N.E.2d 902, 910 (Mass. 1944).

[74] *See* Townsend v. United States, 95 F.2d 352, 358 (D.C. Cir. 1938).

[75] United States v. Murdock, 290 U.S. 389, 395 (1933).

[76] Cheek v. United States, 498 U.S. 192, 200 (1991); *see also* State v. Azneer, 526 N.W.2d 298, 300 (Iowa 1995) ("a voluntary and intentional violation of a known legal duty").

[77] *Ratzlaf v. United States*, 510 U.S. at 141; *see also* United States v. Hayden, 64 F.3d 126, 128 (3d Cir. 1995) ("an intent to violate the law itself").

[78] United States v. Murdock, 290 U.S. 389 (1933), *overruled on other grounds in* Murphy v. Waterfront Commission, 378 U.S. 52 (1964).

[79] *See generally* § 13.02[D][2], *infra*.

[D]   "Negligence" and "Recklessness"[80]

[1]   Overview

Risk-taking is an ever-present aspect of life. Virtually every human act can cause harm to the actor, other persons, property, or non-human life. Nonetheless, society favors some risk-taking (*e.g.*, the doctor who perform risky surgery to save a life). In other circumstances, however, it requires risk-takers to financially compensate those who are harmed by their conduct. And, in still other cases, the law punishes risk-taking.

For current purposes, risk-taking falls into four categories: (1) desirable or, at least, neutral risk-taking; (2) risk-taking that justifies civil liability ("civil negligence"); (3) risk-taking that crosses the civil line and justifies criminal liability ("criminal negligence"); and (4) even more culpable risk-taking that justifies every greater criminal liability ("recklessness"). The lines between these categories are not bright and sometimes in dispute. And, unfortunately, courts have sometimes used the terms "negligence" and "recklessness" interchangeably,[81] particularly before the advent and influence of the Model Penal Code, so it is sometimes difficult to distinguish between these two types of risk-taking in the language of non-modern judicial opinions.

[2]   "Negligence"

[a]   In General

A person's conduct is "negligent" if it constitutes a deviation from the standard of care that a reasonable person would have observed in the actor's situation. Conduct constitutes such a negligent deviation if the actor *fails to appreciate* that he is taking an unjustifiable risk of causing harm to another. Thus, "negligence" constitutes *objective* fault: An actor is not blamed for a wrongful state of mind, but instead is punished for his morally blameworthy *failure to realize* that he is taking an unjustified risk — for his failure, in other words, to live up to the standards of the fictional "reasonable person."[82]

Three factors come into play when determining whether a reasonable person would have acted as the defendant did: (1) the gravity of harm that foreseeably would result from the defendant's conduct; (2) the probability of such harm occurring; and (3) the burden — or loss — to the defendant of desisting from the

---

[80] *See generally* Alexander & Ferzan, Note 27, *supra*; Alexander, Note 27, *supra*; Dressler, Note 27, *supra*; Kimberly Kessler Ferzan, *Opaque Recklessness*, 91 J. Crim. L. & Criminology 597 (2001); George P. Fletcher, *The Theory of Criminal Negligence: A Comparative Analysis*, 119 U. Pa. L. Rev. 401 (1971); Jerome Hall, *Negligent Behavior Should Be Excluded from Penal Liability*, 63 Colum. L. Rev. 632 (1963); Heidi M. Hurd, *The Deontology of Negligence*, 76 B.U.L. Rev. 249 (1996); Samuel H. Pillsbury, *Crimes of Indifference*, 49 Rutgers L. Rev. 105 (1996); A.P. Simester, *Can Negligence Be Culpable?*, *in* Oxford Essays in Jurisprudence (4th Series 2000) (J. Horder ed.), at 85; Kenneth W. Simons, *Culpability and Retributive Theory: The Problem of Criminal Negligence*, 5 J. Contemp. Legal Issues 365 (1994).

[81] Williams v. State, 235 S.W.3d 742, 751 (Tex. Crim. App. 2007).

[82] The nature of the "reasonable person" is considered in § 10.04[D][3][d], *infra*.

risky conduct, which is simply another way of evaluating the reason for taking the risk. Judge Learned Hand described the relationship of these factors "in algebraic terms: if the probability [of harm] be called P; the [gravity of] injury, L; and the burden, B; liability depends upon whether B is less than L multiplied by P: *i.e.*, whether B [is less than] PL."[83] Although this formula cannot be applied with scientific precision, its expression emphasizes the point that, as the gravity and/or probability of harm occurring increases, the more substantial the actor's reason for taking the risk must be, in order to avoid a finding of negligence.

For example, suppose that driver *D* thoughtlessly darts between lanes in his car at a very fast rate of speed on a busy public road, in order to get to a friend's birthday party. As a result, *D* accidently kills *V*. If *D* were civilly sued or criminally prosecuted for negligence in *V*'s death, a jury might find that *D*'s conduct was negligent: The gravity of harm risked was substantial (loss of life); the probability of such harm occurring was not insubstantial (he was driving speedily and there was a great deal of traffic); and the burden to defendant of driving in a safer manner was small (he would have reached his party a bit later). On the other hand, if *D* drives in precisely the same manner in order to get his gravely ill child to the hospital, a jury might determine that *D* took a justifiable — non-negligent — risk, in light of the child's condition.

[b]   Distinguishing Civil from Criminal Negligence

A person who breaches his duty of care to another has acted negligently, as defined in subsection [a]. However, not every breach constitutes a crime. As Jerome Hall has observed, " '[b]lame' is a very wide notion and, like praise, it permeates almost all of daily life. Important differences exist between raising an eyebrow and putting a man in jail."[84] More specifically, the blame expressed in a civil finding of negligence is not the same as the blame communicated by a jury when it returns a verdict of criminal negligence in a criminal prosecution.

Although rare exceptions exist, "civil negligence ordinarily is [considered] an inappropriate predicate by which to define . . . criminal conduct."[85] To establish *criminal* responsibility for negligence, the prosecution must ordinarily show more than mere deviation from the standard of care that would constitute *civil* negligence.[86]

"Criminal negligence" is conduct that represents a *gross* deviation from the standard of reasonable care.[87] Put more precisely, a person is criminally negligent if he takes a *substantial* and unjustifiable risk of causing the social harm that constitutes the offense charged.[88] Applying the Learned Hand formula, *criminal*

---

[83] United States v. Carroll Towing Co., 159 F.2d 169, 173 (2d Cir. 1947).

[84] Hall, Note 80, *supra*, at 641.

[85] Santillanes v. State, 849 P.2d 358, 365 (N.M. 1993).

[86] State v. Jones, 126 A.2d 273, 275 (Me. 1956).

[87] State v. Hazelwood, 946 P.2d 875, 878 (Alaska 1997).

[88] *Williams v. State*, 235 S.W.3d at 751.

negligence exists when "PL" *far* outweighs "B."[89]

Frequently courts describe criminal negligence as "gross negligence," "culpable negligence," or, in early common law, even "recklessness." However, as explained in subsection [3], *infra*, the term "recklessness" today should *not* be equated with criminal negligence.

[c]　　　Should Negligence Be Punished?

Punishment for negligence is controversial. It should be remembered that *"mens rea"* means "guilty mind," and yet the negligent actor is blamed and punished for what *isn't* in (or on) his mind, namely, attention to risk that a reasonable person would display.

Some opponents of punishment for negligence contend that, by definition, a negligent actor fails to perceive the risks of his conduct and, therefore, cannot be deterred. Since utilitarians believe that punishment should be avoided if it will not result in a net reduction in societal pain, negligent harmdoers should not be punished.

The utilitarian defense of punishment for negligence primarily focuses on general deterrence. Holmes has bluntly observed that "public policy sacrifices the individual to the general good."[90] In this context, punishment of an individual negligent actor, even if he was undeterrable on this occasion, may send a useful message to others: "Conduct yourself carefully, or else you will be punished." Punishment of the negligent harmdoer may also have an incidental individual deterrence benefit: The negligent actor who is punished may act more carefully in the future.

Turning away from utilitarianism, retributivists disagree amongst themselves on the moral propriety of punishment for negligence.[91] Retributivists who oppose punishment for negligence reason that the basis for just punishment is voluntary wrongdoing.[92] People who intentionally cause harm choose to act wrongly and, consequently, may properly be punished. Similarly, one who is consciously aware that his planned conduct is unjustifiably risky but proceeds anyway,[93] exercises a choice for which he may fairly be held responsible. The negligent actor's risk-taking, however, is inadvertent: He does not appreciate that his conduct is dangerous, although he *should have been aware*. As a consequence, we cannot blame him for bad choice-making. We can only blame him in the civil tort sense for

---

[89] The common law generally requires proof that the actor took a substantial *and* unjustifiable risk. However, it arguably would be better to say that the actor must take a *substantially* unjustifiable risk. That is, "substantial" should not be an adjective modifying "risk," but an adverb modifying the unjustifiability of the risk. Even a non-substantial risk, if taken for *no* good reason at all, should constitute criminal negligence. Dressler, Note 27, *supra*, at 27–28. Thus, one who, "just for the hell of it," takes a tiny risk of causing death to another should be deemed criminally negligent on the ground that the small risk is substantially outweighed by the virtually non-existent justification for the risk-taking.

[90] Holmes, Note 24, *supra*, at 48.

[91] For a useful discussion of the competing arguments, see Simons, Note 80, *supra*.

[92] Hall, Note 80, *supra*, at 635.

[93] Such a person is acting recklessly. *See* subsection [3], *infra*.

failing to live up to the objective, hypothetical "reasonable person" standard, and even here blame may be unjustifiable if the actor was incapable of living up to such a standard (*e.g.*, low I.Q.).

Retributive defenders of punishment for negligence contend that, in most circumstances, criminal blame *is* justified on the ground that the negligent actor's failure to perceive the riskiness of his conduct constitutes "culpable indifference" to the rights and interests of those around him.[94] If "*mens rea*" implies that the actor is morally blameworthy, or that his conduct demonstrates a character flaw, then the insensitive wrongdoer may possess sufficient "*mens rea*" to deserve punishment for the harm he causes.[95] After all, the negligent actor's explanation for the injury is frequently something like: "But, I just didn't think." Retributive defenders of punishment for negligence argue that if a person can be blamed because he failed to act, there is no reason why he should not be blamed because he failed to think.[96]

[d]   Who *Really* Is the "Reasonable Person"?: Initial Observations[97]

Jurists have struggled for centuries to identify the "reasonable person," or what used to be called the "reasonable prudent *man*." He was once described as "an ideal, . . . the embodiment of all those qualities which we demand of the good citizen."[98] A leading torts treatise once stated that "[h]e is not to be identified with any ordinary individual, who might occasionally do unreasonable things; he is a prudent and careful person, *who is always up to standard.*"[99] According to this questionable description, nobody is a reasonable person; every one of us, at least occasionally, acts "below standard," even if most of us are fortunate enough not to injure others in the process.

Although the stated standard is objective — the defendant's conduct is compared to this external ideal — there are constant pressures on courts to "subjectivize" the "reasonable person," that is, to incorporate into the "reasonable person" some of the mental and/or physical characteristics of the defendant, or by incorporating into the "reasonable person" the defendant's personal life experiences. For example, if the defendant, a man of low education or low mental acuity, is prosecuted for negligently causing the death of his child, the defendant might seek to have his conduct judged by the standard of a reasonable person with a similar level of education and/or mental acuity. Or, suppose that a father fails to obtain traditional medical care for his child because he is a Christian Scientist who

---

[94] Simons, Note 80, *supra*, at 388–90.

[95] Fletcher, Note 80, *supra*, at 416–18.

[96] H.L.A. Hart, Punishment and Responsibility 151–52 (1968).

[97] *See generally* Mayo Moran, Rethinking the Reasonable Person (2003); Tatjana Hornle, *Symposium on the Reasonable Person in Criminal Law*, 11 New Crim. L. Rev. 1–171 (2008); Ronald K.L. Collins, *Language, History and the Legal Process: A Profile of the "Reasonable Man,"* 8 Rutgers-Cam. L.J. 311 (1977); Caroline Forell, *Essentialism, Empathy, and the Reasonable Woman*, 1994 U. Ill. L. Rev. 769. See also the discussion and cites at §§ 18.05[A] and 31.07[B][2][b][ii], *infra*.

[98] A.P. Herbert, Misleading Cases in the Common Law 12 (1930).

[99] Dan B. Dobbs et al., Prosser and Keeton on Torts 175 (5th ed. 1984).

believes that medicine is unnecessary or violative of God's word. He may ask to be judged by the standards of a "reasonable Christian Scientist." Or, a prior mugging victim suddenly confronted by "threatening youths" may seek to have his self-defensive actions, which must be reasonable, measured against the standard of the reasonable prior mugging victim.

The traditional rule, which is undergoing significant modern change, is that, although a defendant's unusual physical characteristics (*e.g.*, blindness), *if relevant to the case*, are incorporated into the "reasonable person" standard, a defendant's mental characteristics are not. Holmes expressed the traditional view that the law does not take "account of the infinite varieties of temperament, intellect and education which make the internal character of a given act so different," and that it "does not attempt to see men as God sees them."[100]

There are few easy or uncontroversial lines drawn in this realm. Just as there is great debate about whether negligence should be punished at all, there is considerable disagreement today on whether the law should "swat the subjectivist bug"[101] or, instead, encourage more subjectivism. This issue is considered in various places in this text, and is more profitably considered in the context of specific legal doctrines. However, it may be noted that one's views of whether the criminal law should primarily be concerned with deterrence or, instead, retributive just deserts, will inevitably color one's approach to the issue of whether (and to what extent) the characteristics and experiences of the person being evaluated should be included in the "reasonable person."

[3] "Recklessness"

In the distant past, "recklessness" was typically a synonym for "criminal negligence." Today, however, a line is usually drawn between these two concepts, with "recklessness" falling on the more culpable side of the line.

As an independent concept, two definitions of "recklessness" have developed. According to the tort law definition, which also had some support in the criminal law, a person acts "recklessly" if he takes a *very* substantial and unjustifiable risk. So understood, "civil negligence," "criminal negligence," and "recklessness" lie on a continuum: Each involves unjustifiable risk-taking; they differ only in respect to the degree of the actor's deviation from the standard of due care. Under this meaning, "recklessness," like "negligence," is an objective form of fault.

Today, however, most jurisdictions apply a different definition of "recklessness": Criminal recklessness requires proof that the actor disregarded a substantial and unjustifiable risk *of which he was aware.*[102] According to the prevailing view, the line between "criminal negligence" and "recklessness" is *not* drawn on the basis of the extent of the actor's deviation from the standard of reasonable care — the deviation is gross or substantial in both cases — but rather is founded on the actor's state of mind in regard to the risk. Criminal negligence involves inadvertent

---

[100] Holmes, Note 24, *supra*, at 108.

[101] Celia Wells, *Swatting the Subjectivist Bug*, 1982 Crim. L. Rev. 209.

[102] Farmer v. Brennan, 511 U.S. 825, 837–38 (1994).

risk-taking (we are saying that the defendant, as a reasonable person, *should have been aware* of the substantial and unjustifiable risk he was taking); in contrast, recklessness implicates *subjective* fault — "a 'devil may care' or 'not give a damn' attitude" — in that the actor was aware of the substantial and unjustifiable risk he was taking, and yet he consciously disregarded it and proceeded with his dangerous conduct.[103]

[E] "Malice"

"Malice" is a critical common law and statutory *mens rea* term. Although the term has a more complicated meaning in the context of murder,[104] in non-homicide circumstances a person acts with "malice" if he *intentionally* or *recklessly* causes the social harm prohibited by the offense.[105] Although language to the contrary can be found in common law treatises,[106] the term "malice" is rarely employed today in its popular, nonlegal sense, as meaning "ill-will," "spite," or "wickedness."

For example, in *Regina v. Cunningham*,[107] *D*, a thief, wrenched a gas meter from gas pipes in the cellar of a building in which *V* resided, in order to steal coins inside the meter. Gases escaped into *V*'s living quarters, unintentionally harming *V*. *D* was prosecuted for "maliciously" causing the injury to *V*. The trial judge defined "malice" in terms of wickedness. In that sense, *D* could be convicted because the harm he caused was the consequence of his immoral efforts to steal money. However, according to the more modern definition of "malice" set out in the last paragraph, which the appellate court said was the appropriate definition, the analysis in *Cunningham* is more complicated. *D* did not intentionally cause the social harm to *V*, but he may have recklessly caused it. By tearing the meter from the gas pipes, *D* arguably took a substantial and unjustifiable risk to *V*'s safety. If so, and *if D was aware of this risk and consciously disregarded it*, then it is correct to state that *D* recklessly caused the social harm and, therefore, acted with "malice." If he did *not* have such foresight — if he *should* have been aware of the risk, but was not — then he acted in a criminally negligent manner, which would fall outside the definition of "malice."

---

[103] Williams v. State, 235 S.W.3d 742, 750–752 (Tex. Crim. App. 2007).

[104] *See* § 31.02[B][2], *infra*.

[105] Regina v. Cunningham, 41 Crim. App. 155, 2 Q.B. 396, 2 All E.R. 412 (1957) (Court of Criminal Appeal).

[106] 4 Blackstone, Note 14, *supra*, at *198–*99 (in the context of common law murder, defining "malice aforethought" as "any evil design in general; the dictate of a wicked, depraved, and malignant heart").

[107] 41 Crim. App. 155, 2 Q.B. 396, 2 All E.R. 412 (1957) (Court of Criminal Appeal). The case is also considered in § 10.02[B], *supra*.

§ 10.05   STATUTORY INTERPRETATION: WHAT ELEMENTS DOES A *MENS REA* TERM MODIFY?[108]

In *United States v. X-Citement Video, Inc.*,[109] the Supreme Court was called upon to interpret a federal statute that makes it a felony to *knowingly* transport, receive, or distribute in interstate or foreign commerce any visual depiction "involv[ing] the use of a minor engaging in sexually explicit conduct."[110] The defendant did not deny that he knowingly transported and distributed sexually explicit materials in interstate commerce. He claimed, however, that he believed the person depicted in the video was an adult, *i.e.*, he did not know that she was a minor.

The issue for the Court was whether such knowledge was required under the statute. A fairly straightforward reading of the statute suggests that the term "knowingly" modifies the conduct or result elements ("transport, receive, or distribute") of the offense. But, does "knowingly" *also* modify the critical statutory attendant circumstance that the person depicted in the videos is underage?

There is no foolproof method for interpreting criminal statutes. The general rule is that if a statute is not clear on its face, the court will seek to interpret the statute in the manner that best gives effect to legislative intent. In determining legislative will, judges often consider the "legislative history of an act and the circumstances surrounding its adoption; earlier statutes on the same subject; the common law as it was understood at the time of the enactment of the statute; and previous interpretations of the same or similar statutes."[111]

Courts also consider the structure of a statute, taking into consideration rules of grammar. For example, if there is only one statutory *mens rea* term, and it is set out at the beginning of the statute, a court may interpret this to mean that the word modifies every *actus reus* element that follows it. A different result would apply, however, if the culpability term *follows* various *actus reus* elements, but *precedes* others, in which case the court will likely conclude that the *mens rea* element applies in a "forward," but not "backward" direction. For example, assume that a statute is drafted in this form: "A person is guilty of a felony if he [does X] with the *intent* of [causing Y and Z]." Here, the term "intent" probably modifies Y and Z, but not X.[112]

---

[108] *See generally* Peter J. Henning, *Statutory Interpretation and the Federalization of Criminal Law*, 86 J. Crim. L. & Criminology 1167 (1996); Eric A. Johnson, *Rethinking the Presumption of Mens Rea*, 47 Wake Forest L. Rev. 769 (2012); John Shepard Wiley Jr., *Not Guilty by Reason of Blamelessness: Culpability in Federal Criminal Interpretation*, 85 Va. L. Rev. 1021 (1999).

[109] 513 U.S. 64 (1994).

[110] 18 U.S.C. § 2252 (2011).

[111] *In re* Banks, 244 S.E.2d 386, 389 (N.C. 1978).

[112] *E.g.*, United States v. Yermian, 468 U.S. 63 (1984) (a federal offense provided that "whoever, in any matter within the jurisdiction of any department or agency of the United States, knowingly . . . makes any false . . . statements . . . shall be fined"; *Y* admitted that he knowingly made false statements in a questionnaire sent by his employer to the Department of Defense, but he denied that he knew that the false statements pertained to "any matter within the jurisdiction of any department or agency of the United States"; held: "knowingly" did not modify the introductory phrase).

Sometimes courts are reluctant to follow the most grammatical reading of a statute if such an interpretation would conflict with "background assumption[s] of our criminal law,"[113] one of which is that a "presumption in favor of a scienter [*mens rea*] requirement should apply to each of the statutory elements that criminalize otherwise innocent conduct."[114] For that reason, the Supreme Court in *X-Citement Video* held that, to convict the defendant, the government had to prove beyond a reasonable doubt that he knew that the person depicted in the video was underage. Distribution of sexually explicit, but non-obscene, videos of *adults* was lawful; therefore, the justices reasoned, it was essential that the government prove that the defendant knew of the underage status of those involved in the sexually explicit activities, as this was what converted otherwise legally innocent conduct into criminality.

§ 10.06 "SPECIFIC INTENT" AND "GENERAL INTENT"

The terms "specific intent" and "general intent" are the bane of criminal law students and lawyers. This is because the terms are critical to understanding various common law rules of criminal responsibility,[115] yet the concepts are so "notoriously difficult . . . to define and apply . . . [that] a number of text writers recommend that they be abandoned altogether."[116] Perhaps the most important message one can provide in regard to these terms is this: There is no way, with confidence, to know what these terms mean except (perhaps) in the context of the law of a given jurisdiction. Tread carefully.

Historically, "general intent" referred to any offense for which the only *mens rea* required was a blameworthy state of mind; "specific intent" was meant to emphasize that the definition of the offense expressly required proof of a particular mental state.[117] In other words, an offense that only required proof of "*mens rea*" in the "culpability" sense of the term was a "general intent" crime; offenses that required "*mens rea*" in the "elemental" sense were "specific intent" in nature.[118] This dichotomy was understandable: The definitions of most common law and early statutory offenses were silent in regard to *mens rea*; those exceptional offenses that did expressly require a particular state of mind — *e.g.*, murder ("malice aforethought"), larceny ("intent to steal"), and burglary ("intent to commit a felony [inside a dwelling]" — stood out, and were thus denominated as "specific intent offenses."

Today, however, most penal statutes expressly include a *mens rea* term, or a particular state of mind is judicially implied, so the line between "general" and "specific" intent is much more difficult to draw. Making matters worse, as noted, there is no universally accepted meaning of the terms. Frequently, courts draw the

---

[113] Liparota v. United States, 471 U.S. 419, 426 (1985).

[114] United States v. X-Citement Video, Inc., 513 U.S. 64, 72 (1994).

[115] *See, e.g.*, §§ 12.03 (mistake of fact); 13.02[D] (mistake of law); 24.03 (voluntary intoxication); 26.02 (diminished capacity), *infra*.

[116] People v. Hood, 462 P.2d 370, 377 (Cal. 1969).

[117] Commonwealth v. Sibinich, 598 N.E.2d 673, 675 n.2, 676 n.3 (Mass. App. Ct. 1992).

[118] For discussion of the "culpability" and "elemental" meanings of "*mens rea*," see § 10.02, *supra*.

following distinction: An offense is "specific intent" if the crime requires proof that the actor's conscious object, or purpose, is to cause the social harm set out in the definition of the offense. In contrast, a crime is "general intent" if the actor can be convicted upon proof of any lesser state of mind, such as when he causes the harm knowingly, recklessly, or negligently.[119]

There is, however, another way the terms are explained. Generally speaking, a "specific intent" offense is one in which the definition of the crime: (1) requires proof of an intention by the actor to perform some future act or achieve some further consequence, beyond the conduct or result that constitutes the social harm of the offense; (2) requires proof of some special motive for the conduct;[120] or (3) provides that the actor must be aware of a statutory attendant circumstance. An offense that does *not* contain one of these features is termed "general intent."

For example, common law burglary is defined as "breaking and entering of the dwelling of another in the nighttime *with intent to commit a felony therein.*"[121] The *actus reus* of this offense is complete when the offender breaks and enters another person's dwelling at night. However, to be guilty of burglary, the actor must intend a further act — commission of a felony inside the dwelling house. But that future act is not part of the social harm of the offense; it does not have to occur. Thus, common law burglary is characterized as a specific-intent offense.

Similarly, larceny is the "trespassory taking and carrying away of the personal property of another *with the intent to permanently deprive the other person of his property.*" That is, a person not guilty of the offense if he, merely, intentionally takes and carries away another person's property. Instead, he must have a particular motive for his wrongful actions, namely, to deprive the owner of the property permanently (and not, simply, temporarily). Therefore, larceny is a specific-intent offense, as defined above.

Another example of a specific-intent crime would be the offense of "receiving stolen property with knowledge that it is stolen." According to this definition, the actor who receives the stolen property (the social harm of the offense) must have knowledge — awareness — of the attendant circumstance that the property was "stolen" in nature.

In contrast to these offenses, consider battery, sometimes defined statutorily as "intentional application of unlawful force upon another." This is a general-intent crime, for the simple reason that the definition does not contain any specific intent. The only mental state required in its definition is the intent to "apply unlawful force upon another," the social harm of the crime.

---

[119] United States v. Bailey, 444 U.S. 394, 405 (1980); United States v. Blair, 54 F.3d 639, 642 (10th Cir. 1995); Harris v. State, 728 A.2d 180, 183 (Md. 1999).

[120] *See People v. Hood*, 462 P.2d at 378; State v. Wilson, 830 N.W.2d 849, 853 (Minn. 2013); Dorador v. State, 573 P.2d 839, 843 (Wyo. 1978).

[121] Mondie v. Commonwealth, 158 S.W.3d 203, 207 (Ky. 2005) (emphasis added).

§ 10.07   MODEL PENAL CODE[122]

No aspect of the Model Penal Code has had greater influence on the direction of American criminal law than Section 2.02 of the Code, which sets out the "General Requirements of Culpability."[123] The purpose of Section 2.02 is to "obliterate[] ill-defined, confusing common law language and concepts and replace[] them with four specifically defined hierarchical levels of culpability . . . used to define crimes."[124]

[A]   Section 2.02: In General

Section 2.02 takes an exclusively "elemental"[125] approach to the concept of *mens rea*. Subsection (1) provides that, except in the case of offenses characterized as "violations,"[126] a person may not be convicted of an offense unless "he acted purposely, knowingly, recklessly or negligently, as the law may require, with respect to *each* material element of the offense." In other words, "violations" aside, the Code requires the prosecution to prove that the defendant committed the social harm of the offense — *indeed, each material ingredient of the social harm of the offense* — with a culpable state of mind, as set out in the specific statute. Furthermore, the legislature may choose to require different levels of culpability for each material element. For example, a statute could be drafted with the following structure: "It is a felony to *purposely* do X and *knowingly* do Y, so as to *recklessly* cause Z."

This provision is noteworthy in various regards. First, a person may not be convicted solely on the ground that he acted with a morally blameworthy state of mind, *i.e.*, the Code eschews the "culpability" meaning of *"mens rea."* Second, the common law distinction between "general intent" and "specific intent"[127] is discarded.

Third, the Model Penal Code removes the clutter of common law and statutory *mens rea* terms, and replaces them with just four carefully defined terms: "purposely"; "knowingly"; "recklessly"; and "negligently."[128] They represent the

---

[122] *See generally* Kimberly Kessler Ferzan, *Don't Abandon the Model Penal Code Yet! Thinking Through Simons's Rethinking*, 6 Buff. Crim. L. Rev. 185 (2002); Ronald L. Gainer, *The Culpability Provisions of the Model Penal Code*, 19 Rutgers L.J. 575 (1988); Paul H. Robinson & Jane A. Grall, *Element Analysis in Defining Criminal Liability: The Model Penal Code and Beyond*, 35 Stan. L. Rev. 681 (1983); Kenneth W. Simons, *Should the Model Penal Code's Mens Rea Provisions Be Amended?*, 1 Ohio St. Crim. L.J. 179 (2003).

[123] For a fairly recent survey of states applying some or all of MPC § 2.02, see John S. Baker, Jr., *Mens Rea* and State Crimes 16–87 (2012).

[124] Dannye Holley, *The Influence of the Model Penal Code's Culpability Provisions on State Legislatures: A Study of Lost Opportunities, Including Abolishing the Mistake of Fact Doctrine*, 27 Sw. U. L. Rev. 229, 230 (1997).

[125] *See* § 10.02[C], *supra*.

[126] A "violation" is an "offense" (but not a "crime"), for which no sentence other than a fine or civil penalty is authorized. Model Penal Code § 1.04(5). Section 2.05, rather than Section 2.02, pertains to violations.

[127] *See* § 10.06, *supra*.

[128] Because "willful" is a commonly used non-MPC statutory term, *see* § 10.04[C], *supra*, the drafters

Code's hierarchy of culpability, in which purposeful misconduct is deemed the most culpable, leading down to negligence, the least culpable.[129]

Fourth, the phrase "material element of the offense," as used in Section 2.02 and throughout the Code, includes "elements" relating to the existence of a justification or excuse for the actor's conduct,[130] *i.e.*, to defenses to crimes. As a consequence, since Section 2.02 states that one of the four culpability terms applies to *every* material element of a crime, this Section is also relevant in determining whether a person is entitled to acquittal on the grounds of an affirmative defense.

[B] Culpability Terms

[1] "Purposely"

The term "purposely" has two definitions in the Code, depending upon whether the material element of the offense under consideration pertains to a *result* or *conduct*, on the one hand, or to an attendant circumstance, on the other. In the context of a *result* or *conduct*, a person acts "purposely" if it his "conscious object to engage in conduct of that nature or to cause such a result."[131] So defined, "purposely" is a mental state comparable to the first — but only the first — of the two alternative common law definitions of the word "intentional."[132] For example, in the airplane bombing hypothetical discussed earlier,[133] the death of V, D's wife, was "purposeful" because it was D's conscious object to take V's life, but the deaths of the remaining passengers were not "purposeful" (although they were "intentional" as the common law defined that term).[134] The Code also follows in *most* respects,

---

of the Code deal with it expressly: A person who acts "knowingly" satisfies the requirement of willfulness. Model Penal Code § 2.02(8).

[129] Some scholars do not believe that the drafters of the Code have drawn proper or sufficient, culpability distinctions. *See, e.g.*, Simons, Note 27, *supra* (dividing mental states into two categories, those that are based on states of desire and others based on states of belief, and arguing that one cannot create a hierarchy of culpability between the two categories).

A recent empirical survey suggests that "most of the *mens rea* assumptions embedded in the MPC are reasonably accurate as a behavioral matter." Francis X. Shen, et al., *Sorting Guilty Minds*, 86 N.Y.U.L. Rev. 1306 (2011). According to the authors of the survey, "[e]ven without the aid of the MPC definitions, subjects were able to distinguish regularly and accurately among purposeful, negligent, and blameless conduct. However, our subjects failed to distinguish reliably between knowing and reckless conduct." *Id.* In a subsequent study by the same authors, even though use of slightly different wording of hypothetical cases improved somewhat the ability of the subjects to draw distinctions between the concepts of knowledge and recklessness, the findings still "raise questions about the normative basis for the knowing/reckless distinction in the MPC's mental state hierarchy." Matthew R. Ginther, et al., *The Language of Mens Rea*, 67 Vand. L. Rev. 1327 (2014).

[130] Model Penal Code § 1.13(10)(ii).

[131] Model Penal Code § 2.02(2)(a)(I).

[132] *See* § 10.04[A], *supra*.

[133] See the example in the text at Note 30, *supra*.

[134] What if an actor's purpose to cause a certain result is conditional? For example, suppose that D threatens to kill V, the driver of an automobile, unless V relinquishes the car to D. Is D guilty of taking a motor vehicle with the "purpose to cause death or serious bodily harm"? The Code provides that "[w]hen a particular purpose is an element of an offense, the element is established although the purpose is conditional, *unless* the condition negatives the harm or evil sought to be prevented by the law defining

the common law "transferred intent" doctrine.[135]

A person acts "purposely" with respect to *attendant circumstances* if he "is aware of the existence of such circumstances or he believes or hopes that they exist."[136] For example, if D enters an unoccupied structure in order to commit a felony inside, he has acted "purposely" regarding the attendant circumstance that the structure was unoccupied if he was aware it was unoccupied or hoped that it would be.

[2] "Knowingly"

The Code provides two definitions of the term "knowingly," one that applies to results, and the second that pertains to conduct and attendant circumstances. A *result* is "knowingly" caused if the actor "is aware that it is practically certain that his conduct will cause such a result."[137] Thus, again in the airplane bombing hypothetical,[138] D *knowingly* killed V's fellow passengers, assuming D was aware that his bomb would almost certainly kill those on board.[139] If D lacked normal mental faculties, or for any other reason had a distorted sense of reality, so that he was not subjectively aware that their deaths were practically certain to result, then a finding of "knowledge" would not be appropriate.

With "attendant circumstances" and "conduct" elements, one acts "knowingly" if he is "aware that his conduct is of that nature or that such [attendant] circumstances exist."[140] For example, suppose D fired a loaded gun in V's direction, and was prosecuted for "knowingly endangering the life of another." D is guilty if he was

---

the offense." Model Penal Code § 2.02(6). In this case, the condition of handing over the car to avoid an assault does not negative the harm sought to be prevented by the carjacking law, which is that an automobile not be taken by the use of force or threat of force. *See generally* Gideon Yaffe, *Conditional Intent and Mens Rea*, 10 Legal Theory 273 (2004).

[135] The common law "transferred intent" doctrine is covered in § 10.04[A][3], *supra*. Section 2.03(2)(a) of the Model Penal Code handles transferred-intent issues. It provides that when purposely causing a particular result is an element of an offense, that element is established if "the actual result differs from that designed or contemplated . . . , *only* in respect that a different person or different property" is harmed. (Emphasis added.) For example, if A's purpose is to kill B, but he accidentally kills C instead, the requisite element of "purpose" is established. Or, if D, intending to set E's house on fire, causes F's home to burn down instead, D may be convicted of an offense prohibiting the purposeful destruction of another's property.

This section of the Code also provides that a defendant is not relieved of liability for an offense if *less* harm occurs than it was the actor's conscious object to cause. For example, if D's conscious object is to kill two persons, but he only succeeds in killing one, the element of "purpose" is established. However, if D intends to kill X and instead kills X *and* Y, D's purpose to kill X would *not* apply as to Y, because he has caused more, not less, harm than was designed. D's liability, if any, for Y's death would have to be based on a different state of mind directly related to Y. Thus, in this regard, the Code applies what appears to be the minority position in non-MPC jurisdictions, but the one this text indicated earlier is the better approach.

[136] Model Penal Code § 2.02(2)(a)(ii).

[137] Model Penal Code § 2.02(2)(b)(ii).

[138] See the text to Note 30, *supra*.

[139] Observe, therefore, that the drafters of the Model Penal Code have taken the common law term "intent" and divided into two Model Penal Code terms, "purposely" and "knowingly."

[140] Model Penal Code § 2.02(2)(b)(i).

aware that his *conduct* endangered the life of another person. If he was not aware (perhaps because he did not see anyone in the vicinity), then *D* did not endanger another knowingly, no matter how obvious *V*'s presence may have been to others.

The same approach is used with attendant circumstances. If *D* purchased stolen property and was prosecuted for "knowingly receiving stolen property," *D* would be guilty of the offense if, when he received the property, he was aware that it had been stolen. In order to deal with the problem of "willful blindness"[141] the Code includes a provision that states that knowledge is established, if "a person is aware of a high probability of . . . [the attendant circumstance's] existence, unless he actually believes that it does not exist."[142] The latter definition is subject to criticisms similar to those generally directed at the willful blindness doctrine.

[3]   "Recklessly" and "Negligently"

[a]   In General

The Code provides that a person acts "recklessly" if he "consciously disregards a substantial and unjustified risk that the material element exists or will result from his conduct." A risk is "substantial[143] and unjustifiable" if "considering the nature and purpose of the actor's conduct and the circumstances known to him, its disregard involves a gross deviation from the standard of conduct that a law-abiding person would observe in the actor's situation."[144]

A person's conduct is "negligent" if the actor "should be aware of a substantial and unjustifiable risk that the material element exists or will result from his conduct."[145] The definition of "substantial and unjustifiable" is the same as that provided for in the definition of "recklessness," except that the term "reasonable person" is substituted for "law-abiding person."

"Negligence" and "recklessness," therefore, require the same degree of risk-taking: "substantial and unjustifiable." The difference between them lies in the fact that the reckless actor "consciously disregards" the risk, whereas the negligent actor's risk-taking is inadvertent.[146] This tracks the modern common law approach to these doctrines; indeed, the Model Penal Code influenced modern courts, and not vice-versa, in this regard.

---

[141] *See* § 10.04[B], *supra*.

[142] Model Penal Code § 2.02(7).

[143] Notice that recklessness involving taking a *substantial risk*, whereas "knowledge" requires that the actor is aware that the outcome is "practically certain." Thus, in the latter situation, the Code does not speak in terms of "risk"-taking, but rather of the virtual certainty of an event. Of course, there is no bright-line way to distinguish between "substantial risk" of X and "virtual certainty" of X. That may be why the knowledge/recklessness line is hard for people to draw. *See* Note 129, *supra*. All that can be said is that "practical certainty" suggests that if X *doesn't* occur, a person might characterize the non-event loosely as "a miracle."

[144] Model Penal Code § 2.02(2)(c).

[145] Model Penal Code § 2.02(2)(d).

[146] State v. Brooks, 658 A.2d 22, 26–27 (Vt. 1995).

[b]   Nature of the "Reasonable Person"

The conduct of the "reasonable person" (and "law-abiding person" in the context of "recklessness") is evaluated from the perspective of a person "in the actor's situation." This phrase is purposely ambiguous, permitting some subjectivism to be incorporated into an otherwise objective standard. The Commentary opines that physical characteristics, such as an actor's blindness, or the fact that he has just suffered a heart attack, "would certainly be facts to be considered in judgment involving criminal liability," but the actor's hereditary factors and matters of intelligence and temperament "would not be held material . . . and could not be without depriving the criterion of all its objectivity." The drafters of the Code did not intend "to displace discriminations of this kind, but rather to leave the issue to the courts."[147] Thus, more than five decades after the American Law Institute adopted the Code, courts continue to struggle to find the proper balance between the opposing poles of pure subjectivism and objectivism.

[C] Principles of Statutory Interpretation

The Model Code provides solutions to some of the perplexing problems of statutory interpretation that have confounded courts dealing with pre-Code statutes.[148] First, according to Section 2.02(4), if a statute defining an offense "prescribes the kind of culpability that is sufficient for the commission of the offense, without distinguishing among the material elements thereof," a court will interpret such culpability provision as applying to *every* material element of the offense, "unless a contrary purpose plainly appears." In other words, a single *mens rea* term — whatever it is — modifies *each actus reus* element of the offense, absent a plainly contrary purpose of the legislature. For example, Section 212.3 (False Imprisonment) provides, in part, that it is an offense to "knowingly restrain another unlawfully." Applying Section 2.02(4), this means that the prosecution must prove that the defendant knowingly restrained the victim, *and* that he knew that the restraint was unlawful.[149]

In contrast, if a single culpability term is placed by the drafters in the middle of the statute — that is, some material elements of the offense precede the culpability term and some come after — this would likely suggest a contrary purpose. For example, Section 221.1 (Burglary) provides in part that it is an offense to "enter an occupied structure with purpose to commit a crime therein." The placement of "purpose" after the phrase "enter an occupied structure" plainly demonstrates the drafters' intention not to require "purpose" as to the preceding phrase, or else it would have placed the word "purposely" at the start.[150]

In the burglary example, does this mean that *no* culpability is required as to the "entry of an occupied structure?" No. It must be remembered that Section 2.02(1) provides that *some* form of culpability — purpose, knowledge, recklessness, or

---

[147] American Law Institute, Comment to § 2.02, at 242.

[148] *See* § 10.05, *supra.*

[149] American Law Institute, Comment to § 2.02, at 245–46.

[150] *See id.* at 246.

negligence — is required for *each* material element of an offense. Therefore, when the definition of a criminal offense is silent regarding the matter of culpability as to a material element of the offense, as in this burglary statute, Section 2.02(3) provides an interpretive solution: The material element "is established if a person acts purposely, knowingly, or recklessly."

In the current burglary example, it should be noted that the phrase "entry of an occupied structure" actually consists of two material elements: (1) the conduct element of "entry"; and (2) the attendant circumstance that the entry be of "an occupied structure." Therefore, in accordance with Section 2.02(3), a person may not be convicted of burglary under the Code unless he purposely, knowingly, or recklessly entered an occupied structure, with the purpose to commit a crime inside. For example, if *D*, with the purpose to commit a crime therein, purposely entered an occupied structure *believing it was unoccupied*, he could *not* be convicted of burglary if he was *negligent* in his belief that the structure was unoccupied. He could be convicted, however, if he was reckless in this regard.

Chapter 11

STRICT LIABILITY

§ 11.01 GENERAL PRINCIPLES[1]

[A] "Strict Liability": Definition

The term "strict liability" is used in various contexts in the criminal law.[2] Generally speaking, however, it is important to distinguish between strict-liability *doctrines* and strict-liability *crimes*. A strict-liability doctrine is a rule of criminal responsibility that authorizes the conviction of a morally innocent person for violation of an offense, even though the crime, by definition, requires proof of a *mens rea*. An example is the rule that a person who is ignorant of, or who misunderstands the meaning of, a criminal law may be punished for violating it, even if her ignorance or mistake of law was reasonable. Strict-liability doctrines of this sort are discussed elsewhere in the text.[3]

The focus of this chapter is on strict-liability offenses, or crimes that, *by definition*, do not contain a *mens rea* requirement regarding one or more elements of the *actus reus*. This chapter considers the nature, wisdom, and constitutionality of such offenses.

[B] Presumption Against Strict Liability

The United States Supreme Court has observed, and as discussed more generally in Chapter 10, that "[t]he contention that an injury can amount to a crime only when inflicted by [*mens rea*] is no provincial or transient notion. It is

---

[1] *See generally* Appraising Strict Liability (A.P. Simester ed. 2005); Douglas N. Husak, *Varieties of Strict Liability*, 8 Can. J.L. & Juris. 189 (1995); Arthur Leavens, *Beyond Blame — Mens Rea and Regulatory Crime*, 46 U. Louisville L. Rev. 1 (2007); Stephen J. Morse, *Inevitable Mens Rea*, 27 Harv. J.L. & Pub. Pol'y 51 (2003); Gerhard O.W. Mueller, *Mens Rea and the Law Without It*, 58 W. Va. L. Rev. 34 (1955); Herbert L. Packer, *Mens Rea and the Supreme Court*, 1962 Sup. Ct. Rev. 107; Francis Bowes Sayre, *Public Welfare Offenses*, 33 Colum. L. Rev. 55 (1933); Kenneth W. Simons, *When Is Strict Liability Just?*, 87 J. Crim. L. & Criminology 1075 (1997); Richard Singer & Douglas Husak, *Of Innocence and Innocents: The Supreme Court and Mens Rea Since Herbert Packer*, 2 Buff. Crim. L. Rev. 859 (1999); Richard G. Singer, *The Resurgence of Mens Rea: III — The Rise and Fall of Strict Criminal Liability*, 30 B.C. L. Rev. 337 (1989); Richard A. Wasserstrom, *Strict Liability in the Criminal Law*, 12 Stan. L. Rev. 731 (1960); John Shepard Wiley, Jr., *Not Guilty by Reason of Blamelessness: Culpability in Federal Criminal Interpretation*, 85 Va. L. Rev. 1021 (1999).

[2] Husak, Note 1, *supra* (discussing seven different ways the term is used).

[3] *See, e.g.*, §§ 13.01 (mistake-of-law) and 19.01 (defense-of-others rule), *infra*.

. . . universal and persistent in mature systems of law."[4] As a consequence, the Supreme Court warned in *United States v. United States Gypsum Co.*[5] that offenses that do not contain a *mens rea* element have a "generally disfavored status" and "at least with regard to crimes having their origin in the common law, an interpretative presumption [exists] that *mens rea* is required" in federal statutes.[6] Indeed, although the Supreme Court has shied away from holding that there is a constitutional requirement of *mens rea*,[7] it frequently will interpret a federal statute, otherwise silent in regard to *mens rea*, as containing an implicit requirement of some culpable mental state. Although the case law is not consistent in this regard, two scholars have declared that the high court has recently "reinvigorated its concern with protecting innocent persons as a bedrock of federal criminal law."[8] Generally speaking, state courts apply the same presumption against strict liability as do federal courts, and they only accept a statute, strict liability on its face, as *truly* strict, if there is clear evidence of legislative intent to dispense with the culpability requirement.[9]

Assuming a statute does not expressly provide that it is strict liability in nature,[10] when will a court interpret it as one of strict liability? Judge (later Justice) Harry Blackmun set out in *Holdridge v. United States*[11] various factors that may overcome the presumption against strict liability: (1) the statutory crime is not derived from the common law; (2) there is an evident legislative policy that

---

[4] Morissette v. United States, 342 U.S. 246, 250 (1952).

[5] 438 U.S. 422 (1978).

[6] *See also* Elonis v. United States, 135 S. Ct. 2001, 192 L. Ed. 2d 1, 13 (2015) (stating that the " 'central thought' [of American criminal law] is that a defendant must be 'blameworthy in mind' before he can be found guilty"); Staples v. United States, 511 U.S. 600, 605–606 (1994) (stating, among other things, that a requirement of *mens rea* is "firmly embedded" in the law, and that an "offenses that require no *mens rea* generally are disfavored").

[7] *See* § 11.03, *infra.*

[8] Singer & Husak, Note 1, *supra*, at 861; *see* Leavens, Note 1, *supra*, at 1 (stating that the Supreme Court has swung "from an almost cavalier endorsement of strict liability at the beginning of the 20th century to a current willingness to find a *mens rea* element in virtually every statute").

[9] *E.g., In re* Jorge M., 4 P.3d 297, 300, 305 (Cal. 2000) (stating that a requirement of *mens rea* "is of such long standing and so fundamental to our criminal law that penal statutes will often be construed to contain such an element despite their failure expressly to state it"; and stating that "at least where the penalties imposed are substantial, [California penal law] can fairly be said to establish a presumption against criminal liability without mental fault " . . . , rebuttable only by compelling evidence of legislative intent to dispense with mens rea entirely.").

An interesting example of the principle set out in the text to this Note is how Florida has handled a statute that criminalized "possession of a controlled substance." The offense is a felony, with significant punishment upon conviction, Although the statute stated no *mens rea* requirement, the Florida Supreme Court applied the presumption against strict liability and interpreted the statute to require proof by the prosecutor of a defendant's knowledge that she was in possession of a controlled substance, as well as knowledge of its illicit nature. Chicone v. State, 684 So. 2d 736 (Fla. 1996); Scott v. State, 808 So. 2d 166 (Fla. 2002). As a result of these decisions, the Florida legislature enacted a new statute, which explicitly provided that such knowledge is not required. This language overcame the presumption in favor of *mens rea*, and the Florida Supreme Court upheld the new law as one of strict liability. State v. Adkins, 96 So. 3d 412 (Fla. 2012).

[10] See the second paragraph of *id.*

[11] 282 F.2d 302, 310 (8th Cir. 1960).

would be undermined by a *mens rea* requirement;[12] (3) the standard imposed by the statute is "reasonable and adherence thereto properly expected of a person"; (4) the penalty for violation of the statute is small; and (5) a "conviction does not gravely besmirch" the defendant.

Unfortunately, "[f]ederal judges have toyed casually and unsystematically with the concept of strict criminal liability."[13] Therefore, one cannot rely on a court to apply the five elements set out above in a consistent or systematic manner; it is often difficult to predict when a court will accept a statute on its own terms and permit it to be strictly enforced.[14]

[C] Public Welfare Offenses

Until the middle of the 19th century, Anglo-American crimes almost exclusively involved conduct *malum in se* (inherently wrongful), such as murder, arson, rape, and robbery. Conviction for such offenses, which required proof of *mens rea*, was gravely stigmatizing, and the penalties for their violation were severe.

imposed by the statute Consequently, Congress and state legislatures began to enact laws, most of which contained no express *mens rea* requirement, that came to be characterized as "public welfare offenses." Such offenses, in contrast to traditional crimes, involve conduct *malum prohibitum* (wrong because it is prohibited). Examples include statutes that prohibit the manufacture or sale of impure food or drugs to the public, anti-pollution environmental laws, as well as traffic and motor-vehicle regulations.

Courts frequently authorize strict criminal liability in the case of public welfare offenses. The factors set out in subsection [B] often support such an outcome: (1) public welfare offenses are not derived from the common law; (2) a single violation of such an offense can simultaneously injure a great number of people, which may explain the legislature's desire to disregard questions of personal moral guilt, in favor of a "sense of the importance of collective interests";[15] (3) the standard imposed by the statute (*e.g.*, "do not sell alcohol to minors," or "be in possession of an unexpired license when driving a motor vehicle") is reasonable; (4) the penalty for violation is relatively minor, sometimes involving only a fine;[16] and (5) conviction rarely damages the reputation of the violator.

---

[12] *E.g.*, a legislature "may . . . create strict liability crimes when there is an 'overriding governmental interest in promoting the health, safety and welfare of its citizens.' " Byrne v. State, 358 S.W.3d 745, 749 (Tex. App. 2011).

[13] Wiley, Note 1, *supra*, at 1161.

[14] *See* Leavens, Note 1, *supra*, at 1 (describing the law as "from murky to incoherent").

[15] Sayre, Note 1, *supra*, at 67.

[16] However, *see* United States v. Flum, 518 F.2d 39 (8th Cir. 1975) (characterizing a public welfare offense with a potential penalty of one year imprisonment as "relatively small").

[D]   Non-Public-Welfare Offenses

A few non-public-welfare offenses are characterized as "strict liability" because they do not require proof that the defendant possessed a *mens rea* regarding a material element of the offense. Perhaps the most common example is statutory rape, *i.e.*, consensual intercourse by a male with an underage female.[17] This offense is characterized in most states as strict liability because the statute does not require, and most courts have refused to imply, any *mens rea* element regarding the defendant's knowledge of the female's underage status.[18] That is, a male may be convicted of statutory rape, even if he honestly and reasonably — and, thus, blamelessly — believed that the female was old enough to consent to intercourse.[19]

Non-public-welfare strict-liability offenses differ from their public welfare counterparts in at least two significant regards, which make them controversial. First, whereas public welfare crimes usually carry only minor penalties, non-public-welfare strict-liability offenses often result in severe punishment.[20] Second, non-public-welfare offenses typically involve conduct considered *malum in se.* Violators of such laws, therefore, are stigmatized despite the absence of proven moral fault.

§ 11.02   POLICY DEBATE REGARDING STRICT-LIABILITY OFFENSES[21]

[A]   Searching for a Justification for Strict Liability

Most modern criminal law scholars look unkindly upon the abandonment of the *mens rea* requirement. As developed elsewhere,[22] the *mens rea* requirement is consistent with the retributive principle that one who does not choose to cause social harm, and who is not otherwise morally to blame for its commission, does not deserve to be punished. In most circumstances, society places the interest of the

---

[17] Felony-murder, *see* § 31.06, *infra*, is also "strict liability" in the sense that a felon, although culpable for committing a felony, may be punished for murder as well, even though the *result* of his felonious conduct — the death of another person — was accidental and unforeseeable.

[18] *E.g.*, State v. Holmes, 920 A.2d 632 (N.H. 2007); Garnett v. State, 632 A.2d 797 (Md. 1993) (authorizing conviction of a 20-year-old male with an I.Q. of 52, who had consensual intercourse with an underage female; holding that the male's mistake regarding the girl's age was immaterial); *see* Catherine L. Carpenter, *On Statutory Rape, Strict Liability, and the Public Welfare Offense Model*, 53 Am. U. L. Rev. 313, 385–91 (2003) (listing 30 states that impose strict liability for sexual activity with an underage female).

[19] Of course, the sexual intercourse itself is intentional, but what makes the conduct criminal is the attendant circumstance that the female is under a specified age. The absence of any *mens rea* requirement in *that* regard is what makes the offense "strict liability."

[20] *E.g.*, Garnett v. State, 632 A.2d 797 (Md. 1993) (statutory rape; maximum punishment is imprisonment for 20 years); State v. Yanez, 716 A.2d 759 (R.I. 1998) (denominating first-degree child molestation as a strict-liability offense because a defendant's mistaken belief as to the victim's age is irrelevant; *minimum* sentence is 20 years' imprisonment).

[21] *See generally* the Note 1 cites to Morse, Simons, Singer, and Wasserstrom.

[22] *See* § 10.03[B], *supra*.

blameless harmdoer above its concern for deterring social harm, by requiring proof of the actor's *mens rea*.

Support for strict liability is largely limited to its use in the enforcement of public welfare offenses, and is premised on utilitarian grounds. In these circumstances, punishing innocent actors is still retributively unfair, but the penalties attached to such offenses usually are slight. Lawmakers, therefore, are willing to permit this "mitigated unfairness"[23] to the individual in order more effectively to deter socially dangerous conduct.

Among the utilitarian arguments for strict liability are: (1) the absence of a *mens rea* requirement may have the desirable effect of keeping people who doubt their capacity to act safely from participating in dangerous activities, such as manufacturing pharmaceutical drugs or using dangerous instrumentalities; (2) those who do choose to engage in the risky activity will act with greater caution in light of the strict liability nature of the law; and (3) an inquiry into the actor's *mens rea* "would exhaust courts, which have to deal with thousands of 'minor' infractions every day."[24]

[B]   Alternatives to Strict Liability

Even if public welfare offenses should be treated differently than traditional crimes, mechanisms other than wholesale abandonment of a culpability requirement are available to legislatures seeking to protect the public. First, a legislature might require proof of negligence or recklessness rather than authorize strict liability, but set higher penalties, including significant prison sentences, for violation of public welfare offenses. This approach might be a more effective means of deterring dangerous conduct than strict liability coupled with small fines or very short jail sentences.

Second, a legislature might retain the minor penalties that apply to public welfare offenses, but require proof of an extremely low level of *mens rea*, such as *civil* negligence. Third, a legislature might continue to define public welfare offenses in strict liability terms, but permit a "lack of *mens rea*" affirmative defense. For example, if a person sold liquor to a minor, she would be convicted unless she persuaded the fact finder by a preponderance of the evidence that she took all reasonable care to determine the customer's age.

---

[23] The unfairness is not really mitigated. If a person has a moral right not to be punished in the absence of moral blameworthiness, as retributivist principles suggest, that right is no less violated simply because the punishment imposed is relatively slight.

[24] Singer, Note 1, *supra*, at 389.

§ 11.03 CONSTITUTIONALITY OF STRICT-LIABILITY OFFENSES[25]

The late professor Herbert Packer once summarized the constitutional law regarding strict-liability offenses this way: "*Mens rea* is an important requirement, but it is not a constitutional requirement, except sometimes."[26] Packer only partially had his tongue in his cheek.

As Packer's remark suggests, generally speaking the Supreme Court has rejected the claim that strict-liability crimes are unconstitutional. In *United States v. Balint*,[27] B and others were indicted for sale of narcotics without a required order form supplied by the Commissioner of Internal Revenue. The maximum penalty for the strict-liability public welfare offense was five years' imprisonment. In a single sentence that cited dictum from an earlier opinion, the Supreme Court held that strict-liability offenses do not violate the Fifth Amendment Due Process Clause. The Court provided no principled explanation for this assertion, however, nor did it mention the offense's potentially substantial prison sentence.

In contrast, in *Morissette v. United States*,[28] the Supreme Court spoke of the common law *mens rea* requirement in glowing terms, stating that it "is no provincial or transient notion. It is . . . universal and persistent in mature systems of law." Nonetheless, the Court observed that, "wisely or not," legislatures usually do not require proof of *mens rea* with public welfare offenses, and that courts, "not . . . without expressions of misgiving," have approved such statutes. With offenses that have evolved from the common law, however, the Court stated that "mere omission . . . of any mention of intent will not be construed as eliminating that element from the [crime]." Thus, in *Morissette*, M was convicted of conversion of government property that he believed had been abandoned. The statute did not expressly require proof of an intent to steal property. However, because the statute evolved from the common law offense of larceny, which contains such a requirement, the Supreme Court construed the conversion statute as requiring this specific intent.

Morissette's finding of a *mens rea* requirement, however, was not constitutionally based. It left *Balint*'s constitutional statements intact in the context of public welfare offenses. Moreover, the *Morissette* Court did *not* suggest that a legislature could not abandon the *mens rea* requirement with *traditional* criminal offenses; it held only that a requirement of *mens rea* would be presumed in such cases in the absence of a contrary legislative purpose.

On a few occasions, the Supreme Court has invalidated a strict-liability law on constitutional grounds. For example, in *Lambert v. California*,[29] the Court overturned L's conviction for failing to register with the city of Los Angeles as a prior convicted felon, as required pursuant to a strict-liability ordinance of which L was

---

[25] *See generally* Alan C. Michaels, *Constitutional Innocence*, 112 Harv. L. Rev. 8289 (1999).

[26] Packer, Note 1, *supra*, at 107; *see also* Singer & Husak, Note 1, *supra*, at 859 (stating that "Packer's assessment still seems valid . . . ").

[27] 258 U.S. 250 (1922).

[28] 342 U.S. 246 (1952).

[29] 355 U.S. 225 (1957).

unaware. Notwithstanding the usual rule that ignorance of the law is no excuse, the Court reversed the conviction on "lack of fair notice" due process grounds.[30] The Court has also occasionally applied the First Amendment to strike down strict-liability legislation in the obscenity field.[31]

§ 11.04 MODEL PENAL CODE

The Model Penal Code "attempted a bold assault upon strict liability."[32] Section 2.02, subsection (1) provides that, subject to one exception, *no* conviction may be obtained unless the prosecution proves some form of culpability regarding *each* material element of an offense. The sole exception is found in Section 2.05, which provides that the voluntary act and *mens rea* requirements need not apply to offenses graded as "violations," rather than "crimes." "Violations" are offenses that cannot result in imprisonment or probation, but may result in fines.[33]

---

[30] *See* § 13.02[C], *infra*, for more discussion of *Lambert.*

[31] Smith v. California, 361 U.S. 147 (1959) (reversing a conviction of a bookstore owner for possessing an obscene book in a place where books were sold, based on a statute that did not require proof of knowledge that the material was obscene).

[32] Sanford H. Kadish, *Fifty Years of Criminal Law: An Opinionated Review*, 87 Cal. L. Rev. 943, 954 (1999); *see also* American Law Institute, Comment to § 2.05, at 282 (the Code "makes a frontal attack on . . . strict liability in the penal law").

[33] Model Penal Code § 1.04(5).

Chapter 12

MISTAKES OF FACT

§ 12.01 PUTTING MISTAKE-OF-FACT IN CONTEXT[1]

D1, a hunter, shoots and kills *V1*, believing he is killing a wild animal. *D2* has nonconsensual sexual intercourse with *V2*, mistakenly believing that *V2* consented. *D3* carries away property belonging to *V3*, incorrectly thinking that he has permission to take it. *D4* drives above the speed limit because his speedometer is inaccurate.

In each of these cases the actor has caused the proscribed social harm. Looking only at their external behavior, one might also initially infer that the defendants intended to cause the harms inflicted. In fact, however, each actor was either unaware of, or mistaken about, a fact pertaining to an element of the offense for which he might be prosecuted. *D1* did not know that he was shooting a human being, yet the death of a human being is an element of murder; *D2* erroneously believed that *V2* was willing to have sexual intercourse with him, which, if true, would have negated the "lack of consent" element of rape; *D3* believed that he had the right to take *V3*'s property, which, if true, would mean that he did not intend to steal the property; and *D4* did not know that he was driving above the speed limit, the *actus reus* of the traffic offense.

This chapter considers why and when a mistake (or ignorance[2]) of a fact relating to an element of an offense[3] exculpates an actor for the social harm he causes. As will become evident, the common law's resolution of this issue is complicated. The Model Penal Code's solution is straightforward.

---

[1] *See generally* George Fletcher, Rethinking Criminal Law §§ 9.1–9.3.3 (1978); Rollin M. Perkins, *Ignorance and Mistake in Criminal Law*, 88 U. Pa. L. Rev. 35 (1939); Kenneth W. Simons, *Mistake and Impossibility, Law and Fact, and Culpability: A Speculative Essay*, 81 J. Crim. L. & Criminology 447 (1990).

[2] "Ignorance" and "mistake" are not synonyms. "Ignorance" implies a total want of knowledge — a blank mind — regarding the matter under consideration, whereas "mistake" suggests a wrong belief about the matter. Because this distinction typically is not drawn in mistake-of-fact cases, no effort will be made in this chapter to distinguish between the terms.

[3] The focus of this chapter, it should be reiterated, is on mistakes pertaining to *elements* in the definitions of crimes. Frequently, however, a defendant will allege that he was mistaken as to the existence of facts that would provide an affirmative defense to his conduct (*e.g.*, *D* kills in "self-defense" because he mistakenly believes *V* is about to kill him). The latter type of mistake is discussed at § 17.04, *infra*.

A person may also be mistaken about some fact unrelated to the *actus reus* of an offense or to an affirmative defense. For example, *D* kills *V*, whom he believes is 25 years of age, when in fact *V* is 24 years of age. As *that* mistake does not pertain to an element of the offense of murder, it is not exculpatory.

§ 12.02   WHY DOES A FACTUAL MISTAKE SOMETIMES EXCULPATE?

Aristotle believed that a person is not morally responsible for his actions unless he acts voluntarily, and that "[b]y the voluntary I mean . . . any of the things in a man's own power which he does with knowledge, *i.e. not in ignorance.*"[4]

Use of the word "voluntary" in this context is potentially misleading because the term has multiple meanings in the criminal law.[5] Nonetheless, it generally points us in the proper direction. An actor who is mistaken about some fact "does not have the same kind of opportunity to avoid doing evil that he would have if he knew what he was doing."[6] Consequently, the mistaken actor's freedom of choice — and ultimately the moral basis for punishing him — is undermined.

A better way to understand why a mistake of fact may exculpate an actor is to observe that what makes a person's mistaken action "involuntary" has to do with his cognition (*i.e.*, what he is aware of) rather than his volition (*i.e.*, his capacity to control his conduct). From this realization, "the trail leads plainly to *mens rea.*"[7]

Unfortunately, if the trail leads to "*mens rea,*" then the common law leads us down two paths. This is because courts use the term "*mens rea*" in two ways: in a general sense to describe the actor's "vicious will," or his moral culpability for causing the social harm; and, in the narrower sense, to describe the particular mental state that is an express element of the offense.[8] A mistake of fact may negate the actor's "*mens rea*" in one or both senses of the term.

In some cases, proof that a person was factually mistaken demonstrates that, despite appearances, he acted in a morally blameless manner and that, therefore, he is not deserving of punishment for causing the social harm. In this sense a mistake of fact negates "*mens rea*" in the "culpability" meaning of the term.

A mistake of fact may also negate "*mens rea*" in the "elemental" sense. That is, because of a mistake, a defendant may not possess the specific state of mind required in the definition of the crime. In such circumstances, the defendant must be acquitted because the prosecutor has failed to prove an express element of the offense.

Once one sees the relationship between mistake and *mens rea* it is easy to see that the rule that a mistake of fact is exculpatory is not a special rule — either the actor had the *mens rea* required to be guilty of the crime or he did not.

Courts frequently characterize mistake-of-fact as a "defense." However, since an exculpatory mistake negates the *mens rea* of an offense — an element of the crime — a mistake-of-fact claim is only a "defense" in the sense that the defendant may

---

[4] Aristotle, *Nicomachean Ethics* 1135a (W.D. Ross trans.), *in* 2 The Complete Works of Aristotle 1791 (Jonathan Barnes ed., 1984) (emphasis added).

[5] *See* § 9.02[C], *supra.*

[6] Michael S. Moore, *Causation and the Excuses*, 73 Cal. L. Rev. 1091, 1149 (1985).

[7] Jerome Hall, General Principles of Criminal Law 360 (2d ed. 1960).

[8] *See* § 10.02, *supra.*

be initially required to produce evidence that he was mistaken.[9] Once the "mistake" issue is raised, however, the defendant "is entitled to have the jury understand that the State must still prove each element of the crime [including *mens rea*] beyond a reasonable doubt and that the burden never shifts to the defendant."[10] Put differently, once the defendant produces some evidence he was mistaken, the prosecutor must prove (beyond a reasonable doubt) that the defendant was *not* mistaken, or that the defendant's mistake did *not* negate the *mens rea*.

§ 12.03   COMMON LAW RULES

[A]   General Approach

The common law rules pertaining to mistakes of fact, although complicated, are understandable if the reader reconsiders the historical context in which the rules developed.[11] Originally, the definitions of most common law crimes omitted any mention of a mental-state requirement: A person was guilty if he committed the *actus reus* under circumstances manifesting his moral culpability. A few crimes, however, included a specific mental-state element in their definitions (typically, "intent" or "knowledge"). The latter offenses came to be known as "specific intent" crimes.

From these two types of crimes and two types of "*mens rea*" came a dual approach to mistakes of fact. With specific-intent crimes,[12] common law jurists developed the rule that a mistake of fact is exculpatory if it negates the particular element of *mens rea* — the "specific intent" — in the definition of the offense. In other words, with specific-intent crimes, the common law adopted an *elemental* approach to mistakes. However, with general-intent offenses — crimes that do not include a specific-intent element — the jurists sought to determine if the actor's mistake negated his moral culpability for the crime. This is the *culpability* approach to mistakes.

This dual system, as sensible as it might have been centuries ago, is unjustifiable today in light of the fact that, strict-liability offenses aside, modern penal codes typically include a *mens rea* element in the definition of all felonies and serious misdemeanors. Logically, therefore, the elemental approach should be followed with *all* non-strict-liability crimes today. Although the trend is in this direction, largely as the result of the promulgation of the Model Penal Code,[13] the common law's two approaches to mistakes — depending on whether the offense charged is

---

[9] "Mistake-of-fact" is properly denominated as a "failure-of-proof" defense. *See* § 16.02, *infra*.

[10] General v. State, 789 A.2d 102, 108 (Md. 2002); State v. Diaz, 241 P.3d 1018, 1021 (Kan. Ct. App. 2010) ("Although termed a 'defense,' the mistake-of-fact doctrine merely encapsulates the State's burden to prove every element of the offense: the State cannot convict the defendant if it fails to show that the defendant had the required mental state when committing the crime."). Regarding burdens of proof generally, see Chapter 7, *supra*.

[11] *See* § 10.02, *supra*.

[12] The concepts of "specific intent" and "general intent" are defined at § 10.06, *supra*, and should be reviewed here.

[13] *See* § 12.04, *infra*.

characterized as general-intent or specific-intent — has largely endured.

As a consequence, the first step in analyzing a mistake-of-fact claim in a jurisdiction that follows common law doctrine is *to identify the nature of the crime for which the defendant is being prosecuted*: That is, is it a strict-liability, specific-intent, or general-intent, crime? The separate rules for each type of offense are described below.

[B] Strict-Liability Offenses

The mistake-of-fact rule for strict-liability crimes is straightforward: Under no circumstances does a person's mistake of fact negate his criminal responsibility for violating a strict-liability offense.

This rule is sensible. By definition, a strict-liability offense is one that does not require proof of any *mens rea*. Inasmuch as the basis for exculpation on the ground of mistake is that it negates the actor's "*mens rea*," the absence of any *mens rea* to negate necessarily precludes the use of this defense. Thus, if *D* drives above the lawful speed limit because his speedometer is inaccurate, he will be convicted of a strict-liability speeding offense, even if the speedometer's faulty calibration was unknown and unforeseeable to him.

Similarly, statutory rape is a strict-liability offense in most states regarding the attendant circumstance of the female's age. Thus, *D*'s erroneous belief, *no matter how reasonable*, that the female with whom he is having intercourse is old enough to consent, will not exculpate him.[14] Any unfairness in this outcome is a function of the strict-liability nature of the offense, and not of the mistake-of-fact rule pertaining to such offenses.

[C] Specific-Intent Offenses

Consider the following two examples of mistake-of-fact claims in the prosecution of specific-intent offenses. First, *D1* takes *V1*'s property, incorrectly believing that the property has been abandoned and, therefore, does not belong to anyone. *D1* is charged with larceny, a specific-intent offense defined at common law as the "trespassory taking and carrying away of the personal property of another with intent to permanently deprive the other of the property (or, in shorthand, the intent to steal)."[15]

In the second case, soldier *D2* attempts to have sexual intercourse in Japan with *V2*. Because of a language barrier, *D2* incorrectly believes that *V2* was a consenting prostitute. *D2* is arrested before the intercourse occurs, so he is charged with the specific-intent crime of assault with the intent to commit rape.[16]

---

[14] *See* § 11.01[D], *supra*.

[15] *E.g.*, People v. Navarro, 99 Cal. App. 3d Supp. 1 (Cal. App. Dep't Super. Ct. 1979); *see also* Hawkins v. United States, 103 A.3d 199 (D.C. 2014) (*H* took a bicycle from a bicycle rack; he claimed he mistakenly believed it had been abandoned); People v. Russell, 144 Cal. App. 4th 1415 (2006) (*R* took an old, rusty motorcycle with expired registration tags lying near some trash bins, believing it had been abandoned).

[16] *See* United States v. Short, 4 U.S.C.M.A. 437 (1954).

In each case, the defendant's mistake relates to the specific-intent portion of the applicable offense. *D1*'s mistaken belief that the property has been abandoned and, therefore, does not belong to anyone, is relevant in determining whether he had the specific intent to steal from *V1*. *D2*'s mistaken belief that *V2* consented to intercourse is pertinent in determining whether he "intended to rape" *V2*, the specific intent in the prosecuted offense.

The rule of law here is simple: A defendant is not guilty of an offense if his mistake of fact negates the specific-intent portion of the crime, *i.e.*, if he lacks the intent required in the definition of the offense. Thus, if *D1* genuinely believed that the property he took had been abandoned, then *D1* did not intend to permanently deprive *V1* of the property; if *D2* truly believed that *V2* was consenting to intercourse, then *D2* did not intend to rape *V2*.[17] It does not matter in these cases that the defendants' mistakes may have been unreasonable — that the defendants may have been reckless or negligent in their beliefs. Acquittal follows inextricably from the fact that a person may not be convicted of an offense unless every element thereof, including the mental-state element (the *intent* to steal and rape, respectively), is proved, which did not occur here assuming the defendants were genuinely mistaken.

On the other hand, suppose that *D3* obtains heroin from *X*, believing that the substance is cocaine, and is prosecuted for "knowingly receiving a controlled substance," a specific-intent offense.[18] In this case, *D3* may properly be convicted, notwithstanding his mistake, because his error, whether reasonable or unreasonable, does not negate the requisite specific intent. *D3* knew that he was receiving a controlled substance; he was only mistaken regarding its nature (heroin versus cocaine).

[D] General-Intent Offenses

[1] Ordinary Approach: Was the Mistake Reasonable?

The ordinary rule is that a person is not guilty of a general-intent crime if his mistake of fact was reasonable, but he is guilty if his mistake was unreasonable.[19] For example, suppose that *D* has nonconsensual sexual intercourse with *V*, whom he incorrectly believes is consenting. *D* is charged with rape, defined for current purposes as "sexual intercourse by a male with a female not his wife, without her consent." Inasmuch as rape is a general-intent offense, courts utilize the *culpability* approach to analyze *D*'s mistake of fact. If his mistake regarding *V*'s "consent" was reasonable, then he is not guilty of the offense.[20] This follows because, although the *actus reus* of the offense has occurred, *D*'s state of mind in regard to the prohibited conduct was *nonculpable*, *i.e.*, his belief that she was consenting was one that a

---

[17] United States v. Langley, 33 M.J. 278 (C.M.A. 1991).

[18] This is a specific-intent offense because it requires proof of the actor's awareness of the attendant circumstance of the offense, *i.e.*, that he has received a "controlled substance."

[19] Hawkins v. United States, 103 A.3d 199, 201 (D.C. 2014); People v. Mayberry, 542 P.2d 1337 (Cal. 1975).

[20] *See* Commonwealth v. Simcock, 575 N.E.2d 1137, 1141 (Mass. App. Ct. 1991).

reasonable person might have harbored. If *D*'s belief as to *V*'s consent was unreasonable, however, then he acted with a culpable state of mind that justifies his conviction of the offense.[21]

The mistake-of-fact rule is not without critics.[22] The practical effect of denying exculpation to those who act on the basis of an *unreasonable* mistake of fact is to permit punishment on the basis of mere negligence. Punishment for negligence is controversial in its own right,[23] but in the mistake context its potential unfairness is aggravated in two ways. First, when a crime is defined in terms of negligence, a person is not ordinarily liable unless his negligence is gross, *i.e.*, he is more negligent than is required for civil liability. With mistakes of fact, however, "unreasonableness" is not always defined to a jury in a manner that requires it to find this heightened degree of fault. Therefore, the unreasonably mistaken actor, although perhaps responsible for conduct that would constitute no more than civil negligence, may be punished as a criminal wrongdoer.

Second, the mistake-of-fact rule permits conviction and punishment of a negligent wrongdoer as if he were guilty of intentional wrongdoing. For example, a male who genuinely, but unreasonably, believes that a female is consenting to intercourse will be convicted of the same degree of offense, and will be subject to the same punishment, as one who has full knowledge that he is acting against the will of the victim. Although the former wrongdoer may be sufficiently culpable to merit criminal punishment, his culpability (and, probably, his dangerousness) is not of the same degree as that of the intentional wrongdoer.

[2] Another (Controversial and Increasingly Uncommon) Approach: Moral-Wrong Doctrine

[a]   The Doctrine Is Explained

As noted in the preceding subsection, in the prosecution of a general-intent offense, the usual approach to a mistake-of-fact claim is to determine the actor's culpability for making the mistake by asking whether the defendant's mistake was reasonable or unreasonable, *i.e.*, whether a reasonable person might, or might not, have made the same mistake. On occasion, however, common law jurists have measured moral blameworthiness in the mistake context differently. According to the "moral wrong" doctrine, a doctrine only very infrequently applied today, a person's *reasonable* mistake regarding an attendant circumstance can still

---

[21] Notice the anomaly in the common law approach: If *D*'s mistake was unreasonable, he is convicted of rape; if he is arrested before the intercourse occurs, and he is charged with the specific-intent offense of assault with intent to commit rape, his unreasonable mistake of fact *will* exculpate him. *See* subsection [C], *supra*.

[22] It is important here to distinguish between criticisms of the mistake-of-fact rule described in the text, a rule which applies to *all* general-intent crimes, and the particular issue of whether and when a reasonable mistake regarding a female's consent should exculpate in rape prosecutions. There is movement by the judiciary to make reasonable-mistake-of-fact claims more difficult to present in rape cases. Rosanna Cavallaro, *A Big Mistake: Eroding the Defense of Mistake of Fact About Consent in Rape*, 86 J. Crim. L. & Criminology 815 (1996). *See* § 33.05, *infra*.

[23] *See* § 10.04[D][2][c], *supra*.

demonstrate moral culpability worthy of punishment.

The basis of the moral-wrong doctrine is that "there should be no exculpation for mistake where, if the facts had been as the actor believed them to be, his conduct would still be . . . immoral."[24] Essentially, according to the moral-wrong doctrine, the intent to commit an act that is immoral furnishes the requisite culpability for the related, but unintended, outcome.[25]

Consider the moral-wrong doctrine in light of the classic case of *Regina v. Prince*.[26] In *Prince*, P was prosecuted for "unlawfully tak[ing] or caus[ing] to be taken, any unmarried girl, being under the age of 16 years, out of the possession and against the will of her father or mother." The girl in question, V, was only 14 years old, but the jury found that P genuinely and *reasonably* believed that she was 18 years of age.

All but one of the judges ruled that P was guilty of the offense, notwithstanding his reasonable mistake of fact as to the female's true age. Judge Blackburn, speaking for a majority, interpreted the offense as one of strict liability as to the statutory element of the girl's age. Under this reading of the offense, of course, P's reasonable mistake *is* properly irrelevant. The remaining judges, however, agreed with Baron Bramwell that *mens rea* had to be proven. The difficulty with this view was that, if the court applied the usual mistake rule pertaining to general-intent offenses, P would have to be acquitted, as P's mistake as to V's age was reasonable. Bramwell voted to affirm P's conviction, however, doing so on the basis of the moral-wrong doctrine.

Pursuant to the moral-wrong doctrine, the first matter to be determined is whether the actor's mistake of fact was reasonable or unreasonable. If it was the latter, the usual mistake rule applies, and he may be convicted.

Here, as P's mistake was reasonable, Bramwell took the second step, which is to look at the factual panorama through the defendant's eyes. Thus, suppose that Bramwell had asked P, "What is it that you (reasonably) thought you were doing?" If P had answered candidly, he would have responded, "I thought that I was taking an *18*-year-old girl out of the possession and against the will of her parents."

The third step with the moral-wrong doctrine is for the court to evaluate the morality of the actor's conduct, *based on the facts as the actor reasonably believed them to be*. According to Bramwell, P's conduct as he supposed it to be — "the taking of a female of such tender years [as age 18] that she is properly called a *girl*" from the care and possession of her father — was morally wrong. Indeed, this conclusion was self-evident to Bramwell: "no argument is necessary to prove [the immorality of P's conduct]; it is enough to state the case."

In light of Bramwell's belief that P's conduct was self-evidently morally wrong, he imputed to P knowledge that he was acting immorally. Pursuant to the moral-wrong doctrine, a person who knowingly performs a morally wrong act assumes

---

[24] Bell v. State, 668 P.2d 829, 833 (Alaska. Ct. App. 1983).

[25] Garnett v. State, 632 A.2d 797, 813 (Md. 1993) (Bell, J., dissenting).

[26] L.R. 2 Cr. Cas. Res. 154 (1875).

the risk that the attendant factual circumstances are not as they reasonably appear to be and that, therefore, his conduct is not merely immoral but also illegal. In *Prince*, therefore, *P* knowingly assumed the risk that *V*, whom he immorally took away from her father, was also underage. *P* was convicted of the offense according to the moral-wrong doctrine.[27]

The moral-wrong doctrine is not triggered unless the defendant's conduct would be immoral had the situation been as he supposed. Suppose, for example, that *P* had known *V*'s true age, but instead had reasonably believed that she was homeless and, therefore, not in anyone's lawful possession. In these circumstances, *P*'s answer to the question, "What did you think you were doing?" would have been, "I thought I was taking a homeless girl of 14 off the streets and into my protective possession." Presumably, this conduct is not by itself immoral. If this assumption is correct, *P* would not assume the risk that he was mistaken about the attendant circumstance that she had a family; as a consequence, he would be acquitted.

[b]   Criticisms of the Doctrine

The moral-wrong doctrine is deservedly controversial.[28] First, it permits conviction of a person who did not know, and had no reason to know, that his conduct would violate the law. In *Prince*, *P* may have known that his behavior was immoral; immorality and illegality, however, are not identical concepts. Even if all offenses involved immoral conduct, which is not the case, it is not true that all immoral conduct is illegal. The moral-wrong doctrine conflates the two concepts in a manner that runs afoul of the principle of legality.[29] That is, if Parliament had wanted to prohibit the "immoral" act of taking an *18*-year-old female away from her parents (which is what *P* reasonably thought he was doing and for which, in essence, he was convicted) it could have done so, but it did not. In today's world, a person should only be punished for conduct that the legislature, the lawmaking branch of government, has prohibited.

Second, the moral wrong doctrine is premised on the assumption that the defendant intentionally committed an immoral act. But, who determines immorality? And, who is to say that the actor *knew* that his conduct was immoral? In *Prince*, Baron Bramwell thought it obvious that taking an 18-year-old female from her parents was immoral and, therefore, he *assumed* that *P* must have known he was acting immorally. Perhaps in the English society in which the doctrine developed, this was a fair assumption. In today's culturally heterogeneous American society, however, it does not inevitably follow that, because a court (or jury) believes particular conduct is immoral, the defendant must have known when he acted that he was crossing the nebulous immorality line.

---

[27] *See also* White v. State, 185 N.E. 64, 65 (Ohio Ct. App. 1933) (*W* abandoned his wife; when he left her she was newly pregnant, although he had no reason to know this; held: *W* was guilty of the offense of "abandoning one's pregnant wife"; according to the court, "[h]e must make sure of his ground when he commits the simple wrong of leaving her at all").

[28] Indeed, the House of Lords has since disapproved of the reasoning found in *Prince*. A Minor v. Director of Public Prosecutions, [2000] A.C. 428 (H.L.). According to Lord Nicholls, *Prince* should not be "reinvograte[d]"; "it is a relic from an age done and gone." *Id.* at 476.

[29] *See* § 5.01, *supra*.

The moral-wrong doctrine deserves to be treated as an unwise relic, one that fortunately is not often invoked in current times.

[3] Still Another Approach: Legal-Wrong Doctrine

[a] The Doctrine Is Explained

What if a state provides that sexual intercourse by an adult with a person under the age of 12 constitutes first-degree rape, but it is the lesser offense of second-degree rape if the victim is older than 12 but under the age of 16.[30] Assume that *D* reasonably believes that the person with whom he is having sexual intercourse is 14 years old (and thus this would constitute second-degree rape), but in fact the victim's age is 11 (first-degree rape). Should *D* be convicted of first-degree or second-degree rape? That is, should we focus on what he did or on what he reasonably believed he was doing?

According to some common law scholars and case law, "[a] mistake of fact relating only to the degree of the crime or gravity of the offense will not shield a deliberate offender from the full consequences of the wrong actually committed."[31] Put differently, if a person's conduct causes the social harm prohibited by More Serious Offense X, he is guilty of *that* offense even if, based on his reasonable understanding of the attendant circumstances, he would be guilty of Less Serious Offense Y if the situation were as he supposed.[32]

This outcome may be characterized as the "legal-wrong doctrine," a less extreme alternative to the moral-wrong doctrine.

[b] Criticism of the Doctrine

The legal-wrong doctrine is not as troubling as the moral-wrong doctrine. It may nonetheless be criticized because it authorizes punishment based on the harm that an actor has caused — *i.e.*, the *actus reus* of the greater offense — while ignoring the fact that the actor's *mens rea* was at the level of a lesser crime. If a society were concerned only with consequences, this outcome would follow. In a society that values the importance of *mens rea* in evaluating guilt, however, punishment should be graduated on the basis of the social harm caused *and* the blameworthiness of the person who caused it. Under some circumstances, therefore, the legal-wrong doctrine will result in punishment disproportional to the offender's blameworthiness.

---

[30] *E.g.*, Ala. Crim. Code §§ 13A-6-61 & 13A-6-62 (2015).

[31] Rollin M. Perkins & Ronald N. Boyce, Criminal Law 916 (3d ed. 1982) (and cases cited therein).

[32] *See* United States v. Jones, 471 F.3d 535 (4th Cir. 2006) (*J* transported a minor across state lines for purposes of prostitution; he was guilty of this offense although he claimed that the government did not prove that he knew the minor was underage; the court stated that "the transportation of *any* individual for purposes of prostitution . . . is already unlawful under federal law"; as *J*'s act would have constituted a federal offense, albeit a lesser one, if she had been older, "he assumed the risk that [she] was a minor") (quoting United States v. Taylor, 239 F.3d 994 (9th Cir. 2001); *see also* American Law Institute, Comment to § 2.04, at 274 (observing that a few states appeared to permit conviction of the greater offense although the defendant's *mens rea* was consistent with the lesser crime).

[E] *Regina v. Morgan*: Common Law in Transition or an Aberration?[33]

Consider the facts in *Regina v. Morgan*:[34] *D*s, three men, were convicted of forcibly raping *V*, *X*'s wife. According to *D*s, *X* invited them to have intercourse with *V*, falsely telling them that if she struggled they should not worry, because she "was 'kinky' and this was the only way in which she could be turned on." At trial, the jury was instructed that *D*s should only be acquitted if their mistake regarding *V*'s consent was reasonable. On appeal, *D*s argued that this instruction was faulty, and that the jury should have been informed that even an unreasonable mistake of fact would exculpate them.

The tendered instruction was proper according to ordinary "mistake" principles.[35] Nonetheless, a majority of the Law Lords ruled that a male who acts on the basis of an honest but *unreasonable* belief that the female consented is *not* guilty of rape, because the mistake prevents the male from possessing the *mens rea* required for that offense. Lord Cross explained the issue raised in the case this way:

> [T]he . . . question to be answered in this case, as I see it, is whether according to the ordinary use of the English language a man can be said to have committed rape if he believed that the woman was consenting to the intercourse and would not have attempted to have it but for his belief, whatever his grounds for so believing. I do not think that he can. Rape, to my mind, imports at least indifference as to the woman's consent.

Lord Cross seems wrong. The average person using the English language in the "ordinary" way would probably say that *V was* raped, even if *D*s believed that she had consented. What Lord Cross may have meant, however, was expressed more cogently by Lord Hailsham:

> [E]ither the prosecution proves that the accused had the requisite intent, or it does not. In the former case it succeeds, and in the latter it fails. Since honest belief clearly negatives intent, the reasonableness or otherwise of that belief can only be evidence for or against the view that the belief and therefore the intent was actually held.

Essentially, Lord Hailsham's remarks demonstrate that he was using the elemental approach to resolve the defendants' mistake claim, a process ordinarily restricted to specific-intent offenses.[36] That is, according to Hailsham, once it is established that the definition of a crime requires proof of "intention," then this *mens rea* term modifies each of the social harm elements, including the attendant

---

[33] *See generally* David Cowley, *The Retreat from Morgan*, 1982 Crim. L. Rev. 198; R.A. Duff, *Recklessness and Rape*, 3 Liverpool L. Rev. 49 (1981); James Faulkner, *Mens Rea in Rape: Morgan and the Inadequacy of Subjectivism, or Why No Should Not Mean Yes in the Eyes of the Law*, 18 Melb. U. L. Rev. 60 (1991).

[34] [1976] A.C. 182.

[35] *See* § 12.03[D][1], *supra*.

[36] *See* §§ 10.02[C], 12.03[A] and [C], *supra*.

circumstance that the intercourse was nonconsensual.[37] Therefore, if *D*s negligently believed that *V* was consenting, they did not possess the requisite *mens rea* of the offense, *i.e.*, the *intention* to act without *V*'s consent.

Morgan seemed at the time to represent an important change in "mistake-of-fact" law because it apparently dispensed with the ordinary "general intent"/"specific intent" dichotomy. *Morgan*, however, proved to be a highly controversial decision. The controversy is hardly surprising in light of the fact that the rule announced in *Morgan* could potentially authorize the acquittal of a male who has nonconsensual intercourse with a female, as long as the male is oblivious of the female's wishes, no matter now obvious they are.[38] As a result of *Morgan*, Parliament redrafted its rape statute, reducing the *mens rea* required, permitting conviction on the basis of an actor's knowledge or recklessness as to the victim's lack of consent.[39]

§ 12.04   MODEL PENAL CODE[40]

[A]   General Rule

The Model Code uses a straightforward elemental approach to matters of *mens rea*, including mistakes of fact. Section 2.02, subsection (1), states the general rule that one is not guilty of an offense unless he acted "purposely, knowingly, recklessly, or negligently, as the law may require, with respect to each material element of the offense." Thus, as to each material element of an offense, there is a particular *mens rea* requirement, be it purpose, knowledge, recklessness, or negligence. Specifically as to mistakes of fact, Section 2.04(1) provides that a mistake is a defense if it negates the mental state required to establish *any* element of the offense. It is irrelevant whether the offense would be identified as general-intent or specific-intent at common law. Put simply, either the actor had the culpable state of mind required in the definition of the offense or he did not.

Consider how the facts in *Morgan*,[41] discussed immediately above in Section 12.03[E], would be analyzed under the Model Penal Code's original Section 213.1: rape occurs when "a male has sexual intercourse with a female not his wife if he

---

[37] Notice: If the word "intentional" modifies the attendant circumstance of "without her consent" in the definition of rape, as Lord Hailsham assumes by his remark, rape is effectively converted into a specific-intent crime! It would be as if rape were defined as follows: "nonconsensual sexual intercourse by a male, with a female, not his wife, *with the knowledge or belief* that she is not consenting." If rape *is* a specific-intent offense, of course, the Lords' elemental approach to the mistake issue is consistent with traditional rules. Historically, however, rape has been treated as a general-intent crime.

[38] Of course, the more unreasonable the claimed mistake, the less likely the jury will believe the defendant's claim of obliviousness.

[39] *See* § 1(1) of the Sexual Offenses (Amendment) Act of 1976.

[40] *See generally* George P. Fletcher, *Mistake in the Model Penal Code: A False False Problem*, 19 Rutgers L.J. 649 (1988); Peter W. Low, *The Model Penal Code, the Common Law, and Mistakes of Fact: Recklessness, Negligence, or Strict Liability?*, 19 Rutgers L.J. 539 (1988).

[41] Regina v. Morgan, [1976] A.C. 182.

compels her to submit by force."[42] Because this definition is silent regarding the applicable *mens rea*, the Code provides that each material element is established if the defendant acted purposely, knowingly, or recklessly with respect thereto.[43]

Therefore, *D*s in *Morgan* could be convicted of rape if they purposely, knowingly, or recklessly compelled the victim to have sexual intercourse by force, but they would not be guilty of rape if they negligently compelled her. For example, if *D*s realized that *X*'s statement to them about his wife's "kinkiness" might be false, and yet they consciously disregarded the substantial and unjustifiable risk that *V* was *not* consenting, then a jury could conclude that they *recklessly* compelled *V*, and their mistaken belief that she consented would be no defense.[44] In contrast, if a jury believed that *D*s were so clueless that they genuinely were unaware of the possibility that her resistance was real, then the defendants would not be guilty of rape. This would be so because, in this latter scenario, *D*s *negligently* compelled *V* by force, whereas the offense requires proof of recklessness or a more culpable state of mind.

[B] Exception to the Rule

The Model Penal Code provides one exception to the general rule stated above. In a variation on the common law legal-wrong doctrine,[45] the Code provides that the defense of mistake-of-fact is not available if the actor would be guilty of another offense, had the circumstances been as he supposed.[46] However, unlike the common law legal-wrong doctrine, which maintains that the defendant is guilty of the higher offense in such circumstances, the Code only permits punishment at the level of the lesser offense.[47]

For example, reconsider the statute that provides that an adult who has sexual intercourse with a person under the age of 12 is guilty of first-degree rape, but is guilty of the lesser offense of second-degree rape if the victim is older than 12 but under the age of 16.[48] In the hypothetical raised earlier, *D* reasonably believed that the person with whom he had intercourse was 14 years old, although in fact she was 11. As we saw, according to the common law legal-wrong doctrine, *D* would be convicted of first-degree rape — based on the *actus reus* of the offense committed. However, if the Model Penal Code rules on mistake-of-fact were applied to this rape statute, *D* would be punished at the level of second-degree rape — based on *D*'s state of mind.

---

[42] As explained more fully in Chapter 33, as this text goes to press the American Law Institute is redrafting its Sexual Offense provisions. When completed, they will almost certainly look very different than the original provisions drafted in the 1950s and adopted by the Institute in 1962.

[43] Model Penal Code § 2.02(3) and (4). *See* § 10.07[C], *supra*.

[44] The Model Code definition of rape does not include the element of "non-consent," but the commentary states that the statutory element of "[c]ompulsion plainly implies non-consent." American Law Institute, Comment to § 213.1, at 306.

[45] *See* § 12.03[D][3], *supra*.

[46] Model Penal Code § 2.04(2).

[47] American Law Institute, Comment to § 2.04, at 273.

[48] *See* § 12.03[D][3][a], *supra*.

Chapter 13

MISTAKES OF LAW

§ 13.01 GENERAL PRINCIPLES[1]

[A] General Rule

"In determining whether a defendant's mistaken belief disproves criminal intent, the courts have drawn a distinction between mistakes of fact and mistakes [or ignorance[2]] of law."[3] Specifically, the law treats mistakes of law more strictly — allows for exculpation of a defendant less easily — than mistakes of fact. Subject to very limited exceptions, the common law mistake-of-law rule is straightforward: *ignorantia legis neminem excusat*, or ignorance of the law is not an excusing defense.[4] This "dogmatic common-law maxim"[5] is deeply imbedded in Anglo-American jurisprudence.[6]

It is also the case that ignorance or mistake of law only rarely serves as a basis for claiming that a defendant lacked the requisite *mens rea* defined in an offense. That is, neither knowledge nor recklessness or negligence as to whether conduct constitutes an offense, or as to its meaning, ordinarily is an element of that offense; therefore, it follows that there typically is no *mens rea* element in an offense capable of being negated by an actor's ignorance or mistake of law.

Put simply, once it is determined that a defendant is asserting a mistake of law, rather than mistake of fact, claim,[7] the default legal position is simple: the

---

[1] *See generally* Jerome Hall, General Principles of Criminal Law 382–414 (2d ed. 1960); Ronald A. Cass, *Ignorance of the Law: A Maxim Reexamined*, 17 Wm. & Mary L. Rev. 671 (1976); Fernand N. Dutile & Harold F. Moore, *Mistake and Impossibility: Arranging a Marriage Between Two Difficult Partners*, 74 Nw. U. L. Rev. 166 (1979); Dan M. Kahan, *Ignorance of Law Is an Excuse — But Only for the Virtuous*, 96 Mich. L. Rev. 127 (1997); Kenneth W. Simons, *Ignorance and Mistake of Criminal Law, Noncriminal Law, and Fact*, 9 Ohio St. J. Crim. L. 487 (2012); Daniel Yeager, *Kahan on Mistakes*, 96 Mich. L. Rev. 2113 (1998).

[2] "Ignorance" and "mistake" involve different states of mind. *See* § 12.01, Note 2, *supra*. However, the terms will be used interchangeably in this chapter, except when distinguishing between them enhances clarity.

[3] People v. Meneses, 165 Cal. App. 4th 1648, 1661 (Ct. App. 2008).

[4] United States v. Int'l Minerals & Chem. Corp., 402 U.S. 558, 563 (1971); People v. Marrero, 507 N.E.2d 1068, 1069 (N.Y. 1987).

[5] *People v. Marrero*, 507 N.E.2d at 1069.

[6] Lambert v. California, 355 U.S. 225, 228 (1957).

[7] A lawyer must be able to distinguish mistake-of-law from mistake-of-fact claims. It is easy to confuse them. For example, in United States v. Shaw, 670 F.3d 360 (1st Cir. 2012), S was prosecuted for

defendant's mistake will not exculpate, subject to the few narrow exceptions described in this chapter.

[B] Rationale of the Rule

[1] Certainty of the Law

It has been said that the law is "definite and knowable."[8] Therefore, it may be argued, there is no such thing as a *reasonable* mistake of law. Anyone who misunderstands the "definite and knowable" law has simply not tried hard enough to learn it and, consequently, is morally culpable for failing to know the law.

At common law, this claim might have had the ring of plausibility. The courts recognized few criminal offenses, and those that existed involved conduct *malum in se.* Few people could seriously allege surprise in learning that stealing another person's property, intentionally burning down another person's house, or unjustifiably taking another person's life, was illegal.

However, even at common law, the principle that laws were definite and knowable was often a fiction. Criminal laws were not enacted by legislatures and published, as they are today. Instead, judges shaped the law on a case-by-case basis, which meant that the criminal law changed incrementally with each new decision. Moreover, the definitions of some common law offenses were not models of clarity.[9]

Whatever its plausibility centuries ago, the "definite and knowable" claim cannot withstand modern analysis. There has been a "profusion of legislation making otherwise lawful conduct criminal (*malum prohibitum*)."[10] Therefore, even a person with a clear moral compass is frequently unlikely to realize that particular conduct is prohibited. Furthermore, many modern criminal statutes are exceedingly intricate. In today's complex society, therefore, an ordinarily law-abiding person can reasonably misunderstand the law or even fail to know of a particular penal law's existence.

"knowingly possessing an unregistered firearm." Under federal law, a firearm less than 18 inches in length must be registered. The barrel of S's firearm was slightly less than 17 inches in length. If *S* had claimed that he did not know he had to register a firearm less than 18 inches in length, this would be a mistake of law claim, which would mean that he would be without a valid defense based on the general principles set out in the text. *S* did not claim this, but rather he asserted that he did not know that his firearm was less than 18 inches in length, *i.e.*, he did not know that his firearm factually possessed the characteristics that brought it within the scope of the registration law. *That* is a mistake of *fact* claim, subject to the broader exculpation rules set out in the last chapter. As concurring District Judge Boudin observed in the case, "[t]his juxtaposition may seem perverse; but a defendant's ignorance of facts may often defeat a criminal charge while ignorance of the law does so only rarely." *Id.* at 368.

[8] 1 J. Austin, Lectures on Jurisprudence 497 (4th ed. 1879); *see* 4 Blackstone, Commentaries on the Laws of England *27 (1769) ("[E]very person of discretion . . . is bound and presumed to know [the law].").

[9] For example, sodomy was considered so shocking an offense that Blackstone not only did not define it with clarity, but he refused to name it, calling it simply "the infamous *crime against nature.*" 4 Blackstone, Note 8, *supra*, at *215. Also, some offenses, *e.g.*, common law larceny, contained exceedingly intricate rules that required judges (and inferentially citizens) to make "hair-splitting distinctions." Rollin M. Perkins & Ronald N. Boyce, Criminal Law 291 (3d ed. 1982).

[10] *People v. Marrero*, 507 N.E.2d at 1075 (Hancock, J., dissenting).

[2] Avoiding Subjectivity in the Law

Jerome Hall once provided a more sophisticated explanation for the common law rule.[11] In stark contrast to the assertion that criminal laws are definite and knowable, Hall claimed that laws are "unavoidably vague" and that persons can "disagree indefinitely regarding the[ir] meaning." At some point, Hall reasoned, debate regarding the meaning of a law must end: certain competent officials and institutions, particularly courts, must determine its meaning. Their official declarations provide an objective definition of penal provisions. If mistake-of-law could excuse, Hall argued, the result would be that the law would lose its objective meaning; the law would mean whatever a person subjectively (and perhaps incorrectly) thought it meant.[12] Yet, a "legal order implies the rejection of such contradiction." The legal system favors "objectivity to subjectivity and judicial process to individual opinion."[13]

Hall's thesis, however, misconceives the nature of a mistake-of-law claim. A person who claims mistake-of-law does not assert, nor would her acquittal imply, that the law means whatever she thinks it does. If a defense were recognized, the meaning of the law would remain stable: Mistake-of-law would simply *excuse* the actor for having violated the law, assuming that an ordinary law-abiding person would also have misunderstood the law in question. To punish one whose mistake of law is reasonable "is contrary to 'the [retributive] notion that punishment should be conditioned on a showing of . . . moral blameworthiness."[14]

[3] Deterring Fraud

A pragmatic justification for the no-excuse rule is that recognition of a mistake-of-law defense would provide "opportunities for wrong-minded individuals to contrive [claims of mistake] . . . solely to get an exculpatory notion before the jury."[15] Courts would become hopelessly enmeshed in insoluble questions regarding the extent of a defendant's true knowledge of the relevant law. Some false claims would doubtlessly succeed because the truth of the allegations "could scarcely be determined by any evidence accessible to others."[16]

---

[11] Hall, Note 1, *supra*, at 382–87.

[12] Empirical studies suggest that "citizens show[] no particular knowledge of the laws of their states." John M. Darley et al., *The Ex Ante Function of the Criminal Law*, 35 Law & Soc'y Rev. 165, 181 (2001). According to the Darley study, respondents guessed that the laws conformed with their moral beliefs: "[P]eople often generate their perceptions of what the law of the state must be from what they think is the morally appropriate form for that law to take. . . . [M]any people are often wrong about what the actual law of their state holds." *Id.* at 183.

[13] Hall, Note 1, *supra*, at 383.

[14] *People v. Marrero*, 507 N.E.2d at 1074 (Hancock, J., dissenting) (quoting Thomas W. White, *Reliance on Apparent Authority as a Defense to Criminal Prosecution*, 77 Colum. L. Rev. 775, 784 (1977)).

[15] *People v. Marrero*, 507 N.E.2d at 1073.

[16] 1 Austin, Note 8, *supra*, at 498.

As Holmes observed, however, "it may be doubted whether a man's knowledge of the law is any harder to investigate than many questions which are gone into,"[17] such as a defendant's *mens rea* or whether the actor suffers from the excusing condition of insanity. Moreover, the risk of fraud could be mitigated by allocating to the defendant the burden of persuasion regarding any mistake-of-law excuse claim.

[4] Encouraging Legal Knowledge

The most commonly accepted explanation for the general no-defense rule — "frankly pragmatic and utilitarian"[18] — comes from Holmes:

> The true explanation of the rule is the same as that which accounts for the law's indifference to a man's particular temperament, faculties, and so forth. Public policy sacrifices the individual to the general good. . . . It is no doubt true that there are many cases in which the criminal could not have known that he was breaking the law, but to admit the excuse at all would be to encourage ignorance . . . and justice to the individual is rightly outweighed by the larger interests on the other side of the scales.[19]

That is, if a reasonable mistake of law were a defense, this rule would foster lawlessness by encouraging ignorance of the law, rather than respect for and adherence to law. The best way to discourage ignorance is to apply the controversial strict liability doctrine that mistakes of law will *never* be countenanced.[20]

Holmes's explanation, however, is also unsatisfactory. As Professor Dan Kahan has argued, when a person "takes reasonable steps to learn the law, there always remains some residual risk" of error.[21] In the strict liability system Holmes defends, the person who tries to learn the law, but errs, is no better off than one who makes no effort at all — the incentive to learn the law is undermined. If the criminal law permitted a *reasonable* mistake of law to serve as a defense while punishing for negligence (for an *unreasonable* mistake), there would be an incentive to learn the law.

§ 13.02 WHEN MISTAKE-OF-LAW IS A DEFENSE: EXCEPTIONS TO THE GENERAL RULE

[A] Putting the Exceptions in Context

Although the no-defense rule stated in Section 13.01 is strict, there are three exceptions to the general rule. The first basis for acquittal is sometimes known as the "reasonable reliance" or "entrapment by estoppel" exception. As discussed below, this defense deals with the situation in which the government provides legal misinformation to the defendant. Because of the defendant's reliance on the

---

[17] Oliver Wendell Holmes, The Common Law 48 (1881).

[18] *People v. Marrero*, 507 N.E.2d at 1074 (Hancock, J., dissenting).

[19] Holmes, Note 17, *supra*, at 48.

[20] For debate regarding strict liability generally, see § 11.02, *supra*.

[21] Kahan, Note 1, *supra*, at 134.

misinformation, the defendant is excused for violation of the offense. Although this exception has its roots in the common law, some courts frame this defense on constitutional grounds.

The second basis for acquittal expressly has its roots in the United State Supreme Court's constitutional ruling in *Lambert v. California*.[22] Here, the basis for acquittal is not misinformation provided by a government official, but rather something about the nature of the criminal statute itself that prevents a citizen from receiving fair notice of the existence of the statute itself. Thus, the basis of *this* defense is not *mistake* of law, but *ignorance* of law.

The third exception is a so-called "failure-of-proof" claim.[23] Essentially, here, the defendant claims that, because of a mistake of law (almost always it is a mistake regarding a law other than the one for which she is being prosecuted), she did not have the requisite *mens rea* to be convicted of the offense charged. To the extent that this type of claim is exculpatory, it is a defense for the same reason a mistake-of-*fact* claim acquits: the government has failed to satisfy its burden of proof regarding an essential element of the offense.

These three exceptions are explained below.

[B]   Reasonable-Reliance Doctrine (Entrapment by Estoppel)[24]

Under limited circumstances, a person may rely on an interpretation of the law later determined to be erroneous. We start, however, with two situations in which such reliance is *not* permitted.

[1]   No Defense: Reliance on One's Own Interpretation of the Law

A person is *not* excused for committing a crime if she relies on her own erroneous reading of the law, even if a reasonable person — even a reasonable law-trained person — would have similarly misunderstood the law. For example, in *People v. Marrero*,[25] *M*, a federal corrections officer, was arrested for possession of a loaded .38 caliber automatic pistol, in violation of a statute that prohibited the carrying of a handgun without a permit. *M* sought dismissal of his indictment on the ground that the law expressly exempted peace officers from liability under the statute. The statutory definition of "peace officers" included any official or guard of "any state prison or *of any penal correctional institution.*" As a federal corrections officer, *M* said that he believed that he was exempt under the law.

---

[22] 355 U.S. 225 (1957).

[23] For an explanation of the meaning "failure-of-proof" defense, see § 16.02, *infra.*

[24] *See generally* Gabriel J. Chin, et al., *The Mistake of Law Defense and an Unconstitutional Provision of the Model Penal Code*, 93 N.C.L. Rev. 139 (2014); John T. Parry, *Culpability, Mistake, and Official Interpretations of Law*, 25 Am. J. Crim. L. 1 (1997).

[25] 507 N.E.2d 1068 (N.Y. 1987).

M's reading of the statute was not self-evidently unreasonable. Indeed, the trial judge agreed with *M*'s interpretation of the law. Nonetheless, an appellate court concluded, by a 3-2 vote, that he was not a "peace officer" within the meaning of the statute. Although this means that three of the six judges who considered the exemption interpreted it as *M* did, *M* was not entitled to claim mistake-of-law at his subsequent trial to the extent that his mistake was founded solely on his own understanding of the law. In such circumstances, the ordinary no-defense rule applies: One is never excused for relying on a personal — even reasonable — misreading of a statute.

[2] No Defense: Advice of Private Counsel[26]

Reliance on erroneous advice provided by a private attorney is not a defense to a crime.[27] This blanket rejection of a defense is controversial. Society arguably is better off if a person acts on the basis of a lawyer's advice than if she acts on her own untutored reading of the applicable law. A rule that encourages a citizen to seek a lawyer's assistance would likely promote, rather than discourage, knowledge of the law.

Occasionally it is suggested that if reliance on private legal advice could excuse a person's unlawful conduct, she might purposely turn to an unethical lawyer or one of questionable competency in order to obtain advice that authorizes the improper conduct.[28] However, this argument exaggerates the dangers in permitting an excuse. Unqualified lawyers exist, but courts presume that attorneys are competent, absent evidence to the contrary.[29] Nor is the risk of fraud substantial: An attorney is subject to professional discipline or criminal prosecution for fraudulent conduct.[30]

Probably the most serious problem with permitting the defense in these circumstances is one of line-drawing. Should the advice of any lawyer qualify, or only advice from a specialist in the field? Must a person turn to an experienced lawyer, or may she turn to a new member of the Bar? Ultimately, however, any reliance that would result in exculpation would have to be reasonable. A jury could determine whether the defendant made reasonable efforts to obtain accurate legal

---

[26] *See generally* Miriam Gur-Arye, *Reliance on a Lawyer's Mistaken Advice — Should It Be an Excuse from Criminal Liability?*, 29 Am. J. Crim. L. 455 (2002).

[27] State v. Huff, 36 A. 1000 (Me. 1897). There are exceedingly rare cases that have ruled to the contrary. *E.g.*, Long v. State, 65 A.2d 489 (Del. 1949) (permitting *L*, prosecuted for bigamy, to show that he consulted with, and relied upon incorrect legal information of, a reputable attorney who stated that *L*'s earlier divorce in Arkansas was valid and, therefore, that *L* could remarry in Delaware). It should be noted that, although a person in such circumstances cannot successfully claim mistake of law in a criminal prosecution, she may sue the attorney in a civil action for legal malpractice. Winstock v. Galasso, 64 A.3d 1012 (N.J. Super Ct. App. Div. 2013).

[28] *See* State v. Downs, 21 S.E. 689, 689 (N.C. 1895); *see also* Gur-Arye, Note 26, *supra*, at 466 (permitting the excuse "might lead to people purchasing custom-tailored legal opinions in order to acquire immunity from criminal prosecution").

[29] *See* Strickland v. Washington, 466 U.S. 668, 687–91 (1984).

[30] A lawyer who purposely gives incorrect advice so that her client can assert a mistake-of-law defense could be prosecuted for obstruction of justice, conspiracy with her client to violate the statute in question, and/or be convicted as an accomplice in the criminal act perpetrated by her client.

advice. Nonetheless, no such defense is recognized.

[3]　Faulty Interpretation of the Law by the Government

There is no agreed-upon way of describing the required elements of the "reasonable reliance" or "entrapment by estoppel" exception to the no-defense rule. Although a person is not excused for relying on her own interpretation of a criminal statute or that of a private attorney, one court has stated that the defense applies "when an official assures a defendant that certain conduct is legal, and the defendant reasonably relies on that advice and continues or initiates the conduct."[31] Another court has stated that the defense applies if a government official "misleads a party as to the state of the law and that party proceeds to act on the misrepresentation," as long as the defendant's reliance is reasonable "in light of the identity of the agent, the point of law misrepresented, and the substance of the misrepresentation."[32] Other courts have described the common law defense in a manner similar to the Model Penal Code.[33] Some courts characterize this defense as finding its source not merely in common law principles, but also in principles of constitutional due process.[34]

This defense may be justified on various grounds. First, the threat of punishment can have little deterrent effect on an individual whose conduct has been authorized by an appropriate party or legal body. Second, a person who acts on the basis of an official, albeit erroneous, interpretation of the law has acted as we would want her to act, i.e., in obedience of the law as it was explained to her by a proper party. Third, there is a "clean hands" justification for the rule: It is fundamentally unfair for a government agent to authorize conduct and then seek to have the individual who relied on that authorization prosecuted, even if it later turns out that the original authorization was incorrect.

This defense is narrowly applied. In general, a person may only reasonably rely on a statement of the law contained in: (1) a statute later declared to be invalid;[35] (2) a judicial decision of the highest court in the jurisdiction, later determined to be erroneous;[36] or (3) an erroneous interpretation of the law, secured from a public officer in charge of its interpretation, administration, or enforcement, such as the Attorney General of the state[37] or, in the case of federal law, of the United States.

---

[31]　United States v. Smith, 940 F.2d 710, 714 (1st Cir. 1991).

[32]　United States v. Nichols, 21 F.3d 1016, 1018 (10th Cir. 1994).

[33]　Commonwealth v. Twitchell, 617 N.E.2d 609, 619 (Mass. 1993). The Model Penal Code formulation is described in § 13.03[B][1], infra.

[34]　E.g., Miller v. Commonwealth, 492 S.E.2d 482, 484–87 (Va. Ct. App. 1997); for fuller discussion of the constitutional basis for the defense, see Chin, et al., Note 24, supra.

[35]　E.g., Claybrook v. State, 51 S.W.2d 499 (Tenn. 1932).

[36]　State v. O'Neil, 126 N.W. 454 (Iowa 1910). The law is divided on whether a person may also rely on a lower court ruling. E.g., State v. Chicago, Milwaukee & St. Paul Ry., 153 N.W. 320 (Minn. 1915) (recognizing the excuse); United States v. Barker, 546 F.2d 940 (D.C. Cir. 1976) (recognizing the excuse, in dictum); State v. Striggles, 210 N.W. 137 (Iowa 1927) (rejecting the defense).

[37]　See Commonwealth v. Twitchell, 617 N.E.2d 609 (Mass. 1993).

According to these narrow principles, *D1*, an ex-felon in possession of a muzzle-loading hunting rifle, who is charged with "possession of a firearm by a person previously convicted of a felony" may defend her actions if she was assured by her probation officer than she could possess the weapon, but she cannot rely on assurances of a state Department of Game and Fisheries official who lacked authority to interpret the penal law in question.[38] For the same reason, *D2*, a motorist charged with disobeying a lawful police order, cannot rely on a 911 telephone operator's advice received by *D2* on a car phone, to ignore a police officer's order to pull over in her car.[39]

Even if a person obtains an interpretation of the law from a proper source, one should look at the context in which the misinformation was given. For example, a person may rely on an official "opinion letter" from the state Attorney General, formally interpreting the statute in question.[40] However, a highly informal interpretation of the law will typically not do. For example, a fisherman may not reasonably rely on an extemporaneous interpretation of a fishing regulation, provided by a Fish and Wildlife Patrol Officer at the scene.[41]

[C] Fair Notice and the *Lambert* Principle[42]

At common law, it is said that "every one is *conclusively* presumed to know the law."[43] This means not only that citizens are presumed to understand the law, but more fundamentally to be aware of the *existence* of each criminal law. On occasion, however, there will be an exceptional case in which it is so grossly unjust to assume that a citizen is aware of a penal law's existence that one might expect that a court would provide some common law dispensation.[44] And, as it turns out, the Supreme Court held in *Lambert v. California*[45] that, under limited circumstances, a person who is unaware of a duly enacted and published criminal statute may successfully assert a constitutional defense in a prosecution of that offense.

In *Lambert*, *L* was a Los Angeles resident and convicted felon. A local ordinance required felons residing in the city for more than five days to register their presence with the police. Violation of the ordinance was punishable by a maximum sentence of six months in jail, $500, or both. *L* never registered and was prosecuted under the ordinance. She was convicted after the trial court barred evidence of her claim that she was unaware of the law.

---

[38] *See* Miller v. Commonwealth, 492 S.E.2d 482 (Va. Ct. App. 1997).

[39] State v. DeCastro, 913 P.2d 558 (Haw. Ct. App. 1996).

[40] Commonwealth v. Twitchell, 617 N.E.2d 609 (Mass. 1993).

[41] *See* Haggren v. State, 829 P.2d 842 (Alaska Ct. App. 1992), *overruled on other grounds*, Allen v. Municipality of Anchorage, 168 P.3d 890 (Alaska Ct. App. 2007).

[42] *See generally* Peter W. Low & Benjamin Charles Wood, Lambert *Revisited*, 100 Va. L. Rev. 1603 (2014).

[43] State v. Woods, 179 A. 1, 2 (Vt. 1935) (emphasis added).

[44] *E.g.*, Rex v. Bailey, 168 Eng. Rep. 651 (Crown Cases 1800) (affirming *B*'s conviction, but recommending that a pardon be issued, for violating a statute enacted while *B* was in a sailing ship along the coast of Africa and, therefore, without possible knowledge of the statute's existence).

[45] 355 U.S. 225 (1957).

The Supreme Court ruled that her conviction violated the Due Process Clause of the Constitution. The high court acknowledged that the common law rule that ignorance of the law is no excuse is "deep in our law." Nonetheless, it warned that the Constitution places limits on this doctrine. Specifically, "actual knowledge of the duty to register or proof of the probability of such knowledge" was a constitutional prerequisite to conviction for violation of the registration statute.

It is important to determine what features of the Los Angeles ordinance troubled the Supreme Court. Perhaps the Court's most significant observation was that L's situation was atypical because "we deal here with conduct that is wholly passive — mere failure to register. It is unlike the commission of acts, or the failure to act under circumstances that should alert the doer to the consequences of his deed."

Looking at that observation, three aspects of the ordinance may have concerned the justices: (1) it punished an omission (failure to register); (2) the duty to act was imposed on the basis of a status (presence in Los Angeles), rather than on the basis of an activity; and (3) the offense was *malum prohibitum*. The key to *Lambert*, however, is not these three factors, *as such*, but that, especially when these factors are present, there may be nothing to alert a law-abiding person to the need to inquire into the law. As one judge has put it, "[i]t is wrong to convict a person of a crime if [s]he had no reason to believe that the act for which [s]he was convicted *was* a crime, or even that it was wrongful."[46] Such statutes are particularly susceptible to arbitrary enforcement, to "law by cop, not law by law."[47]

Few statutes are apt to fall within the *Lambert* exception, but some do. For example, a District of Columbia statute makes it a felony for a person to be present in a motor vehicle if she knows that the vehicle contains a firearm, even if she has no connection to, or control of, the weapon, and even if she is not involved in any wrongdoing. As a practical matter, this statute creates a duty of a passenger to leave a motor vehicle if she becomes aware of the firearm's presence. Antwaun Coney was prosecuted under this statute in 2010. Here, arguably all three *Lambert* factors are present: it punishes an omission (failure to exit the vehicle); the duty to act is imposed on the basis of a statute (presence in a motor vehicle containing a firearm); and the offense is *malum prohibitum*. Conley's conviction was overturned on the basis of the principles of *Lambert*.[48]

Similarly, a growing list of jurisdictions have held that a person, charged with the offense of failing to register, or re-register due to a change of address, as a convicted sex offender, is entitled to a jury instruction requiring the prosecutor to prove, in the language of *Lambert*, "actual knowledge of the duty to register or . . . probability of such knowledge" on the defendant's part.[49]

---

[46] United States v. Wilson, 159 F.3d 280, 293 (7th Cir. 1998) (Posner, J., dissenting).

[47] Low & Wood, Note 42, *supra*, at 1605.

[48] Conley v. United States, 79 A.3d 270 (D.C. 2013).

[49] Bartlett v. Alameida, 366 F.3d 1020 (9th Cir. 2004); State v. Giorgetti, 868 So. 2d 512 (Fla. 2004); and Garrison v. State, 950 So. 2d 990 (Miss. 2006).

[D] Ignorance or Mistake That Negates *Mens Rea*

[1] General Approach

As noted in § 13.01[A], neither knowledge nor recklessness or negligence as to whether conduct constitutes an offense, or as to the meaning of an offense, is ordinarily an element of that offense. Therefore, a mistake of law, whether reasonable or unreasonable, will not usually negate any *mens rea* element found in the definition of a crime.

On very rare occasion, knowledge that the prohibited conduct constitutes an offense *is* itself an express element of the crime.[50] Somewhat more often, however, a defendant's lack of knowledge of, or misunderstanding regarding the meaning or application of, *another* law — typically, a non-penal law — will negate the *mens rea* element in the definition of the criminal offense.[51]

Consider these three cases. *D1* takes her automobile to *X*, a mechanic, for repair. Upon receiving what she believes to be an excessive bill, she refuses to pay, whereupon *X* refuses to deliver the car. That night *D1* returns to *X*'s lot, finds her car, and drives it away. She is prosecuted for larceny.[52] Here, *D1* is unaware of the fact that a non-penal state lien law provides that a mechanic may retain possession of a repaired automobile until the bill is paid.

D2 is charged with rape after he has nonconsensual sexual intercourse with *V.* At the time of his actions, *D2* believed that *V* legally was his wife, thus taking his conduct outside the proscription of common law rape, which prohibits nonconsensual intercourse with a female "not his wife." In fact, the marriage ceremony in which he and *V* participated was legally invalid, so *V* was not legally his wife.

D3 is prosecuted for bigamy. She responds that she believed that she had obtained a legally valid divorce before remarrying.

What do these cases have in common? Each defendant presumably was aware of, and understood the meaning of, the criminal statute (larceny, rape, or bigamy) that was the basis of her or his prosecution. At the same time, however, each defendant was unaware of, or misunderstood the import of, another law (mechanics' lien law, marriage law, or divorce law), under circumstances in which this mistake of law arguably is relevant to the defendant's criminal liability. For shorthand purposes, a mistake-of-law claim of the sort described here may be termed a *different-law mistake*, because the claimed mistake relates to a law other than the offense for which the defendant has been charged.

---

[50] For example, the Michigan Campaign Finance Act makes it illegal for any person to make or accept a campaign cash contribution in excess of $20. The statute further provides that "[a] person who knowingly violates this section is guilty of a misdemeanor." Mich. Comp. Laws § 169.241. It is a defense under this statute, therefore, that the defendant, a campaign contributor, did not know it was against the law for her to make a cash contribution in excess of $20. People v. Weiss, 479 N.W.2d 30 (Mich. Ct. App. 1991).

[51] People v. Hagen, 967 P.2d 563, 568 n.4 (Cal. 1998).

[52] *See* State v. Cude, 383 P.2d 399 (Utah 1963).

When a defendant seeks to avoid conviction for a criminal offense by asserting a different-law mistake, on the ground that the different-law mistake negates her *mens rea*, the first matter for determination is whether the offense charged is one of specific-intent (as in *D1*'s case), general-intent (*D2*), or strict-liability (*D3*).

[2]   Specific-Intent Offenses

A different-law mistake, whether reasonable or unreasonable, is a defense in the prosecution of a specific-intent offense, if the mistake negates the specific intent in the prosecuted offense.[53] This doctrine parallels the rule relating to mistakes-of-*fact* in the prosecution of specific-intent crimes.[54]

For example, in *D1*'s larceny prosecution described in the preceding subsection, the prosecutor must prove that *D1* had the specific intent "to steal the property of another." For purposes of larceny law, the automobile belonged to the mechanic,[55] so *D1* committed the *actus reus* of larceny when she drove away in "*X*'s" car. However, because *D1* was unaware of the lien law, she erroneously believed that she had a right to possession of the vehicle without paying the bill. Therefore, this different-law mistake negated *D1*'s "intent to steal the *property of another.*" As she understood the law, she was simply taking lawful possession of what rightfully was hers. *D1*, therefore, is not guilty of the offense, even if her mistake of law was unreasonable.

Cheek v. United States[56] provides another example of this rule. In *Cheek*, *C*, an anti-tax activist, failed to file federal income tax returns for six years, although he received wages each year as an airline pilot. As a result, *C* was charged with six counts of "willfully" failing to file federal income tax returns. For purposes of this tax statute, "willfully" means "a voluntary and intentional violation of a known legal duty."

C testified in his own defense at trial. He admitted that he had not filed personal income tax returns during the years in question, but he explained that during this period he attended seminars sponsored by an anti-tax organization that provided advice on tax matters. *C* introduced evidence that an attorney from that group indicated, among other things, that wages did not constitute "income" under the Internal Revenue Code. Therefore, *C* testified, he believed that he was not required to report his wages to the Internal Revenue Service. As a consequence, *C* requested the judge to instruct the jury that he was not guilty of the offense if he believed, even unreasonably, that he was not legally required to report his wages.

The trial court did not instruct the jury as *C* requested, but the Supreme Court held that it should have done so: If the jury believed *C*'s outlandish testimony, his mistake regarding the meaning of the term "income" under the Revenue Code

---

[53] *Id.*; State v. Varszegi, 635 A.2d 816 (Conn. App. Ct. 1993).

[54] *See* § 12.03[C], *supra.*

[55] Ownership of property is not determinative in larceny law. The offense is intended to protect the person in lawful *possession* of personal property. *See* Chapter 32, *infra.* In this case, the mechanic was in lawful possession of the car.

[56] 498 U.S. 192 (1991); *accord* United States v. Montgomery, 747 F.3d 303 (5th Cir. 2014).

disproved that he "intentionally violated a *known* legal duty."

[3]   General-Intent Offenses

Although there is very little case law on point, a different-law mistake, whether reasonable or unreasonable, apparently is not a defense to a general-intent crime.[57] Thus, in the rape hypothetical described in subsection [1], *D2* may be convicted of *V*'s rape because the *D2-V* marriage was legally invalid. Even if *D2*'s mistake regarding the legality of the marriage was reasonable — and, thus, *D2* did not intend to have intercourse with a "female not his wife" — the common law probably does not exculpate *D2*.

This result does not conform with the comparable mistake-of-*fact* rule.[58] Presumably, the difference in result is a function of the strong policy-based presumption against recognizing a mistake-of-law "loophole." However, the outcome is inconsistent with the general principle that people should not be punished in the absence of culpability, since one who acts on the basis of a reasonable mistake of law lacks moral blameworthiness.

[4]   Strict-Liability Offenses

A different-law mistake, whether reasonable or unreasonable, is not a defense to a strict-liability offense. This result is sensible: If liability is strict, there is no *mens rea* to negate. Thus, in the bigamy case noted in subsection [1], *D3* will be convicted of bigamy even though she believed, perhaps reasonably, that she had obtained a proper divorce before she remarried.[59]

§ 13.03   MODEL PENAL CODE

[A]   General Rule

Unless the definition of a crime so provides, "[n]either knowledge nor recklessness or negligence as to whether conduct constitutes a crime or as to the existence, meaning or application of the law determining the elements of an offense is an element of such offense."[60] Under limited circumstances, a mistake-of-law defense is recognized.

---

[57] *E.g.*, People v. Snyder, 652 P.2d 42 (Cal. 1982) (*S* was prosecuted for the general-intent offense of "possession of a concealable firearm by a convicted felon"; *S* was denied the opportunity to prove at trial that she believed that her prior conviction for marijuana possession was a misdemeanor; held: the trial court's ruling was correct; *S*'s mistake, *i.e.*, the status of marijuana possession as a felony, was irrelevant to her guilt for the firearm-possession charge).

[58] *See* § 12.03[D][1], *supra.*

[59] *See* State v. Woods, 179 A. 1 (Vt. 1935) (despite *W*'s reasonable belief in the lawfulness of a prior divorce, she may be convicted of violation of a statute prohibiting a person to be "found in bed" with another person's spouse).

[60] Model Penal Code § 2.02(9).

[B]   Exceptions to the General Rule

[1]   Reasonable-Reliance Doctrine

A person's belief that her conduct is lawful constitutes a defense if: (1) she relies on an official,[61] but erroneous, statement of the law; (2) the statement of law is found in a statute, judicial decision, administrative order or grant of permission, or an official interpretation by a public official or body responsible for the interpretation, administration, or enforcement of the law; and (3) the reliance is otherwise reasonable.[62] A person is excused in these circumstances because, according to the Commentary, she has acted in law-abiding fashion, the danger of fraud is slight, and her claim is not unduly difficult to prove or disprove.[63]

Because of the danger of collusion, the Model Code, like the common law, does not recognize an excuse for reliance on the advice of a private attorney. The Commentary concedes, however, that cases can "be imagined in which a client is unfairly taxed with his lawyer's bad advice."[64]

[2]   Fair Notice

The Model Penal Code provides that a defendant is not guilty of an offense if she does not believe that her conduct is illegal, and the statute defining the offense: (1) is not known to her; and (2) was "not published or otherwise reasonably made available" to her before she violated the law.[65]

The Model Code antedates *Lambert v. California.*[66] The Code defense applies only if the statute was neither published nor otherwise made reasonably available to the actor before she committed the crime. *Lambert* would apply to a situation in which the statute or ordinance *was* published and available to be read by a citizen, but in which the prohibited conduct itself would not alert an actor to the need to investigate whether there is a relevant published statute.

[3]   Ignorance or Mistake That Negates *Mens Rea*

The Model Penal Code requires proof of some culpable state of mind regarding every material element of an offense.[67] Furthermore, Section 2.04(1) provides that a mistake of law *is* a defense if it negates a material element of the offense (or if the law expressly provides for a mistake-of-law defense).

---

[61] Notice: The Model Penal Code expressly provides that the person may only rely on an *official* interpretation of the law. Non-Code jurisdictions do not always add this word. *E.g.*, United States v. W. Indies Transp. Inc., 127 F.3d 299, 313 (3d Cir. 1997) (only stating that the government official "told" the defendant that her conduct was legal). Because of this potential difference, some scholars argue that the Model Penal Code provision is unconstitutionally narrow. Chin, et al., Note 24, *supra*.

[62] Model Penal Code § 2.04(3)(b).

[63] American Law Institute, Comment to § 2.04, at 275.

[64] *Id.* at 280.

[65] Model Penal Code § 2.04(3)(a).

[66] 355 U.S. 225 (1957). *See* § 13.02[C], *supra*.

[67] Model Penal Code § 2.02(1).

As noted in subsection [A], however, Section 2.02(9) of the Code states that, unless the definition of an offense so provides, "neither knowledge nor recklessness or negligence as to whether conduct constitutes a crime, or as to the existence, meaning, or application of the law determining the elements of an offense, is an element of such offense." So, ordinarily, any mistake-of-law claim in this area will relate to a *different*-law mistake.[68]

A claim that a different-law mistake negates the *mens rea* of the offense is handled in the same manner as a claim of mistake-of-*fact* under the Code.[69] For example, in *State v. Wickliff*, W was a bail collection agent attempting to apprehend a fugitive who had "jumped bail." In the process, W came to a residence in which he believed the fugitive lived. Although the resident said the fugitive was not present, W asserted a legal right to enter to look, which he did. He was prosecuted for criminal trespass, which statute provided that "if, *knowing that he is not licensed or privileged to do so*, he enters . . . any structure." In view of the fact W believed he had a legal right to enter that residence to perform his duties, the court held that he was entitled to a mistake-of-law jury instruction on these facts.[70]

---

[68] For the meaning of "different-law mistakes," see § 13.02[D][1], *supra.*

[69] *See* § 12.04, *supra.*

[70] State v. Wickliff, 875 A.2d 1009 (N.J. Super. Ct. App. Div. 2005).

Chapter 14

CAUSATION

§ 14.01 GENERAL PRINCIPLES[1]

[A] "Causation": An Element of Criminal Responsibility

D points a gun at *V*, intending to kill *V*. A few seconds before *D* pulls the trigger, *X*, independently[2] of *D*, shoots and instantly kills *V*. The bullet in *D*'s gun strikes the already dead *V*. Is *D* guilty of murder?

The answer, of course, is "no." A crime (here, murder) is composed of an *actus reus* and, almost always, a *mens rea*. As described elsewhere,[3] the "*actus reus*" of an offense consists of a voluntary act (or an omission, when there is a duty to act) that results in the social harm prohibited by the offense. The "*mens rea*" is the culpable state of mind.

In the hypothetical, *D*'s conduct included a voluntary act — pulling the trigger of the gun. The social harm of murder — the killing of a human being by another human being — occurred. Moreover, *D* intended to kill *V*, a sufficient *mens rea* for murder. It would appear, then, that everything is in place for *D*'s murder conviction. Common sense, however, tells us that *D* is only guilty of attempted murder, rather than murder.

Common sense is confirmed by another prerequisite to criminal responsibility: causation. Analytically, "causation" is an ingredient of a crime's *actus reus*.[4] A careful look at the definition of "*actus reus*," provided above, indicates that there must be a link between the voluntary act (or omission) and social harm. That link is "causation"; the defendant's voluntary act (or omission) must "result in" — cause — the social harm. And, as explained in this chapter, "causation" consists of *two* constituent parts, "actual cause" (or "cause in fact"), and "proximate cause" (or

---

[1] *See generally* Jerome Hall, General Principles of Criminal Law 247–95 (2d ed. 1960); H.L.A. Hart & Tony Honoré, Causation in the Law (2d ed. 1985); Sanford H. Kadish, *The Criminal Law and the Luck of the Draw*, 84 J. Crim. L. & Criminology 679 (1994); Michael S. Moore, *Causation*, *in* 1 Encyclopedia of Crime & Justice 150 (Joshua Dressler ed., 2d ed. 2002); Paul K. Ryu, *Causation in Criminal Law*, 106 U. Pa. L. Rev. 773 (1958); Stephen J. Schulhofer, *Harm and Punishment: A Critique of Emphasis on the Results of Conduct in the Criminal Law*, 122 U. Pa. L. Rev. 1497 (1974).

[2] Throughout this chapter the word "independently" is used to describe a person who is not acting in concert with (*i.e.*, is not an accomplice or co-conspirator of) another actor.

[3] *See* § 9.01[A], *supra*.

[4] Albin Eser, *The Principle of "Harm" in the Concept of Crime: A Comparative Analysis of the Criminally Protected Legal Interests*, 4 Duq. L. Rev. 345, 386 (1965).

"legal cause").[5]

"Causation" is an implicit component of all crimes.[6] It must be proved by the prosecution, as with all other elements of an offense, beyond a reasonable doubt.[7] As a practical matter, however, "causation" only turns up as an issue in the prosecution of "result" crimes, *i.e.*, when the social harm of an offense is an unwanted result (*e.g.*, the death of another human being).[8] Indeed, causation problems seldom arise outside the context of homicide prosecutions.

Returning to the initial hypothetical, D will not be guilty of murder for the simple reason that X — not D — caused V's death. D is not legally responsible for a result that he did not cause. He may be held responsible, however, for the harm he *did* cause, for example, the social harm that results from the commission of an attempted murder.

[B] "Causation": Its Role in Criminal Law Theory

Causation analysis is so common a part of everyday thought processes that it is easy to ignore or downplay its importance in the criminal law. In fact, however, "causation" is a concept deeply imbedded "in human thought and expressed even among the most [ancient] people in their effort to understand 'the way of things.' "[9]

The role of causality in the criminal law is the same as it is in the evaluation of any everyday event: to determine why something occurred. More specifically, principles of causation assist us in deciding who or what among the various people and forces existing in the world should be held responsible for resulting harm.

The value of "causation" in determining criminal responsibility is virtually irrefutable. Imagine a law that provided that any person in physical proximity to an accident could be punished for the resulting harm, even if he had nothing to do with causing the injury. Such a draconian rule would have immense negative social consequences. People would rationally fear that the lightning bolt of the law might strike them at any time; therefore, they would be deterred from socially desirable, and not simply unduly dangerous, activities.

This utilitarian argument, however, does not adequately explain the moral importance of the causation requirement in the criminal law. It does not explain why, in the hypothetical at the beginning of this chapter, D should not be held responsible for V's death, even though X intervened a split second earlier and killed

---

[5] Burrage v. United States, 134 S. Ct. 881, 887 (2014).

[6] Moore, Note 1, *supra*, at 151.

[7] People v. Tims, 534 N.W.2d 675, 680 (Mich. 1995).

[8] Where is the causation requirement with a "conduct" crime? For example, if D is charged with attempted murder of V in the hypothetical shooting episode, isn't D guilty of an attempt precisely because he did *not* cause the social harm of the offense? Yes, if "social harm" is defined exclusively in terms of tangible injury. However, as discussed in § 9.10, *supra*, "social harm" may be defined more broadly to include the *endangerment* of any socially valuable interest. As discussed in Chapter 27, the social harm of attempted murder might be described as conduct by an actor that brings him in "dangerous proximity" to taking another's life.

[9] Hall, Note 1, *supra*, at 248.

V. After all, *D* is *not* an innocent party selected at random for punishment. Presumably, he is as dangerous as *X*; certainly he is no less dangerous than he would have been but for the fortuity of *X*'s involvement in the events. Yet, *D* will only be convicted of attempted murder, a lesser offense than murder. The reason for this is *D*'s lack of causal connection to the death.

The role of causation in the criminal law finds its primary moral justification in retributive concepts of just deserts. Unlike tort law, in which morally innocent parties are frequently held vicariously responsible for the wrongful acts of others, the criminal law is wedded to the concept of personal responsibility for crimes. This notion is rooted in the "inarticulate, subconscious sense of justice of the man on the street."[10]

The principle of causation is the instrument society employs to ensure that criminal responsibility is personal. It is the basis that links the actor to the social harm. Moreover, "causation" serves as the mechanism for determining how much the wrongdoer owes society and ought to repay it, *i.e.*, causation principles help quantify his just deserts. According to one school of retributive thought, a wrongdoer's punishment should not exceed the harm that he has caused.[11]

[C]　"Causation": Criminal Law Versus Tort Law

Causation is a litigated issue in both tort and criminal law. However, causal problems are fewer and often less factually complex in criminal cases. Consequently, much that we think we know about causation in the criminal law springs from tort law and from scholarly literature focused on that area. Nonetheless, "[a]s a matter of historical fact, the rules of causation in criminal cases are *not* tied to the rules of causation in civil cases."[12] This is particularly the case when one considers issues of "proximate" or "legal" causation.[13]

There is justification for treating criminal law conceptions of causation separately from tort law. Tort law seeks to identify the most suitable party on whom to place financial responsibility for negligently or innocently caused harm. In contrast, the criminal law seeks to determine whether and to what extent a wrongdoer, typically an intentional one, ought to be condemned by the community and have his liberty restricted.

Because of the higher stakes in the criminal law, and its especially strong commitment to personal, rather than vicarious, responsibility, some courts expressly provide that a tort conception of causation — in particular, *proximate* causation — is insufficient to impose criminal responsibility.[14] Instead, a stricter

---

[10] Francis Bowes Sayre, *Criminal Responsibility for the Acts of Another*, 43 Harv. L. Rev. 689, 717 (1930).

[11] This principle may explain why, for example, an attempted murder is punished less severely than a murder at common law. *See* § 27.04[B], *infra*.

[12] People v. Tims, 534 N.W.2d 675, 684 (Mich. 1995) (emphasis added).

[13] *See* § 14.03, *infra*.

[14] *E.g.*, State v. Bauer, 329 P.3d 67, 71 (Wash. 2014) ("Most states that have addressed the question agree that [proximate] causation is defined more narrowly in criminal law than it is in tort law.");

test, requiring a closer connection between the defendant's conduct and the resulting harm, is applied.

§ 14.02 ACTUAL CAUSE (OR "FACTUAL CAUSE")

[A] "But-For" ("*Sine Qua Non*") Test

Causation analysis is divisible into two parts: "actual cause" (also called "factual cause" or "cause-in-fact") and "proximate cause" (or "legal cause"). The first causal issue that might be determined is that of "actual cause." That is, there can be no criminal liability for resulting social harm "unless it can be shown that the defendant's conduct was a cause-in-fact of the prohibited result."[15] In order to make this determination, courts traditionally apply the "but-for" or "*sine qua non*" test, *i.e.*, " 'that the harm would not have occurred' in the absence of — that is, but for — the defendant's conduct."[16] This test may also be stated as follows: "*But for D's voluntary act(s),*[17] *would the social harm have occurred when it did?*" If the answer to this question is "no" — if the social harm would *not* have occurred when it did in the absence of *D*'s voluntary conduct — *D* is an actual cause of the result.

The but-for test serves a limited, but essential, purpose. It functions to exclude certain forces, potentially including human ones, from potential causal responsibility for ensuing harm. That is, subject to one possible controversial and very limited exception,[18] *D* cannot be held criminally responsible for social harm unless the prosecution proves beyond a reasonable doubt that *D* is a (not necessarily "the"[19]) but-for cause of the harm.

The fact that *D*'s conduct is determined to be an actual cause of a result does not mean that he will be held criminally responsible for the harm. To be guilty, *D* must have also acted with the requisite *mens rea*,[20] and he must also be the *proximate* cause of the social harm, the latter issue of which is considered in § 14.03.

Commonwealth v. Root, 170 A.2d 310, 314 (Pa. 1961) (stating that the "tort liability concept of proximate cause has no proper place in prosecutions for criminal homicide and more direct casual connection is required for conviction").

[15] Velazquez v. State, 561 So. 2d 347, 350 (Fla. Dist. Ct. App. 1990).

[16] University of Tex. Southwestern Medical Center v. Nassar, 133 S. Ct. 2517, 2525 (2013) (quoting Restatement of Torts § 431).

[17] In the prosecution of a culpable omission, this test would be rephrased to begin "but for *D*'s *omission.*"

[18] *See* § 14.02[C][2][b], *infra.*

[19] To prove that a person is an actual cause of harm, it is not necessary to show that he was the exclusive cause-in-fact of the resulting harm. Rogers v. State, 232 P.3d 1226, 1233 (Alaska Ct. App. 2010).

[20] *Id.* at 1235 ("[S]tanding alone, the fact that the law views the defendant's conduct as having caused the result specified in a criminal statute does not mean that the defendant can be convicted of violating that criminal statute. The government must prove that the defendant acted with the culpable mental state(s) required by the statute.").

[B]   "Causes" Versus "Conditions"

D pulls the trigger of a gun, and a bullet is propelled from the gun into *V*'s chest, causing *V*'s death. Common sense tells us that *D* was the cause of the death: But for *D*'s voluntary act of pulling the trigger of the gun, *V* would not died when he did.

In fact, however, there are additional "actual causes" of *V*'s death. For example, *V* would not have died but for the fact that his heart muscle was too weak to withstand the intrusion of the bullet. Other causes of the death are found in certain principles of physics that explain how and why the pulling of the trigger results in a bullet moving at a fast rate of speed. The law will either ignore these latter "causes" or identify them more realistically as necessary "conditions" for the harm to occur. Although conditions may technically meet the *sine qua non* test of causation, their exclusion from the latter category is consistent with a common sense view of the issue.[21]

In determining causation, people focus on what is interesting in an event. They focus on the abnormal, the matters that seem out of the ordinary.[22] "Conditions" are normal events or circumstances that, although necessary for the result to occur, do not positively contribute to it. *D*'s firing of the gun is the act that is interesting and out of the ordinary. It is *D*'s conduct, therefore, and not the basic laws of physics or the structure of *V*'s heart that affirmatively contributed to the death.

[C]   Special "Actual Cause" Problems

[1]   Confusing "Causation" with "*Mens Rea*"

The common law treats "actual causation" and "*mens rea*" as independent concepts, each of which must be proven in a criminal prosecution. Frequently, however, this point is forgotten, resulting in improper analysis.

[a]   Causation Without *Mens Rea*

D has a minor argument with her husband, *V. V*, upset about the argument, decides to leave the house. He walks across the street. As he does, he is struck and killed by an automobile driven by *X*. Is *D* an actual cause of *V*'s death? Based on

---

[21] Supreme Court Justice Scalia provides a nice example of the point made in the text:

> Consider a baseball game in which the visiting team's leadoff batter hits a home run in the top of the first inning. If the visiting team goes on to win by a score of 1 to 0, every person competent in the English language and familiar with the American pastime would agree that the victory resulted from the home run. That is so because it is natural to say that one event is the outcome or consequence of another when the former would not have occurred but for the latter. It is beside the point that the victory also resulted from a host of *other* necessary causes, such as skillful pitching, the coach's [sic] decision to put the leadoff batter in the lineup, and the league's decision to schedule the game.

Burrage v. United States, 134 S. Ct. 881, 888 (2014).

[22] Hall, Note 1, *supra*, at 249–50; Hart & Honoré, Note 1, *supra*, at 32–37.

the facts just described, the answer is "yes": But for D having the argument with V, V would not have crossed the street at that moment and, therefore, would not have been struck and killed by X.

It does not necessarily follow, however, that D may be convicted of a crime pertaining to V's death. First, D was not the sole cause of the harm. X's conduct was another cause. So, too, was V's decision to leave the house and cross the street. "Actual cause," it will be remembered, serves only to *eliminate* candidates for responsibility; it does not resolve the matter of ultimate causal responsibility, which awaits proximate causation analysis. Second, and more immediately to the point, the facts do not suggest that D possessed a culpable state of mind — any *mens rea* — regarding V's death. Thus, this is a case of but-for causation without a *mens rea*.

[b]   *Mens Rea* Without Causation

Just as a person may be an actual cause of resulting harm without having a *mens rea*, it is also possible to possess a culpable state of mind without being the actual cause of the harm. For example, suppose that $D1$, intending to kill V, shoots at V, missing him. Simultaneously, $D2$, independently and accidentally, shoots V in the heart. V dies instantly. Here, $D1$ intended to kill V, but did not cause the death; thus, $D1$ is not legally responsible for V's death.[23] $D2$ is the only potential candidate for homicide prosecution, but he may also be acquitted for lack of *mens rea*!

[2]   Multiple Actual Causes

[a]   Accelerating a Result

$D1$ intentionally shoots V in the stomach. Assume that medical testimony would prove that V would have died from the wound in one hour. However, simultaneously and independently of $D1$, $D2$ intentionally shoots V in the stomach. Medical evidence would show that V would have died from the latter wound, by itself, in one hour. As a result of the two wounds, however, V dies in five minutes.

Who is the cause of V's death? At first glance it may appear that application of the but-for test will result in the conclusion that *neither D1 nor D2* was an actual cause of the death. In fact, however, *both* actors may properly be described as actual causes of V's death.

A careful application of the but-for test supports this conclusion. It must be remembered that this test asks whether, but for the voluntary act of the defendant, the harm would have occurred *when it did*. The italicized words are essential to the correct application of the test. After all, ultimately everyone dies. No act can do more than accelerate that process.[24]

---

[23] Of course, he may be convicted of attempted murder.

[24] People v. Phillips, 414 P.2d 353, 358 (Cal. 1966) ("Murder is never more than the shortening of life; if a defendant's culpable act has . . . decreased the span of a human life, the law will not hear him say that his victim would thereafter have died in any event."), *overruled on other grounds*, People v. Flood, 957 P.2d 869 (Cal. 1998).

With this point in mind it is evident that *D1* accelerated *V*'s death. Ask the *sine qua non* question: "But for *D1*'s voluntary act [firing the gun], would *V* have died *when he did* [in five minutes]?" The answer is that he would *not* have died *when he did* — he would have died in one hour as the result of the wound inflicted by *D2*. Because *D1*'s actions accelerated the death process, *D1* is *an* (not "the") actual cause of the death. One need only substitute *D2* for *D1* in this analysis to reach the same causal conclusion regarding *D2*.

Or, consider the facts in *Oxendine v. State*.[25] *V* was the tragic victim of two separate acts of child abuse: First, he sustained *mortal* injuries from a beating inflicted by *X*; one day later, *D*, *V*'s father, inflicted additional injuries. *V* died later that day. *X* and *D* were prosecuted for *V*'s death. The government introduced evidence regarding the cause of death: One physician testified that he could not determine whether *V* died as the result of the acts of one person (*X*) or of both; a second doctor stated that the injury inflicted by *X* was the underlying cause of the death and he could not state whether *D*'s subsequent actions accelerated the process.

Based on this evidence, the court ruled that *D* was entitled to a directed verdict of acquittal, because the prosecutor failed to prove beyond a reasonable doubt that *D* hastened *V*'s death. If the state had introduced evidence that the beating inflicted by *D* had shortened his child's life even by a short time, *D* could properly have been declared an actual cause of the death along with *X*.[26]

[b]   Concurrent Sufficient Causes

D1 shoots *V* in the heart; simultaneously and independently, *D2* shoots *V* in the head. *V* dies instantly. Medical evidence indicates that either attack alone would have killed *V* instantly.

In the real world such events rarely occur. If two people simultaneously shoot a victim, the shooters very likely were acting in concert, not independently of each other, in which case their joint conduct may be analyzed as if they were one party. Or, one of the actor's wound will accelerate the result caused by the other. Another possibility in a dual attack is that neither wound will be mortal, but in combination they result in the death. As the facts are described here, however, *D1* and *D2* are concurrent *sufficient* causes of *V*'s death. That is, each act alone was sufficient to cause the result that occurred *when it did*.

Our intuitions probably suggest that both actors should be convicted of murder. Yet, the but-for test *seems* to fail us here: But for *D1*'s act of shooting *V* in the heart, *V* would have died when he did (instantly) as the result of *D2*'s gunshot to *V*'s head. Because *D1* did *not* accelerate *V*'s death, *D1* is not (it seems) the cause of the death. Applying the same test to *D2*'s conduct, *D2* also is relieved of responsibility. If this analysis is correct, and if no other principle applies, *D1* and *D2* could be convicted of attempted murder, but of no more.

---

[25] 528 A.2d 870 (Del. 1987).

[26] Jefferson v. State, 276 S.W.3d 214, 220 (Ark. 2008) ("Our law is well settled that, where there are concurrent causes of death, conduct which hastens . . . a person's death is a cause of death.").

There are two ways to avoid this counter-intuitive result. First, some criminal law courts import from tort law its solution in comparable circumstances, which is to rephrase the causation test in this circumstance to ask whether the defendant was a "substantial factor" in causing the prohibited harm.[27] The difficulty with this solution is not only that the critical term — "substantial factor" — is sometimes left undefined, but also that it is hard to comprehend how a person's conduct can ever be a "substantial factor" in contributing to a result that was going to occur when it did *even without his contribution.*[28] The only way it may sensibly be said that a concurrent sufficient cause (*e.g., D1*) is a substantial factor in an outcome is to point out that the force *would have been* the cause of the harm if circumstances had been different (*i.e.,* if the *other* sufficient cause, *D2's* lethal act, had not materialized). However, this is not the way we ordinarily talk about causation. If it were, the would-be killer in the example that began this chapter — *D* shoots to kill *V*, but *X* kills *V* before *D's* bullet strikes *V* — would be guilty of murder, rather than of attempted murder, but that is not how the example is resolved (nor, sensibly, should it be).

A preferable method of resolving the causal quandary is to retain the but-for test in these circumstances, but to elaborate on the test. Two extra words are added, so that the test becomes: "But for *D's* voluntary act would the social harm have occurred when *and as* it did."[29] In essence, this technique refines the description of the result for which the defendants are prosecuted. Thus, in the present example, the result would not be described as "the death of *V*," but more precisely as "the death of *V by two simultaneous mortal wounds.*" Applying the but-for test to *this* "result," both *D1* and *D2* satisfy the causation standard, because the result — death from two mortal wounds — could not have occurred without the presence of both actors.

[3] Obstructed Cause

D1 shoots *V* in the stomach. Simultaneously and independently, *D2* shoots *V* three times in the head, killing him instantly.

Although it may appear that *D1* is causally linked to *V's* death, this depends on more facts. Let's assume a coroner testifies that the wound inflicted by *D1* did not contribute to *V's* death — that the three bullets to the head from *D2's* weapon would have killed *V* instantly even in the absence of the abdominal wound. Under such circumstances, *D1* is no more the cause of *V's* death than if, just a split-second before *D1* fired the gun, *V* had been struck by a bolt of lightning that killed him instantly. In the latter case we would not say that *D1* killed *V*; rather, we would say that he *attempted* to kill *V*, but that his efforts were obstructed by a separate force (the lightning), which actually caused the result. The same analysis applies to *D1*

---

[27] Anderson v. Minneapolis, St. Paul & Sault Marie Ry., 179 N.W. 45, 46 (Minn. 1920), *overruled on other grounds*, Borsheim v. Great N. Ry., 183 N.W. 519 (Minn. 1921); State v. Christman, 249 P.3d 680, 687 (Wash. Ct. App. 2011) (stating that "[t]he 'substantial factor' test is generally applied in multiple causation cases"; "[u]nder the substantial factor test, all parties whose actions contributed to the outcome are held liable").

[28] State v. Montoya, 61 P.3d 793, 799 (N.M. 2002) (quoting this text).

[29] *See id.* at 797.

and *D2* in this hypothetical: *D1* attempted to take *V*'s life; he was thwarted in this goal because *D2* was a more effective killer.

§ 14.03 PROXIMATE CAUSE (OR "LEGAL CAUSE")

[A] Putting "Proximate Cause" in Context

"Mankind might still be in Eden, but for Adam's biting an apple."[30] The present point of this remark is to remind us that the purpose of the but-for test of causation is to identify the *candidates* for responsibility for an event. From this pool, which may include other human actors and non-human forces stemming over an extended period of time,[31] the "proximate" or "legal" cause of the social harm must be selected.[32] Thus, we might ask: Is Adam's decision to eat the apple the proximate cause of a murder that occurs today, or should we hold someone or something else responsible? The answer is obvious: Adam may have been an actual cause of today's murder, but he is not the proximate cause. For that determination, we will look elsewhere — focusing on a less remote actual cause.[33]

The concept of "proximate causation" is obscure. In the process of determining proximate causation, courts and lawyers frequently bandy about conclusory terms like "superseding intervening cause," "direct cause," and "remote cause." An observer might assume from this language that a scientific formula exists to produce uniform and reliable results in proximate causation analysis. In fact, however, courts and juries don't *discover* the proximate cause of harm — they *select* it. The decision to attach causal responsibility for social harm to one, rather than to another, factor is made in a common sense manner, or by application of moral intuitions, public policy considerations, and/or a sense of justice.[34]

---

[30] Welch v. State, 235 So. 2d 906, 907 (Ala. Crim. App. 1970).

[31] *E.g.*, State v. Govan, 744 P.2d 712 (Ariz. Ct. App. 1987) (*G* shot *V*, paralyzing *V* from the neck down; *G* was charged with assault, but the charge was dropped when *V* married *G*; five years later, *V* contracted pneumonia and died; *G* was charged with her murder, based on the initial shooting, and convicted of manslaughter; held: a jury could properly find that *G*'s conduct five years earlier was the proximate cause of *V*'s death, despite subsequent events that also affected her health).

[32] Typically, there will be only one proximate cause of a result, but this is not always so. For example, in the case of concurrent sufficient causes, see § 14.02[C][2][b], *supra*, each cause-in-fact is also a proximate cause. Likewise, it is theoretically possible for two negligent wrongdoers, acting independently of each other, to be the proximate cause of resulting harm.

[33] Paroline v. United States, 134 S. Ct. 1710, 1719 (2014) (the concept of proximate cause "serves, *inter alia*, to preclude liability in situations where the causal link between conduct and result is so attenuated that the consequence is more aptly described as mere fortuity").

Mathematician Edward Lorenz once used a numerical computer model to conduct a weather prediction. However, when he repeated the process, this time inputting the number ".506" for the proper number (.506127), he got an entirely different weather scenario, causing him later to present a scientific paper entitled, "Does the Flap of a Butterfly's Wings in Brazil Set Off a Tornado in Texas?" His point is that even the slightest act has a ripple effect on later events. That Brazilian butterfly that flapped its wings might be an actual cause of the tornado in Texas, but are we prepared to say it is the *proximate* case? Obviously not.

[34] *See* Paroline v. United States, 134 S. Ct. at 1719 (stating that "[t]he idea of proximate cause . . . defies easy summary"; it is "a flexible concept"); People v. Schaefer, 703 N.W.2d 774, 774 (Mich. 2005) ("A

[B] Direct Cause

In many cases, no serious litigable issue of proximate causation arises. For example, suppose that D shoots V, and V dies instantly. Or, suppose that D shoots V, and V is taken to the hospital where he dies after proper medical care. In both cases, courts are apt to say that D was the "direct" cause of the result. That is, no event of causal significance intervened between D's conduct and the social harm for which he is being prosecuted. In the first case, the death occurred instantly; in the second hypothetical, nothing done by the medical personnel aggravated V's injuries or accelerated V's death.

The closest thing to a bright-line rule in the realm of proximate cause is this: *An act that is a direct cause of social harm is also a proximate cause of it.* This makes sense. A "direct cause" is a force already determined to be an "actual cause" of the undesired result. Inasmuch as no other causal factor has intervened, there is no more proximate party to whom to shift legal responsibility for the result.

[C] Intervening Causes

[1] Overview

An "intervening cause" is an independent force — another "but for" cause — that operates in producing social harm, but which only comes into play *after* the defendant's voluntary act has been committed or his omission has occurred.[35] Although not exhaustive of the circumstances in which intervening causes arise, many criminal cases fit the following pattern: (1) D negatively affects V in some manner; (2) a second causal force intervenes; and (3) the latter intervening cause aggravates V's injuries or accelerates the inevitable (*e.g.*, V's death). The intervention usually comes in the form of: wrongdoing by a third party; the victim's own contributory negligence[36] or suicidal act; or a natural force ("an act of God").[37]

The legal issue for consideration in such cases is the following: When is the intervening conduct — of a third party, the victim, or a natural force — sufficiently out-of-the-ordinary that "it no longer seems fair to say that the [social harm] was 'caused' by the defendant's conduct?"[38] Framing the issue more precisely: Under what circumstances should D, who acts with the requisite *mens rea*, and who commits a voluntary act that *is* a cause-in-fact of the social harm, be relieved of criminal responsibility because of an intervening but-for cause? When an interven-

---

proximate cause is simply a factual cause 'of which the law will take cognizance.' ") (quoting 1 Torcia, Wharton's Criminal Law (15th ed.), § 26, pp. 147–48).

[35] State v. Marti, 290 N.W.2d 570, 586 (Iowa 1980).

[36] In the criminal law, a victim's contributory negligence is *not* a defense to a criminal homicide charge, but may be a factor in determining whether the defendant's conduct was a proximate cause of the death. State v. Farner, 66 S.W.3d 188, 203 (Tenn. 2001). *See* Jefferson v. State, 276 S.W.3d 214, 220 (Ark. 2008) ("The doctrine of contributory negligence recognized in civil actions is inapplicable in a criminal case.").

[37] State v. Munoz, 659 A.2d 683, 692–93 (Conn. 1995).

[38] State v. Malone, 819 P.2d 34, 37 (Alaska Ct. App. 1991); *see also* United States v. Main, 113 F.3d 1046, 1049 (9th Cir. 1997).

ing cause *does* relieve the defendant of criminal responsibility, the law generally describes that intervening event as the "superseding cause" of the social harm.

One early 20th century scholar observed that all efforts to set down universal tests that explain the law of causation are "demonstrably erroneous."[39] There are no hard-and-fast rules for rendering the commonsense "community justice" determination of when an intervening cause supersedes the defendant's conduct. However, there are various factors that assist the factfinder in the evaluative process, discussed immediately below.

[2] Factor 1: *De Minimis* Contribution to the Social Harm

Sometimes, a defendant's causal responsibility for ensuing harm is exceptionally insubstantial in comparison to that of an intervening cause. For example, suppose that D strikes V. Although the injury is minor, it requires non-emergency medical attention, so V drives himself to the doctor. On the way, his car is struck by lightning. V dies instantly.

From a causal perspective, D was an actual cause of the ensuing death-by-lightning: But for D's wrongful actions, V would not have been in the car driving to the doctor, and thus would not have been at the spot where the lightning struck. Nonetheless, the law will very likely treat D's causal connection as *de minimis*, and relieve him of criminal liability for V's death.[40]

This outcome conforms with our common sense analysis of causal events. If a small pebble is followed immediately by a giant meteor striking Jupiter, our attention focuses on the meteor. Although the pebble may have contributed slightly to the ensuing damage, we treat the giant force as the "real" cause of the harm. The same principle applies in the criminal law: Some wrongdoers have too minor a causal role to justify criminal punishment.[41] The law will treat the substantial, intervening cause as the proximate cause of the social harm.

[3] Factor 2: Foreseeability of the Intervening Cause

[a]   In General

According to many courts, the "linchpin"[42] of proximate causation is whether the intervening party's acts were reasonably foreseeable. This is an overstatement, but it is certainly true that foreseeability is a matter of considerable significance in proximate-causation analysis.

---

[39] Jeremiah Smith, *Legal Cause in Actions of Tort*, 25 Harv. L. Rev. 303, 317 (1912); *see* People v. Rideout, 727 N.W.2d 630, 635 (Mich. Ct. App. 2006) (quoting this text), *affirmed in part and reversed in part on other grounds*, 728 N.W.2d 459 (Mich. 2007).

[40] Of course, D may be prosecuted for the original battery.

[41] *Jefferson v. State*, 276 S.W.3d at 220 (stating that to find proximate cause, a court "must find more than that a given result would not have happened but for the prior occurrence of fact 'A'; rather we must find that fact 'A' was a substantial . . . factor in bringing about the result in question."); State v. Montoya, 61 P.3d 793, 799 (N.M. 2002) (citing this text).

[42] State v. Dunn, 850 P.2d 1201, 1215 (Utah 1993).

Cases can be found in which it is said, simply, that the defendant cannot escape liability if the intervening act was reasonably foreseeable,[43] whereas an unforeseeable intervening cause is "superseding" in nature. Proper analysis, however, is more sophisticated than this. The criminal law tends to distinguish between "responsive" (or "dependent") and "coincidental" (or "independent") intervening causes,[44] as these concepts are clarified below.

[b] Responsive (Dependent) Intervening Causes

A responsive intervening cause is an act that occurs in reaction or response to the defendant's prior wrongful conduct. For example, suppose that *D1* operates his boat at an unsafe speed, causing it to capsize. *V1*, his drunken passenger, drowns foolishly attempting to swim to shore.[45] *V1*'s actions constitute a responsive intervening cause in his own death, *i.e.*, his life-saving efforts were a response to *D1*'s initial improper conduct. Or, suppose that *D2* seriously wounds *V2*. *V2* is taken to a hospital where he receives poor medical treatment by physician *X* and dies. In *D2*'s prosecution for the death, *X*'s negligent conduct constitutes a responsive intervening cause: *X*'s medical actions were in response to *D2*'s act of wounding *V2*.

Generally speaking, a responsive intervening cause does *not* relieve the initial wrongdoer of criminal responsibility, unless the response was abnormal and, if abnormal, also unforeseeable.[46] This outcome is justifiable. The defendant's initial wrongdoing caused the response. Since he is responsible for the presence of the intervening force, the defendant should not escape liability unless the intervening force was bizarre and unforeseeable.

Applying this analysis, case law generally provides that the accused bears criminal responsibility for the death of, or injury to, a person who seeks to extricate himself or another from the dangerous situation created by the defendant, even if the victim was contributorily negligent in his efforts.[47] Similarly, many cases provide that one who wrongfully injures another is responsible for the ensuing death, notwithstanding subsequent negligent medical treatment that contributes to the victim's death or accelerates it.[48] On the other hand, grossly

---

[43] *Id.* at 1216.

[44] In his treatise, Professor LaFave use the "responsive/coincidental" terms, Wayne R. LaFave, Criminal Law 364–65 (5th ed. 2010), whereas Professors Perkins and Boyce describe intervening causes as "dependent/independent." Rollin M. Perkins & Ronald N. Boyce, Criminal Law 791, 809 (3d ed. 1982).

[45] People v. Armitage, 194 Cal. App. 3d 405 (Ct. App. 1987).

[46] *E.g.*, Kibbe v. Henderson, 534 F.2d 493, 498 n.6 (2d Cir. 1976), *reversed on other grounds*, 431 U.S. 145 (1977); State v. Malone, 819 P.2d 34, 37 (Alaska Ct. App. 1991).

[47] People v. Armitage, 194 Cal. App. 3d 405 (Ct. App. 1987) (see the facts described in the text accompanying Note 45); State v. Leopold, 147 A. 118 (Conn. 1929) (one who knowingly sets fire to a building is responsible for the death or injury of another who enters the building to save his property); People v. Kern, 554 N.E.2d 1235 (N.Y. 1990) (*D*s chased *V* with a baseball bat, with the intention of beating or killing him; *V* attempted to escape by running onto a highway, where he was struck and killed by a third party; held: *D*s are responsible for *V*'s death); State v. Johnson, 615 A.2d 132 (Vt. 1992) (*J* attempted to kill *V*; *V*, fearing for his life, walked into a river to escape, and drowned; held: *J* is guilty of murder).

[48] *E.g.*, State v. Shabazz, 719 A.2d 440 (Conn. 1998); Fairman v. State, 513 So. 2d 910 (Miss. 1987); State v. Baker, 742 P.2d 633 (Or. Ct. App. 1987).

negligent or reckless medical care is sufficiently abnormal and unforeseeable to supersede the initial wrongdoer's causal responsibility.[49]

[c]   Coincidental (Independent) Intervening Causes

A coincidental intervening cause is a force that does not occur in response to the initial wrongdoer's conduct. The only relationship between the defendant's conduct and the intervening cause is that the defendant placed the victim in a situation where the intervening cause could independently act upon him. For example, suppose that *D1* robs *V1*, a passenger in *D1*'s car, and then abandons *V1* on a rural road. Sometime later, driver *X1* strikes and kills *V1*, who is standing in the middle of the road.[50] *X1*'s conduct is a coincidental intervening cause: *D1*'s actions did not cause *X1* to drive down that road on that particular occasion; *D1* simply put *V1* on the road where *X1*'s independent conduct could act upon *V1*.

Or, suppose that *D2* wounds *V2*. *V2* is taken to a hospital for medical treatment, where he is killed by *X2*, a "knife-wielding maniac" who is running through the hospital killing everyone in sight.[51] Again, *X2* is a coincidental intervening cause: *X2* was running through that hospital killing persons whether or not *V2* was there. This is a case in which *V2* was in the wrong place at the wrong time, put there by *D2*'s original wrongdoing.

The common law rule of thumb is that a coincidental intervening cause relieves the original wrongdoer of criminal responsibility unless the intervention *was* foreseeable. In the present examples, therefore, it would be necessary to determine whether *D1* and *D2*, as reasonable people, should have foreseen, respectively, that *V1* would be struck by another car, and that *V2* would be the victim of a criminal intermediary. In the first case, it may have been quite foreseeable that another car would drive down that road and strike *V1*. In the second hypothetical, *X2*'s criminal activities were probably abnormal enough to relieve *D2* of liability for the ensuing death, unless, for example, the events occurred in a high-security penal institution.[52]

[4]   Factor 3: The Defendant's *Mens Mea* (Intended Consequences Doctrine)

"The legal eye reaches further in the examination of intentional crimes than in those in which this element is wanting."[53] A voluntary act intended to "bring about what in fact happens, and in the manner in which it happens, has a special place in

---

[49] Regina v. Jordan, 40 Cr. App. R(S). 152 (1956).

[50] Kibbe v. Henderson, 534 F.2d 493 (2d Cir. 1976).

[51] This is an embellishment on hypothetical 6(c) in Sanford H. Kadish et al., Criminal Law and Its Processes 518 (8th ed. 2007).

[52] One other example: As the result of negligence, *D* strikes *V*'s car, leaving *V* pinned in his car, where he is later eaten by a bear. United States v. Main, 113 F.3d 1046, 1049 (9th Cir. 1997) (suggesting the hypothetical). The bear is a coincidental intervening cause. Barring unusual facts, *D* would not be causally responsible for the death.

[53] State v. Cummings, 265 S.E.2d 923, 927 (N.C. Ct. App. 1980) (emphasis omitted) (Clark, J., dissenting) (quoting Perkins, Criminal Law 693 (2d ed. 1969)).

causal inquiries."[54] That special place is this: *We often trace the cause of social harm backwards through other causes until we reach an intentional wrongdoer.* Or, as is sometimes said, although too strongly: "Intended consequences can never be too remote."[55]

For example, in a classic case,[56] *M*, intending the death of *V* (her child), furnished poison to *X*, a home nurse, falsely informing *X* that the substance was medicine to be administered to *V*. *X* did not believe that *V* needed the "medicine," so she did not administer it. Instead, she placed the substance on a mantel where, some time later, *C* (a young child) discovered it and gave it to *V*, killing *V*. *M* was prosecuted for murder.

Notice: *M* intended *V*'s death by poisoning. Her voluntary act of providing the poison to *X* was a but-for cause of *V*'s death. On the other hand, at least two other causes intervened: *X*'s negligent act of placing the "medicine" where it could be reached by *C*; and *C*'s innocent act of administering it to *V*. Despite these intervening acts, *M* was declared to be the proximate cause of *V*'s death.

This outcome is hardly surprising. *M* wanted her child dead by poisoning, which is *exactly* what she got.[57] As a matter of moral intuitions, the intervening actions — *X*'s possible negligence and *C*'s innocent conduct — should not override *M*'s intentional wrongdoing. It is as if the jurors were to say: "You got *exactly* what you wanted. What right do you have to complain if we hold you responsible for the intended consequence?"[58]

[5] Factor 4: Dangerous Forces That Come to Rest (Apparent Safety Doctrine)

One scholar has observed that when a "defendant's active force has come to rest in a position of apparent safety, the court will follow it no longer."[59] For example, consider a somewhat simplified version of the facts in *State v. Preslar*:[60] *P* threatened the life of *V*, his spouse. As a consequence, *V* was forced to leave the house on a freezing night in order to protect herself. *V* reached within 200 yards of her father's home, where she would have been welcome, but she chose to spend the night in the extreme cold, rather than bother him by entering the house. *V* froze to death during the night. Clearly, *P* was an actual cause of *V*'s death: But for his threatening conduct, *V* would not have gone out into the cold. But, *V*'s decision to sleep outside was also a but-for cause of her own death. Is *P* the proximate cause

---

[54] Hart & Honoré, Note 1, *supra*, at 42.

[55] *Id.* at 170 (emphasis omitted); *see* Henry T. Terry, *Proximate Consequences in the Law of Torts*, 28 Harv L. Rev. 10, 17 (1914).

[56] Regina v. Michael, 169 Eng. Rep. 48 (1840).

[57] The intended consequences doctrine is most often applied when the result *and the means of its commission* were intended by the defendant.

[58] *See also* State v. Ruane, 912 S.W.2d 766 (Tenn. Crim. App. 1995) (*R* intentionally shot *V* in the neck, intending to kill *V*; *V*'s spinal column was severed, requiring permanent life support; subsequently, *V* requested to be removed from the life support; *V* died minutes later; held: *R* is guilty of murder).

[59] Joseph H. Beale, *The Proximate Consequences of an Act*, 33 Harv. L. Rev. 633, 651 (1920).

[60] 48 N.C. 421 (1856).

of *V*'s death? The court in *Preslar* answered this question in the negative.

The result may be explained in terms of the apparent safety doctrine. *P* did not follow *V* from their home. When *V* reached the vicinity of her father's house, she knew that she could enter and be free from immediate harm. Therefore, her decision to sleep outside constituted a superseding intervening cause.[61]

[6] Factor 5: Free, Deliberate, Informed Human Intervention

A defendant is far more apt to be relieved of criminal responsibility in the case of a "free, deliberate, and informed"[62] — that is, a voluntary, knowing, and intelligent — intervening human agent than in the case of the intervention of a natural force or the actions of a person whose conduct is not fully free. The result in the *Preslar* case,[63] described in the last subsection, can also be explained in terms of this factor. *V* chose to sleep in the cold rather than to enter her father's home. Her decision arguably was free, deliberate, and with full knowledge of the fact that it was exceedingly cold outside. Under these circumstances, the responsibility for her death is shifted from *P* to *V.* This outcome is consistent with the retributive principle that accords special significance to the free-will actions of human agents.

The same analysis applies if, for example, *D* and *V* recklessly participate in drag race, at the end of which race *V* voluntarily turns his car around and speeds through a guardrail, killing himself or another. Regardless of *D*'s initial responsibility for the race, *V*'s decision to continue the race after it was over relieves *D* of responsibility for the ensuing harm.[64]

Of course, the critical issue in applying the present factor is whether the human intervention *was* "free, deliberate, and informed." Sometimes, it is not. For example, if *V* escapes *B*, a home-intruder, by jumping out of a second-story window of his house, his actions would not be considered voluntary. Therefore *B* would be liable for *V*'s injuries or death from the jump.[65] Likewise, if *S* kidnaps and rapes *V*, after which highly despondent *V* commits suicide, *S* could be held responsible for her death.[66] Or, if *R* shoots *V*, requiring *V* to survive on a ventilator, *V*'s decision to be removed from life support and be allowed to die is not sufficiently free to break the causal chain of criminal liability.[67]

---

[61] *Compare* Commonwealth v. Rementer, 598 A.2d 1300 (Pa. Super. Ct. 1991) (*R* assaulted *V*, his girlfriend, in a bar; *R* continued to pursue *V* when she left; *V* fell to the ground and was run over by a car as she approached *X* for aid; held: *R*'s conduct remained an operative force that justified holding him criminally responsible for *V*'s death).

[62] Hart & Honoré, Note 1, *supra*, at 326.

[63] State v. Preslar, 48 N.C. 421 (1856).

[64] Velazquez v. State, 561 So. 2d 347 (Fla. Dist. Ct. App. 1990).

[65] Rex v. Beech, 23 Cox Crim. Cas. 181 (1912).

[66] Stephenson v. State, 179 N.E. 633 (Ind. 1932).

[67] State v. Ruane, 912 S.W.2d 766 (Tenn. Crim. App. 1995). Compare this, however, to *Regina v. Blaue*, [1975] 1 W.L.R. 1411. In *Blaue*, *B* seriously wounded *V. V*, informed that she needed a blood transfusion, which presumably would have saved her, refused it on religious grounds. The court, stating that *B* had

[7]   Factor 6: Omissions

"Doing nothing . . . is just that — nothing — so far as the law is concerned."[68] Therefore, an omission will rarely supersede an earlier, operative wrongful act. For example, if D drives his automobile in a negligent manner, causing the death of V, a passenger in D's car, V's failure to wear a seat belt, although causally related to his own death,[69] will not absolve D from liability for the death.[70]

This principle operates even if the intervening actor has a duty to act. Therefore, a father's failure to intervene to stop a stranger from beating his child will usually not absolve the attacker for the ensuing homicide, although the father may also be responsible for the death on the basis of omission principles.

§ 14.04   MODEL PENAL CODE[71]

[A]   Actual Cause

The Model Penal Code applies the but-for (*sine qua non*) rule. To be guilty of an offense, a person's conduct must cause the prohibited result. "Cause" is defined under the Code as "an antecedent but for which the result in question would not have occurred."[72]

The common law principles that clarify the meaning of this test also apply in Code jurisdictions. In the case of concurrent sufficient causes[73] — *e.g.*, when $D1$ and $D2$ independently inflict immediately-lethal wounds on V — the Commentary to the Code states that "the result in question" should be described as "death from two mortal wounds."[74] Thus, the jury would determine whether "but for [$D1$'s]/[$D2$'s] act, the result [death from two mortal wounds] would have occurred

---

to take his victim (including V's religious views) as he found her, concluded that he was the proximate cause of V's death.

This result might be wrong. Arguably, V's decision to refuse medical treatment should be accorded the respect of being treated as a free, deliberate, and informed decision. Although it is often said, as in *Blaue*, that a wrongdoer takes his victim as he finds him, this doctrine is typically applied in cases in which the victim has a pre-existing and hidden medical condition, such as hemophilia or a weak heart. In such circumstances, it cannot be said that the victim chooses for his blood not to coagulate, or that he chooses to have a heart attack. In contrast, V in *Blaue* chose to "suffer" from a pre-existing religious "condition," and to act upon it.

[68] Perkins & Boyce, Note 44, *supra*, at 820.

[69] There is philosophical debate regarding whether an omission can ever "cause" a resulting event. *See* Michael S. Moore, Act and Crime 267–78 (1993). How can nothing be the "cause" of something? The criminal law, however, accepts the view that omissions *can* be causally relevant. *See* Model Penal Code § 1.13(5) (defining "conduct" as an "act *or omission* and its accompanying state of mind"); and § 2.03(1)(a) (providing the circumstances under which "conduct" is the "cause" of a result).

[70] Bowman v. State, 564 N.E.2d 309 (Ind. Ct. App. 1990), *aff'd in part, vacated in part*, 577 N.E.2d 569 (Ind. 1991); People v. Clark, 431 N.W.2d 88 (Mich. Ct. App. 1988).

[71] *See generally* David J. Karp, Note, *Causation in the Model Penal Code*, 78 Colum. L. Rev. 1249 (1978).

[72] Model Penal Code § 2.03(1)(a).

[73] *See* § 14.02[C][2][b], *supra*.

[74] American Law Institute, Comment to § 2.03, at 259.

when it did." This way, each party is a but-for cause of the result, and a court need not apply the "substantial factor" test.

[B] Proximate Cause (Actually, Culpability)

Unlike the common law, the Model Penal Code treats but-for causation as the exclusive meaning of "causation" in the criminal law. The Code treats matters of "proximate causation" as issues relating instead to the actor's culpability.

Specifically, subsections (2)(b) and (3)(b)[75] of Section 2.03 deal with situations in which the actual result of the defendant's conduct (considering both the precise harm caused and the manner in which it occurred) diverges from that which was designed, contemplated, or risked. In such circumstances, the issue in a Model Code jurisdiction is not whether, in light of the divergences, the defendant was a "proximate cause" of the resulting harm, but rather whether it may still be said that he caused the prohibited result with the level of culpability — purpose, knowledge, recklessness, or negligence — required by the definition of the offense.

Under the Code, the defendant has *not* acted with the requisite culpability unless the actual result, including the way in which it occurred, was not "too remote or accidental in its occurrence to have a [just] bearing on the actor's liability or on the gravity of his offense."[76] Thus, the "varying and sometimes inconsistent"[77] proximate causation factors developed by the common law are replaced with a single standard, which expressly invites the jury to reach a commonsense, or just, result.

In the rare circumstance of an offense containing no culpability requirement,[78] the Code provides that causation "is not established unless the actual result is a probable consequence of the actor's conduct."[79] This would mean that in a jurisdiction that recognizes the felony-murder rule, but which applies Model Penal Code causation principles,[80] a defendant may not be convicted of felony-murder if the death was not a probable consequence of his felonious conduct. For example, if D attempted to rob a bank, and the bank teller was accidentally electrocuted pressing the burglar alarm switch, D would not be liable for the death because the actual result — death by electrocution — was not a probable consequence of

---

[75] Subsection (2)(b) applies to crimes in which purposely or knowingly causing a result is the requisite element; subsection (3)(b) applies to crimes of recklessness or negligence.

[76] The word "just" was placed in brackets by the American Law Institute as a possible addition to the formulation. Disagreement existed among its members regarding the desirability of submitting undefined questions of justice to a jury. American Law Institute, Comment to § 2.03, at 261 n.16.

[77] *Id.* at 256.

[78] Under the Code, some element of culpability is required regarding *every* material element of an offense, except in the case of a "violation." Model Penal Code §§ 2.02(1), 2.05. *See* §§ 10.07[A] and 11.04, *supra.*

[79] Model Penal Code § 2.03(4).

[80] The felony-murder rule permits a person to be convicted of murder for an accidental (even non-negligent) killing that occurs during the commission of a felony. *See* § 31.06, *infra.* The Model Penal Code has rejected this doctrine. *See* § 31.10[B], *infra.* However, some states have retained the felony-murder doctrine but follow the Code causation approach.

robbing a bank.[81]

Chapter 15

CONCURRENCE OF ELEMENTS

§ 15.01 GENERAL PRINCIPLES

A crime contains an *actus reus* and, usually, a *mens rea*. More specifically, a person may not be convicted of an offense unless the prosecutor proves beyond a reasonable doubt that the defendant, with the requisite mental state, performed a voluntary act that actually and proximately caused the proscribed social harm. Implicit in this statement is an additional prerequisite to criminal liability: the *concurrence* of the *actus reus* and the *mens rea*.[1]

The principle of concurrence contains two components, discussed in the next two sections of this chapter. First, there must be temporal concurrence. That is, the defendant must possess the requisite *mens rea* at the same moment that her voluntary conduct (or omission) causes the social harm (the *actus reus*).[2] Second, there must be motivational concurrence: The defendant's conduct that caused the social harm must have been set into motion or impelled by the thought process that constituted the *mens rea* of the offense.

§ 15.02 TEMPORAL CONCURRENCE

Lack of temporal concurrence occurs when the *mens rea* of an offense exists before or after, but not during, the commission of the *actus reus*.

[A] *Mens Rea* Preceding *Actus Reus*

Occasionally, a defendant's *mens rea* will precede the *actus reus* of the offense, but be absent when she acts. For example, suppose that *D* intends to kill *V*, plans the killing, but never has the opportunity to implement the plan. Later, she changes her mind, abandons the scheme, and befriends *V*. Thereafter, *D* and *V* go hunting, during which time *D* innocently (non-negligently) kills *V*. On these facts, *D* is not guilty of criminal homicide. When she had the *mens rea*, there was no *actus reus*. When she subsequently killed *V*, she had no culpable state of mind.

---

[1] The concurrence principle is codified in a few state penal codes. *E.g.*, Cal. Penal Code § 20 (2015), which provides that "[i]n every crime . . . there must exist a *union, or joint operation* of act and intent, or criminal negligence" (emphasis added). The Model Penal Code also requires concurrence, albeit inferentially, by defining "conduct" as "an action or omission and *its accompanying* state of mind." Model Penal Code § 1.13(5) (emphasis added).

[2] State v. Cobb, 743 A.2d 1, 62–63 (Conn. 1999).

The concurrence principle is satisfied, however, if the *voluntary act* that causes the social harm concurs with the *mens rea*, although the social harm itself occurs later. For example, suppose that *D*, intending to kill *V*, mortally wounds *V*. *V* dies in the hospital three months later, by which time *D* has expressed genuine remorse, and no longer wants *V* to die. Here, *D* is guilty of murder. The critical issue is whether the lethal act — the firing of the gun — concurred with the *mens rea*, and not whether the *mens rea* was present at the time of the death.

[B] *Actus Reus* Preceding *Mens Rea*

Temporal concurrence is absent if the *actus reus* precedes the *mens rea*. For example, suppose that *D1* breaks into and enters *V1*'s home at night in order to escape the cold. After she enters, *D1* decides to steal *V1*'s property. *D1* is prosecuted for burglary, defined as "breaking and entering the dwelling house of another at night, with intent to commit a felony therein." On these facts, *D1* is not guilty of burglary because the specific intent of the offense ("intent to commit a felony therein") arose *after* the occurrence of the voluntary acts that caused the social harm of burglary ("breaking and entering the dwelling house of another at night").[3] Likewise, *D2* is not guilty of murder if she innocently takes *V2*'s life, after which she decides that she is glad that she killed *V2*.[4]

§ 15.03   MOTIVATIONAL CONCURRENCE

The impelling force or motivation behind the act that causes the social harm must be the *mens rea* of the offense, and not some other thought process, such as the mental state of preparing to commit the offense.

For example, suppose that *D* intends to shoot and kill her domestic partner, *V*, as soon as *V* arrives home. Incorrectly believing the gun is still unloaded, *D* tests the trigger by pulling it. As she does, *V* unexpectedly enters the house and is struck and killed by the bullet. Based on these facts, the requisite motivational concurrence is missing. Although *D* had the intent to kill *V* as she voluntarily performed the act that caused the death (*i.e.*, *temporal* concurrence existed), the *mens rea* — the intent to kill — was not the actuating force behind the conduct. The lethal act of pulling the trigger was intended as a preparatory act; it was "not done in order to give effect to [the] desire to kill."[5]

---

[3] *See* Cooper v. People, 973 P.2d 1234 (Colo. 1999), *overruled on other grounds*, Griego v. People, 19 P.3d 1 (Colo. 2001) (*C* claimed he broke into his elderly mother's home to get out of the cold; only later, after he got into an altercation with his mother, did he decide to commit a felony; held: if the jury believes *C*'s claim, he is not guilty of burglary).

[4] *See also* State v. Allen, 875 A.2d 724 (Md. 2005) (*A* stabbed *V*, mortally wounding him; *A* thereafter decided to steal *V*'s car; *V* died; *A* was charged with felony-murder based on the felonious taking of the vehicle; held: *A* is not guilty of felony-murder if the intent to commit the felony, the *mens rea* for murder in this case, is an afterthought of the lethal act of killing); Nay v. State, 167 P.3d 430 (Nev. 2007) (*N* claimed that he killed the victim in self-defense and only thereafter decided to rob the victim; held: *N* was entitled to a jury instruction that a robbery committed as an afterthought cannot support a felony-murder conviction).

[5] 1 W. Russell, Crime 54 (12th ed. 1964).

§ 15.04 SPECIAL PROBLEM: TEMPORALLY DIVISIBLE ACTS AND/OR OMISSIONS

In most cases application of the concurrence principle is straightforward. Difficulties arise, however, when a person commits temporally divisible acts only one of which causes the social harm, or when the defendant's *mens rea* concurs with an omission that follows an innocent act.

For example, in *State v. Rose*,[6] *R*, an automobile driver, was prosecuted for negligent homicide, in the death of *V*, a pedestrian. The evidence apparently showed that *R* non-negligently struck *V*, whose body wedged underneath *R*'s car. *R* negligently continued to drive some distance, dragging *V*'s body along. Medical experts could not determine whether *V* died at impact or as the result of being dragged.

Based on this evidence, the court properly reversed *R*'s conviction. Although all of the elements of manslaughter were present — *R* committed a voluntary act; she caused the death of *V*; and as to her post-impact conduct, *R* acted with the requisite negligent *mens rea* — the prosecutor did not prove beyond a reasonable doubt that the elements of manslaughter concurred. Essentially, *R* committed two divisible voluntary acts or series of acts: First, she collided with *V*; second, she dragged *V*'s body after impact. Regarding the first voluntary act, *R* lacked a *mens rea*. Regarding the second voluntary act (or, if you will, *R*'s omission of failing to stop), *R* was criminally negligent. There was insufficient medical testimony, however, to prove beyond a reasonable doubt that *this* negligent conduct/omission caused the death.[7]

In exceptional factual circumstances, courts have been known to ignore the concurrence requirement. In one case *D1*, intending to kill *V1*, poisoned *V1*. Although the poison left *V1* unconscious, it did not kill her. Thereafter, believing that *V1* was dead, *D1* decapitated *V1*, causing her death.[8] In another case, *D2* struck *V2* over the head; thinking that *V2* was now dead, *D2* threw *V2* over a cliff, in order to make it appear that *V2* had died from an accident. *V2* died from exposure after the fall.[9]

In both cases, a defendant, with the intent to kill the victim, performed a voluntary act (poisoning *V1*; striking *V2*) that did *not* cause death, and then committed a second voluntary act (decapitating *V1*; throwing *V2* over a cliff) that *did* cause death but without the requisite intent to kill (because the defendant thought that the deed had already been completed). Nonetheless, the murder convictions in both cases were affirmed, presumably because the defendant's

---

[6] 311 A.2d 281 (R.I. 1973).

[7] Sometimes a court will stretch to meet the concurrence requirement by finding a "continuing act." *See* Fagan v. Commissioner of Metropolitan Police, [1969] 1 Q.B. 439 (*F*, perhaps accidentally, drove his car onto *V*'s toes; thereafter, *F* purposely failed to move his vehicle off *V*'s toes; held: "There was an act constituting a battery which at its inception was not criminal because there was no element of intention but which became criminal from the moment the intention was formed to produce the apprehension [of a battery] which was flowing from the continuing act.").

[8] Jackson v. Commonwealth, 38 S.W. 422 (Ky. 1896).

[9] Thabo Meli v. Regina, [1954] 1 W.L.R. 228, 1 All E.R. 373.

culpability was that of a murderer, and "[o]rdinary ideas of justice and common sense require that such [cases] . . . be treated as murder,"[10] rather than attempted murder.

---

[10] Glanville Williams, Criminal Law: The General Part 174 (2d ed. 1961).

Chapter 16

DEFENSES: AN OVERVIEW

§ 16.01 DEFENSES: IN CONTEXT[1]

In criminal trials in the United States, the prosecution has the burden of producing evidence, and of persuading the fact finder beyond a reasonable doubt, of the concurrence of four ingredients of criminal responsibility: (1) a voluntary act (or an omission when there is a duty to act) by the defendant; (2) the social harm specified in the definition of the offense; (3) the defendant's *mens rea* (strict-liability crimes aside); and (4) an actual and proximate causal connection between elements (1) and (2).

Even if the prosecution proves the concurrence of these four elements, the defendant may seek to raise one or more defenses, which, if proven, will result in his acquittal of the offense charged.[2] This chapter sets out the various categories of defenses recognized in the criminal law.

Generally speaking, a legislature may allocate to the defendant the burden of persuasion regarding criminal law defenses.[3] When the defendant shoulders the burden, he is usually required to convince the fact finder of his claim by a preponderance of the evidence. But, there is one category of defenses — failure-of-proof defenses — that is a "defense" in only a loose sense of the term.[4] As to defenses that fall in *this* category, as will be explained, the legislature may *not* properly place the burden of persuasion on the defendant.

Two categories of defenses described briefly below — "justification" and "excuse" defenses — are of such fundamental significance that they are considered in greater detail in Chapter 17.

---

[1] *See generally* 1 Paul Robinson, Criminal Law Defenses 62–200 (1984). The categorization of defenses set out in this chapter is largely based on the influential work of Professor Robinson.

[2] Some defenses result in the defendant's conviction of a lesser offense. They are sometimes described as "partial defenses." For example, the "heat of passion" (or "provocation") defense to murder, if successfully proven, results in conviction of the defendant for voluntary manslaughter. *See* § 31.07, *infra.* Partial defenses are complete, however, in the sense that the defendant is acquitted of the crime originally charged, *e.g.,* murder.

[3] *See* Chapter 7, *infra.*

[4] Loosely speaking, a defense is "any set of identifiable conditions or circumstances that may prevent conviction for an offense." 1 Robinson, Note 1, *supra*, at 70.

§ 16.02   FAILURE-OF-PROOF DEFENSES

A failure-of-proof defense is one in which the defendant introduces evidence at his trial that demonstrates that the prosecution has failed to prove an essential element of the offense charged. For example, assume *D1*, charged with an intentional homicide, seeks to prove that he mistakenly believed that the object at which he fired his gun was a tree stump rather than a human being. Or, *D2* claims that he was sleepwalking when he killed *V*. Or, *D3* introduces evidence that he was not at the scene of the crime and, therefore, was misidentified as the wrongdoer. Each of these defendants is raising what courts often describe as a "defense": *D1* is claiming a mistake-of-fact "defense"; *D2* is asserting an unconsciousness "defense"; *D3* alleges an alibi "defense."

Although courts may characterize such claims as defenses, the purpose of the defendants' evidence in these examples is to raise a reasonable doubt regarding an element of the prosecutor's case-in-chief. The mistake-of-fact "defense" would negate the *mens rea* of the crime; *D2*'s unconsciousness would demonstrate that the prosecutor has failed to prove beyond a reasonable doubt that *D2*'s conduct included a voluntary act; and the alibi "defense" calls into question whether *D3* performed the *actus reus* of the offense.

The prosecution must shoulder the burden of disproving beyond a reasonable doubt a defendant's failure-of-proof claim. This conclusion follows from the fact that the prosecutor has the constitutional duty to prove every element of a criminal offense.[5]

§ 16.03   JUSTIFICATION DEFENSES

A justification defense is one that defines conduct "otherwise criminal, which under the circumstances is socially acceptable and which deserves neither criminal liability nor even censure."[6] Justified conduct is conduct that is "a good thing, or the right or sensible thing, or a permissible thing to do."[7] That is, a justified act is an act that is right or, at least, not wrong.

For example, killing a human being ordinarily is wrongful conduct. When *D* kills *V* in self-defense, however, society says that *D*'s conduct is "justified." Although *D* has committed the *actus reus* of criminal homicide, the special circumstance of the situation — *D* killed *V* because *V* was unlawfully attacking him — renders the homicide socially acceptable. By providing *D* with the justification defense of self-defense, society announces that *D*'s act of killing *V* was the right or, at least, a permissible, thing to do. Or, put differently, the result of *D*'s conduct — *V*'s death — was not a socially undesirable outcome under the circumstances.

---

[5] *See* § 7.03[B], *supra.*

[6] Peter D. W. Heberling, Note, *Justification: The Impact of the Model Penal Code on Statutory Reform*, 75 Colum. L. Rev. 914, 916 (1975).

[7] J.L. Austin, *A Plea for Excuses, in* Freedom and Responsibility 6 (Herbert Morris ed., 1961).

§ 16.04   EXCUSE DEFENSES

An excuse defense differs fundamentally from a justification defense. Whereas a justification claim generally focuses upon an *act* (*i.e.*, *D*'s conduct), and seeks to show that the result of the act was not wrongful, an excuse centers upon the *actor* (*i.e.*, *D*), and tries to show that the actor is not morally culpable for his wrongful conduct. Thus, an excuse defense "is in the nature of a claim that although the actor has harmed society, [he] should not be blamed or punished for causing that harm."[8] A defendant who asserts an excuse defense claims, "in essence, 'I admit, or you have proved beyond a reasonable doubt, that I did something that I should not have done, but I [still] should not be held criminally accountable for my actions.' "[9]

An insane actor, for example, does not deny that the prosecutor has proved the essential elements of the crime nor that, all things considered, his conduct was wrongful, intolerable, and censurable (*i.e.*, unjustified). He seeks to avoid criminal liability, however, by demonstrating that, as a result of his mental disease or defect, he lacks the moral blameworthiness ordinarily attached to wrongdoers.

§ 16.05   SPECIALIZED DEFENSES ("OFFENSE MODIFICATIONS")

Justification and excuse defenses apply to all crimes. Some defenses, however, pertain to just one or a few crimes. For example, "legal impossibility" is a common law defense to the crime of attempt. In some jurisdictions "abandonment" or "renunciation" is a defense to the crimes of attempt and conspiracy. And, "Wharton's Rule" is a defense peculiar to the crime of conspiracy.[10]

Crime-specific defenses have a common feature: They authorize acquittal of a defendant, even though his conduct satisfies the elements of the offense, when the underlying purpose for prohibiting the conduct is negated by the conditions that constitute the defense.

For example, a criminal attempt serves the utilitarian purpose of providing society with a basis for arresting and punishing a person who has demonstrated his culpability and dangerousness by taking a substantial step toward committing a criminal offense. Suppose, however, *D* purposely takes a substantial step toward committing a murder (*i.e.*, he commits the *actus reus* and *mens rea* of an attempted murder), but then voluntarily and irrevocably abandons his criminal enterprise. In such a case, the Model Penal Code recognizes the defense of renunciation. This defense applies, although the elements of an attempt have been proven, because the underlying reason for punishing *D* no longer applies. His decision to abandon his criminal goal negates his culpability and dangerousness and, therefore, renders his punishment unnecessary.

---

[8] Joshua Dressler, *Justifications and Excuses: A Brief Review of the Concepts and the Literature*, 33 Wayne L. Rev. 1155, 1162–63 (1987).

[9] *Id.* at 1163.

[10] *See* §§ 27.07[D] (legal impossibility), 27.08 (renunciation of an attempt), 29.09[B] (abandonment of a conspiracy), and 29.09[C] (Wharton's Rule), *infra*.

§ 16.06 EXTRINSIC DEFENSES ("NONEXCULPATORY DEFENSES")

Justification, excuse, and offense-modification defenses are similar in this regard: These defenses relate to the culpability or dangerousness of the defendant or to the wrongfulness of his conduct. Some defenses, however, bar a defendant's conviction, *or even his prosecution,* for reasons unrelated to these factors. These latter claims involve public policy factors extrinsic to substantive criminal law doctrine. Examples of such defenses are the statute of limitations, diplomatic immunity, and incompetency to stand trial.

A nonexculpatory defense serves an important public policy interest unrelated to the social harm committed by the actor or to his blameworthiness for causing it. Legislative recognition of such a defense implies that the social interest served by it outweighs the utilitarian and/or retributive reasons for punishing the offender.

Chapter 17

JUSTIFICATIONS AND EXCUSES

§ 17.01 HISTORICAL OVERVIEW[1]

Two categories of criminal law defenses are the subject of this chapter: justifications and excuses. In very early English legal history, the distinction between justifications and excuses was a matter of profound practical significance. In the case of felonies, a justified actor was acquitted of the offense; an excused actor, however, was subject to the same punishment as a convicted offender (the death penalty and forfeiture of property), although he could escape the death sentence with a pardon from the Crown.

This dichotomy blurred over time, as excused actors were pardoned by the Crown on an increasingly *pro forma* basis; and they were allowed to regain their property by means of a writ of restitution.[2] Nonetheless, the excused wrongdoer was not on the same footing as the justified actor, since the excused party was subject to incarceration while petitioning for a pardon and for restitution of his property. The justified actor was free of all legal impediments.

Today, justified and excused actors are treated the same by the criminal courts: Each is acquitted of the offense and neither is punished for her conduct (although a person excused on the ground of insanity is subject to civil commitment). As a result, many courts, legislatures, and commentators have become inattentive to the differences between the two classes of defenses, even to the point of using the terms "justification" and "excuse" interchangeably.[3]

---

[1] *See generally* George P. Fletcher, Rethinking Criminal Law 759–875 (1978); Marcia Baron, *Justifications and Excuses*, 2 Ohio St. J. Crim. L. 387 (2005); Mitchell N. Berman, *Justification and Excuse, Law and Morality*, 53 Duke L.J. 1 (2003); Joshua Dressler, *Justifications and Excuses: A Brief Review of the Concepts and the Literature*, 33 Wayne L. Rev. 1155 (1987); Kent Greenawalt, *Distinguishing Justifications from Excuses*, 49 Law & Contemp. Probs., Summer 1986, at 89; Heidi M. Hurd, *Justification and Excuse, Wrongdoing and Culpability*, 74 Notre Dame L. Rev. 1551 (1999); Eugene R. Milhizer, *Justification and Excuse: What They Were, What They Are, and What They Ought to Be*, 78 St. John's L. Rev. 725 (2004).

[2] 4 Blackstone, Commentaries on the Law of England *188 (1838). Forfeiture was statutorily abolished in 1838. 9 Geo. 4, c. 13, § 10 (1838).

[3] *E.g.*, State v. Cozzens, 490 N.W.2d 184, 189 (Neb. 1992) ("Therefore, the *justification* . . . defense operates to legally *excuse* conduct that would otherwise subject a person to criminal sanctions.") (emphasis added). Sometimes, as well, a judge will use the term "excuse" in discussing a justification defense, as when United States Supreme Court Justice Samuel Alito, joined by Justice Clarence Thomas, wrote that the "traditional defense of necessity" — a justification defense, see Chapter 22, *infra* — "*excuses* a violation of the law if 'the harm which will result from compliance with the law is greater than that which will result from violation of it.'" Rosemond v. United States, 134 S. Ct. 1240, 1254 (2014). For citations to other judicial, legislative, and scholarly misuses of the terms, see Joshua Dressler, *New*

This inattention has not gone without objection by a cadre of scholars. These writers have sought to clarify the concepts of "justification" and "excuse," to demonstrate how the two defenses differ, and to explain why lawyers should care about the distinctions. Because of renewed interest in the subject, including greater sensitivity to the distinction among some courts,[4] this chapter provides a closer inspection of these concepts.

§ 17.02 UNDERLYING THEORIES OF "JUSTIFICATION"[5]

[A] Searching for an Explanatory Theory

As explained in the last chapter,[6] justified conduct is conduct that under ordinary circumstances is criminal, but which under the special circumstances encompassed by the justification defense is not wrongful and is even, perhaps, affirmatively desirable.[7] A justified act is one that "the law does not condemn, or even welcomes."[8]

The question for consideration in this section is: What makes ordinarily bad conduct justifiable? Why is it, for example, that *D* is justified in killing *V* to protect herself from *V*'s unlawful lethal assault or from *V*'s intrusion into her home, but that she is not justified in killing *V* to protect her dog or her television set from theft? Are the justification defenses of self-defense, defense-of-habitation, and defense-of-property, for example, no more than a conglomeration of rules unrelated to one another, or is there a single moral theory that unifies the various

---

Thoughts About the Concept of Justification in the Criminal Law: A Critique of Fletcher's Thinking and Rethinking, 32 UCLA L. Rev. 61, 65–66 (1984); Paul H. Robinson, *A Theory of Justification: Societal Harm as a Prerequisite for Criminal Liability*, 23 UCLA L. Rev. 266, 276 (1975).

[4] *E.g.*, State v. Edwards, 717 N.W.2d 405, 413 n.4 (Minn. 2006) ("While the term[s] . . . are often used interchangeably, they are distinct legal concepts."); State v. Leidholm, 334 N.W.2d 811, 814–15 (N.D. 1983) (defining the terms and indicating that they are not synonyms); United States v. Lopez, 662 F. Supp. 1083 (N.D. Cal. 1987) (seeking to determine whether *L*'s actions were justified or excused, and explaining why the distinction affected an evidentiary motion made by the prosecutor).

[5] *See generally* Fletcher, Note 1, *supra*, at 759–98; Dressler, Note 1, *supra*; R. A. Duff, *Rethinking Justifications*, 39 Tulsa L. Rev. 829 (2004); Milhizer, Note 1, *supra*; Robinson, Note 3, *supra*; Paul H. Robinson & John M. Darley, *Testing Competing Theories of Justification*, 76 N.C. L. Rev. 1095 (1998).

[6] *See* § 16.03, *supra.*

[7] Notice that "justification," as defined in the text, may imply a positive judgment about conduct (it is right, good, or desirable), or it might constitute a weaker value judgment (that the conduct is tolerable or not wrongful). Some scholars believe that the concept of "justification" necessarily implies the stronger meaning; others favor an interpretation broad enough to include both characterizations. *E.g.*, *compare* George P. Fletcher, *The Right and the Reasonable*, 98 Harv. L. Rev. 949 (1985), and George P. Fletcher, *Should Intolerable Prison Conditions Generate a Justification or an Excuse for Escape?*, 26 UCLA L. Rev. 1355 (1979) (favoring the view that "justification" implies "right" conduct), *with* Dressler, Note 3, *supra*, and Kent Greenawalt, *The Perplexing Borders of Justification and Excuse*, 84 Colum. L. Rev. 1897 (1984) (favoring the vew that "justification" can mean "permissible" or "not wrongful" conduct).

The significance of this debate is more than semantic. For example, if "justification" signifies that conduct is morally desirable, and if one believes (as some do) that killing in self-defense is tolerable but not affirmatively good, then the defense of self-defense should be an excuse defense, rather than a justification. This, in turn, can have practical implications. *See* § 17.05, *infra.*

[8] H.L.A. Hart, Punishment and Responsibility 13 (1968) (footnote omitted).

justification defenses — some principle that explains why something bad (socially harmful) becomes good or, at least, tolerable?

It would be convenient if there were a single, unifying principle of justification, but there is none. What follows is a brief summary of various justification principles. These principles can and should be considered when evaluating the wisdom of recognizing particular "justificatory" claims.

[B] "Public Benefit" Theory

At early common law, justification defenses had a strong public-benefit cast to them. Generally speaking, conduct was not justified unless it was performed in the public's interest, and in most cases was limited to the actions of public officers.

For example, Blackstone identified three sets of circumstances in which homicides were justifiable:[9] (1) when a public officer was commanded to take a life (*e.g.*, when the warden executed a convicted felon); (2) when a public officer, although not commanded to do so, took a life in order to advance the public welfare (*e.g.*, when an officer killed a felon resisting arrest); and (3) when a private party took a life in order to prevent the commission of a forcible, atrocious felony.[10]

A homicide in these circumstances is considered justifiable because society benefits from the actor's conduct. But, there is more to this justification principle: The benefit to society is not incidental to some self-interested goal of the actor; it is the underlying motivation for the actor's conduct. Although strands of the public-benefit concept remain today, it is no longer the dominant theory of justification.

[C] "Moral Forfeiture" Theory

The public-benefit justification principle discussed in the preceding subsection attaches to conduct that benefits society. Some theories of justification, however, are more limited in their focus: A person's conduct is justified as long as it does not result in a socially undesirable outcome. The moral-forfeiture principle of justification fits this category. It is based on the view that people possess certain moral rights or interests that society recognizes through its criminal laws, *e.g.*, the right to life, but which may be forfeited by the holder of the right.

The *forfeiture* of a right must be distinguished from its *waiver.* Some moral interests are not waivable. For example, a person may not legally consent to her own death. The right to life is inviolable in this sense. Nonetheless, even this nonwaivable right can be *forfeited* — nonconsensually lost — as the result of an actor's voluntary decision to violate the rights of another. In such circumstances, society may determine unilaterally that it will no longer recognize the wrongdoer's interest in her life.

---

[9] 4 Blackstone, Note 2, *supra*, at *177–88.

[10] A person who killed another to prevent a rape, robbery, burglary, or other forcible felony acted justifiably, presumably because she was benefitting others; however, if a person killed in self-defense, this conduct constituted excusable, rather than justifiable, homicide.

The moral-forfeiture doctrine is frequently called upon to explain why an aggressor or fleeing felon may justifiably be killed: As a result of V's freely-chosen decision to wrongfully threaten D's life or to commit a dangerous felony, V forfeits her right to life; consequently, when D kills V in self-defense or in order to prevent V's escape, no socially recognized harm has occurred. From the law's perspective, V's life is worth no more than that of an insect or inanimate body.[11]

The forfeiture principle, although widespread in the common law, is morally troubling to some people because it involves the nonconsensual loss of a valued right. When the forfeiture principle is applied to the interest in human life, it runs counter to the "good and simple moral principle that human life is sacred."[12] To equate human life with that of an insect or an inanimate object is troubling to those who believe in the sanctity of human life.

[D] "Moral Rights" Theory

Conduct may be justified on the ground that the actor has a right to protect a particular moral interest. This theory of justification differs significantly from the moral-forfeiture principle described in the preceding subsection. The forfeiture doctrine focuses on the wrongdoing of the "victim" (e.g., the aggressor) whereas the moral-rights theory focuses on the interests of the innocent defendant. Whereas forfeiture works in a negative way to deny that there is a socially protected interest harmed when the wrongdoer is injured or killed, the moral-rights theory works in a positive sense to provide the actor with an affirmative right to protect her threatened moral interest.

For example, when D kills or seriously injures V, a lethal aggressor, her conduct may be justified because she was enforcing a natural right of autonomy that V's conduct threatened. D is a right-holder protecting her interest against V, the wrongdoer who would violate her right. This principle of justification does not treat V's death as socially irrelevant, as the forfeiture doctrine does; rather, it views D's conduct as affirmatively proper.

This theory is not without critics or, at least, persons who express what may be characterized as a proportionality concern. Because this justification principle focuses on the innocent person whose rights are being threatened by a wrongdoer, some commentators fear that it "filters out shades and nuances and transforms all situations into black and white relief."[13] That is, once it is determined that V has intruded on a right belonging to D, it is plausible to contend that D may do whatever is necessary to enforce her right, no matter how minor the intrusion. After all, D is in the right, and V is in the wrong, and (some say) Right should

---

[11] Hugo Bedau, *The Right to Life*, 1968 Monist 550, 570 ("[The wrongdoer] no longer merits our consideration, any more than an insect or a stone does.").

[12] Working Party, Board for Social Responsibility, Church of England, On Dying Well — An Anglican Contribution to the Debate on Euthanasia 24 (1975), *quoted in* Sanford H. Kadish, *Respect for Life and Regard for Rights in the Criminal Law*, 64 Cal. L. Rev. 871, 878 (1976).

[13] George P. Fletcher, *Proportionality and the Psychotic Aggressor: A Vignette in Comparative Criminal Theory*, 8 Israel L. Rev. 367, 381 (1973).

never give way to Wrong.[14] Unless limits are placed on this justification theory, it could authorize a disproportional response to the right being threatened.

[E] "Superior Interest" (or "Lesser Harm") Theory

Another theory of justification authorizes conduct when the interests the defendant seeks to protect outweigh those of the person whom she harms. Pursuant to this principle, the interests of the parties, and, more broadly, the values that they seek to enforce, are balanced. In each case there is a superior, or at least a non-inferior, interest. As long as such an interest is pursued the conduct is justified.

For example, if *D* trespasses by entering *V*'s house in order to avoid a tornado, her conduct is justified. Protection of human life is more important than property protection. Similarly, the use of nonlethal force upon a lethal aggressor is justifiable because preservation of life is more important than prevention of moderate injury to another. As these examples suggest, the superior-interest theory of justification is consistent with the utilitarian goal of promoting individual conduct that reduces overall social harm. It is also consistent with the non-utilitarian concept of weighing moral rights and identifying the superior one.

§ 17.03 UNDERLYING THEORIES OF "EXCUSE"[15]

[A] Searching for an Explanatory Theory

An excuse defense "is in the nature of a claim that although the actor has harmed society, she should not be blamed or punished for causing that harm."[16] The question that must be answered here is: Is there a single principle that determines when the law will abstain from blaming a person who has caused social harm and, as a result, not hold her legally accountable in a criminal prosecution?

As with justifications, no single theory explains every excuse defense. Moreover, some of the theories partially overlap. However, unlike justification defenses, which are often (but need not) be explained on utilitarian grounds, excuses in the criminal

---

[14] Edmond Coke, Third Institute *55 (1644) (no "man shall [ever] give way to a thief, etc., neither shall he forfeit anything").

[15] *See generally* Fletcher, Note 1, *supra*, at § 10.3; Peter Arenella, *Convicting the Morally Blameless: Reassessing the Relationship Between Legal and Moral Accountability*, 39 UCLA L. Rev. 1511 (1992); Michael Corrado, *Notes on the Structure of a Theory of Excuses*, 82 J. Crim. L. & Criminology 465 (1991); Joshua Dressler, *Reflections on Excusing Wrongdoers: Moral Theory, New Excuses and the Model Penal Code*, 19 Rutgers L.J. 671 (1988); Sanford H. Kadish, *Excusing Crime*, 75 Cal. L. Rev. 257 (1987); Anders Kaye, *Objectifying and Identifying in the Theory of Excuse*, 39 Am. J. Crim. L. 175 (2012); Anders Kaye, *Resurrecting the Causal Theory of Excuses*, 83 Neb. L. Rev. 1116 (2005); Michael S. Moore, *Causation and the Excuses*, 73 Cal. L. Rev. 1091 (1985); Stephen J. Morse, *Diminished Rationality, Diminished Responsibility*, 1 Ohio St. J. Crim. L. 289 (2003); Samuel H. Pillsbury, *The Meaning of Deserved Punishment: An Essay on Choice, Character, and Responsibility*, 67 Ind. L.J. 719 (1992); Paul H. Robinson, *A System of Excuses: How Criminal Law's Excuse Defenses Do, and Don't, Work Together to Exculpate Blameless (and Only Blameless) Offenders*, 42 Tex. Tech. L. Rev. 259 (2009); George Vuoso, *Background, Responsibility, and Excuse*, 96 Yale L.J. 1661 (1987).

[16] Dressler, Note 1, *supra*, at 1162–63.

law are far more plausibly defended in non-utilitarian terms. As Professor Sanford Kadish has observed, "[s]omething is missing" in the utilitarian account of excuses, namely, "concern for the innocent person who is the object of a criminal prosecution." As Kadish points out:

> To blame a person is to express a moral criticism, and if the person's action does not deserve criticism, blaming him is a kind of falsehood and is, to the extent the person is injured by being blamed, unjust to him. It is this feature of our everyday moral practices that lies behind the law's excuses.[17]

After brief comment on the utilitarian theory of excuses, various nonconsequentialist moral theories are surveyed.

[B] Deterrence Theory

Jeremy Bentham, the leading classical utilitarian, explained that excuses are recognized in the criminal law because they identify the circumstances in which conduct is undeterrable, *e.g.*, when a person is insane or coerced to commit an offense. In such situations, punishment of the actor is wrong because it is inefficacious.[18]

This argument has rightly been denounced as a "spectacular *non sequitur.*"[19] The *threat* of punishment may not deter a person who is suffering from a mental illness or is acting under duress, but its *infliction* may deter misconduct by "normal" persons who might otherwise believe that they could fraudulently convince a jury of their undeterrability. Abolition of all excuses, therefore, might be socially useful: The pain inflicted on the undeterrable actor might be outweighed by the prevention of harm caused by the law's imposition of a stricter form of liability.[20]

Professor H.L.A. Hart has offered a more sophisticated utilitarian account of excuses. He has argued that excuses "function as a mechanism for . . . maximizing within the framework of coercive criminal law the efficacy of the individual's informed and considered choice in determining the future and also his power to predict that future."[21] That is, the rule that criminal liability is limited to voluntary wrongdoing allows each person to derive satisfaction from being able to plan her life with reasonable confidence that she can avoid the sanctions of the law, as long as she chooses to obey society's dictates.

---

[17] Kadish, Note 15, *supra*, at 264.

[18] Jeremy Bentham, An Introduction to the Principles of Morals and Legislation 160–62 (J. Burns & H.L.A. Hart eds., 1970).

[19] Hart, Note 8, *supra*, at 19.

[20] *Id.* at 19–20; Fletcher, Note 1, *supra*, at 813–17.

[21] Hart, Note 8, *supra*, at 46.

[C]   Causation Theory

Perhaps the broadest excuse theory states that a person should not be blamed for her conduct if it was caused by factors outside her control.[22] For example, according to a causal theorist, D should be excused if she commits a crime because of a mental illness or a coercive deadly threat: Since she is not to blame for being ill or the victim of coercion — the cause of her actions — she is not to blame for the crime itself. On the other hand, she *is* to blame and punishable if her criminal conduct was caused by *self-induced* intoxication or by any other factor for which she is responsible.

Although this principle is plausible on its face, it does not accurately describe current excuse law. For example, as is developed elsewhere,[23] only a single, largely discredited, definition of insanity applies the causation principle; most people who commit criminal offenses due to mental disease *are* held criminally responsible. As another example, if a person commits a crime solely because she is threatened with economic ruin, her conduct is nonetheless *not* legally excused.[24]

It is also not evident that the causation principle conforms with our moral intuitions. A person who commits a crime due to self-induced intoxication, for example, may be able to show that her propensity to become intoxicated was the result of genetic or environmental factors over which she had no control; yet we do not consider such a wrongdoer morally blameless. Indeed, acceptance of the causal principle of excuses could threaten to lead society down "the cul-de-sac of . . . determinism,"[25] in which *nobody* can be blamed or punished for any wrongful conduct.

[D]   Character Theory

Various theorists treat a person's moral character as central to the concept of deserved punishment. According to one character theory, punishment should be proportional to a wrongdoer's moral desert, and that desert should be measured by the actor's character.[26] Normally, we infer bad character from an actor's wrongful conduct; these character theorists argue that excuses should be recognized in the law in those circumstances in which bad character cannot be inferred from the offender's wrongful conduct.

For example, if D robs a bank, we would ordinarily infer that she is a greedy person who lacks concern for the rights of others, *i.e.*, that she possesses a bad character. However, we would not infer bad character if we learned that she robbed the bank because terrorists threatened to kill her child if she did not cooperate. In such circumstances, we assume that even a person of good moral character would probably violate the law. Therefore, we excuse her actions.

---

[22] For a full exposition of this theory, which the author ultimately rejects, see Moore, Note 15, *supra*, at 1101–12.

[23] *See* § 25.04[C][4], *infra*.

[24] *See* § 23.01[B], *infra*.

[25] Fletcher, Note 1, *supra*, at 801.

[26] *Id.* at 800.

This theory may conform with our moral intuitions. We assume that people who commit crimes are "bad people." When a "good person" commits a "bad act" we sometimes say that her act was "out of character." We look for some explanation independent of her character that explains and excuses her conduct.

Nonetheless, critics raise various objections to this and other versions of the character theory of excuses. First, if excuse law were genuinely based on character, a court would need to look at a person's entire life, and not solely at the circumstances surrounding the particular criminal act, in order to evaluate her moral desert. But, as philosopher Jeffrie Murphy has pointed out, "there are staggering obstacles in the way of our making [character] judgments about others." God, it may be argued, can judge our character, but mortals lack "the knowledge required to impute deep character depravity to others with any degree of reliability"; therefore, "we act recklessly in inflicting misery on people as the suffering they deserve for their inner wickedness."[27]

Second, the character theory does not explain why we *do* punish people of *good* character who commit out-of-character offenses. For example, suppose that *D*, unemployed, unjustifiably batters an innocent stranger in a moment of frustration with her plight. Even if *D* is a person of good character, she has acted in a blameworthy manner and is (and, most people would probably say, should be) held accountable for her actions.

Third, causal theorists argue that the character theory assumes that people are responsible for their character — and, thus, may be blamed for their actions stemming from their bad character — but this may not be the case. They argue that one's character is shaped by powerful genetic and environmental factors beyond the individual's control. Defenders of the character theory argue, however, that a person *may* properly be held responsible for her character traits, even if she did not initially choose them, because she is responsible for *retaining* them.[28]

[E] "Free Choice" (or Personhood) Theory

Advocates of the free choice principle claim that a person may properly be blamed for her conduct "if, but only if, [s]he had the capacity and fair opportunity to function in a uniquely human way, *i.e.*, freely to choose whether to violate the moral/legal norms of society."[29] According to this account, "free choice" exists if, at the time of the wrongful conduct, the actor has the substantial capacity and fair opportunity to: (1) understand the facts relating to her conduct; (2) appreciate that her conduct violates society's mores; and (3) conform her conduct to the dictates of the law. A person lacking the *substantial capacity* in any of these regards

---

[27] Jeffrie G. Murphy, *Moral Epistemology, the Retributive Emotions, and the "Clumsy Moral Philosophy" of Jesus Christ, in* The Passions of Law 149, 157–58 (Susan A. Bandes ed., 1999).

[28] Pillsbury, Note 15, *supra*, at 730–31. For variations on the character theory described in the text, see *id.*, at 730–34 (describing, but ultimately rejecting all of the character theories).

[29] Dressler, Note 15, *supra*, at 701 (footnote omitted); *see* Hart, Note 8, *supra*, at 181 ("Thus a primary vindication of the principle of responsibility could rest on the simple idea that unless a man has the capacity and a fair opportunity . . . to adjust his behaviour to the law its penalties ought not to be applied to him.").

essentially suffers from some serious *internal disability* (*e.g.*, severe mental illness) and, therefore, does not deserve to be punished because she lacks the basic attributes of personhood that qualify her as a moral agent. Alternatively, a person who lacks "free choice" under the *no-fair-opportunity* prong does not deserve punishment because some *external* factor (*e.g.*, a deadly threat) is acting upon her on this particular occasion such that it is unjust to blame her for her wrongful conduct.

Some critics believe the choice theory is too narrow. Causal theorists argue, for example, that because "free choice" is defined in terms of the actor's capacity and opportunity *at the moment of the criminal act* to obey the law, morally significant events arising earlier are improperly excluded from the picture. For example, although a person may have had free choice regarding whether to rob a particular liquor store on a particular occasion, she may not have had a fair opportunity to avoid the conditions that hardened her character and made committing the crime seem inevitable.

Professor Peter Arenella is also critical, but for a different reason.[30] He contends that the free choice theory provides too "thin" an account of what it means to be a moral agent. He argues that one cannot be a moral decisionmaker, and thus qualify as a morally accountable actor, unless the person possesses certain abilities and attributes, including the ability to care for the interests of other human beings, *i.e.*, the capacity to empathize. Arenella contends that one who lacks *this* capacity, as is said to be the case with people once called "sociopaths," is missing such an important human attribute that she is undeserving of blame, even if she "freely" causes harm as "free choice" is defined above.

§ 17.04 JUSTIFICATION DEFENSES AND MISTAKE-OF-FACT CLAIMS[31]

[A] General Rule

Consider the following hypothetical: *D* intentionally kills *V.* At trial, *D* claims that she killed *V* because she believed that *V* was about to kill her. In fact, *V* was *not* about to kill *D.* This very common scenario involves the convergence of two "defense" concepts: a traditional justification defense (here, self-defense) and a mistake-of-fact claim (*D*'s erroneous belief that *V* posed an imminent unlawful deadly threat).

Two questions arise when a defendant asserts a justification defense, and yet also claims a mistake of fact: (1) Is a defendant entitled to be acquitted if she was mistaken regarding the facts that would justify her conduct?; and (2) If she *is*

---

[30] *See* Arenella, Note 15, *supra.*

[31] *See generally* Fletcher, Note 1, *supra*, at 762–68; 2 Paul H. Robinson, Criminal Law Defenses § 184 (1984); Baron, Note 1, *supra*; Russell L. Christopher, *Mistake of Fact in the Objective Theory of Justification: Do Two Rights Make Two Wrongs Make Two Rights . . . .?*, 85 J. Crim. L. & Criminology 295 (1994); Dressler, Note 3, *supra*; Greenawalt, Note 7, *supra*; Richard Singer, *The Resurgence of Mens Rea: II — Honest but Unreasonable Mistake of Fact in Self-Defense*, 28 B.C. L. Rev. 459 (1987).

entitled to be acquitted, should the law describe her conduct as justified or excused? For current purposes, these questions will be answered in relation to self-defense (considered fully in Chapter 18), but the principles here have application to the other justification defenses, as well.

The law is clear-cut in situations of the sort described here. A defendant *is* entitled to be acquitted on the basis of self-defense if her mistake of fact regarding the threat was reasonable. However, she will be convicted of some form of criminal homicide if her mistake was unreasonable.[32] More specifically, the rule is that a defendant is justified — and not merely excused — in using deadly force if, at the time of the homicide, she genuinely and reasonably believed that she was in imminent danger of death or grievous bodily injury, and that deadly force was necessary to repel the threat, although it turned out later that these appearances were false.

[B] Criticisms of the General Rule

There is little disagreement with the principle that a defendant who acts on the basis of reasonable appearances should be acquitted, but there is debate about the propriety of treating such a mistaken actor's conduct as justifiable, rather than excusable. In the self-defense hypothetical at the beginning of this section, how can it be that D is *justified* in taking V's life if V was, in fact, an innocent person?

Critics of the general rule that a person is *justified* in acting on the basis of reasonable, albeit inaccurate, appearances, argue that it confuses the difference between justifications, which go to the propriety of the defendant's *act*, and excuses, which relate to the blameworthiness of the *actor.* These critics maintain that a reasonable-but-mistaken *actor* is morally blameless and, therefore, should be excused; but it is wrong to suggest that the *act* of killing an innocent person (one who does not pose a threat to the life of the actor) is ever justifiable.

These critics are making more than a semantic argument. As discussed more fully in the next section of this chapter, the justification/excuse distinction may have practical implications. Critics of the general rule contend that it is wrong to authorize D (in the hypothetical) to kill innocent V, because this would seemingly leave V without her own right of self-defense against D, who is now attacking *her.* Alternatively, the law would have to recognize conflicting justifications: That is, D would be justified in killing V based on incorrect-but-reasonable appearances; and, meanwhile, V would be justified in killing D based on the reality that D is (justifiably) trying to take V's life! To critics, this is an anomalous outcome. They reason that one, and only one, person — specifically, here, V — should be justified in killing the other. Moreover, they argue, unless the law properly characterizes D's and V's conduct, a third person who arrives on the scene will not know whether she may come to the aid of D, V, both, or neither.[33]

---

[32] Under traditional common law principles, she is guilty of murder if her mistake was unreasonable; in some jurisdictions today, however, she would be convicted of manslaughter. *See* §§ 18.01[E] and 18.03, *infra.* Under the Model Penal Code, she is guilty of manslaughter or negligent homicide, depending on whether she was reckless or negligent as to her mistake. *See* § 18.06[B], *infra.*

[33] *See* § 17.05[E], *infra.*

[C] Defense of the General Rule

Defenders of the general rule point out that "[t]he criminal law does not demand ideal behavior from people."[34] All that the law can fairly expect of a person is that she make a conscientious effort to determine the true state of affairs before acting. If she does this, defenders of the general rule claim, her conduct is justifiable, although the result of her conduct (in the hypothetical, innocent *V*'s death) may be tragic.

The defenders of the rule may be right. Consider that a police officer is legally entitled to arrest a person if she has probable cause to believe that the suspect has committed a felony. An officer acting on probable cause is justified in making the arrest, even if the suspect later turns out to be innocent. Critics of the general rule would say that an officer in such circumstances has acted *un*justifiably, no matter how carefully she has investigated the situation. Yet, few would agree that a police officer is acting outside the law, *i.e.*, unjustifiably, simply because her knowledge of the circumstances proves to be humanly imperfect.

Defenders of the general rule also argue that there is no inherent anomaly in recognizing incompatible justifications. For example, in the arrest situation, suppose that a police officer has probable cause to make an arrest, but the suspect is factually innocent of the crime, so she uses nondeadly force to resist her own arrest. If she is later charged with battery upon the officer, there is no reason why the law must inflexibly deny a justification defense to her, even though the officer was also legally justified in making the arrest. The point here is not that the law *should* permit a justification defense to the citizen in this hypothetical, but rather that it is not irrational to permit one.

Finally, defenders of the general rule point out that, at least according to some of the justification theories set out earlier in this chapter, a person *can* be justified in acting on the basis of reasonable, but mistaken, appearances. For example, it is plausible to argue that a person's natural right to defend her autonomy should apply in any situation in which her life reasonably appears to be in imminent jeopardy, even if later events demonstrate that such appearances were false.

The reader should appraise these competing arguments, and their practical effects, while considering the specifics of the justification defenses, as set out in Chapters 18–22.

---

[34] Greenawalt, Note 7, *supra*, at 1905.

§ 17.05   JUSTIFICATION v. EXCUSE: WHY DOES IT MATTER?[35]

[A]   In General

Why should the legal profession care about the conceptual differences between justification and excuse defenses, if they both result in acquittal of a defendant? Not everyone believes that the distinctions are sufficiently important to merit close attention. The drafters of the Model Penal Code, for example, were skeptical that they could draw sensible lines between justifications and excuses; and, even if they could, they concluded that the resulting increased complexity of the statutory system would have outweighed the benefits from drawing distinctions.[36]

Advocates of drawing distinctions offer a number of justifications for their position, a few of which are summarized below.[37]

[B]   Sending Clear Moral Messages

The criminal law represents a crude, but nonetheless important, moral compass that can assist people in deciding which of various potential paths they should take in particular circumstances. For example, if a battered woman is considering whether to kill her abusive partner while he is asleep, should the law tell her that her proposed action is justifiable, excusable, or neither?[38] People should take justifiable, rather than wrongful-but-excusable, paths. If the law does not label the paths clearly, the system has failed to provide adequate guidance. Just as importantly, if the justification/excuse distinction is ignored or misapplied, the law may inadvertently express a moral falsity by characterizing improper-but-excusable conduct as proper, or vice-versa. In short, the criminal law ought to send the moral messages we intend to send.

[C]   Providing Theoretical Consistency in the Criminal Law

Appreciation of the justification/excuse distinction can help lawmakers coherently define criminal defenses. For example, as discussed more fully later in the Text,[39] the common law heat-of-passion defense to murder suffers from a lack of proper attention to the justification/excuse distinction: Some elements of the defense are best explained in justificatory terms, while others seem excuse-based. The law is not well-served when a defense is composed of a set of inconsistent — perhaps contradictory — principles.

---

[35] *See* Fletcher, Note 1, *supra*, at 664–70, 759–69; Berman, Note 1, *supra*; Gabriel J. Chin, *Unjustified: The Practical Irrelevance of the Justification/Excuse Distinction*, 43 U. Mich. J.L. Reform 79 (2009); Dressler, Note 1, *supra*; Dressler, Note 3, *supra*; Fletcher, *Intolerable Prison Conditions*, Note 7, *supra*; Greenawalt, Note 7, *supra*; Robinson, Note 3, *supra*.

[36] American Law Institute, Comment to art. 3, at 2–4.

[37] *See also* § 17.04, *supra*.

[38] *See* § 18.05[B], *infra*.

[39] *See* § 31.07[C], *infra*.

[D] Accomplice Liability

Suppose that *D* wishes to perform conduct A. *D* needs assistance to do so, so she turns to *X* for aid. If *X* assists, what is *her* criminal responsibility? If conduct A is justified, *D* has acted properly. *X*, therefore, should be acquitted as she is an "accomplice" in the commission of a justified — lawful — act.[40] Thus, if *X* provides *D* with a gun used to kill *V* in justifiable self-defense, *X* should be guilty of no crime.

Suppose, however, that *D* kills *V* due to an insane delusion. *X*, who is sane, assists *D* by providing the gun used in the killing. Although *D* may be acquitted on the basis of insanity, no logical reason precludes the conviction of *X* for the murder in which she sanely assisted. After all, a wrongful act has occurred, *i.e.*, the death of *V*. The fact that *D* is relieved of responsibility due to mental illness should not bar conviction of a sane person who assists in the wrongful act. As one court has explained, "[b]ecause excuses relate to a condition that is peculiar to the actor, such defenses are generally considered to be non-delegable and, thus, unavailable to an accomplice."[41]

[E] Third Party Conduct

Generally speaking, justifications are universalized, whereas excuses are individualized.[42] That is, if *D* is *justified* in performing act A to protect her own rights, a third person, *X*, is also justified in doing A to protect *D*. An *excuse*, however, may only be invoked by the individual who suffers from the excusing condition.

In some cases this generalization works easily and straightforwardly. For example, if *D* is justified in killing *V*, an aggressor, in self-defense, it would ordinarily follow that *X*, an onlooker, is justified in killing *V* in order to save *D*. On the other hand, if *D* is only excused in killing *V*, *e.g.*, if *D* is insane, no right attaches to *X* to kill *V*.

Some cases are more difficult to resolve. Consider the case of a person who kills a morally innocent aggressor in self-defense.[43] Assume *V*, a very young child (a child too young to understand the consequences of her actions) points a loaded gun at *D* under circumstances in which *D* realizes that her life is in imminent jeopardy and that the only way to protect herself is to take *V*'s life. If *D* kills *V*, *D* will be acquitted, but should her defense be treated as one of justification or excuse? She

---

[40] United States v. Lopez, 662 F. Supp. 1083 (N.D. Cal. 1987), *aff'd*, 885 F.2d 1428 (9th Cir 1989).

[41] Taylor v. Commonwealth, 521 S.E.2d 293, 297 (Va. Ct. App. 1999), *aff'd*, 537 S.E.2d 592 (Va. 2000).

[42] *See* Fletcher, Note 1, *supra*, at 810–13. Some commentators believe that this proposition, although generally accurate, is not true in all circumstances or would lead to undesirable conclusions if it were followed without exception. *See* Dressler, Note 3, *supra*, at 95–98; Greenawalt, Note 7, *supra*, at 1915–16.

[43] *See generally* Fletcher, Note 13, *supra*; Mordechai Kremnitzer, *Proportionality and the Psychotic Aggressor: Another View*, 18 Israel L. Rev. 178 (1983); Jeff McMaham, *Self-Defense and the Problem of the Innocent Attacker*, 104 Ethics 252 (1994); Michael Otsuka, *Killing the Innocent in Self-Defense*, 23 Phil. & Pub. Aff. 74 (1994).

is *justified* in killing the youth under the moral-right theory of justification,[44] since her right of autonomy is being threatened. She is *not justified*, however, in killing the youth under the moral-forfeiture doctrine,[45] since the child is too young to know what she is doing and, therefore, has not forfeited her right to life.

Arguably, the legal position of *X*, a stranger who comes upon the situation when *V* is about to kill *D*, depends on the label attached to *D*'s defense. If *D* is justified in killing *V*, it would seemingly follow from the universalization premise[46] that *X* is also justified in killing *V* to save *D*. If *D* is merely excused in killing *V*, however, *X* could be convicted if she killed the youth, unless *X* demonstrates some excuse personal to her.

[F] Retroactivity

Suppose that φ constitutes a defense (*e.g.*, self-defense or insanity) when *D* acts, but that the defense is repealed before *D*'s trial. Should *D* be entitled to assert φ as a defense at her trial? The answer arguably should depend on whether φ was a justification or excuse defense.

D should be entitled to raise any justification defense legally recognized at the time of her conduct. A justification defense defines conduct that society wishes to encourage or, at least, permit. People should be allowed to rely on these representations when they act. To deny *D* the opportunity at trial to justify her conduct on the basis of the subsequently-repealed defense (*e.g.*, self-defense) would be unjust and counter-utilitarian.

It is submitted that the same cannot be said for excuses. Excuse defenses are not directives to would-be actors regarding the permissibility of particular conduct; excuses identify the circumstances under which a person ought to be relieved of criminal responsibility for her conduct because she is undeterrable or is not morally to blame for her wrongful conduct. Any person who investigates excuse law and relies on it *before* she acts, however, is not the type of person to whom the excuses are meant to apply. Therefore, to the extent that retroactivity principles are based on conceptions of justifiable reliance, it is fair to deny her the opportunity to raise a repealed excuse (*e.g.*, insanity).

[G] Burden of Proof

As a matter of constitutional law, a legislature may allocate to the defendant the burden of persuasion regarding any justification or excuse defense.[47] Conceptually, however, a plausible case can be made for the proposition that the government should carry the burden of persuasion regarding justification defenses, but that the defendant should be required to persuade the factfinder regarding excuses.

---

[44] *See* § 17.02[D], *supra*.

[45] *See* § 17.02[C], *supra*.

[46] *But see* Note 42, *supra*.

[47] *See* § 7.03[B], *supra*.

The theory behind this distinction would proceed as follows. The prosecutor is allocated the burden of persuasion regarding the elements of a crime because nobody should be punished if a reasonable doubt exists whether the defendant has committed an unlawful act. Justified conduct, in turn, is conduct that society has determined is desirable or, at least, permissible. In short, it is lawful conduct. If the defendant is allocated the burden of persuasion regarding a justification, she may be punished although the jury is not satisfied beyond a reasonable doubt that she has done anything wrong.

In contrast, with excused conduct, all of the elements of the crime have been proven *and* it has been determined that the conduct was unjustifiable. Under these circumstances, it is fair to expect the defendant to persuade the jury that she is not to blame for her wrongful conduct.

Chapter 18

SELF-DEFENSE

§ 18.01 GENERAL PRINCIPLES

[A] Overview

Every state in the United States recognizes a defense for the use of force, including deadly force, in self-protection. Abolition of the defense — "thereby leaving one a Hobson's choice of almost certain death through violent attack now or statutorily mandated death [or life imprisonment] through trial and conviction of murder later"[1] — seems impossible to imagine. Indeed, if a state legislature *were* to abolish the defense of self-defense, it would likely violate the United States Constitution.[2]

Most issues regarding the application of defensive force arise in the context of homicide and attempted murder prosecutions. Therefore, this chapter focuses primarily on the question of when *deadly* force may be used in self-defense.

[B] Elements of the Defense

At common law, a non-aggressor is justified in using force upon another if he reasonably believes such force is necessary to protect himself from imminent use of unlawful force by the other person.[3] Specifically, however, *deadly* force is only justified in self-protection if the actor reasonably believes that its use is necessary to prevent imminent and unlawful use of *deadly* force by the aggressor.[4]

These principles are subject to substantial clarification, as discussed in the next chapter section. However, it should be noted at the outset that the defense of self-defense, as is the case with other justification defenses, contains: (1) a "necessity"

---

[1] Griffin v. Martin, 785 F.2d 1172, 1186 n.37 (4th Cir.), *aff'd en banc and opinion withdrawn,* 795 F.2d 22 (4th Cir. 1986).

[2] *See* District of Columbia v. Heller, 554 U.S. 570 (2008) (holding that the Second Amendment to the United States Constitution provides an individual the right to possess a firearm, and to use that weapon for traditional lawful purposes, including self-defense within the home); *see also* Eugene Volokh, *State Constitutional Rights of Self-Defense and Defense of Property,* 11 Tex. Rev. L. & Pol. 399, 400 n.2 (2007) (reporting that 44 of the 50 *state* constitutions "secure either a right to defend life or a right to bear arms in defense of self" and, therefore, concluding that "a constitutional right to self-defense is firmly established in American legal traditions").

[3] People v. Dunlap, 734 N.E.2d 973, 981 (Ill. App. Ct. 2000); State v. Gheen, 41 S.W.3d 598, 606 (Mo. Ct. App. 2001).

[4] *E.g.,* United States v. Peterson, 483 F.2d 1222, 1229–31 (D.C. Cir. 1973); State v. Smullen, 844 A.2d 429, 440 (Md. 2004); Commonwealth v. Sepulveda, 55 A.3d 1108, 1124 (Pa. 2012).

component; (2) a "proportionality" requirement; and (3) a reasonable-belief rule that overlays the defense.

[C]   The Necessity Component

The *necessity* rule provides that force should not be used against another person unless, and only to the extent that, it is necessary. One aspect of this requirement — one which is increasingly controversial — is that self-defense is limited at common law to *imminent* threats.[5] Moreover, a person may not use deadly force to combat an imminent deadly assault if some *non*deadly response will apparently suffice. For example, if *V*, an elderly or infirm aggressor, attempts to stab *D*, *D* may not kill *V* if *D* knows or should know that he could avoid death by disarming *V*, or by using *non*deadly force.[6] And, in some jurisdictions, a person may not use deadly force against an aggressor if he knows that he has a completely safe avenue of retreat.[7]

[D]   The Proportionality Component

The *proportionality* rule provides that a person is not justified in using force that is excessive in relation to the harm threatened.[8] Assuming all of the other elements of the defense apply, a person *may* use *non*deadly force to repel a *non*deadly threat; he may also use *non*deadly force against a *deadly* threat (and, in some circumstances may be required to do so, as noted above). However, a person ordinarily is *not* permitted to use *deadly* force[9] to repel what he knows is a *nondeadly* attack, even if deadly force is the only way to prevent the battery. For example, if *V* threatens to strike *D* on a public road, and the only way *D* can avoid the battery is to push *V* into the street in front of a fast-moving car, *D* must abstain and seek compensation for the battery after the fact.

[E]   The "Reasonable Belief" Component

A self-defense claim contains a subjective and an objective component.[10] First, the jury must determine that the defendant subjectively believed that he needed to use deadly force to repel an imminent unlawful attack. Second, the defendant's belief in this regard must be one that a reasonable person in the same situation would have possessed. Notice, however, the implication of the latter component: A defendant is justified in killing a supposed aggressor if the defendant's belief in this regard is objectively reasonable, *even if appearances prove to be false, i.e.*, even if

---

[5] *See* § 18.02[D][1], *infra*.

[6] People v. Riddle, 649 N.W.2d 30, 34 (Mich. 2002); *see* State v. Garrison, 525 A.2d 498 (Conn. 1987) (*V*, intoxicated, moved menacingly toward *G* with a gun in his waistband; *G* disarmed *V*; *V* then pulled out a knife; *G* shot *V* to death; *G*'s conviction was upheld, in part on the ground that *G* knew, or should have known, that he could have disarmed *V* again).

[7] *See* § 18.02[C], *infra*.

[8] State v. Warren, 794 A.2d 790, 793 (N.H. 2002).

[9] For the definition of "deadly force," see § 18.02[A], *infra*.

[10] People v. Watie, 100 Cal. App. 4th 866, 877 (Ct. App. 2002); State v. Clark, 826 A.2d 128, 134–35 (Conn. 2003).

the decedent did *not* represent an imminent threat to the defendant.[11]

On the other hand, the defense is unavailable to one whose self-defense belief, although genuine, was *unreasonable*. In such circumstances, the traditional rule is that the *un*reasonably mistaken actor completely loses his self-defense claim and, therefore, is guilty of murder. An increasing number of jurisdictions, however, now permit an unreasonably mistaken actor to assert an "imperfect" or "incomplete" claim of self-defense, which mitigates the offense to manslaughter.[12]

§ 18.02 DEADLY FORCE: CLARIFICATION OF THE GENERAL PRINCIPLES

As stated in § 18.01, a person who is not the aggressor in a conflict is justified in using deadly force upon another if he reasonably believes that such force is necessary to protect himself from imminent use of unlawful deadly force by the other party. This rule is examined here in detail.

[A] "Deadly Force": Definition

Statutes vary in their definition of the term "deadly force." However defined, it ordinarily applies whether one is describing the force used by the aggressor or the innocent person threatened.

As summarized by one court,[13] some states define the term on the basis of the likelihood that the force will result in death or serious bodily injury.[14] Thus, "deadly force" is, for example, force "likely" or "reasonably expected" to cause death or serious bodily injury. Under this approach, the actor's state of mind in regard to the likely outcome is irrelevant — what matter is, objectively, what is likely to occur.[15] Other jurisdictions include a mental-state element in the definition. Thus, "deadly force" is, for example, force "intended" to cause death or serious bodily injury, regardless of the likelihood of such a result occurring. Other definitions, while including a mental-state element, tie it to the likelihood of a result (*e.g.*, the actor "knew" or "reasonably should have known" that the force used was likely to cause death or serious injury).

---

[11] State v. Simon, 646 P.2d 1119, 1120–21 (Kan. 1982); People v. Goetz, 497 N.E.2d 41, 46–48 (N.Y. 1986); Fresno Rifle & Pistol Club, Inc. v. Van de Kamp, 746 F. Supp. 1415, 1421 (E.D. Cal. 1990). For more discussion of the "reasonable belief" topic, see § 17.04, *supra*.

[12] *See* § 18.03, *infra*.

[13] People v. Vasquez, 148 P.3d 326, 328–29 (Colo. Ct. App. 2006).

[14] Notice: The definition of "deadly force" is broadly defined to include serious bodily injury (or, alternatively, "grievous bodily injury" or "life-threatening injury"), and not just death.

[15] *E.g.*, if D stabs V with a knife, this constitutes "deadly force," even if D only intended to wound V slightly, and regardless of whether V dies from the wounds. On the other hand, applying this definition, a minor battery does not ordinarily constitute deadly force, even if death unexpectedly results. *E.g.*, D, in self-defense against a minor battery, protects himself by lightly pushing V away; V falls and unexpectedly dies. D may successfully claim self-defense because he used force proportional to the threat — he used nondeadly force (force *unlikely* to cause death or serious bodily injury) to repel a nondeadly attack.

[B]   The "Non-Aggressor" Limitation

[1]   Definition of "Aggressor"

An aggressor "has no right to a claim of self-defense."[16] Although there is no universally accepted definition of the term, an "aggressor" has been defined by one court as one whose "affirmative unlawful act [is] reasonably calculated to produce an affray foreboding injurious or fatal consequences."[17] For example, if A unlawfully brandishes a weapon and threatens to kill B, A is *not* justified in defending himself if B responds to A's threats by use of self-protective force.[18]

On the other hand, courts are split on whether words alone can render a person the aggressor. Some courts hold that words by themselves never make the speaker an aggressor.[19] Other courts, however, indicate that words can constitute aggression,[20] although a few jurisdictions explicitly distinguish between merely provocative (insulting) words and threatening words, holding that the latter but not the former can constitute aggression.[21]

Courts frequently state that a person is not privileged to use force to resist an attack unless he is, in essence, "free from fault in the difficulty,"[22] but that is an overstatement.[23] For example, if D asks V, an acquaintance, "how in the world can you be a stupid Yankee fan?" to which V take such umbrage that he pulls out a gun and threatens D with it, V is the aggressor, although D was not entirely free from fault in the conflict.

Three other features of the concept of "aggression" merit brief attention here. First, a person is an aggressor even if he merely starts a *non*deadly conflict. Second, it is *incorrect* to state that the first person who *uses* force is *always* the aggressor.[24] One who unlawfully brandishes a weapon in a threatening manner, but who does not use it, is an aggressor; the person threatened, although he may be the first to use actual force, can still potentially claim self-defense. Third, the issue of whether a

---

[16] Bellcourt v. State, 390 N.W.2d 269, 272 (Minn. 1986); *see* Loesche v. State, 620 P.2d 646, 651 (Alaska 1980) ("The law of self-defense is designed to afford protection to one who is beset by an aggressor and confronted by a necessity not of his own making.").

[17] United States v. Peterson, 483 F.2d 1222, 1233 (D.C. Cir. 1973).

[18] State v. Riley, 976 P.2d 624, 627 (Wash. 1999).

[19] *E.g., id.* at 628, 629 (and citing cases from other jurisdictions).

[20] *E.g.*, State v. Brown, 450 S.E.2d 538, 541 (N.C. Ct. App. 1994) (stating that one is at fault in a conflict if he " 'has provoked a present difficulty by language or conduct towards another that is calculated and intended to bring' about the assault on the defendant") (quoting State v. Crisp, 87 S.E. 511 (N.C. 1916)); *see also* People v. Dunlap, 734 N.E.2d 973 (Ill. App. Ct. 2000) (*D* beat on *V*'s apartment window, threatening *V*; the court noted that "[e]ven the mere utterance of words may be enough to qualify one as an initial aggressor").

[21] *E.g.*, People v. Gordon, 636 N.Y.S.2d 317 (N.Y. App. Div. 1996). For an excellent article on the distinction between being a provocateur and an aggressor, see Kimberly Kessler Ferzan, *Provocateurs*, 7 Crim. L. & Philos. 597 (2013).

[22] United States v. Peterson, 483 F.2d 1222, 1231 (D.C. Cir. 1973).

[23] State v. Corchado, 453 A.2d 427, 433 (Conn. 1982) (stating that "[i]t is not difficult to visualize self-defense situations where . . . there is some fault on both sides.").

[24] State v. Jones, 665 A.2d 910, 913–14 (Conn. App. Ct. 1995).

defendant is the aggressor ordinarily is a matter for the jury to decide, based on a proper instruction on the meaning of the term.[25]

[2]　Removing the Status of "Aggressor"

The initial aggressor in a conflict may purge himself of that status and regain the right of self-defense. The issue always is: Who was the aggressor *at the time the defensive — in this context, deadly — force was used*? In this regard, it is important to distinguish between "deadly" (or "felonious") and "nondeadly" aggressors.

[a]　　Deadly Aggressor

A "deadly" aggressor is a person whose acts are reasonably calculated to produce fatal consequences. The only way such a person may regain the right of self-defense is by withdrawing in good faith from the conflict and fairly communicating this fact, expressly or impliedly, to his intended victim.[26]

This rule is strictly applied. For example, suppose that *D* initiates a deadly attack on *V* in the street, whereupon *V* responds with sufficient force that *D* is now fearful for his own life. If *D* runs behind a parked car, and *V* pursues him, *D* is still not entitled to act in self-defense, unless by actions or words *D* puts *V* on actual or reasonable notice that he no longer is a threat to *V*, *i.e.*, that *D*'s retreat is not simply a temporary strategic act of avoiding *V*'s resistance. In the absence of fair notice to *V* of the termination of the conflict, *D* is guilty of murder if he kills *V* in "self-defense."

[b]　　Nondeadly Aggressor

Suppose that *D* wrongfully attempts to slap *V. V* improperly responds to the threat by pulling out a knife and attempting to kill *D*. In this conflict, *D* was the initial aggressor. On the other hand, *V*'s response was disproportional to *D*'s attack, as he wrongfully converted a minor altercation into a deadly one. Thus, *V* is also an aggressor, indeed, a worse one than *D*. May *D*, therefore, now kill *V* in self-defense?

Case law in these circumstances is not uniform. Some courts provide that when the victim of a nondeadly assault responds with deadly force, the original aggressor immediately regains his right of self-defense, *i.e.*, he is freed of the "aggressor" status.[27] Thus, in the hypothetical, although *D* was the initial aggressor — *and is subject to prosecution, therefore, for the original assault* — he may defend himself (assuming he satisfies the other requirements for self-defense), including by use of deadly force if required.

The other approach is that *D*, the initial nondeadly aggressor, does *not* have an

---

[25] Swann v. United States, 648 A.2d 928, 933 (D.C. 1994).

[26] People v. Watie, 100 Cal. App. 4th 866, 877 (Ct. App. 2002); State v. Miller, 868 So. 2d 239, 243 (La. Ct. App. 2004); State v. Morrow, 41 S.W.3d 56, 59 (Mo. Ct. App. 2001).

[27] *E.g.*, Watkins v. State, 555 A.2d 1087, 1088 (Md. Ct. Spec. App. 1989).

automatic right of self-defense.[28] In these jurisdictions, *D* is not entitled to use deadly force against *V* unless and until he withdraws from the affray by availing himself of an obviously safe retreat, if one exists.[29] If no safe place exists, or if *D* *does* retreat and *V* pursues him, then *D* may resort to deadly force. If *D* does *not* retreat when he obviously could do so, he does *not* lose his status as an aggressor, and is not justified in killing *V*. However, in such circumstances, *D* may be convicted in some jurisdictions of manslaughter, rather than of murder.[30]

The rationale for reducing the offense to manslaughter in such circumstances is not always explained. Frequently, *D*'s manslaughter verdict can be explained on grounds unrelated to self-defense: *V*'s deadly response to *D*'s nondeadly assault constitutes "adequate provocation," which brings *D*'s conduct within the "sudden heat of passion" doctrine of homicide law.[31] Sometimes, however, a court will treat the nondeadly aggressor as possessing an "imperfect" or "incomplete" right of self-defense, which results in the manslaughter conviction.[32]

[C]   Necessity Requirement: The Special Issue of Retreat[33]

[1]   Explanation of the Issue

The general rule is that self-defense "is measured against necessity."[34] Thus, a victim of a deadly attack may only use deadly force in self-protection if it reasonably appears necessary, *i.e.*, he should respond with *non*deadly force if such lesser force will reasonably prevent the threatened harm. Likewise, one may ordinarily only use force when a threat has become imminent, a controversial requirement considered later in the text.[35] At issue in *this* subsection is the question of whether an actor, under attack, must retreat before using deadly force. In other words, if an innocent person is attacked, and if he has only two realistic options — use deadly force or retreat to a place of safety — must he choose the latter option? As discussed immediately below, the law in this area is in flux.

---

[28] *See* American Law Institute, Comment to § 3.04, at 50–51.

[29] Rollin M. Perkins & Ronald N. Boyce, Criminal Law 1128–29 (3d ed. 1982).

[30] *Id.*

[31] *See* § 31.07[B][2], *infra.*

[32] *See* § 18.03, *infra.*

[33] *See generally* Joseph H. Beale, *Retreat from a Murderous Assault*, 16 Harv. L. Rev. 567 (1903); Catherine L. Carpenter, *Of the Enemy Within, the Castle Doctrine, and Self-Defense*, 86 Marq. L. Rev. 653 (2003); Tamara Rice Lave, *Shoot to Kill: A Critical Look at Stand Your Ground Laws*, 67 U. Miami L. Rev. 827 (2013); Jeannie Suk, *The True Woman: Scenes from the Law of Self-Defense*, 31 Harv. J. L. & Gender 237 (2008); Cynthia V. Ward, *"Stand Your Ground" and Self Defense*, 42 Am. J. Crim. L. ___ (2015).

[34] State v. Abbott, 174 A.2d 881, 884 (N.J. 1961).

[35] *See* § 18.02[D][1], *infra.*

[2] Contrasting Approaches

If a person can safely retreat and, therefore, avoid killing the aggressor, deadly force is, objectively speaking, unnecessary. Nonetheless, American jurisdictions are split on the issue of whether an innocent person, outside his home, must retreat when this can be done in complete safety. A majority of jurisdictions today apply a "no retreat" rule: a non-aggressor[36] is permitted to use deadly force to repel an unlawful deadly attack, even if he is aware of a place to which he can retreat in complete safety.[37]

The no-retreat position has gained additional recent support as the result of successful efforts, particularly by the National Rifle Association, to broaden self-defense law.[38] Between 2005 and 2007, "thirty states . . . considered altering their laws on self-defense to replace the retreat element with a right to 'stand your ground.'"[39] Although not all of these states changed their law, by 2010, 27 jurisdictions had significantly expanded the scope of their self-defense provisions, allowing victims of aggression to use deadly force under circumstances that might have subjected them to prosecution for murder under former law.[40]

The rule that a person is not required to retreat is justified on various grounds. First, it is claimed that the law "should not denounce conduct as criminal when it accords with the behavior of reasonable men. . . . [T]he manly thing is to hold one's ground, and hence society should not demand what smacks of cowardice."[41] Second, "Right" should never give way to "Wrong," yet this is what the retreat doctrine demands of those in the right. Third, the no-retreat rule sends a positive, utilitarian message to criminals that they threaten innocent persons at their own risk. As one legislator put it, "[i]t's going to give the crooks second thoughts about carjackings and things like that. They're going to get a face full of lead."[42] Some advocates, as well, have sought to argue that a non-retreat rule provides greater protection to women outside the home, who otherwise might be subjected to serious attack.[43]

---

[36] *Aggressors* who wish to defend themselves *are* required to retreat, even in no-retreat jurisdictions. See § 18.02[B][2], *supra*.

[37] *See* State v. Anderson, 631 A.2d 1149, 1154, 1155 (Conn. 1993) (stating, but rejecting, what it characterized as the majority "no retreat" rule); Wayne R. LaFave, Criminal Law 578 (5th ed. 2010) (describing the no-retreat rule as the majority view, but also indicating there is a "strong minority" position).

[38] Joshua Dressler, *Feminist (or "Feminist") Reform of Self-Defense Law: Some Critical Reflections*, 93 Marq. L. Rev. 1475, 1483 (2010).

[39] P. Luevonda Ross, *The Transmogrification of Self-Defense by National Rifle Association-Inspired Statutes: From the Doctrine of Retreat to the Right to Stand Your Ground*, 35 S.U. L. Rev. 1, 2 (2007).

[40] Lave, Note 33, *supra*; Dressler, Note 38, *supra*, at 1482.

[41] State v. Abbott, 174 A.2d 881, 884 (N.J. 1961).

[42] Robert Tanner, *States Signing on to Deadly Force Law*, Associated Press, May 24, 2006. A recent study casts doubt on this prediction. Cheng Cheng & Mark Hoekstra, *Does Strengthening Self-Defense Law Deter Crime or Escalate Violence? Evidence from Expansions to Castle Doctrine*, 48 J. Human Resources 821 (2013) (showing that the laws do not deter the offenses of burglary, robbery, or aggravated assault, and that there was an 8% increase in the number of murders and non-negligent manslaughters).

[43] This claim is rebutted by Mary Anne Franks, *Real Men Advance, Real Women Retreat: Stand Your Ground, Battered Women's Syndrome, and Violence as Male Privilege*, 68 U. Miami L. Rev. 1099 (2014); Suk, Note 33, *supra*, see also Dressler, Note 38, *supra*, at 1483.

A minority of jurisdictions provide that an innocent person threatened by deadly force outside one's home must retreat rather than use deadly force if he is aware that he can do so in complete safety.[44] Defenders of the retreat rule state that the defense of self-protection — and especially the necessity doctrine — is based on the principle that *all* human life, even that of an aggressor, should be preserved if reasonably possible. The retreat requirement properly places protection of human life above the supposedly "manly" response of standing up to aggression.[45]

Moreover, defenders of the retreat requirement contend that the retreat rule should not increase the risk of harm to innocent persons because retreat is never demanded when it would imperil the would-be defender.[46] Indeed, in retreat jurisdictions, the duty to retreat is not triggered unless there is a place of *complete* safety to which the non-aggressor can turn.[47] Furthermore, the issue is not simply whether a place of such safety exists and that a reasonable person would have been aware of its presence: The duty to retreat only exists if the person under siege is *subjectively* aware of its existence.[48] The practical effect of these conditions is that a person under attack rarely is compelled to retreat, especially when the aggressor is armed with a gun: There is almost never a place of complete safety to which one can turn when confronted by a gun; and even when a place of safety exists, the person is apt to be unaware of it because of the attendant excitement of the situation.[49]

[3] The "Castle" Exception to the Retreat Rule

Even in jurisdictions that ordinarily require a person to retreat to a known place of safety before using deadly force, a universally recognized exception — the so-called "castle doctrine" — exists. This doctrine provides that a non-aggressor is not ordinarily required to retreat from his dwelling,[50] even though he knows he could do so in complete safety, before using deadly force in self-defense.[51]

As one scholar has explained,[52] the castle doctrine is justified on two grounds. Sometimes courts view the rule, although used in self-defense cases, as a form of

---

[44] *E.g.*, Wilson v. State, 7 A.3d 197, 203 (Md. 2010); People v. Riddle, 649 N.W.2d 30, 34 (Mich. 2002).

[45] *See* Beale, Note 30, *supra*, at 581 (stating that a "really honorable man . . . would perhaps always regret the apparent cowardice of a retreat, but he would regret ten times more . . . the thought that he had the blood of a fellow-being on his hands").

[46] State v. Gardner, 104 N.W. 971, 975 (Minn. 1905) ("Self-defense has not, by statute nor by judicial opinion, been distorted, by an unreasonable requirement of the duty to retreat, into self-destruction.").

[47] State v. Anderson, 631 A.2d 1149, 1155 (Conn. 1993) (holding that a judge's "retreat" instruction to the jury was erroneous because it failed to include the word "complete").

[48] Redcross v. State, 708 A.2d 1154, 1158 (Md. Ct. Spec. App. 1998).

[49] State v. Abbott, 174 A.2d 881, 884–86 (N.J. 1961).

[50] For purposes of the castle doctrine, the "dwelling" typically includes a porch physically attached to the home, People v. Canales, 624 N.W.2d 439, 442 (Mich. Ct. App. 2000), but not the lobby or common stairway in a person's apartment building, People v. Hernandez, 774 N.E.2d 198, 201–03 (N.Y. 2002). *See also* State v. Marsh, 593 N.E.2d 35, 38 (Ohio Ct. App. 1990) (*M*'s tent at a campground constituted a home, for purposes of the castle doctrine).

[51] Wilson v. State, 7 A.3d 197, 204 n.3 (Md. 2010).

[52] Carpenter, Note 33, *supra*, at 667.

"defense of habitation,"[53] in that the home-dweller is permitted to kill to protect the sanctity of his home, which has been intruded upon. Second, the home, as castle, is viewed as a person's final sanctuary from external attack. Therefore, "[h]aving retreated as far as possible, the actor should not be compelled to leave the sanctuary."[54]

May a person in his home stand his ground, even if the assailant is a co-dweller, with an otherwise equal right to be there? This is a matter of considerable significance, in view of the fact that "[i]n the great majority of homicides the killer and the victim are relatives or close acquaintances."[55] More to the point, many in-home self-defense cases involve a female who needs to defend herself from an abusive domestic partner. As recent courts have increasingly observed, "imposing a duty to retreat from the home may adversely impact victims of domestic violence."[56] Particularly in the case of a battered woman who has attempted to leave her abusive partner — in essence, she has tried to retreat *permanently* from the situation — but has been dragged back home, literally or figuratively, it seems especially unjust to deny her the right of self-defense because she did not retreat *again* from her home, when she would have no such legal duty if her assailant was a stranger in the dwelling.[57]

Many retreat jurisdictions in recent years have grown more sensitive to the problem of domestic violence and have adopted the rule that the assailant's status as a co-dweller is irrelevant, *i.e.*, the innocent person need *not* retreat from the home, even if the aggressor also lives there.[58] The contrary position is that, in the absence of express legislation, a court will not conclude that a "legislature intended to sanction the reenactment of the climactic scene from 'High Noon' in the familial kitchens of this state."[59]

---

[53] *See generally* § 20.03, *infra.*

[54] Carpenter, Note 33, *supra*, at 667; *see also* People v. Aiken, 828 N.E.2d 74, 77 (N.Y. 2005) ("Our contemporary castle doctrine grew out of a turbulent era when retreat from one's home necessarily entailed increased peril and strife . . . . [O]ne should not be driven from the inviolate place of refuge that is the home.").

[55] State v. Shaw, 441 A.2d 561, 566 (Conn. 1981).

[56] Weiand v. State, 732 So. 2d 1044, 1052 (Fla. 1999).

[57] State v. Gartland, 694 A.2d 564, 570–71 (N.J. 1997) (calling on the state legislature to reconsider its retreat rules in this context).

[58] State v. Glowacki, 630 N.W.2d 392, 400 (Minn. 2001) (characterizing the no-retreat rule among co-dwellers as the majority rule).

[59] *State v. Shaw*, 441 A.2d at 566. As Professor Carpenter has observed, these jurisdictions may be especially influenced by the defense-of-habitation, rather than home-as-sanctuary self-defense, rationale of the castle doctrine: These courts "choose to emphasize the shared property interest of the deadly aggressor," rather than "the defender's right of protection in the sanctuary." Carpenter, Note 33, *supra*, at 671.

[D] Nature of the Threat: "Imminent, Unlawful Deadly Force"

[1] "Imminent"[60]

According to the common law, a person who wishes to use force in self-defense must reasonably fear that the threatened harm is imminent.[61] In the context of self-defense, force is said to be "imminent" if it will occur "immediately,"[62] or "at the moment of . . . danger."[63] The danger must be "pressing and urgent."[64] Force is *not* imminent if an aggressor threatens to harm another person at a later time: " 'later' and 'imminent' are opposites."[65] Indeed, even if it seems clear that harm at the hands of another is inevitable, use of force is premature until the threat is immediate.[66]

The common law imminency requirement is controversial. Some scholars advocate its abolition on the ground that it is nothing more than "an imperfect proxy to ensure that the defendant's force is necessary."[67] This argument has gathered greater support and attention in recent years because of society's increased awareness of domestic violence and, in particular, the plight of battered women, who are victims of repeated, seemingly inevitable, but not always imminent, beatings.[68]

According to Professor Richard Rosen, because imminency "serves only to further the necessity principle, if there is a conflict between imminence and necessity, necessity must prevail."[69] Therefore, he reasons, if it is truly necessary for a person, such as a battered woman, to use deadly force before a threat is imminent, she should be justified in doing so, just as the law should *disallow* the use of force, even if harm *is* imminent, if it is *un*necessary. Essentially, the argument here is that the criminal law should apply the "anticipatory self-defense" concept of international law, which provides that a country may act before a threat is imminent "if a targeted country has been victimized by prior attacks and learns more attacks

---

[60] *See generally* Larry Alexander, *A Unified Excuse of Preemptive Self-Protection*, 74 Notre Dame L. Rev. 1475 (1999); Joshua Dressler, *Battered Women and Sleeping Abusers: Some Reflections*, 3 Ohio St. J. Crim. L. 457 (2006); Kimberly Kessler Ferzan, *Defending Imminence: From Battered Women to Iraq*, 46 Ariz. L. Rev. 213 (2004); Whitley R.P. Kaufman, *Self-Defense, Imminence, and the Battered Woman*, 10 New Crim. L. Rev. 342 (2007); Jane Campbell Moriarty, *"While Dangers Gather": The Bush Preemption Doctrine, Battered Women, Imminence, and Anticipatory Self-Defense*, 30 N.Y.U. Rev. L. & Soc. Change 1 (2005); Richard A. Rosen, *On Self-Defense, Imminence, and Women Who Kill Their Batterers*, 71 N.C. L. Rev. 371 (1993).

[61] Ha v. State, 892 P.2d 184, 190 (Alaska Ct. App. 1995).

[62] State v. Norman, 378 S.E.2d 8, 13 (N.C. 1989).

[63] Sydnor v. State, 776 A.2d 669, 675 (Md. 2001).

[64] *Ha v. State*, 892 P.2d at 191.

[65] United States v. Haynes, 143 F.3d 1089, 1090 (7th Cir. 1998).

[66] *Ha v. State*, 892 P.2d at 191.

[67] Alafair S. Burke, *Rational Actors, Self-Defense, and Duress: Making Sense, Not Syndromes, Out of the Battered Woman*, 81 N.C. L. Rev. 211, 271 (2002).

[68] The subject of self-defense in the battered-woman context is considered in detail at § 18.05[B], *infra*.

[69] Rosen, Note 60, *supra*, at 380.

are planned. When a prior aggressor threatens to commit future violence, international law treats the threat as real. So should domestic criminal law."[70]

There may be good reason to enlarge the defense of self-defense. The Model Penal Code provides an alternative that narrowly expands on the common law.[71] Professor Stephen Morse would take the matter further, suggesting that "[i]f death or serious bodily harm in the relatively near future is a virtual certainty *and* the future attack cannot be adequately defended against when it is imminent *and* if there really are *no* reasonable alternatives, traditional self-defense doctrine ought to justify the pre-emptive strike."[72]

Professor Morse's characterization of the use of deadly force as a "pre-emptive strike" — what Professor Moriarty describes as "anticipatory self-defense" — is a valuable one. In some sense, all self-defense cases involve pre-emptive strikes.[73] Seen this way, the issue becomes *how prematurely or anticipatorily* the perceived aggression may be pre-empted. The difficulty is that when one moves away from an imminency requirement to something less — or to *no* temporal requirement of any kind, as some advocate — the risks of error in predicting the future *and* in predicting whether options less extreme than deadly force may be available are greatly enhanced. Weather forecasters predict the future, but "even funnel clouds sometimes turn around, and human beings sometimes defy predictions."[74] Indeed, because humans have the capacity for free choice, humans are less predictable than funnel clouds — there is very little "virtual certainty" about human behavior. One benefit of the imminency requirement, therefore, is that it reduces the risk of unnecessary use of deadly force.

There are two other defenses of the imminency requirement, both of which understand imminence as more than a proxy for necessity. First, according to Professor Kim Ferzan, "[s]elf-defense is uniquely justified by the fact that the defender is responding to aggression. Imminence, far from simply establishing necessity, is conceptually tied to self-defense by staking out the type of threats that constitute aggression."[75] In short, in the absence of imminence there is no aggression, and "we blur the distinction between offense and defense."[76]

Second, the imminence requirement is defended on political theory grounds: "The basic idea is that the state claims a monopoly on force, under which no individual or non-state group is permitted to resort to force without the state's

---

[70] Moriarty, Note 60, *supra*, at 25. *But see* Sanford H. Kadish, *Respect for Life and Regard for Rights in the Criminal Law*, 64 Cal. L. Rev. 871, 880 (1976) (stating the traditional view of the law that "[t]he life of the good man and the bad stand equal, because how a man has led his life may not affect his claim to continued life.").

[71] *See* § 18.06[A], *infra*, for details.

[72] Stephen J. Morse, *The "New Syndrome Excuse Syndrome,"* 14 Crim. Just. Ethics (Winter/Spring 1995), at 3, 12.

[73] Alexander, Note 60, *supra*, at 1477.

[74] Albert W. Alschuler, *Preventive Pretrial Detention and the Failure of Interest-Balancing Approaches to Due Process*, 85 Mich. L. Rev. 510, 557 (1986).

[75] Ferzan, Note 60, *supra*, at 262.

[76] *Id.* at 252.

authorization."[77] This requirement of authorization, which controls the use of violence in society, "rests on the venerable natural law principle . . . that no one should be a judge in his own case; the decision to use force against another person must be made by an objective and disinterested authority."[78] The exception is when "danger is present and immediate, and there is no time to resort to a central authority."

[2] "Unlawful Force"

A person may not defend himself against the imposition of *lawful, i.e.,* justified, force. For example, a robber may not assert self-defense if he shoots and kills his intended robbery victim when the latter responds with force to prevent the robbery.[79] Likewise, reasonable force applied by a police officer in the performance of his duties is justified. Consequently, a citizen may not use deadly force to resist an officer's proper use of force against him.[80]

Conduct that would constitute a crime or a tort is "unlawful," even if the actor could escape conviction or liability by assertion of an *excuse* defense. For example, if *V*, an insane person or an infant, uses unjustifiable force upon another, this constitutes "unlawful force," notwithstanding *V*'s potential excuse claim.

§ 18.03 DEADLY FORCE: "IMPERFECT" SELF-DEFENSE CLAIMS

In general, the defense of self-defense is a full defense, resulting in exoneration of the person acting in self-protection. However, the traditional common law rule is that if *any* of the elements of the defense are missing, the defense is *wholly* unavailable to a defendant,[81] and thus the defendant may be convicted of murder. Various states, however, now recognize a so-called "imperfect" defense of self-defense to murder, which results in conviction for manslaughter.

There are two versions of imperfect self-defense. First, some courts provide that a *nondeadly* aggressor who is the victim of a *deadly* response must retreat to any known place of complete safety before using deadly force; if he fails to do so, his right of self-defense is considered imperfect.[82]

---

[77] Kaufman, Note 60, *supra*, at 354.

[78] *Id.* at 359.

[79] State v. Amado, 756 A.2d 274, 282–84 (Conn. 2000).

[80] However, in the absence of special legislation restricting his rights, a person may defend himself against excessive (and, therefore, unlawful) police force. *See* § 18.05[D], *infra*.

[81] State v. Morris, 22 So. 3d 1002, 1012 (La. Ct. App. 2009) (applying the all-or-nothing rule).

[82] *E.g.*, People v. Amos, 414 N.W.2d 147, 150 (Mich. Ct. App. 1987); State v. McAvoy, 417 S.E.2d 489, 497 (N.C. 1992). *See* § 18.02[B][2][b], *supra*.

Second, many states now provide by case law[83] or statute[84] that one who kills another because he *unreasonably* believes that the factual circumstances justify the killing, is guilty of manslaughter, rather than murder. That is, *D* is guilty of manslaughter if he kills *V* because: (1) *D* unreasonably believes that *V* is about to use deadly force although, in fact, *V* intends no harm or intends only nondeadly harm; or (2) *V* intends to use deadly force, but *D* fails to realize, as a reasonable person, that nondeadly protective force will suffice. In short, "[i]mperfect self-defense consists of the same elements [as "perfect" self-defense], except that the defendant need not have had an *objectively reasonable* belief that he was in . . . imminent danger of death or serious bodily harm . . . , requiring the use of deadly force."[85]

§ 18.04　DEADLY FORCE IN SELF-PROTECTION: RATIONALE FOR THE DEFENSE[86]

[A]　Self-Defense as an Excuse

Although dispute about the matter exists, use of deadly force in self-defense apparently constituted an excuse, rather than a justification, in early English legal history. It is not difficult to appreciate why the use of deadly force in such circumstances is, at least, excusable.

Each of the three non-utilitarian moral theories of excuse outlined elsewhere[87] can explain self-defense as an excuse. First, under the causation theory of excuses, an innocent person is not responsible for the condition that caused him to commit the crime: but for the aggressor's actions, the defendant would not have taken a life. Therefore, the innocent person is not to blame for the killing. Second, a character theorist would point out that it is the aggressor, and not the innocent person acting in self-defense, whose actions manifest a bad moral character.

Third and most plausibly, the choice theory supports an excuse for self-defense. An innocent person figuratively, if not literally, with his back to the wall, lacks a fair opportunity to choose *not* to kill. Moreover, as Blackstone suggested, the common

---

[83] *E.g., In re* Christian S., 872 P.2d 574, 575 (Cal. 1994); Wilson v. State, 7 A.3d 197, 204 (Md. 2010); Young v. State, 99 So. 3d 159, 165 (Miss. 2012); Commonwealth v. Sepulveda, 55 A.3d 1108, 1124–25 (Pa. 2012).

[84] *E.g.,* Kan. Stat. Ann. § 21-3403(b) (2011).

[85] State v. Peterson, 857 A.2d 1132, 1148 (Md. Ct. Spec. App. 2004).

[86] *See generally* George P. Fletcher, A Crime of Self-Defense: Bernhard Goetz and the Law on Trial (1988); Suzanne Uniacke, Permissible Killing: The Self-Defence Justification of Homicide (1994); A.J. Ashworth, *Self-Defence and the Right to Life,* 34 Cambridge L.J. 282 (1975); Kimberly Kessler Ferzan, *Self-Defense and the State,* 5 Ohio St. J. Crim. L. 449 (2008); Claire Oakes Finkelstein, *On the Obligation of the State to Extend a Right of Self-Defense to Its Citizens,* 147 U. Pa. L. Rev. 1361 (1999); George P. Fletcher, *Punishment and Self-Defense,* 8 Law & Phil. 201 (1989); George P. Fletcher, *Proportionality and the Psychotic Aggressor: A Vignette in Comparative Criminal Theory,* 8 Isr. L. Rev. 367 (1973); Sanford H. Kadish, Note 70, *supra*; Whitley Kaufman, *Is There a "Right" of Self-Defense?,* 23 Crim. Just. Ethics, Winter/Spring 2004, at 20; Judith Jarvis Thomson, *Self-Defense,* 20 Phil. & Pub. Aff. 283 (1991).

[87] *See* § 17.03, *supra.*

law "respects the passions of the human mind."[88] Killing in self-defense, therefore, may be "excusable from the great universal principle of self-preservation, which prompts every man to save his own life preferably to that of another."[89] The act of killing another person to save one's own life is nearly instinctual; it represents the "the primary law of nature."[90]

The latter argument can also explain self-defense as an excuse according to individual deterrence principles. One who is threatened with immediate death is not deterrable by the threat of criminal sanction. Therefore, his punishment is inefficacious.

[B]   Self-Defense as a Justification

[1]   Utilitarian Explanations

Killing in self-defense may be socially desirable. A utilitarian may reason that if someone must die in a deadly conflict it is better that the aggressor, whose anti-social nature is manifested by his conduct, is the victim.[91] If it were otherwise, a dangerous person would remain alive and a continuing threat to others unless and until he is taken into custody.

This argument might somewhat overstate the case. Many self-defense homicidal conflicts occur between mutually intoxicated actors, or start with fisticuffs and escalate into deadly affairs. In such self-defense circumstances, therefore, it is hard to argue convincingly that the aggressor is the "bad" or dangerous person, and the defender is the "good" or more socially desirable individual. Matters are often not so clear-cut.

Another utilitarian claim is that the rules of self-defense will function over time to preserve life because the permission to kill provided to innocent people will operate as a sanction against unlawful aggression.[92] At least in a fair number of cases, the aggressor will be deterred by the fear that his intended victim will resist the attack.

The difficulty with this argument is the basis for *excusing* deadly force in self-defense: It is doubtful that *any* rule of self-defense can successfully affect the actions of parties involved in deadly confrontations. Self-preservation is the "primary law of nature." Therefore, what will deter an aggressor from attacking another person is his expectation that the person being assailed will follow the law of nature, irrespective of the law of society.

---

[88] 3 William Blackstone, Commentaries on the Laws of England *3 (1768).

[89] 4 William Blackstone, Commentaries on the Laws of England *186 (1769).

[90] 3 Blackstone, Note 88, *supra*, at *4.

[91] *See* Kadish, Note 70, *supra*, at 882.

[92] Herbert Wechsler & Jerome Michael, *A Rationale of the Law of Homicide: I*, 37 Colum. L. Rev. 701, 737 (1937).

[2] Non-Utilitarian Explanations

Various non-utilitarian theories have been invoked to justify the use of deadly force in self-defense. First, it is said that a defensive killing is justifiable because the aggressor, by his culpable act of threatening an innocent person's life, forfeits his moral right to life.[93] As a result, the aggressor's death constitutes no cognizable social harm.[94]

Second, "[t]he idea of physical security as one of the 'natural rights' of mankind has a long history."[95] Consequently, when an aggressor "breaches an implicit contract among autonomous agents . . . to respect the living space of all others,"[96] he creates a "state of war" between himself and the person wrongfully threatened,[97] which justifies the innocent person vindicating his autonomy by taking the aggressor's life.

A third rationale of self-defense is that the right of an innocent person to life is morally superior to an aggressor's right to life. Therefore, by balancing moral interests, the safety of the innocent person represents the greater moral good; the aggressor's death is the lesser social evil.[98] Ultimately, however, this argument returns to the principle of forfeiture: Ordinarily, human beings are deserving of equal protection, so this theory only makes sense if the aggressor's interest in life is, at least partially, forfeited by his culpable conduct.

Fourth, self-defense is sometimes justified as a form of private punishment of a wrongdoer, in which the individual being threatened "acts in the place of the state in inflicting on wrongdoers their just deserts."[99] Self-defense as punishment "avoid[s] the injustice of suffering unsanctioned crime."[100]

---

[93] *E.g.*, Ashworth, Note 86, *supra*, at 283; Kadish, Note 70, *supra*, at 883.

[94] For criticisms of the forfeiture doctrine, see § 17.02[C], *supra*.

[95] Ashworth, Note 86, *supra*, at 282.

[96] Fletcher, *Proportionality and the Psychotic Aggressor*, Note 86, *supra*, at 380.

[97] John Locke, Second Treatise of Civil Government: An Essay Concerning the True Original, Extent, and End of Civil Government 23 (DeKoster ed., 1978).

[98] Of course, a *utilitarian* balancing of social interests is also possible, as is discussed in subsection [1], *supra*.

[99] Fletcher, A Crime of Self-Defense, Note 86, *supra*, at 27–28.

[100] Fletcher, *Punishment and Self-Defense*, Note 86, *supra*, at 215.

§ 18.05 SELF-DEFENSE: SPECIAL ISSUES

[A] The Reasonable-Belief Standard: More Reflections About the "Reasonable Person"[101]

[1] The Issue

The law of self-defense represents a compromise. The right of self-defense is not based on objective reality (*i.e.*, whether the person about to be killed represents a real threat to the life of the actor), but neither is it based solely on the actor's subjective impressions. A person may only defend himself if he subjectively believes that deadly force is required *and* a reasonable person would also believe that it is appropriate under the circumstances. The crux of the issue is this: who is the "reasonable person" to whom the defendant is compared? Or, put slightly differently: to what extent should courts permit juries, as factfinders, to incorporate the defendant's own characteristics or life experiences into the "reasonable person" standard?[102]

Consider in this regard two controversial self-defense cases. In *People v. Goetz*,[103] *G* shot and wounded four African-American youths on a New York City subway after one or two of them approached him and requested five dollars. *G*, a prior mugging victim, claimed that he shot the youths because he believed that their request for money was a precursor to an armed robbery. At his trial,[104] *G* claimed that a reasonable person would have believed, as he did, that deadly force was necessary to repel impending use of deadly force by the youths. Among the

---

[101] *See generally* Cynthia Lee, Murder and the Reasonable Man: Passion and Fear in the Criminal Courtroom (2003); Jody D. Armour, *Race Ipsa Loquitur: Of Reasonable Racists, Intelligent Bayesians, and Involuntary Negrophobes*, 46 Stan. L. Rev. 781 (1994); Stephen P. Garvey, *Self-Defense and the Mistaken Racist*, 11 New Crim. L. Rev. 119 (2008); Mark Kelman, *Reasonable Evidence of Reasonableness*, 17 Critical Inquiry 798 (1991); V. F. Nourse, *A Comment on Switching, Inequality, and the Idea of the Reasonable Person*, 2 Ohio St. J. Crim. L. 361 (2004); Kenneth W. Simons, *Self-Defense, Mens Rea, and Bernhard Goetz*, 89 Colum. L. Rev. 1179 (1989); Richard Singer, *The Resurgence of Mens Rea: II — Honest but Unreasonable Mistake of Fact in Self Defense*, 28 B.C. L. Rev. 459 (1987); Michael Vitiello, *Defining the Reasonable Person in the Criminal Law: Fighting the Lernaean Hydra*, 14 Lewis & Clark L. Rev. 1435 (2010); Peter Westen, *Individualizing the Reasonable Person in Criminal Law*, 2 Crim. L. & Phil. 137 (2008). *See also* §§ 10.04[D][2][d], *supra* ["initial observations" on the topic] and 31.07[B][2][ii.], *infra* [the issue in regard to the provocation doctrine in manslaughter cases], and the cites therein.

[102] Some scholars believe that this is a false issue. Professor Victoria Nourse has asked the "near-heretical question: Would we really lose so much if we were to eliminate the reasonable person" from the law? Nourse, Note 101, *supra*, at 371. She contends that much of the debate — for example, whether a "reasonable woman," "reasonable man," or "reasonable person" standard should be used in particular cases — "is a bit of a diversion," *id.*, and that the law ought to "eliminate the implied metaphor of personhood." *Id.* at 373. For an exposition of Professor Nourse's position, see *id.*; V.F. Nourse, *Self-Defense and Subjectivity*, 68 U. Chi. L. Rev. 1235 (2001); and Victoria Nourse, *After the Reasonable Man: Getting over the Subjectivity/Objectivity Question*, 11 New Crim. L. Rev. 33 (2008).

[103] 497 N.E.2d 41 (N.Y. 1986).

[104] *G* originally claimed that his indictment was invalid because the prosecutor instructed the grand jurors to measure the accused's actions against an objective standard. According to *G*, the question under New York law was simply whether he, *G*, subjectively believed that he acted reasonably. The New York Court of Appeals rejected this argument.

questions that one may pose about the "reasonable person" in this case are: (1) Is the "reasonable person," like *G*, a prior mugging victim?; (2) Is the "reasonable person" an experienced New York subway user?; and (3) To what extent would a "reasonable person" consider the race, age, sex, body language, and/or wearing apparel of the victims in determining whether deadly force was necessary?

In the second case, *State v. Wanrow*,[105] *W*, a 5'4" woman with a broken leg and using crutches, killed *V*, a large and visibly intoxicated man, in her home. Although *V* did not menace *W* at the moment of the shooting, *W* suspected *V* of a prior attempted sexual molestation of her son. Furthermore, a neighbor girl had identified *V* as the man who had molested her, and *W* had previously been told that *V* was a former inmate of a mental institution. At trial, the judge instructed the jury on self-defense, but used the male pronoun "he" in describing the circumstances under which deadly force could properly be used. Among the questions that one may pose in this case are: (1) Is the "reasonable person" male or female?; (2) Is (s)he diminutive and on crutches?; and (3) What knowledge or beliefs would (s)he possess regarding *V*'s background?

These cases pose difficult problems for the law. For example, the traditional description of the "reasonable person" is in male — "reasonable *man*" — terms.[106] Yet, such an approach to self-defense is unfair when the defender is a small woman and the aggressor is a large man, as in *Wanrow*. The effect of a "reasonable man" instruction, if taken literally by a jury, is that a woman in *W*'s situation would be held to the standard of a person whose size, weight, strength, and experience in combat exceeds her own. A strong male, for example, might be able to repel an attack with nondeadly force under circumstances in which a woman might be unable to protect herself except by use of a deadly weapon.[107] Therefore, at first (and, perhaps, later) glance, it seems fairer to test a woman's conduct by the standards of a "reasonable woman." On the other hand, some women are taller, stronger, and better able to defend themselves than some men. Is it fair to hold a diminutive and weak man who lacks self-defense skills to the standard of a "reasonable man," if the latter standard assumes that all males are tall, strong, and experienced in combat?

On rare occasions, a court has permitted near-total subjectivization of the "reasonable person." For example, according to one court, the "accused's actions are to be viewed from the standpoint of a person whose mental and physical characteristics are like the accused's and who sees what the accused sees and knows what the accused knows."[108] Another court has stated that since "guilt is personal, . . . the conduct of an individual is to be measured by that individual's equipment mentally and physically. He may act in self-defense, not only when a reasonable person would so act, but when one with the particular qualities that the individual

---

[105] 559 P.2d 548 (Wash. 1977).

[106] In light of the subordinate position of women in early Anglo-American society, it is unrealistic to assume that the common law used the gender-specific term "man" in a gender-neutral sense.

[107] *State v. Wanrow*, 559 P.2d at 558 (footnote omitted) ("In our society women suffer from a conspicuous lack of access to training in and the means of developing those skills necessary to effectively repel a male assailant without resorting to the use of deadly weapons.").

[108] State v. Leidholm, 334 N.W.2d 811, 818 (N.D. 1983).

himself has would so do."[109] Under such a standard, a timid, diminutive male would be judged by the standard of a reasonable timid, diminutive male; and a "strong, courageous and capable female" would be judged by the latter standard.[110]

Subjectivization of the standard sometimes seems morally attractive. For example, in *State v. Hampton*,[111] the defendant, out of fear for his life, preemptively used deadly force in a confrontation. He sought to introduce evidence of his "psycho-social history," including the fact that as a 6-year-old boy he had witnessed his mother shoot another person on the way to a bar, later observed her kill the father of three of her children, and was once strung up by his neck by his godfather. Essentially, his argument was that anyone who has experienced as much trauma and violence as he had in growing up would respond differently than the ordinary "reasonable person." Therefore, he should be measured by a standard of one who has lived *his* life.

However, where does such a subjective standard leave the law? Consider *State v. Simon*:[112] *S*, an elderly man, fired a weapon at *V*, a young Asian-American male, although *V* was not acting aggressively. According to trial testimony, *S* was a "psychological invalid" who feared persons of Asian ancestry, and who believed that by virtue of *V*'s racial heritage the young man was an expert in martial arts. If a judge were to instruct the jury to incorporate *S*'s beliefs and mental characteristics into the "reasonable person," it would be inviting the jury to measure him by the standard of a "reasonable psychological invalid who fears Asian-Americans and believes that they are all experts in the martial arts." Is this not equivalent of the oxymoronic standard of the "reasonable unreasonable person," "reasonable racist," or "reasonable mentally ill person"?

It is one thing to take into consideration an actor's physical characteristics in determining how a reasonable person would respond to a physical threat; it is quite another to incorporate the actor's mental or emotional characteristics — perhaps the result of a terrible childhood or some other factor beyond his control — into the "reasonable person." The risk is that the normative message of the criminal law will be lost if the reasonableness of an actor's conduct — if, indeed, "reasonableness" is a proper term to use in this context — is measured by the standard of one who may be unreasonable by nature. At some point, a defendant's real claim is not that he is acting *justifiably*, but rather that he should be *excused* because he has done the best he can given his unusual mental or emotional characteristics.

[2] The Law

The law is undergoing uneven change in this area. In general, the law provides that, in determining whether the defendant's self-protective acts were reasonable, the factfinder should hold the accused to the standard of the "reasonable person in

---

[109] State v. Thomas, 468 N.E.2d 763, 765 (Ohio Ct. App. 1983) (quoting Nelson v. State, 181 N.E. 448 (Ohio. Ct. App. 1932)).

[110] *Leidholm*, 334 N.W.2d at 818; *see also* State v. Wheelock, 609 A.2d 972, 976 (Vt. 1992) ("Our law does not hold a nervous coward and fearless bully to an identical reasonable person standard.").

[111] 558 N.W.2d 884 (Wis. Ct. App. 1996).

[112] 646 P.2d 1119 (Kan. 1982).

the actor's situation." This language derives from the Model Penal Code definitions of the terms "recklessness" and "negligence."[113] As the Commentary to the Code concedes, however, the word "situation" in this context is ambiguous — inevitably and designedly so.[114]

Most courts have rejected the wholesale subjectivization of the "reasonable person" standard.[115] Nonetheless, in the self-defense context, in determining what a reasonable person in the actor's situation or circumstances would believe or do — that is, in comparing the defendant's conduct and beliefs to that of the "reasonable person" — modern juries typically *are* entitled to consider

> more than the physical movements of the potential assailant. . . . [The] terms ["situation" and "circumstances"] include any relevant knowledge the defendant had about that person [the supposed aggressor]. They also necessarily bring in the physical attributes of all persons involved, including the defendant. Furthermore, the defendant's circumstances encompass any prior experiences he had which could provide a reasonable basis for a belief that another person's intentions were to [harm] . . . him or that the use of deadly force was necessary under the circumstances.[116]

Thus, *G*'s prior mugging experience (in *Goetz*) might be relevant in determining the reasonableness of his belief that he was about to be attacked again,[117] and *W* was properly measured by a standard of a woman of her height, weight, strength, and physical handicap (in *Wanrow*). And, applying this standard, as well, a battered woman who uses deadly force against her abusive partner should be held to a standard of a reasonable woman who has experienced the same abuse as the battered woman has experienced.

This standard still leaves many issues open. For example, returning to *Wanrow*, would a reasonable person in *W*'s situation consider *V* a child molester and former resident of a mental hospital, although *W* had no first-hand knowledge of these alleged "facts"? The answer should be that a reasonable person would only consider allegations that are based on reliable information. If this is so, reconsidering *Goetz*, to what extent is it appropriate for the reasonable person in *G*'s shoes to take into consideration the race, age, sex, clothing, and body language of the youths in the subway, in order to measure *their* dangerousness? This remains a difficult and sensitive issue,[118] one that the "designedly ambiguous" standard of the "reasonable

---

[113] *See* § 10.07[B][3], *supra.*

[114] American Law Institute, Comment to § 2.02, at 242; ("[t]here is an inevitable ambiguity in 'situation' "); *id.*, Comment to § 210.3, at 62 ("[t]he word 'situation' is designedly ambiguous").

[115] *E.g.*, People v. Romero, 69 Cal. App. 4th 846, 848 (Ct. App. 1999) (holding that the trial court was correct in refusing to permit expert testimony offered by the defense on "the role of honor, paternalism, and street fighters in the Hispanic culture," because "we are not prepared to sanction a 'reasonable street fighter standard' ").

[116] People v. Goetz, 497 N.E.2d 41, 52 (N.Y. 1986).

[117] This would not be so if *G*'s prior mugging occurred in quite different factual circumstances.

[118] On this subject, see especially the articles by Armour and Kelman, cited in Note 101, *supra.* These articles identify the arguments that a person in *G*'s situation might make at trial. First, *G* could claim that he is a "reasonable racist." That is, he is a "product of a particularly racist subculture that led him to overestimate the risk of violence by young black males." Kelman, Note 101, *supra*, at 804. This

person in the actor's situation" apparently leaves to jurors to resolve for themselves.

[B] Battered Women and "Battered Woman Syndrome"[119]

[1] Issue Overview

Men are more prone to violence than are women.[120] Although the number of women incarcerated has risen in recent years,[121] it is still true that "[w]omen rarely kill" and, to the extent that they do, "[f]emale homicide is so different from male homicide that women and men may be said to live in two different cultures, each with its own 'subculture of violence.' "[122]

When women *do* kill, their target frequently is an abusive husband or domestic partner.[123] In many of these cases, women have sought exculpation by asserting the defense of self-defense, and in the past few decades they have frequently attempted to introduce evidence of so-called "battered woman syndrome" (BWS, for short)

---

argument must fail. Even if G is empirically correct — that his subculture *is* racist — it would defeat the normative message of the criminal law, and would conflict with the fact that self-defense is a justification defense, to treat the "reasonable person" as a racist.

Alternatively, G might claim "that his racial fears rest on a valid factual basis, rather than on a racial basis." Armour, Note 101, *supra*, at 809. That is, it may be that people fitting the victims' description — black young males, dressed in a specific manner, acting in concert — represented a disproportionate threat to New York subway passengers at the time of the events. G might claim that when reasonable people have to make split-second decisions, they take race, gender, age, wearing apparel, and body language into account. Professor Armour contends, however, that a defendant should not be allowed overtly to raise race as a factor, in part because it enhances the risk of racial bias in the jury box.

[119] *See generally* Charles Ewing, Battered Women Who Kill: Psychological Self-Defense as Legal Justification (1987); Cynthia Gillespie, Justifiable Homicide: Battered Women, Self-Defense, and the Law (1989); Lenore E. Walker, The Battered Woman Syndrome (1984); Dressler, Note 60, *supra*; Ferzan, Note 60, *supra*; Kaufman, Note 60, *supra*; Kit Kinports, *Defending Battered Women's Self-Defense Claims*, 67 Or. L. Rev. 393 (1988); Joan H. Krause, *Distorted Reflections of Battered Women Who Kill: A Response to Professor Dressler*, 4 Ohio St. J. Crim. L. 555 (2007); Holly Maguigan, *Battered Women and Self-Defense: Myths and Misconceptions in Current Reform Proposals*, 140 U. Pa. L. Rev. 379 (1991); Sue Osthoff & Holly Maguigan, *Explaining Without Pathologizing, in* Current Controversies on Family Violence (Donilee R. Loseke et al. eds., 2d ed. 2005); Rosen, Note 58, *supra*; Stephen J. Schulhofer, *The Feminist Challenge in Criminal Law*, 143 U. Pa. L. Rev. 2151 (1995).

[120] U.S. Dep't of Justice, Sourcebook of Criminal Justice Statistics Online, http://www.albany.edu/sourcebook/pdf/t31292006.pdf (among single offender criminal homicides in 2006 about which the sex of the offender was known, 86.5% were males).

[121] *See* http://www.bjs.gov/content/pub/pdf/cpus13.pdf (reporting that at yearend 2013, females represented a slightly larger share (18%) of the total correctional population than in 2000).

[122] Laurie J. Taylor, Comment, *Provoked Reason in Men and Women: Heat-of-Passion Manslaughter and Imperfect Self-Defense*, 33 UCLA L. Rev. 1679, 1680, 1681 (1986) (footnotes omitted); *see also* James Q. Wilson & Richard J. Herrnstein, Crime & Human Nature 114 (1985) ("The male and female style of offending was so different even within crime categories that [criminologists] concluded 'that female criminality is a separate and distinct order of criminal behavior.' ").

[123] Although societal attention has focused on the plight of women who are battered by their male partners, some men are victims of recurrent abuse from their female partners. Also, gay men and lesbians are "as likely [as heterosexual couples], proportionally, to encounter violence in their intimate relationships." Denise Bricker, Note, *Fatal Defense: An Analysis of Battered Woman's Syndrome Expert Testimony for Gay Men and Lesbians Who Kill Abusive Partners*, 58 Brook. L. Rev. 1379, 1383–84 (1993).

(also called "battered spouse syndrome")[124] or, more generally, about battering and its effects on the victim.

Battered women cases, and the legal issues that arise in the prosecutions, may be divided into three categories. First, there are "confrontational" homicides, *i.e.,* cases in which the battered woman kills her partner during a battering incident.[125] Most prosecutions fall into this category.[126] The primary issue in these cases is whether the defendant is entitled to introduce history-of-abuse evidence and offer expert testimony regarding the effects of battering.

In a relatively few circumstances, the battering victim has killed her abuser while he was asleep[127] or during a significant lull in the violence (a "nonconfrontational" homicide).[128] Two inter-related legal issues commonly arise in these cases. First, in view of the imminent threat requirement,[129] is the defendant entitled to a jury instruction on self-defense in the absence of proof of some aggressive act by the decedent at the time of the killing? Second, in order to cure any problem raised by the first question, may the defendant introduce BWS or other evidence of the effects of battering in order to show that she *subjectively* and *reasonably* believed that the threat was imminent, or that her actions were necessary, notwithstanding the lack of an immediate threat?

Finally, in a very few cases, the battered woman has hired[130] or importuned[131] a third party to kill her husband, and then pled self-defense at trial. In these cases, the defendant seeks to introduce evidence of BWS in order to show that her response — soliciting a homicide — was reasonable under the circumstances.

---

[124] As discussed more fully below, the term "syndrome" can have the effect of pathologizing the battered woman in the eyes of jurors, so experts are increasingly avoiding this terminology.

[125] *E.g.,* State v. Hundley, 693 P.2d 475 (Kan. 1985) (during a long battering incident, the batterer hit, choked, raped, and threatened to kill *H*; *H* picked up a gun and demanded that the decedent leave; decedent laughed and said, "You are dead, bitch, now," and reached for a beer bottle; *H* closed her eyes and fired the gun, killing the decedent).

[126] In one study of appellate court decisions, 75% of the prosecutions involved confrontational homicides. Maguigan, Note 119, *supra,* at 394–97.

[127] *E.g.,* State v. Norman, 378 S.E.2d 8 (N.C. 1989); State v. Leidholm, 334 N.W.2d 811 (N.D. 1983).

[128] *E.g.,* State v. Gallegos, 719 P.2d 1268 (N.M. Ct. App. 1986) (abuser shot while lying in bed); State v. Peterson, 857 A.2d 1132 (Md. Ct. Spec. App. 2004) (abuser shot while watching television); *see also* State v. Urena, 899 A.2d 1281 (R.I. 2006) (boyfriend not abusive on that occasion, but was drunk and "talking . . . aggressively").

[129] *See* § 18.02[D][1]. As discussed there, some advocates for battered women recommend abolition of the imminency rule. *See also* Chester v. State, 471 S.E.2d 836, 841 (Ga. 1996) (Sears, J., concurring) ("It is incomprehensible to me to permit such severely battered individuals existing in such a deeply troubled state of mind to justifiably use defensive force only when the use or threat of unlawful force against them is in fact 'imminent.' ").

[130] *E.g.,* People v. Yaklich, 833 P.2d 758 (Colo. Ct. App. 1991); State v. Leaphart, 673 S.W.2d 870 (Tenn. Crim. App. 1983).

[131] People v. Erickson, 57 Cal. App. 4th 1391 (Ct. App. 1997) (abused woman solicited son to kill her sleeping husband).

[2]   Jury Instructions on Self-Defense

A trial court must give an instruction on a defense if it determines that a jury reasonably *could* (not necessarily *will*) be persuaded, based on the evidence introduced, that all of the elements of the defense have been proven. In confrontational battered woman cases, an instruction on self-defense is virtually always given, as it should be. In these cases, by the very nature of the confrontation, there are sufficient grounds to support a jury instruction.[132]

In the absence of special evidence — such as evidence relating to BWS, a matter considered immediately below — nearly all courts hold that a jury instruction on self-defense should not be given if no evidence is introduced at the trial of threatening conduct by the abuser at the time of the homicide, *i.e.*, in nonconfrontational circumstances.[133]

But, are there ways around this problem? We turn to that question.

[3]   Evidentiary Issues

[a]   Prior Abuse by the Decedent

Courts do not ordinarily allow a defendant to put the victim of a homicide on trial, because it improperly focuses the jury's attention on the decedent's character, rather than on the events occurring at the time of the homicide. Nonetheless, it is now routine for a court to permit a battered woman to introduce evidence of the decedent's prior abusive treatment of her, in support of her claim of self-defense.[134]

The courts' willingness to allow such evidence is appropriate, especially in those cases in which the decedent's conduct at the time of the homicide was not overtly threatening. A decedent's prior aggressive and violent behavior is relevant to show that the actor reasonably feared deadly force at the decedent's hands on the present occasion.[135] A reasonable person in the abused victim's shoes would surely take into consideration an abuser's prior violence against her, as well as other actions that have been a regular precursor to violence,[136] in determining whether he represents a deadly threat on the present occasion.

---

[132] For example, consider the facts in State v. Hundley, 693 P.2d 475 (Kan. 1985), set out in Note 125, *supra*. A prior victim of domestic violence, in *H*'s shoes, could reasonably have believed that her life was in imminent jeopardy, based on the aggressor's words ("You are dead, bitch, *now*") and actions (reaching for a beer bottle, which could serve as a weapon).

[133] *E.g.*, Ha v. State, 892 P.2d 184 (Alaska Ct. App. 1995); People v. Yaklich, 833 P.2d 758 (Colo. Ct. App. 1991);State v. Stewart, 763 P.2d 572 (Kan. 1988); State v. Norman, 378 S.E.2d 8 (N.C. 1989); *contra* State v. Leidholm, 334 N.W.2d 811 (N.D. 1983) (permitting a jury instruction on self-defense in a non-confrontational circumstance); *see also* State v. Peterson, 857 A.2d 1132 (Md. Ct. Spec. App. 2004) (permitting an instruction for *imperfect* self-defense).

[134] Maguigan, Note 119, *supra*, at 423–24.

[135] *See* People v. Hawkins, 696 N.E.2d 16, 19–20 (Ill. App. Ct. 1998).

[136] State v. Urena, 899 A.2d 1281, 1284–85 (R.I. 2006) (in a case in which the decedent-abuser was drunk but not attacking *U* at the time of her self-defensive actions, *U* testified that when her abusive partner drank alcohol, "everything changes," and that it was often a precursor to the decedent's violent behavior).

[b] Expert Testimony Regarding Battered Woman Syndrome

According to Dr. Lenore Walker,[137] battering relationships go through cycles commencing with comparatively minor incidents of abuse, escalating to the "acute battering incident," followed by a period of time when the abuser expresses contrition and love for the partner, after which the abuse resumes. Dr. Walker also reported that battered women have low self-esteem and suffer from "learned helplessness" as the result of their inability to prevent the abuse. As a consequence of the latter condition, a battered woman is apt to remain in her relationship rather than seek to escape. Once Walker's research became known, defense lawyers in battered-woman homicide cases began to seek out experts to provide BWS testimony, including testimony that the defendant suffered from the condition and acted pursuant to it.

How might BWS evidence be helpful to a battered woman charged with criminal homicide of her batterer? First, such evidence may enhance the defendant's credibility when she testifies about the decedent's prior abuse. Evidence of learned helplessness, for example, is useful in explaining to jurors why the defendant did not leave the abusive relationship. In the absence of such an explanation, especially in a nonconfrontational homicide, jurors may disbelieve the defendant's claim of prior abuse ("if she really was abused, why didn't she leave?"), blame the woman for her plight, and/or conclude that deadly force was unnecessary given the option of escape. Second, in non-confrontational cases, such testimony can help explain why the defendant *subjectively* believed that the decedent was about to kill her even though he was asleep or otherwise passive, and to demonstrate that this belief was *objectively* reasonable to a person suffering from the syndrome.

Today, despite some dissenting scholarly opinion regarding Dr. Walker's research,[138] "battered woman's syndrome has . . . gained general acceptance in the scientific community. . . . Equally compelling is the clear trend across the United States towards admissibility of expert testimony on battered woman's syndrome"[139] in appropriate self-defense cases.[140]

Although BWS evidence is admissible in most battered woman self-defense

---

[137] *See* Walker, Note 119, *supra*, at 75–85; Lenore Walker, Battered Woman 32–51 (1979).

[138] *E.g.*, David L. Faigman & Amy J. Wright, *The Battered Woman Syndrome in the Age of Science*, 39 Ariz. L. Rev. 67 (1997); David L. Faigman, Note, *The Battered Woman Syndrome and Self-Defense: A Legal and Empirical Dissent*, 72 Va. L. Rev. 619 (1986); and Robert F. Schopp et al., *Battered Woman Syndrome, Expert Testimony, and the Distinction Between Justification and Excuse*, 1994 U. Ill. L. Rev. 45.

[139] Rogers v. State, 616 So. 2d 1098, 1098–99 (Fla. Dist. Ct. App. 1993) (footnotes omitted). At least 41 states expressly permit introduction of BWS evidence for some purpose to support a self-defense claim. (This is based on the excellent research of my assistant Lisa Herman (Moritz 2014), whose work for me was and is deeply appreciated.)

[140] A few states have passed legislation expressly providing for the general admissibility of expert testimony "regarding intimate partner battering and its effects, including the nature and effect of physical, emotional, or mental abuse on the beliefs, perceptions, or behavior of victims of domestic violence." Cal. Evid. Code § 1107(a) (2015); *see also* Md. Code Ann., Cts. & Jud. Proc. § 10-916 (2015).

cases, states vary as to the purposes for which it may be introduced.[141] Some courts permit evidence of the syndrome, but do not permit the expert to testify as to whether the defendant suffers from the syndrome or what its effect may have been on the defendant at the time of the homicide.[142] Other courts allow the expert to state an opinion as to whether the defendant *subjectively* believed that deadly force was necessary under the circumstances, but will not allow the evidence to be used to show that her conduct was *objectively* reasonable under the circumstances.[143] Still other courts permit syndrome evidence to assist the jury in determining whether the defendant's perceptions were objectively reasonable.[144]

The proposition that BWS testimony should be admitted to show that the defendant reasonably believed that the decedent was about to kill her is questionable in *nonconfrontational* cases. Seemingly, such expert testimony pathologizes the battered woman in the eyes of the jury: it shows that the defendant suffers from a condition that renders her unable to appreciate objective reality (the reality being that her currently passive, perhaps even sleeping, abuser does *not* represent an *imminent* threat). Indeed, BWS evidence arguably demonstrates the battered woman's abnormal mental condition, which is why courts frequently characterize the battered woman as one "suffering" from battered woman syndrome.[145] As Professor Anne Coughlin has put it, syndrome evidence suggests that "women in battering relationships lose their mental capacity to make rational choices," and the evidence "marks the woman as a collection of mental symptoms and behavioral abnormalities."[146] This evidence might support a claim that the battered woman should be *excused* for her conduct due to her mental condition, or that she is entitled to claim imperfect self-defense (*i.e.*, that she actually but *un*reasonably believed that she was repelling an *imminent* threat), but it arguably should have nothing to do with whether her act of killing her sleeping (or otherwise passive) partner was *justifiable*, under current self-defense law requiring proof of imminency.[147]

The issue as to whether a battered woman's self-defense claim should be

---

[141] *See* Maguigan, Note 119, *supra*, at 429–31.

[142] *E.g.*, People v. Wilson, 487 N.W.2d 822, 825 (Mich. Ct. App. 1992); State v. Hennum, 441 N.W.2d 793, 799 (Minn. 1989).

[143] *E.g.*, State v. Kelly, 478 A.2d 364, 377 (N.J. 1984).

[144] *See, e.g.*, People v. Humphrey, 921 P.2d 1, 8–9 (Cal. 1996); State v. Peterson, 857 A.2d 1132, 1150 (Md. Ct. Spec. App. 2004); Boykins v. State, 995 P.2d 474, 476 (Nev. 2000); State v. Kelly, 685 P.2d 564, 570 (Wash. 1984).

[145] *E.g.*, *Boykins v. State*, 995 P.2d at 476; *see also* State v. Edwards, 60 S.W.3d 602, 614, 615 (Mo. Ct. App. 2001) (describing "reasonable battered woman" as "something of an oxymoron" because a "battered woman is a terror-stricken person whose mental state is distorted").

[146] Anne M. Coughlin, *Excusing Women*, 82 Cal. L. Rev. 1, 71, 76 (1994). Some scholars disagree with the "*abnormal* mental condition" characterization. Kinports, Note 119, *supra*, at 417. Essentially, they believe that the syndrome "is more appropriately understood as a normal response to an abnormally stressful situation." Schopp et al., Note 62, *supra*, at 95 (reporting, but rejecting, this view).

[147] Because of all of these concerns and the belief that syndrome testimony "fails to capture the full experience of battered women," lawyers and researchers now increasingly avoid the "syndrome" label and provide "more comprehensive testimony" about the effects of domestic violence. Osthoff & Maguigan, Note 119, *supra*, at 228–31, 232–37.

characterized as a justification or excuse is not without deep moral and practical significance, as discussed immediately below.

[4]　Nonconfrontational Battered Woman Self-Defense?: Some Reflections

Battered women who kill in confrontational circumstances can assert a relatively traditional self-defense claim. It is worth reflecting, however, on the question of whether a battering victim who kills in *non*confrontational circumstances, or who solicits a third party to kill her abuser, should also be able to claim self-defense (or some newly crafted defense). Notice that this question may be asked independent of BWS. Perhaps a battered woman, *syndrome or no syndrome*, is justified in killing (or obtaining another to kill) her abuser, independent of any traditional imminent-based self-defense claim that might be made. Let's consider this.

A utilitarian might defend the killing of an abuser on the ground that he constitutes an ongoing danger to the woman and, very possibly, to other persons. Therefore, his immediate death results in a net social benefit. However, ultimately, a more socially acceptable utilitarian solution is for society to offer abused persons places of sanctuary from abusers, as well as to devise more efficient mechanisms for bringing abusers to justice. Therefore, at least from a rule-utilitarian perspective — that is, from the perspective of what *rule* will result in the best outcome over the course of time — it seems difficult to justify nonconfrontational homicides.

A non-utilitarian justification for killing the abuser, even when he is not an imminent threat, may be found in the principle of moral forfeiture: As a result of the abuser's ongoing culpable conduct, he has forfeited his right to life. This may have been what Justice Harry C. Martin of the North Carolina Supreme Court had in mind when he said about one abuser, who was killed by his wife while he was asleep:

> By his barbaric conduct over the course of twenty years, [he] reduced the quality of the defendant's life to such an abysmal state that, given the opportunity to do so, the jury might well have found that she was justified in acting in self-defense for the preservation of her tragic life.[148]

Even if the controversial moral-forfeiture doctrine is an otherwise acceptable principle,[149] its application here is troubling. First, in the traditional self-defense context, an aggressor only temporarily forfeits his right to life. If he withdraws from the conflict, or once the aggression is thwarted, his right to protect himself is restored. In the case of the abuser, however, the implication is that the constancy of his immoral conduct renders his right to life constantly (permanently?) forfeited. He becomes fair game for killing day or night, awake or asleep, in ambush or otherwise. Second, the *logic* of the forfeiture position is that the abuser is fair game for killing *by anyone*, at least by anyone who acts for the purpose of protecting the woman's autonomy. Does a battered woman, therefore, have a right to solicit her son[150] or another relative to kill her husband? After all, if the abuser has no right

---

[148]　State v. Norman, 378 S.E.2d 8, 21 (N.C. 1989) (dissenting opinion).

[149]　*See* § 17.02[C], *supra.*

[150]　People v. Erickson, 57 Cal. App. 4th 1391 (Ct. App. 1997).

to life, why should it matter *who* kills him? It is unlikely that many people would want to take the forfeiture doctrine to its logical conclusion.

An alternative rationale for a battered woman defense starts from the principle that "a state that denies the opportunity for self-defense, that asks its citizens to die rather than protect themselves, []creates the . . . fear that citizens will become the slavish victims of the strong."[151] Therefore, it may be argued, an abused woman should be permitted to kill her tormenter whenever the opportunity arises — a pre-emptive strike — in order to protect her natural right of autonomy. This argument, which would justify abolishing the imminency rule (and either replacing it with a different temporal standard, such as that provided by the Model Penal Code, or rejecting any temporal limitation) is considered elsewhere in this chapter.[152]

A different approach to the issue, but one which is criticized by some advocates of abused women, is to provide a full or partial *excuse* to the battered woman who kills her abusive partner, either on traditional grounds of insanity, duress, diminished capacity, or provocation, or by carefully crafting a new excuse defense.[153]

The question of whether a battered woman should be justified or only excused for her actions raises intriguing moral questions, but also practical ones. Suppose that the abused party is about to shoot or set on fire[154] her sleeping husband, when he unexpectedly awakens. What are *his* rights of self-defense at that moment? If she is justified in killing him, the traditional rule would be that he is not justified in killing her because he would be combating an imminent, *lawful* exercise of deadly force. If she is *excused* (partially or wholly) in killing him, however, he would be *justified* in taking her life in self-defense, assuming that the other elements of the defense are satisfied. How we feel about *his* rights, therefore, is linked to the question of how we should characterize *her* situation.

Also, how should we deal with the person who helps her commit the crime, such as a person who, knowing her intentions, provides the abused woman with the gasoline? *His* legal position will likely depend on whether *her* actions are justified or merely excused.[155]

---

[151] Nourse, *Self-Defense and Subjectivity*, Note 102, *supra*, at 1300–01.

[152] *See* § 18.02[D][1], *supra*.

[153] The concern with the excuse theory is that a battered woman's claim should not be demeaned by suggesting that she is sick or "crazy" for killing her abuser. Ironically, there is some evidence that introduction of battered woman syndrome evidence has the very effect of pathologizing the abused woman in the minds of jurors. Regina A. Schuller & Patricia A. Hastings, *Trials of battered Women Who Kill: The Impact of Alternative Forms of Expert Evidence*, 20 Law & Hum. Behav. 167, 169 (1996). For an argument in favor of recognizing an excuse defense that does not run this risk, see Dressler, Note 60, *supra*, (arguing for a duress-type excuse claim).

[154] This was the method of killing by Francine Hughes in a famous battered woman case recounted in an NBC-TV movie, *The Burning Bed*, and in a 1980 book of the same name, written by Faith McNulty.

[155] *See* § 30.06[B][2], *infra*.

[C]   Risk to Innocent Bystanders

Assume that *D* (perhaps a police officer) is justified in killing *V* in self-defense. *D* fires a gun at *V* (perhaps a criminal shooting at the officer) but misses him, instead killing or wounding *X*, an innocent bystander (or perhaps more than one bystander). May *D* use his self-defense right against *V* as a basis of exculpation for the harm he inflicted on *X* (and *Y*)?

Courts have only infrequently confronted this issue and few non-Model Code jurisdictions have statutes dealing expressly with the problem.[156] In general, however, courts apply a transferred-justification doctrine, similar to the transferred-intent rule:[157] That is, a defendant's right of self-defense "transfers" (just as his intent to kill does) from the intended to the actual victim(s).[158]

Not all courts treat this rule as absolute. If the defendant, acting justifiably in self-defense against an aggressor — intending to kill him — fires a weapon "wildly or carelessly,"[159] thereby jeopardizing the safety of known bystanders, some courts may hold the defendant guilty of manslaughter of the bystander, or of reckless endangerment if no bystander is killed, but not of intent-to-kill murder.[160] Some courts, however, provide an absolute defense, even in such circumstances.[161]

From a utilitarian perspective, the right to act in self-defense should not be absolute, at least when a defender's conduct jeopardizes multiple innocent bystanders. If the actor's self-protective behavior creates an unjustifiable risk of death to others, it may be socially desirable for him to choose some less dangerous (albeit less protective) means of defending himself.[162]

A non-absolute rule is also consistent with at least one non-utilitarian rationale of self-defense, namely, the moral-forfeiture doctrine: The death of an innocent bystander is unjustified, because he is not guilty of any culpable act that would merit loss of his life. On the other hand, the absolute rule seems consistent with the "moral right" theory that one has a natural right to protect one's own life, even if innocent people are unintentionally harmed.

---

[156] The Model Penal Code resolution of this issue is discussed at § 18.06[C], *infra*.

[157] *See* § 10.04[A][3], *supra*.

[158] People v. Mathews, 91 Cal. App. 3d 1018, 1023–24 (Ct. App. 1979); Smith v. State, 419 S.E.2d 74, 75 (Ga. Ct. App. 1992); People v. Adams, 291 N.E.2d 54, 55–56 (Ill. App. Ct. 1972).

[159] *People v. Adams*, 291 N.E.2d at 56.

[160] *See id.* (dictum); People v. Jackson, 212 N.W.2d 918 (Mich. 1973).

[161] Commonwealth v. Fowlin, 710 A.2d 1130, 1134 (Pa. 1998) ("[W]e do not share the lower court's concern that random wild self-defense shootings will injure large numbers of innocent people.").

[162] It seems unlikely, however, that such a rule would have any deterrent effect on a person "acting within his instinct for self-preservation." *Id.* Therefore, arguably, a utilitarian would favor *excusing* such an actor.

[D]   Resisting an Unlawful Arrest[163]

Suppose that *V*, a police officer, attempts to arrest *D*. Assume the arrest is unlawful. Therefore, *D* uses force to resist the arrest, and is subsequently prosecuted for the harm caused to *V* by his resistance, *e.g.*, battery or murder. May *D* defend his actions on the ground that he had a right to resist the unlawful arrest?

An arrest may be unlawful for various reasons. First, an arrest is unlawful if the officer uses excessive force in effectuating it. Under common law doctrine, an officer may use only as much force as necessary to make an arrest, and may never use deadly force to arrest a misdemeanant.[164] Therefore, if a police officer uses excessive force in making an arrest, he is to that extent the aggressor, and the citizen is justified in protecting himself. The common law rule here is simple: general self-defense doctrines apply. That is, the victim of excessive police force is entitled to use reasonable force to protect himself, *including deadly force if his life reasonably appears to be in jeopardy.*[165]

Many unlawful arrests, however, do not implicate self-defense concerns. For example, an arrest is unlawful (even if reasonable force is used) if the arresting officer lacks probable cause to believe that the suspect is guilty of the crime for which he is being taken into custody.[166] And, even if an officer has probable cause, he must respect other constitutional and statutory arrest procedures, such as obtaining a warrant to make an arrest in a suspect's home,[167] and knocking and demanding admittance before entering the residence.[168]

The common law rule as to this second type of "unlawful arrest" was that a person could use as much force as reasonably necessary, *short of deadly force*, to resist the illegal arrest.[169] If the arrestee used deadly force, he was potentially guilty of manslaughter, rather than murder.[170] However, there is some question as to whether the manslaughter result applied to all non-excessive-force unlawful arrests or only to those that occurred under particularly provocative circumstances, *i.e.*, in which the arrestee became enraged because he was actually aware of the illegality of the arrest (in which case ordinary provocation rules came into play).[171]

---

[163] *See generally* Paul G. Chevigny, *The Right to Resist an Unlawful Arrest*, 78 Yale L.J. 1128 (1969).

[164] *See generally* § 21.03, *infra*.

[165] *E.g.*, Commonwealth v. French, 611 A.2d 175, 178 (Pa. 1992).

[166] *See* Dunaway v. New York, 442 U.S. 200, 207–08 (1979).

[167] Payton v. New York, 445 U.S. 573 (1980).

[168] Wilson v. Arkansas, 514 U.S. 927 (1995).

[169] *See* People v. Curtis, 450 P.2d 33, 35 (Cal. 1969).

[170] Davis v. State, 102 A.2d 816, 820–21 (Md. 1954).

[171] Chevigny, Note 163, *supra*, at 1129–32 (interpreting early Anglo-American law as requiring provocation); Davis v. State, 102 A.2d at 820–21 (summarizing the contrasting rules). The provocation doctrine in homicide cases is consider in § 31.07, *infra*.

Today, the right to resist an excessive-force arrest remains untrammeled. However, most states by statute[172] or case law[173] have abolished or limited the defense in non-excessive-force circumstances.[174] The argument for retrenchment is that the original reasons for the defense no longer apply. At common law, a person who was unlawfully arrested had little hope for early release. Moreover, jail conditions were harsh; death from disease and maltreatment in jails were not uncommon. When these evils were balanced against the social harm of a battery upon an officer, resistance could be viewed as justifiable.

Today, the balancing process supposedly results in a different conclusion. Jail conditions, although harsh, "are no longer the pestilential death traps"[175] of old. Moreover, pre-trial release is somewhat easier to obtain than it was centuries ago, and the lawfulness of an arrest can now be determined comparatively rapidly (usually within 48 hours), so that the extent of wrongful incarceration is reduced. Finally, it is much more difficult today than it was in the past to successfully resist an unlawful arrest without using deadly force. In light of these changes, it may be preferable for the arrestee to forego all resistance, even the non-deadly variety, and seek post-custodial remedies.

These arguments for abandonment of the common law rule apply if the defense is perceived to be a justification defense, based on a balancing of utilities. Under non-utilitarian analysis, however, the case for retention of the defense is stronger. It may be argued that a person should be permitted to use non-deadly force to protect his natural right of autonomy. This right is no less applicable today than it was centuries ago.

Moreover, perhaps the common law defense (in non-excessive-force cases) should be treated as an excuse, rather than a justification. That is, the "right" to resist unlawful arrests may be a misnomer; perhaps the underlying basis for the rule should be that when one is patently mistreated by government officials, he is apt to become enraged, and that his response (expressed in the form of nondeadly resistance to the arrest) is morally blameless under the circumstances.

---

[172] *E.g.*, Cal. Penal Code § 834a (Deering 2015) (abolishing the defense).

[173] State v. Wright, 162 S.E.2d 56, 62 (N.C. Ct. App.), *aff'd*, 163 S.E.2d 897 (N.C. 1968) (no defense if the officer is acting under authority of a warrant, even if it is defective or irregular in some respect); State v. Valentine, 935 P.2d 1294 (Wash. 1997) (a person may not use force if he is faced only with a loss of freedom).

[174] *State v. Valentine*, 935 P.2d at 1302 (stating that, in 1997, only 20 states recognized a defense).

[175] *Id.* at 1301.

§ 18.06   MODEL PENAL CODE

[A]   General Rules

[1]   Force, in General

[a]   Permissible Use

Subject to various limitations, a person is justified in using force upon another person if he believes that such force is immediately necessary to protect himself against the exercise of unlawful force[176] by the other individual on the present occasion.[177] (Special issues relating to use of *deadly* force in self-protection are considered in subsection [2])

This rule diverges from the common law in two noteworthy ways. First, it is drafted in terms of the actor's subjective belief in the need to use force; his belief need not be reasonable. However, nearly all of the Code justification defenses, including the defense of self-protection, are modified by Section 3.09, which re-incorporates a reasonableness component, although not in the fashion of the common law. This feature of the Code is discussed in subsection [B] below.

Second, and quite significantly, the Code substitutes the phrase "immediately necessary . . . on the present occasion," for the common law imminency requirement. This shift in language authorizes self-protective force sooner than may be allowed at common law. This is because the issue under the Code is *not* how soon the aggressor's force will be used, but rather whether the innocent person's *need* to use defensive force exists immediately. For example, suppose that V, an abusive husband, tells D, his wife, while they are in the kitchen, that he is going to the bedroom to get a gun and kill her. In response, V picks up a kitchen knife and, when V turns his back on her to go to the bedroom to obtain the gun, she stabs him to death. Under traditional common law principles, D's self-defense claim would likely fail because V did not yet represent an imminent threat: he is unarmed; therefore, she would likely have to wait until he returned with the weapon. In contrast, under the Code, D's self-defensive act of stabbing V in the back would be justifiable, if she believed that she could not afford to wait until V returned with the weapon — *i.e.*, that force was *immediately* necessary.[178]

---

[176] The Model Penal Code definition of "unlawful force" (§ 3.11(1)) is cumbersome. The definition, however, does not appreciably differ from the meaning accorded to the phrase at common law. *See* § 18.02[D][2], *supra*. One difference, however, is that "force" under the Code includes "confinement." That is, if the other provisions of the defense are met, a person may use force to resist an unlawful effort to imprison him, even if he is aware that the imprisoner will not touch him in order to confine him. For example, D may use force to prevent V from unlawfully locking him in a room.

[177] Model Penal Code § 3.04(1).

[178] *See* American Law Institute, Comment to § 3.04, at 39–40. It must be remembered, however, that if her belief in this regard was wrong, her mistake-of-fact could partially undermine her defense. *See* § 18.06[B], *infra*.

[b]   Impermissible Use: Resisting an Unlawful Arrest

In a departure from common law principles but in accord with the modern trend, a person may not use force to resist an arrest that he knows is being made by a police officer (thus, arrests by undercover officers do not apply), even if the arrest is unlawful (*e.g.*, without probable cause).[179] However, this rule, which was opposed by a substantial minority of the members of the American Law Institute,[180] does *not* prohibit use of force by an arrestee who believes that the officer intends to use excessive force in effectuating the arrest.[181]

[2] Deadly Force, in General

[a]   "Deadly Force": Definition

Section 3.11, subsection (2), of the Code provides that "deadly force" is force used for the "purpose of causing or that [the actor] knows to create a substantial risk of causing death or serious bodily injury." The section expressly provides that the act of purposely firing a gun in the direction of a person or of a vehicle that the actor believes is occupied constitutes "deadly force." However, courts applying the Code have generally held that a mere threat (without the purpose) to cause death or serious injury to another is not "deadly force," even if the actor brandishes a weapon to back up his spurious threat.[182]

[b]   Permissible Use

Deadly force is unjustifiable unless the actor believes that such force is immediately necessary to protect himself on the present occasion against: (1) death; (2) serious bodily injury; (3) forcible rape; or (4) kidnapping.[183]

The first three categories in which deadly force may be used are not problematic. The provision regarding kidnapping, however, is controversial. As the Commentary concedes,[184] the appropriateness of its inclusion in the Code will depend on how kidnapping is defined by state law. A kidnapping need not involve a threat of death or great bodily injury to the kidnap victim, for example, when a parent abducts a child from the custody of another parent. In such circumstances, deadly force would be a disproportional (yet, under the Code, permissible) response.

---

[179] Model Penal Code § 3.04(2)(a)(i).

[180] For a summary of the minority's position, see American Law Institute, Comment to § 3.04, at 43.

[181] *Id.*

[182] State v. Moore, 729 A.2d 1021, 1027 (N.J. 1999) (and cases cited therein).

[183] Model Penal Code § 3.04(2)(b).

[184] American Law Institute, Comment to § 3.04, at 48.

[c]   Impermissible Use

Even if deadly force is otherwise permitted, as described immediately above, the Code prohibits its use in two key circumstances.

[i]   Deadly Force by Aggressors

The Code prohibits the use of deadly force by a person who, "with the purpose of causing death or serious bodily injury, provoked the use of force against himself in the same encounter."[185] This concept of aggression is narrower than the common law version because it does not include within its scope the "nondeadly aggressor," *i.e.*, the actor who provokes a *non*deadly conflict. Therefore, in a Model Code jurisdiction, if *D* unlawfully starts a *non*lethal conflict, he does not lose his privilege of self-defense if *V* escalates it into a lethal assault.

It should be observed that an actor only loses his privilege to use deadly force in self-protection if he is the aggressor "in the same encounter." That is, if *D* unlawfully commences a deadly assault upon *V*, he may regain the right of self-protection if he breaks off the struggle, and *V* continues to threaten him. In these circumstances, *V*'s threat is viewed as a "distinct engagement."[186]

[ii]   Retreat

The Code comes down on the side of those who favor retreat. A person may not use deadly force against an aggressor if he "knows that he can avoid the necessity of using such force with complete safety by retreating."[187] As a result of policy disagreements among members of the American Law Institute and subsequent compromising,[188] the retreat rule is subject to various exceptions and counter-exceptions.[189] The most significant exception is that, as in common law retreat jurisdictions, retreat is not necessary if the actor would have to retreat from his home, or even from his place of work.

This exception, however, is subject to its own exception, which is that retreat from the home or office *is* required: (1) if the actor was the initial aggressor, and wishes to regain his right of self-protection; or (2) even if he was not the aggressor, if he is attacked by a co-worker in their place of work. However, the Code does not require retreat by a non-aggressor in the home, even if the assailant is a co-dweller, a result beneficial to a battering victim involved in a domestic dispute.[190]

[iii]   Summarizing the MPC Deadly-Force Rules

The Code's deadly-force rules add up to this. First, if *D* did not start the unlawful conflict, he may use deadly force against *V* if he believes that such force is

---

[185] Model Penal Code § 3.04(2)(b)(i).

[186] American Law Institute, Comment to § 3.04, at 52.

[187] Model Penal Code § 3.04(2)(b)(ii).

[188] *See generally* American Law Institute, Comment to § 3.04, at 52–57.

[189] *See* Model Penal Code § 3.04(2)(b)(ii).

[190] *See* § 18.02[C][3], *supra*.

immediately necessary on the present occasion to combat an unlawful deadly assault by *V*, assuming one of the following circumstances exists: (1) *D* has retreated, and *V* continues to pursue him; (2) *D* knows of no safe place to retreat; or (3) even if *D* could have retreated, if *D* is in his home or place of work, and *V* is not in his place of work.

Second, if *D* *did* start the unlawful conflict but did so with*out* the purpose of provoking a deadly conflict — *e.g.*, he lightly struck *V*, but *V* escalated matters by menacing *D* with a knife — *D* may still use deadly force in all of the circumstances noted above. *D* may be prosecuted, however, for the initial unlawful assault or battery that commenced the conflict.[191]

Third, *D* may *not* kill *V* in self-defense if he started the conflict with the intent to cause death or great bodily harm, unless he withdraws from the conflict. If he does so, *D*'s privilege to kill is restored, although he may be charged with a crime pertaining to the initial acts that commenced the conflict.

[B]　Mistake-of-Fact Claims and Model Penal Code Justification Defenses[192]

As previously explored, the common law rule is that a person is justified in acting on the basis of reasonable, albeit erroneous, appearances.[193] A common law justification defense is not available, however, to one who acts on the basis of an unreasonable belief, although some states recognize an "imperfect" defense in such circumstances.[194]

The Model Penal Code recognizes an imperfect defense, but it takes a two-step process to get to this point. Initially each justification defense dealing with the use of defensive force is defined *solely* in terms of the defendant's subjective belief in the necessity of using the force, or in terms of his subjective belief regarding other circumstances that are material to the particular justification claimed.

Each of these defenses, however, is subject to the provisions of Section 3.09(2), which provides that when the defendant is reckless or negligent in regard to the facts relating to the justifiability of his conduct, the justification defense is unavailable to him in a prosecution for an offense for which recklessness or negligence suffices to establish culpability. For example, if *D* purposely kills *V* because he *unreasonably* (let us assume, negligently) believes that *V* is about to kill him, the defense of self-protection is available to *D* if he is charged with purposely, knowingly, or recklessly killing *V*, but the defense is unavailable to him if he is prosecuted for negligent homicide, in light of his negligent mistake of fact. Or, if *D* *consciously* disregards a substantial and unjustifiable risk that *V* is not an

---

[191] American Law Institute, Comment to § 3.04, at 50.

[192] The concepts described in this section apply to the defenses of execution of public duty (§ 3.03), self-protection (§ 3.04), protection of other persons (§ 3.05), protection of property (§ 3.06), law enforcement (§ 3.07), and use of force by persons with special responsibility for care, discipline, or safety of others (§ 3.08).

[193] *See* §§ 17.04 (justification defenses generally) and 18.01[E] (self-defense), *supra.*

[194] *See* § 18.03, *supra.*

aggressor, *D*'s recklessness as to the relevant facts would render him guilty of an offense based on a reckless state of mind.

The Code's approach is sensible. In the hypotheticals above, the traditional common law rule, which does not recognize an imperfect defense, authorizes *D*'s conviction for a more serious offense than his overall culpability — he may be convicted of a crime of intent, although he is really a negligent or reckless wrongdoer (in light of his negligent or reckless mistake). The Code approach permits conviction of an offense in accord with the culpability of his mistake.[195]

[C] Justification Defenses and Risks to Innocent Bystanders

If a person justifiably uses force against an aggressor, but uses such force in a reckless or negligent manner in regard to the safety of an innocent bystander, the justification defense, although available to the person in regard to the *aggressor*, is *unavailable* to him in a prosecution for such recklessness or negligence as to the *bystander.*[196] For example, if *D* shoots at *A*, an aggressor, in a crowded subway, thereby recklessly causing *X*'s death or recklessly endangering the lives of *X* and others, *D* may successfully assert self-protection as a defense in prosecution for his actions against *A*, but he is not entitled to use this defense in a prosecution for manslaughter of *X*, or for the offense of reckless endangerment of the bystanders.

However, convictions in this regard are difficult to obtain. In order to show that a defendant acted recklessly or negligently as to a bystander, the prosecution must show that he took an *unjustifiable* risk to others in protecting himself, because "unjustifiability" is an element in the definition of both "recklessness" and "negligence."[197] And, and as the Commentary explains, "in assessing . . . a charge of reckless or negligence, the actor's justifying purpose [*e.g.*, self-protection] must . . . be given weight in determining whether the risk to innocent persons was sufficient to establish a gross deviation from proper standards of conduct."[198]

---

[195] American Law Institute, Comment to § 3.09, at 151–52.

[196] Model Penal Code § 3.09(3).

[197] *See* § 10.07[B][3], *supra.*

[198] *See* American Law Institute, Comment to § 3.09, at 154–55.

Chapter 19

DEFENSE OF OTHERS

§ 19.01 GENERAL RULE

Generally speaking, a person is justified in using force to protect a third party from unlawful use of force by an aggressor.[1] The intervenor's right to use force in such circumstances parallels the third party's right of self-defense;[2] that is, the intervenor may use force when, and to the extent that, the third party would apparently be justified in using force to protect herself.[3] Thus, deadly force is justified if the intervenor has reasonable grounds for believing that such force is necessary to prevent the danger of imminent death or grievous bodily injury to the innocent third party.[4]

Some potential limits to this rule exist. First, the defense originally was limited to protection of persons[5] related to the intervenor by consanguinity, marriage, or employment relation.[6] This limitation no longer applies.

Second, a majority of jurisdictions once applied the "alter-ego rule": An intervenor could only use force to defend a third party if the latter party would *in fact* have been justified in using force, and force in the same degree, in *self*-defense.[7] This means that *D*, the intervenor, was placed in the shoes of *X*, the person being defended, and *acted at her peril*. That is, if *X* had no right of self-defense, even though a reasonable person would have believed that *X* did, this rule provided that *D* was not justified in using force to protect *X*. The alter-ego doctrine, when applied, represents an exception to the common law rule that an actor is justified in using force based on reasonable appearances.

The justification for the alter-ego rule is understood if one considers the following not-uncommon scenario: *D* comes upon an apparently unlawful attack by *V* on *X*; *D* defends *X*; *D* subsequently learns that *V* was an undercover police officer using

---

[1] Commonwealth v. Martin, 341 N.E.2d 885, 889–90 (Mass. 1976).

[2] State v. Cook, 515 S.E.2d 127, 133 (W. Va. 1999).

[3] State v. Bolden, 371 S.W.3d 802, 805 (Mo. 2012).

[4] *E.g.*, Utah Code § 76-2-402(1)(a) (2015); Maye v. State, 49 So. 3d 1124, 1130 (Miss. 2010).

[5] May a pregnant mother respond to a threatened punch to her stomach with deadly force to protect the life of her fetus? Courts are split on this, largely depending on whether the state defines a fetus as a "person." *Compare* People v. Kurr, 654 N.W.2d 651 (Mich. Ct. App. 2002) (permitting the defense), *with* Ogas v. State, 655 S.W.2d 322 (Tex. App. 1983) (disallowing the defense).

[6] *Commonwealth v. Martin*, 341 N.E.2d at 891–92.

[7] *See* People v. Young, 183 N.E.2d 319, 319–20 (N.Y. 1962) (stating and applying the then-majority rule), *superseded by statute*, N.Y. Penal Law § 35.15.

lawful force against an unlawfully resistant X. Permitting D in such circumstances to act on reasonable appearances, it is said, creates "a dangerous precedent . . . that plain-clothes police officers attempting lawful arrests over wrongful resistance are subject to violent interference by strangers ignorant of the facts."[8]

Largely due to the influence of the Model Penal Code, the modern majority view today is that an intervenor *may* use force to the extent that such force *reasonably appears* to the intervenor to be justified in defense of the third party.[9] Advocates of the reasonable-appearance rule justify it on both utilitarian and retributive grounds.

From a utilitarian perspective, a consequence of the alter-ego doctrine is that onlookers may hesitate to intervene in disputes. As one court explained, "[e]ven if their hearts had been stout enough to enter the fray in defense of a stranger being violently assaulted, the fear of legal consequences chilled their basic instincts."[10] The reasonable-appearance rule seeks "to afford protection to a defender who acts while injury may still be prevented."[11]

The alter-ego rule also violates retributive concepts of just deserts, because it results in liability and punishment without fault.[12] The reasonable-appearance rule ensures that people who act reasonably, albeit mistakenly, are not punished for their good motives.

§ 19.02 MODEL PENAL CODE

Under the Model Code, subject to retreat provisions discussed in the next paragraph, an intervenor (D) is justified in using force upon another person in order to protect a third party (X) if three conditions are met: (1) D uses no more force to protect X than D would be entitled to use in *self*-protection, based on the circumstances as D believes them to be; (2) under the circumstances as D believes them to be, X would be justified in using such force in her self-defense; and (3) D believes that intervention is necessary for X's protection.[13]

Some of the Code's self-protection retreat rules[14] have limited applicability in the context of the defense of another person. First, if D would be required to retreat to a place of known safety if she were protecting *herself* in such circumstances, she is *not* required to retreat before using force in X's protection, except in the unlikely circumstance that she knows that such retreat will assure X's complete safety.[15] Second, D is required to attempt to secure X's retreat if X would be required to

---

[8] People v. Young, 210 N.Y.S.2d 358, 367 (App. Div. 1961) (Valente, J., dissenting), *rev'd*, 183 N.E.2d 319 (N.Y. 1962).

[9] *E.g.*, Alexander v. State, 447 A.2d 880, 885–87 (Md. Ct. Spec. App. 1982); State v. Cook, 515 S.E.2d at 135–37.

[10] Alexander v. State, 447 A.2d at 881.

[11] *Id.* at 887.

[12] American Law Institute, Comment to § 3.05, at 65–66.

[13] Model Penal Code § 3.05(1).

[14] *See* § 18.06[A][2][c][ii], *supra*.

[15] Model Penal Code § 3.05(2)(a).

retreat under the rules of self-protection, but this requirement only applies if D knows that X can reach complete safety by retreating.[16] Third, neither D nor X is required to retreat "in the other's dwelling or place of work to any greater extent than in [her] own."[17]

As with other justification defenses,[18] the applicability of the defense-of-others provision is based on the intervenor's subjective beliefs. Thus, if D is prosecuted for purposely killing V, an undercover officer lawfully pointing a gun at X, D is entitled to raise a defense-of-others claim if she believed that V was an unlawful attacker.[19] However, as with other justification defenses, if D's belief in this regard was negligent or reckless, the justification defense is unavailable to her in a prosecution for negligent or reckless homicide.

---

[16] Model Penal Code § 3.05(2)(b).

[17] Model Penal Code § 3.05(2)(c).

[18] *See* § 18.06[B], *supra.*

[19] Notice the interesting possibility of conflicting justifications in this example: D is justified in using deadly force upon V, based on her reasonable but mistaken belief that she is acting in X's defense; simultaneously, officer V would be justified under § 3.04(1) in killing D in self-protection if *she* (V) reasonably but mistakenly believes that D is X's accomplice. (In such circumstances, V would be acting on the reasonable belief that she is repelling *unlawful* force by D.)

Chapter 20

DEFENSE OF PROPERTY AND HABITATION

§ 20.01 PROPERTY AND HABITATION: COMPARISON AND CONTRAST

This chapter focuses on two related defenses. The first is the *defense of property*, which is implicated when a person uses force to prevent another person from dispossessing him of real or personal property, or in order to regain possession of the property immediately after dispossession. The second is the *defense of habitation*, which is involved when the dweller of a home uses force to prevent unlawful entry into the actor's "castle" by an intruder. This defense is distinguishable from the property defense in that its purpose is to safeguard the dweller's bodily security and privacy in his home; dispossession of the home or its contents need not be implicated.

Some courts and statutes treat the habitation defense as part of a broader property defense. It is easy to see why: When *V* enters *D*'s home wrongfully and forcibly in order to dispossess him or to take property from within it, *D* simultaneously has the right to protect his property from dispossession (defense of property) *and* to protect his right to inhabit his home in privacy and safety (defense of habitation). Realistically, there is often no way to separate the two interests. Nonetheless, it is preferable to distinguish the claims because the common law treats them differently in one significant respect: Deadly force is *never* permitted to protect property, as such; deadly force *is* justified in certain circumstances, however, in order to defend habitation.

These two defenses often overlap other justification claims, as well. For example, one who uses force in his residence might simultaneously claim one or more of the following defenses: defense of property; defense of habitation; crime prevention (which itself subsumes multiple defenses); self-defense; and defense of others. Frequently, some of these defenses overlap nearly completely; sometimes, however, subtle differences exist, so it is important to distinguish between the claims.

§ 20.02 DEFENSE OF PROPERTY

[A] General Rule

Despite the high value placed on property rights in Anglo-American society, the law prefers the resolution of property disputes by nonforcible means, including the use of judicial orders. Forcible self-help is discouraged. Nonetheless, in narrow circumstances, a person may use force to protect his property.

As more fully examined in subsection [B], a person in possession of real or personal property is justified under the common law and modern statutes in using nondeadly force against a would-be dispossessor if he reasonably believes that such force is necessary to prevent imminent, unlawful dispossession of the property.[1] Subject to one exception considered in subsection [B][6] below, once a person is dispossessed of his property, his right to use force to defend his interest in it is extinguished.

[B] Clarification of the Rule

[1] Possession Versus Title to Property

The privilege of defense-of-property entitles a person to use necessary force to retain rightful possession of, as distinguished from title to, personal or real property.[2] For example, assuming the other aspects of the defense are satisfied, D, a mechanic repairing X's car, may use nondeadly force against V, a thief, in order to prevent V from taking the vehicle. Similarly, T, a tenant in an apartment, may use nondeadly force, if necessary, to prevent L, the owner of the property, from wrongfully evicting him from the premises.

[2] Necessity for the Use of Force

A person may use no more force than reasonably appears necessary to defend his possessory interest in the property. Some early common law courts further specified that a person could not properly use force until he sought to avoid a physical conflict by requesting desistance by the would-be dispossessor.[3] A request was unnecessary, however, if it would be futile or would jeopardize the defender's or another person's safety (*e.g.*, the wrongdoer attempts to take property by force rather than by stealth). And, it also follows from the necessity requirement that nondeadly force should not be used if one can seek assistance by law enforcement agents already on the scene.[4]

[3] Deadly Force

Deadly force is not permitted in defense of property, even if it is the only means available to prevent the loss.[5] However, the right to use *non*deadly force to protect property is sometimes transformed into an independent right to use *deadly* force in

---

[1] *E.g.*, Pike v. Commonwealth, 482 S.E.2d 839, 840 (Va. Ct. App. 1997) (right to expel trespasser to property, but not if force endangers human life); State v. Trammel, 672 P.2d 652, 654 (N.M. 1983) (no right to use force if attempt to dispossess is lawful); Fla. § 776.031 (2015).

[2] *See* State v. Rullis, 191 A.2d 197 (N.J. Super. Ct. App. Div. 1963).

[3] *E.g.*, State v. Elliot, 11 N.H. 540, 544–45 (1841). Today, even if a request for desistance is not an express element of the defense, the failure of a person to request desistance may constitute evidence in a given case that subsequent use of force was unnecessary. *E.g.*, State v. Bellinger, 278 P.3d 975 (Kan. Ct. App. 2012) (*D* only ordered *X* off his rural property seconds before he used force against *X*, who had not otherwise interfered with *D*'s property or posed an imminent threat to it).

[4] Gatlin v. United States, 833 A.2d 995 (D.C. 2003).

[5] People v. Ceballos, 526 P.2d 241, 249 (Cal. 1974); Commonwealth v. Alexander, 531 S.E.2d 567, 568 (Va. 2000).

self-protection or defense of a third party. For example, assume this scenario: *V* threatens to steal *D*'s property; *D* resists by use of moderate nondeadly force; in an effort to overcome *D*'s lawful resistance, *V* pulls a knife and threatens to stab *D*. In these circumstances, *D* may now use deadly force against *V*. This right, however, is based on *D*'s privilege to protect himself from an imminent, unlawful deadly attack, and not on the basis of his interest in the property.

[4] Threat to Use Deadly Force

Although a person may not *use* deadly force to protect his property, may he *threaten* it as a way to prevent interference with, or dispossession of, his property? For example, suppose that *D* discovers *V* about to steal *D*'s briefcase. May *D* point a gun at *V* and, although he has no intention of using the weapon (perhaps it is even unloaded), threaten *V* with it, to prevent the theft? If *D* is charged with assault on these facts,[6] and asserts the claim of defense-of-property, should he be denied the defense because he threatened to perform a forbidden act?

There is relatively little case law on point. A few cases, especially old ones, apparently authorized the threatened use of deadly force to prevent unlawful dispossession of property.[7] The prevailing modern position, however, is that a person may not threaten to do that which he is not permitted to do in fact.[8]

Those who would permit the defense in such cases contend that a threat of deadly force will often deter a wrongdoer without harming him. Thus, a *threat* of *deadly* force may be preferable to *implementation* of *non*deadly force, which the common law permits. On the other hand, a threat of deadly force is itself a highly dangerous act because it may provoke a deadly response, so it is arguably desirable to deter threats that the issuer has no right to implement.

[5] Claim of Right

Occasionally, a person may assert a "claim of right" to possession of property and, therefore, seek to dispossess another person of the disputed property. For example, *V*, a landlord, may have a right to retake real property from *D*, a tenant; or *V* may seek to recapture an automobile from *D*, who has failed to make timely car payments.

V's claim of right to possession of the property is relevant to *D*'s claim of defense-of-property in one circumstance: If *D* knows, believes, or as a reasonable person should believe, that *V* has a legitimate claim of right to possession of the property in question, it follows that *D* cannot reasonably believe that *V* represents a threat to dispossess him *unlawfully*. From *D*'s (or the reasonable person's)

---

[6] At common law, an assault is an attempted battery. *See* § 27.02[E], *infra*. In the present hypothetical, *D* did not intend to batter *V*, so *D* is not guilty of common law assault, regardless of the defense-of-property claim. However, most states have redefined the offense of assault to include the tort definition (*i.e.*, intent to place another person in reasonable apprehension of an imminent battery). *E.g.*, Ariz. Rev. Stat. § 13-1203(A)(2) (2015). Under such a statute, *D* would be guilty of assault, subject to any applicable defense.

[7] State v. Yancey, 74 N.C. 244, 245 (1876).

[8] *Commonwealth v. Alexander*, 531 S.E.2d at 568.

perspective, *V*'s threatened act of dispossession is *lawful*. Therefore, in these circumstances, *D* is not privileged to use force against *V*.

[6]   Recapture of Property

In order to discourage self-help and consequent breaches of the peace, a person may not ordinarily use force to recapture property of which he has been unlawfully dispossessed.[9]

One exception to this rule exists. A person who acts *promptly* after dispossession may use nondeadly force, as reasonably necessary, to regain or recapture his property. Thus, a person wrongfully evicted from his land may immediately re-enter the property and attempt to retake it; likewise, one who is unlawfully dispossessed of his personal property may follow the dispossessor in hot pursuit and use nondeadly force, if necessary, to recapture it.[10]

§ 20.03   DEFENSE OF HABITATION

[A]   Rationale of the Defense

If jurists have treated the use of force in defense of property with considerable caution, they have always treated the related interest of safe and private habitation of one's home with reverence. The reason for the difference in attitude — as with the rule permitting people to kill in self-defense rather than to retreat from their home — is that the home represents the person's "castle." As with a castle, the home is a dweller's fortress, "as well for his defence against injury and violence, as for his repose."[11] The house serves as a sanctuary from external attack, "for where shall a man be safe if it be not in his house?"[12]

The home is also a source of privacy where the most intimate activities in life are conducted, and from which people seek to exclude the prying eyes and ears of strangers and of the government. The Supreme Court has observed:

> The [Constitution] protects the individual's privacy in a variety of settings. In none is the zone of privacy more clearly defined than when bounded by the unambiguous physical dimensions of an individual's home — a zone that finds its roots in clear and specific constitutional terms: "The right of the people to be secure in their . . . houses . . . shall not be violated."[13]

---

[9] The 14th century English Statute of Forcible Entry made it a crime for one entitled to possession of land to regain it by use of force. 5 Rich. 2, ch. 8 (1381). This statute "has been substantially reenacted by nearly all the states." American Law Institute, Comment to § 3.06, at 86.

[10] Woodward v. State, 855 P.2d 423, 428 n.14 (Alaska Ct. App. 1993).

[11] Semayne's Case, 5 Co. Rep. 91a, 91b, 77 Eng. Rep. 194, 195 (1620); *see* State v. Pellegrino, 577 N.W.2d 590, 594 (S.D. 1998) ("The feudal concept of home as castle was borne of an age when inhabitants were compelled to turn their dwellings into fortified strongholds. The idea endures into modern times.").

[12] Edmond Coke, Third Institute *162 (1644).

[13] Payton v. New York, 445 U.S. 573, 589 (1980).

Although this quotation concerns a person's right to be free from unreasonable intrusions by the government, the constitutional right is itself based on the pre-constitutional common law reverence for the home as a place of security.

When a wrongdoer seeks to enter another person's dwelling, therefore, more than property is invaded. In common law terms, the fortress has been attacked; a person's primary source of safe and private habitation has been jeopardized.

[B] Rules Regarding Use of Deadly Force

A person may use deadly force to defend his home. The scope of this privilege has changed over time, and no single rule universally applies today.[14] Three general approaches will be noted.

[1] Early Common Law Rule

The broadest right to use deadly force is found in the original common law principle that a home-dweller could justifiably use deadly force upon another person if he reasonably believed that such force was necessary to prevent an imminent and unlawful[15] entry of his dwelling.[16]

A careful look at the elements of this version of the defense demonstrates its wide scope. The right to use deadly force under this approach is triggered by the immediacy of the unlawful entry. The unlawful purpose of the intruder, and the degree to which he constitutes a threat to the physical safety of the occupants, is immaterial. For example, D may kill V, an apparent intruder, whether V is an armed burglar intending to kill him or to steal his property, an unarmed intruder seeking to dispossess him of his property, or even an unarmed and intoxicated neighbor mistakenly entering what he thinks is his own home.[17] Indeed, pursuant to this rule, the right to kill would apparently exist even if D *knows* that V is his intoxicated neighbor, as long as D reasonably believes that deadly force is the only way of preventing the entry.

---

[14] Two warnings: First, the law in this area is changing rapidly, along with changes in "retreat" law in the context of self-defense. *See* § 18.02[C], *supra*. Second, some modern statutes very broadly define "habitation" in relation to this defense. For example, Georgia defines the term to include "any dwelling, motor vehicle, or place of business." Official Code Ga. Ann. § 16-3-24.1 (2015). Obviously, this latter definition is largely inconsistent with the common law "home-as-castle-and-last-fortress" rationale of the defense.

[15] Courts or statutes sometimes state that deadly force is only permitted if the unlawful entry itself is forcible. *E.g.*, People v. Stombaugh, 284 N.E.2d 640, 643 (Ill. 1972) (applying the state statute, deadly force is not justifiable unless the intruder enters in a "violent, riotous or tumultuous manner"); Official Code Ga. Ann. § 16-3-23(1) (2011) (*id.*).

[16] State v. Reid, 210 N.E.2d 142 (Ohio Ct. App. 1965).

[17] Notice the irony: Pursuant to the common law property defense, D may *not* use deadly force to prevent V from stealing his car in the driveway, nor may he kill a trespasser on his land (but outside the dwelling). According to this early common law rule, however, if D is inside the dwelling and V is on the outside, D has the right to use deadly force regardless of V's purpose for the apparently wrongful entry. Technically — but only technically — this is because D is protecting his habitation and not his possessory interest in property per se.

[2] "Middle" Approach

A less broad approach to the defense of habitation provides that a person may only use deadly force if he reasonably believes that: (1) the other person intends an unlawful and imminent entry of the dwelling; (2) the intruder intends to injure him or another occupant, or to commit a felony therein; and (3) deadly force is necessary to repel the intrusion.[18]

This rule is narrower than the original common law defense. Under this formulation, for example, *D* may not justifiably shoot *V* if he knows or should know that the intruder is *D*'s intoxicated neighbor mistakenly attempting to enter his own house. Under such circumstances, *V* (presumably) does not represent a threat to an occupant's physical well-being, and *V*'s entry would not constitute a burglary[19] or any other felony.

[3] "Narrow" Approach

A narrow version of the defense provides that a person is only justified in using deadly force upon another if he reasonably believes that: (1) the other person intends an unlawful and imminent entry of the dwelling; (2) the intruder intends to commit a forcible felony therein;[20] and (3) such force is necessary to prevent the intrusion.[21] A "forcible" felony is one "committed by forcible means, violence, and surprise, such as murder, robbery, burglary, rape, or arson."[22]

This version of the defense differs from the immediately preceding one in two significant respects. First, deadly force is impermissible if the occupant knows or should know that the intruder only intends to commit a minor battery. Second, the resident may not use deadly force if he knows or should know that the intruder's purpose is to commit a nonforcible felony, such as larceny.

---

[18] N.C. Gen. Stat. § 14-51.1 (2015); State v. Pendleton, 567 N.W.2d 265 (Minn. 1997); State v. Pellegrino, 577 N.W.2d 590 (S.D. 1998); *see* Mondie v. Commonwealth, 158 S.W.3d 203 (Ky. 2005) (statute interpreted to permit use of deadly force, when reasonably necessary, to prevent unlawful entry for *any* criminal purpose, including petty theft and simple assault).

[19] Burglary requires a specific intent to commit a felony inside the dwelling; in the example, neighbor *V* does not intend to commit a crime inside.

[20] Some states are making the defense easier to prove. Florida, for example, provides that a "person who unlawfully and by force enters or attempts to enter a person's dwelling [or occupied vehicle] . . . is presumed to be doing so with the intent to commit an unlawful act involving force or violence." Fla. Stat. § 776.013(4) (2015). Moreover, when a home dweller uses deadly force in such circumstances, he is "presumed to have held a reasonable fear of imminent peril of death or great bodily harm to himself or herself or another." Fla. Stat. § 776.013(1)(a) (2011).

[21] N.C. Gen. Stat § 14-51.1(a) (2015); State v. Boyett, 185 P.3d 355, 358–60 (N.M. 2008).

[22] Crawford v. State, 190 A.2d 538, 542 (Md. 1963) (quoting 1 F. Wharton, Wharton's Criminal Law and Procedure § 206, at 453–55 (Anderson ed., 1957)).

[C]   Looking at the Rules in Greater Depth

[1]   May the Occupant Use Force After the Intruder Has Entered?

The defense of defense-of-habitation is triggered when an intruder attempts to enter the dwelling unlawfully. Suppose, however, that *D* awakens at night and finds *V* already in the house, or he returns home and finds *V* on the premises. Does the defense still apply?

Case law is split in this regard. Some courts consider the defense inapplicable once the entry has occurred.[23] In these states, if *D* uses deadly force, he must assert some other defense, such as self-defense (once the threat of unlawful attack is imminent) or crime prevention.

Many jurisdictions permit application of the defense, however, even after the intruder's forcible entry has occurred.[24] It must be remembered, however, that the fact that entry has already occurred may affect the dweller's right: Once *V* is in the dwelling, *D* may know more about the intruder's intentions than he would have known prior to entry. In some circumstances, *e.g.*, if *D* observes that the intruder is his well-meaning but intoxicated neighbor, the occupant's right to use deadly force will no longer be available.

[2]   Are the Differences in the Habitation Rules Significant?

The differences among the rules set out in subsection [B] regarding use of deadly force in defense of habitation are more theoretical than real. First, as with all other justification defenses, the right to defend the dwelling is based on reasonable appearances rather than on objective reality. This is an especially significant point in the application of the habitation defense because the right to use force is triggered *before* the intruder's entry of the dwelling and, therefore, often before the occupant is able to determine the intruder's intentions. In these days of ready access to weapons, an occupant can reasonably believe that nearly *any* intruder represents a serious threat to the dwellers' safety. In most cases, therefore, a home-dweller who uses deadly force will be able to satisfy the elements of even the narrowest version of the habitation defense.

Second, even under the narrowest version of the defense, a home-dweller will often be permitted to kill an intruder whom he knows intends to commit a *non*violent felony, such as larceny. This result follows from the usual inclusion of burglary in the category of forcible felonies. At common law, a person who intends to enter another person's home in order to commit larceny is a burglar if he breaks in at night. Indeed, many modern burglary statutes dispense with the nighttime

---

[23]   *E.g.*, State v. Brookshire, 353 S.W.2d 681 (Mo. 1962) (after the intruder crosses the "protective barrier," deadly force is only justified on the basis of some other defense, such as self-defense, or prevention of a felony therein).

[24]   *E.g.*, N.C. Gen. Stat. § 14-51.1 (2015) (deadly force is available "to prevent a forcible entry . . . or to terminate the intruder's unlawful entry"); State v. Boyett, 185 P.3d 355, 359 (N.M. 2008).

requirement, thus expanding the right to use deadly force still further.[25]

[3] Relationship of the Defense to Other Defenses

[a]   Self-Defense and Defense-of-Others

The common law defense of habitation is broader than the right to kill in self-defense or to protect a third person. First, under the original common law and "middle" approaches to habitation, a home-dweller may properly use deadly force against an intruder, even if the dweller does not reasonably believe that his life or that of an occupant is jeopardized. The habitation defense, therefore, permits use of force disproportional to the physical harm threatened.

Second, the traditional defense of self-defense is not triggered until physical harm to the dweller is imminent. The right to defend the home begins when *entry* of the dwelling is imminent, which may be well before the dweller's physical well-being is in imminent jeopardy;[26] the defense of habitation is a form of "accelerated self-defense."[27]

[b]   Law Enforcement Defenses

The privilege to use deadly force to defend one's house will often overlap one of the law enforcement defenses discussed in the next chapter. To the extent that an occupant reasonably believes that the intruder intends to commit a felony inside the home, the resident's right to use deadly force to defend his habitation will coincide with his right to kill in order to prevent commission of a felony (*i.e.*, the defense of "crime prevention").[28]

§ 20.04 SPRING GUNS[29]

[A] The Issue

A "spring gun" or "trap gun" is a mechanical device that can be set off when a person opens a door or other entryway into or within a building equipped with such a device. A spring gun ordinarily has the capacity to kill or seriously injure the intruder. Such devices may be placed in an unoccupied home (*e.g.*, while the residents are on vacation) or other structure (*e.g.*, garages, barns, etc.).

---

[25] *Contra* People v. Ceballos, 526 P.2d 241 (Cal. 1974) (concluding that deadly force is impermissible in order to prevent an intruder from committing a burglary, unless the burglar intends to commit some forcible or dangerous act within the dwelling).

[26] State v. Johnson, 54 S.W.3d 598, 603 (Mo. Ct. App. 2001); State v. Rye, 651 S.E.2d 321, 323 (S.C. 2007).

[27] State v. Ivicsics, 604 S.W.2d 773, 777 (Mo. Ct. App. 1980).

[28] Sometimes, however, deadly force in crime prevention is limited to prevention of forcible felonies, whereas the habitation defense might authorize deadly force against intruders intending to commit nonforcible crimes. In these circumstances, the defenses will not perfectly overlap.

[29] The issue discussed in this section applies to the privileges of defense-of-property, defense-of-habitation, self-defense, defense-of-others, and crime prevention.

Historically, they were sometimes placed in an occupied home, in order to wound or kill an intruder while the occupant is asleep.

The problem with these devices springs from their advantage: They act mechanically — "without mercy or discretion."[30] A trap gun will as quickly kill an innocent child as an armed robber; it will kill an intoxicated neighbor mistakenly entering the premises, as well as a police officer or firefighter lawfully entering. Moreover, the device cannot determine whether deadly or nondeadly force is needed, or even whether a warning to desist would be sufficient. The lives of innocent people, therefore, may needlessly be lost by use of such devices.

Advocates of spring guns have argued that as long as the law permits use of deadly force to protect a dweller of a home, the means used to inflict it — personally or by his "agent," the spring gun — should not matter. Indeed, from the occupant's perspective, a mechanical device may provide special protection: It will stop the intruder immediately upon entry, before a confrontation can occur; in the case of an elderly or infirm resident, or one untrained in firearm use, the spring gun may be an especially effective mechanism for limiting unlawful entries.

The risks and benefits of spring guns are amply demonstrated by the facts reported in *People v. Ceballos*.[31] *C* placed a spring gun in his garage, a structure in which he kept valuable property and sometimes slept at night, after an unknown intruder attempted unsuccessfully to enter. One afternoon thereafter, while *C* was absent, two unarmed teenagers, after looking in a window to make sure that nobody was present, entered the garage in order to steal property. As they did so, the spring gun fired, striking one youth in the face.

C was charged with assault with a deadly weapon. He raised several claims in support of his right to use the spring gun, including defense-of-property, defense-of-habitation, crime prevention, and apprehension of a felon. The applicability of these defenses are considered below.

[B] Common Law Rule

At common law, a mechanical device may be used "where the intrusion is, in fact, such that the person, were he present, would be justified in taking the life or inflicting the bodily harm with his own hands."[32]

The words "in fact" in this rule are significant. One who deliberately places a spring gun on his property acts at his peril: His right to use force by this means is based on reality, rather than on reasonable appearances. Thus, if *D* is present and reasonably believes that *V*, a police officer, is a felonious intruder, he may kill *V* in defense of his habitation. If *D*'s spring gun kills the same officer, however, *D* is *not* entitled to the defense.

How does the common law rule apply to the events in *Ceballos*, described in subsection [A]? The answer depends on whether *C* would have been justified in

---

30 People v. Ceballos, 526 P.2d 241, 244 (Cal. 1974).

31 *Id.*

32 *Id.* at 244.

using deadly force "by his own hands," when the youths entered the garage. The answer to *that* question depends, in turn, on the nature of the defense being claimed. For example, *C* would not have been justified in using deadly force to defend his property in the garage, so a spring gun, as well, would be impermissible for *that* purpose.

C's privilege to use deadly force in defense of habitation was more problematic. Assuming that the garage is determined to be part of his dwelling (on the basis that he sometimes slept in it, or because it was physically connected to the house), he could justifiably have used deadly force by his own hands under the original, "middle," and perhaps "narrow," versions of the habitation defense.[33] In light of this, *C* had a common law right to use a deadly mechanical device in his absence.[34]

The common law rule regarding spring guns is changing. An increasing number of states now support the proposition that a resident may not justifiably use a mechanical device designed to kill or seriously injure an intruder, even if he would be permitted to use deadly force in person.[35]

§ 20.05   MODEL PENAL CODE

[A]   Permissible Use of Nondeadly Force

[1]   Force to Protect Property

Subject to the limitations described in subsection [B], the Code provides that a person may use nondeadly force upon another person to prevent or terminate an entry or other trespass upon land, or to prevent the carrying away of personal property, if he believes[36] that three conditions exist: (1) the other person's interference with the property is unlawful; (2) the intrusion affects property in the actor's possession, or in the possession of someone else for whom he acts; and (3) nondeadly force is immediately necessary.[37] In general, this provision conforms

---

[33] Under the narrow habitation defense, a home-dweller must reasonably believe that the intruder intends to commit a forcible felony upon entry. See § 20.03[B][3], *supra*. The youths intended to commit larceny, a nonforcible crime; and, as it was daytime when they entered, they were not guilty of common law burglary, a forcible felony. Under the law in *C*'s jurisdiction, however, entry of a garage in the daytime constituted statutory burglary; as a result, deadly force by *C* would have been allowed, even under the narrow version of the habitation defense. However, the state supreme court in *Ceballos* took a different approach, ruling that deadly force may not be used unless a burglar's entry creates a reasonable apprehension of serious harm to human life.

[34] The justifiability of the use of spring guns in crime prevention depends on the class of crimes for which deadly force may be used in such circumstances. See § 21.03[B][1], *infra*.

[35] *E.g.*, People v. Ceballos, 526 P.2d 241 (Cal. 1974); Falco v. State, 407 So. 2d 203, 208 (Fla. 1981) (the "arbitrary brutality" of spring guns "should necessarily be prohibited under any circumstance"); State v. Britt, 510 So. 2d 670 (La. Ct. App. 1987).

[36] As with other MPC justification defenses, the Code's "protection of property" defense is based on the actor's subjective beliefs. However, as with other MPC justification defenses, if the actor's relevant beliefs were negligent or reckless, the justification defense is unavailable to him in a prosecution for an offense based on negligence or recklessness. See *generally* § 18.06[B], *supra*.

[37] Model Penal Code § 3.06(1)(a).

with the common law.

[2]   Force to Recapture Property

Subject to the limitations described in subsection [B], the Code provides that a person may use nondeadly force to re-enter land or to recapture personal property if: (1) he believes that he or the person for whom he is acting was unlawfully dispossessed of the property; and either (2a) the force is used immediately after dispossession; or (2b) even if it is not immediate, he believes that the other person has no claim of right to possession of the property. In the (2b) situation, however, re-entry of land (as distinguished from recapture of personal property) is *not* permitted unless the actor also believes that it would constitute an "exceptional hardship" to delay re-entry until he can obtain a court order.[38]

This recapture provision is broader than the common law. It extends the right to use nondeadly force to circumstances in which hot pursuit of the dispossessor has ended, namely, when the actor believes that he was dispossessed at an earlier time by one who had no claim of right to the property. In this situation, the American Law Institute believes that the law "should not deny a privilege that a well conducted person would expect to have."[39] However, force may *not* be used to regain property if the dispossessed party believes that the dispossessor acted on the basis of a claim of right to the property, even if the dispossessed party believes that the other's claim ultimately will be rejected by the courts. In the latter circumstance, the Institute agrees with the common law that absent immediacy, the best approach is for the parties to resolve their conflicting claims in court.

[B]   Impermissible Use of Nondeadly Force

Nondeadly force that is otherwise permitted in defense of property is unjustified in three circumstances. First, force is not "immediately necessary" unless the defender first requests desistance by the interfering party. A request is not required, however, if the defender believes that a request would be useless, dangerous to himself or to another, or would result in substantial harm to the property before the request can effectively be made.[40]

Second, a person may not use force to prevent or terminate a trespass to personal or real property if he knows that to do so would expose the trespasser to a substantial risk of serious bodily injury.[41] For example, it would be impermissible to evict a trespasser from a moving vehicle.[42]

---

[38] Model Penal Code § 3.06(1)(b). "Exceptional hardship" would exist, for example, if the land contained a crop that would be lost if it were not immediately harvested, or if the land were the site of a small business that would suffer substantial economic damage if the owner could not enter to carry on his duties. American Law Institute, Comment to § 3.06, at 87.

[39] American Law Institute, Comment to § 3.06, at 85.

[40] Model Penal Code § 3.06(3)(a).

[41] Model Penal Code § 3.06(3)(b).

[42] American Law Institute, Comment to § 3.06, at 91.

Third, the Code addresses the situation in which both the dispossessor of land or personal property (call him "A") and the person seeking to regain it ("B") believe that they have a right to the property in dispute. For example, suppose that A, believing that he has a lawful right to an automobile in B's possession, dispossesses B of it. B, unaware that A claims a right to the car, immediately seeks to recapture his property. Pursuant to the Code's recapture provisions described above, B would be justified in using nondeadly force to retake the property. However, since A's original dispossession was based on a claim of right to the property, the Code would appear to authorize A to use nondeadly force against B to protect his newly-obtained possessory interest in the vehicle from what he (A) believes is B's wrongful efforts at recapture! Thus, without a special rule to deal with the situation, the Code seems to allow both parties, justifiably, to fight over the property.

In such circumstances, the Code prefers that the original dispossessor (in the hypothetical, A) forego the use of force and permit the recapture to occur. Specifically, the Code provides that A, a prior dispossessor, may *not* use force to resist re-entry or recaption of property by B, even if he believes that B is acting unlawfully, if B's re-entry or recaption is otherwise justifiable.[43]

[C] Use of Deadly Force[44]

[1] In General

Deadly force in defense of property is prohibited except in two circumstances.

[a] Dispossession of a Dwelling

A person may use deadly force upon an intruder if he believes that: (1) the intruder is seeking to dispossess him of the dwelling; (2) the intruder has no claim of right to possession of the dwelling; and (3) such force is immediately necessary to prevent dispossession.[45] The actor may use deadly force although he does not believe that his or another person's physical well-being is jeopardized.

Notice that the right to use deadly force under this provision is *not* predicated on the actor's right to personal safety or privacy, as such, but rather is founded on the actor's right to avoid eviction from the dwelling. The Commentary to this Code section concedes that "[t]o kill a man is, on a dispassionate view, an evil both more serious and more irrevocable than the loss of possession of a dwelling for a period during which a court order is being obtained."[46] Nonetheless, describing an illegal ouster from one's home as a "provocation that is not to be depreciated," the

---

[43] Model Penal Code § 3.06(3)(c). For further explanation of this complicated provision, see American Law Institute, Comment to § 3.06, at 89–90.

[44] *See generally* Comment, *The Use of Deadly Force in the Protection of Property Under the Model Penal Code*, 59 Colum. L. Rev. 1212 (1959).

[45] Model Penal Code § 3.06(3)(d)(i).

[46] American Law Institute, Comment to § 3.06, at 93.

Institute determined that the right to use deadly force should be permitted in this class of cases.

Notice, as well, that, unlike the original common law position, this provision does *not* authorize deadly force merely to prevent an unlawful entry into the home, as such. Instead, the actor must believe two things: that the intruder's *purpose* for entry is to dispossess him of the dwelling, *and* that the intruder is acting without a claim of right.

[b]   Prevention of Serious Property Crimes

A person may use deadly force in protection of property interests inside a dwelling, *or anywhere else*, if he believes that: (1) the other person is attempting to commit or consummate arson, burglary, robbery, or felonious theft or property destruction; (2) such force is immediately necessary to prevent commission or consummation of the offense; and either (3a) the other person previously used or threatened to use deadly force against him or another person in his presence, or (3b) use of nondeadly force to prevent commission or consummation of the offense would expose him or another innocent person to substantial danger of serious bodily injury.[47]

This provision is highly controversial. It justifies use of deadly force in protection of property, under circumstances that go well beyond any concern relating to habitation. Moreover, the right to kill is not based upon the actor's perceived need to protect his or another person's life. For example, if *F*, a burglar or a robber on the street, uses or threatens to use deadly force against *D* or *X*, but is disarmed by *D* and seeks to flee with the fruits of his crime, *D* may kill *F* if he believes that this is the only way to prevent *F* from successfully consummating the crime. As the Institute puts it, "deadly force may be used in order to prevent [*V*] from capitalizing upon his offense."[48]

The Model Code's position is surprising. Another section of the Code[49] provides that a private person (*i.e.*, one who is neither a law enforcement officer nor a person assisting him) may *not* use deadly force in order to effectuate a felony arrest. Yet, when the actor's justification for using deadly force is protection of personal property — presumably, a less socially valuable interest than law enforcement — the Code authorizes its use. The Commentary recognizes that this result is inconsistent with the judgment underlying the arrest provisions.[50]

---

[47] Model Penal Code § 3.06(3)(d)(ii). This provision in some regards overlaps the Code's law enforcement provisions discussed in the next chapter. However, in other regards, it is broader. *See* § 21.05[B][2], *infra*.

[48] American Law Institute, Comment to § 3.06, at 96.

[49] Model Penal Code § 3.07(2)(b). *See* § 21.05[C][2], *infra*.

[50] American Law Institute, Comment to § 3.06, at 96–97.

[2] Spring Guns

The Model Code prohibits the use of a mechanical device to protect property if it is intended to cause, or is known by the user to create a substantial risk of causing, death or serious bodily injury.[51] Thus, in those circumstances in which deadly force is permitted in defense of property, the actor must personally commit the lethal acts rather than use a spring gun.

---

[51] Model Penal Code § 3.06(5)(a).

Chapter 21

LAW ENFORCEMENT

§ 21.01 WHAT ARE THE "LAW ENFORCEMENT" DEFENSES?

Society wants its criminal laws enforced. Ideally, crimes should be prevented, people involved in criminal activity arrested, and suspects who attempt to flee restrained so that their innocence or guilt can be determined by due process of law. In order to meet these goals, police officers must perform acts that ordinarily would be criminal: they must apply force upon suspected criminals, and deprive them of their liberty or even life in the process.[1] When such acts occur in the reasonable enforcement of the criminal laws, they are legally justified. When the police use excessive force given the circumstances, criminal liability should follow, as it would for any private citizen.

The label attached to the defense that authorizes such conduct is problematic. Sometimes, courts speak generically of a "law enforcement" defense. This term, however, encompasses three sub-defenses, which will be described here as: (1) public authority; (2) crime prevention; and (3) effectuation of an arrest. This third defense may itself be sub-divided into two temporal components: (3a) the arrest; and (3b) prevention of the escape of the arrestee.

As considered below, common law "law enforcement" rules (today, typically codified by statute) often differentiate between police officers and private individuals. In general, the law enforcement defenses provide broader authority to police officers than to private persons to make arrests and use force in doing so.

---

[1] Of course, other harm can occur in the law enforcement context. For example, the police may trespass on land in order to make an arrest, or drive above the posted speed limit on a highway in the apprehension of a fugitive. These comparatively unproblematic issues are not considered in this chapter.

§ 21.02 RESTRAINT ON LIBERTY IN LAW ENFORCEMENT: "PUBLIC AUTHORITY" DEFENSE[2]

[A] By Police Officers

[1] Common Law

At common law, a police officer was authorized to make an arrest, whether for a felony or misdemeanor, if it was based upon "reasonable" or "probable" cause.[3] Felony arrests could be made with or without an arrest warrant.[4] Warrantless misdemeanor arrests, however, were valid only if the offense occurred in the officer's presence.[5]

[2] Constitutional Limits on the Common Law

The Fourth Amendment to the United States Constitution prohibits unreasonable searches and seizures. Generally speaking, this provision protects an individual's legitimate expectations of privacy against unreasonably intrusion.[6] Nowhere is the zone of privacy more clearly defined and more rigorously protected than in a person's home. Consequently, in contrast to the common law, warrantless felony arrests in the home are unconstitutional in the absence of an emergency or consent.[7] Moreover, warrantless *misdemeanor* arrests in the home are frowned upon, except in hot pursuit.[8]

[B] By Private Persons

Private persons have common law authority to make "citizen arrests" and, therefore, defend against a criminal charge of false imprisonment. The common law provides that a private citizen may arrest another person for a felony, or for a misdemeanor involving a breach of the peace,[9] if: (1) the crime actually occurred;

---

[2] *See generally* Rollin M. Perkins, *The Law of Arrest*, 25 Iowa L. Rev. 201 (1940).

[3] "Probable cause" exists when the facts and circumstances within an officer's knowledge and of which she has reasonably trustworthy information are sufficient in themselves to cause a person of reasonable caution to believe that an offense has been committed and that the person to be arrested committed it. Carroll v. United States, 267 U.S. 132 (1925).

[4] *See* United States v. Watson, 423 U.S. 411, 418–19 (1976); Balt. & Ohio R.R. v. Cain, 31 A. 801 (Md. 1895).

[5] *Watson*, 423 U.S. at 418–19. "Presence" has been broadly construed to mean that commission of the offense is "apparent to the officers' senses." People v. Brown, 290 P.2d 528, 529 (Cal. 1955). For example, this would include hearing the offense committed over a telephone. People v. Cahill, 328 P.2d 995, 998 (Cal. Ct. App. 1958).

[6] Katz v. United States, 389 U.S. 347 (1967).

[7] Payton v. New York, 445 U.S. 573 (1980).

[8] Welsh v. Wisconsin, 466 U.S. 740, 753 (1984) (stating the general rule against warrantless entry for minor offenses); Stanton v. Sims, 134 S. Ct. 3 (2013) (seemingly narrowing the no-warrant rule to cases in which the officers are not acting in hot pursuit of the misdemeanant).

[9] "Breach of the peace" is conduct that causes or tends to cause a disturbance of the peace and

and (2) she reasonably believes that the suspect committed the offense.[10] With misdemeanors, the offense must also occur in the arresting person's presence.[11]

Under this rule, the arresting party acts at her peril regarding the first element of the defense, but is permitted a reasonable mistake of fact regarding the second element. For example, suppose that D observes V flee from a bank as the bank alarm goes off. D believes that V robbed the bank and, therefore, arrests V. If it later turns out that V did not rob the bank, and D is prosecuted for false imprisonment of V, D may *not* successfully assert a public authority defense unless the bank was, in fact, robbed. If it was robbed, however, D may successfully claim the defense, even if V was not the robber (*e.g.*, she was a customer fleeing the scene), as long as D's belief in V's guilt was a reasonable one.

The Fourth Amendment only applies to the actions of public officers.[12] Therefore, private parties who make arrests are not subject to the constitutional rules that apply to police officers, discussed above in subsection [A][2].

§ 21.03 FORCE USED IN LAW ENFORCEMENT: COMMON AND STATUTORY LAW

[A] Nondeadly Force

A police officer or private citizen may use force in law enforcement, either to prevent the commission or consummation of a crime, or to make an arrest after the offense has been committed. Criminal prosecutions for use of nondeadly force in such circumstances are rare.

The common law rule regarding use of nondeadly force in law enforcement may be summarized simply: A police officer or private person is justified in using nondeadly force upon another if she reasonably believes that: (1) such other person is committing or has committed a felony, or a misdemeanor amounting to a breach of the peace; and (2) the force used is necessary to prevent commission of the offense, or to effectuate an arrest, *i.e.*, to make the arrest or to prevent the arrestee's escape.[13]

---

tranquility of other persons. Cantwell v. Connecticut, 310 U.S. 296, 308 (1940). Sometimes, "breach of the peace" is a specific offense; in other cases, it is a general term that encompasses crimes such as "disorderly conduct" and "disturbing the peace."

[10] Rollin M. Perkins & Ronald N. Boyce, Criminal Law 1094–95 (3d ed. 1982).

[11] *See* State v. Johnson, 930 P.2d 1148, 1154 (N.M. 1996).

[12] Burdeau v. McDowell, 256 U.S. 465 (1921).

[13] *See* Durham v. State, 159 N.E. 145 (Ind. 1927); *In re* C.L.D., 739 A.2d 353, 354–55 (D.C. 1999) (citing this text); Restatement (Second) of Torts §§ 141–43 (1965).

[B] Deadly Force

Deadly force may *never* be used to prevent commission of a misdemeanor offense, or to effectuate an arrest of a misdemeanant.[14] The following discussion relates to use of deadly force in *felony* cases.

[1] Crime Prevention

Deadly force is permitted to prevent commission of felonies. A split of authority exists regarding the scope of this right.

[a] Broad Defense: Minority Rule

The broad, largely outdated, version of the crime prevention defense provides that a police officer or private person is justified in using deadly force upon another if she reasonably believes that: (1) such other person is committing any felony; and (2) deadly force is necessary to prevent commission of the crime.[15] This version of the defense is remarkably broad in that it authorizes use of necessary deadly force to prevent nonviolent felonies. Thus, D may kill V, a would-be felonious thief, if it is the only means to prevent her from taking the personal property of D or a third person, even though no life is jeopardized by V's criminal activities.

The right to use deadly force in crime prevention, as stated here, is broader than the scope of the common law justification of defense-of-property, which bars the use of deadly force to protect a person's possessory interest in property.[16] This difference results in an undesirable anomaly: If a defendant kills an intended thief, she may avoid conviction if she claims the defense of crime prevention, but may be convicted of murder if she raises a defense-of-property claim.

[b] Narrow Defense: Majority Rule

In modern times, the right to use deadly force is usually limited to the prevention of "forcible" or "atrocious" felonies, *i.e.*, felonies involving the use or threat of physical force or violence against any person.[17] Thus, under this rule, a store owner may shoot a would-be robber, if necessary, to prevent the commission of the offense, but she may not justifiably kill one who takes property and attempts to leave without paying for it, as the latter offense is a misdemeanor or, at most, the nonviolent felony of larceny.[18]

---

[14] *See* Tennessee v. Garner, 471 U.S. 1, 12 (1985); *Durham v. State*, 159 N.E. at 147.

[15] State v. Rutherford, 8 N.C. (1 Hawks) 457 (1821).

[16] *See* § 20.02[A], *supra*.

[17] *E.g.*, 4 William Blackstone, Commentaries on the Laws of England *180 (1769); 1 Matthew Hale, History of the Pleas of the Crown *488 (1736); Ga. Code Ann. § 16-3-204 (2008).

[18] *See* Laney v. State, 361 S.E.2d 841 (Ga. Ct. App. 1987), *overruled on other grounds*, Holmes v. State, 543 S.E.2d 688 (Ga. 2001) (upholding L's conviction for manslaughter in the death of V, who attempted to leave L's convenience store with a beer without paying for it; but stating that deadly force *would* have been permitted if L had reasonably believed that V was planning to rob the store).

[2]   Effectuation of an Arrest

[a]   By Police Officers

[i]   Early Common Law Rule

Until the 14th century, a law enforcement officer had the right (perhaps even the duty) to use deadly force against any person whom the officer reasonably believed had committed *any* felony. The officer was justified in killing the felon *even if deadly force was unnecessary to effectuate the felon's detention.*

This extreme approach was based on the premise that felons were outlaws at war with society.[19] Society was justified, therefore, in treating them as dangerous combatants whose lives could be taken for the community's benefit. This view was strengthened by the fact that all felonies were subject to the penalty of death and forfeiture of property. Thus, it was said, by committing a capital offense, a felon forfeited his right to life;[20] his killing was merely "a premature execution of the inevitable judgment."[21]

[ii]   Modification of the Rule

The stark approach of pre-14th century England is no longer followed. Necessity, not part of the original common law rule, is now included as an element of the defense. Thus, deadly force is permitted only as a last resort.[22] Nonetheless, under the modified common law rule, a person may use deadly force upon another if she reasonably believes: (1) the suspect committed a forcible *or nonforcible* felony; and (2) such force is necessary to make the arrest or to prevent the suspect from escaping. It should be observed that this rule is broader than the majority common law rule pertaining to the use of deadly force in crime prevention, which only authorizes the use of deadly force to repel *forcible* felonies.

[b]   By Private Persons

A private person may use deadly force, if reasonably necessary, to arrest or apprehend a felon, but the defense ordinarily is narrower than the comparable right held by police officers. The special limitations are the result of lawmakers' concerns about "uncontrolled vigilantism and anarchistic actions . . . [as well as] the danger of death or injury of innocent persons at the hands of untrained volunteers using firearms."[23]

Although the rules vary among the states, some of the special requirements that often must be satisfied before a private person may justifiably use deadly force in

---

[19] *See* Schumann v. McGinn, 240 N.W.2d 525, 532–33 (Minn. 1976).

[20] Petrie v. Cartwright, 70 S.W. 297, 299 (Ky. Ct. App. 1902).

[21] Note, *Legalized Murder of a Fleeing Felon*, 15 Va. L. Rev. 582, 583 (1929).

[22] *Schumann v. McGinn*, 240 N.W.2d at 533; 4 Blackstone, Note 17, *supra*, at *289; 1 Hale, Note 17, *supra*, at *85.

[23] Commonwealth v. Klein, 363 N.E.2d 1313, 1317–18 (Mass. 1977).

connection with a felony arrest include: (1) the offense must be a forcible felony;[24] (2) the arresting party must give the suspect notice of her intention to make the arrest;[25] and (3) the arresting party must be correct in her belief that the person against whom the force is used actually committed the offense in question, *i.e.*, a reasonable mistake of fact in this regard neither justifies nor excuses the use of deadly force.[26]

§ 21.04   FORCE USED IN LAW ENFORCEMENT: CONSTITUTIONAL LIMITS[27]

[A]   Background: The Controversy

Many commentators have criticized the breadth of the common law "law enforcement" defense set out above, which authorizes the use of deadly force, when reasonably necessary, to arrest or prevent the escape of persons suspected of *non*forcible felonies. And, critics have maintained that police officers too often kill or seriously injure individuals who do not even fall within the scope of justifiable force, *i.e.*, unarmed persons innocent of any offense or suspected of some very minor offense.[28]

Besides the loss of life involved in police shootings, police use of lethal force may have an undesirable effect on police-community relations. Police shootings can appear racially motivated[29] or the result of "trigger-happy" law enforcement

---

[24] *E.g., id.* at 1319.

[25] *E.g.,* Commonwealth v. Chermansky, 242 A.2d 237, 240 (Pa. 1968).

[26] *E.g., id; see also* Perkins & Boyce, Note 10, *supra,* at 1099–1100 ("a *private person* was never privileged to use deadly force to stop the flight of one he was seeking to arrest . . . if that one was in fact innocent").

[27] *See generally* Steven E. Barkan & Steven F. Cohn, *Racial Prejudice and Support by Whites for Police Use of Force: A Research Note,* 15 Just. Q. 743 (1998); Karen M. Blum, *Scott v. Harris: Death Knell for Deadly Force Policies and Garner Jury Instructions,* 58 Syracuse L. Rev. 45, 59 (2007); Rachel A. Harmon, *When Is Police Violence Justified?,* 102 Nw. U. L. Rev. 1119 (2008); Abraham N. Tennenbaum, *The Influence of the Garner Decision on Police Use of Deadly Force,* 85 J. Crim. L. & Criminology 241 (1994); H. Richard Uviller, *Seizure by Gunshot: The Riddle of the Fleeing Felon,* 14 N.Y.U. Rev. L. & Soc. Change 705 (1986).

[28] Data on killings *of* police officers are carefully compiled, but data on killing *by* police have not been the subject of systematic official recordkeeping. For the best recent effort to deal with this problem, see Franklin E. Zimring & Brittany Arsiniega, *Trends in Killings of and by Police: A Preliminary Analysis,* 13 Ohio St. J. Crim. L. ___ (Fall 2013). One early study based on data obtained from newspaper reports in four cities found substantial increases in reported killings and woundings from 1977 through 1988. In a two-year period, for example, 250 bystanders were killed or wounded in the four cities. The study stated that such shootings "rank[ed] at the top of public outrage." Illinois v. Wardlow, 528 U.S. 119, 131 n.6 (2000) (Stevens, J., concurring in part and dissenting in part) (directly quoting from Sherman et al., *Stray Bullets and "Mushrooms": Random Shootings of Bystanders in Four Cities, 1977–1988,* 5 J. Quantitative Criminology 297, 303 (1989)).

[29] *See* The President's Commission on Law Enforcement and Administration of Justice Task Force Report: The Police 183–90 (1967) (documenting the belief among racial minorities that police act abusively on racial grounds, and that such conduct is a principal reason for friction between the police and minority communities); *see also* Barkan & Cohn, Note 27, *supra* (noting significant attitudinal differences, between white and non-white communities, regarding police use of force).

officers.[30] Even when these appearances are inaccurate, police use of deadly force can increase tension between them and the communities they serve, resulting in citizen disrespect for the law.

Critics have also claimed that the underlying justifications for the broad defense no longer apply. The law no longer considers a felon an outlaw whose life may be taken at any time, regardless of necessity. Nor does the forfeiture theory withstand modern scrutiny: Only the crime of murder carries the penalty of death today, and even here it is not mandatory. It cannot be said, therefore, that any felon's "execution" on the street merely speeds up an inevitable process.[31]

Perhaps as a consequence of criticisms of police shootings, law enforcement agencies in some large American cities began in the late 1970s to develop policies limiting police use of firearms to circumstances in which a threat of death or serious bodily injury is posed to police or bystanders.[32] Then, beginning in 1985, the issue of police use of deadly force in law enforcement reached the United States Supreme Court. The Supreme Court case law is summarized below.

One important point must be noted here, however. As discussed below, the cases in this field have come to the courts, including the Supreme Court, in a civil context. That is, a victim or victim's family has sought damages under a federal statute, which prohibits violations by government officers of federal constitutional rights.[33] There is serious doubt, however, that the rules discussed below apply in a *criminal* case in which a police officer is prosecuted for using excessive force against a private party. That is, if a state provides a criminal law defense to a police officer who uses deadly force in circumstances that, under the constitutional law discussed below, would result in *civil* damages against the officer or police department, it is not clear that a criminal conviction of the officer for the homicide is permitted. If a state wishes to provide *criminal law* immunity to a police officer, even though she has acted in violation of the Constitution and, therefore, is subject to *civil* liability for such violation, this may be within the power of the state.[34]

[B]　Constitutional Law

The Fourth Amendment of the United States constitution prohibits "unreasonable searches and seizures" of persons and property. An arrest is a seizure of a person. Consequently, police officers must make arrests in a reasonable manner. An arrest is not reasonable if the officer lacked probable cause to make the arrest *or* if she used excessive force in effectuating the arrest. The

---

[30]　Eric Lichtblau, *LAPD Officers Faulted in 3 of 4 Shooting Cases*, L.A. *Times*, Aug. 14, 1994, at A1 (reporting that, according to a review of nearly 700 shooting reports in Los Angeles in 1989, officers succumbed to "the John Wayne Syndrome" and, in 75% of the cases, fired their weapons inappropriately).

[31]　Of course, the forfeiture justification could never withstand analysis when the suspected felon was innocent of the crime.

[32]　Tennessee v. Garner, 471 U.S. 1, 18–19 (1985).

[33]　42 U.S.C. § 1983 (2015).

[34]　At least a few courts have said or hinted that this is the case. State v. Clothier, 753 P.2d 1267, 1271 (Kan. 1988); People v. Couch, 461 N.W.2d 683, 684 (Mich. 1990).

question here is: When is deadly force to effectuate an arrest unreasonable and, therefore, in violation of the Fourth Amendment?

In *Tennessee v. Garner*,[35] the Supreme Court provided its first answer to this question. In *Garner*, *O*, an officer, was dispatched to a home on a "prowler inside call." He observed *G* fleeing in the direction of a six-foot-high chain-link fence. By use of his flashlight, *O* could tell that *G* was young, 5'5" to 5'7" tall, and apparently unarmed. He ordered *G* to halt; when the youth began to scale the fence, *O* shot him in the back of the head, killing him. A federal civil suit was brought. The Supreme Court held that *O*'s use of deadly force to prevent the escape of *G*, an apparently unarmed felon, violated the Fourth Amendment. It stated that "[t]he use of deadly force to prevent the escape of all felony suspects, whatever the circumstances, is constitutionally unreasonable. It is not better that all felony suspects die than that they escape."

Garner seemingly announced a relatively clear rule applicable to all civil suits in which deadly force is used by police officers[36] to prevent suspects from escaping arrest: Deadly force is unreasonable, even if there is probable cause for the arrest, unless two conditions are met: (1) the officer must have "probable cause to believe that the suspect poses a significant threat of death or serious physical injury to the officer or others"; and (2) the officer must reasonably believe that deadly force is necessary to make the arrest or prevent escape. This is the rule lower courts applied following *Garner*.[37]

The Supreme Court returned, however, to the issue in 2007, in *Scott v. Harris*.[38] In doing so, it effectively rewrote the lesson of *Garner*.[39] In *Scott*, police officers rammed a fleeing motorist's car from behind during a high-speed chase that began when they sought to ticket the motorist for speeding. The motorist survived the incident, but brought suit against the police under *Tennessee v. Garner*, asserting that the officers failed to meet the two preconditions to use of deadly force set out in that case.

The *Scott* Court agreed that the police action here "posed a high likelihood of serious injury or death" to the motorist and, therefore, constituted deadly force. They further acknowledged that the police could have avoided the risk of killing the motorist by terminating pursuit of him. Nonetheless, the Court held that the officers' action did *not* violate the Fourth Amendment, and further stated:

> *Garner* does not establish a magical on/off switch that triggers rigid preconditions whenever an officer's actions constitute "deadly force." *Garner* was simply an application of the Fourth Amendment's "reasonable-ness" test . . . to the use of a particular type of force in a particular

[35] 471 U.S. 1 (1985).

[36] The Fourth Amendment only applies to governmental conduct. Therefore, common law and statutory provisions relating to the use of deadly force *by private persons* are not affected by *Garner*.

[37] Harmon, Note 27, *supra*, at 1128.

[38] 550 U.S. 372 (2007).

[39] Harmon, Note 27, *supra*, at 1135–36 (In *Scott*, "the Supreme Court waved away what every federal court since *Garner* . . . had taken to be clear criteria for determining the reasonableness of the use of deadly force against fleeing suspects during an arrest.").

situation. . . . Whatever *Garner* said about the factors that *might have* justified shooting the suspect in that case, such "preconditions" have scant applicability to this case, which has vastly different facts.[40]

Although the Court did not back off from its specific holding in *Garner*, it warned that "in the end we must still slosh through the factbound morass of 'reasonableness.'" That is, in determining whether the police acted reasonably in using deadly force to effectuate an arrest, a court must balance the interests of the defendant against society's interest in effectuating the particular arrest in question. This means that there is no bright-line rule for determining precisely when deadly force crosses the line from legitimate to unconstitutionally excessive force.[41]

§ 21.05   MODEL PENAL CODE

[A]   Authority to Arrest

The Model Penal Code defense of "execution of public duty" provides that conduct is justified when it is required or permitted by: (1) a law defining the duties of a government officer; (2) a law pertaining to the execution of legal process; (3) an order of a court; or (4) any other law imposing a public duty on the actor.[42]

This defense is also available in two circumstances in which an actor *lacks* legal authority to act, but believes that she does. Essentially, these two situations constitute special mistake-of-law rules. First, a law enforcement officer acts justifiably if she believes, albeit incorrectly, that her conduct is authorized "by the judgment or direction of a competent court or tribunal or in the lawful execution of legal process."[43] For example, if *D* makes an arrest based on a warrant (*i.e.*, legal process) that later proves to be defective (*e.g.*, it was issued on less than probable cause), she is not subject to criminal prosecution for restricting the arrestee's liberty in an unlawful manner.

Second, the defense is available to a private individual who believes that she is authorized to assist a public officer in the performance of her duties, although it turns out that the officer was acting beyond her authority.[44] For example, if an officer requests assistance from a bystander in making an arrest, the private citizen is not subject to prosecution if the officer lacked authority to arrest the

---

[40] 550 U.S. at 382–83; *see* Blum, Note 27, *supra*, at 59 (describing this statement by the Court as "simply wrong, or, at best misguided, and reflects an exercise in reconstruction of a case that has clearly stood for more than its particular facts for over twenty years").

[41] In recent years, the Supreme Court has hesitated to uphold excessive-force civil suits that have reached it. For example, in Plumhoff v. Rickard, 134 S. Ct. 2012 (2014), another case involving a high-speed chase after a driver was stopped for a traffic violation and then sped away, the police fired 12 shots at the car, killing the driver and his passenger. The Court held that, in light of the driver's "outrageously reckless driving," and the genuine risk to innocent drivers, the officers acted reasonably in using deadly force to bring the car to a halt.

[42] Model Penal Code § 3.03(1).

[43] Model Penal Code § 3.03(3)(a).

[44] Model Penal Code § 3.03(3)(b).

suspect, *e.g.*, lacked probable cause for the arrest or did not have a required warrant.

[B] Crime Prevention

[1] Use of Force, In General

A police officer or private person is justified in using force upon another if she believes that: (1) such other person is about to commit suicide, inflict serious bodily injury upon herself, or commit a crime involving or threatening bodily injury, damage to or loss of property, or a breach of the peace; and (2) the force is immediately necessary to prevent commission of the aforementioned act.[45] Deadly force is impermissible except as discussed below.

The Code does not impose any special limitations on the use of nondeadly force in crime prevention. Instead, it provides that the limitations on the use of force imposed by the other justification provisions of the Code apply to the use of force in crime prevention.[46]

[2] Use of Deadly Force

A police officer or private person may not use deadly force to prevent the commission of a crime unless she believes that: (1) a substantial risk exists that the suspect will cause death or serious bodily injury to another person unless she prevents the suspect from committing the offense; and (2) use of deadly force presents no substantial risk of injury to bystanders.[47]

This provision should be compared to the Code's deadly-force provisions in analogous circumstances. First, it largely parallels the effectuation-of-arrest defense discussed below, except that the crime prevention defense applies to all persons, public or private, whereas only public officers and those aiding them may use deadly force in the arrest process. The Institute's justification for this distinction is that "[i]n modern conditions, the arrest of suspected criminals is peculiarly the concern of the police. The prevention of crime, on the other hand, is properly the concern of everybody."[48]

Second, the crime prevention defense is somewhat narrower than the rules regarding defense of property.[49] The present defense, but not the defense of property, prohibits the use of deadly force if it would jeopardize the safety of bystanders. Moreover, deadly force may be used in defense of property in some circumstances in which the safety of the actor is no longer threatened,[50] but deadly force is *not* permitted in crime prevention unless the actor believes that there is a

---

[45] Model Penal Code § 3.07(5)(a).

[46] Model Penal Code § 3.07(5)(a)(i).

[47] Model Penal Code § 3.07(5)(a)(ii)(A).

[48] American Law Institute, Comment to § 3.07, at 132.

[49] *Id.*, Comment to § 3.06, at 95 n.48.

[50] *See* § 20.05[C][1][b], *supra*.

related threat of death or serious bodily injury connected to the commission of the crime.

[C] Effectuation of an Arrest

[1] Use of Force, In General

A police officer or private person is justified in using force upon another to make or assist in making an arrest, or to prevent the suspect's escape, if the actor: (1) believes that force is immediately necessary to effectuate a lawful arrest or to prevent the suspect's escape;[51] and (2a) makes known to such other person the purpose of the arrest or (2b) believes that such other person understands the purpose of the arrest or that notice cannot reasonably be provided.[52] Deadly force is impermissible except as discussed immediately below.

[2] Use of Deadly Force

Deadly force may never be used by a private person, acting on her own, to make an arrest or to prevent a suspect's escape. However, deadly force may be employed by a police officer, or a private person assisting someone whom she believes is a law enforcement officer, to make an arrest or to prevent the suspect's escape if: (1) the arrest is for a felony; (2) the requirements for the use of force set out in subsection [C][1] of the text immediately above are satisfied; (3) the actor believes that the use of deadly force creates no substantial risk of harm to innocent bystanders; and either (4a) the actor believes that the crime included the use or threatened use of deadly force; or (4b) the actor believes that a substantial risk exists that the suspect will kill or seriously harm another if her arrest is delayed or if she escapes.[53]

This Code provision is considerably narrower than the common law. First, the common law permitted private citizens acting alone to use deadly force in making arrests. Second, deadly force may not be used unless the actor affirmatively believes that its use will not seriously jeopardize the safety of bystanders. For example, assume *D*, a police officer, purposely shoots and kills *V*, a dangerous fleeing felon, on a crowded street. At common law, *D*'s conduct as to *V* would be justified; under the Code, *D* would be denied the law enforcement defense, and could be convicted of purposely killing *V*, unless she believed that her actions did not jeopardize the bystanders' safety.[54]

---

[51] The defense is not available, however, if the arrest or degree of force used was unlawful and if the actor's belief in its lawfulness was the result of a mistake of law regarding provisions of the criminal law or the law governing the scope of her power to arrest. Model Penal Code § 3.09(1). *See generally* American Law Institute, Comment to § 3.07, at 107.

[52] Model Penal Code §§ 3.07(1), 3.07(2)(a), 3.07(3).

[53] Model Penal Code § 3.07(2)(b).

[54] This provision represents a departure from the rule set out in Model Penal Code § 3.09(3), as discussed at § 18.06[C], *supra*. Under § 3.09, a person whose conduct in relation to *V* is justified, but whose conduct recklessly or negligently threatens the safety of *X*, a bystander, is entitled to the defense in a prosecution for use of force against *V*, but may be convicted of an offense based on recklessness or negligence regarding *X*. Under § 3.07, however, *D*'s recklessness regarding the safety of *X* results in the loss of the defense *in relation to V*. The drafters of the Code believed that this was an appropriate way

Third, unlike the common law, the Code does not permit use of deadly force in making arrests for nonforcible felonies in the absence of special circumstances. Essentially, the Code does not justify use of deadly force in effectuating an arrest for a felony unless the arrestee poses such a high level of risk to the safety of others, should she remain free, that her immediate capture by use of deadly force overrides her right to life.[55]

---

of emphasizing the priority that police officers must accord to the safety of bystanders. American Law Institute, Comment to § 3.07, at 118.

[55] American Law Institute, Comment to § 3.07, at 120.

Chapter 22

NECESSITY

§ 22.01 BASIC NATURE OF THE DEFENSE[1]

This chapter considers the defense of necessity, also called the "lesser evil" or "choice of evils" defense. Unfortunately, "[t]he origins and present status of the defense . . . are shrouded in uncertainty and confusion."[2] Indeed, at the foundational level, there is uncertainty whether the defense should be classified as a justification defense, an excuse, or as having characteristics of both. Also, this defense is often confused with, or is treated as part of, a broader defense encompassing the defense of duress. The excuse characteristics of "necessity" (to the extent that they might exist) and the relationship of necessity to the defense of duress, are considered in the next chapter.[3] This chapter considers only necessity as a justification defense.

The defense of necessity can arise in a myriad of circumstances, but is rarely successful. It is most often invoked successfully when an actor encounters the following dilemma: As a result of some natural (non-human) force or condition, he must choose between violating a relatively minor offense, on the one hand, and suffering (or allowing others to suffer) substantial harm to person or property, on the other hand. For example, the necessity defense applies if a seaman violates an embargo by putting into a foreign port due to dangerous and unforeseeable weather conditions,[4] a person drives on a suspended license in order to take a loved one to the hospital in a life-endangering emergency,[5] or a motorist exceeds the speed limit in order to pass another car and move to the right lane, so that an emergency vehicle can pass.[6]

---

[1] *See generally* George Fletcher, Rethinking Criminal Law § 10.2 (1978); Kent Greenawalt, Conflicts of Law and Morality 286–310 (1987); Glanville Williams, Criminal Law: The General Part §§ 229–39 (2d ed. 1961); Edward B. Arnolds & Norman F. Garland, *The Defense of Necessity in Criminal Law: The Right to Choose the Lesser Evil*, 65 J. Crim. L. & Criminology 289 (1974); Monu Bedi, *Excusing Behavior: Reclassifying the Federal Common Law Defenses of Duress and Necessity Relying on the Victim's Role*, 101 J. Crim. L. & Criminology 575 (2011); P.R. Glazebrook, *The Necessity Plea in English Criminal Law*, 30 Cambridge L.J. 87 (1972); Rollin M. Perkins, *Impelled Perpetration Restated*, 33 Hastings L.J. 403 (1981).

[2] Greenawalt, Note 1, *supra*, at 288; *see also* Toops v. State, 643 N.E.2d 387, 388 (Ind. Ct. App. 1994) ("The origins of the necessity defense are lost in antiquity.").

[3] *See* §§ 23.03, 23.05–.06, *infra*.

[4] The William Gray, 29 F. Cas. 1300 (C.C.D.N.Y. 1810).

[5] State v. Baker, 579 A.2d 479 (Vt. 1990).

[6] State v. Messler, 562 A.2d 1138 (Conn. App. Ct. 1989); *see also* Toops v. State, 643 N.E.2d 387 (Ind. Ct. App. 1994) (defense is available where *T*, an intoxicated passenger, assumed control of a moving,

Not all litigated necessity cases fit the preceding, relatively easy, paradigm. For example, courts have been required to determine whether it is justifiable for a homeless person to violate a city ordinance banning sleeping in designated public areas,[7] or for a person to do any of the following: possess marijuana for use to reduce the effects of a serious disease;[8] distribute clean hypodermic needles to drug addicts in an effort to combat the spread of AIDS;[9] escape confinement because of intolerable prison conditions;[10] to possess a firearm (otherwise in violation of law) because of an unlawful imminent threat to life;[11] forge a check to pay for food out of economic necessity;[12] kidnap a person in order to remove her from the influence of a "religious cult";[13] drive an automobile in an intoxicated condition in order to escape an angry, threatening abusive husband;[14] or kill an innocent person in order to save several innocent lives.[15] Occasionally, too, the defense is raised when a person commits civil disobedience in order to signal his opposition to a law or governmental policy.[16]

Generally speaking, "necessity" may be characterized as a "residual justification defense." That is, it is a defense of last resort: It legitimizes technically illegal conduct that common sense, principles of justice, and/or utilitarian considerations convince us is justifiable, but which is not dealt with — neither authorized nor disallowed — by any other recognized justification defense. Thus, the necessity defense serves as "a supplement to legislative judgment."[17] It comes into play in relatively unique instances in which it may fairly be assumed that lawmakers *would* have authorized the conduct if they could have considered the matter in advance.

The principle of necessity — that, if circumstances require a choice among various evils, an actor is justified if he chooses the least harmful option — is one so "essential to the rationality and justice of the criminal law, [that it] is appropriately

---

careening vehicle, when the original driver dove into the back seat in a panic).

[7] *In re* Eichorn, 69 Cal. App. 4th 382 (Ct. App. 1998) (permitting consideration of the defense).

[8] *E.g.*, State v. Kurtz, 309 P.3d 472 (Wash. 2013) (permitting a medical necessity defense); State v. Bonjour, 694 N.W.2d 511 (Iowa 2005) (barring such a defense); *see also* United States v. Oakland Cannabis Buyers' Coop., 532 U.S. 483 (2001) (not recognizing the defense in a federal prosecution for manufacturing and distributing marijuana).

[9] Commonwealth v. Leno, 616 N.E.2d 453 (Mass. 1993) (disallowing the defense).

[10] *See* § 23.05, *infra.*

[11] United States v. Gomez, 92 F.3d 770 (9th Cir. 1996) (allowing the defense).

[12] People v. Fontes, 89 P.3d 484 (Colo. App. 2003) ("While we are not without sympathy for the downtrodden, the law is clear that economic necessity alone cannot support a choice of crime."); *but see* Rosemond v. United States, 134 S. Ct. 1240, 1255 (2014) (Alito, J., dissenting) (suggesting that Victor Hugo's famous *Les Misérables* character, Jean Valjean, "had he been living in American today, . . . may have pleaded necessity as a defense" to stealing the loaf of bread to feed his starving family).

[13] People v. Brandyberry, 812 P.2d 674 (Colo. App. 1991) (disallowing the defense).

[14] Axelberg v. Commissioner of Public Safety, 848 N.W.2d 206 (Minn. 2014) (disallowing the defense); *but see* Greenwood v. State, 237 P.3d 1018 (Alaska 2010) (allowing the defense when she heard that her former boyfriend threatened to burn her parent's house, so she drove to the house to warn them).

[15] *See* § 22.04, *infra.*

[16] *See* § 22.03, *infra.*

[17] Greenawalt, Note 1, *supra*, at 289.

addressed in a penal code."[18]

§ 22.02   GENERAL RULES

Necessity may not have been a common law defense in England,[19] but it is a part of the common law tradition of the United States.[20] Despite this, the defense has no single accepted definition. Indeed, at any given time in history it was exceedingly difficult to determine the standing and scope of the defense in any particular jurisdiction.[21]

Today, 19 states statutorily recognize the defense.[22] Some of the statutes define "necessity" in general terms; others are more specific in their descriptions. In states without a statutory defense, the vague contours of the common law presumably apply.[23]

The parameters of the common law defense may be deduced from its purpose as described in the preceding chapter section. Subject to three potential limitations mentioned below, generally speaking, a person is justified in violating a criminal law if the following six conditions are met.

First, the actor must be "faced with a clear and imminent danger."[24] For example, in *United States v. Paolello*,[25] *X*, unjustifiably fired a weapon in the air, threatening *P*, a convicted felon. To protect himself, *P* wrested the gun from *X* and ran away with it. *P* was prosecuted for violation of a statute that made it an offense for a convicted felon to possess a firearm. Based on these facts, however, *P* was entitled to an instruction on the necessity defense, because the danger to him was clear and imminent. In contrast, in *Commonwealth v. Leno*,[26] *L* participated in a needle exchange program run by AIDS activists, in which he and others furnished clean needles to drug addicts in order to reduce the spread of the then-deadly disease. *L* was charged with possession and distribution of hypodermic needles without a prescription. The Supreme Judicial Court of Massachusetts held that *L* was not entitled to a jury instruction on the defense necessity because the harm — spread of AIDS — was not imminent in any given case in which the needles were exchanged.

---

[18] American Law Institute, Comment to § 3.02, at 9.

[19] Glanville Williams states "somewhat confidently" that it was a defense in England. Williams, Note 1, *supra*, at § 231. Others disagree. *See* English Law Commission, No. 83, Criminal Law Report on Defences of General Application 20 (1977).

[20] American Law Institute, Comment to § 3.02, at 10.

[21] *Id.* at 10–11.

[22] Michael H. Hoffheimer, *Codifying Necessity: Legislative Resistance to Enacting Choice-of-Evils Defenses to Criminal Liability*, 82 Tul. L. Rev. 191, 232 (2007).

[23] However, in the *federal* courts, it is now considered "an open question whether federal courts ever have authority to recognize a necessity defense not provided by statute." United States v. Oakland Cannabis Buyers' Coop., 532 U.S. 483, 490 (2001) (dictum).

[24] Commonwealth v. Brugmann, 433 N.E.2d 457, 461 (Mass. App. Ct. 1982).

[25] 951 F.2d 537 (3d Cir. 1991).

[26] 616 N.E.2d 453 (Mass. 1993).

Second, the defendant must expect, as a reasonable person, that his action will be effective in abating the danger that he seeks to avoid, *i.e.*, there must be a direct causal relationship between his action and the harm to be averted.[27] For example, an inmate who flees confinement because of a raging prison fire, has chosen a path that will directly save his life.

Third, there must be no effective *legal* way to avert the harm.[28] For example, in *Nelson v. State*,[29] N drove his truck onto a side road off the highway, where it became stuck in a marsh. After spending an hour trying to free the vehicle, N and a friend went to a nearby Highway Department Yard where they took a dump truck without permission, and unsuccessfully used it to try to pull N's vehicle out of the mud, thereby damaging the dump truck. N was prosecuted for reckless destruction of the Highway Department's property and of driving the truck without consent. The court held that the facts did not support a defense of necessity, in part because N had lawful alternatives in his situation — on several occasions strangers offered to help pull the vehicle out of the marsh or by calling for a tow truck or the police.

Fourth, the harm that the defendant will cause by violating the law must be less serious than the harm that he seeks to avoid.[30] Two features of this lesser-harm principle must be understood. First, in balancing the harms, the defendant's actions "should be weighed against the harm reasonably foreseeable at the time, rather than the harm that actually occurs."[31] For example, if D's car loses its brakes and D must choose between striking one of two parked automobiles, one of which is occupied by one person (who will likely be injured by the collision) and another that apparently is unoccupied, D should choose the latter option. He would not lose the defense, however, if it later turns out that the "unoccupied car" in fact contained two children inside, not visible to D or any reasonable person when he had to make the emergency decision. Second, given the facts as they reasonably appear, the issue is not whether the *defendant* believes that he made the right choice, but rather the question is "whether the defendant's value judgment was [in fact] correct,"[32] as determined by the judge or the jury. What is less clear is whether the value judgment should be made on utilitarian grounds[33] or on the basis "of what is [morally] right and proper conduct under the circumstances."[34]

A fifth condition of the necessity defense is that lawmakers must not have previously "anticipated the choice of evils and determined the balance to be struck between the competing values" in a manner in conflict with the defendant's choice.[35] For example, a defendant may not defend his illegal use of marijuana for medical purposes if the legislature previously "weighed the competing value of medical use

---

[27] *Id.* at 455; United States v. Schoon, 971 F.2d 193, 195 (9th Cir. 1991).

[28] *Commonwealth v. Leno*, 616 N.E.2d at 455; People v. Gray, 571 N.Y.S.2d 851, 853 (Crim. Ct. 1991).

[29] 597 P.2d 977 (Alaska 1979).

[30] State v. Cram, 600 A.2d 733, 735 (Vt. 1991).

[31] *Nelson v. State*, 597 P.2d at 980.

[32] *Id.* at 980 n.6.

[33] *United States v. Schoon*, 971 F.2d at 196 ("Necessity is, essentially, a utilitarian defense.").

[34] *Id.* at 200 (Fernandez, J., concurring).

[35] State v. Tate, 505 A.2d 941, 946 (N.J. 1986); *Commonwealth v. Leno*, 616 N.E.2d at 455.

of marijuana against the values served by prohibition of its use or possession," and rejected the former claim.[36]

The final feature of the necessity defense is that the defendant must come to the situation with clean hands. That is, he must not have "substantially contribute[d] to the emergency"[37] or wrongfully "placed himself in a situation in which he would be forced to engage in criminal conduct."[38] For example, suppose that D recklessly starts a fire. He realizes that the fire is likely to spread quickly and burn down a number of residences, so he purposely burns V's farm land in order to create a "fire line" that will prevent a major conflagration. Although D's act satisfies the other elements of the defense, he may be denied the defense of necessity because he was responsible for creating the emergency.[39]

Even if these elements of the necessity defense are proven, three limitations on the application of the necessity defense may come into play. First, some states limit the defense to emergencies created by natural (as distinguished from human) forces.[40] Thus, in these jurisdictions, D may trespass on property in order to avoid a tornado, but not to escape an armed robber. Likewise, D, a prison inmate, may be able to claim necessity if he flees a prison as the result of a conflagration, but not if another inmate threatens to assault him. Assuming that the defendant has chosen the lesser of two evils, and the other elements of the defense are satisfied, this natural-versus-human distinction is indefensible.

Second, the necessity defense may not apply in homicide cases.[41] Third, some states limit the defense to protection of persons and property; in such jurisdictions a person may not act, for example, to protect reputation or economic interests, no matter what the circumstances.[42]

---

[36] *State v. Tate*, 505 A.2d at 946.

[37] People v. Pepper, 41 Cal. App. 4th 1029, 1035 (Ct. App. 1996).

[38] United States v. Paolello, 951 F.2d 537, 541 (3d Cir. 1991).

[39] From a utilitarian perspective, this requirement is unwise. The law should provide D with an incentive, *i.e.*, the necessity defense, to save the houses from the fire. D remains liable in tort for his original reckless conduct, and he would be subject to criminal prosecution for any offense (*e.g.*, reckless endangerment) committed by his recklessness, but he should be encouraged to stop the conflagration. From a retributivist perspective, as well, the rule is unsound, for it may result in an actor being punished in excess of his culpability. In the current example, D will be convicted of *purposely* setting fire to V's land, although his true culpability is that of recklessness for setting the original fire. *See* Paul H. Robinson, *Causing the Conditions of One's Own Defense: A Study in the Limits of Theory in Criminal Law Doctrine*, 71 Va. L. Rev. 1, 3–4, 8–10 (1985).

[40] *E.g.*, Wis. Stat. § 939.47 (2015) ("[p]ressure of natural physical forces").

[41] This is a matter of controversy. *See* § 22.04, *infra*.

[42] *E.g.*, State v. Moe, 24 P.2d 638, 640 (Wash. 1933) ("Economic necessity has never been accepted as a defense to a criminal charge").

§ 22.03   CIVIL DISOBEDIENCE[43]

"Civil disobedience" may be defined as a nonviolent act, publicly performed and deliberately unlawful, that has as its purpose to protest a law, government policy, or action of a private body whose conduct has serious public consequences.[44]

Civil disobedience may be direct or indirect. Direct civil disobedience involves protesting a particular law by breaking it or "by preventing the execution of that law in a specific instance."[45] For example, in the early 1960s civil rights demonstrators "sat-in" all-white lunch counters in the South to protest, and ultimately to prove the unconstitutionality, of segregationist laws that barred their presence.

In contrast, indirect civil disobedience involves the violation of a law that is not the object of the protest. In this category, for example, are protesters who violate a trespass statute, although they have no objection to trespass laws, in order to express their opposition to the construction of a nuclear power plant[46] or the performance of abortions in a nearby clinic,[47] or who sit in a Congressman's office in order to protest governmental actions in a foreign country.[48]

Do the facts alleged in a typical indirect civil disobedience case state a credible claim of necessity, so as to justify a jury instruction on the defense? The issue usually arises prior to trial as part of a prosecutor's motion "*in limine*" ("on or at the threshold") to bar evidence on the necessity claim, or during trial when the prosecutor objects to introduction of such evidence. If the prosecutor's motion or objection is granted, which it nearly always is,[49] the defendant is left without any realistic basis to avoid conviction. Therefore, on appeal from the conviction, the defendant will argue that he was improperly denied the opportunity to raise the necessity claim with the jury.

Appellate courts consistently reject the claim that a defendant is entitled to assert a necessity defense in cases of indirect civil disobedience.[50] Indeed, one federal circuit court has ruled that the defense is unavailable as a matter of law in

---

[43] *See generally* Carl Cohen, Civil Disobedience (1971); Abe Fortas, Concerning Dissent and Civil Disobedience (1968); Greenawalt, Note 1, *supra*; Steven M. Bauer & Peter J. Eckerstrom, Note, *The State Made Me Do It: The Applicability of the Necessity Defense to Civil Disobedience*, 39 Stan. L. Rev. 1173 (1987); Itzhak Kugler, *On the Possibility of a Criminal Law Defence for Conscientious Objection*, 10 Can. J. L. & Jurisprudence 387 (1997).

[44] *See* Cohen, Note 43, *supra*, at 39–40.

[45] United States v. Schoon, 971 F.2d 193, 196 (9th Cir. 1991).

[46] Commonwealth v. Capitolo, 498 A.2d 806 (Pa. 1985) (defense is inapplicable).

[47] *E.g.*, United States v. Lucero, 895 F. Supp. 1421 (D. Kan. 1995) (defense is inapplicable); City of Wichita v. Tilson, 855 P.2d 911 (Kan. 1993) (same); Jones v. City of Tulsa, 857 P.2d 814 (Okla. Crim. App. 1993) (same).

[48] People v. Craig, 585 N.E.2d 783 (N.Y. 1991) (protesting governmental policy in Nicaragua; held: defense is inapplicable); State v. Cram, 600 A.2d 733 (Vt. 1991) (protest of shipment of guns to El Salvador; held: same).

[49] On rare occasions, a trial judge permits the defendant to raise the claim. *E.g.*, Terry Wilson, *26 Found Not Guilty of Trespassing at Base*, Chi. *Trib.*, May 18, 1988, at 3 (twenty-six protesters were acquitted of trespassing to dramatize their opposition to United States policy in Central America).

[50] *E.g.*, State v. Warshow, 410 A.2d 1000 (Vt. 1979); United States v. Kroncke, 459 F.2d 697 (8th Cir. 1972); *see also* the citations in Notes 46–48, *supra*.

all such cases.[51] Typically, the requisites of a traditional necessity claim are lacking in indirect civil disobedience cases: the harm to be avoided is not imminent; the protest cannot directly abate the danger; protesters have legal options, such as the ballot box, to seek change in the disputed policy; and the legislature (or, in the case of issues such as abortion, the judiciary) has calculated the comparative harms differently than the protesters and its value determination may not be overridden.

As a matter of technical application of the necessity defense, the claim should be unavailable to protesters. However, advocates of a "political necessity" defense contend that such a defense should be recognized because it "empowers the individual primarily by presenting a forum in which stifled minority or unheeded majority viewpoints receive a public hearing."[52] Also, the defense empowers the jury, by giving them an opportunity to nullify the law[53] and "weigh in" on a controversial subject. Some would argue, as well, that the criminal law should not be used against those who — in contrast to ordinary criminals — are impelled by conscience and not avarice or some similar improper motive, to nonviolently violate the law.

Opponents of such a defense believe that recognition of a defense would undesirably erode the principle of traditional civil disobedience, which is that people who are compelled by conscience to violate the law, but who also believe in a democratic system, should accept their punishment (as Gandhi and Martin Luther King did) as part of their protest.[54] As one philosopher put it, "[w]e must pay a certain price to convince others that our actions have . . . a sufficient moral basis in the political convictions of the community."[55] And, for some critics, a civil disobedient *does* demonstrate his own character flaw, namely, moral arrogance, by believing that his value judgments are better than society's. Therefore, the reasoning goes, the law violator should accept punishment as the price of choosing to break the law, rather than using the democratic processes.

§ 22.04   "NECESSITY" AS A DEFENSE TO HOMICIDE[56]

[A]   The Issue

Assume for a moment that *A*, *B*, and *C*, are riding in a horse-drawn carriage that is being pursued by a pack of very hungry wolves. If it becomes clear to the passengers that the horse cannot outrun the wolves and that all of them will likely

---

[51]   United States v. Schoon, 971 F.2d 193 (9th Cir. 1991).

[52]   Bauer & Eckerstrom, Note 43, *supra*, at 1184.

[53]   The jury nullification principle is discussed at § 1.02[C], *supra*.

[54]   Bauer & Eckerstrom, Note 43, *supra*, at 1194.

[55]   John Rawls, A Theory of Justice 367 (1971).

[56]   *See generally* A.W. Brian Simpson, Cannibalism and the Common Law (1984); Joshua Dressler, *Reflections on Dudley and Stephens and Killing the Innocent: Taking a Wrong Conceptual Path, in* The Sanctity of Life and the Criminal Law: The Legacy of Glanville Williams (Dennis J. Baker & Jeremy Horder, eds. 2012); Lon L. Fuller, *The Case of the Speluncean Explorers*, 62 Harv. L. Rev. 616 (1949); S.E. Marshall, *Life or Death on a Plank — Ripstein and Kant*, 2 Ohio St. J. Crim. L. 435 (2005); Arthur Ripstein, *In Extremis*, 2 Ohio St. J. Crim. L. 415 (2005); Tom Stacy, *Acts, Omissions, and the Necessity*

be devoured by the animals, may A push B out of the carriage, so that the wolves devour him, thereby saving the lives of A and C?[57]

Or, suppose that D, a surgeon, wants to save the lives of five critically ill patients, one of whom needs a new heart, two of whom each need a healthy lung, and two of whom require a kidney transplant to survive. Each of his patients is likely to die within 24 hours without the needed operation. Along comes E, who possesses two good lungs, two good kidneys, and a very healthy heart. Amazingly, E has the proper blood type and tissue-match to serve as an organ donor for D's patients. May D harvest E's organs, on the ground that he has saved five people at the expense of just one?[58]

Or, consider the recent tragic British case of conjoined infant twins, Jodie and Mary.[59] Jodie, the stronger twin, provided oxygenated blood to her own body and sister Mary through a shared artery. According to their doctors, Jodie's heart could not continue to support both bodies for longer than a few more months, at which time both would certainly die; if the twins were surgically separated, however, Jodie could live a full life, but Mary would die immediately. Thus, without surgery, two would die; with surgery, one would die. The parents opposed surgically separating the twins for religious reasons; the physicians sought and secured judicial authorization to conduct the surgery. As expected, Mary died. Jodie survived and is living a relatively normal life.

Finally, what if the government had realized on September 11, 2001, that one of the hijacked planes was going to crash into one of the Twin Towers in New York City, ultimately taking the lives of more than 1,000 persons. Would the government have been justified in shooting down the plane, thereby killing hundreds of innocent passengers?

Each of these hypotheticals seemingly raises the same issue: Assuming that all of the requirements for a necessity defense are otherwise satisfied, may a person justifiably kill an innocent person — or more than one — in order to save a greater number of innocent lives? Fortunately, this issue rarely arises. The most celebrated criminal case involved a lifeboat containing four hungry individuals.

[B] *Regina v. Dudley and Stephens*[60]

Three adult seamen and a 17-year-old youth were forced to survive on an open boat after their sailing vessel sank. After 20 days on the boat, the last nine days of which were without food, and the last seven of which were without water, the seamen were exceedingly weak. The boy was seriously ill, as well, from drinking seawater. As a consequence, two of the men, D and S, killed V, the youth, in order

---

of Killing Innocents, 29 Am. J. Crim. L. 481 (2002); Judith Jarvis Thomson, *The Trolley Problem*, 94 Yale L.J. 1395 (1985); Glanville Williams, *A Commentary on* R. v. Dudley and Stephens, 8 Cambrian L. Rev. 94 (1977).

[57] Perkins, Note 1, *supra*, at 406.

[58] Thomson, Note 56, *supra*, at 1396.

[59] Re A, [2000] 4 All E.R. 961.

[60] 14 Q.B.D. 273 (1884); *see generally* Dressler, note 56, *supra*.

to eat his flesh to survive.[61] Four days later, the three survivors were discovered and saved. *D* and *S* were prosecuted for *V*'s murder. They raised the defense of necessity, arguing that they reasonably believed (and the jury so found) that, had they not killed *V*, all of the occupants of the boat probably would have perished.

Their defense claim was rejected. Lord Coleridge, describing the argument as "new and strange," canvassed common law authority, and concluded that no decided case or scholar, with one possible exception,[62] supported the claim that "in order to save your own life you may lawfully take the life of another, when that other is neither attempting nor threatening [to take] yours, nor is guilty of any illegal act whatever toward you or any one else."

Lord Coleridge stated that, although "preserv[ing] one's life is generally speaking a duty, . . . it may be the plainest and highest duty to sacrifice it. . . . [I]t is enough in a Christian country to remind ourselves of the Great Example whom we profess to follow." Although Coleridge conceded that the principle he was espousing was harsh, he remarked that "[w]e are often compelled to set up standards that we cannot reach ourselves, and to lay down rules which we could not ourselves satisfy." And, on a more pragmatic level, Coleridge also feared the potential for abuse: "[I]t is quite plain that such a principle [as *D* and *S* were espousing] once admitted might be made the legal cloak for unbridled passion and atrocious crime."

D and *S* were convicted of murder and sentenced to death, although the sentence was commuted by the Crown to six months' imprisonment.

Based on *Dudley and Stephens*, and an American case that also rejected the necessity defense in somewhat similar circumstances,[63] most, but not all, English commentators have concluded that the common law bars the defense of necessity in intentional homicide prosecutions, and some American courts and statutes expressly so state.[64]

---

[61] The third man did not approve of, or participate in, the homicide, but he joined in eating the flesh.

[62] Lord Coleridge discounted the views of Lord Bacon, who asserted that one is justified by necessity to thrust another person off a plank in the ocean to save one's own life. Coleridge stated that if Bacon intended "to lay down a broad proposition that man may save his life by killing . . . an innocent and unoffending neighbour, it certainly is not law at the present day." In any case, Bacon's example involves the taking of one innocent life to save another (one's own) innocent life. If human lives are equally valued — if, for example, a person is not entitled to weigh his own life or that of a family member above that of a stranger — this becomes an "equal evil," and not a "lesser evil," hypothetical.

[63] *United States v. Holmes*, 26 F. Cas. 360 (C.C.E.D. Pa. 1842), was a case "replete with incidents of deep romance, and of pathetic interest." *Id.* at 363. Holmes and other crew-members of an American ship threw 14 male passengers of a lifeboat overboard after it began to leak. The trial judge told the jurors that "in applying the law, we must look, not only to the jeopardy in which the parties are, but also to the relations to which they stand." *Id.* at 366. He explained that the sailors were bound to sacrifice their own lives to save the passengers. He also expressed the view that when the life of one person must be taken "to appease the hunger of others, the selection is by lot." *Id.* at 367. The defendants were convicted of manslaughter, sentenced to a term of six months, although the maximum potential penalty was three years' imprisonment. President Tyler refused to grant a pardon, despite public pleas on their behalf.

[64] *E.g.*, Ky RS § 503.030 (2015) (recognizing the defense "except that no justification can exist under this section for an intentional homicide"); Wis. Stat. § 939.47 (2015) (but reducing the offense to second-degree murder).

[C]   What Does *Dudley and Stephens* Really Say?

Some commentators believe that *Dudley and Stephens* did not categorically reject the defense of necessity in homicide cases.[65] The argument may be made that *D* and *S* acted precipitously; in necessity terms, the harm they were seeking to avoid was not yet imminent. In support of this view, Lord Coleridge focused on the special finding of the jury that it was only "probable" that the three men would have died had they not killed the youth. As Coleridge weighed the evils, *D* and *S* "with certainty" deprived *V* of his life, merely "upon the chance" of preserving their own lives. If the seamen's plight had been more extreme, some argue, the defendants might have received more favorable treatment.[66]

The weaknesses in the defendants' case are highlighted by comparing it to the following hypothetical:[67] *D* and *V* are mountaineers tied together by a rope. *V* loses his footing, falls off the cliff, and is about to drop to his certain death, pulling *D* down with him. *D* holds on as long as he can. When *D* feels himself about to be pulled over the cliff, may he justifiably cut the rope and permit *V* to fall?

Dudley and Stephens need not compel a negative answer to this hypothetical. First, unlike the facts in the lifeboat, climber-*D*'s plight is clear: the threat is imminent; he must act now or never. Second, *V*'s status is different from that of the "unoffending" youth in the lifeboat. *V* may fairly be characterized as an aggressor (*i.e.*, by slipping, *V* threatened *D*'s life), albeit an innocent one.[68]

Third, in *Dudley and Stephens*, the means of selection of the potential victim troubled the court. The youth was likely, but not doomed, to die. He died because *D* and *S* *chose* to kill him. Selection by lot would have been fairer. Climber-*V*'s death, however, was a certainty. *D* did not choose for him to die; circumstances did.[69]

Finally, and closely related to the previous point, *D* and *S* *caused* the boy to die. They chose him for death, and they shortened his life by more than a *de minimis* amount. In light of the certainty of mountaineer-*V*'s death, however, it seems preferable to say that *D*'s act of cutting the line on the rope merely *permitted* nature to take its course.[70]

---

[65] *E.g.*, Glazebrook, Note 1, *supra*, at 114.

[66] On the other hand, there is language in the Coleridge judgment — most notably, his statement regarding the "Great Example" (Jesus), quoted in the last subsection — that supports the categorical no-defense interpretation of most scholars.

[67] *See* American Law Institute, Comment to § 3.02, at 15.

[68] A court might choose to bring this hypothetical within an expansive version of self-defense *or* characterize this as a "lesser harm" necessity case, as the Model Penal Code Commentary does.

[69] This would also distinguish the September 11 nightmare, as the passengers on the plane were doomed, no matter what.

[70] Notice, too, the differences that can be drawn between *Dudley and Stephens* and the conjoined twins case noted in subsection [A]. As in the mountain-climbing hypothetical, it can be said that "Mary was making use of Jodie's body in a way that put Jodie's life at risk," Stacy, Note 56, *supra*, at 498, so Mary might be characterized as an innocent aggressor (or, more accurately, innocent *threatener*), unlike the youth killed in the lifeboat. Also, the doctors did not choose Mary's life over Jodie's, whereas *D* and *S* chose the youth to be the victim. Mary's death was inevitable; the doctors only accelerated the process.

[D]   How Should *Dudley and Stephens* Have Been Decided?

To repeat, the issue is this: Assuming that all of the requirements for a necessity defense are satisfied (which arguably they were not in *Dudley and Stephens*), may a person justifiably (*not excusably*) kill an innocent person in order to save a greater number of innocent lives?

A utilitarian might say yes. The calculus would seem simple: In *Dudley and Stephens*, one person's life should be taken so that three may survive. Indeed, the calculus may be put more starkly: The choice was between doing nothing, in which case all four occupants of the lifeboat were likely to die (based on the unforeseeability of their rescue at the moment at issue), and acting, in which case only one life would be lost. To utilitarians, the end (reduction in aggregate harm) seemingly justifies the means (an intentional homicide).

But this calculus is too simple. First, if *D* and *S* were justified in taking *V*'s life to save three lives, would they not also have been justified in taking the third person's life to save their own, assuming that they were not rescued in time? If so, two lives would be taken to save two lives, although the calculus looked different at each step along the way. Second, even if the killing of an innocent person might be justified in a particular case, a *rule* authorizing such behavior might be abused (as Lord Coleridge feared) or, at least, misapplied, in other cases, thus ultimately resulting in more, not less, social harm. And a rule that justifies killing innocent people in extreme circumstances might weaken general moral strictures against taking human life, which again could have a counter-utilitarian effect. "Rule-utilitarians" — those who look at the big picture, and seek to devise rules that will result in a net reduction of harm over time — would need to consider these possibilities.

A negative answer to the question posed here is more easily made from a non-utilitarian, perhaps Kantian, moral perspective. The imperative would be that each person is an end in himself, and should not be treated merely as a means to an end, as *D* and *S* used *V*. *V* was "unoffending"; he did not forfeit his moral right to life by any misconduct. Therefore, a non-consequentialist might conclude that an innocent person's life may *never* justifiably be taken, even to save a larger number of lives.

But, notice: This does *not* mean that a retributivist would necessarily punish *D* and *S*. A plausible argument can be made that *D* and *S* should be *excused*, on the ground that, as a result of the extraordinary natural circumstances in which they found themselves, they were compelled to take a life. Therefore, they should not be blamed for giving in to the coercive circumstances. This points up that "necessity" should sometimes serve as an excuse, rather than a justification.[71]

Finally, in *Dudley and Stephens*, persons in jeopardy determined who amongst themselves would live or die. In the conjoined twins case, however, the "killers" — the physicians — were not in jeopardy. They could not sacrifice themselves for the babies, and Mary could not choose to sacrifice herself for Jodie.

[71] For the view that Lord Coleridge failed to show proper sensitivity to the justification/excuse distinction, see Dressler Note 56, *supra*. See also § 23.06, *infra*.

§ 22.05 MODEL PENAL CODE[72]

The Model Code recognizes a "choice of evils" defense. A person's conduct is justified if: (1) he believes that his conduct is necessary to avoid harm to himself or another; (2) the harm to be avoided by his conduct is greater than that sought to be avoided by the law prohibiting his conduct; and (3) no legislative intent to exclude the conduct in such circumstances plainly exists.[73] The determination of what constitutes a lesser harm is not left to the actor's evaluation, but rather to the judge or jury at trial. The Code does not resolve whether the balancing-of-harms should be determined by the judge, as a matter of law, or should be submitted to the jury for its evaluation.[74]

This defense is broader than the common law in various respects. First, the Code rejects the common law imminency requirement. Second, a person does not automatically lose the defense because he was at fault in creating the necessitous situation. Instead, the Code provides that the defense is unavailable if the actor is prosecuted for a crime of recklessness or negligence and he acted recklessly or negligently, as the case may be, in bringing about the emergency or in evaluating the necessity of his conduct.[75] For example, in the hypothetical discussed earlier in this chapter,[76] in which *D recklessly* started a fire that threatened to burn down a number of homes, *D* would be justified in *purposely* burning *V*'s property, although he could be prosecuted for criminal mischief,[77] due to his original reckless act.

Third, the Code provision is one of general applicability. All forms of necessity qualify — the defense is not limited to emergencies created by natural forces, is not limited to physical harm to persons or property, and, most controversially, may be employed in homicide prosecutions. The Commentary states that it would be "particularly unfortunate" to deny the defense in appropriate homicide cases; it contends that the sanctity of human life is promoted by a law that permits an actor to kill to save a larger number of lives.[78]

---

[72] According to Professor Hoffheimer, "[o]nly two states have enacted the Model Penal Code's version of the defense verbatim — a third has adopted it with modifications." Hoffheimer, Note 22, *supra*, at 196.

[73] Model Penal Code § 3.02(1).

[74] American Law Institute, Comment to § 3.02, at 12.

[75] Model Penal Code § 3.02(2).

[76] See the text accompanying Note 39, *supra*.

[77] Model Penal Code § 220.3(1) ("damag[ing] tangible property of another . . . *recklessly* . . . in the employment of fire") (emphasis added).

[78] American Law Institute, Comment to § 3.02, at 14–15.

Chapter 23

DURESS

§ 23.01 GENERAL PRINCIPLES[1]

[A] Overview

"Duress" or "coercion" is a common law defense to criminal conduct. As it has been written about the defense:

> Our society has a love-hate relationship with the . . . defense. Although "of venerable antiquity," the defense was frequently condemned as illegitimate, narrowly defined at common law, comparatively rarely invoked in criminal prosecutions, and not often successfully pleaded. [¶] . . . Nonetheless, our society also seems to love the plea or, at least, to be intrigued by it. Despite criticisms, our society has retained the defense, expanded it over the years, and paid close attention to the calls of those who would apply the defense in novel ways.[2]

[B] Elements of the Defense

The contours of the duress defense differ by jurisdiction. However, very generally speaking, a person will be acquitted of any offense *except murder*[3] if the criminal act was committed under the following circumstances: (1) another person threatened to kill or grievously injure the actor or a third party, particularly a near relative, unless she committed the offense; (2) the actor reasonably believed that the threat was genuine; (3) the threat was "present, imminent, and impending" at the time of the criminal act;[4] (4) there was no reasonable escape from the threat

---

[1] *See generally* Joshua Dressler, *Duress, in* Oxford Handbook of the Philosophy of Criminal Law (John Deigh & David Dolinko ed., 2011); Jerome Hall, General Principles of Criminal Law 436–48 (2d ed. 1960); Glanville Williams, Criminal Law: The General Part §§ 242–50 (2d ed. 1961); Joshua Dressler, *Exegesis of the Law of Duress: Justifying the Excuse and Searching for Its Proper Limits*, 62 S. Cal. L. Rev. 1331 (1989); Herbert Fingarette, *Victimization: A Legalist Analysis of Coercion, Deception, Undue Influence, and Excusable Prison Escape*, 42 Wash. & Lee L. Rev. 65 (1985); Claire O. Finkelstein, *Duress: A Philosophical Account of the Defense in Law*, 37 Ariz. L. Rev. 251 (1995); John Lawrence Hill, *A Utilitarian Theory of Duress*, 84 Iowa L. Rev. 275 (1999); Kyron Huigens, *Duress Is Not a Justification*, 2 Ohio St. J. Crim. L. 303 (2004); Peter Westen & James Mangiafico, *The Criminal Defense of Duress: A Justification, Not an Excuse — And Why It Matters*, 6 Buff. Crim. L. Rev. 833 (2003).

[2] Dressler, *Exegesis*, Note 1, *supra*, at 1331–32 (footnotes omitted).

[3] Regarding murder, see § 23.04, *infra*.

[4] State v. Crawford, 861 P.2d 791, 797 (Kan. 1993); State v. Toscano, 378 A.2d 755, 760 (N.J. 1977); *see also* United States v. Zayac, 765 F.3d 112, 120 (2d Cir. 2014).

except through compliance with the demands of the coercer; and (5) the actor was not at fault in exposing herself to the threat.[5]

As this description of the common law (and, sometimes, statutory) defense suggests, a person will not be acquitted unless she acts as a result of a very specific type of threat. First, the threat must come from a human being. For example, if *D* breaks into *V*'s home because a rabid dog is threatening her in the street, or a severe lightning storm is underway, she might be able to claim the defense of *necessity* if she is charged with criminal trespass,[6] but the defense of duress is inapplicable.

Second, the coercer must threaten to cause death or serious bodily harm.[7] Force that is likely to cause death *or serious bodily harm* is commonly termed "deadly force" in the criminal law;[8] therefore, it is accurate to state, as a shorthand, that a person may not claim common law duress unless she is the victim of a threat of "deadly force." A lesser threat, such as a threat to cause property damage, economic hardship, or to damage another person's reputation, is insufficient.[9]

Third, the deadly force threatened must be imminent, or as some courts put it, "present, imminent, and impending." The word "present" suggests that the threat must be operating on the actor's will at the time of the criminal act.[10] The remaining requirement is that the threatened harm will occur immediately, unless the actor complies. Courts rarely explain this requirement, except to state that a threat of future harm is insufficient; the harm must be likely to occur so quickly that there is no realistic way for the actor to escape the situation.[11] For example, in *State v. Rosillo*,[12] *R*, a police informant, agreed to testify against a suspected drug dealer. Prior to trial, however, armed assailants threatened him, and he was nearly run over on the street. As a consequence of his fear for his life and that of his family, *R* gave false testimony at the trial of the alleged narcotics dealer. *R*, prosecuted for perjury, claimed duress. The court held, however, that the facts did not support the claim, as he was not in fear of *imminent* harm at the moment he testified falsely at the trial. According to the court, however, a duress claim *would* have been available if *D* had reasonably feared being shot through a courthouse window.

---

[5] *See* People v. Merhige, 180 N.W. 418, 422 (Mich. 1920); Dressler, *Exegesis*, Note 1, *supra*, at 1335–43; Fingarette, Note 1, *supra*, at 67 n.9.

[6] *See* § 22.02, *supra*.

[7] Although there are few cases on point, an implicit threat should be sufficient to entitle a defendant to a jury instruction on duress. State v. Harvill, 234 P.3d 1166 (Wash. 2010) (*X*, known by *H* to be a violent person who had once smashed a person's head with a beer bottle, and stabbed another, insisted "in an aggressive tone" that *H* provide him with cocaine; held: if *H*'s perception of an implicit threat is reasonable under the circumstances, an instruction on duress is appropriate).

[8] *See* § 18.02[A], *supra*.

[9] *E.g.*, United States v. Palmer, 458 F.2d 663 (9th Cir. 1972) ("financial ruin" insufficient threat); People v. Ricker, 262 N.E.2d 456 (Ill. 1970) (threat of loss of job insufficient).

[10] People v. Luther, 232 N.W.2d 184, 187 (Mich. 1975).

[11] *See* United States v. Contento-Pachon, 723 F.2d 691, 694 (9th Cir. 1984).

[12] 282 N.W.2d 872 (Minn. 1979).

Fourth, at original common law, the threat must be directed at the defendant or a family member.[13]

Even if all of the preceding criteria are satisfied, the duress defense is unavailable to a defendant if she was at fault for finding herself in the coercive situation. For example, if D voluntarily joins a criminal organization that she knows or has reason to know is likely to subject her to coercive threats at a later time, she will not be permitted to claim the defense if that foreseeable event arises.[14]

If the elements of the defense *are* satisfied, the coerced actor will be acquitted of the non-homicide offense for which she was prosecuted. The *coercing* party, however, is responsible for the coerced victim's conduct and, therefore, may be convicted of the offense committed.[15]

[C]　Duress: Justification or Excuse?

Some scholars, courts, and statutes characterize duress as a subspecies of the *justification* defense of necessity, or treat the two defenses interchangeably.[16] There is superficial (but only superficial) logic in this position: According to common law principles, the duress defense only applies if the coercing party threatens to use deadly force; and the defense is only available if the coerced actor commits a *non*-homicide offense. Therefore, at first blush, it appears that a coerced party *always* commits the lesser of two evils; therefore, she is *justified* in acceding to the threat. Following this reasoning, the only potential significant difference between necessity and duress is that the former defense (at least, at common law) entails natural threats like fires and tornadoes, whereas the latter involves human threats.

It is not true, however, that *every* common law example of duress involves a lesser-evils situation. For example, if C threatens to cut off D's left arm unless D cuts off V's left arm, the harms are of equal severity, yet D is entitled to raise the duress defense if she complies with C's demand.[17]

---

[13] Modern courts have broken from this limitation. *E.g.*, United States v. Haney, 287 F.3d 1266, 1272 (10th Cir. 2002) (characterizing a "family members only" limitation as "unprincipled," and stating that "[w]e know of no federal case categorically declining to apply the duress defense in the third party context"), *vacated and remanded on rehearing en banc*, 318 F.3d 1161 (10th Cir. 2003). States that follow the Model Penal Code, as well, extend the defense to threats to all third parties. *See* § 23.08[B][1], *infra*.

[14] Williams, Note 1, *supra*, at 758–59; American Law Institute, Comment to § 2.09, at 379 n.47.

[15] In common law terminology, the coercer is a "principal in the first degree" who used the coerced party as her "innocent instrumentality" in committing the offense. *See* § 30.03[A][2][b], *infra*.

[16] *E.g., United States v. Haney*, 287 F.3d at 1270 (describing duress as a lesser-harm defense); Westen & Mangiafico, Note 1, *supra*, at 947–48 (characterizing duress as a justification defense, because "society regards [the coerced actor's conduct] as acceptable under the circumstances"); Wayne R. LaFave, Criminal Law 467, 476–77 (3d ed. 2000) (treating duress as a subspecies of the necessity defense); United States v. Bailey, 444 U.S. 394, 410 (1980) (observing that "[m]odern cases have tended to blur the distinction between duress and necessity," and thereafter treating the two defenses alike); Ariz. Rev. Stat. § 13-412 (2015) (describing duress in justificatory language).

[17] It is plausible to argue that a person may properly value her own (and family's) well-being over that of a stranger. Therefore, under this view, the harms are *not* equal in this hypothetical. But, even if one

Furthermore, it is unlikely that the concept of duress as a justification for criminal activity conforms with common moral intuitions. For example, suppose that C orders D to rape V, and backs up the order by threatening grievous harm to X, D's young child — *e.g.*, C threatens to cut off X's left hand or blind X. If D complies with C's threat and rapes V, it is highly unlikely that the decision whether to acquit D of rape would be based on the balancing of the harms threatened and inflicted. Are we *really* prepared to say that V's rape is a lesser harm than X's loss of an arm or eyesight? More likely, our intuitions suggest that the real issue is whether, in view of the threats, D should be blamed — excused — for the injuries inflicted on V.

In conformity with this analysis, most scholars, courts, and states' criminal codes that draw distinctions between justifications and excuses, treat duress as an excuse defense.[18]

§ 23.02   RATIONALE OF THE DEFENSE (AS AN EXCUSE)

[A]   Utilitarian Arguments

The traditional utilitarian argument in support of the duress defense is straightforward: When a person is "in thrall to some [coercive] power" the threat of criminal punishment is ineffective.[19] As Hobbes has reasoned:

> If a man, by the terror of present death, be compelled to do a fact against the law, he is totally excused, because no law can oblige a man to abandon his own preservation. And supposing such a law were obligatory, yet a man would reason thus: *If I do it not, I die presently; if I do it, I die afterwards; therefore by doing it, there is time of life gained.*[20]

Moreover, a utilitarian may argue that the victim of coercion is just that — a victim. The coercing party, and not she, possesses a criminal disposition. Therefore, the coercing party, and not she, requires incapacitation and rehabilitation.

Not all utilitarian arguments support the defense. Sir James Stephen has presented the most famous (although not generally accepted) utilitarian argument against the excuse. According to Stephen, recognition of the defense dangerously undermines the moral clarity of the criminal law and invites fraud: "Surely it is at the moment when the temptation to [commit] crime is strongest . . . that the law should speak most clearly and emphatically to the contrary." He conceded that it is unfortunate when an innocent person is "placed between two fires," but he believed that it is a much greater misfortune for society if the coercing party could confer immunity on her "agents by threatening them with death or violence if they refused to execute . . . [her] commands." Such a rule would open "a wide door . . . to

---

accepts this idea, there will be cases in which the harm threatened *is* equal to the harm caused, in which case the lesser-harm thesis fails.

[18] *E.g.*, Dressler, *Exegesis*, Note 1, *supra*; Huigens, Note 1, *supra*; Model Penal Code § 2.09. The Model Penal Code approach to duress, which has influenced the law, is considered in § 23.08, *infra*.

[19] Williams, Note 1, *supra*, at 756.

[20] Thomas Hobbes, Leviathan, Pt. II, ch. 27 (1651).

collusion, and encouragement would be given to associations of malefactors, secret or otherwise."[21]

[B] Retributive Arguments

Most arguments in support of the duress defense are founded on the retributive principle that a coerced actor does not deserve to be punished for her actions. In order to understand why this is so, it is useful first to consider various *incorrect* or potentially misleading explanations frequently given in support of the defense.

First, some courts suggest that a coerced actor lacks the requisite *mens rea* to be convicted of an offense.[22] Exceptional circumstances aside, however, this explanation is false.[23] Ordinarily, one who acts under duress *intends* to cause the result in question, for the simple reason that she wants to avoid the harm threatened by the coercer. Therefore, a coercive threat *creates* the intent; it does not negate it. The only exception to this proposition is when the coercive threat negates a specific intent or motive of the actor that may be required in the definition of an offense. For example, suppose that *C* coerces *D* to steal a Picasso painting from City Museum. *D* does as she is told, but as soon as the coercion is removed, she contacts the police and leads them to *C*. Under such circumstances, although *D* intended to take and carry away the Picasso, the prosecutor may be unable to prove beyond a reasonable doubt that *D* did do so with the intent to *permanently* deprive the museum of its property. As this motive is an element of larceny, *D* may be acquitted.

Second, courts sometimes state that a coerced party should be excused because "commission of the alleged offense was no longer the voluntary act of the accused."[24] In the narrow willed-contraction-of-a-muscle sense of the term "voluntary act,"[25] however, this statement is flatly incorrect. Stephen has correctly observed:

> A criminal walking to execution is under compulsion if any man can be said to be so, but his motions are just as much voluntary actions as if he was going to leave his place of confinement and regain his liberty. He walks to his death because he prefers it to being carried.[26]

That is, the coerced actor wills her muscles to commit the crime, *e.g.*, to strike *V* or to steal *V*'s automobile. Coercion, therefore, does not negate the voluntary act

---

[21] 2 James Stephen, A History of the Criminal Law in England 107–08 (1883).

[22] *E.g.*, State v. Tanner, 301 S.E.2d 160, 163 (W. Va. 1982) (" '[I]n general an act which would otherwise constitute a crime may be excused on the ground that it was done under compulsion or duress, since the necessary ingredient of intention . . . is then lacking.' ") (quoting 22 C.J.S. Criminal Law § 44 (1961)).

[23] State v. Rios, 980 P.2d 1068, 1071 (N.M. Ct. App. 1999) ("A defendant pleading duress is *not* attempting to disprove a requisite mental state."); Hibbert v. The Queen, [1995] 999 C.C.C.3d 193, 205 (Can.) ("[S]ituations where duress will operate to 'negate' *mens rea* will be exceptional, for the simple reason that the types of mental states that are capable of being 'negated' by duress are not often found in the definitions of criminal offences.").

[24] Regina v. Hudson, [1971] 2 All E.R. 244, 246.

[25] *See* § 9.02[C][2], *supra.*

[26] 2 Stephen, Note 21, *supra*, at 102.

requirement of the criminal law.

Third, it is not precisely correct to say that a person is excused for violating the law because she "lacked free will." The coerced actor has the *capacity* to choose, *i.e.*, she is not an automaton controlled by the coercing party. More to the point, the coerced actor *in fact* chooses to violate the law; she chooses to commit an offense rather than to suffer the threatened consequences. She "self-consciously subordinates [the law] to the primacy of the person who is the subject of desire,"[27] *i.e.*, she chooses to make the coercing party's desires her own for present purposes.

Although the free-will explanation is not precisely on target, it brings us very close to understanding why it is unjust to punish one who acts under duress. Although the coerced actor possesses free will, she does not possess a *fair opportunity* to exercise her will to act lawfully.[28] Of course, society does not excuse an actor for violating the law whenever she must make a hard choice. Duress only excuses when the available choices are not only hard but also deeply unfair.[29] Choice-making opportunities are unfair when the alternative to committing an offense is so awful that "judges are not prepared to affirm that they . . . could comply with [the law] if their turn to face the problem should arise."[30] The defense of duress recognizes that all humans have breaking points; society is prepared to excuse a coerced actor's unlawful conduct if she accedes to a threat that, upon honest self-reflection, most of us doubt we would have the moral fortitude to resist either.[31]

§ 23.03   DISTINGUISHING DURESS FROM NECESSITY

As noted earlier,[32] some commentators and courts treat duress as a subspecies of the justification defense of necessity, in which case the only true distinction between the defenses is that duress involves human threats, whereas the necessity defense applies to natural forces.

As long as duress is recognized as an excuse defense, which it should be, it is important to see how the two defenses differ.[33] The necessity defense — as one of its alternative names ("lesser evil" defense) reminds us — applies "when a person is faced with a choice of two evils and must then decide whether to commit a crime

---

[27] Alan Brudner, *A Theory of Necessity*, 7 Oxford J. Legal Stud. 339, 349 (1987).

[28] This is an example of the "free choice" or "personhood" theory of excuses. *See* § 17.03[E], *supra.*

[29] Dressler, *Exegesis*, Note 1, *supra*, at 1365.

[30] American Law Institute, Comment to § 2.09, at 374–75.

[31] Contrast these remarks to Lord Coleridge's observation in Regina v. Dudley and Stephens, 14 Q.B.D. 273 (1884), in which he stated that judges "are often compelled to set up standards that we cannot reach ourselves, and to lay down rules which we could not ourselves satisfy." *See* § 22.04[B], *supra.* In the context of *justification* defenses, this might be an appropriate observation, but with duress we are talking about *excusing* people; it is wrong to blame and punish people for being unable to live up to standards that nobody but the most "saintly" individual could satisfy.

[32] *See* § 23.01[C], *supra.*

[33] The assumption here is that necessity is a *justification* defense. Necessity may be an excuse defense in some circumstances. *See* § 23.06, *infra.*

or an alternative act that constitutes a greater evil,"[34] and the person makes the right choice. In contrast, duress applies even when the coercer's threats overwhelm the actor's will so that she makes the wrong choice, *i.e.*, perpetrates a greater evil.[35]

This potential difference has practical consequences. When a person commits the lesser of two evils, nobody should be subject to prosecution for the outcome, because the outcome is socially desirable or, at least, not undesirable. For example, suppose that *D1* justifiably exceeds the speed limit in order to drive a gravely injured child to the hospital. Even if it later turns out that the child was in that condition as the result of wrongful conduct by *X*, it would be odd to say that *X* should be held criminally responsible for *D1's justified* act of speeding. *X* should be prosecuted for any crime she committed in relation to the child, but that is all.

If a defendant is *excused* on the basis of duress, however, the person who coerced her may be prosecuted for the harm caused. For example, if *D2* robs a bank because *C* threatened immediate serious physical harm to *D2's* husband, *D2* may be excused for the crime; *C*, however, may be prosecuted for the robbery. This result follows from the fact that duress is an excuse rather than a justification, and there is a culpable human being who may properly be held accountable for the social harm caused.[36]

§ 23.04   DURESS AS A DEFENSE TO HOMICIDE

[A]   General Rule

The common law rule, stemming from antiquity, and expressly adopted by statute in 17 states,[37] is that duress is not a defense to an intentional killing.[38] A few states recognize an imperfect duress defense, which reduces the offense of the coerced actor to manslaughter.[39]

There is a division of law regarding whether the duress defense may be raised in a felony-murder prosecution. Some states provide that a person coerced to commit a felony, during which she or an accomplice kills the victim, may raise the duress defense as to the felony and, therefore, is not guilty of felony-murder.[40] Other

---

[34] United States v. Contento-Pachon, 723 F.2d 691, 695 (9th Cir. 1984).

[35] *See* United States v. Lopez, 662 F. Supp. 1083, 1086 (N.D. Cal. 1987), *aff'd*, 885 F.2d 1428 (9th Cir. 1989).

[36] The necessity/duress distinction may have additional practical implications beyond those stated in this paragraph. *See* § 23.05[C][2], *infra*.

[37] *E.g.*, Wash. Rev. Code 9A.16.060(2) (2015).

[38] According to this author's research, at least 14 states have, by case law, also excluded duress as a full defense to murder. *E.g.*, People v. Anderson, 50 P.3d 368, 370–73 (Cal. 2002); Wright v. State, 402 So. 2d 493, 498 (Fla. Dist. Ct. App. 1981); People v. Henderson, 854 N.W.2d 234, 238 (Mich. Ct. App. 2014); Commonwealth v. Jackson, 28 N.E.3d 437, 440–41 (Mass. 2015); *see* Regina v. Howe, [1987] 2 W.L.R. 568, 575 ("[A]n unbroken tradition of authority dating back to Hale and Blackstone seems to have been . . . that duress was not available to a defendant accused of murder.").

[39] Wentworth v. State, 349 A.2d 421, 427–28 (Md. Ct. Spec. App. 1975); Minn. Stat. § 609.20(3) (2015).

[40] *E.g.*, People v. Anderson, 50 P.3d at 379; State v. Hunter, 740 P.2d 559, 568 (Kan. 1987); McMillan v. State, 51 A.3d 623, 635 (Md. 2012); Pugliese v. Commonwealth, 428 S.E.2d 16, 24 (Va. Ct. App. 1993).

states disallow the defense in all murder prosecutions, regardless of the defendant's *mens rea* regarding the death.[41]

[B] Is the No-Defense Rule Sensible?

What are the arguments for the common law rule that duress does not excuse a murder? Why is a defendant entitled to claim duress if she complies with a gun-to-the-head demand that she steal a car, rob a bank, or sexually assault another person, but the defense is unavailable to her if she kills as the result of precisely the same threat? From a utilitarian perspective, it would seem that the traditional basis for the defense — that a threat of future punishment will not deter an actor confronted by an immediate deadly threat[42] — potentially applies to coerced murders as it does to coerced thieves, robbers, and assaulters.

Some scholars, however, defend the no-defense rule on utilitarian grounds. According to Jerome Hall, it is wrong to assume that "the drive of self-preservation is irresistible, that conduct in such situation is inexorably fixed for all human beings."[43] Lord Hailsham of the English House of Lords agrees:

> Doubtless in actual practice many will succumb to temptation [and kill] . . . . But many will not . . . . I have known in my own lifetime of too many acts of heroism by ordinary human beings of no more than ordinary fortitude to [reject the common law position].[44]

The California Supreme Court, as well, recently observed:

> [W]hen confronted with an apparent kill-an-innocent-person-or-be-killed situation, a person can always choose to resist. As a practical matter, death will rarely, if ever, inevitably result from a choice not to kill. *The law should require people to choose to resist rather than kill an innocent person.*[45]

But this argument sounds more like a reason not to *justify* a coerced killing. The issue, however, is — or, at least, should be[46] — whether a person who accedes to a deadly threat should be *excused* for her actions.

The nonconsequentialist argument for the common law no-defense position is also questionable. Blackstone offered a religious explanation for the rule: Murder is a crime against God; human laws, therefore, can never excuse such a crime.[47] In non-religious terms, the no-defense rule supports the moral imperative that, "if a

---

[41] *E.g.*, State v. Ng, 750 P.2d 632, 636 (Wash. 1988).

[42] *See* § 23.02[A], *supra.*

[43] Hall, Note 1, *supra*, at 445–46.

[44] Regina v. Howe, [1987] 2 W.L.R.568, 579.

[45] People v. Anderson, 50 P.3d 368, 371 (Cal. 2002) (emphasis added).

[46] Unfortunately, courts are often insensitive to the justification/excuse distinction. It is noteworthy, for example, that the court in *Anderson, id.*, stated that the "basic rationale behind allowing the defense of duress for other crimes 'is that the defendant, faced with a choice of evils, choose to do the lesser evil . . . ' " (quoting LaFave, Note 16, *supra*); *see also* People v. Henderson, 854 N.W.2d 234, 239 (Mich. Ct. App. 2014) ("a defendant may not *justify* homicide with a claim of duress") (emphasis added).

[47] 4 William Blackstone, Commentaries on the Law of England *30 (1769).

man be desperately assaulted, and in peril of death, and cannot otherwise escape, unless to satisfy his assailant's fury he will kill an innocent person then present . . . he ought rather to die himself than kill an innocent."[48] The difficulty with this argument is, again, that it supports the proposition that a coerced actor is *unjustified* in taking an innocent life; it does not demonstrate that she should not be *excused* for violating the moral imperative.

From a retributive perspective, the question should come down to "whether a coerced person who unjustifiably violates the moral principle [against taking an innocent life] *necessarily, unalterably,* and *unfailingly* deserves to be punished as a murderer, as the common law insists."[49] The answer would seem to be that she does not always deserve to be treated as a murderer: If a person of reasonable moral strength would comply with a kill-or-be-killed threat (or, perhaps more compellingly, a kill-or-I-will-kill-a-loved-one threat), the case for denying the defense, as a matter of law, is weakened considerably.

At a minimum, a person who kills under duress should have her offense mitigated to manslaughter. Why should a person who kills in sudden *anger* as the result of adequate provocation be permitted to mitigate her offense to manslaughter,[50] while one who kills out of *fear* for her own or another person's safety receives no formal mitigation? Sometimes this apparent inconsistency is explained in terms of the victims: In the case of duress the homicide victim is innocent; in the provocation case, the homicide victim is to blame for provoking her own death. The difficulty with this reasoning, however, is that by focusing on whether the *victim* is innocent or not, rather than on the *defendant's* capacity or opportunity to make the right decision, the law treats the two defenses as if they were justification defenses (focusing on whether the victim deserves to die) rather than excuse defenses (focusing on whether the defendant deserves to be blamed).

§ 23.05   ESCAPE FROM INTOLERABLE PRISON CONDITIONS[51]

[A]   The Issue

Supreme Court Justice Harry Blackmun once wrote that "[t]he atrocities and inhuman conditions of prison life in America are almost unbelievable; surely they are nothing less than shocking."[52] Among the conditions that prisoners face are physical and sexual assaults from fellow inmates,[53] brutality at the hands of prison

---

[48] 1 Matthew Hale, History of the Pleas of the Crown *51 (1736).

[49] Dressler, *Exegesis*, Note 1, *supra*, at 1372.

[50] *See generally* § 31.07, *infra*.

[51] *See generally* David Dolinko, Comment, *Intolerable Conditions as a Defense to Prison Escapes*, 26 UCLA L. Rev. 1126 (1979); Fingarette, Note 1, *supra*; George P. Fletcher, *Should Intolerable Prison Conditions Generate a Justification or an Excuse for Escape?*, 26 UCLA L. Rev. 1355 (1979); Martin R. Gardner, *The Defense of Necessity and the Right to Escape from Prison — A Step Towards Incarceration Free from Sexual Assault*, 49 S. Cal. L. Rev. 110 (1975).

[52] United States v. Bailey, 444 U.S. 394, 421 (1980) (dissenting opinion).

[53] Justice Blackmun stated: "A youthful inmate can expect to be subjected to homosexual gang rape

guards, fires in their cells, excessive cold and heat, and inadequate medical attention.

Occasionally, a prisoner seeks to avoid harsh prison conditions by escaping confinement. She may later be prosecuted for the crime of escape; in such circumstances, the escapee may defend her conduct on the ground that she fled due to intolerable prison conditions. Sometimes such a claim is based on the defense of duress; other times the justification defense of necessity is advanced.

[B] The Law

At the policy level, courts are concerned that if an inmate who flees due to alleged intolerable prison conditions avoids conviction on this ground, other inmates will be emboldened to attempt to escape. As a result, some courts originally refused to recognize any defense in such circumstances.[54] Most modern courts, however, recognize the right of an escapee to assert an intolerable-prison-condition claim. They split, however, on whether the inmate should raise the defense of necessity[55] or of duress.[56]

As either a necessity or duress defense, courts almost always place special restrictions on its use.[57] From a practical perspective, the most significant limitation placed on the defense is the requirement that the escapee make "a bona fide effort to surrender or return to custody as soon as the claimed duress or necessity ha[s] lost its coercive force."[58] That is, once the prisoner attains a point of safety outside the prison, the escapee must turn herself in; if she fails to do so, the defense of duress or necessity is unavailable as a matter of law.[59] A few courts do not go this far, instead treating the actor's failure to turn herself in as merely one factor in assessing the escapee's claim.[60]

---

his first night in jail, or, it has been said, even in the van on the way to jail." *Id.*

[54] *E.g.*, State v. Davis, 14 Nev. 439, 444–45 (1880).

[55] *E.g.*, Lacey v. State, 54 P.3d 304 (Alaska Ct. App. 2002); People v. Lovercamp, 43 Cal. App. 3d 823 (Ct. App. 1974); People v. Unger, 362 N.E.2d 319 (Ill. 1977); State v. Reese, 272 N.W.2d 863 (Iowa 1978); Spakes v. State, 913 S.W.2d 597 (Tex. Crim. App. 1996).

[56] *E.g.*, State v. Kinslow, 799 P.2d 844 (Ariz. 1990); People v. Harmon, 220 N.W.2d 212 (Mich. Ct. App. 1974), *aff'd*, 232 N.W.2d 187 (Mich. 1975); State v. Tuttle, 730 P.2d 630 (Utah 1986).

[57] *Contra Spakes v. State*, 913 S.W.2d at 598 (holding that an escapee is entitled to an instruction on necessity if she presents evidence satisfying the ordinary statutory elements of the defense).

[58] United States v. Bailey, 444 U.S. 394, 415 (1980).

[59] According to a 1996 survey, at least 30 jurisdictions require an escapee to attempt to surrender or report to authorities as a precondition for asserting the defense. *See Spakes v. State*, 913 S.W.2d at 599 (Keller, P.J., dissenting).

[60] *E.g.*, People v. Mendoza, 310 N.W.2d 860 (Mich. Ct. App. 1981) (duress); State v. Miller, 313 N.W.2d 460 (S.D. 1981) (necessity).

[C] Necessity Versus Duress

[1] The Conceptual Problem

Neither necessity nor duress neatly covers all intolerable-prison-condition cases. For example, when an inmate flees as the result of a threatened sexual assault, a necessity claim is inappropriate in jurisdictions that still limit that defense to emergencies created by non-human forces. On the other hand, the defense of duress ordinarily is triggered when a coercer orders another person to commit the crime for which the latter individual is prosecuted. In prison cases, however, threats may spur an inmate to flee, but nobody commands her to escape.

[2] Why the Nature of the Defense Is Significant

[a]   The Message of Acquittal

An inmate does not care whether she is acquitted on the basis of necessity or duress. Courts, lawyers, and prison officials, however, understandably worry about the message sent in prison escape cases.

The two defenses send different messages. Acquittal on the basis of necessity implies that it is right or, at least, tolerable, for a prisoner to escape confinement in specified circumstances; acquittal on the ground of duress implies only that the escapee should not be blamed for fleeing. A prison official is apt to consider the label of justification unacceptable; advocates of prison reform are likely to prefer this description.

[b]   Ability of the Defendant to Obtain Acquittal

A necessity claim may be a harder defense to prove than a claim of duress. With necessity, the prisoner must convince the jury that her flight from confinement was a lesser evil than what was facing her behind bars. Once the balancing process begins, many factors weigh against the inmate. For example, prison escapes jeopardize discipline within the institution, a factor that a jury may weigh against the defendant. Also, if the inmate is a habitual violent criminal, her prior criminal record, which ordinarily would be inadmissible at her trial, arguably is relevant to her lesser-evil defense claim. Juries are likely to conclude that it is better that a dangerous criminal suffer in prison, than that she be free from confinement, even for a short time.

In duress cases, juries are not asked to balance evils. Neither prison discipline nor the inmate's prior criminal record is material. The determinative factor ought to be whether the conditions in the prison that motivated the flight were so extreme and immediate that the jurors could reasonably imagine themselves fleeing under similar circumstances.

[c]   Liability of Those Who Assist in the Escape

The line between duress and necessity may be critical in determining the criminal responsibility of persons who assist escapees. Consider *United States v. Lopez*:[61] *L* landed a helicopter on the grounds of a women's prison in order to assist the escape of *X*, his girlfriend, whose life allegedly had been unlawfully threatened by prison officials. *L* and *X* were apprehended 10 days later. As a consequence of their actions, *X* was charged with escape, and *L* was charged with aiding in *X*'s escape. The prosecution agreed that *X* was entitled to introduce evidence supporting her claim that her life was threatened in prison; but it sought to bar *L* from introducing the same evidence on his own behalf.

Conceptually, the propriety of a prosecutor's motion to bar such evidence depends on whether *X*'s intolerable-prison-condition claim is properly identified as one of necessity (justification) or of duress (excuse). A justified act is a proper, or at least non-wrongful, act. Therefore, assuming arguendo that *X* was justified in escaping, *L* was also justified in assisting in the escape. In such circumstances, *L* should be permitted to raise *X*'s necessity claim on his own behalf.

In contrast, with excuse defenses, the result is wrongful, but the actor is not held responsible for it because she was the victim of an excusing condition. An excuse defense, however, is personal to the actor suffering from the condition. Therefore, since *L*'s life was not threatened — he did not personally experience the excusing condition — he should not be allowed to assert *X*'s duress claim as a basis for exculpation. Under such circumstances — if *X*'s flight from prison was only excusable — *L* may properly be convicted of aiding and abetting *X*'s wrongful-but-excusable act.[62]

[d]   Liability of Those Who Resist the Escape

Assume the following scenario: *D* seeks to escape confinement due to an intolerable prison condition; *X*, a prison guard, exercises her authority to prevent the escape. Is *X* acting justifiably? If *X* uses force to stop *D*, should *X* be prosecuted for battery? May *D* use force against *X* in self-defense to the battery? The answers to these questions may depend on the nature of *D*'s defense.

If the proper defense to escape is duress, *X* is justified in preventing *D* from committing the wrongful act of escaping. *X* should also be allowed to use reasonable force to prevent the escape, and *D* would not be entitled to use force against her in the conflict.

If *D*'s escape is justifiable, however, the analysis become more complicated. There are two possible solutions. Either the law must recognize incompatible justifications — justify *D*'s escape, yet also justify *X*'s effort to prevent *D*'s justified flight — or it must deny *X*, the prison guard, the right to use force to resist the escape. Following the latter reasoning, *D* would also be justified in using

---

[61] 662 F. Supp. 1083 (N.D. Cal. 1987).

[62] In *Lopez*, the trial court concluded that *X*'s defense "most clearly resemble[d]" a necessity claim. Therefore, it permitted *L* to introduce evidence at his trial regarding the purported threats on *X*'s life.

reasonable force, if necessary, to prevent resistance by the guard.[63]

[3] Concluding Comments

There is no reason why a jurisdiction should fit all prison escape cases within just one defense category. Occasionally, an escapee will wish to assert that she acted properly in escaping, in which case the necessity defense should be permitted, whether or not the threat was human or natural in origin. For example, in *People v. Unger*,[64] *U* was a thief serving his sentence on an honor farm when his life was threatened by a fellow inmate. The *Unger* court considered necessity to be the appropriate defense in the case.

But, why should an inmate always be forced to prove that the escape was the lesser of two evils? An inmate should be permitted to raise a duress claim instead of, or in conjunction with, the necessity claim. If a jury is unwilling to treat an escape as the lesser of two evils, but it does not believe that the inmate should be blamed for escaping, the jury should be allowed this option.

§ 23.06 SITUATIONAL DURESS: BRIEF OBSERVATIONS

[A] The Simplest Case: Necessity as an Excuse[65]

Reconsider *Dudley and Stephens*,[66] in which desperately hungry survivors on a lifeboat killed one of their number — a sick, defenseless youth — in order to eat his remains to survive. The two defendants were denied a necessity defense. One can defend this outcome, although not all do, on the ground that it is never morally justifiable to kill an innocent person or, in a more limited manner, for example, on the ground that no justifiable method was used to choose the victim.

But, even if the defendants in that case did act unjustifiably, does it follow that they should also be denied an *excuse* defense? Under traditional doctrine, the duress defense does not apply. Not only is duress not a common law defense to murder, but even if it were, it would not apply here because the duress defense only applies to human threats, whereas *Dudley and Stephens* involved a threat emanating from a natural source.

Is a conviction for murder morally just in such circumstances? If a defense were recognized in the lifeboat case, it might be called "situational duress" (or "duress by circumstances," a phrase used in English law), to distinguish it from duress claims involving human-induced coercion. Or, the defense of necessity could be enlarged to include an excuse component, to deal with natural forces that compel a person to commit an equal or greater evil, rather than a lesser one.

---

[63] For discussion of these competing solutions, see Dolinko (arguing for the legitimacy of incompatible justifications) and Fletcher (arguing against such an analysis), Note 52, *supra*.

[64] 362 N.E.2d 319 (Ill. 1977).

[65] *See generally* Dressler, *Duress*, Note 1, *supra*; Edward M. Morgan, *The Defence of Necessity: Justification or Excuse?*, 42 U. Toronto Fac. L. Rev. 165 (1984).

[66] Regina v. Dudley and Stephens, 14 Q.B.D. 273 (1884). *See* § 22.04[B], *supra*.

Opponents of such a new defense argue that in ordinary duress cases "the basic interests of the law may be satisfied by prosecution of the agent of unlawful force,"[67] namely, the coercer. Thus, if C compels D to rob a bank, D is excused, but C can be convicted of the crime. However, in a situational duress case — where the "coercer" is a natural force — there is nobody who can be subjected to the law's application. Therefore, critics maintain, society's valid interest in punishing *someone* for wrongful behavior requires that the law not recognize a situational duress defense. The difficulty with this argument is that it fails to explain why we legally excuse the insane person, since nobody *there* is subjected to punishment for the social harm caused by the mentally ill offender.

The argument for recognizing such a defense is that natural threats can be as compelling as human ones. Therefore, situational duress should excuse in precisely the same circumstances that human coercion excuses conduct. Of course, at the present time, duress is not available in homicide cases, a highly controversial rule, but if the defense *were* available in human-threat duress cases, it should also apply in natural-threat "situational duress" circumstances. Thus, in a *Dudley and Stephens*-type case (or, at least in some exceptionally extreme circumstances), the defendants should be excused because of the compelling natural threat to their lives.[68]

[B]   Going Beyond Natural Threats

Assume that a situational duress defense *is* recognized to deal with coercive natural threats. Suppose, then, that X uses physically and psychologically coercive techniques over an extended period of time in order to render D1 submissive to X's beliefs (what once was called "brainwashing" but more properly described as "coercive persuasion"). Later, X noncoercively suggests to D1 that she rob State Bank. D1 — not out of fear but devotion to the values espoused by D1 — commits the crime. Should D1 be excused?

Or, suppose that D2, whose father has abandoned her and whose mother is a drug addict, lives in a neighborhood dominated by vicious gangs.[69] D2 spends most of her waking hours with gang members, who teach her a code of conduct including robbery, arson, and murder. One day, D2 decides to prove her devotion to gang ideals by robbing a liquor store, during which offense she kills the owner. Should D2 be excused for her crimes?

At common law, of course, neither defendant would be acquitted. D1 and D2 knew what they were doing; they intended to violate the law; and their actions were voluntary in the willed-contraction-of-a-muscle sense of that term. Moreover, the defense of duress — even situational duress as posited in subsection [A] — is unavailable to them. In the first case, D1 acted on the basis of X's uncoerced

---

[67]   American Law Institute, Comment to § 2.09, at 379.

[68]   *See* Perka v. The Queen, [1984] 2 S.C.R. 232 (Can.) (recognizing a residual excuse defense of necessity, the essential criterion of which is the moral involuntariness of the actor's conduct, as measured by society's expectation of appropriate and normal resistance to pressure).

[69]   This example is a variation on one provided by Richard Delgado, *A Response to Professor Dressler*, 63 Minn. L. Rev. 361, 365 (1979).

suggestion and her now-existing similar values. In *D2*'s case, there was no threat or suggestion of any kind; the decision to commit the offense was *D2*'s.

Are convictions in these cases morally just? Some would say that they are not. *D1* seems to be of a victim of "brainwasher" *X*, and not a criminal. *D2*, too, is a victim, if not of a particular person, then of an environment that shaped her anti-social attitudes. Few people can say with genuine confidence that, but for the luck of being born into a better environment, they would not have turned out as *D2* did.

Some commentators believe that the law should recognize new defenses, *e.g.*, "brainwashing"[70] and "rotten social background,"[71] to deal with the particular excusing conditions suggested here. Another solution is to recognize a more general excuse, which would provide that a person is excused for committing a crime if, through no fault of her own, she is placed in a situation so harsh that a person of ordinary moral firmness in her situation would have committed the crime.[72] In essence, this defense would be founded on the principle that a person is not responsible for her conduct if it is the result of a condition beyond her control.[73]

Critics argue that recognition of such a defense would undermine the most basic principle of the criminal law, namely, that humans ordinarily possess sufficient free will to be held responsible for their actions. Although we should feel compassion for *D1* and *D2*, critics maintain, there is nothing inconsistent with the claim that victims can also be victimizers who deserve to be blamed and punished for their unjustifiable conduct.[74] According to this view, society has a moral duty to right social wrongs, but jurors have the simultaneous duty to hold individuals responsible for their immediate actions.[75]

§ 23.07   BATTERED WOMEN UNDER DURESS[76]

A battered woman who kills her abusive living partner may seek to defend her actions on the basis of self-defense. Self-defense law has undergone significant change as a result of a flurry of battered woman self-defense cases that have made

---

[70] *Compare* Richard Delgado, *Ascription of Criminal States of Mind: Toward a Defense Theory for the Coercively Persuaded ("Brainwashed") Defendant*, 63 Minn. L. Rev. 1 (1978) (favoring exculpation), *with* Joshua Dressler, *Professor Delgado's "Brainwashing" Defense: Courting a Determinist Legal System*, 63 Minn. L. Rev. 335 (1979) (rejecting Delgado's reasoning).

[71] Richard Delgado, *"Rotten Social Background": Should the Criminal Law Recognize a Defense of Severe Environmental Deprivation?*, 3 Law & Ineq. 9 (1985).

[72] Richard L. Lippke, *Chronic Temptation, Reasonable Firmness and the Criminal Law*, 34 Oxford J. Legal Stud. 75 (2014) (arguing that some living conditions create a chronic temptation to offend, which can wear down a person, such that only a person of extraordinary, rather than ordinary, self-control, would be able to resist giving in to the temptations).

[73] This is an application of the highly questionable causation theory of excuses. *See* § 17.03[C], *supra.*

[74] *See* Joshua Dressler, *Reflections on Excusing Wrongdoers: Moral Theory, New Excuses and the Model Penal Code*, 19 Rutgers L.J. 671, 682–89 (1988).

[75] Samuel H. Pillsbury, Judging Evil 47–61 (1998).

[76] *See generally* Alafair S. Burke, *Rational Actors, Self-Defense, and Duress: Making Sense, Not Syndromes, Out of the Battered Woman*, 81 N.C. L. Rev. 211 (2002); Laurie Kratky Doré, *Downward Adjustment and the Slippery Slope: The Use of Duress in Defense of Battered Offenders*, 56 Ohio St. L.J. 665 (1995); Beth I.Z. Boland, *Battered Women Who Act Under Duress*, 28 New Eng. L. Rev. 603 (1994).

their way through the appellate courts in the past two decades.[77] Now, a new legal problem is developing: How should the law deal with a battered woman who commits a violent crime[78] or even participates in a crime spree,[79] as the result of domination by her abuser?

Battered women who wish to claim duress typically confront various legal obstacles. First, the abuser may order or simply expect the woman to commit a crime or assist him in its commission, without issuing an immediate (or any) coercive threat. The woman interprets his remarks or actions as threatening, in light of her battering experiences. Second, under ordinary duress principles, a person is not excused for committing a crime if she could have escaped the situation. Likewise, the defense is unavailable to one who is at fault in exposing herself to the coercive situation. In some of these cases, the prosecutor will argue that the battered woman had an avenue of escape from committing the crimes, yet she did not take it.

The key issue in most battered woman duress cases is whether the defendant will be permitted to introduce expert testimony regarding battered woman syndrome, or other evidence relating to the experience of being a battered person, to buttress her duress claim. The potential purposes of such testimony include: demonstrating that the battered woman subjectively feared her abuser even in the absence of an expressed threat; that fear of imminent harm was reasonable; and, in order to explain her failure to escape, the expert might testify regarding "learned helplessness," a common symptom of the syndrome, or seek to show that the woman effectively was trapped by her batterer.

Case law is still comparatively slight, and the rulings on battered woman syndrome are mixed, but the trend is to admit battered woman syndrome evidence, although the proper purposes for its use vary. Courts are more likely to permit the syndrome evidence to support subjective claims by the battered woman (*e.g.*, lack of intent to assist in a crime, or her subjective fear of imminent harm if she did not cooperate with her abuser)[80] than to support the claim that her fear of imminent

---

[77] *See* § 18.05[B], *supra*.

[78] Wonnum v. State, 942 A.2d 569 (Del. 2007) (*M* regularly abused *W*; on particular occasion, *M* gave *W* a loaded revolver and told her to rob somebody because he needed money, which she did; held: conviction reversed because trial judge refused to give a duress instruction to the jury); Neelley v. State, 642 So. 2d 494 (Ala. Crim. App. 1993) (*N* killed a girl whom she procured for her abusive husband, after he raped and sexually abused her; *N* was convicted and sentenced to death; held: conviction and sentence affirmed).

[79] State v. Dunn, 758 P.2d 718 (Kan. 1988), *habeas granted*, Dunn v. Roberts, 768 F. Supp. 1442 (D. Kan. 1991), *aff'd*, 963 F.2d 308 (10th Cir. 1992) (*D* participated with *X* in two-and-a-half-week crime spree involving multiple kidnappings, murder, and a robbery; *D* was convicted; the state supreme court affirmed the conviction; her conviction was overturned by a federal court on the ground that she was entitled to payment for expert psychiatric services in support of her battered woman syndrome claim).

[80] *E.g.*, State v. Dunn, 758 P.2d 718 (Kan. 1988), *habeas granted*, Dunn v. Roberts, 768 F. Supp. 1442 (D. Kan. 1991), *aff'd*, 963 F.2d 308 (10th Cir. 1992) (BWS evidence relevant to prove *D* lacked the specific intent to assist in her abuser's crime-spree); People v. Romero, 26 Cal. App. 4th 315, 326 (Ct. App. 1992), *rev'd on procedural grounds*, 883 P.2d 388 (Cal. 1994) (BWS relevant to *R*'s credibility, and to support her testimony she entertained a good faith belief her abuser represented an imminent threat.); United States v. Marenghi, 893 F. Supp. 85 (D. Me. 1995) (BWS evidence relevant "to assist the jury in reviewing the evidence.").

harm, where no threat is issued, was reasonable.[81]

§ 23.08 MODEL PENAL CODE

[A] General Rule

Duress is an affirmative defense to unlawful conduct by the defendant if: (1) she was compelled to commit the offense by the use, or threatened use, of unlawful force by the coercer upon her or another person;[82] and (2) a person of reasonable firmness in her situation would have been unable to resist the coercion.[83] The defense of duress is recognized in such circumstances, the Commentary explains, because the "law is ineffective in the deepest sense, indeed . . . it is hypocritical if it imposes on the actor . . . a standard that . . . judges are not prepared to affirm that they should and could comply with."[84]

The defense is unavailable if the actor recklessly placed herself in a situation in which it was probable that she would be subjected to coercion. If she negligently placed herself in such a situation, however, the defense is available to her for all offenses except those for which negligence suffices to establish culpability.[85] This provision differs from Section 3.02, the MPC choice-of-evils defense, which is available in some circumstances to a person who recklessly causes the emergency.[86]

[B] Comparison to the Common Law

[1] In General

The Code's duress defense is broader than the common law in various respects. First, it abandons the common law requirement that the defendant's unlawful act be a response to an imminent deadly threat. Under the Code, the defendant may plead duress as a result of non-deadly and non-imminent threats — or even as the result of *prior* use of *non*-deadly force — as long as a person of reasonable firmness would have committed the offense in the defendant's circumstances.

Second, the defense is one of general applicability, so the defense may be raised in murder prosecutions.[87] Third, the Code does not require that the imperiled

---

[81] *E.g.*, United States v. Willis, 38 F.3d 170 (5th Cir. 1994) (BWS testimony demonstrates why *W* was unusually susceptible to coercion; therefore, it is irrelevant to whether a person of ordinary firmness would succumb.).

[82] Although the Code does not expressly so provide, the defense is also available if the defendant reasonably, but erroneously, believed that a threat to use unlawful force was issued. The defense is unavailable, however, if her mistake in this regard was reckless or negligent, and she is prosecuted for a crime of similar culpability. American Law Institute, Comment to § 2.09, at 380.

[83] Model Penal Code § 2.09(1).

[84] American Law Institute, Comment to § 2.09, at 374–75.

[85] Model Penal Code § 2.09(2).

[86] *See* § 22.05, *supra.*

[87] Even if a murder defendant is not acquitted, her duress claim may result in conviction of the lesser

person be the defendant or a member of her family.

The Code defense is similar to the common law in two significant ways. First, the defense is limited to threats or use of "unlawful" force; therefore, it does not apply to coercion arising from natural sources. This results in an anomaly: If D is compelled by X to run her car over the body of V, who is lying on a narrow mountain road, D may claim duress; but if she runs over V because her brakes give out and she prefers to kill V than to die herself by driving over the cliff, D may be convicted of criminal homicide.[88]

Second, in conformity with the common law, the Code does not recognize the defense when an interest other than bodily integrity is threatened. The Commentary simply states that other threats, such as to property or reputation, "cannot exercise sufficient power over persons of 'reasonable firmness' to warrant consideration."[89]

[2]   Escape from Intolerable Prison Conditions[90]

The common law duress defense applies when the coercer orders another person to commit a specific crime. Under the Code, however, the defense *also* applies if the coercer's use of unlawful force causes the coerced party to perform a different criminal act, one not ordered by the coercer. Therefore, the Model Code defense of duress applies in the typical intolerable-prison-condition escape case.

For example, if X threatens to sexually assault D, a prison inmate, D may be excused for committing the different criminal act of escaping confinement, assuming that a person of reasonable firmness in D's situation would have fled.[91] Moreover, the Code provides that a coerced act may also be *justified* under Section 3.02, the Code's choice-of-evils provision.[92] Therefore, a prisoner may be able to assert *both* defenses in an escape prosecution.

[3]   "Situational Duress"[93]

Because the duress defense only applies to human threats, "situational duress" claims based on compelling natural circumstances fall outside the scope of the defense. The drafters permitted this gap because they were concerned that if a person were excused as the result of a compelling natural threat, no one would be subject to prosecution for unjustified conduct.[94]

---

offense of manslaughter, on the ground that she committed the crime due to an "extreme emotional disturbance" for which there was a "reasonable explanation or excuse." Model Penal Code § 210.3(1)(b). *See* § 31.10[C][3], *infra.*

[88]   American Law Institute, Comment to § 2.09, at 378.

[89]   *Id.* at 375.

[90]   *See* § 23.05, *supra.*

[91]   American Law Institute, Comment to § 2.09, at 377.

[92]   Model Penal Code § 2.09(4).

[93]   *See* § 23.06, *supra.*

[94]   American Law Institute, Comment to § 2.09, at 379.

On the other hand, a brainwashing ("coercive persuasion") claim of duress might be available in a Model Penal Code jurisdiction. The duress defense applies if the actor commits an offense in response to prior use of unlawful force, assuming that a person of reasonable firmness in the actor's situation would have committed the crime. Therefore, a victim of brainwashing could claim coercion on the ground that prior force by a captor rendered her subconsciously fearful of more force if she did not accede to the suggestion that she commit a crime.[95]

[4]   Battered Women and the Nature of the "Person of Reasonable Firmness"

A battered woman should find features of the Code's duress defense helpful to her coercion claim. First, as there is no imminency requirement, she may defend herself on the basis of an earlier threat by the abuser. Second, as with the brainwashing cases discussed immediately above, a person who has suffered from prior abuse — prior unlawful force — may be able to excuse her conduct when she commits a crime at the "suggestion" of her abusive partner. Third, a battered women who kills her abuser in non-confrontational circumstances, and thus arguably when a self-defense claim will fail,[96] should be able to have the jury consider her claim under the Code's duress defense, by arguing that the abuser's prior use of force would cause a "person of reasonable firmness" to kill her abuser in such circumstances.[97]

A battered woman's conduct, however, is measured against the objective standard of a "person of reasonable firmness" in the defendant's situation. Does this mean that the "reasonable person" is a woman suffering from battered woman syndrome? Apparently not, as the Code intends for the overall standard to remain objective.[98] The Commentary provides that a defendant's incapacity should be "based upon the incapacity of men *in general* to resist the coercive pressures."[99] The Code drafters believed that it was impractical to "vary legal norms with the individual's capacity to meet the standards they prescribe." Except when a person suffers from a "gross and verifiable" disability that may otherwise establish irresponsibility, *e.g.*, insanity, the Code leaves consideration of an actor's subjective weaknesses to the discretion of the sentencing judge.

---

[95] American Law Institute, Comment to § 2.09, at 376–77.

[96] *See* § 18.05[B], *supra*, for discussion of the issues arising when battered women seek to assert the defense of self-defense when they kill their abuser when he does not represent an imminent threat.

[97] Joshua Dressler, *Battered Women and Sleeping Abusers: Some Reflections*, 3 Ohio St. J. Crim. L. 457 (2006).

[98] *E.g.*, State v. B.H., 870 A.2d 273 (N.J. 2005) (BWS testimony is admissible for the purpose of assisting the factfinder in its assessment of whether the battered woman was reckless in not leaving her abuser, and in understanding her subjective fear of her abuser, but such evidence is properly excluded in determining whether a person of reasonable firmness in her situation would have succumbed); United States v. Willis, 38 F.3d 170 (5th Cir. 1994) (*see* Note 82, *supra*).

[99] American Law Institute, Comment to § 2.09, at 374 (emphasis added).

Chapter 24

INTOXICATION

§ 24.01 INTOXICATION AND THE CRIMINAL LAW: AN OVERVIEW[1]

[A] "Intoxication": Definition

The term "intoxication" may be defined as a "disturbance of mental or physical capacities resulting from the introduction of any substance into the body."[2] As this definition suggests, the law pertaining to intoxication does not distinguish between alcohol and other foreign substances, including prescribed medications and illegal drugs.

[B] Intoxication Law in Its Social and Historical Context

Intoxicants distort judgment. They also reduce an actor's ability to control his aggressive feelings and anti-social impulses, resulting in criminal conduct, especially of a violent nature.[3] Persons addicted to narcotics, as well, often commit crimes (even when not intoxicated) in order to support their illegal habit.

In light of the social damage caused by intoxicated actors, it is unsurprising that Anglo-American common law has provided wrongdoers very little opportunity to avoid conviction on the basis of intoxication, and the modern legislative trend is to reduce the scope of any intoxication defense still further.[4] Indeed, in a few

---

[1] *See generally* Jerome Hall, *Intoxication and Criminal Responsibility*, 57 Harv. L. Rev. 1045 (1944); Phil Handler, *Intoxication and Criminal Responsibility in England, 1819–1920*, 33 Oxford J. Legal Stud. 243 (2013); Meghan Paulk Ingle, Note, *Law on the Rocks: The Intoxication Defenses Are Being Eighty-Sixed*, 55 Vand. L. Rev. 607 (2002); Mitchell Keiter, *Just Say No Excuse: The Rise and Fall of the Intoxication Defense*, 87 J. Crim. L. & Criminology 482 (1997); Monrad G. Paulsen, *Intoxication as a Defense to Crime*, 1961 U. Ill. L.F. 1.

[2] People v. Low, 732 P.2d 622, 627 (Colo. 1987) (quoting Model Penal Code § 2.08(5)(a)). The term "substance" is not often litigated, but one court interestingly held that a virus is not a "substance" for purposes of an intoxication defense. People v. Voth, 312 P.3d 144 (Colo. 2013).

[3] Montana v. Egelhoff, 518 U.S. 37, 49 (1996); *see also* Director of Public Prosecutions v. Majewski, [1976] 2 All E.R. 142, 146 ("Self-induced alcoholic intoxication has been a factor in crimes of violence . . . throughout the history of crime in this country."); Farmer v. State, 411 S.W.3d 901, 911 (Tex. Crim. App. 2013) (stating that "people, at least historically, consider [the condition of voluntary intoxication] . . . a sin, or at least a personal weakness"). Some studies, although quite dated, have suggested that as many as one-half of all homicides in the United States are committed by intoxicated persons. *Egelhoff, supra* (citing studies).

[4] *See* Ingle, Note 1, *supra*, at 608 (stating that the "health" of the defense "appears questionable," and, with some hyperbole, describing the intoxication defense as "an increasingly endangered species

jurisdictions now, the law has taken on "a certain Alice-in-Wonderland quality," by requiring prosecutors to prove the *mens rea* required in the definition of offenses, but then preventing defendants from introducing evidence of intoxication that might rebut its presence.[5]

[C] Intoxication Cases: Issues to Consider

When a defendant is intoxicated at the time of the alleged criminal conduct, a lawyer must consider at least three questions. First, how did the defendant become intoxicated? Intoxication law is divisible into two general categories: rules pertaining to conduct that was the result of "voluntary" (or "self-induced") intoxication, and the law pertaining to "involuntary" (or "innocent") intoxication. The vast majority of cases concern the former condition.

Second, in what way does the defendant claim that his intoxication affected his culpability? In almost all cases, the actor claims that he did not form the statutorily required state of mind to be convicted of the offense. Occasionally, however, the defendant's intoxication is so severe that he may seek to show that he was unconscious when he acted, *i.e.*, that his conduct did not include a voluntary act. Or, the defendant may assert that the intoxicants rendered him temporarily insane.

Third, of what type of offense is the defendant charged — general intent, specific intent, or strict liability? The common law rules differ considerably depending on the nature of the *mens rea*, if any, that must be proved, although this distinction is less relevant in states that apply Model Penal Code provisions.

[D] Intoxication Claims: Relationship to Other Defenses

Intoxication claims can confusingly parallel or overlap other defenses. First, as the previous comments suggest, under very limited circumstances an intoxication — not insanity — defense is recognized when an actor becomes "temporarily insane" as the result of the introduction of drugs, alcohol, or other foreign substances into the body.[6] In other cases, as the result of *long-term* intoxication, a person may suffer from permanent (or, at least, continuing) insanity; in the latter situation a traditional insanity defense claim may lie.[7]

Second, in some states, the defenses of diminished capacity[8] and intoxication operate similarly, except that the former defense applies when the actor suffers from mental illness rather than intoxication. However, occasionally, a state will permit evidence on one, but not the other, factor.[9]

---

within the American criminal law landscape, threatening soon to go the way of the dinosaur").

   [5] Sanford H. Kadish, *Fifty Years of Criminal Law: An Opinionated Review*, 87 Cal. L. Rev. 943, 955 (1999). See § 24.03, *infra*.

   [6] *See* § 24.06[B], *infra*.

   [7] *See* § 24.05[B], *infra*.

   [8] *See* Chapter 26, *infra*.

   [9] State v. Bias, 653 So. 2d 380 (Fla. 1995) (permitting evidence of voluntary intoxication in limited circumstances, but precluding expert testimony on diminished capacity).

Third, claims of intoxication and mistake-of-fact[10] very frequently overlap. For example, in *Regina v. Cogan and Leak*,[11] *L* fraudulently convinced *C*, who was intoxicated, that *V*, *L*'s wife, desired intercourse with *C*, despite *V*'s protestations to the contrary. Charged with rape, *C* claimed a mistake of fact regarding *V*'s lack of consent. Because *C* was intoxicated, however, his claim could also be described as an "intoxicated mistake"[12] claim. Often the two defenses operate similarly, so that the label attached to the claim will not matter. However, in some jurisdictions, the "mistake" defense is broader than the counterpart "intoxication" claim, so that the mixture of the two claims may result in conceptual confusion.

§ 24.02   VOLUNTARY INTOXICATION: GENERAL PRINCIPLES[13]

[A]   Definition of "Voluntary Intoxication"

[1]   In General

The term "voluntary intoxication" rarely is defined by the courts, which prefer instead to provide examples of the very few circumstances in which intoxication is *in*voluntary. Basically, intoxication is "voluntary" if the actor is culpable for becoming intoxicated. Such culpability exists if the person knowingly ingests a substance that he knows or should know can cause him to become intoxicated, unless the substance was a prescribed medication or he was coerced to ingest it.[14]

Once an actor voluntarily ingests a known intoxicant, courts are unsympathetic to claims that the substance had an unexpected effect on the actor. For example, in *People v. Velez*,[15] *D* knowingly puffed on a marijuana cigarette at a social gathering, unaware that it was laced with phencyclidine (PCP). *D*, while in an unconscious state precipitated by the PCP, assaulted *V* with a deadly weapon. The court held that for purposes of intoxication law, *D* was "voluntarily" intoxicated, because it was "common knowledge that unlawful street drugs do not come with warranties of purity or quality associated with lawfully acquired drugs, such as alcohol."

---

[10] *See* Chapter 12, *supra.*

[11] [1976] Q.B. 217.

[12] Kenneth L. Campbell, *Intoxicated Mistakes*, 32 Crim. L.Q. 110 (1989).

[13] *See generally* Alan R. Ward, *Making Some Sense of Self-Induced Intoxication*, 45 Cambridge L.J. 247 (1986); Peter Westen, *Egelhoff Again*, 36 Am. Crim. L. Rev. 1203 (1999); see also the sources in Note 1, *supra.*

[14] *See* Model Penal Code § 2.08(5)(b) (defining "self-induced intoxication").

[15] 175 Cal. App. 3d 785 (Ct. App. 1985).

[2] Alcoholism, Drug Addiction, and "Voluntary Intoxication"[16]

The common law treats intoxication resulting from alcoholism or drug addiction as voluntary. In general, "an irresistable [sic] compulsion to consume intoxicants caused by a physiological or psychological disability does not render the ensuing intoxication involuntary."[17] The law treats the alcoholic's first drink of the day, and the drug addict's first use of narcotics on a particular occasion, no differently than it does the actions of the ordinary drinker and casual user of drugs.

As a matter of constitutional law, a state may not punish a person for the *status* — the condition — of being addicted to narcotics[18] or, presumably, of being an alcoholic. On the other hand, an alcoholic may be punished for conduct resulting from intoxication, such as public drunkenness;[19] and a drug addict may not use his condition as a defense to the crime of drug possession or offenses committed in support of his drug habit.[20] Constitutional law in this regard is discussed elsewhere in the text.[21]

[B] General Rules

[1] No Excuse

Courts commonly state that voluntary intoxication never excuses criminal conduct.[22] This is a somewhat misleading statement: Although it is true that self-induced intoxication *as such never* excuses wrongdoing, the condition that intoxication causes, *e.g.*, a clouded mental state, unconsciousness, or insanity, *may* serve as an exculpatory basis in *very limited* circumstances. Nonetheless, the no-excuse rule is a good starting point from which to appreciate how few are the circumstances in which a voluntarily intoxicated actor may avoid criminal conviction.

---

[16] *See generally* Herbert Fingarette, Heavy Drinking — The Myth of Alcoholism as a Disease (1988); Richard C. Boldt, *The Construction of Responsibility in the Criminal Law*, 140 U. Pa. L. Rev. 2245 (1992); Douglas N. Husak, *Addiction and Criminal Liability*, 18 Law & Phil. 655 (1999); Warren Lehman, *Alcoholism, Freedom, and Moral Responsibility*, 13 Int'l. J.L. & Psychiatry 103 (1990); Steven S. Nemerson, *Alcoholism, Intoxication, and the Criminal Law*, 10 Cardozo L. Rev. 393 (1988).

[17] See v. State, 757 S.W.2d 947, 950 (Ark. 1988); *see* State v. Bishop, 632 S.W.2d 255, 258 (Mo. 1982) ("We have examined the laws of each of those states which deal with the question of whether and to what extent intoxication is a defense to a criminal charge. We find nothing in that examination which causes us to conclude that those statutory provisions are intended to provide that the taking of drugs by a drug addict produces intoxication which is involuntarily produced so as to provide a defense.").

[18] Robinson v. California, 370 U.S. 660 (1962).

[19] Powell v. Texas, 392 U.S. 514 (1968).

[20] *See* United States v. Moore, 486 F.2d 1139, 1147–48 (D.C. Cir. 1973).

[21] *See* § 9.04, *supra.*

[22] *E.g.*, State v. Cameron, 514 A.2d 1302, 1304 (N.J. 1986) ("Under the common law intoxication was not a defense to a criminal; charge."); People v. Langworthy, 331 N.W.2d 171, 172 (Mich. 1982) ("Every jurisdiction in this country recognizes the general principle that voluntary intoxication is not any excuse for crime.") (footnote omitted); Farmer v. State, 411 S.W.3d 901, 911 (Tex. Crim. App. 2013) ("Voluntary intoxication is virtually never a defense to crime.").

The early English common law rule was that voluntary intoxication did not serve in any way to exculpate a wrongdoer. Hale wrote that an intoxicated person "shall have no privilege by this voluntarily contracted madness, but shall have the same judgment as if he were in his right senses."[23] Put differently, "a man who by his own voluntary act debauches and destroys his will power [should] be no better situated in regard to criminal acts than a sober man."[24] Indeed, Blackstone viewed intoxication "as an aggravation of the offence, rather than as an excuse for any criminal misbehaviour."[25]

[2] When Voluntary Intoxication May Be Exculpatory

Beginning in the 19th century, very narrow exceptions to the early common law no-exculpation rule began to take root.[26] First (and subject to considerable clarification), in most jurisdictions, a person may be acquitted of certain offenses if, as the result of self-induced intoxication, he did not harbor the state of mind provided for in the definition of the offense. Second, there is limited authority for the proposition that one who acts in a state of unconsciousness brought on by voluntary intoxication may seek to avoid conviction on this ground. Third, a person who suffers from long-term intoxication-induced "fixed" (or "settled") insanity may be acquitted. These principles are discussed below.

§ 24.03 VOLUNTARY INTOXICATION: *MENS REA*

[A] In General

The most common voluntary intoxication "defense" raised in criminal trials is not an excuse defense at all, but rather is a failure-of-proof claim,[27] namely that, as a result of the actor's intoxication, he lacked the mental state required in the definition of the offense.

Today, there are various common law and statutory approaches to *mens rea* claims, ranging from the rule that voluntary intoxication that negates an actor's *mens rea* is a defense to all crimes, to the opposite and increasingly popular position that it is not recognized for any offense.[28] The traditional common law rule — the rule that took root in the 19th century and remains the most common approach — is one that distinguishes between general-intent and specific-intent

---

[23] 1 Matthew Hale, History of the Pleas of the Crown *32–*33 (1736).

[24] Director of Public Prosecutions v. Beard, [1920] A.C. 479, 494 (H.L.) (opinion of Lord Birkenhead); *see also* People v. Lewis, 36 Cal. 531, 531–32 (1869), *overruled on other grounds*, People v. Gorshen, 336 P.2d 492 (Cal. 1959) (the law should "not allow [the defendant] to avail himself of the excuse of his own gross vice and misconduct to shelter himself from the legal consequences of [his] crime").

[25] 4 William Blackstone, Commentaries on the Laws of England *25–*26 (1769).

[26] Montana v. Egelhoff, 518 U.S. 37, 46–47 (1996).

[27] See § 16.02, *supra*, for a definition of a "failure-of-proof" defense.

[28] Mowery v. State, 247 P.3d 866, 872 (Wyo. 2011) (noting that "many jurisdictions have chosen to abandon the . . . defense altogether"); *see also* Note 4, *supra*.

crimes.[29]

[B] Traditional Common Law Rule

[1] Overview

In matters relating to voluntary intoxication, the common law draws a distinction between general-intent and specific-intent crimes. Indeed, as the California Supreme Court once pointed out, the concepts of "general intent" and "specific intent" "evolved as a judicial response to the problem of the intoxicated offender." The distinction, it said, represents the law's "compromise between the conflicting feelings of sympathy and reprobation for the intoxicated offender."[30]

[2] General-Intent Offenses

According to ordinary common law principles, and overwhelmingly followed today, voluntary intoxication is not a defense to general-intent crimes.[31] For example, if *D* rapes *V*, he will not be entitled to claim that, as a result of voluntary intoxication, his mind was so clouded that he did not or could not form the intent to have sexual intercourse with *V*.[32]

This rule made sense when the intoxication doctrine was first formulated. At that time, "general intent" referred to an offense for which the only *mens rea* required was a culpable state of mind.[33] Consistent with this meaning of the term *"mens rea,"* the voluntary act of impairing one's mental faculties with intoxicants is a morally blameworthy course of conduct that renders the actor culpable for the ensuing harm.[34] By this view, a person's voluntary intoxication *proves*, rather than negates, his *"mens rea."*

In modern language, self-induced intoxication typically constitutes reckless conduct.[35] The effect of alcohol and drugs on the human body is now sufficiently well known that the law can safely assume that when an ordinary adult chooses to ingest intoxicating substances, he knows that he will suffer temporary impairment of his

---

[29] According to a somewhat outdated 1997 survey of statutory and case law, 10 states did not admit intoxication evidence as a defense to any crime; two states only admitted such evidence to reduce first-degree murder to a lower degree; in one state, voluntary intoxication was a defense to all crimes; in the remaining 37 states, voluntary intoxication was a defense to some, but not all, non-homicide crimes. Twenty-one of these states drew the line on the "specific intent"/"general intent" basis. Keiter, Note 1, *supra*, at 518–20.

[30] People v. Hood, 462 P.2d 370, 377 (Cal. 1969).

[31] *E.g.*, State v. Dwyer, 757 A.2d 597, 604 (Conn. App. Ct. 2000); State v. Erickstad, 620 N.W.2d 136, 144 (N.D. 2000); Mowery v. State, 247 P.3d 866, 872 (Wyo. 2011); United States v. Sewell, 252 F.3d 647, 650–51 (2d Cir. 2001).

[32] *See* State v. McDaniel, 515 So. 2d 572, 575 (La. Ct. App. 1987); People v. Langworthy, 331 N.W.2d 171, 177 (Mich. 1982).

[33] *See* §§ 10.02[B] and 10.06, *supra*.

[34] Hendershott v. People, 653 P.2d 385, 396 (Colo. 1982).

[35] People v. Register, 457 N.E.2d 704, 709 (N.Y. 1983), *overruled on other grounds*, Policano v. Herbert, 859 N.E.2d 484 (N.Y. 2006); Director of Public Prosecutions v. Majewski, [1976] 2 All E.R. 142, 150 (Lord Elwyn-Jones, L.C.).

powers of perception, judgment, and control; therefore, he knows that he may jeopardize the safety of others while in that condition.

[3] Specific-Intent Offenses

The traditional rule is that voluntary intoxication *is* a defense to specific-intent crimes.[36] That is, a person is not guilty of an offense if, as the result of his intoxication at the time of the crime, he was incapable of forming[37] or did not in fact form,[38] the specific intent required in the definition of the offense.[39]

For example, suppose that *D* becomes intoxicated and sexually assaults *V*, a woman. He is arrested during the assault and charged with the specific-intent crime of assault with intent to commit rape. Under the common law, *D* is entitled to introduce evidence regarding his intoxication in order to prove that, because of his condition, he lacked the specific intent to rape *V*, either because he was too intoxicated to know what he was doing, or because he mistakenly believed that *V* was consenting.[40] *D* is entitled to introduce this evidence because, the reasoning goes, "[w]here the legislature, in its definition of a crime, has designated a particular state of mind as a material element of the crime, evidence of intoxication becomes relevant if the degree of inebriation has reached that point" where he did not form the required intent.[41]

[4] Criticism of the Traditional Approach

[a]   Why Draw a Distinction?

Notice the apparent anomaly with the present law. If *D* has nonconsensual sexual intercourse with *V* because he drunkenly believes *V* is consenting, *D* may *not* introduce evidence of his intoxication to support his *mens rea* claim in the prosecution of the general-intent offense of rape. However, if *D* is arrested *before* the intercourse occurs, and he is charged with the specific-intent offense of "assault with intent to rape," *D* may now introduce evidence of his drunkenness in order to negate the specific intent ("intent to rape").

---

[36] *E.g.*, State v. Cameron, 514 A.2d 1302, 1304 (N.J. 1986); State v. Dwyer, 757 A.2d at 604; State v. Erickstad, 620 N.W.2d at 143–44; Mowery v. State, 247 P.3d at 872.

[37] United States v. Zink, 612 F.2d 511, 515 (10th Cir. 1980); Commonwealth v. Henson, 476 N.E.2d 947, 953 (Mass. 1985); State v. Hicks, 538 N.E.2d 1030, 1034 (Ohio 1989).

[38] Cal. Penal Code § 22(b) (2015).

[39] The difference in language between "lacking capacity to form" and "not forming" a specific intent is potentially significant. Logically, one who lacks the capacity to form a specific intent, does not in fact form it. The converse, however, does not necessarily follow. Logically, acquittal should be more difficult to obtain in an "incapacity" jurisdiction because intoxication rarely renders a person so insensible that he lacks the ability to intend. The "incapacity" language is undesirable, however, because a jury might improperly convict because it determines that the defendant *had* the capacity to form the specific intent, without resolving the pertinent question — *did* the defendant form the intent?

[40] *See* People v. Guillett, 69 N.W.2d 140, 143 (Mich. 1955), *overruled on other grounds*, People v. Carines, 597 N.W.2d 130, 140 (Mich. 1999).

[41] Commonwealth v. Graves, 334 A.2d 661, 663 (Pa. 1975), *overruled by statute, as noted in* Commonwealth v. Pickett, 368 A.2d 799, 801 (Pa. Super. Ct. 1976).

At least in a modern penal code, in which *mens rea* terms are expressly set out in the definition of offenses, nothing commends this dual approach. *D*'s intoxication is the same in both cases. He is equally drunk. He is equally culpable for becoming drunk. His mind is equally clouded. His capacity to form a mental state is equally undermined (or not undermined). And, "neither common experience nor psychology knows of any such phenomenon as 'general intent' distinguishable from 'specific intent.' "[42] Nor do utilitarian concerns favor separate approaches: *D* is equally dangerous in the two cases; and principles of general deterrence demand equal treatment.

[b]   Should the Defense Be Abolished?

Most critics of the current law would resolve the perceived anomaly by disallowing *any mens rea*-based voluntary intoxication defense. Supreme Court Justice Antonin Scalia has expressed the arguments for this position as follows:

> Disallowing consideration of voluntary intoxication has the effect of in-creasing the punishment for all unlawful acts committed in that state, and thereby deters drunkenness or irresponsible behavior while drunk. The rule also serves as a specific deterrent, ensuring that those who prove incapable of controlling violent impulses while voluntarily intoxicated go to prison. And finally, the rule comports with and implements society's moral perception that one who has voluntarily impaired his own faculties should be responsible for the consequences.[43]

Justice Scalia's utilitarian arguments are based on the proposition that "the aim of the law is to protect the innocent from injury by the sick as well as the bad."[44] Therefore, it follows, the intoxication defense is detrimental to the welfare and safety of the citizenry. Unlike insane people, who are usually institutionalized on the basis of an insanity acquittal,[45] intoxicated persons who are acquitted, many of whom are alcoholics and drug addicts, return to the street where they may commit new offenses.

Those who favor an intoxication defense[46] disagree with Scalia's "moral percep-tion" argument. Even if an intoxicated actor is dangerous, they contend, this fact does not prove that he possessed the state of mind required in the definition of the offense. When a lawmaking body expressly includes a mental state in the definition of a crime, as common law courts did with specific-intent offenses and which modern criminal codes now do with most non-strict-liability crimes, it does so because it

---

[42] People v. Kelley, 176 N.W.2d 435, 443 (Mich. Ct. App. 1970); *see also* Mowery v. State, 247 P.3d 866, 872 (Wyo. 2011) (noting the "tenuous logic" of the distinction).

[43] Montana v. Egelhoff, 518 U.S. 37, 49–50 (1996).

[44] State v. Maik, 287 A.2d 715, 720 (N.J. 1972), *overruled on other grounds by*, State v. Krol, 344 A.2d 289 (N.J. 1975).

[45] *See* § 25.05, *infra.*

[46] Some commentators who favor a defense contend that voluntary intoxication should serve as a potential basis for exculpation for *any* offense, regardless of its characterization as "general" or "specific" intent. Others would retain the common law distinction between general-intent and specific-intent offenses.

believes that the particular *mens rea* incorporated therein renders the actor more deserving of punishment than if that mental state were absent.

Supreme Court Justice Sandra O'Connor has explained the pro-defense position on the ground that there is a "fundamental incompatibility" with imposing a mental-state requirement in the definition of an offense, and then disallowing "consideration of evidence that might defeat establishment of that mental state."[47] It is not that voluntary intoxication *excuses* commission of a crime, but, as she explains, "rather, an element of the crime, the requisite mental state, was not satisfied and therefore the crime [has] not been committed." Put simply, "where a subjective mental state [is] an element of the crime to be proved, the defense must be permitted to show, by reference to intoxication, the absence of that element."[48] Notwithstanding the latter arguments, statutes that bar evidence of voluntary intoxication do not inevitably offend constitutional principles.[49]

[C] Special Problem: Intoxication and Homicide

The voluntary intoxication rules pertaining to criminal homicide merit special attention. Many jurisdictions separate murder into degrees, in which first-degree murder includes "wilful, deliberate, premeditated" killings.[50] In virtually all states with this type of statutory system, a defendant may introduce evidence that, because his mental faculties were clouded by intoxicants, he did not premeditate or deliberate the killing.[51] In such circumstances, the defendant is entitled to have his crime reduced to second-degree murder.[52]

A defendant's intoxication may also arise as an issue in a felony-murder prosecution.[53] For example, suppose that *D*, in an extremely intoxicated condition, takes property from *V* by force. *V* dies of a heart attack brought on by the robbery. Robbery is a specific-intent offense. In a jurisdiction that recognizes the voluntary intoxication defense in specific-intent prosecutions, what should happen if *D* is so intoxicated that he does not form the specific intent to steal *V*'s property? The answer should be that *D* is not guilty of robbery and, therefore, not guilty of felony-murder.[54]

---

[47] *Montana v. Egelhoff*, 518 U.S. at 69 (dissenting opinion).

[48] *Id.* at 70.

[49] Montana v. Egelhoff, 518 U.S. 37 (1996). See § 7.03[B][4][b], *supra*, for examination of *Egelhoff*.

[50] *See* §§ 31.02[D] and 31.03[C], *infra*.

[51] *E.g.*, State v. Ludlow, 883 P.2d 1144, 1147–50 (Kan. 1994); Commonwealth v. Henson, 476 N.E.2d 947, 953 (Mass. 1985); State v. Stasio, 396 A.2d 1129, 1131 (N.J. 1979).

[52] The offense is only reduced to second-degree murder because a person who becomes so intoxicated that he cannot form the requisite state of mind for first-degree murder has acted recklessly in becoming so insensible. Therefore, his actions fall within the recklessness or "depraved heart" form of murder that typically constitutes second-degree murder. *See* § 31.05, *infra*. Rarely, a court will hold that voluntary intoxication can also negate depraved-heart murder. State v. Brown, 931 P.2d 69, 73–75 (N.M. 1996) (in a state in which depraved-heart murder is *first*-degree, held: excessive consumption of alcohol can negate the statutory requirement of subjective or actual knowledge of the high degree of risk involved in the actor's conduct). The Model Penal Code rejects this approach. *See* § 24.07[B][1][b], *infra*.

[53] The felony-murder doctrine is considered at § 31.06, *infra*.

[54] *E.g.*, Commonwealth v. Parker, 522 N.E.2d 924, 926 (Mass. 1988).

§ 24.04 VOLUNTARY INTOXICATION: VOLUNTARY ACT

Occasionally, a person will become so intoxicated that he is rendered unconscious, in which condition his body may move in an automatic, *i.e.*, unwilled manner and cause harm to others. If so, may a defendant seek to avoid conviction by asserting the general principle of criminal responsibility that a person may not be convicted of a crime unless his conduct includes a voluntary act, *i.e.*, a willed, conscious, muscular contraction?[55]

There are relatively few cases that deal directly with this issue, since an unconscious person will almost certainly also assert a voluntary-intoxication *mens rea* defense as well, assuming the jurisdiction permits such claims. Where courts have spoken to the issue, the general approach appears to be that, although unconsciousness ordinarily precludes criminal liability, it is *not* a defense if the condition was itself brought on by voluntary consumption of alcohol or drugs.[56]

Unconsciousness may serve as a basis for acquittal in another manner, however. Courts sometimes state that evidence of unconsciousness produced by voluntary intoxication may be introduced by a defendant when "his defense is that he did not physically accomplish the act of which he is accused."[57] In other words, the defendant may use his intoxication-induced unconsciousness to prove that he did not commit the criminal act at all, as distinguished from claiming that he committed it involuntarily.

§ 24.05 VOLUNTARY INTOXICATION: INSANITY[58]

[A] "Temporary" Insanity

Suppose that a person becomes so intoxicated that, at the time he commits an offense, he is so out of touch with reality that he does not appreciate the wrongfulness of his conduct, or he cannot conform his conduct to the law. Assume further that if his state of mind were caused by a mental disease, rather than by intoxication, he could successfully raise the excuse of insanity.[59] As mental illness is not involved, however, the defendant may wish to claim that because of his voluntary ingestion of drugs or alcohol, he experienced something like "temporary insanity," or what Hale called "temporary phrenzy."[60]

---

[55] *See* § 9.02[A], *supra*.

[56] *E.g.*, Schlatter v. State, 891 N.E.2d 1139, 1143 (Ind. Ct. App. 2008); State v. Utter, 479 P.2d 946 (Wash. Ct. App. 1971); *see* People v. Boyer, 133 P.3d 581, 622 (Cal. 2006) ("[V]oluntary intoxication, even if it induced unconsciousness, is not a defense to crime as such, though it may be relevant to whether the defendant formed a specific intent necessary for its commission.").

[57] Linehan v. State, 442 So. 2d 244, 250 (Fla. Dist. Ct. App. 1983), *overruled on other grounds*, Coicou v. State, 39 So. 3d 237 (Fla. 2010).

[58] *See generally* Lawrence P. Tiffany, *The Drunk, The Insane, and the Criminal Courts: Deciding What to Make of Self-Induced Insanity*, 69 Wash. U. L.Q. 221 (1991).

[59] The definition of "insanity" varies by jurisdiction. *See* § 25.04[C], *infra*.

[60] 1 Hale, Note 23, *supra*, at *32.

The common law does not recognize such a defense. To the extent that an actor's intoxication was voluntary, "any degree of insanity thus produced would be a part of the consequences of such voluntary intoxication."[61] In contrast to mental illness, which is a condition that ordinarily is contracted involuntarily, one who voluntarily introduces alcohol or drugs into his system is the victim of "artificial voluntarily contracted madness."[62] As such, he is not entitled to the law's dispensation.[63]

[B] "Fixed" ("Settled") Insanity

Long-term use of intoxicants can result in a substance-induced mental disorder that persists, *i.e.*, the disorder remains even when the actor is not under the influence of intoxicants.

The law distinguishes between mental impairment that does not extend beyond the period of voluntary intoxication, for which no defense is available, and insanity resulting from long-term use of drugs or alcohol. If the unsoundness of mind, although produced by long-term alcohol or drug abuse, has become "fixed" or "settled," the general, but not universal, rule is that the defendant may assert a traditional insanity defense.[64] Although the defense is usually asserted when the defendant was not intoxicated at the time of the offense, the insanity defense applies even if the actor was intoxicated at the time of the crime.[65]

In light of the unsympathetic view of common law jurists regarding intoxication-caused criminal conduct, it is surprising that "madness . . . contracted by the vice and will of the party"[66] would excuse. Indeed, one court that has rejected the defense has asserted:

> There is no principled basis to distinguish between the short-term and long-term effects of voluntary intoxication by punishing the first and excusing the second. If anything, the moral blameworthiness would seem to be even greater with respect to the long-term effects of many, repeated instances of voluntary intoxication occurring over an extended period of time.[67]

The law's general willingness to recognize the defense is sometimes defended on the theory that it would constitute an impossible task to trace the chain of causation back to the original misconduct of abusive drinking or narcotics usage.[68] More likely, however, the law recognizes the fact that at some point a person's earlier

---

[61] Roberts v. People, 19 Mich. 401, 422 (1870); *see* Evans v. State, 645 P.2d 155, 158–60 (Alaska 1982); State v. Wicks, 657 P.2d 781, 782 (Wash. 1983).

[62] 4 Blackstone, Note 25, *supra*, at *25.

[63] However, a person suffering from such a mental condition may be incapable of forming a required *mens rea*, and be able to avoid conviction on *that* ground, as considered in § 24.03, *supra*.

[64] 1 Hale at *32; Berry v. State, 969 N.E.2d 35, 38 (Ind. 2012); Jones v. State, 648 P.2d 1251, 1255 (Okla. Crim. App. 1982).

[65] People v. Chapman, 418 N.W.2d 658, 659 (Mich. Ct. App. 1987).

[66] 1 Hale at *32.

[67] Bieber v. People, 856 P.2d 811, 817 (Colo. 1993).

[68] Paulsen, Note 1, *supra*, at 23.

voluntary decisions become morally remote.[69] One should not be blamed for every harmful act that can be linked to a much earlier transgression.

§ 24.06 INVOLUNTARY INTOXICATION[70]

[A] Definition

Intoxication is "involuntary" (or "innocent") if the actor is not to blame for becoming intoxicated.[71] According to one scholar, if we judge the state of legal affairs from court opinions, involuntary intoxication is "simply and completely non-existent."[72] Although this is an exaggeration, cases of successful assertion of involuntary intoxication claims are exceedingly uncommon.

As described in *City of Minneapolis v. Altimus*,[73] intoxication is characterized as "involuntary" in four circumstances.[74] First, if the person is coerced to ingest an intoxication, such as when B, a youth, was told that he would be left in the desert if he did not drink alcohol.[75] Second, if the person ingests an intoxicant by innocent mistake, *e.g.*, X fraudulently induces P to ingest cocaine by telling him that it is a "breath freshener."[76]

Third, blame is inappropriate if the actor becomes unexpectedly intoxicated from a prescribed medication, *i.e.*, he does not know, and has no reason to know, that the medication is likely to have an intoxicating effect.[77] However, if the actor purposely takes more than the prescribed medication, the jury may find that the intoxication is voluntary.[78]

---

[69] Parker v. State, 254 A.2d 381, 388 (Md. Ct. Spec. App. 1969) (distinguishing between "the direct results of drinking, which are voluntarily sought after, and its remote and undesired consequences")

[70] *See generally* Lawrence P. Tiffany & Mary Tiffany, *Nosologic Objections to the Criminal Defense of Pathological Intoxication: What Do the Doubters Doubt?*, 13 Int'l J.L. & Psychiatry, 49 (1990).

[71] Mendenhall v. State, 15 S.W.3d 560, 565 (Tex. App. 2000) (involuntary intoxication is an affirmative defense when "the accused has exercised no independent judgment or volition in taking the intoxicant").

[72] Jerome Hall, General Principles of Criminal Law 539 (2d ed. 1960).

[73] 238 N.W.2d 851, 856 (Minn. 1976).

[74] *See also* Farmer v. State, 411 S.W.3d 901, 912–15 (Tex. Crim. App. 2013) (providing a nice recent national survey of involuntary intoxication cases).

[75] Burrows v. State, 297 P. 1029, 1035 (Ariz. 1931), *overruled on other grounds by* State v. Hernandez, 320 P.2d 467, 469 (Ariz. 1958).

[76] People v. Penman, 110 N.E. 894, 900 (Ill. 1915).

[77] *City of Minneapolis v. Altimus*, 238 N.W.2d at 856–57; Commonwealth v. Darch, 767 N.E.2d 1096, 1098–99 (Mass. App. Ct. 2002); *e.g.*, Mendenhall v. State, 15 S.W.3d 560, 565 (Tex. App. 2000) (*M*, a diabetic, failed to eat appropriately in conjunction with a self-administered prescribed insulin injection; he had not been provided sufficient information from medical personnel on the appropriate diet for his condition and the effects of taking insulin on an empty stomach).

[78] People v. Chaffey, 25 Cal. App. 4th 852 (Ct. App. 1994) (taking an overdose of prescription medicine in order to commit suicide may be deemed *voluntary* intoxication); *contra* People v. Turner, 680 P.2d 1290 (Colo. App. 1983) (as in the past, *T* took more than the prescribed medication for migraine headaches; in the past, he suffered drowsiness from the overdose; on the present occasion it had an intoxicating effect; held: because the doctor had never warned him that an overdose might cause intoxication, and it had not caused this effect in the past, a jury could find that the intoxication was *involuntary*).

Fourth, "pathological intoxication" is involuntary. Pathological intoxication is "intoxication grossly excessive in degree, given the amount of the intoxicant, to which the actor does not know he is susceptible."[79] It is often the result of some pre-disposing mental or physical condition, *e.g.*, temporal lobe epilepsy, encephalitis, or a metabolic disturbance.[80]

[B] General Rule

A person who is involuntarily intoxicated is entitled to acquittal in all of the circumstances in which *voluntary* intoxication is a defense. Although there is exceedingly little case law on the matter, it would seem that because the actor's intoxication was contracted in a nonculpable manner, he should also be acquitted of any general-intent offense.[81]

In contrast to the principles relating to voluntary intoxication,[82] a defendant is also excused for his conduct if, as the result of involuntary intoxication, he is "temporarily insane," *i.e.*, he suffers from a temporary intoxication-induced mental condition that satisfies that jurisdiction's definition of insanity.[83]

§ 24.07 MODEL PENAL CODE

[A] General Rule

An actor's intoxicated condition at the time of a crime may generally exculpate him in two circumstances. First, with one exception, any form of intoxication is a defense to criminal conduct if it negates an element of the offense.[84] Second, pathological intoxication and intoxication that was not self-induced[85] are affirmatives defenses, if the intoxication causes the actor to suffer from a mental condition comparable to that which constitutes insanity under the Code.[86] These

---

[79] *City of Minneapolis v. Altimus*, 238 N.W.2d at 855 (quoting Model Penal Code § 2.08(5)(c)).

[80] Tiffany & Tiffany, Note 70, *supra*, at 49.

[81] To the extent that involuntary intoxication is a defense because it negates the required *mens rea* of an offense, it should not be a defense to a strict-liability crime, because there is no *mens rea* to negate. *E.g.*, State v. Miller, 788 P.2d 974 (Or. 1990) (*M* drank coffee fixed for him by *X*, without knowledge that it had been spiked with alcohol; held: *M* may *not* claim involuntary intoxication in a strict-liability prosecution for driving under the influence of alcohol); Aliff v. State, 955 S.W.2d 891 (Tex. App. 1997) (same holding, driving while intoxicated); *contra* Commonwealth v. Darch, 767 N.E.2d 1096 (Mass. App. Ct. 2002) (driving while intoxicated); People v. Koch, 294 N.Y.S. 987 (App. Div. 1937) (same).

[82] *See* § 24.05[A], *supra*.

[83] People v. Turner, 680 P.2d 1290, 1292 (Colo. App. 1983); People v. Caulley, 494 N.W.2d 853, 859 (Mich. Ct. App. 1992); State v. Bauman, 689 A.2d 173, 182 (N.J. Super. Ct. App. Div. 1997); State v. Voorhees, 596 N.W.2d 241, 250 (Minn. 1999); Mendenhall v. State, 15 S.W.3d 560, 565 (Tex. App. 2000); State v. Gardner, 870 P.2d 900, 901–02 (Utah 1993); State v. Gardner, 601 N.W.2d 670, 673 (Wis. Ct. App. 1999).

[84] Model Penal Code § 2.08(1).

[85] The Code defines "self-induced intoxication" as "intoxication caused by substances that the actor knowingly introduced into his body, the tendency of which to cause intoxication he knows or ought to know, unless he introduces them pursuant to medical advice." Mode Penal Code § 2.08(5)(c).

[86] Model Penal Code § 2.08(4).

exculpatory claims are explained below.

[B] Negation of an Element of an Offense

[1] Mental State

[a]   In General

The Code does not distinguish between "general intent" and "specific intent" offenses.[87] Consequently, with one exception, a person is not guilty of an offense — regardless of whether it would be characterized as "general intent" or "specific intent" at common law — if, as the result of intoxication — self-induced or not — he lacked the state of mind required in respect to an element of the crime.

For example, assume that under state law "rape" occurs when a male "knowingly has nonconsensual sexual intercourse with a female not his wife." Under this statute, *D* would be entitled to acquittal if, because of self-induced intoxication, he did not have the knowledge required for the offense, *e.g.*, he did not know that he was having intercourse, he did not know that the female did not consent, or he did not know that the victim was a "female not his wife."

[b]   Exception to the Rule[88]

The Code recognizes one exception to the rule described above. The exception relates to crimes defined in terms of recklessness. Ordinarily, a person acts "recklessly" as defined by the Code if "he consciously disregards a substantial and unjustifiable risk that the material element of the offense exists or will result from his conduct."[89] However, the Code provides that if a person "due to self-induced intoxication is unaware of a risk of which he would have been aware had he been sober, such unawareness is immaterial" in a prosecution for which recklessness establishes criminal liability.[90] In other words, in a prosecution for recklessness, a voluntarily intoxicated defendant cannot negate proof of recklessness by introducing evidence of his *intoxication-caused* lack of awareness of a risk. As a practical matter, this means that a negligent actor may be convicted of a crime of recklessness, in violation of ordinary Model Penal Code culpability principles.

The Commentary to the Code concedes that criticism of this rule is "worthy of respect," but the drafters concluded:

> [A]wareness of the potential consequences of excessive drinking on the capacity of human beings to gauge the risks incident to their conduct is by now so dispersed in our culture that it is not unfair to postulate a general equivalence between the risks created by the conduct of the drunken actor and the risks created by his conduct in becoming drunk. Becoming so

---

[87] *See* § 10.07[A], *supra*.

[88] *See generally* Gideon Yaffe, *Intoxication, Recklessness, and Negligence*, 9 Ohio St. J. Crim. L. 545 (2012).

[89] Model Penal Code § 2.02(2)(c).

[90] Model Penal Code § 2.08(2).

drunk as to destroy temporarily the actor's powers of perception and judgment is conduct that plainly has no affirmative social value to counter-balance the potential danger.[91]

[2]   Voluntary Act

The Code provides that a person is entitled to acquittal if his intoxication negates *any* element of the offense. Under the Code, a person is not guilty of an offense unless his conduct includes a voluntary act (or an omission in limited circumstances).[92]

Conduct during unconsciousness is involuntary. Therefore, a person who is unconscious as the result of intoxication, even if the intoxication is self-induced, may raise an involuntariness claim. However, the requisite voluntary act may sometimes be found in conduct prior to the unconsciousness.[93]

[C]   Intoxication as an Affirmative Defense

Even if all of the elements of a crime are proved, the Code recognizes an affirmative defense based on intoxication if, at the time of his conduct: (1) the actor suffered from pathological intoxication[94] or intoxication that was not self-induced; and (2) the actor's condition qualifies under the American Law Institute's test of insanity.[95]

If the criteria for the defense are satisfied, the actor's defense is that of intoxication, rather than insanity. The Code expressly provides that intoxication does not "in itself, constitute mental disease."[96] As is the case in common law jurisdictions, however, an actor is entitled to raise an *insanity* claim if, at the time of his conduct, he suffered from a mental disease caused by long-term use of alcohol or drugs.[97]

---

[91] American Law Institute, Comment to § 2.08, at 359.

[92] Model Penal Code § 2.01(1). *See* § 9.05[A], *supra.*

[93] American Law Institute, Comment to § 2.08, at 353. Is the voluntary ingestion of the known intoxicant sufficient to prove that the actor's conduct "included" a voluntary act? According to the Commentary, "the act of drinking itself, though perhaps 'voluntary,' would not suffice to meet this requirement unless it were undertaken with the requisite culpability as to the actual result that ensued." *Id.*

[94] See § 24.06[A], *supra*, for the definition of "pathological intoxication."

[95] For the Code definition of insanity, see Model Penal Code § 4.01(1), discussed at § 25.04[C][3], *infra.*

[96] Model Penal Code § 2.08(3). The key words here are "in itself." The Institute does not preclude the possibility that experts will someday conclude that there is a disease giving rise to an uncontrollable urge to drink, in which case, an alcoholic whose intoxicated conduct meets the Code test of "insanity" would be entitled to raise the latter defense. American Law Institute, Comment to § 2.08, at 361.

[97] American Law Institute, Comment to § 2.08, at 362.

Chapter 25

INSANITY

§ 25.01 INSANITY: AN OVERVIEW[1]

"The insanity defense exists in criminal law not to identify the mentally ill, but rather to determine who among the mentally ill should be held criminally responsible for their conduct."[2]

Few doctrines of criminal law engender more controversy than the insanity defense. Since the time of Edward III in the 14th century, when "madness" became a complete defense to criminal charges,[3] English and American courts and, more recently, legislatures have struggled to define "insanity." No sooner is a definition propounded than critics, often from conflicting philosophical vantage points, attack it. Some criticism runs deeper, in the form of calls for outright abolition of the defense.

The issue of the proper relationship of mental illness to criminal responsibility is controversial for various reasons. First, although the insanity defense is rarely raised,[4] it is offered in some unusually heinous[5] and well-publicized cases — in attacks upon public officials (such as when John Hinckley attempted to kill President Ronald Reagan[6]), in mass and serial killings, and in especially bizarre homicides. These crimes shock the community, but the persons who commit these

---

[1] See generally Herbert Fingarette, The Meaning of Criminal Insanity (1972); Herbert Fingarette & Ann Fingarette Hasse, Mental Disabilities and Criminal Responsibility (1979); Abraham S. Goldstein, The Insanity Defense (1967); Michael S. Moore, Law and Psychiatry: Rethinking the Relationship (1984); Norval Morris, Madness and the Criminal Law (1982); Michael L. Perlin, The Jurisprudence of the Insanity Defense (1994); and Stephen J. Morse & Morris B. Hoffman, The Uneasy Entente Between Legal Insanity and Mens Rea: Beyond Clark v. Arizona, 97 J. Crim. L. & Criminology 1071 (2007).

[2] State v. Singleton, 48 A.3d 285, 294 (N.J. 2012).

[3] Rollin M. Perkins & Ronald N. Boyce, Criminal Law 950 (3d ed. 1982).

[4] Remarkably, "data concerning such a fundamental issue as frequency of insanity pleas and acquittals" have historically been exceptionally hard to obtain, because states have failed to keep suitable records. Carmen Cirincione & Charles Jacobs, Identifying Insanity Acquittals: Is It Any Easier?, 23 Law & Hum. Behav. 487, 487 (1999). However, contrary to the common impression that the insanity defense is raised virtually exclusively in homicide cases, it was once estimated that as many as 86% of insanity pleas occur in the prosecution of nonviolent felonies and misdemeanors. National Mental Health Association, Myths & Realities: A Report of the National Commission on the Insanity Defense 20–21 (1983).

[5] E.g., Andrea Yates, a loving mother, drowned each of her five children in a bathtub in 2001. Phillip J. Resnick, The Andrea Yates Case: Insanity on Trial, 55 Clev. St. L. Rev. 147 (2007).

[6] Hinckley v. United States, 163 F.3d 647 (D.C. Cir. 1999) (summarizing the facts of the much-litigated case stemming from the 1981 attempted assassination of the President and subsequent insanity acquittal of John Hinckley).

acts are mentally ill. The issue for the jury (and society) is to distinguish between the mad and the bad, between sickness and evil.[7] If such a line exists, it is a difficult one to identify.

Second, the insanity defense suffers from the conceptual intermingling of psychiatry and the law, or of what one mental health professional has called the "war between lawyers and psychiatrists."[8] The two groups, it is said, "speak two different languages in regard to professional matters."[9] A *legal* defense based at its core on a *medical* conception, therefore, is inevitably difficult to administer, because the legal standard must satisfy several sometimes conflicting objectives. It must reflect underlying principles of criminal responsibility, comport with the current scientific understanding of mental disease, permit mental health experts reasonable opportunity to provide their insights to the court, and yet also preserve to the trier of fact the ultimate and full authority to render a verdict on criminal responsibility.[10]

This chapter addresses the principal issues regarding the insanity defense in its various forms, and considers the underlying arguments regarding its abolition or reform.

§ 25.02 INSANITY DEFENSE: PROCEDURAL CONTEXT

[A] Competency to Stand Trial[11]

[1] General Rule

The criminal trial of an incompetent defendant violates the Due Process Clause of the United States Constitution.[12] A person is incompetent if, during the criminal proceedings, she: (1) lacks the capacity to consult with her attorney "with a reasonable degree of rational understanding"; or (2) lacks "a rational as well as factual understanding of the proceedings" against her.[13] Incompetency may be the result of a physical handicap (*e.g.*, an inability to speak), or temporary or permanent mental disability (*e.g.*, mental illness, mental retardation, or amnesia).

Competency to stand trial is constitutionally required because an incompetent person is unable to provide needed assistance to her attorney, *e.g.*, to discuss

---

[7] Consider Anders Behring Breivik, a Norwegian man who killed 69 people, mostly teenagers, at a Labor Party summer youth camp. He also planned to film the beheading of Norway's Prime Minister. He was a political fanatic. He also was mentally ill. Was he insane, as well? For more on the case, see Michael S. Moore, *The Question for a Responsible Responsibility Test: Norwegian Insanity Law After Breivik*, forthcoming in Criminal Law & Philosophy journal

[8] Karl Menninger, The Crime of Punishment ch. 4 (1966). *See* § 25.06[A][3], *infra.*

[9] *Id.* at 96.

[10] State v. Johnson, 399 A.2d 469, 471 (R.I. 1979).

[11] *See generally* Bruce J. Winick, *Restructuring Competency to Stand Trial*, 32 UCLA L. Rev. 921 (1985).

[12] Medina v. California, 505 U.S. 437, 453 (1992).

[13] Dusky v. United States, 362 U.S. 402, 402 (1960).

strategy, explain her side of the case, and provide the names of potential witnesses. She is also unable meaningfully to confront her accusers at trial, and rationally to testify in her own behalf.[14] Moreover, two justifications for punishment of offenders, retribution and individual deterrence may be frustrated if an incompetent defendant does not understand the nature of the proceedings against her.[15]

[2]   Procedures for Determining Competency

The issue of competency to stand trial may be raised by the prosecutor, the defense, or by the trial judge on her own motion,[16] and is independent of any insanity plea that the defendant might later raise.

Typically, a defendant's competency to stand trial is treated as an issue of law to be determined by the trial judge, rather than a question of fact for jury consideration.[17] Whenever the issue of competency is raised, the defendant is required to submit to a psychiatric examination during which time she may be committed to a mental facility. The report of the examination is filed with the court.

If the findings of the report are not disputed by the parties, the judge may act on it. If the findings are disputed, a hearing is held at which the parties may present evidence on the matter of competency. State laws vary on the burden of proof at the hearing: some states require the prosecutor to demonstrate the defendant's competency once the issue is credibly raised; other states place the burden on the defendant to prove by preponderance of the evidence[18] that she is not competent to stand trial; and still other jurisdictions allocate the burden of proof to whichever party raised the competency issue.[19]

[3]   Effect of an Incompetency Finding

If it is determined that the defendant is incompetent to stand trial, criminal proceedings must be suspended until she is competent.[20] In some cases, particularly if the defendant's incompetency is based on a permanent condition, such as severe mental retardation, a criminal trial may never be held.

An incompetency ruling usually results in the defendant's commitment to a mental facility. The Supreme Court has held, however, that the Due Process Clause is violated when a criminal defendant is committed indefinitely solely on the basis

---

[14] Riggins v. Nevada, 504 U.S. 127, 139–40 (1992) (Kennedy, J., concurring).

[15] American Law Institute, Comment to § 4.04, at 230 n.1. Individual deterrence by intimidation (see § 2.03[B][2], *supra*) will fail if the party is so irrational that she cannot see the cause-and-effect relation between her conduct and the pain that would be inflicted.

[16] The defendant's competency must be investigated, even over her objection, if the trial judge believes that she may be incompetent. Pate v. Robinson, 383 U.S. 375, 385–86 (1966).

[17] Model Penal Code § 4.06(1). Prior to the promulgation of the Code, most states allowed a jury trial on the issue. American Law Institute, Comment to § 4.06, at 241–42.

[18] *See* Cooper v. Oklahoma, 517 U.S. 348 (1996) (state law requiring the defendant to prove incompetency by clear and convincing evidence violates due process).

[19] Medina v. California, 505 U.S. 437, 447 (1992) (summarizing state laws at the time).

[20] Model Penal Code § 4.06(2).

of her incompetency to stand trial.[21] A person may not be restrained "more than the reasonable period of time necessary to determine whether there is a substantial probability that [s]he will attain . . . capacity in the foreseeable future."[22] If it is determined that this is likely, her continued commitment "must be justified by progress toward that goal." If not, the defendant must be released or committed pursuant to customary civil procedures.[23] Even with these protections, the length of pretrial commitment will frequently extend beyond the possible maximum sentence for the crime.[24]

[B]   Pre-Trial Assertion of the Insanity Plea

Many states and federal rules require a defendant to provide the prosecutor with notice prior to trial of her intention to raise the defense of insanity.[25] She may also be required to provide the prosecutor with a list of witnesses who will testify on behalf of her insanity claim. The purpose of these rules is to provide the prosecutor adequate time to prepare a rebuttal to the defense at trial, and to allow the court an opportunity to require the defendant to submit to a psychiatric examination.

In virtually all states, a trial court has statutory authority to order a defendant to submit to a pretrial psychiatric examination if she plans to raise an insanity defense.[26] Under such rules, the defendant is committed to a mental facility for a specified period of time, for example, 60 to 90 days, during which period the examination is conducted. In some states, a psychiatrist retained by the defendant may witness or even participate in the examination process.[27] In order to avoid the possibility of violating the defendant's constitutional privilege against compelled self-incrimination at trial, some jurisdictions prohibit the introduction at trial of the defendant's statements to the government's psychiatrist, except on the matter of insanity.[28] If the court-ordered psychiatric report supports the defendant's claim of insanity, the prosecutor will frequently dismiss the charges against the defendant, on the condition that the accused agrees to civil commitment to a mental facility.

---

[21] Jackson v. Indiana, 406 U.S. 715, 731 (1972).

[22] *Id.* at 738.

[23] As a result, Model Penal Code § 4.06(2), which authorizes indefinite commitment without a civil hearing, is unconstitutional. American Law Institute, Explanatory Note to § 4.06, at 241; *see* Foucha v. Louisiana, 504 U.S. 71, 83 n.6 (1992).

[24] Winick, Note 11, *supra*, at 926.

[25] *E.g.*, Model Penal Code § 4.03(2); Fed. R. Crim. P. 12.2(a).

[26] *E.g.*, Model Penal Code § 4.05(1); Fed. R. Crim. P. 12.2(c).

[27] *See* Model Penal Code § 4.05(1).

[28] *E.g.*, Model Penal Code § 4.09; Fed. R. Crim. P. 12.2(c).

[C] Jury Verdicts

In most states, the fact finder may return one of three verdicts in a criminal trial in which the defendant pleads insanity: "not guilty" (NG); "not guilty by reason of insanity" (NGRI); or "guilty."[29]

A verdict of NGRI implies that the prosecution proved all of the elements of the crime, including the defendant's *mens rea*, beyond a reasonable doubt, and that all of the defendant's non-insanity defenses were rejected, but that the accused was insane at the time of the crime.

Logically, a jury should consider a NG verdict before it considers a NGRI verdict. Indeed, an instruction to the jury to consider the insanity defense *before* it considers the accused's guilt or innocence should be considered inappropriate,[30] because it permits the jury to reach a NGRI verdict, which usually results in civil commitment of the insanity acquittee,[31] without determining whether the prosecution has proven every element of the crime beyond a reasonable doubt.

[D] Bifurcated Trial

A few states[32] require, and other states permit, a trial court to bifurcate a criminal trial in which the insanity defense is raised. In a bifurcated system, all aspects of the case except the defendant's sanity are litigated at the first phase of the trial. At the completion of this first phase, the fact finder deliberates and returns a verdict of guilty or not guilty (NG). If the verdict is NG, the defendant is acquitted and the trial is over.

If the defendant is found guilty, the second phase is conducted. Here, the sole issue is the accused's insanity claim. After introduction of the testimony, most notably expert psychiatric evidence, the fact finder deliberates and returns a second verdict of guilty or, instead, not guilty by reason of insanity.[33]

The purpose of bifurcation is four-fold. First, time may be saved. If the jury returns a NG verdict in the first phase, time consuming psychiatric testimony is avoided. Second, confusion may be reduced. The jury can reach a verdict in the first phase without considering complicated psychiatric evidence.

Third, the bifurcated system may decrease the possibility of compromise verdicts. In a unitary system, the jury deliberates once. If it has reasonable doubt regarding the defendant's involvement in the crime, but is convinced that she is

---

[29] The jury may return a fourth verdict, "guilty but mentally ill," in a few states. *See* § 25.07, *infra.*

[30] *See* State v. McMullin, 421 N.W.2d 517, 518 (Iowa 1988).

[31] *See* § 25.05, *infra.*

[32] *E.g.*, Cal. Penal Code § 1026(a) (2015); Wis. Stat. § 971.165 (2015).

[33] Although psychiatric testimony, frequently conflicting, typically dominates a trial during the insanity phase, the jury as fact finder not only may disregard the testimony of some experts in favor of others, but may disregard *all* of the expert testimony. Although uncommon, an insanity verdict can be justified solely on the basis of non-expert testimony of the defendant's mental condition. Pacheco v. State, 770 S.W.2d 834, 835 (Tex. App. 1989). Conversely, a jury may disregard psychiatric testimony that a defendant is insane and rely entirely upon lay testimony of sanity. Dashield v. State, 110 S.W.3d 111, 115 (Tex. App. 2003).

insane, the jury may improperly compromise and find her insane, rather than acquit her outright, as it should.

Finally, the bifurcated system protects a defendant's privilege against compelled self-incrimination. In a unitary system, she may be forced to testify about her mental condition at the time of the crime in order to support her insanity defense. In the process, she opens herself up to questioning on issues unrelated to her mental condition. In a bifurcated system she may remain silent during the first phase, and force the prosecutor to prove her participation in the crime by independent evidence.

The bifurcated system has not worked as intended. The primary problem is that evidence of mental illness sometimes needs to be introduced by the defense at the first phase in order to demonstrate that the defendant lacked the mental state required in the definition of the offense. The same evidence, therefore, is introduced twice, although the testimony is phrased slightly differently at each stage. In the first phase, the psychiatrist may testify regarding whether, as the result of a mental disease or defect, the defendant was capable of forming or did form the requisite intent for the criminal offense, e.g., whether D intended to kill V. In the second phase, the same witness is questioned regarding whether the accused was insane at the time of the crime, e.g., whether D knew right from wrong when she intentionally killed V. The effect of this process is that time is wasted, not saved; and juries are apt to be confused, not benefitted, by the system.

[E] Burden of Proof

Insanity is an affirmative defense. The defendant has the initial burden of producing evidence regarding her mental condition in order to raise the insanity defense. Furthermore, the legislature may constitutionally require the defendant to persuade the jury that she was insane at the time of the crime.[34]

Until the 1980s, most states and the federal courts required the prosecutor to prove the defendant's sanity beyond a reasonable doubt.[35] However, as the result of the insanity acquittal of John Hinckley for the attempted murder of President Ronald Reagan,[36] a majority of states and the federal system now require the defendant to shoulder the burden of persuasion regarding her insanity claim.[37]

Most states that require a defendant to prove her insanity provide that she must do so by a preponderance of the evidence. Since 1984, however, defendants in federal courts have been required to prove insanity by clear and convincing evidence.[38] No state presently requires the defendant to prove her insanity beyond a reasonable doubt, although such a burden may be constitutional.[39]

---

[34] Leland v. Oregon, 343 U.S. 790, 799 (1952); see generally § 7.03[B], supra.

[35] 2 Paul H. Robinson, Criminal Law Defense 284–85 (1984); e.g., Model Penal Code § 4.03(1).

[36] See Note 6, supra.

[37] In 2004, only 10 states placed the burden of persuasion on the prosecution in insanity claims. U.S. Dept. of Justice, State Court Organization 204 (NCJ 212351 2006), Table 35, at 199–201.

[38] 18 U.S.C. § 17(b) (2011).

[39] Leland v. Oregon, 343 U.S. at 798–99 (upholding such a burden); but see Jones v. United States, 463

§ 25.03   RATIONALE OF THE INSANITY DEFENSE[40]

The insanity defense is controversial. The arguments for abolition of the defense are set out in Section 25.06 of this chapter. But, what are the arguments *for* the defense that explain its recognition and retention?

[A]   Utilitarian Theory

To the extent that the insanity defense is limited to persons who suffer from serious cognitive or volitional disorders,[41] punishment of an insane person may be "pointless or counter-productive."[42] A person who does not know what she is doing or who cannot control her conduct cannot be deterred by the threat of criminal sanction.

Incapacitation of an insane person normally is socially desirable, but acquittal by reason of insanity need not, and ordinarily does not, result in her liberty, inasmuch as the acquittal almost always serves as the basis for civil commitment.[43] There is no need, therefore, to convict and stigmatize an insane person in order to ensure her segregation from society.

Similarly, rehabilitation is not furthered by convicting an insane person and sending her to prison. It is rational to separate her from the penal system and treat her condition as a medical problem.

[B]   Retributive Theory

One scholar has observed that "[w]e . . . put up with the bother of the insanity defense because to exclude it is to deprive the criminal law of its chief paradigm of free will."[44]

The role that free will plays in recognition of the insanity defense can be appreciated by focusing on our feelings and intuitions. First, we make judgments about people based on their actions. We condemn people who commit crimes, and blame them for their wrongdoing. At the same time, we applaud courage; we praise those who perform acts of benevolence. These reactions, however, are unjustifiable unless we acknowledge the concept of free will — that people can and do choose to do good or to do evil, that human behavior is not scripted by other persons or by non-human forces.

U.S. 354, 368 n.17 (1983) (describing the law in somewhat more cautious terms: "[a] defendant [may] be required to prove his insanity *by a higher standard than a preponderance of the evidence*") (emphasis supplied).

[40] *See generally* R.B. Brandt, *The Insanity Defense and the Theory of Motivation*, 7 Law & Phil. 123 (1988); Stephen J. Morse, *Excusing the Crazy: The Insanity Defense Reconsidered*, 58 S. Cal. L. Rev. 777 (1985).

[41] A *cognitive* disorder is one that undermines a person's ability to perceive reality accurately. A *volitional* disorder is one that undermines a person's ability to control her conduct.

[42] American Law Institute, Comment to § 4.01, at 168 n.12.

[43] *See* § 25.05, *infra.*

[44] Herbert L. Packer, The Limits of the Criminal Sanction 132 (1968).

Another human feeling cannot be denied — severely mentally ill people do not appear to be like the rest of us. They seem odd or "crazy." We pity them (sometimes, too, we fear them), because they lack the capacity to do what other humans are able to do: to act rationally and to control their behavior. Ordinarily, we do not blame the "crazy" person for her wrongdoing or, if we do, we sense that such negative expressions are wrong. To blame such an individual for her acts is much like blaming a sick person for sneezing or an infant for dropping her glass of milk.

Our impressions of the mentally diseased actor reinforce our basic belief in human free will. The exception of the insane person serves as proof of the general rule. The fact that we do not blame the insane person serves to justify the fact that we blame the sane wrongdoer. The insanity defense, therefore, serves as a distinguishing point between the bad and the mad, between evil and sickness, between those who possess free choice and those whose free choice is seriously undermined.

We can place these feelings into a rational set of retributivist premises: just punishment is dependent on moral desert; moral desert is dependent on moral responsibility for one's actions; and moral responsibility for one's actions is dependent on the essential attributes of personhood, namely rationality[45] and self-control. Insane people, however, lack essential attributes of personhood. Therefore, they are "no more the proper subjects of moral evaluation than are young infants, animals, or even stones."[46] Or, as one court put it: "To punish a man who lacks the power to reason is as undignified and unworthy as punishing an inanimate object or an animal. A man who cannot reason cannot be subject to blame. Our collective conscience does not allow punishment where it cannot impose blame."[47]

---

[45] Morse, Note 40, *supra*, at 783; Morse & Hoffman, Note 1, *supra*, at 1117.

[46] Michael S. Moore, *Causation and the Excuses*, 73 Cal. L. Rev. 1091, 1137 (1985).

[47] Holloway v. United States, 148 F.2d 665, 666–67 (D.C. Cir. 1945).

§ 25.04   DEFINITIONS OF "INSANITY"[48]

[A]   Putting the Insanity Tests in Historical and Legal Context

Generally speaking, five tests of insanity, discussed in subsection [C], *infra*, have gained support at one time or another in the United States: the *M'Naghten*[49] rule; the "irresistible impulse" (or "control") test; the "product" standard; the American Law Institute's (ALI) Model Penal Code definition; and the federal statutory definition of insanity.

The first insanity test of modern relevance was enunciated by the English House of Lords in the *M'Naghten* case. It quickly became the generally accepted standard in this country. Criticism of the *M'Naghten* rule, however, was immediate[50] and has been unending. As a result of the perceived narrowness of the test, a few courts expanded the standard of insanity, by coupling the *M'Naghten* rule with an "irresistible impulse" test.

In 1954, the influential United States Court of Appeals for the District of Columbia promulgated the "product" or *Durham* rule of insanity.[51] Based on an 1870 New Hampshire case,[52] the *Durham* test was exceedingly broad, and was intended to bring insanity law more in accord with modern psychiatric knowledge. *Durham* represented a dramatic departure in the jurisprudence of insanity, and consequently received tremendous scholarly attention. No other court, however, adopted the standard.

The *Durham* court itself encountered problems with the product rule, which it struggled to resolve. In 1972, however, it abandoned the rule and substituted for it a version of the ALI Model Penal Code insanity defense, originally promulgated by the Institute in 1962. The ALI test quickly attracted support from courts and legislatures. In less than two decades, it was adopted by 10 of the 11 federal circuit courts and by a majority of the states.[53]

---

[48] *See generally* Jodie English, *The Light Between Twilight and Dusk: Federal Criminal Law and the Volitional Insanity Defense*, 40 Hastings L.J. 1 (1988); Christopher Slobogin, *The Integrationist Alternative to the Insanity Defense: Reflections on the Exculpatory Scope of Mental Illness in the Wake of the Andrea Yates Trial*, 30 Am. J. Crim. L. 315 (2003); see also the sources in Note 1, *supra*.

For discussion of juror responses to insanity instructions, see generally Norman J. Finkel & Sharon F. Handel, *How Jurors Construe "Insanity,"* 13 Law & Hum. Behav. 41 (1989); James R.P. Ogloff, *A Comparison of the Insanity Defense Standards on Juror Decision Making*, 15 Law & Hum. Behav. 509 (1991); Michael L. Perlin, *Psychodynamics and the Insanity Defense: "Ordinary Common Sense" and Heuristic Reasoning*, 69 Neb. L. Rev. 3 (1990); Caton F. Roberts & Stephen L. Golding, *The Social Construction of Criminal Responsibility and Insanity*, 15 Law & Hum. Behav. 349 (1991).

[49] M'Naghten's Case, 10 Cl. & F. 200, 8 Eng. Rep. 718 (1843).

[50] *See* Isaac Ray, A Treatise on the Medical Jurisprudence of Insanity 42 (Winfred Overholder ed., 1962) (originally published in 1833).

[51] Durham v. United States, 214 F.2d 862 (D.C. Cir. 1954), *overruled by* United States v. Brawner, 471 F.2d 969 (D.C. Cir. 1972).

[52] State v. Pike, 49 N.H. 399 (1870).

[53] Michael L. Perlin, Mental Disability Law: Civil and Criminal 302 (1989); American Law Institute, Comment to § 4.01, at 175–76.

The trend in favor of the ALI test seemed unstoppable until the attempted assassination of President Ronald Reagan. Public fury following John Hinckley's acquittal on the ground of insanity[54] resulted in pressure to abolish the defense.[55] Although the abolitionist movement generally failed, it had a significant effect on the law. Courts and legislatures began to reconsider their support for the comparatively broad ALI rule. "When the dust cleared, the sun of the Model Penal Code test had set."[56] For example, California, which originally adopted the *M'Naghten* test, and then shifted to the ALI standard, reversed itself again and returned to *M'Naghten.*[57] Congress, too, enacted a *M'Naghten*-like definition of insanity, thereby overriding the nearly unanimous adoption of the ALI test in the federal system. A few states abolished the insanity defense.[58]

One must put the controversy over the insanity tests in context. There is social science literature suggesting that jurors either do not consider or fail to understand the insanity instructions they are given. Jurors apparently come to a trial with their own implicit standards of criminal responsibility. These standards involve a mixtures of factors, such as the defendant's motive for her conduct, history of mental illness, degree of remorse, as well as the specific psychiatric diagnosis.[59] According to one empiricist, "jurors apply their own sense of justice when determining whether a defendant" should be found not guilty by reason of insanity.[60] And, according to him, the insanity test most consistent with jurors' intuitions is one that has never been accepted by a court, namely, the so-called "justly responsible" test suggested by one federal judge.[61]

---

[54] *See* Note 5, *supra.*

[55] For example, an Associated Press-National Broadcasting Company poll found that 69% of the respondents favored abolition of the insanity defense. Minneapolis Trib., Oct. 25, 1981, at 9a. *See generally* Valerie P. Hans, *An Analysis of Public Attitudes Toward the Insanity Defense*, 24 Criminology 393 (1986).

[56] Sanford H. Kadish, *Fifty Years of Criminal Law: An Opinionated Review*, 87 Cal. L. Rev. 943, 960 (1999).

[57] The saga of California's insanity law, culminating in the passage of a statewide initiative designed to eliminate the ALI standard, is chronicled in People v. Skinner, 704 P.2d 752 (Cal. 1985).

[58] *See* § 25.06[B], *infra.*

[59] *See* Jocelyn A. Lymburner & Ronald Roesch, *The Insanity Defense: Five Years of Research (1993–1997)*, 22 Int'l J.L. & Psychiatry 213, 293–94 (1999) (and studies cited therein).

[60] Ogloff, Note 48, *supra*, at 527.

[61] United States v. Brawner, 471 F.2d 969, 1032 (D.C. Cir. 1972) (Bazelon, C.J., concurring in part and dissenting in part) (proposing the follow instruction: "a defendant is not responsible *if at the time of his unlawful conduct his mental or emotional processes or behavior controls were impaired to such an extent that he cannot justly be held responsible for his act*").

[B]　"Mental Disease or Defect"[62]

[1]　In General

The terms "mental illness," "mental disorder," and "mental disease or defect," on the one hand, and "insanity," on the other hand, are not synonymous. The first set of terms is used by the mental health community; the word "insanity" is a legal term. Thus, it is incorrect to say that "mental illness" is a criminal defense; "insanity" is the excusing defense.

"Mental illness" is a more encompassing term than "insanity." A person can be mentally ill without being insane; insanity, however, presupposes a mental disease or defect.

[2]　Medical Definition of "Mental Disorder"

The American Psychiatric Association's manual of mental disorders concedes that "no definition [of 'mental disorder'] can capture all aspects" of the concept[63] A mental disorder is not a discrete entity. There are no sharp boundaries between "mental disorder" and "no mental disorder." That being said, the manual currently provides that a "mental disorder" is a:

> syndrome characterized by clinically significant disturbance in an individual's cognition, emotion regulation, or behavior that reflects a dysfunction in the psychological, biological, or developmental processes underlying mental functioning. Mental disorders are usually associated with significant distress or disability in social, occupational, or other important activities.[64]

[3]　Legal Definition of "Mental Disease or Defect"

All of the insanity tests presuppose that the actor suffers from a "mental disease or defect" or "disease of the mind," yet courts rarely define the terms.[65] The Model Penal Code insanity defense, as well, provides no general definition of the critical phrase, preferring instead to leave the issue "open to accommodate developing medical understanding."[66]

Only an earlier, now virtually defunct, test of insanity included a definition of the term: It defined a mental disease or defect as "any abnormal condition of the mind which substantially affects mental or emotional processes and substantially impairs behavior controls."[67] Under this definition, a "disease" is a condition capable of improving or deteriorating; a "defect" is a condition incapable of changing, which

---

[62] *See generally* Bruce J. Winick, *Ambiguities in the Legal Meaning and Significance of Mental Illness*, 1 Psychol. Pub. Pol'y & L. 534 (1995).

[63] American Psychiatric Association, Diagnostic and Statistical Manual of Mental Disorders 20 (5th ed. 2013).

[64] *Id.* at 20.

[65] *See* Goldstein, Note 1, *supra*, at 47–48.

[66] American Law Institute, Explanatory Note to § 4.01, at 164.

[67] McDonald v. United States, 312 F.2d 847, 851 (D.C. Cir. 1962).

may be congenital (*e.g.*, low intelligence), the result of injury to the brain, or the residual effect of a physical or mental illness.[68]

[C]   The Tests

[1]   *M'Naghten* Test[69]

[a]   Rule

The *M'Naghten* test of insanity is cognitive-based. According to *M'Naghten*, a person is insane if, at the time of her act,[70] she was laboring under such a defect of reason, arising from a disease of the mind, that: (1) she did not know the nature and quality of the act that she was doing; or (2) if she did know it, she did not know that what she was doing was wrong, *i.e.*, the accused at the time of doing the act did not know the difference between right and wrong. According to a decade-old survey, 17 states and the federal government apply this standard in its entirety; one state has adopted only the first prong of *M'Naghten*; and 10 states apply only the second prong.[71] Various features of the test are discussed immediately below.

[i]   "Know": Broad or Narrow?

The word "know" used in both prongs of the test may be defined narrowly or broadly. Sometimes the word is used narrowly: A person may be found sane if she can describe what she is doing ("I was strangling her") and can acknowledge the forbidden nature of her conduct ("I knew I was doing something wrong"). This may be referred to as "formal cognitive knowledge." It is the type of limited knowledge that one might expect a child to have. But, there is a potentially deeper meaning of "knowledge" ("affective knowledge"), which is absent unless the actor can evaluate her conduct in terms of its impact on others and appreciate the total setting in which she acts, *i.e.*, can "internalize the enormity of the[ir] criminal act" and, thus, "emotionally appreciate its wrongfulness."[72] One may expect prosecutors to emphasize the narrow sense of knowledge, whereas defense attorneys focus on the latter.

[ii]   "Nature and Quality of the Act"

The phrase "nature and quality of the act" in the first prong of the *M'Naghten* test potentially is an exceedingly narrow concept. If *D* squeezes *V*'s neck, believing that she is squeezing a lemon, she does not know the nature and quality of her act.

---

[68]   Durham v. United States, 214 F.2d 862, 875 (D.C. Cir. 1954), *overruled by* United States v. Brawner, 471 F.2d 969 (D.C. Cir. 1972).

[69]   M'Naghten's Case, 10 Cl. & F. 200, 8 Eng. Rep. 718 (1843).

[70]   The issue with *any* definition of insanity is whether the actor was insane at the time of the offense. Theoretically, at least, an actor may be sane before and after the crime, and yet be insane at the time of the criminal act and, therefore, be entitled to acquittal on the basis of insanity. *See* Miller v. State, 911 P.2d 1183, 1185–87 (Nev. 1996).

[71]   Clark v. Arizona, 548 U.S. 735, 750–751 (2006).

[72]   Slobogin, Note 48, *supra*, at 324.

However, if she knows that she is squeezing the neck of a human being, but does not appreciate that her act is causing pain, she is sane insofar as the first prong of *M'Naghten* is concerned in jurisdictions that apply a narrow meaning of the word "knowledge," as discussed immediately above. Frequently, this prong is omitted from jury instructions or statutes because anyone who does not know what she is doing (*e.g.*, cannot distinguish a neck from a lemon) will also "fail" the right-and-wrong test, the second prong of the insanity definition.[73]

[iii]   "Right from Wrong"

A question exists whether the word "wrong" in the right-and-wrong prong refers to legal or moral wrongdoing. There is language in *M'Naghten* to support either interpretation. Lord Tindal, for example, stated early in the opinion that *M'Naghten* could be punished if he "knew . . . that he was acting contrary to law; by which expression we . . . mean the law of the land." Subsequently, however, he stated that if the jury were instructed "exclusively with reference to the law of the land it might tend to confound the jury by inducing them to believe that an actual knowledge of the law was essential." Rather, Lord Tindal stated, the question is whether *M'Naghten* knew that his "act was one which he ought not to do, and if the act was at the same time contrary to the law of the land, he is punishable." American law is sharply divided on the legal-versus-moral distinction.[74]

The distinction will rarely affect the outcome of a trial. However, suppose that *D*, due to mental illness, believes that God has given her permission to kill *V*, an act that *D* knows violates the secular law. In view of God's permission, however, *D* believes that it is morally proper to kill *V*. On these facts, *D* is sane if the right-and-wrong test is based on awareness of the *illegality* of an act. However, subject to one important clarification noted in the next paragraph, *D* is insane if *M'Naghten* requires knowledge of the *immorality* of her actions.

The important clarification is this: In jurisdictions that apply a "moral right-and-wrong" standard, the issue is not whether the defendant *personally* believed that her conduct was morally proper. Rather, the question is whether she knowingly violated *societal* standards of morality.[75] That is, *D* is sane under this prong of *M'Naghten* if she commits an offense that she knows society will condemn, even if (as a result of mental illness) she is personally convinced her conduct is morally proper.[76]

---

[73] *Clark v. Arizona*, 548 U.S. at 753–54.

[74] *See* People v. Serravo, 823 P.2d 128, 135 (Colo. 1992) (noting the division of American courts).

[75] *Id.* at 137; Wallace v. State, 766 So. 2d 364, 367 (Fla. Dist. Ct. App. 2000); United States v. Ewing, 494 F.3d 607, 621 (7th Cir. 2007).

[76] Notice, however, that the line drawn in the text can be blurred to near extinction. Presumably, in determining whether the defendant knew that society would consider her actions morally wrong, we have to look at the circumstances as she (in her mentally disturbed mind) believes them to be. *See* State v. Wilson, 700 A.2d 633, 653 (Conn. 1997). For example, a mentally disturbed person is apt to know that society considers it generally morally wrong to kill, but if she is acting pursuant to a delusional belief that God has given her permission to kill, she might also believe that society would agree with her God-endorsed actions if it knew what she knows.

[iv]　　　　**The "Deific Decree" Doctrine**

Reconsider the hypothetical discussed in the last subsection, but with one significant change: What if a mentally ill person believes that God has done more than give her permission to kill (or commit some other offense), but has *ordered* her to do so. For more than two centuries, some courts, particularly in *M'Naghten* jurisdictions, have recognized the so-called "deific decree" doctrine in applying the "know moral-right-or-wrong" standard.[77] Under this doctrine, a mentally disordered individual who believes that what she is doing "is by the command of a superior power, which supersedes all human laws, and the laws of nature,"[78] is considered legally insane. Sometimes this doctrine is treated as an exception to the general rule, *i.e.*, it applies when "a party performs a criminal act, knowing it is morally and legally wrong, but believing, because of a mental defect, that the act is ordained by God."[79] However, other courts believe that the doctrine "is not so much an exception to the right-wrong test measured by the existing societal standards of morality as it is an integral factor in assessing a person's cognitive ability to distinguish right from wrong with respect to the act charged."[80] That is, a person who believes that God has commanded her act is likely to believe that society would approve of her conduct.

[b]　　　　Criticisms of the Rule

The *M'Naghten* rule has been persistently criticized. First, the test is considered "grossly unrealistic" because, by its terms, it does not recognize degrees of incapacity. A person must wholly lack cognition. Yet, "our mental institutions, as any qualified psychiatrist will attest, are filled with people who *to some extent* can differentiate between right and wrong,"[81] or who can tell the difference between a human neck and a lemon, but who still are significantly out of touch with reality. Because of the apparent absolutism of the test, some psychiatrists are tempted to shape their testimony to fit the definition of insanity, although few of them believe that incapacity is ever complete.

Second, some critics believe that *M'Naghten* places "unrealistically tight shackles"[82] upon expert psychiatric testimony. If a trial court refuses to permit a psychiatrist to testify on any matter that falls outside the narrow confines of the test, the jury is unable to learn the full background of the defendant's state of mind.

---

[77] For an excellent survey of cases applying this doctrine, see Lundgren v. Mitchell, 440 F.3d 754 (6th Cir. 2006).

[78] Grant H. Morris & Ansar Haroun, *"God Told Me to Kill": Religion or Delusion?*, 38 San Diego L. Rev. 973, 1004 (2001).

[79] State v. Crenshaw, 659 P.2d 488, 494 (Wash. 1983).

[80] People v. Serravo, 823 P.2d 128, 139 (Colo. 1992); *see also* State v. Potter, 842 P.2d 481, 486–89 (Wash. Ct. App. 1992) (concluding that notwithstanding language in prior Washington cases treating the deific-decree doctrine as an "exception," the doctrine is instead an "elaboration[] of the second prong of the insanity rule").

[81] United States v. Freeman, 357 F.2d 606, 618 (2d Cir. 1966) (emphasis added).

[82] *Id.* at 619.

Third, the test is outdated in that it disregards mental illnesses that affect *volition*.[83] By focusing solely on cognitive disability, the rule disregards the possibility that a person may be able to distinguish right from wrong, and yet be unable to control her behavior.

Finally, closely tied to the latter point is the suggestion that the test is too narrow in terms of penological theory. If a person knows what she is doing but cannot control her conduct, she is undeterrable; therefore, punishment is inefficacious. Moreover, it is morally wrong to punish a person who, due to mental illness, lacks sufficient free will to control her conduct.

[2] "Irresistible Impulse" ("Control") Test

[a] Rule

In order to broaden the scope of *M'Naghten*, three states[84] have added a third prong to the insanity test, which encompasses mental illnesses affecting volitional capacity. The latter prong has come to be known as the "irresistible impulse" or "control" test.

The precise language of the test varies by jurisdiction. Generally speaking, a person is insane if, at the time of the offense: (1) she "acted from an irresistible and uncontrollable impulse";[85] (2) she "lost the *power to choose* between the right and wrong, and to avoid doing the act in question, as that [her] free agency was at the time destroyed";[86] or (3) the "[defendant's] will . . . has been otherwise than voluntarily so completely destroyed that [her] actions are not subject to it, but are beyond [her] control."[87]

[b] Criticisms of the Rule

Criticisms of this rule run in both directions — that it is too narrow and, to the contrary, that it should be abolished. Those who believe the test is too narrow state that it is improper to exclude from its coverage non-impulsive behavior (*i.e.*, behavior that is the result of brooding and reflection), and that it is psychologically naive to require total incapacity (*i.e.*, an *irresistible* impulse).[88] These criticisms are not ordinarily relevant in practice. The label "irresistible impulse" has proven to be a misnomer.[89] Many courts permit use of the test even if the defendant planned her behavior, as long as the defendant lacked the ability to control her conduct; and most courts do not require proof of total volitional incapacity.

Both principled and pragmatic arguments have been made for abolition of any

---

[83] *See* United States v. Pollard, 171 F. Supp. 474, 478 (E.D. Mich. 1959), *rev'd on other grounds*, Pollard v. United States, 282 F.2d 450 (6th Cir. 1960).

[84] *See* Clark v. Arizona, 548 U.S. 735, 751 (2006).

[85] Commonwealth v. Rogers, 48 Mass. 500, 502 (1844).

[86] Parsons v. State, 81 Ala. 577 (1887).

[87] Davis v. United States, 165 U.S. 373, 378 (1897).

[88] *United States v. Pollard*, 171 F. Supp. at 478.

[89] Goldstein, Note 1, *supra*, at 67–79.

test based on an actor's lack of volition. Some abolitionists argue that if an exceptionally strong urge to commit a crime should excuse, it should excuse whether the person suffers from a mental illness or not:

[T]he psychotic individual who hears voices telling him to kill may experience a powerful urge to commit crime. But that claim is also true of pedophiles, repeat rapists, . . . serial murderers . . . , and thieves who steal to feed an addiction. It may even be true of the greedy corporate executive who manipulates accounts, or of the teenage boy who, on Friday night, wants to have intercourse with an underage girlfriend. The subjectively experienced urges of a person with mental illness are not provably greater than the urges of people we would never think of excusing.[90]

The pragmatic criticism of the "irresistible impulse" test is that "a majority of psychiatrists now believe that they do not possess sufficient accurate scientific bases for measuring a person's capacity for self-control or for calibrating the impairment of that capacity."[91] According to the American Psychiatric Association, "[t]he line between an irresistible impulse and an impulse not resisted is probably no sharper than between twilight and dusk."[92]

[3] American Law Institute (Model Penal Code) Test

[a]   Rule

The Model Penal Code provides that a person is not responsible for her criminal conduct if, at the time of the conduct, as the result of a mental disease or defect, she lacked substantial capacity to: (1) appreciate the "criminality" (or, in the alternative, at the option of the legislature adopting the Code, the moral "wrongfulness") of her conduct; or (2) to conform her conduct to the requirements of the law.[93] This is a revised version of the *M'Naghten* and irresistible-impulse tests. It consists of the second, and more significant, cognitive prong of the former test, and restates the volitional aspects of the latter standard. In 2006, 14 states reportedly applied this standard of insanity.[94]

Notice the differences between the ALI test and its antecedents. First, it uses the term "appreciate" rather than "know," in order to avoid a narrow interpretation of the *M'Naghten*-like cognitive prong.[95] Second, the test avoids the word "impulse," in order to sidestep the potential pitfalls arising from using that word. Third, both prongs of the test are modified by the words "lacks substantial capacity." This avoids the criticism that the earlier tests unrealistically required total incapacity.

---

[90] Slobogin, Note 48, *supra*, at 322 (footnotes omitted).

[91] United States v. Lyons, 731 F.2d 243, 248 (5th Cir. 1984).

[92] American Psychiatric Association, Statement on the Insanity Defense 11 (Dec. 1982).

[93] Model Penal Code § 4.01(1).

[94] *See* Clark v. Arizona, 548 U.S. 735, 751 (2006).

[95] *See* § 25.04[C][1][a][i], *supra*.

[b]   Criticisms of the Rule

The ALI test has received little criticism independent of the objections raised regarding the earlier tests on which it is founded. Those who favor a broader test and who believe that psychiatric knowledge is unduly restricted in the courtroom have criticized the ALI definition because they believe that it is based on an outdated psychological assumption that the human mind is divisible into "volitional" and "cognitive" functions. In contrast, persons who favor a narrow definition of insanity are critical of the fact that the ALI standard includes a volitional prong, even though psychiatrists now question their ability to provide reliable data on the subject.

[4] The Product Test

[a]   Rule

The product test of insanity, first adopted in New Hampshire,[96] gained national attention when David Bazelon, one of the country's most respected judges, announced recognition of the product rule in the District of Columbia in *Durham v. United States.*[97] This standard provided, quite simply, that a person should be excused if her unlawful act was the product of a mental disease or defect. Pursuant to this rule, the jury would determine whether the defendant was suffering from a mental disease or defect at the time of the offense and, if so, whether the disease caused the criminal conduct in a but-for sense. If the answer was yes, the person is deemed legally insane.

Advocates of this test believed that it brought the insanity standard into modern times. The test was intended to permit mental health professionals to testify without the volitional/cognitive strictures of the other insanity standards. In turn, the product rule would give jurors the critical information they needed to decide whether to hold a defendant criminally accountable for her actions.

These observations about the product test are stated in the past tense because difficulties with, and criticisms of, the test (as discussed below) led the *Durham* court ultimately to abandon it.[98] Only New Hampshire retains a product rule.

[b]   Criticisms of the Rule

An early criticism of the *Durham* version of the product test was that it failed to define the critical phrase "mental disease or defect." As such, it left the matter solely in the hands of mental health professionals. If a mental health professional testified that the condition that caused the defendant's behavior was a mental disease, the accused was entitled to acquittal; if the expert stated that the same condition fell outside the parameters of any recognized disease model, the defendant lost her insanity claim. Yet, the causal connection between the condition

---

[96] State v. Pike, 49 N.H. 399 (1870); State v. Fichera, 903 A.2d 1030 (N.H. 2006); John Reid, *Understanding the New Hampshire Doctrine of Criminal Insanity*, 69 Yale L.J. 367 (1960).

[97] 214 F.2d 862 (D.C. Cir. 1954).

[98] United States v. Brawner, 471 F.2d 969 (D.C. Cir. 1972).

and the conduct was the same in both circumstances. After an embarrassing situation, in which a psychiatrist's testimony as to whether a particular condition was a mental illness changed over a weekend,[99] the Court of Appeals for the District of Columbia provided a working definition, set out elsewhere in this chapter.[100]

Second, some lawyers criticized the test because they believed it allowed psychiatrists to usurp the jury's authority. As the *Durham* rule was applied, psychiatrists were called by the defense and the prosecution; the competing psychiatrists would testify that D suffered (or did not suffer) from condition X, that condition X was (or was not) a mental disease or defect, and that D would not (or would) have committed the crime but for condition X. Essentially, the expert's testimony "proved" that D was (or was not) insane. There was nothing for the jury to do other than to decide which expert to believe. The jury's moral judgment regarding D's conduct was suppressed. The federal court later acknowledged this problem and set limits on psychiatric testimony by preventing experts from testifying directly in terms of "products," "results," or "causes."[101] Thus, a test intended to let experts testify freely now was restricting them.

A third and more basic criticism of the product test is that it excludes from criminal responsibility some deterrable and morally blameworthy actors. For example, assume that Alice suffers from a delusion (brought on by a mental disease) that Bob will marry her if Carla, Bob's wife, is dead. As a result, Alice kills Carla. Pursuant to the product rule, Alice is insane: but for her delusion, she would not have killed Carla. Alice's acquittal on these facts, however, is arguably penologically indefensible. Alice knew what she was doing, knew that her conduct was legally and morally wrong, and, presumably, could have controlled her conduct. Therefore, Alice was deterrable. From a retributive perspective, as well, she may be blamed for her conduct. According to the free-choice theory of excuses,[102] a person who appreciates the illegality or immorality of her conduct, and is able to control her behavior, is a moral agent who may properly be held accountable for her actions.

[5]   Federal Test

The United States Congress enacted a statutory definition of insanity in 1984. In federal courts, a person is excused if she proves by clear and convincing evidence that, at the time of the offense, as the result of a severe mental disease or defect, she was unable to appreciate: (1) the nature and quality of her conduct; or (2) the wrongfulness of her conduct.[103]

---

[99] *In re* Rosenfield, 157 F. Supp. 18 (D.D.C. 1957) (a psychiatrist testified on Friday that R's condition was not a mental disease; over the weekend, as the result of an administrative change in the witness's hospital policy, the condition was reclassified as a mental disease).

[100] *See* § 25.04[B][3], *supra.*

[101] Washington v. United States, 390 F.2d 444, 455–56 (D.C. Cir. 1967).

[102] *See* § 17.03[E], *supra.*

[103] 18 U.S.C. § 17(a) (2015).

Various features of the federal test are noteworthy. First, unlike prior standards, the federal law requires proof that the actor suffers from a "severe" mental disease or defect. However, this word may be superfluous, since any mental disease or defect that satisfies either of the two prongs of the test is apt to be severe. Second, like *M'Naghten*, but unlike the ALI standard, the test appears to require that cognitive incapacity be total.

One feature of the federal rule is patterned on the ALI test — the word "appreciate," rather than "know," modifies both prongs of the defense. This should render the test broader than *M'Naghten* in this regard.

§ 25.05   EFFECT OF AN INSANITY ACQUITTAL

[A]   Mental Illness Commitment Procedures

[1]   Automatic Commitment

Contrary to a common conception, a person found not guilty by reason of insanity (NGRI) is rarely released upon acquittal.[104] One scholar has gone so far as to state that the defense of insanity is not an excuse in the ordinary sense, but is actually a direction to punish the insane person in a noncriminal context.[105]

In many states, a person found NGRI is automatically committed to a mental facility on the basis of the verdict.[106] Under automatic-commitment laws, the NGRI-acquittee is not entitled to a pre-commitment hearing to determine whether she continues to suffer from a mental illness, or to determine whether her institutionalization is necessary for her protection or for that of society.

In this respect, NGRI-acquittees are provided fewer procedural rights than are granted to people who may otherwise be subjected to civil commitment. The Supreme Court has held that a person may *not* be committed to a mental institution in a civil proceeding unless the state proves by clear and convincing evidence that she is presently mentally ill and that she is dangerous to herself or others.[107] In contrast, with NGRI-acquittees in automatic-commitment jurisdictions, the insanity verdict at the criminal trial is considered a sufficiently reliable finding of current mental illness and dangerousness to dispense with a hearing.[108]

---

[104] National Mental Health Association, Myths & Realities: A Report of the National Commission on the Insanity Defense 24–25 (1983). Making matters worse, most states provide that a defendant is not entitled to a jury instruction that informs it of the consequences of a NGRI verdict. *E.g.*, State v. Okie, 987 A.2d 495, 497 (Me. 2010). The reason for keeping jurors in the dark is that the their role is only to determine whether the defendant factually committed the offense and is or is not insane; issues of sentencing and other post-verdict matters are considered outside the jury's province. *Id.* at 498.

[105] Packer, Note 44, *supra*, at 134; *see also* Joseph Goldstein & Jay Katz, *Abolish the "Insanity Defense" — Why Not?*, 72 Yale L.J. 853, 868 (1963) ("[T]he insanity defense is not a defense, it is a device for triggering indeterminate restraint.").

[106] *E.g.*, Model Penal Code § 4.08(1).

[107] Addington v. Texas, 441 U.S. 418, 426–27 (1979).

[108] Jones v. United States, 463 U.S. 354, 363–64 (1983).

[2] Discretionary Commitment

In some jurisdictions, commitment of an insanity-acquittee is not automatic. Instead, the trial judge has authority to require a person found NGRI to be detained temporarily in a mental facility for observation and examination, in order to determine whether she should be committed indefinitely.

Under federal law, a commitment hearing must be held within 40 days of an NGRI verdict, during which time the acquittee is detained in a mental hospital.[109] If the offense for which the defendant was acquitted involved bodily injury to another, serious damage to property, or a substantial risk to either, she must prove by clear and convincing evidence that she is entitled to release, *i.e.*, that "release would not create a substantial risk of bodily injury to another person or serious damage of property of another due to a present mental disease or defect."[110] With less serious crimes, she must meet the same standard by a preponderance of the evidence.

[B] Release After Commitment for Mental Illness

[1] Criteria for Release

An insanity-acquittee may be detained as long as she is *both* mentally ill and dangerous to herself or others. Put differently, she is constitutionally entitled to release from a mental facility if she is no longer mentally ill — even if she remains dangerous to herself or others[111] — or is no longer dangerous, even if she continues to suffer from a mental illness.[112] In this regard, state laws based on the Model Penal Code,[113] which authorizes the continued commitment of dangerous persons who are *not* mentally ill, violate the Due Process Clause of the United States Constitution.[114]

[2] Length of Confinement

An insanity-acquittee's commitment is of an indeterminate length, *i.e.*, until she meets the criteria for release. In practice and as a constitutional matter,[115] she may remain in a mental hospital for a longer period of time than she would have served in a prison had she been convicted of the crime that triggered her commitment. The concept of proportionality between a criminal offense and the length of detention is irrelevant in such circumstances, because the purpose of her confinement is "treatment," rather than "punishment."

---

[109] 18 U.S.C. § 4243(c) (2015).

[110] 18 U.S.C. § 4243(d) (2015).

[111] *But see* § 25.05[C], *infra*, in regard to sexual predators, which apparently represents an exception to the rule that a person may not be civilly committed if she is not mentally ill.

[112] Foucha v. Louisiana, 504 U.S. 71, 80–83 (1992).

[113] Model Penal Code § 4.08.

[114] *See Foucha v. Louisiana*, 504 U.S. at 83 n.6.

[115] Jones v. United States, 463 U.S. 354, 370 (1983).

[3]   Release Procedures

Release procedures vary by jurisdiction.[116] In many states, the court that ordered the insanity-acquittee's commitment retains jurisdiction over her. She or the mental facility may petition the court to release her based on that jurisdiction's criteria for release.[117] In most jurisdictions, the acquittee may not petition for release for a specified period of time, ranging from 90 days to 1 year after initial commitment.[118] Thereafter, subsequent petitions for release may be limited to stated time intervals.

The institutionalized party is entitled to a hearing on her petition for release. In nearly all states, the burden of proof is placed on the committed party to demonstrate that she is either no longer mentally ill or dangerous. The burden of proof varies from a preponderance of the evidence to clear and convincing evidence.

[C]   A Different Form of Commitment: Sexual Predator Laws[119]

By 2006, about one-third of the states enacted laws, so-called "sexual predator" or "sexual offender" statutes, which authorize civil commitment of individuals who are considered dangerous but who do not necessarily suffer from a mental disease or defect.[120] Since 2006, more states have followed suit.

Sexual predator laws vary in scope and procedure by jurisdiction, but a brief overview is possible. For example, the State of Kansas established procedures for the "long-term care and treatment" of "sexually violent predators."[121] A "sexually violent predator" was defined as "any person who has been convicted of or charged with a sexually violent offense and who suffers from a mental abnormality or personality disorder which makes the person likely to engage in repeat acts of sexual violence." A "mental abnormality" was defined as a "congenital or acquired condition affecting the emotional or volitional capacity which predisposes the person to commit sexually violent offenses in a degree constituting such person a menace to the health and safety of others."

Notice that this statute applies to any one "convicted of or charged with" specific sexual offenses. Thus, the law covers those who have been convicted of a sexual offense, but also those who have been charged and acquitted on the ground of insanity, *those acquitted generally*, and even those who, although charged with an offense, have not been brought to trial. Also, a "mental abnormality or personality

---

[116] *See generally* American Law Institute, Comment to § 4.08, at 262–65.

[117] Model Penal Code § 4.08(2)–(3).

[118] *E.g.*, Model Penal Code § 4.08(5) (providing a six-month waiting period).

[119] *See generally* Sex Offender Laws: Failed Policies, New Directions (Richard G. Wright ed. 2009); Catherine L. Carpenter, *Legislative Epidemics: A Cautionary Tale of Criminal Laws That Have Swept the Country*, 58 Buff. L. Rev. 1 (2010); Michael Vitiello, *Punishing Sex Offenders: When Good Intentions Go Bad*, 40 Ariz. St. L.J. 651 (2008).

[120] Christopher Slobogin, *Dangerousness and Expertise Redux*, 56 Emory L.J. 275, 276 (2006).

[121] Kan. Stat. Ann. §§ 59-29a01 to 59-29a21 (2015).

disorder" is a broader concept than "mental disease or defect," the triggering mechanism for an insanity defense.

To invoke the law, a prosecutor files a petition in a state court seeking the individual's involuntary commitment.[122] If there is probable cause to believe that the person is a sexual predator as defined, the individual is transferred to a mental facility for evaluation, after which a full hearing is held. If the court determines beyond a reasonable doubt that the individual is a sexually violent predator, she is civilly committed until she "is safe to be at large." Currently, such persons are not generally thought to be amenable to existing mental health treatment modalities, so the practical effect of sexual predator laws may be the life-long commitment of the person.

§ 25.06 ABOLITION OF THE INSANITY DEFENSE[123]

[A] Abolitionist Arguments

Opponents of the insanity defense (abolitionists, for short) come from different ideological and philosophical vantage points. Some abolitionists are political "hawks" who favor abolition of the defense as part of a broader effort to reduce the number of excuse defenses recognized in the criminal law. In contrast, "dove" abolitionists would like to *expand* the law of excuses, but for reasons of equity do not want to treat mentally ill people more leniently than others whom the critics consider equally morally blameless but who are punished for their wrongdoing. Public opinion surveys also suggest that abolitionism is founded on both retributive and utilitarian grounds.[124]

[1] Abuse

Some abolitionists assert that the insanity defense results in abuse of the criminal justice system. They claim that the defense is frequently asserted and too often successful.[125] Implicit in this argument is that insanity claims, including successful ones, are often fraudulent in nature. As a result, wrongdoers "walk free" because they are able to persuade psychiatrists and gullible juries of their nonexistent madness.

---

[122] This may occur, for example, as a person convicted of a sexual offense is about to be released from prison after serving the criminal sentence, or immediately after acquittal or dismissal of charges for a sexual offense.

[123] See generally Morris, Note 1, supra; National Mental Health Association, Note 104, supra; Goldstein & Katz, Note 105, supra; Norval Morris, The Criminal Responsibility of the Mentally Ill, 33 Syracuse L. Rev. 477 (1982); Morse, Note 40, supra; Stephen J. Morse, Justice, Mercy, and Craziness, 36 Stan. L. Rev. 1485 (1984); Morse & Hoffman, Note 1, supra; Michael L. Perlin, Unpacking the Myths: The Symbolism Mythology of Insanity Defense Jurisprudence, 40 Case W. Res. L. Rev. 599 (1990); Jonas Robitscher & Andrew Ky Haynes, In Defense of the Insanity Defense, 31 Emory L.J. 9 (1982); Ernest van den Haag, The Insanity Defense, Criminal Just. Ethics, Winter-Spring 1984, at 3.

[124] See Hans, Note 55, supra.

[125] See National Mental Health Association, Note 104, supra, at 14–15. A national survey in 1981 found that 87% of the public believed that the defense was over-used and too often successful. Minneapolis Trib., Oct. 25, 1981, at 9a.

There is virtually no empirical support for this proposition.[126] According to one team of commentators, "[a]ll empirical analyses . . . have been consistent: the public, legal profession and . . . legislators 'dramatically' and 'grossly' overestimate both the frequency and the success rate of the insanity plea."[127]

Although statistics regarding use of the insanity plea are sketchy,[128] it appears that the defense is rarely invoked; when it is invoked, there is often agreement among the experts that the defendant suffers from a mental illness; and the success rate for the insanity plea, although variable, is usually extremely low.[129] For example, in one reported New Jersey study, NGRI verdicts were secured in only half of one percent of all cases handled by the Office of Public Defenders.[130] In a survey of 36 states for the years 1970–1995, there were only 16,379 insanity acquittals, or an average of 33.4 acquittals per state per year in the many hundreds of thousands of felony and misdemeanor prosecutions during that period, including a modest decline in such acquittals beginning in the late 1980s.[131] As a result of jury antipathy to insanity claims, many criminal defense lawyers view the defense as a plea of last resort.

[2] Counter-Deterrence

Although the insanity defense may serve a valid utilitarian purpose with genuinely insane people,[132] there is abolitionist fear that the defense may have a negative impact on those who are *not* mentally ill, and on those whose illnesses are not severe enough to qualify for acquittal. They reason that awareness by such people that the law recognizes an insanity defense may reduce the deterrent effect of the criminal sanction. A would-be wrongdoer may believe, although perhaps inaccurately, that if she is caught for her crime she will be able to avoid conviction or commitment by raising the insanity defense.

Defenders of the insanity plea contend that even if this argument is correct, which they dispute, the solution is not to abolish the defense, but instead is to educate the public regarding the true effect of the insanity defense (*e.g.*, that long-term civil commitment usually follows the rare acquittal), and/or place the burden of proof on the defense to prove insanity, rather than on the prosecution to prove the defendant's sanity.[133]

---

[126] American Law Institute, Comment to § 4.01, at 182.

[127] Joseph H. Rodriguez et al., *The Insanity Defense Under Siege: Legislative Assaults and Legal Rejoinders*, 14 Rutgers L.J. 397, 401 (1983) (footnotes omitted).

[128] *See* Note 4, *supra.*

[129] *See* Perlin, Note 123, *supra*, at 648–49, 651–53.

[130] National Mental Health Association, Note 104, *supra*, at 15.

[131] *See* Cirincione & Jacobs, Note 5, *supra*, at 490, 494.

[132] *See* § 25.03[A], *supra.*

[133] Most states do not place the burden of persuasion on the prosecution in insanity claims. *See* § 25.02[E], *supra.*

[3] Conflict of Perspectives

Some abolitionists contend that the criminal law and psychiatry cannot mix any more than oil and water does. They point out that the criminal law and psychiatry look at human conduct from different philosophical perspectives.[134] The law is premised on the concept of free will, whereas psychiatry typically is deterministic regarding human conduct. From the psychiatric point of view, "[t]he study of man . . . has an undoubted tendency to make him, in the eyes of his investigator, a creature of forces beyond its control. . . . Law, on the other hand, stands pre-eminently for the freedom of the will."[135] The distinction the criminal law seeks to draw between the mad and the bad, therefore, is an illusion.

Psychiatrist Karl Menninger agreed with the claim that lawyers and psychiatrists have conflicting perspectives on human conduct. He stated that "[t]he Law — with a capital L — has no real relation to the affairs of men." He observed disparagingly that lawyers are interested in placing or rebutting "blame," and that "the word *justice*, which is so dear to lawyers, is one which the doctor *qua* scientist simply does not use or readily understand."[136]

The conflict-of-perspectives argument has much to commend it, but it arguably proves too much. Although psychiatrists are less apt to blame wrongdoers than are lawyers and the general public, the idea that some people are too sick to be blamed for their conduct is not antithetical to the criminal law, nor does it endanger the paradigm of free will. The criminal law is based on the view that, although humans *generally* possess free will, some people are so irrational that they lack the basic attributes of personhood that make them morally accountable for their actions. Therefore, the present claim is more an argument for limiting the scope of psychiatric testimony at trial than it is for abolishing the insanity defense.

[4] "Mental Illness": Merely a Deviation from a Cultural Norm

Some abolitionists[137] believe that the term "mental illness" is little more than a pseudo-scientific term for describing abnormal behavior. And, the argument proceeds, "abnormality" means no more than that the conduct is unusual or odd in a particular cultural environment. Ultimately, the term "mental disease" is attached to behavior that society considers strange, frightening, or disagreeable.

Historical support for this premise can be found. For example, when slavery was the norm in the Southern U.S.A., slaves who fled were characterized as mentally ill.[138] Likewise, in a pre-feminist age, some Freudian psychologists described

---

[134] United States v. Pollard, 171 F. Supp. 474, 479 (E.D. Mich. 1959).

[135] Gino C. Speranza, *The Medico-Legal Conflict over Mental Responsibility*, 13 Green Bag 123, 125 (1901).

[136] Menninger, Note 8, *supra*, at 96.

[137] *E.g.*, Thomas S. Szasz, The Myth of Mental Illness (1961); Thomas S. Szasz, Ideology and Insanity (1970).

[138] Emily Eakin, *Bigotry as Mental Illness or Just Another Norm*, N.Y. Times, Jan. 15, 2000, at A9 (quoting from an 1851 report of Dr. Samuel A. Cartwright, a Louisiana psychologist).

female advocates of women's rights as "neurotics . . . compensating for masculine trends . . . [or] more or less successfully sublimating sadistic and homosexual [trends]."[139] Also, the psychiatric establishment labeled homosexuality as a mental disease until 1973, at which time the Board of Trustees of the American Psychiatric Association voted to remove homosexuality from that category. Politics and changing social attitudes, not new science, is credited for the change — "[a] more recent moral judgment simply replaced an older one."[140]

Advocates of the insanity defense assert that even if the preceding criticism of psychiatry is valid, it is beside the point. In the typical case in which the insanity defense is raised in a criminal proceeding, *e.g.*, in which the defendant hears voices in her head or experiences exceedingly strong urges to commit criminal acts, there is little doubt that she is suffering from an aberrant mental or physical condition, and is not simply a person out of place in her culture.

[5]　Equity

Some abolitionists contend that various conditions, *e.g.*, abuse as a child or growing up in a bad social environment, are equally or even more criminogenic than psychoses, and yet they are not considered legitimate bases for exculpation. Advocates of the equity position concede that a defense based on such factors is politically unacceptable at this time. Therefore, since morally similar cases should be treated alike, they contend that until society recognizes an excuse for persons suffering from non-medical criminogenic factors, insane people should also be punished.[141]

Advocates for an insanity defense believe that critics are comparing apples with oranges. "Identification of the correlates of crime . . . does not mean the crime is compelled";[142] "[c]ausation is not compulsion."[143] That is, a person from a bad social environment knowingly commits a crime and could choose to act otherwise; in contrast, one who suffers from a mental disease or defect that prevents her from knowing right from wrong lacks the basic attributes of a moral agent and, therefore, should be declared morally blameless.

[B]　Legislative Efforts to Abolish the Defense[144]

After the attempted assassination of President Ronald Reagan in the 1980s, a few legislatures abolished the insanity defense.[145] These states, however, permit a defendant to introduce evidence of her mental disease or defect in order to rebut

---

[139]　*See* Mary P. Ryan, Womanhood in America 276 (1975) (quoting H.W. Frink).

[140]　Ernest van den Haag, Note 123, *supra*, at 4; *see also* Eakin, Note 138, *supra* (quoting the views of Dr. Alvin Poussaint, professor of psychiatry at Harvard Medical School).

[141]　Norval Morris & Gordon Hawkins, The Honest Politician's Guide to Crime Control 179 (1970).

[142]　Slobogin, Note 48, *supra*, at 321–22.

[143]　Moore, Note 46, *supra*, at 1131; *see generally* § 17.03[C], *supra*.

[144]　Daniel J. Nusbaum, Note, *The Craziest Reform of Them All: A Critical Analysis of the Constitutional Implications of "Abolishing" the Insanity Defense*, 87 Cornell L. Rev. 1509 (2002).

[145]　Idaho Code § 18-207 (2015); Kan. Stat. Ann § 22-3220 (2015); Mont. Code Ann. § 46-14-102 (2015); Utah Code Ann. § 76-2-305(1) (2015). The Nevada legislature abolished the defense in 1995, but this

the prosecution's claim that she possessed the mental state required in the definition of the crime.

For example, if *D* is prosecuted for intentionally killing *V*, *D* may introduce evidence that, due to mental illness, she believed that she was killing a wolf and, therefore, lacked the intent to kill a human being. Evidence of *D*'s mental condition would be inadmissible, however, to show that she killed *V* because the wolf told her to do so![146]

These state laws have been declared constitutional.[147] Although defendants have argued that "the insanity defense is so embedded in our legal history that it should be afforded status as a fundamental right,"[148] the United States Supreme Court has stated that:

> The doctrines of *actus reus, mens rea,* insanity, . . . justification, and duress have historically provided the tools for a constantly shifting adjustment of the tension between the evolving aims of the criminal law and changing religious, moral, philosophical, and medical views of the nature of man. This process of adjustment has always been thought to be the province of the States.[149]

More recently, the Supreme Court observed in dictum that "[w]e have never held that the Constitution mandates an insanity defense, nor have we held that [it] . . . does *not* so require."[150]

Since the federal Due Process Clause does not prohibit a legislature from abandoning the basic requirement of *mens rea,*[151] it would seem to follow that a state may take the less drastic approach of retaining the element of *mens rea,* while repealing the *defense* of insanity, as long as the prosecution is required to prove beyond a reasonable doubt that the defendant had the requisite mental state. Nor does abolition of the defense currently constitute unconstitutionally disproportionate punishment because, except in death penalty cases, legislatures have nearly

---

legislation was declared violative of the Due Process Clauses of the state constitution. Finger v. State, 27 P.3d 66 (Nev. 2001).

[146] *See* Delling v. Idaho, 133 S. Ct. 504, 505 (2012) (Breyer, Ginsburg, and Sotomayor, JJ., dissenting from a denial of a writ of certiorari),

[147] State v. Searcy, 798 P.2d 914 (Idaho 1990) (abolition of the defense does not violate the Due Process Clause); State v. Korell, 690 P.2d 992 (Mont. 1984) (abolition does not violate Due Process Clause or Eighth Amendment bar on cruel and unusual punishment); State v. Herrera, 895 P.2d 359 (Utah 1995) (abolition does not violate due process or equal protection rights of the defendant); State v. Mace, 921 P.2d 1372 (Utah 1996) (abolition does not constitute cruel and unusual punishment).

[148] *State v. Korell,* 690 P.2d at 998 (stating, but rejecting, the argument); *but see* Finger v. State, 27 P.3d 66, 84 (Nev. 2001) ("We conclude that legal insanity is a well-established and fundamental principle of the law of the United States. It is therefore protected by the Due Process Clauses of both the United States and Nevada Constitutions."); State v. Joyner, 625 A.2d 791, 800 (Conn. 1993) (stating in dictum that "[w]e agree with the defendant that our common law tradition provides considerable support for the proposition that . . . the state could not entirely eradicate such a defense from the penal code.").

[149] Powell v. Texas, 392 U.S. 514, 536 (1968).

[150] Clark v. Arizona, 548 U.S. 735, 752 n.20 (2006) (emphasis added).

[151] *See* § 11.03, *supra.*

unfettered discretion in determining appropriate penalties for serious crimes.[152]

These rulings by the Supreme Court are controversial and may be unwise, but unless and until the Supreme Court reverses itself on these matters, state legislatures are seemingly not barred by the federal[153] constitution from abolishing the insanity defense, as long as the defendant is entitled to a *mens rea* "defense."

§ 25.07 "GUILTY BUT MENTALLY ILL"[154]

In response to criticisms of the insanity defense, some states have adopted an alternative verdict, "guilty but mentally ill" (GBMI). In all but two of these states, the insanity defense has been retained, but a jury may now choose from among four, rather than the usual three, verdicts: guilty, not guilty, not guilty by reason of insanity (NGRI), and GBMI.[155] In these states, the jury returns a NGRI verdict if the defendant was insane at the time of the crime; it returns a GBMI verdict if she is guilty of the offense, was sane at the time of the crime, but is "mentally ill" at the time of trial, as the latter term is defined by statute.

The effect of a GBMI verdict is that the convicted party receives the sentence that would otherwise be imposed if she were found guilty; after sentencing, however, she may receive psychiatric care in the prison setting or in a mental institution. If she is cured while in custody, she must complete her prison sentence.

Proponents of the GBMI verdict claim the following benefits of the system: (1) inappropriate insanity findings will be reduced; (2) treatment of mentally ill, but sane, offenders is provided; and (3) the public receives greater protection from mentally disordered and dangerous offenders.

Critics of the verdict raise the following objections. First, the distinction between mental illness and insanity may be too fine for a jury to distinguish. Second, the GBMI verdict is unnecessary: Any person convicted of a crime may receive psychiatric care if the state wishes to provide it. Third, persons who are found GBMI are not guaranteed treatment. Especially during state budgetary crises, insufficient funds may be allocated to mental health agencies. Finally, juries may compromise and return GBMI verdicts when NGRI verdicts should be reached, *i.e.*, the GBMI alternative may reduce the number of *appropriate* insanity acquittals.[156]

---

[152] *See* § 6.05, *supra*.

[153] This does not preclude a state from enforcing its own constitution in a manner more protective of defendants' rights. *See* Note 145, *supra*.

[154] *See generally* Ingo Keilitz et al., The Guilty but Mentally Ill Verdict: An Empirical Study (1984); R.D. MacKay & Jerry Kopelman, *The Operation of the "Guilty but Mentally Ill" Verdict in Pennsylvania*, 16 J. Psychiatry & L. 247 (1988); Donald W. Morgan et al., *Guilty but Mentally Ill: The South Carolina Experience*, 16 Bull. Am. Acad. Psychiatry & L. 41 (1988); Gare A. Smith & James A. Hall, Project, *Evaluating Michigan's Guilty but Mentally Ill Verdict: An Empirical Study*, 16 U. Mich. J.L. Reform 77 (1982).

[155] *E.g.*, Mich. Comp. Laws § 768.36 (2015).

[156] With one exception, however, studies have found that the GBMI option has not resulted in a decrease in NGRI verdicts. *See* MacKay & Kopelman, Note 154, *supra* (reviewing four previous studies that found no reduction in insanity acquittals, but reporting a reduction in Pennsylvania).

Chapter 26

DIMINISHED CAPACITY

§ 26.01 "DIMINISHED CAPACITY": A TERM OF CONFUSION[1]

The term "diminished capacity" is used and misused by courts and commentators to describe two different concepts, neither one of which is adequately characterized by the term. Although the problem is less severe than in the past,[2] one scholar has aptly depicted the state of affairs in this field as "undiminished confusion in diminished capacity."[3] Because of the confusion pervading this area of the law, any generalization about it is just that — a generalization subject to exceptions and inconsistencies.

With this caveat in mind, it may be said that "diminished capacity" is a term used to describe two categories of circumstances in which an actor's abnormal mental condition, short of insanity, will occasionally exonerate him or, far more often,[4] result in his conviction of a less serious crime or degree of crime than the original charge.

First, there is a *mens rea* form of diminished capacity. As explained below, the *mens rea* model of diminished capacity functions as a failure-of-proof defense. That is, evidence of mental abnormality is *not* offered by the defendant to partially or fully *excuse* his conduct, but rather as evidence to negate an element of the crime charged,[5] almost always the *mens rea* element.[6]

---

[1] *See generally* Peter Arenella, *The Diminished Capacity and Diminished Responsibility Defenses: Two Children of a Doomed Marriage*, 77 Colum. L. Rev. 827 (1977); Joshua Dressler, *Reaffirming the Moral Legitimacy of the Doctrine of Diminished Capacity: A Brief Reply to Professor Morse*, 75 J. Crim. L. & Criminology 953 (1984); Arlie Loughnan, *Mental Incapacity Doctrines in Criminal Law*, 15 New Crim. L. Rev. 1 (2012); Stephen J. Morse, *Diminished Capacity*, *in* Action and Value in Criminal Law 239 (Stephen Shute et al. eds., 1993); Stephen J. Morse, *Undiminished Confusion in Diminished Capacity*, 75 J. Crim. L. & Criminology 1 (1984).

[2] Morse, *Diminished Capacity*, Note 1, *supra*, at 240 n.8.

[3] Morse, *Undiminished Confusion*, Note 1, *supra*.

[4] State v. Joseph, 590 S.E.2d 718, 723 (W. Va. 2003).

[5] Jackson v. State, 160 S.W.3d 568, 573 (Tex. Crim. App. 2005).

[6] In extremely rare circumstances, evidence of the defendant's mental condition may be introduced to prove that he acted in an unconscious state, thereby negating the voluntary act requirement of a criminal offense. Of course, proof of lack of a voluntary act will also demonstrate lack of *mens rea*, but the "voluntary act" approach will result in a better outcome for a defendant in a prosecution of a strict liability offense (where there is no *mens rea* element to negate), as well as in jurisdictions that (as discussed in the text *infra*) bar evidence of mental abnormality to negate *mens rea*. *E.g.*, Reed v. State, 693 N.E.2d 988, 992 n.6 (Ind. Ct. App. 1998) (although evidence of diminished capacity may not be

The second form of diminished capacity, which partially excuses or mitigates a defendant's guilt even if he has the requisite *mens rea* for the crime, will be called here "partial responsibility." This version of the defense is now recognized in only a few states, and only for the crime of murder, to mitigate the homicide to manslaughter.

§ 26.02 DIMINISHED CAPACITY: *MENS REA* DEFENSE

[A] Nature of the Defense

Consider three hypothetical cases. First, *D1* is charged with first-degree murder based on the claim that he intentionally killed *V*. *D1* wishes to introduce expert testimony that at the time he killed *V* he was suffering from a mental illness. Although the testimony will not show that *D1* was insane at the time of the crime, it is intended to prove that, as a result of his abnormal mental condition, he did not form the intent to kill *V*.

Second, suppose that *D2* is prosecuted for rape and wishes to introduce evidence that as a result of mental disability, he genuinely believed that the female with whom he was having intercourse consented.

Finally, suppose that *D3* is prosecuted for assault with intent to commit rape, but wishes to prove that due to a delusion he believed that the woman he was forcibly attacking was his wife.

In each of these cases, the proffered expert testimony forms the basis of the *mens rea* version of the diminished capacity defense. The testimony that each defendant seeks to introduce speaks to the "question of whether the defendant in fact possessed a particular mental state [intent to kill, by *D1*; intent to have nonconsensual intercourse, by *D2*; intent to rape, by *D3*] which is an element of the charged offense."[7]

The word "defense," as used here, is a "legal colloquialism," because the doctrine "is not designed to defeat a case the State has otherwise established."[8] Indeed, it is potentially "confusing to refer to [the *mens rea* version of] diminished capacity as a 'defense'."[9] This is because "the 'diminished capacity defense' . . . does not provide any grounds for acquittal not provided in the definition of the offense. Properly understood, [diminished capacity] is . . . not a defense at all but merely a rule of evidence."[10] As one court put it, "[f]or the purpose of determining criminal guilt, diminished capacity either negates the state of mind required for a particular offense, if successful, or it does not."[11]

---

introduced to disprove criminal intent, *R* was entitled to introduce evidence that she suffered from a small stroke and, therefore, acted unconsciously, thereby disproving that she voluntarily committed a theft).

[7] United States v. Pohlot, 827 F.2d 889, 896 (3d Cir. 1987).

[8] State v. Humanik, 489 A.2d 691, 697 (N.J. Super. Ct. App. Div. 1985).

[9] State v. Joseph, 590 S.E.2d 718, 723 (W. Va. 2003).

[10] *United States v. Pohlot*, 827 F.2d at 897.

[11] State v. Breakiron, 532 A.2d 199, 208–09 (N.J. 1987).

[B] Law

[1] Overview

Because of judicial confusion regarding the concept of diminished capacity, and legislative imprecision in the enactment of relevant statutes, the law of "diminished capacity" is unclear in many states. However, certain observations and a general summary are possible.

American law is sharply divided regarding the extent to which evidence of an abnormal mental condition not amounting to legal insanity may be introduced for the purpose of negating the *mens rea* of an offense. As examined below, some states, primarily those that follow the Model Penal Code, permit introduction of such evidence, when relevant,[12] to negate the *mens rea* of *any* crime. Other states limit the admissibility of such evidence to some or all specific-intent offenses. A third group bars "diminished capacity" evidence in prosecutions of all offenses.

[2] Defense-to-All-Crimes (Model Penal Code) Approach

Perhaps as many as 15 states, consistent with the Model Penal Code,[13] provide that evidence that the defendant suffered from a mental disease or defect at the time of his conduct is admissible if it is relevant to prove that he lacked a mental state that is an element of the charged offense.[14] The Colorado Supreme Court in *Hendershott v. People*[15] has succinctly explained the reasoning behind this rule:

> Once we accept the basic principles that an accused is presumed innocent and that he cannot be adjudicated guilty unless the prosecution proves beyond a reasonable doubt the existence of the mental state required for the crime charged, it defies both logic and fundamental fairness to prohibit a defendant from presenting reliable and relevant evidence that, due to a mental impairment beyond his conscious control, he lacked the capacity to entertain the very culpability which is indispensable to his criminal responsibility in the first instance.

---

[12] Even in jurisdictions that recognize a defense of diminished capacity, a jury instruction on the issue is inappropriate unless the proffered evidence is legally relevant, *i.e.*, evidence of the defendant's abnormal mental condition must tend to support the claim that it "impaired the defendant's ability to form the culpable mental state to commit the crime charged." State v. Atsbeha, 16 P.3d 626, 632 (Wash. 2001). Thus, in State v. Guilliot, 22 P.3d 1266 (Wash. Ct. App. 2001), *G* was not entitled to a diminished capacity instruction, although he offered to prove that he suffered from narcissistic personality traits; this mental condition, even if supported by expert testimony, would not have prevented *G* from forming the mental state required to be convicted of murder.

[13] Model Penal Code § 4.02(1).

[14] According to Professor Paul Robinson, in 1984, 12 states followed the rule set out in the text. 1 Paul H. Robinson, Criminal Law Defenses § 64(a)–(b) (1984). Recent Pocket Part supplements to the treatise and this author's own research demonstrate that a few states seemingly have joined this list, but others have dropped off. Because of ambiguities in judicial opinions and dicta, however, it is uncertain how many jurisdictions now apply the equivalent of the Model Penal Code standard, but the figure seems not to exceed 15 states.

[15] 653 P.2d 385, 393–94 (Colo. 1982).

Applying the Model Penal Code rule to the hypotheticals posited in subsection [A], the defendants in each case would be entitled to introduce evidence of their respective mental abnormalities. The effect of the evidence — if believed or, at least, if it created a reasonable doubt as to the defendants' *mens rea* — would be to acquit them of the crimes charged, although they might be guilty of a lesser offense.[16] In contrast, as an example, a murder defendant who seeks to show that he is very mildly disabled and, as a consequence, is a follower of stronger-willed persons, would not be permitted to introduce expert evidence in *this* regard in an intent-to-kill prosecution, because such testimony, even if believed, would not negate the required element of intent.[17]

[3] Limited-Use Approach

A few states arbitrarily limit the introduction of mental-condition evidence to murder prosecutions.[18] Thus, in the hypotheticals in subsection [A], *D1* would be permitted to introduce evidence of his mental illness in order to avoid a first-degree intent-to-kill conviction of murder, but *D2* and *D3* would not be allowed to introduce evidence of their abnormal mental conditions.

A far more common distinction is one drawn between specific-intent and general-intent offenses: Evidence of an abnormal mental condition may be introduced if it tends to show that the defendant could not, or did not, form a *specific* intent specified in the offense, but such evidence is inadmissible in the prosecution of a *general*-intent crime.[19] Thus, *D1* could raise his diminished capacity claim to prove that he lacked the capacity to form, or did not in fact form,[20] the specific intent to kill. *D3*, as well, could introduce evidence to prove that he lacked the specific intent to rape *V*. *D2*, however, would not be permitted to introduce evidence of his mental condition to disprove rape, because rape is a general-intent crime.[21]

As a practical matter, this version of diminished capacity functions only as a partial defense, because there is almost always a crime for which a person with

---

[16] *D1* could be convicted of any form of criminal homicide for which intent to kill is not an element.

D2's situation is more problematic. Because of his mental condition, *D2* believed he was having consensual intercourse, so he is not guilty of rape. Therefore, he would be guilty of no offense unless the state recognizes an offense such as fornication or some strict-liability offense.

D3 would be guilty of assault or battery since, as he perceived the situation, he was sexually attacking his own wife. Only the specific intent to rape would be negated by his mental condition. (This latter analysis assumes that rape is defined as it was at common law, namely as sexual intercourse by a man with a woman, *not his wife*, without her consent. *See generally* Chapter 33, *infra*.)

[17] State v. Watson, 618 A.2d 367, 372 (N.J. Super. Ct. App. Div. 1992).

[18] *E.g.*, Commonwealth v. Garcia, 479 A.2d 473, 476 (Pa. 1984) (evidence admissible to negate the first-degree murder requirement of specific intent to kill).

[19] *E.g.*, State v. Jacobs, 607 N.W.2d 679, 684 (Iowa 2000); State v. Lancaster, 527 S.E.2d 61, 66–67 (N.C. Ct. App. 2000).

[20] As with voluntary intoxication, see § 24.03[B][3], *supra*, some jurisdictions speak of the defense in "lack of capacity" terms, *e.g.*, State v. Galloway, 628 A.2d 735, 743 (N.J. 1993) ("[T]he claimed deficiency . . . affect[ed] the defendant's cognitive capacity to form the mental state necessary for the commission of the crime."), whereas other states are concerned, simply, with whether the actor *actually* formed the state of mind in question.

[21] *See* State v. Lopez, 892 P.2d 898 (Idaho Ct. App. 1995).

diminished capacity can be convicted, even if he succeeds in proving that he lacked a specific intent.[22] Thus, the defense will reduce a defendant's guilt from one degree of murder to a lower degree of criminal homicide, or from a non-homicide specific-intent offense to a general-intent crime, *e.g.*, from burglary to criminal trespass. Outright acquittal is exceedingly rare.

[4] No-Defense Approach

Some jurisdictions permit introduction of evidence of a defendant's mental illness or defect in order to prove insanity, but prohibit introduction of the same evidence for the purpose of showing that the defendant may have lacked the capacity to, or did not in fact, form the required mental-state element of the offense charged.[23]

In some states, this rule leads to an anomaly: A defendant may introduce evidence of his self-induced, and thus culpable, *intoxication* in order to show that he lacked the specific intent to commit an offense, but he is barred from introducing expert testimony regarding an abnormal mental condition — which he did not culpably contract — for the same purpose.[24] A stated justification for this distinction is that "[u]nlike the notion of partial or relative insanity, conditions such as intoxication, medication, epilepsy, infancy, or senility are, in varying degrees, susceptible to quantification or objective demonstration."[25]

Anomalies aside, is it constitutional to prohibit introduction of expert mental-health evidence to disprove a defendant's *mens rea*? The United States Supreme Court recently answered this question, mostly in the affirmative. In *Clark v. Arizona*,[26] C shot to death a police officer. He was charged with first-degree murder, which was defined under Arizona law as "intending or knowing that the person's conduct will cause death to a law enforcement officer, [and] the person causes the death of a law enforcement officer who is in the line of duty."

C freely admitted the shooting, but he sought to introduce undisputed mental-health evidence that he suffered from paranoid schizophrenia, that he demonstrated bizarre behavior at the time of the incident and long before, and that he suffered from a delusion that the police officer he shot was, in fact, a non-human "alien." C

---

[22] Some jurisdictions expressly limit the defense in this regard. *E.g.*, State v. Doyon, 416 A.2d 130, 137 (R.I. 1980) ("Acceptance of the doctrine requires that there must be some lesser-included offense which lacks the requisite specific intent of the greater offense charged.").

[23] *E.g.*, Chestnut v. State, 538 So.2d 820, 820 (Fla. 1989); State v. Wise, 128 So. 3d 1220, 1225 (La. Ct. App. 2013); People v. Carpenter, 627 N.W.2d 276, 283 (Mich. 2001); Bethea v. United States, 365 A.2d 64, 89–90 (D.C. 1976).

[24] State v. Joseph, 590 S.E.2d 718, 724 (W. Va. 2003) (quoting State v. Simmons, 309 S.E.2d 89, 98 n.18 (1983)) (characterizing such an approach as illogical and unjust).

[25] *Bethea v. United States*, 365 A.2d at 88. Based on this purported distinction, Florida bars "mental abnormality" evidence, Chestnut v. State, 538 So. 2d 820 (Fla. 1989), but permits evidence of epilepsy, Bunney v. State, 603 So. 2d 1270, 1273 (Fla. 1992), to prove lack of specific intent.

[26] 548 U.S. 735 (2006). *Clark* is analyzed in Ronald J. Allen, Clark v. Arizona: *Much (Confused) Ado About Nothing*, 4 Ohio St. J. Crim. L. 135 (2006); Stephen J. Morse & Morris B. Hoffman, *The Uneasy Entente Between Legal Insanity and Mens Rea: Beyond* Clark v. Arizona, 97 J. Crim. L. & Criminology 1071 (2007); Peter Westen, *The Supreme Court's Bout with Insanity:* Clark v. Arizona, 4 Ohio St. J. Crim. L. 143 (2006).

argued that this evidence was relevant to show that he did not "intend" or "know" that he was killing a human being, more specifically under the murder statute, a law enforcement officer.

In considering the matter, the Supreme Court distinguished between three types of *mens rea* evidence that might be proffered in a criminal case: (1) *observational evidence* "in the everyday sense," which could include testimony from lay people who could describe *C*'s actions and words, and which could also include "testimony that an expert witness might give about [*C*]'s tendency to think in a certain way and his behavioral characteristics"; (2) *mental disease evidence*, here in the form of expert testimony that *C* suffered from paranoid schizophrenia, with an explanation of what the characteristics are of this disease; and (3) *capacity evidence*, also in the form of expert testimony, about *C*'s capacity to form the requisite *mens rea*, here, the intent to kill a police officer (or knowledge that his actions would cause such a result). Arizona did *not* prohibit a defendant from introducing evidence of the first sort (observational evidence), but it did prohibit categories (2) and (3) evidence in order to disprove *mens rea*, although it permitted introduction of such evidence on the issue of insanity.[27]

According to the Supreme Court, Arizona was within its constitutional right to limit the introduction of expert mental-disease and capacity testimony to insanity claims. The justices stated that "[a]s [*C*] recognizes, . . . the right to introduce relevant evidence can be curtailed if there is good reason for doing that." Here, the Court found good reasons for the Arizona approach. First, a state has the right to presume that people are sane and, therefore, to place the burden of persuasion on the defendant to prove insanity; but, if *C* could introduce evidence of his mental disease to create a reasonable doubt as to his *mens rea*, this would effectively permit *C* "the opportunity to displace the presumption of sanity."

The Court noted other reasons why a state might wish to limit mental-disease and capacity evidence to insanity claims: "the controversial character of some categories of mental disease[;] . . . the potential of mental-disease evidence to mislead[;] and . . . the danger of according greater certainty to capacity evidence than experts claim for it."[28] As one scholar has explained this aspect of the Court's opinion, "[i]n short, mental health professionals often talk gibberish, and the evidence they provide is often lousy, both being true enough so that the state's limitation of the use of this type of evidence [to insanity claims, where the burden of proof can be placed on the defendant] . . . is permissible under the due process clause."[29]

---

[27] State v. Mott, 931 P.2d 1046 (Ariz. 1997).

[28] *See also* State v. Wong, 641 N.E.2d 1137, 1150–51 (Ohio Ct. App. 1994) (a legislature may reasonably "find psychiatric testimony to be a useful tool in the determination of insanity, yet not be convinced that the sciences of psychiatry and psychology are advanced enough to 'fine-tune' among sane defendants and find whether they possess[] the specific intent necessary for commission of a crime"); State v. Wilcox, 436 N.E.2d 523, 530 (Ohio 1982) ("The ability [of jurors] to assimilate and apply the finely differentiated psychiatric concepts associated with diminished capacity demands a sophistication (or as critics would maintain a sophistic bent) that jurors (and officers of the court) ordinarily have not developed.").

[29] Allen, Note 26, *supra*, at 140.

The dissenters did not agree: "Either [C] knew he was killing a police officer or he did not." If he did not, C "needs no excuse, as then he did not commit the crime as Arizona defines it." Although the dissenters agreed with the majority that a state has a legitimate interest in barring unreliable evidence, that interest "does not extend to per se exclusions that may be reliable in an individual case."[30] As for the risk of jury confusion, the dissenters observed that "[w]e have always trusted juries to sort through complex facts in various areas of law."[31]

§ 26.03   DIMINISHED CAPACITY: "PARTIAL RESPONSIBILITY" DEFENSE

[A]   Rule

[1]   In General

Few states recognize the "partial responsibility" defense. Where it does apply, it is only a defense to murder to mitigate the offense to manslaughter. As discussed below, the California Supreme Court promulgated the United States judicial version of the doctrine in the 1960s.[32] Only four other state courts adopted the defense.[33] The drafters of the Model Penal Code developed a different version of the partial responsibility doctrine. Although legislatures and courts only rarely recognize the doctrine as a partial defense, "it has long been applied, at least implicitly, by judges during sentencing."[34]

[2]   The Largely Discredited California Approach

The partial responsibility defense was adopted "through the judicial back door,"[35] in order to allow mitigation of some homicides from first-degree to second-degree murder. Later the mitigation process extended to reducing murder to manslaughter. California courts led the judicial movement.

In order to avoid the appearance of encroaching on legislative authority, the California Supreme Court dressed the partial responsibility defense in "*mens rea* clothing."[36] That is, the judges developed strained definitions of *mens rea* terms;

---

[30] *Clark*, 548 U.S. at 792 (quoting Rock v. Arkansas, 483 U.S. 44, 61 (1987)).

[31] Despite *Clark*, which ruled on whether Arizona's law violated the *federal* constitution, a state court has authority to hold that its own *state* constitution requires admission of relevant mental-disease and capacity *mens rea* evidence. *E.g.*, State v. Evans, 62 P.3d 220, 225 (Kan. 2003) (holding that, applying the state constitution, "a defendant is entitled to present the theory of his or her defense and . . . exclusion of evidence that is *integral* part of that theory violates a defendant's fundamental right to a fair trial").

[32] The common law defense was first recognized in the 19th century in Scotland, to reduce the offense of the "partially insane" from murder to the non-capital offense of "culpable homicide." Arenella, Note 1, *supra*, at 830 n.16. It was codified in England in the Homicide Act of 1957, 5 & 6 Eliz. 2, c. 11, pt. I, § 2.

[33] American Law Institute, Comment to § 210.3, at 70 n.77.

[34] United States v. Leandre, 132 F.3d 796, 802 (D.C. Cir. 1998).

[35] Morse, *Undiminished Confusion*, Note 1, *supra*, at 24.

[36] Arenella, Note 1, *supra*, at 831.

then the courts concluded that mentally impaired actors lacked the requisite mental state (under the new strained definitions) to be convicted of first-degree or second-degree murder. In fact, however, the true rationale of the partial responsibility doctrine was — and is — that a person who does not meet the state's definition of insanity, but who suffers from a mental abnormality, is less blameworthy, and therefore less deserving of punishment, than a killer who acts with a normal state of mind.[37]

For example, in *People v. Conley*,[38] *C* shot his ex-lover and her husband after planning their deaths over a weekend. According to psychiatric testimony, *C* suffered from "personality fragmentation" and was in a "dissociative state" on the fatal weekend. Nonetheless, the jury found that at the time of the crime, *C* killed the victims intentionally and with premeditation and deliberation. In short, the *mens rea* variant of the diminished capacity defense apparently did not apply.

The California Supreme Court overturned *C*'s first-degree murder conviction, although it accepted the jury's findings. It stated that the judge had failed to instruct the jury properly on the element of "malice aforethought," the mental element of murder that distinguishes it from manslaughter. To act with "malice aforethought," the court stated, a person must be aware of his "obligation to act within the general body of laws regulating society." If *C*, although sane, lacked this awareness, he did not act with malice aforethought and, therefore, lacked the required *mens rea* of murder and was guilty only of manslaughter. Of course, a person who is unaware of his obligation to act within the law because he suffers from a mental disease or defect is probably insane because he does not know right from wrong. What the court really was doing was creating a mini-insanity defense, so that a jury could mitigate a defendant's guilt when it was unwilling to find insanity.

Subsequently, the California Supreme Court extended the doctrine. Probably because the state legislature had not codified the irresistible-impulse test of insanity, the court further redefined "malice," by including a volitional feature. According to the court, "malice" is absent if, as the result of a mental abnormality, the defendant is "unaware of or *unable to act* in accordance with the law."[39]

In response to controversial verdicts involving the diminished capacity defense, the California legislature and the state's electorate abolished the partial responsibility form of the diminished capacity doctrine in the 1980s.[40]

---

[37] *See* United States v. Skodnek, 896 F. Supp. 60, 63 (D. Mass. 1995) ("[M]ental illness is not like a spigot, to be turned on and off, but exists in varying degrees in different individuals.").

[38] 411 P.2d 911 (Cal. 1966).

[39] People v. Poddar, 518 P.2d 342, 348 (Cal. 1974) (emphasis supplied).

[40] Cal. Penal Code §§ 28(b), 188 (2015); State v. Congress, 114 A.3d 1128 (Va. 2014) (deviating from earlier state case law, the court holds that partial responsibility form of diminished capacity defense is no longer recognized). For a thorough discussion of California law, including the abandonment of the doctrine, see People v. Saille, 820 P.2d 588 (Cal. 1991).

[3]   The Model Penal Code Approach

The Model Penal Code provides that a homicide that would otherwise constitute murder is manslaughter if it is committed as the result of "extreme mental or emotional disturbance for which there is a reasonable explanation or excuse." The reasonableness of the actor's explanation or excuse for the "extreme mental or emotional disturbance" (EMED) is "determined from the viewpoint of a person in the actor's situation under the circumstances as he believes them to be."[41]

The EMED provision has two purposes: (1) it codifies and expands on the common law "sudden heat of passion" doctrine;[42] and (2) it permits, but does not require, courts in states that adopt the EMED language to recognize a partial responsibility defense.[43] It is unclear how many states that have codified the EMED provision allow for a partial responsibility defense, but courts in at least two jurisdictions expressly recognize the defense.[44] The Commentary to the Code explains the partial responsibility doctrine this way:

> [The defense] looks into the actor's mind to see whether he should be judged by a lesser standard than that applicable to ordinary men. It recognizes the defendant's own mental disorder or emotional instability as a basis for partially excusing his conduct . . . . To the extent that the abnormal individual is judged as if he were normal, to the extent that the drunk man is judged as if he were sober, to the extent, in short, that the defective person is judged as if he were someone else, the moral judgment underlying criminal conviction is undermined.[45]

As a practical matter, the EMED provision is very difficult to apply in the context of diminished capacity, because the latter concept is subjective — the defendant is not like an ordinary person because he suffers from an abnormal mental condition — yet the EMED standard is partially objective, *i.e.*, the provision includes the "*reasonable* explanation or excuse" language. More specifically, the issue in partial responsibility cases is not whether there is a reasonable explanation or excuse for the defendant's homicidal act, but rather whether there is a reasonable explanation or excuse for the defendant's EMED that caused him to take a life.[46]

To see how the EMED doctrine works in the context of mental abnormalities, consider *State v. Dumlao*:[47] *D* introduced testimony at his trial that he suffered from "paranoid personality disorder," a condition that caused him to experience "unwarranted suspiciousness" of other people's actions and to be hypersensitive to criticism. As a result of his condition, *D* irrationally believed that his wife was being unfaithful to him, and he became enraged when his brother-in-law and father

---

[41] Model Penal Code § 210.3(1)(b).

[42] *See* §§ 31.07 (common law) and 31.10[C][3] (Model Penal Code), *infra*.

[43] American Law Institute, Comment to § 210.3, at 72'73.

[44] State v. Perez, 976 P.2d 379 (Haw. 1999); State v. Counts, 816 P.2d 1157 (Or. 1991).

[45] American Law Institute, Comment to § 210.3, at 71.

[46] *See* People v. Casassa, 404 N.E.2d 1310, 1316 n.2 (N.Y. 1980).

[47] 715 P.2d 822 (Haw. Ct. App. 1986).

sought to counsel him about his suspicions. *D* took a life while in the preceding emotional state.

According to the appellate court, this evidence was sufficient to justify an instruction on EMED manslaughter. In determining whether there was a reasonable explanation or excuse for *D*'s disturbance, the court concluded that the jury should consider "the subjective, internal situation in which the defendant found himself and the external circumstances as he perceived them at the time, however inaccurate that perception may have been, and assess[] from that standpoint whether the explanation . . . for his emotional disturbance was reasonable."[48]

To summarize: The issue is not whether there was a reasonable explanation or excuse for the homicide *or* for *D*'s paranoid condition.[49] Instead, the issue is whether there was a reasonable explanation or excuse, *based on D's psychological characteristics*, for his emotional disturbance (here, his suspicion-based rage) at the time of the crime. *D*'s psychological makeup is relevant because the Code provides that the reasonableness of the actor's explanation for his rage should be considered "from the viewpoint of a person *in the actor's situation*," which includes his paranoid delusions and hypersensitivity, "under the circumstances as he believes them to be," which includes his paranoid belief that his wife was unfaithful to him.

The Commentary to the Code warns that the fact that an actor suffers from a mental disorder does not preclude a finding that he is morally depraved. Moreover, it states that "surely" cases will exist (although it offers no examples) in which a defendant's mental condition, although abnormal, "should be regarded as having no just bearing on his liability" for the intentional homicide.[50]

[B] Controversy Regarding the Defense[51]

As the American Law Institute concedes, the partial responsibility defense "brings formal guilt more closely into line with moral blameworthiness, but only at the cost of driving a wedge between dangerousness and social control."[52] Indeed, the very factor that mitigates an actor's blameworthiness — his mental abnormality — aggravates his dangerousness.[53]

Critics of psychiatry are troubled by the recognition of this defense. Even if agreement exists that at some gross level mental disease can be so severe that it is fair to excuse the defendant, they believe that the subtle gradations that this defense implies — the distinction between full, partial, and no mental abnormality — cannot reliably be determined.

---

[48] *Id.* at 830 (quoting *People v. Casassa*, 404 N.E.2d at 1316).

[49] As to the latter condition, unless a defendant can be blamed for "contracting" a mental abnormality, there will *always* be a reasonable explanation or excuse.

[50] American Law Institute, Comment to § 210.3, at 72.

[51] Dressler, Note 1, *supra*; Stephen J. Morse, *Diminished Rationality, Diminished Responsibility*, 1 Ohio St. J. Crim. L. 289 (2003); and Morse, *Undiminished Confusion*, Note 1, *supra*.

[52] American Law Institute, Comment to § 210.3, at 71–72.

[53] Arenella, Note 1, *supra*, at 857.

As a normative matter, as well, it has been argued that the partial responsibility doctrine is unjustified. A leading law and mental health scholar, Professor Stephen Morse, once opposed the defense. The criminal law does not require people to live up to a high moral standard; all it demands of citizens is that they *not* rob, rape, kill, and commit other serious offenses. Morse reasoned, therefore, that even if a person has a mental health problem (short of insanity), it is not difficult for him to avoid offending society's laws. Therefore, Morse called for abolition of *all* partial excuses to murder (*e.g.*, heat of passion and partial responsibility). He would have treated *all* sane intentional killers alike, "without regard to differences in background, mental or emotional condition, or other factors often thought to necessitate mitigation."[54]

However, even though it is true that it is not hard to avoid killing persons, it remains true that it *is* harder for some people to avoid violating the law than it is for others. For example, in *Fisher v. United States*,[55] *F*, an African-American of subnormal intelligence and a victim of an abnormal condition that made him highly aggressive, intentionally strangled *V* to death, after *V* uttered a racial epithet. *F* was convicted of murder. An advocate of the partial responsibility defense might respond that, although *F* assuredly deserved to be punished for his conduct, his mental condition, for which he was not culpable, rendered him less blameworthy than a "normal" person, because it was harder for *F* to avoid taking a life than for an ordinary person.[56] In the case of murder, in which the most severe penalties are imposed (in *Fisher*, *F* was executed), it may be appropriate to investigate an actor's mental condition with great care, and mitigate the offense when justice seems to require it, *i.e.*, when the defendant's choice-making capacities are undermined by a mental disease or defect.

And, indeed, on further reflection, Professor Morse now believes "that the moral claim [for a partial responsibility defense] is sufficiently weighty to justify bearing the potential practical costs."[57] Indeed, he now "proposes that the criminal law . . . include a generic, doctrinal mitigating excuse of partial responsibility that would apply to all crimes," and not simply murder.[58] Morse now agrees that such an excuse "is a moral imperative for a just criminal law that attempts never to punish defendants more than they deserve."[59]

---

[54] Morse, *Undiminished Confusion*, Note 1, *supra*, at 30.

[55] 328 U.S. 463 (1946).

[56] For a fuller exposition of this argument see Dressler, Note 1, *supra*.

[57] Stephen J. Morse, *Excusing and the New Excuse Defenses: A Legal and Conceptual Review*, 23 Crime and Just. 329, 397 (1998).

[58] Morse, Note 51, *supra*, at 289 (and thereafter laying out the specifics of the defense).

[59] *Id.* at 290. Morse continues, however, to oppose the specific partial excuse of "heat of passion." *Id.*

Chapter 27

ATTEMPT

§ 27.01 CRIMINAL ATTEMPTS: AN OVERVIEW TO INCHOATE CONDUCT[1]

When a person intentionally commits a crime, it is the result of a six-stage process.[2] First, the actor conceives the idea of committing a crime. Second, she evaluates the idea, in order to determine whether she should proceed. Third, she fully forms the intention, *i.e.*, resolves, to go forward and commit the crime. Fourth, she prepares to commit the crime, for example, by obtaining any instruments necessary for its commission. Fifth, she commences commission of the offense. Sixth, she completes her actions, thereby achieving her immediate criminal goal.[3] In some cases, of course, this process takes only seconds to transpire; in other circumstances, the six stages may take days, weeks, or even years, to complete.

Anglo-American law does not punish a person during the first three stages of the process. Until the third step occurs, the actor lacks a *mens rea*. Even after the *mens rea* is formed, she is not punished if there is no *actus reus* — people are not punished for thoughts alone.[4]

Activity in the middle ranges, *i.e.*, after the formation of the *mens rea* but short of attainment of the criminal goal, is described as "inchoate" — imperfect or incomplete — conduct. Anglo-American law recognizes various inchoate offenses, the most notable of which are attempt, solicitation, and conspiracy. This chapter focuses on the inchoate crime of attempt.

---

[1] *See generally* R. A. Duff, Criminal Attempts (1996); Jerome Hall, General Principles of the Criminal Law 558–99 (2d ed. 1960); Glanville Williams, Criminal Law: The General Part §§ 197–209 (2d ed. 1961); Joseph H Beale, Jr., *Criminal Attempts*, 16 Harv. L. Rev. 491 (1903); Douglas N. Husak, *The Nature and Justifiability of Nonconsummate Offenses*, 37 Ariz. L. Rev. 151 (1995); Rollin M. Perkins, *Criminal Attempt and Related Problems*, 2 UCLA L. Rev. 319 (1955); Francis Bowes Sayre, *Criminal Attempts*, 41 Harv. L. Rev. 821 (1928).

[2] *See* Hall, Note 1, *supra*, at 576.

[3] The actor may not have achieved her *ultimate* goal. For example, *D1* may hit *V1* in the eye in order to give her a black eye, but the eye does not bruise; or *D2* may kill *V2*, her business rival's husband, to cause the rival to sell her business, but the rival refuses to do so. In these cases, the actors have failed in their ultimate goals but the crimes of battery and murder have been committed. For criticism of this six-stage analysis, see Husak, Note 1, *supra*, at 166–67.

[4] Should this be so? Consider Stephen P. Garvey, *Are Attempts like Treason?*, 14 New Crim. L. Rev. 173, 212 (2011) ("[A]n actor who chooses to form the intent to commit a crime, and who perhaps in addition resolves to commit it, has violated a duty of loyalty to his fellow citizens, and a state should be permitted to punish him for that breach.").

Criminal attempts are of two varieties: "complete" (but "imperfect"); and "incomplete." A complete-but-imperfect attempt occurs when the actor performs all of the acts that she set out to do, but fails to attain her criminal goal. For example, if D, intending to kill V, purchases a gun, loads it, drives to V's home, waits for V to arrive, and then fires the weapon at V, but misses her target, this is a complete attempt. In contrast, an incomplete attempt occurs when the actor does some of the acts necessary to achieve the criminal goal, but she quits or is prevented from continuing, *e.g.*, a police officer arrives before completion of the attempt.

Inchoate conduct, including attempts, raise special enforcement issues that do not arise with successfully completed offenses. The earlier the police intervene to arrest for inchoate conduct, the greater the risk that suspicious looking, but innocent, conduct (and persons) will be punished, or that a person with a less than fully-formed criminal intent will be arrested before she has had the opportunity to reconsider and voluntarily desist. On the other hand, the longer the law requires police officers to abstain from intervention, the greater the risk that an actor will successfully complete an offense.[5]

§ 27.02 GENERAL PRINCIPLES

[A] Historical Background

Although language favoring punishment of inchoate conduct can be found in judicial opinions as early as the middle of the 14th century, the general offense of attempt was not recognized until 1784.[6] Until then, "in those forthright days, a miss was as good as a mile."[7]

Early on, a common law attempt was a misdemeanor, regardless of the nature or seriousness of the offense that the person sought to commit (*i.e.*, the "target" or "substantive" offense).

[B] Definition of "Attempt"

Until the Model Penal Code was drafted, most states punished, but did not expressly define, criminal attempts.[8] However, subject to substantial clarification in this chapter, a criminal attempt occurs when a person, with the intent to commit an offense, performs "some act done towards carrying out the intent."[9] Not just any act will do, however. The action must constitute a substantial step, beyond mere preparation, toward commission of the offense.[10] The term "substantial step" is a

---

[5] *See* § 27.06[A], *infra.*

[6] Rex v. Scofield, Caldecott 397 (1784).

[7] Hall, Note 1, *supra*, at 560.

[8] American Law Institute, Comment to § 5.01, at 300.

[9] United States v. Resendiz-Ponce, 549 U.S. 102, 127 S. Ct. 782, 787 (2007) (quoting Edwin R. Keedy, *Criminal Attempts at Common Law*, 102 U. Pa. L. Rev. 464, 468 (1954)).

[10] Dabney v. State, 858 A.2d 1084, 1089 (Md. Ct. Spec. App. 2004); State v. Reid, 679 S.E.2d 194, 198 (S.C. Ct. App. 2009).

term of art in the Model Penal Code,[11] but for current purposes, the "substantial step" required for a criminal attempt is, simply, any conduct that has reached the fifth stage of criminality described in Section 27.01, *i.e.*, conduct that has passed the *preparatory* stage and moved to the point of *perpetration* of the target offense.

In common law parlance, attempt is a specific-intent crime.

[C] Punishment of Attempts

As noted in subsection [A], a criminal attempt was a misdemeanor at common law, even when the target offense was a felony. Thus, an attempt to commit a felony was punished less severely than the target crime.

Today, an attempt to commit a felony is graded as a felony, but typically is treated as a lesser offense than the substantive crime.[12] Almost always, the penalty for an attempt to commit a capital crime or an offense for which the penalty is life imprisonment is set at a specific term of years of imprisonment. An attempt to commit a less serious felony is often punished at one-half of the maximum allowed for the target crime (or by some similar formula).

[D] Relationship of an Attempt to the Target Offense

A criminal attempt is "an adjunct crime; it cannot exist by itself, but only in connection with another crime,"[13] the so-called "target" or "substantive" offense.

Most jurisdictions provide in some form that a "person is guilty of a criminal attempt when, with intent to commit a crime, the person engages in conduct which constitutes a substantial step toward the commission of that crime *whether or not his intention is accomplished.*"[14] The implication of this quote is that, with crimes of intent, the successful commission of the target crime logically includes an attempt to commit it.

This point is significant for two reasons: (1) in a prosecution for a crime of intent (*e.g.*, rape), assuming appropriate facts, a jury may instead return a guilty verdict for the lesser offense of an attempt to commit the substantive crime (*e.g.*, attempted rape); and (2) in every case where an attempt is charged, proof of the commission of the target offense establishes the attempt.[15] However, if a person commits the target offense, she may *not* be convicted of both it and the criminal attempt.[16] If she was charged with the target offense, and the jury convicts her of this offense, the criminal attempt "merges" with the substantive crime; the lesser offense of attempt is absorbed by the greater one.

---

[11] *See* § 27.09[D], *infra.*

[12] This is not generally the case in jurisdictions that follow the lead of the Model Penal Code. *See* § 27.09[F][1], *infra.*

[13] Cox v. State, 534 A.2d 1333, 1335 (Md. 1988).

[14] Grill v. State, 651 A.2d 856, 857 (Md. App. 1995) (emphasis added); Crump v. State, 287 N.E.2d 342, 345 (Ind. 1972).

[15] Townes v. State, 548 A.2d 832, 834 (Md. 1988); Berry v. State, 280 N.W.2d 204, 209 (Wis. 1979).

[16] United States v. York, 578 F.2d 1036, 1040 (5th Cir. 1978).

In contrast to the preceding analysis, a few statutes and court opinions provide that *failure* to consummate the target offense is an essential element of a criminal attempt.[17] The implication of *this* statement is that a criminal attempt and the substantive offense are mutually exclusive crimes. A wrongdoer may commit the target offense or, perhaps, unsuccessfully attempt to commit it, but she can never do both.

[E] "Assault": "Attempt" in Different Clothing

[1] "Assault" Versus "Attempt"

In the early common law, a criminal assault was defined as an "attempted battery."[18] Today, most states have broadened the offense to include the tort version of assault, *i.e.*, intentionally placing another in reasonable apprehension of an imminent battery.[19] Thus, today an assault ordinarily is proved if *D* attempts to batter *V* or, even if she does not, if she intentionally places *V* in apprehension of an imminent battery. Today, as at common law, a simple assault is a misdemeanor. Aggravated assaults, *e.g.*, "assault with the intent to kill" and "assault with the intent to rape," are felonies.

Although a common law assault is an attempted battery, the law pertaining to criminal attempts does not apply to assaults. This is the result of an historical accident — assault law developed earlier and, therefore, independently of the crime of attempt. Specifically, for a criminal assault (attempted battery) to occur, a greater degree of proximity to completion of the offense is required than in the case of non-assault attempts. For example, although an attempted murder may occur before the victim is in the would-be assailant's sights, a common law assault does not occur until the defendant is within apparent reach of the victim.[20]

Another difference between assault and attempt pertains to the doctrine of "impossibility." As described more fully below,[21] a person may be convicted of an attempt even if consummation of the target offense is factually impossible. For example, *D* may be convicted of attempted murder if, with the intention of killing *V*, she pulls the trigger of an unloaded gun. In contrast, some statutes define "assault" as "an unlawful attempt, *coupled with a present ability*, to commit [a battery]."[22] Under this definition, *D* would not be guilty of *assault* if she fired an unloaded weapon at *V*.

---

[17] *E.g.*, Cal. Penal Code § 664 (2015) ("Every person who attempts to commit any crime, but fails, . . . is punishable."); People v. Lardner, 133 N.E. 375, 376 (Ill. 1921) ("The essentials of the attempt are the intent to commit the crime, the performance of some overt act towards its commission, and a failure to consummate the crime.").

[18] Rollin M. Perkins & Ronald N. Boyce, Criminal Law 159 (3d ed. 1982). A battery is any unlawful application of force to the person of another. American Law Institute, Comment to § 211.1, at 175.

[19] Carter v. Commonwealth, 594 S.E.2d 284, 288 (Va. Ct. App. 2004), *aff'd*, 606 S.E.2d 839 (Va. 2005).

[20] *E.g.*, State v. Boutin, 346 A.2d 531 (Vt. 1975) (in a scuffle, *B* walked toward *V* with a bottle raised over his head, apparently with the intention of striking *V* with it; the police intervened when *B* and *V* were 10 feet apart; held: assault conviction was reversed).

[21] *See* § 27.07, *infra*.

[22] *E.g.*, Cal. Penal Code § 240 (2015) (emphasis added).

[2] Attempted Assault

Inasmuch as a criminal attempt is a substantial step, beyond mere preparation, toward the commission of any offense, and assault is a criminal offense, the question arises whether a person may be convicted of "attempted assault." Since a common law assault is an attempted battery, an attempted assault would be an attempt to attempt to commit a battery, *i.e.*, a substantial step beyond mere preparation toward committing a substantial step beyond mere preparation toward committing a battery!

Some courts have upheld convictions for attempted common law assault.[23] They reason that because an assault does not occur unless the assailant is near enough to the victim that she can immediately batter her, it should be possible to convict a person of *attempted* assault if she endeavors to place herself in such a position, but fails to do so.

Other courts, however, do not recognize the offense of an attempted (common law) assault.[24] Such jurisdictions fear "a perversion of the law of attempt":[25] If an attempt to commit an attempt were permitted, "there could be a never ending domino effect backward from the targeted crime. . . . [T]here might then be urged upon [a court] an attempted attempt, and so on *ad infinitum* until the *actus reus* would completely disappear into the bare *mens rea*."[26] Or, if such a "double inchoate" offense were permitted, a person might be convicted on the basis of innocent, albeit suspicious appearing, conduct.[27]

[F] Inchoate Crimes in Disguise

Some common law and statutory offenses, although defined as if they were complete crimes, are inchoate offenses in disguise. Indeed, some such offenses prohibit conduct less proximate to completion than is required for a criminal attempt. For example, common law burglary is defined as "breaking and entering the dwelling house of another at night with the intent to commit a felony therein." Thus, a fully consummated burglary is "inchoate to a theft or to some other crime intended to be committed on the inside" of the dwelling.[28]

---

[23] *E.g.*, People v. O'Connell, 14 N.Y.S. 485 (1891); State v. Wilson, 346 P.2d 115, 121 (Or. 1959) (applying state law since superseded by statute).

[24] *E.g.*, Allen v. People, 485 P.2d 886 (Colo. 1971); *see* Wilson v. State, 53 Ga. 205, 206 (1874) (suggesting that such an offense "is like conceiving of the beginning of eternity or the starting place of infinity"). An "attempted assault" of the tort variety is recognized, however.. *E.g.*, People v. Jones, 504 N.W.2d 158, 164 (Mich. 1993).

[25] American Law Institute, Comment to § 211.1, at 179.

[26] Dabney v. State, 858 A.2d 1084, 1097 (Md. 2004).

[27] *E.g.*, McQuirter v. State, 63 So. 2d 388, 390 (Ala. Ct. App. 1953) (*M* was convicted of "attempted assault with intent to rape," based on evidence that he, an African-American man, followed *V*, a white woman, somewhat closely down the street; the court affirmed the conviction, stating that "the jury may consider social conditions and customs founded upon racial differences, such as that the prosecutrix was a white woman and defendant was a Negro man").

[28] *Dabney v. State*, 858 A.2d at 1098; *see generally* Helen A. Anderson, *From the Thief in the Night to the Guest Who Stayed Too Long: The Evolution of Burglary in the Shadow of the Common Law*, 45 Ind. L.J. 629 (2012).

The crime of burglary serves the purpose of compensating for stringencies found in the law of attempt. The act of breaking into another person's home in order to commit a felony inside may sometimes fall short of a criminal attempt to commit the in-dwelling crime. For example, suppose *D* intends to break into *V*'s residence, obtain a kitchen knife, and then enter *V*'s second-floor bedroom and kill her. On these facts, *D* might not be guilty of attempted murder when she breaks into the home. Recognition of the substantive crime of burglary, therefore, allows a police officer who observes *D*'s conduct to arrest her as she enters the dwelling, while she still is within the practical reach of the officer. Indeed, recognition of the crime of burglary allows for preventive law enforcement even before *D* enters, when she is guilty of an *attempted* burglary!

The common law offense of larceny, as well, has an inchoate aspect to it. A person is guilty of larceny if she takes and carries away the personal property of another with the intent to permanently deprive the other of the property.[29] In essence, larceny occurs the instant the thief wrongfully moves the property even an inch, long before the permanent loss — the *ultimate* harm — results.

Other offenses of a statutory nature include such double or triple inchoate crimes as possession of burglars' tools,[30] stalking,[31] and child luring.[32]

§ 27.03 "SUBJECTIVISM" AND "OBJECTIVISM"[33]

According to Austin, "[g]enerally, attempts are perfectly innocuous, and the party is punished . . . in respect of what he intended to do."[34] In other words, a person who attempts a crime is punished for possessing a *mens rea*; no harm is required.

On its face, Austin's perception seems correct. Many incomplete attempts, and even some complete but imperfect ones,[35] appear to be harmless. For example, suppose that *D1* lies in wait with a loaded gun outside *V1*'s house, intending to kill *V1* when she returns home. Just as *V1* shows up, and *D1* points the gun at *V1*, a police officer drives by and arrests *D1* for attempted murder. Or, suppose that *D2*,

---

[29] *See* Chapter 32, *infra.*

[30] *E.g.*, Cal. Penal Code § 466 (2015).

[31] *E.g.*, Ala. Code § 13A-6-90(a) (2015) ("A person who intentionally and repeatedly follows or harasses another person and who makes a credible threat . . . with the intent to place that person in reasonable fear of death or serious bodily harm is guilty of the crime of stalking.").

[32] *E.g.*, N.J. Stat. Ann. § 2C:13-6 (2015) ("A person commits a crime . . . if he attempts . . . to lure or entice a child . . . into a motor vehicle . . . with a purpose to commit a criminal offense . . . against the child.").

[33] *See generally* George P. Fletcher, Rethinking Criminal Law 115–22, 135–84 (1978); Andrew Ashworth, *Criminal Attempts and the Role of Resulting Harm Under the Code, and in the Common Law*, 19 Rutgers L.J. 725 (1988); Lawrence Crocker, *Justice in Criminal Liability: Decriminalizing Harmless Attempts*, 53 Ohio St. L.J. 1057 (1992); Garvey, Note 4, *supra*; Paul H. Robinson & John M. Darley, *Objectivist Versus Subjectivist Views of Criminality: A Study in the Role of Social Science in Criminal Law Theory*, 18 Oxford J. Legal Studies 409 (1998); Thomas Weigend, *Why Lady Eldon Should Be Acquitted: The Social Harm in Attempting the Impossible*, 27 DePaul L. Rev. 231 (1977).

[34] 1 John Austin, Lectures on Jurisprudence 523 (4th ed. 1873).

[35] For the definition of "incomplete" and "complete" attempts, see § 27.01, *supra.*

intending to kill spouse *V2*, who is asleep in bed, points a gun at *V2* and pulls the trigger, only to discover that the gun is unloaded. *V2* sleeps through the attempt, and goes on with her life oblivious of *D2*'s efforts. *D1* and *D2* are guilty of attempted murder, but *V1* and *V2* have suffered no apparent harm.

But, this does not end the analysis. As earlier defined,[36] there is social harm whenever a person "negates, *endangers* or destroys" an individual, group, or state interest that is socially valuable. When a person lies in wait in order to kill another, or pulls the trigger of a gun, she endangers another person's bodily security, jeopardizes the interests of loved ones of the intended victim, and impairs society's interest in a safe community in which to live. Likewise, when a person comes close to violating one of society's moral and legal commandments, she tears the fabric of society, if only slightly. Contrary to Austin's assertions, therefore, criminal attempts are *not* innocuous; criminal attempts *do* cause social harm, even if only intangible.

Notwithstanding the deficiency, Austin's statement serves as a useful starting point for considering two conflicting perceptions of the proper roles of social harm and personal culpability in criminal attempt law. The competing philosophies may be characterized as "subjectivism" and "objectivism." As will become evident in later sections of this chapter, the criminal attempt provisions of the Model Penal Code are largely based on subjectivist conceptions of inchoate liability, whereas the common law of attempts includes many strands of objectivist thought, as well as some subjectivism.

Subjectivists assert that, in determining guilt and calibrating punishment, the criminal law in general, and attempt law in particular, should focus nearly exclusively on an actor's subjective intentions (her *mens rea*) — her choice to commit a crime — rather than on her conduct, which may or may not result in injury. The subjective intentions of an actor simultaneously bespeak her danger-ousness and bad character (or, at least, her morally culpable choice-making). With inchoate offenses, a subjectivist believes that "the act of execution is important [only] so far as it verifies the firmness of the [actor's] intent."[37] In a subjectivist system, therefore, any act — no matter how innocuous — that verifies the actor's commitment to carry out a criminal plan, or which corroborates her confession or other incriminating evidence, is sufficient to justify punishment for an inchoate offense.[38]

In contrast, objectivists believe that conduct should not be punished unless the defendant's "acts performed, without any reliance on the accompanying *mens rea*, mark [her] . . . conduct as criminal in nature."[39] According to George Fletcher, with objectivism, "[t]he assumption is that a neutral third-party observer could recognize the activity as criminal even if [she] had no special knowledge about the offender's intention."[40] For an objectivist, criminal liability only occurs when the inchoate conduct manifests criminality and, therefore, causes social harm by "disturb[ing]

---

[36] *See* § 9.10[B], *supra.*

[37] Fletcher, Note 33, *supra*, at 138.

[38] Indeed, why wait for *any* act if we know his thoughts from some reliable source? *See* Note 4, *supra.*

[39] United States v. Oviedo, 525 F.2d 881, 885 (5th Cir. 1976).

[40] Fletcher, Note 33, *supra*, at 116.

the public repose,"[41] "unnerving . . . the community,"[42] or by causing apprehension, fear or alarm in the community because the actor has patently "set out to do serious damage . . . and to break the accepted rules of social life."[43] Once *this* social harm has been observed, the actor's *mens rea* is relevant in order to determine whether she should be held accountable for the societal harm that she has caused.

Subjectivists and objectivists will frequently reach the same result regarding criminal liability, but for different reasons. For example, reconsider the two hypotheticals at the beginning of this chapter section. Subjectivists and objectivists alike would convict *D1* (who was lying in wait) and *D2* (with her unloaded gun) of attempted murder. Subjectivists would favor conviction on the basis of the defendants' *mens rea*, *i.e.*, her decision to break the law. The actors' conduct would be of limited significance, *i.e.*, to verify the fact that their homicidal intentions were genuine and fixed. Conduct considerably less proximate to the outcome would be sufficient to justify punishment.

From an objectivist perspective, the criminality of the defendants' conduct is easily discernible to a hypothetical observer on the basis of their conduct alone. Therefore, assuming sufficient corroboration of the actors' *mens rea*, objectivists would also punish *D1* and *D2*. However, if the actors' conduct had terminated at an earlier stage — *e.g.*, while *D1* was driving to *V1*'s house, or after *D2* loaded the gun but before she pointed it at her spouse[44] — the criminality of their conduct might not have been manifest, in which case objectivists would not favor conviction.

The difference between subjectivism and objectivism may be seen more dramatically if one considers the following simple event: *D3* puts sugar in spouse-*V3*'s coffee. Is this attempted murder? Of course not. Suppose, however, that we learn that *D3* had told a friend a day earlier that she intended to put a lethal dose of poison in *V3*'s coffee the next morning, and suppose further that *D3* oddly thought that the sugar was arsenic. If we are convinced beyond a reasonable doubt from this new information that *D3* intended to kill *V3*, and that the act of putting sugar in the coffee was a misguided act in execution of this murderous plan, the subjectivist would punish *D3* for attempted murder. The innocuous conduct of putting sugar in *V3*'s coffee verifies *D3*'s criminal intent.

An objectivist seemingly would *not* convict *D3*. An objectivist would look at the conduct, without consideration of *D3*'s prior incriminating statements or subjective belief that the substance was arsenic. Based on conduct alone, the act of placing sugar in coffee does not demonstrate criminality. Therefore, in the absence of knowledge of *D3*'s intentions and beliefs, her conduct would not cause public alarm or unnerve the hypothetical observer.[45] Notwithstanding other evidence of *D3*'s

---

[41] Clark v. State, 8 S.W. 145, 147 (Tenn. 1888).

[42] Fletcher, Note 33, *supra*, at 144.

[43] Weigend, Note 33, *supra*, at 264 (footnote omitted).

[44] Since *D2* and *V2* live in the same house together, as wife and husband, there is nothing manifestly criminal about one spouse loading a firearm in their home.

[45] Of course, the issue will rarely be as simple for the objectivist as is described in the text. How does the hypothetical observer know that the white substance put in the coffee is sugar, rather than arsenic? Suppose that the sugar is spooned into the coffee cup from a container labeled "poison," but which

mens rea — and thus of her dangerousness and moral culpability — the objectivist would not punish *D3*, for want of social harm from the conduct itself.

§ 27.04   PUNISHING ATTEMPTS: WHY, AND HOW MUCH?[46]

[A]   Rationale for Punishing Attempts

[1]   Utilitarian Analysis

Professor H.L.A. Hart has written that "[i]t is not obvious . . . on some versions of utilitarian theory, why attempts should be punishable, as they are, in most legal systems."[47] After all, an attempt is merely conduct targeted at commission of a substantive crime. Those who set out to commit a crime expect to succeed. Therefore, any deterrent effect of threatened punishment emanates from the target offense; the penalty threatened for an attempt has no additional influence. As it is inefficacious, it should not be inflicted.

As Hart has demonstrated, this utilitarian argument is fallacious. First, a person may assume that if she is successful in her conduct she will avoid detection, so she will be willing to risk the penalty for the targeted crime. On the other hand, she may figure that if she fails in her attempt it will be because she executed the crime poorly, in which case her poor execution may result in arrest. Therefore, she may be deterred by the punishment imposed for an attempt.

Second, applying subjectivist theories,[48] anyone who attempts to commit a crime is dangerous. Whether or not she succeeds in her criminal venture, she is likely to represent an ongoing threat to the community. Therefore, her incapacitation and/or rehabilitation is justifiable, even if she fails in her criminal plans.

Third, criminal attempt laws serve a valuable preventive law enforcement purpose: If there were no inchoate offenses in a penal code, police officers would lack legal authority to stop criminal activities before they are consummated.

---

strangely contains sugar? Would the hypothetical observer know that the substance is sugar, or would she believe that it is poison? One scholar has suggested that "our hypothetical observer, if he is to be of any help at all, must be thought of as having a correct notion of all objective circumstances of the defendant's act which can be observed from outside." Weigend, Note 33, *supra*, at 267. Under this view, the observer would know that the substance is sugar, although it is being removed from a poison container.

[46] Ashworth, Note 33, *supra*; Theodore Y. Blumoff, *A Jurisprudence for Punishing Attempts Asymmetrically*, 6 Buff. Crim. L. Rev. 951 (2003); Björn Burkhardt, *Is There a Rational Justification for Punishing an Accomplished Crime More Severely than an Attempted Crime?*, 1986 BYU L. Rev. 553; Russell Christopher, *Does Attempted Murder Deserve Greater Punishment than Murder? Moral Luck and the Duty to Prevent Harm*, 18 Notre Dame J.L. Ethics & Pub. Pol'y 419 (2004); Michael Davis, *Why Attempts Deserve Less Punishment than Complete Crimes*, 5 Law & Phil. 1 (1986); Joel Feinberg, *Equal Punishment for Failed Attempts: Some Bad but Instructive Arguments Against It*, 37 Ariz. L. Rev. 117 (1995); Marcelo Ferrante, *Deterrence and Crime Results*, 10 New Crim. L. Rev. 1 (2007); Barbara Herman, *Feinberg on Luck and Failed Attempts*, 37 Ariz. L. Rev. 143 (1995); Sanford H. Kadish, *The Criminal Law and the Luck of the Draw*, 84 J. Crim. L. & Criminology 679 (1994).

[47] H.L.A. Hart, Punishment and Responsibility 128 (1968).

[48] *See* § 27.03, *supra*.

[2] Retributive Analysis

Punishment of attempts makes sense under retributive theory, although retributivists differ in their basis for defending attempt laws. Some retributivists focus on the culpability of criminal attempters. These *culpability-retributivists* argue that a person who, for example, shoots but misses her intended victim is as morally culpable as one who succeeds in her endeavor. After all, she has done everything in her control to consummate the target offense. The only difference between her and the successful wrongdoer is her bad aim or the fortuity of the victim's movement. The attempter, therefore, deserves to be punished.

A second group of retributivists, *harm-retributivists*, focus instead on the harm caused by at attempter. A person who attempts to commit a crime, by her actions, endangers the community; she "disturbs the order of things ordained by law."[49] By disturbing the public's repose and causing any other social harm that flows from the attempt, "punishment is necessary so as to restore, at least symbolically," the public order.[50]

[B] Less or Equal Punishment?

[1] Overview to the Issue

Once it is determined that inchoate conduct should be punished, the question turns to one of grading. At common law and in most jurisdictions today, an attempt to commit a felony is considered a less serious crime and, therefore, is punished less severely, than the target offense. Is this traditional "differential punishment" approach justifiable, or should an attempt be graded and punished at the same level as a successful criminal enterprise, as is generally the case in states following the Model Penal Code?[51] It is here that the subjectivist/objectivist debate[52] comes into clearer focus. As the discussion below suggests, in general, subjectivists favor equal punishment; objectivists do not.

Social science studies suggest that most persons in the United States intuitively are "objectivist-grading subjectivist[s]."[53] That is, people tend to be subjectivist (they focus on an actor's state of mind) in determining what the minimum criteria should be for holding an actor criminally responsible for her inchoate conduct, but once it is determined that punishment is appropriate and the issue is how much punishment to inflict, they tend to become objectivist (they focus on resulting harm) and favor the common law lesser-punishment result. Are these intuitions defensible?

---

[49] Ashworth, Note 33, *supra*, at 735.

[50] *Id.*

[51] *See* § 27.09[F][1], *infra*.

[52] *See* § 27.03, *supra*.

[53] Robinson & Darley, Note 33, *supra*, at 430.

[2]   Utilitarian Analysis

Utilitarian advocates of equal punishment argue that a person who attempts to commit a crime is no less dangerous and no less in need of rehabilitation than one who succeeds in her criminal endeavor. Assume three persons, A, B, and C, each intending to kill another person. A aims a gun at V1, but is arrested before she pulls the trigger. B shoots V2, but through the heroic efforts of hospital personnel, V2 survives the attack. C kills V3. Utilitarian advocates for equal punishment, applying subjectivist criteria, say that nothing distinguishes the actors here except simple luck. The actors' intentions are the same; their criminal resolve is the same; they are equally dangerous. Punishment, therefore, should be the same.

This argument may prove too much. Blackstone has reasoned that "[f]or evil, the nearer we approach it, is the more disagreeable and shocking, so that it requires more obstinacy and wickedness to perpetrate an unlawful action, than barely to entertain the thought of it."[54] If it takes more "obstinacy" and "wickedness" — which can also be characterized as dangerousness — to come closer to committing an offense than to "barely entertain the thought of it," then it may follow that "from the moment the defendant's conduct crosses the threshold of an attempt [and, therefore, merits punishment], up until the completion of the attempt, the punishments should ideally be graded with increasing severity."[55] In other words, a complete, but imperfect, attempt should be punished at the same level as the target offense, whereas incomplete attempts would require less punishment. But, this argument may itself fail, since the only reason that an attempt is incomplete may be factors outside the actor's control (e.g., the presence of a police officer and/or absence of the victim), and not factors that demonstrate a less dangerous character.

The better utilitarian argument for lesser punishment is that mitigated punishment provides "an encouragement to repentance and remorse,"[56] i.e., reduced punishment serves as an incentive to the actor to desist before completing the attempt. For example, if a person entering a bank to rob it already is subject to the punishment imposed for a successful robbery, she has one less reason to stop short. The same reasoning would apply to some completed attempts: If D sends V a mail bomb which is set to explode the next day, the attempt is complete (she has done every act in her power to commit the offense); but if punishment for attempted murder is less than for murder, D has a powerful incentive to prevent detonation of the bomb.[57]

[3]   Retributive Analysis

Culpability-retributivists[58] generally believe that a failed attempt should be punished as severely as an accomplished crime. They reason that luck — whether the attempt succeeds or fails — should play no role in setting the punishment of a

---

[54] 4 William Blackstone, Commentaries on the Laws of England *14 (1769).

[55] Ashworth, Note 33, *supra*, at 739.

[56] 4 Blackstone, Note 54, *supra*, at *14.

[57] *See also* Ferrante, Note 46, *supra* (based on social and psychological findings, the author provides a deterrence-based argument for differential punishment).

[58] See § 27.04[A][2], *supra*, for the definition of this term.

wrongdoer. A person should be punished depending on her moral desert; and, as Professor Sanford Kadish puts it, "desert [is] the same whether or not the harm occurs."[59] A person deserves punishment proportional to her culpability, and "fault depends on [the] choice to do the wrongful action, not on what is beyond [her] control," namely, whether the harm intended occurs.

Harm-retributivists disagree.[60] They reason that punishment should be apportioned according to culpability *and* harm. After all, the criminal law punishes for external results, not merely for culpable thoughts; it is the harm that an actor culpably causes that generates the debt that she must repay through her punishment. Put another way, the criminally successful actor and the unsuccessful one "have done different things. They are indeed equally morally blameworthy, but that fact determines not the degree of punishment that is appropriate, but their equal eligibility for penal sanction."[61] Since the harm caused by a failed attempt is less than that caused by the successful commission of the targeted crime, the debt owed by the attempter is less than that of the successful wrongdoer. Therefore, the traditional approach to attempt law is correct: A criminal attempt should always be a lesser offense than the consummated crime.

§ 27.05 *MENS REA* OF CRIMINAL ATTEMPTS[62]

[A] General Rule

It is sometimes said that the mental state required for a criminal attempt is "the intent to commit some other crime."[63] This is an accurate statement, as far as it goes. It is more complete to say, however, that a criminal attempt involves two "intents": the actor (1) must intentionally commit the acts that constitute the *actus reus* of an attempt (as the latter concept is explained in Section 27.06), that is, she must intentionally perform acts that bring her in proximity to commission of a substantive offense; and (2) she must perform these acts with the specific intention of committing the target crime. As the latter intent suggests, an attempt is a specific-intent offense,[64] *even if the target offense is a general-intent crime.*

To see how the dual "intents" work, suppose that *D*, a hunter, fires a gun in the woods, wounding *V. D* is guilty of attempted murder of *V* if: (1) she intentionally pulled the trigger of the gun (as this would satisfy the first "intent" required above); and (2) she did so intending to kill *V* (the second, and specific, intent). If *D* intentionally pulled the trigger of the gun, but she did *not* intend to kill *V* by her intentional acts, then *D* is *not* guilty of attempted murder.

---

[59] Kadish, Note 46, *supra*, at 688.

[60] See § 27.04[A][2], *supra*, for the definition of this term.

[61] Herman, Note 46, *supra*, at 149; Duff, Note 1, *supra*, at 337–38.

[62] *See generally* Larry Alexander & Kimberly D. Kessler, *Mens Rea and Inchoate Crimes*, 87 J. Crim. L. & Criminology 1138 (1997); Michael T. Cahill, *Attempt, Reckless Homicide, and the Design of Criminal Law*, 78 U. Colo. L. Rev. 879 (2007); Arnold N. Enker, *Mens Rea and Criminal Attempt*, 1977 Am. B. Found. Res. J. 845.

[63] State v. Green, 480 A.2d 526, 534 (Conn. 1984).

[64] State v. Reid, 679 S.E.2d 194, 198 (S.C. Ct. App. 2009).

Although this rule seemingly is straightforward, various issues arise that require clarification.

[B] "Result" Crimes

[1] In General

A "result" crime is an offense defined in terms of a prohibited result. For example, the offense of murder prohibits the result of the death of a human being at the hands of another. For crimes of this nature, the ordinary rule is that a person is not guilty of an attempt unless her actions in furtherance of the prohibited result are committed with the specific purpose[65] of causing the unlawful result.

Because of the specific-intent nature of a criminal attempt, the prosecutor in an attempt prosecution is sometimes required to prove that the actor possessed a *higher degree* of culpability than is required to commit the target offense. For example, if *D* blindfolds herself and fires a loaded pistol into a room that she knows is occupied, she may be convicted of murder if someone is killed. Such a killing, although unintentional, constitutes malice aforethought (the *mens rea* of murder), because it evinces a reckless disregard for the value of human life.[66] However, if *D*'s reckless act does *not* kill anyone in the room, almost all jurisdictions would rule that she is *not* guilty of *attempted* murder[67] (although she could be guilty of a statutory offense, such as reckless endangerment): *D* purposely aimed and fired the gun — she intentionally performed the acts that brought her close to taking human life — but she lacked the specific intent to kill anyone in the room.

Similarly, if *D* intends to severely injure *V*, *D*'s state of mind constitutes malice, so she may be convicted of murder if she unintentionally kills *V*. If *V* does not die from the attack, however, *D* is not guilty of attempted murder, as she lacked the

---

[65] Suppose that a person does not want the result to occur but knows that it will take place. Is knowledge, rather than purpose, sufficient *mens rea* to be convicted of attempt? Reconsider a hypothetical discussed earlier in the text at § 10.04[A][1], *supra*: *D* plants a bomb in an airplane so that it will explode in air and kill *V*, *D*'s spouse. *D* knows that, short of a miracle, every other passenger on the airplane will also die. At common law, a person causes a result "intentionally" if it is her conscious object to cause the result (she causes it "*purposely*") or if she *knowingly* causes the result. Therefore, if the bomb explodes, *D* may be convicted of "intentionally" killing each passenger. If the bomb fails to go off, however, is *D* guilty of *attempted* murder of the passengers. (*D* is clearly guilty of attempted murder of *V*, as *V*'s death was *D*'s conscious object.) The common law answer to this question is uncertain. American Law Institute, Comment to § 5.01, at 305. The Model Penal Code resolution of this hypothetical is described at § 27.09[C], *infra*.

[66] *See* § 31.05, *infra*.

[67] Thacker v. Commonwealth, 114 S.E. 504, 506 (Va. 1922) (shooting into a tent without the specific intent to kill does not constitute attempted murder); People v. Lee, 738 P.2d 752, 754 (Cal. 1987) (specific intent to kill is a required element of attempted murder; lesser forms of malice are insufficient); Commonwealth v. Foster, 522 A.2d 277, 282 (Conn. 1987) (same); People v. Gentry, 510 N.E.2d 963, 966 (Ill. App. Ct. 1987) (same); Dominguez v. State, 840 N.W.2d 596, 600 (N.D. 2013) (same); State v. Casey, 82 P.3d 1106, 1115 (Utah 2003) (same); *contra*, People v. Thomas, 729 P.2d 972 (Colo. 1986) (recognizing the offense of attempted reckless manslaughter, and reinstating a conviction for this offense in a case in which *T* fired a gun three times in *V*'s direction, hitting him twice accidentally); People v. Castro, 657 P.2d 932 (Colo. 1983) (recognizing the offense of attempted extreme-indifference murder).

specific intent to kill.[68]

[2] Rationale of Intent Requirement: Does It Make Sense?

Why does the law not punish unintentional "attempts"? One answer could be purely etymological: The word "attempt" means "to try," which in turn means "to seek to do." This basis for the intent requirement, however, cannot take us very far. If the only obstacle to permitting guilt for unintentional "attempts" is the meaning of the word "attempt," legislators can simply change the name of the crime. The more important question is whether the requirement of specific intent makes good penal sense. Should the law be changed, for example, to permit the conviction of a person for an attempt as long as she acts with the same level of culpability regarding the prohibited result as would be sufficient to convict her for the completed offense? Or, why not at least permit conviction for criminal attempts if the actor's conduct constitutes recklessness?

Those who defend the intent requirement sometimes focus on the supposed heightened dangerousness of intentional wrongdoers. One who intends to commit an offense and takes substantial steps in that direction, but who fails in its commission or is required temporarily to desist, remains an ongoing threat, *i.e.*, "the actor's unspent intent is itself a source of harm independent of his conduct."[69] The danger is that after the failed attempt or involuntary desistance, the actor will try again to commit the crime. In contrast, one who acts recklessly or negligently is less apt to represent an ongoing threat. For example, one who drives recklessly or negligently in order to get to the airport for a flight, but who fortunately kills nobody in the process, has no "unspent" intent to kill that is apt to recur. Although the law may choose to punish the driver for her reckless driving, her conduct should not be equated with an attempted — intentional — harmdoer.

Critics of the intent requirement contend that the policies underlying the target offense should apply to criminal attempts. They "emphasize[] the illogic of requiring the state to prove an intent for successful prosecution of an attempt to commit a crime when no such degree of proof is necessary for successful prosecution of the completed crime."[70] If the common law or a legislature considers reckless indifference to the value of human life a sufficiently culpable frame of mind to justify a murder conviction when a person dies, it should be adequate for conviction of attempted murder, if nobody dies.[71]

Various scholars have advocated a recklessness *mens rea* for criminal attempts: "[A]ctors are culpable because they choose to impose risks on others for insufficient reasons. When an actor chooses to engage in risky conduct, she does so by willing the movement of her body. . . . [I]t is her volition that is the appropriate locus of culpability."[72] Following this reasoning, once a person chooses to risk harm to

---

[68] State v. Hawkins, 631 So. 2d 1288, 1290 (La. Ct. App. 1994).

[69] Enker, Note 62, *supra*, at 855.

[70] Gentry v. State, 437 So. 2d 1097, 1098 (Fla. 1983).

[71] This is the rule in Colorado. See the Colorado cites in Note 67, *supra.*

[72] Larry Alexander & Kimberly Kessler Ferzan, Crime and Culpability: A Theory of Criminal Law 230 (2009).

another by, for example, voluntarily pulling the trigger of a gun, she should be guilty of an attempt (if the bullet fails to kill) or murder (if it does take life).[73] It is submitted, however, that if the law were to be changed in this manner, a "reckless attempt" should be punished less severely than the traditional intentional attempter.

[3]   Special Homicide Problems

[a]   Attempted Felony-Murder

Suppose that *D intentionally* commits a felony, during the perpetration of which another person *unintentionally* dies. At common law, *D* is guilty of murder as the result of the felony-murder rule.[74] Suppose, however, *D accidentally* fires a gun during the felony, and *V* is wounded. May *D* be convicted of *attempted* felony-murder?

All but two states[75] that have considered this issue have held that attempted felony-murder is not a cognizable offense.[76] This is consistent with the general rule that the offense of attempted murder requires a specific intent to kill; the defendant's intent to commit a felony does not substitute for the intent to kill a human being.

If a jurisdiction is going to recognize the offense, it is difficult to determine at what instant an attempted felony-murder occurs. Presumably, the doctrine would apply if the actor unintentionally wounds a person during the commission of the felony. But, in one state in which the offense is recognized, an attempted felony-murder conviction was allowed when a rapist fired his weapon but struck nobody.[77] Indeed, one may ask whether firing a weapon is necessary. Suppose that an attempted rapist displays a gun or knife and *V* suffers an unforeseeable non-lethal heart-attack as a result? In Florida, "attempted felony murder" occurs when one "commits, aids or abets an intentional act that is not an essential element of the felony and that could, but does not, cause the death of another."[78] It would seem that conviction under this remarkable statute would be possible in the latter hypothetical. Indeed, it is not clear that the victim would have to suffer the cardiac attack in order for an attempted felony-murder conviction to be allowed!

---

[73] For further, thoughtful discussion of this topic, see Cahill, Note 62, *supra.*

[74] *See* § 31.06, *infra.*

[75] White v. State, 585 S.W.2d 952 (Ark. 1979); Fla. Stat. ch. § 782.051 (2015).

[76] Among the states that have ruled that attempted felony-murder is not a cognizable offense are People v. Meyer, 952 P.2d 774 (Colo. Ct. App. 1997); State v. Robinson, 883 P.2d 764, 767 (Kan. 1994); State v. Lea, 485 S.E.2d 874, 877 (N.C. Ct. App. 1997); State v. Nolan, 25 N.E.3d 1016, 1017 (Ohio 2014); State v. Kimbrough, 924 S.W.2d 888, 892 (Tenn. 1996); and Goodson v. Commonwealth, 467 S.E.2d 848, 855 (Va. Ct. App. 1996).

[77] White v. State, 585 S.W.2d 952 (Ark. 1979).

[78] Fla. Stat. ch. § 782.051(1) (2015).

[b] Attempted Manslaughter

A person who intentionally kills another in sudden heat of passion, as the result of adequate provocation, is guilty of voluntary manslaughter.[79] If a person in such an emotional state attempts to kill the provoker, but fails, the actor may properly be convicted of attempted voluntary manslaughter.[80] No reason of logic precludes this result, as the provoked actor possesses the specific intent to kill.

The overwhelming rule is that a person may not be convicted of attempted *involuntary* manslaughter, as the latter offense is based on a *mens rea* of criminal negligence or, perhaps, recklessness.[81] As long as attempt is understood to be a specific intent offense, it is illogical to say that a person can intentionally commit an unintentional crime.[82]

[C] "Conduct" Crimes

The issues described in the preceding subsection — convicting a person for a result crime on the basis of a lesser *mens rea* than intent — should be distinguished from prosecutions pertaining to "conduct" crimes, *i.e.*, crimes defined in terms of conduct rather than injurious results. For example, the offense of "reckless endangerment" punishes dangerous conduct, even if such endangering conduct does not result in further physical harm to others.

Although very little case law exists on the point, it is submitted that there is no logical reason why a person should not be convicted of an attempt to commit such a conduct crime, as long as she possesses the specific intent to engage in the conduct which, if performed, would constitute the substantive offense. For example, suppose that *D* drives her car blindfolded, as a practical joke. This conduct, it may be assumed, would constitute reckless endangerment of others. Therefore, it follows that if *D* enters her car, blindfolds herself, turns on the ignition, but is arrested at that moment, she should be convicted of *attempted* reckless endangerment: She has intentionally committed the *actus reus* of the attempt by purposely blindfolding herself and turning on the car ignition; and she has the specific intent to drive the car on the road in a manner that a jury could conclude is reckless.[83]

[D] Attendant Circumstances

Suppose that *D*, believing that *V* is 18 years of age, has sexual intercourse with her. In fact, *V* is 15, under the age of legal consent for intercourse. In the vast majority of jurisdictions, in a prosecution for statutory rape, *D*'s mistake of fact, even if reasonable, will not excuse him. This is because statutory rape laws are

---

[79] *See* § 31.07[B][2], *infra*.

[80] *E.g.*, Cox v. State, 534 A.2d 1333, 1336 (Md. 1988); State v. Robinson, 643 A.2d 591, 597 (N.J. 1994).

[81] *Cox v. State*, 534 A.2d at 1336.

[82] *Id.*

[83] *Contra* Minshew v. State, 594 So. 2d 703, 713 (Ala. Crim. App. 1991) (holding that the offense of attempted reckless endangerment "is legally impossible").

interpreted to be strict-liability in nature in regard to the attendant circumstance of the female's age.

Suppose, however, that *D* is arrested immediately before intercourse occurs. Is *D* guilty of *attempted* statutory rape? That is, what *mens rea* regarding an attendant circumstance (here, the female's age) is required for the offense of attempt? There is relatively little case law on point, but virtually all commentators agree that the ordinary specific-intent requirement of attempt law should not apply to attendant circumstances.[84] Some commentators favor the proposition that a person should be convicted of a criminal attempt if she is reckless with regard to any attendant circumstance.[85] Thus, in the statutory rape case, *D* would not be guilty of attempted statutory rape unless he knew that there was a substantial risk that the female was underage.

Other commentators would not impose a special *mens rea* requirement regarding attendant circumstances in attempt prosecutions.[86] For them it is sufficient that the actor is as culpable regarding the attendant circumstance as is required for the completed offense. These scholars reason that as long as the actor has the specific intent to engage in the conduct, or to cause the result, that is prohibited by the statute defining the substantive crime, the law should not artificially require culpability regarding an attendant circumstance greater than is necessary to commit the target offense. The policy supporting the latter offense should preempt attempt doctrines. Following this reasoning, *D* would be guilty of attempted statutory rape: The target offense is one of strict liability with regard to the female's age, so the same analysis would apply to the attempt.[87]

§ 27.06 *ACTUS REUS* OF CRIMINAL ATTEMPTS[88]

[A] Policy Context

Neither the common law nor most statutes provide a clear vision of the *actus reus* aspect of a criminal attempt. Unhelpful conclusory statements are frequently expressed. For example, an attempt involves "perpetration" rather than "preparation"; or the defendant's conduct must be "proximate" to completion, rather than "remote." Beyond this, courts have developed a myriad of sometimes overlapping rules or tests meant to identify the point, or line, past which conduct constitutes a criminal attempt. One court has conceded "that the line of

---

[84] *See* Enker, Note 62, *supra*, at 867 n.58.

[85] *E.g.*, Williams, Note 1, *supra*, at 619–20.

[86] *E.g.*, J.C. Smith, *Two Problems in Criminal Attempts Reexamined — I*, 1962 Crim. L. Rev. 135, 143.

[87] Neal v. State, 590 S.E.2d 168 (Ga. Ct. App. 2003) (*N* was not entitled to a mistake-of-fact instruction in attempted statutory rape prosecution as it is not a defense to the crime of statutory rape).

[88] *See generally* Robert Batey, *Minority Report and the Law of Attempt*, 1 Ohio St. J. Crim. L. 689 (2004); Herbert Wechsler et al., *The Treatment of Inchoate Crimes in the Model Penal Code of the American Law Institute: Attempt, Solicitation, and Conspiracy [Pt. 1]*, 61 Colum. L. Rev. 571, 586–592 (1961); Gideon Yaffe, *Criminal Attempts*, 124 Yale L.J. 92 (2014).

demarkation is not a line at all but a murky 'twilight zone.' "[89] Indeed, the crime of attempt "expands and contracts and is redefined commensurately with the substantive offense"[90] — the more serious the offense, the sooner a criminal attempt will likely be found.

A major difficulty in drawing a line between noncriminal preparation and a criminal attempt is that courts are torn by competing policy considerations.[91] On the one hand, there is the understandable desire of courts and legislators to ease the burden on the police, whose goal it is to prevent crimes from occurring. Thus, as one court has candidly put it, an attempt occurs when "acts of preparation when coupled with intent have reached a point at which they pose a danger to the public so as to be worthy of law's notice."[92] On the other hand, if courts authorize too early police intervention, innocent persons, as well as those with still barely formed criminal intentions — persons who might voluntarily turn back from criminal activity — may improperly or needlessly be arrested.

The struggle to find the proper demarcation line is also a function of the debate between subjectivists and objectivists.[93] Generally speaking, subjectivists favor an *actus reus* test of attempt that allows for early attachment of guilt. This generalization follows from the underlying premises of the doctrine. For subjectivists, proof of an actor's dangerousness, as evidenced by her *mens rea*, is paramount. Intention, however, can be proved through confessions, independent evidence of the actor's motive to commit the offense, and/or third-party testimony regarding the defendant's state of mind. It follows from this that any conduct, no matter how slight, that corroborates the defendant's alleged *mens rea*, should suffice for a criminal attempt.

For objectivists, the *actus reus* element has independent significance, because adherents to this theory do not believe that society should use its coercive power against inchoate conduct unless the actor has caused some social harm, at least in the form of societal apprehension of criminal activity. Often, however, conduct does not lose its ambiguity and result in societal apprehension until well into the criminal transaction.

Objectivists believe that unchecked subjectivism, with its emphasis on *mens rea* and de-emphasis on conduct, endangers civil liberties, and too easily results in conviction of innocent persons. They fear that subjectivism may result in criminal liability for little more than bad thoughts. Moreover, guilt may too often be based on unreliable confessions, and other circumstantial evidence of an actor's alleged motivations. In contrast, subjectivists reason that if a society must wait until conduct unambiguously demonstrates its criminality, crime prevention will be frustrated.

---

[89] United States v. Williamson, 42 M.J. 613, 617 n.2 (N.M. Ct. Crim. App. 1995).

[90] Cox v. State, 534 A.2d 1333, 1335 (Md. 1988).

[91] State v. Reid, 679 S.E.2d 194, 198 (S.C. Ct. App. 2009) ("A competition among policy considerations exists in this realm of the law.").

[92] State v. Otto, 629 P.2d 646, 653 (Idaho 1981) (Bakes, C.J., dissenting).

[93] For an explanation of these doctrines, see § 27.03, *supra.*

[B] The Tests

[1] General Observations

"Much ink has been spilt in an attempt to arrive at a satisfactory standard for telling where preparation[] ends and attempt begins."[94] Generally speaking, the "attempt" tests that have developed over the years fall into two categories: those that focus on how much remains to be done before the crime is committed; and those that consider how much has already occurred.

In light of the conflicting policy considerations relating to attempt law discussed above, there is little or no way to predict with certainty where a court will draw the critical line between preparation and perpetration in a particular case. However, various factors come into play, including: (1) whether the act[95] in question appears to be dangerously close to causing tangible harm, so that police intervention cannot realistically be delayed;[96] (2) the seriousness of the threatened harm, *i.e.*, "the more serious the crime attempted . . . , the further back in the series of acts leading up to the consummated crime should the criminal law reach in holding the defendant guilty for an attempt";[97] and (3) the strength of the evidence of the actor's *mens rea*, *i.e.*, the more clearly the intent to commit the offense is proven, the less proximate the acts need to be to consummation of the offense.[98]

The most frequently used common law tests or factors are described below. (The "substantial step" test, formulated by the American Law Institute and included in the Model Penal Code, is described at § 27.09, *infra*.) It should be noted at the outset, however, that: (1) most states rarely adopt a single test as the exclusive basis for determining when an attempt has occurred;[99] and (2) the names of the tests (if, indeed, they are provided) and their descriptions vary by jurisdiction.

---

[94] Mims v. United States, 375 F.2d 135, 148 (5th Cir. 1967).

[95] Wait! What if there is *no* act, and the prosecutor seeks to prove a criminal attempt by pointing to an omission? *E.g.*, State v. Smith, 870 So. 2d 618 (La. Ct. App. 2004) (*S* was convicted of attempted "cruelty to the infirm" because she failed to bathe or otherwise aid her elderly mother who laid on a sofa for over a month). The criminal attempt statutes in 24 states directly or indirectly appear to permit convictions for omissions. Michael T. Cahill, *Attempt by Omission*, 94 Iowa L. Rev. 1207, 1222–1224 (2009). Professor Cahill reports, however, that there are only two appellate opinions (both in Louisiana) involving prosecution of attempts by omission.

[96] Arnold N. Enker, *Impossibility in Criminal Attempts — Legality and the Legal Process*, 53 Minn. L. Rev. 665, 674 (1969).

[97] Sayre, Note 1, *supra*, at 845.

[98] *See* People v. Berger, 280 P.2d 136, 138 (Cal. Ct. App. 1955).

[99] *E.g.*, Hudson v. State, 745 So. 2d 997, 1000 n.3 (Fla. Dist. Ct. App. 1999) (noting that Florida has not expressly adopted a particular "attempt" test, and stating that "[a]dopting one approach to the exclusion of the other[s] . . . may not be advisable").

[2] "Last Act" Test

Some courts used to state that a criminal attempt only occurred when the person performed all of the acts that she believed were necessary to commit the target offense.[100] Applying this standard, an attempted murder-by-shooting does not occur until D pulls the trigger of the gun; an attempted theft of a museum painting does not take place until D begins to remove the property from the wall; and an attempted arson does not occur unless D sets fire to the dwelling that she hopes to destroy. Today, there is general agreement that an attempt occurs *at least* by the time of the last act, but no jurisdiction *requires* that it reach this stage on all occasions.

As a practical matter, little commends the last-act standard, except for its bright-line nature. The police would be stymied by such a rule; it would virtually be impossible to prevent commission of a substantive crime.[101] To the extent that subjectivist principles are important, an actor's dangerousness can be identified well before the last act; and, from an objectivist viewpoint, social harm can occur, and the criminality of an actor's conduct can often be discerned, before the final act.[102]

[3] "Physical Proximity" Test

Some courts state that, while an actor's conduct need not reach the last act, it must be "proximate" to the completed crime, in that "it must approach sufficiently near to it to stand either as the first or some subsequent step in a *direct movement* towards the commission of the offense after the preparations are made."[103] Or, as another court has explained, for an act to constitute an attempt, "it must go so far that it would result, or apparently result in the actual commission of the crime it was designed to effect, if not extrinsically hindered or frustrated by extraneous circumstances."[104]

In essence, according to this test, an attempt does not arise unless an actor has it within her power to complete the crime almost immediately. For example, D would be guilty of attempted robbery if, weapon in hand, she has her victim in view and can immediately proceed to rob her, absent external factors, such as the intervention of the police. On the other hand, applying this test, an attempt does *not* occur if two men, intending to trick the victim out of his money, convince him to go to the bank and withdraw some of his cash, but the culprits are arrested before the

---

[100] *E.g.*, Regina v. Eagleton, 6 Cox Crim. Cas. 559, 571 (1855).

[101] "[T]he law of attempts would be largely without function if it could not be invoked until the trigger was pulled, the blow struck, or the money seized." People v. Dillon, 668 P.2d 697, 703 (Cal. 1983).

[102] However, Alexander and Ferzan, Note 72, *supra*, at 216, favor the last-act rule. They argue that until the last act is performed, a person "retains complete control over whether she will actually so act. The law still influences her, and she may decide to reconsider or to stop at any moment." Only when she engages in the last act does she "cease[] to be guided by her reason and will."

[103] State v. Dowd, 220 S.E.2d 393, 396 (N.C. Ct. App. 1975) (emphasis added); *see* State v. Reid, 679 S.E.2d 194 (S.C. Ct. App. 2009) (affirming conviction of R for attempted criminal sexual conduct, when he arranged a time and meeting location with a person whom he believed was underage, and arrived at the location within 15 minutes of the agreed meeting time; the fact that the female was not present did not bar conviction).

[104] Commonwealth v. Kelley, 58 A.2d 375, 377 (Pa. Super. Ct. 1948).

victim withdraws the cash, and before they can make overtures to secure the money from him.[105]

[4] "Dangerous Proximity" Test

In a series of cases,[106] Justice Oliver Wendell Holmes formulated a test that incorporates the just-discussed "physical proximity" standard, but in a somewhat more flexible form: According to this standard, a person is guilty of an attempt when her conduct is in "dangerous proximity to success,"[107] or when an act "is so near to the result that the danger of success is very great."[108] There is no clear point of proximity — "[e]very question of proximity must be determined by its own circumstances"[109] — but Holmes observed that courts consider three factors: the "nearness of the danger, the greatness of the harm, and the degree of apprehension felt."[110] Thus, in a prosecution for attempted murder by poisoning, Holmes observed that

> the gravity of the crime, the uncertainty of the result, and the seriousness of the apprehension, coupled with the great harm likely to result from poison, even if not enough to kill, would warrant holding the liability for an attempt to begin at a point more remote from the possibility of accomplishing what is expected than might be the case with lighter crimes.[111]

Applying the dangerous-proximity standard, one state court has held that a person who, with intent to possess cocaine, orders contraband from a supplier, meets a courier at her home, examines the goods, but rejects them on quality grounds, is guilty of attempted possession of a controlled substance;[112] in contrast, a person who tells the courier that she will buy the drugs once she obtains sufficient funds, and schedules a later meeting to consummate the sale, but who is arrested immediately, is not guilty of an attempt.[113]

One of the most famous — and controversial — applications of this standard occurred in *People v. Rizzo*,[114] in which four armed men drove around looking for *V*, whom they expected would be withdrawing a large sum of money from the bank. They entered various buildings looking for their victim. Suspicious, two police officers placed the men under surveillance. Finally, the suspects were arrested when one of them entered another building. *V* was not present where the arrest occurred.

---

[105] *Id.* at 376–77.

[106] Commonwealth v. Kennedy, 48 N.E. 770 (Mass. 1897); Commonwealth v. Peaslee, 59 N.E. 55 (Mass. 1901); Hyde v. United States, 225 U.S. 347 (1912) (dissenting opinion).

[107] *Hyde v. United States*, 225 U.S. at 388 (Holmes, J., dissenting).

[108] People v. Rizzo, 158 N.E. 888, 889 (N.Y. 1927).

[109] *Commonwealth v. Kennedy*, 48 N.E. at 771.

[110] Oliver Wendell Holmes, Jr., The Common Law 68 (1881).

[111] *Commonwealth v. Kennedy*, 48 N.E. at 771.

[112] People v. Acosta, 609 N.E.2d 518, 519 (N.Y. 1993).

[113] People v. Warren, 489 N.E.2d 240, 241–42 (N.Y. 1985).

[114] 158 N.E. 888 (N.Y. 1927).

With apparent embarrassment, the court overturned the conviction. While commending "[t]he police of the city of New York [for their] excellent work in this case by preventing the commission of a serious crime," and expressing their "great satisfaction to realize that we have such wide-awake guardians of our peace," the court concluded that in the absence of a victim, the armed suspects were not dangerously close to success.

[5]   "Indispensable Element" Test

In determining proximity, some courts "emphasize[] any indispensable aspect of the criminal endeavor over which the actor has not yet acquired control."[115] For example, according to this standard, an actor who does not yet possess a necessary instrumentality for the crime, *e.g.*, a gun for a murder or the equipment needed to manufacture illegal drugs, has not yet crossed the line from preparation to perpetration;[116] and an offense that requires action by an innocent person cannot be attempted until such action is completed.[117]

This test, although easier to apply than the dangerous-proximity standard, is arbitrary. The presence or absence of an indispensable element often says little regarding the actor's culpability, the firmness of her intentions, or the degree to which prior conduct may have disturbed the public's repose.

[6]   "Probable Desistance" Test

The preceding tests focus on the actor's proximity to successful completion of the crime, *i.e.*, on how much remains to be done. In contrast, the Commentary to the American Law Institute has described (but not endorsed) another standard, which it terms the "probable desistance" test, that centers on how far the defendant has already proceeded. Specifically, a court will find an attempt when, in the ordinary course of events, without interruption from an external source, "the actor . . . reached a point where it was unlikely that he would have voluntarily desisted from his effort to commit the crime."[118]

According to this standard, a man who induced a youth to come to his house for improper sexual relations and met the intended victim as the latter exited a taxicab, was guilty of attempted lewd and lascivious acts on a minor.[119] However, a woman who altered a prescription form for "Tylenol 3" (containing codeine) so that she could obtain "11" refills rather than the "1" specified by the doctor, and who brought it to a pharmacy to fill the prescription for the first time, was not guilty of attempted fraudulent acquisition of a controlled substance, because there existed reasonable

---

[115] Wechsler et al., Note 88, *supra*, at 587.

[116] *See also* State v. Addor, 110 S.E. 650 (N.C. 1922) (holding: there was no attempt to manufacture "spiritous liquors" because the defendants did not yet possess a still, necessary for production of the illegal whiskey).

[117] *E.g.*, *In re* Schurman, 20 P. 277 (Kan. 1889) (*S*, intending to defraud a life insurance company, feigned death; *X*, the beneficiary under the policy, and an innocent party to the scheme, had not yet filed a claim; held: *S* is not guilty of an attempt to defraud the company).

[118] American Law Institute, Comment to § 5.01, at 325.

[119] Hudson v. State, 745 So. 2d 997, 1000 n.3 (Fla. Dist. Ct. App. 1999).

doubt whether she would have returned twice more (once to get the refill to which she was entitled, and then to obtain a refill to which she was *not* entitled).[120]

Factfinders called upon to make the necessary judgment pursuant to this test are not usually called upon to determine whether the defendant reached her own psychological point of unlikely desistance; instead they try to identify the "point of no return" of an ordinary person in the actor's shoes.[121] What is unclear is how a jury, presumably composed of law-abiding persons, determines when an ordinary would-be criminal would or would not desist.

[7] "Unequivocality" Test

According to the unequivocality (or *res ipsa loquitur*) test, an act does not constitute an attempt until it ceases to be equivocal. That is, an attempt occurs when a person's conduct, standing alone, unambiguously manifests her criminal intent.[122] It is as if the jury observed the conduct in video form with the sound muted (so as not to hear the actor's potentially incriminating remarks), and sought to decide from the conduct alone whether the accused was attempting to commit the offense for which she was prosecuted.[123]

For example, in *People v. Miller*,[124] M threatened to kill V, whom M accused of harassing his wife. Later that day, M came armed with a rifle to a field where C, the local constable, and V, standing approximately 30 yards further away, were working. M walked in the direction of both C and V, stopped, loaded his rifle but did not aim it, and resumed his approach. At some point either before or after M loaded his weapon, V fled at a right angle from M's line of approach. C took possession of M's rifle without resistance. The court remarkably held that M was not guilty of attempted murder, because "up to the moment the gun was taken from the defendant, no one could say with certainty whether [he] had come into the field to carry out his threat to kill [V] or merely to demand his arrest by [C]."

The unequivocality test is in general harmony with the objectivist goal of reserving criminal liability for those whose conduct manifests criminality and, as a consequence, causes social apprehension. The test, however, has been attacked as impractical. For example, in a leading case in support of the doctrine,[125] the court stated that buying a box of matches to burn a haystack is too ambiguous to justify conviction for attempted arson, but that "he who takes matches to a haystack and there lights one of them," acts unambiguously. However, as one scholar has

---

[120] State v. Henthorn, 581 N.W.2d 544, 547 (Wis. Ct. App. 1998).

[121] Berry v. State, 280 N.W.2d 204, 209 (Wis. 1979) ("The defendant's conduct must pass that point where most men, holding such an intention as the defendant holds, would think better of their conduct and desist.").

[122] People v. Staples, 6 Cal. App. 3d 61, 67 (1970) (an attempt occurs "when it becomes clear what the actor's intention is and when the acts done show that the perpetrator is actually putting his plan into action").

[123] *See* J.W. Cecil Turner, *Attempts to Commit Crimes*, 5 Cambridge L.J. 230, 236–38 (1934).

[124] 42 P.2d 308 (Cal. 1935).

[125] King v. Barker, [1924] N.Z.L.R. 865.

shown,[126] the unequivocality standard fails to work in this case, because a person who lights a match near a haystack may only intend to light a pipe. Thus, in this example, either we must say that the actor's conduct is equivocal (in which case, police intervention would be improper until the last act occurs, *e.g.*, when the match is tossed into the hay), or we must concede that after conduct manifests criminality, a later act may render it ambiguous again (in which case the standard may not adequately protect the innocent from arrest).

§ 27.07 DEFENSE: IMPOSSIBILITY[127]

[A] The Issue

D wants to kill *V.* Standing outside *V*'s house, she fires a gun through a window at the bed in which she believes *V* is sleeping. *V* is not killed because she is not at home. Is *D* guilty of attempted murder, even though it was impossible for *D* to kill *V* under these circumstances?

Our intuitions almost certainly tell us that *D* should be convicted of an attempt. She has the requisite *mens rea*, and she has performed every act in her power to kill *V.* From a policy perspective, too, *D* merits punishment — she is dangerous, culpable, and has acted in a manner that would cause societal apprehension. The law seemingly confirms our moral intuitions and legal analysis: *D* almost certainly is guilty of attempted murder.[128]

However, suppose that we change the facts slightly. Suppose that when *D* fires the gun, *V* is in the bed, but is already dead from a coincidental heart attack. That is, *V* is a corpse, rather than a "human being," as defined by homicide law. Is *D now* guilty of attempted murder? No, according to dicta in various court opinions.[129] Is this dicta wrong, or can this example be distinguished in a principled manner from the "empty bed" case?

---

[126] Williams, Note 1, *supra*, at 630.

[127] *See generally* Larry Alexander, *Inculpatory and Exculpatory Mistakes and the Fact/Law Distinction: An Essay in Memory of Myke Bayles*, 12 Law & Phil. 33 (1993); Fernand N. Dutile & Harold F. Moore, *Mistake and Impossibility: Arranging a Marriage Between Two Difficult Partners*, 74 Nw. U. L. Rev. 166 (1979); John Hasnas, *Once More unto the Breach: The Inherent Liberalism of the Criminal Law and Liability for Attempting the Impossible*, 54 Hastings L.J. 1 (2002); Graham Hughes, *One Further Footnote on Attempting the Impossible*, 42 N.Y.U. L. Rev. 1005 (1967); Ken Levy, *It's Not Too Difficult: A Plea to Resurrect the Impossibility Defense*, 45 N.M. L. Rev. 225 (2014); Ira P. Robbins, *Attempting the Impossible: The Emerging Consensus*, 23 Harv. J. on Legis. 377 (1986); Kenneth W. Simons, *Mistake and Impossibility, Law and Fact, and Culpability: A Speculative Essay*, 81 J. Crim. L. & Criminology 447 (1990); Peter Westen, *Impossibility Attempts: A Speculative Thesis*, 5 Ohio St. J. Crim. L. 523 (2008); Yaffe, Note 88, *supra*.

[128] *E.g.*, State v. Mitchell, 71 S.W. 175, 177 (Mo. 1902). The words "seemingly" and "almost certainly" are used in the text because one English trial judge, in giving instructions to a jury in a case *not* involving these facts, suggested a contrary conclusion. Rex v. Osborn, 84 J.P. 63, 63 (Central Crim. Ct. 1919) (suggesting that if *O*, intending to kill *V*, enters *V*'s bedroom and strikes the pillow with a hatchet, but *V* is not in bed and miles away, *O* is *not* guilty of attempted murder because *O* "has not yet got at the thing near enough to attempt it").

[129] State v. Taylor, 133 S.W.2d 336, 341 (Mo. 1939); State v. Guffey, 262 S.W.2d 152, 156 (Mo. Ct. App. 1953).

Or, suppose that we move our case to a forest. D and V are hunting together; D wants to use this opportunity to kill V, so she shoots at V in the woods. As it turns out "V" — the object at which she aimed and fired her gun — is a tree stump. Or V, wisely sensing danger, displays a wax facsimile of herself, and it is *this* object that hunter-D shoots. Attempted murder? No, according to dicta and a holding in equivalent circumstances.[130]

Now, consider an increasingly frequent Internet scenario. Suppose that D enters an Internet chat room and communicates with V, whom D believes is an underage female, but who actually is an undercover male decoy. If D sends V an obscene photograph by electronic mail, he cannot be convicted of distribution of obscene materials to a minor, since V was not a minor, but may he be convicted of *attempted* distribution to a minor?[131] Or, if D makes plans over the Internet with V to have her perform nude dancing, may D be convicted of "attempted sexual performance by a child" when he arrives at the planned site only to learn that the 13-year-old female is a 47-year-old male Internet undercover officer?[132]

Finally consider these two cases. In each one, a male has sexual intercourse with a 17-year-old female in a jurisdiction that sets the age of consent for intercourse at 16. In other words, in both cases statutory rape has *not* occurred. *D1*, however, believed that the girl was 15, so he thought that he was committing statutory rape.[133] *D2* knew that the girl was 17, but he incorrectly believed that the lawful age of consent was 18, so he also thought he was committing statutory rape.[134] Should either or both of these cases constitute *attempted* statutory rape?

The real cases, and imaginative hypotheticals, go on and on. In each of these cases, the actor presumably has the requisite *mens rea*, and has gone far enough for her conduct to constitute an attempt (indeed, usually has done everything in her power to commit the target offense). But, in each of these cases, the desired outcome is predestined to fail — for one reason or another, it was impossible for the actor to succeed in consummating the offense. Therefore, these cases raise the same issue: whether a person should be convicted for an attempt that cannot succeed. In other words, is "impossibility" a defense to the crime of attempt?

---

[130] *See* State v. Guffey, 262 S.W.2d 152, 156 (Mo. Ct. App. 1953) (*G*, a hunter, was not guilty of attempting to kill a deer out of season when he shot at a wax-dummy deer); Regina v. M'Pherson, 7 Cox Crim. Cas. 281, 284 (1857) (dictum, tree stump); *Rex v. Osborn*, 84 J.P. at 64 (*id.*).

[131] People v. Thousand, 631 N.W.2d 694 (Mich. 2001).

[132] Chen v. State, 42 S.W.3d 926 (Tex. Crim. App. 2001); *see also* United States v. Tykarsky, 446 F.3d 458 (3d Cir. 2006) (*T* conversed in a chat room with an undercover male FBI agent posing as a 14-year-old girl; *T* solicited sexual activities with the "girl" and made arrangements to meet with "her"; when *T* arrived at the scene, he was charged with the federal offense of attempted "persuasion of a minor to engage in illicit sexual activity").

[133] Notice that this is a mirror image of the typical mistake-of-fact case, in which D believes that the female is old enough to consent, but she is not. In the typical case, therefore, the *actus reus* of statutory rape is committed; at issue is D's *mens rea*. In the present case, however, the *actus reus* of statutory rape did not occur, but D possessed a culpable mental state.

[134] Notice that this is a mirror image of the usual mistake-of-law case, in which an actor believes that her conduct is lawful, but it is not; here, D believed that he was violating a law, but he was wrong. If ignorance of the law does not ordinarily exculpate, may it nonetheless inculpate?

[B] General Rule

The common law rule regarding impossible attempts is easy to state. It distinguishes between two types of impossibility: "factual impossibility" and "legal impossibility." *At common law, legal impossibility is a defense; factual impossibility is not.*[135]

When one moves from the hornbook rule to specific cases, however, the law becomes exceedingly complex. Many pages of court opinions and scholarly literature have been filled in a largely fruitless effort to explain and justify the difference between factual and legal impossibility. Perhaps no aspect of the criminal law is more confusing and confused than the common law of impossible attempts.

In part because of the confusing nature of the law, and as a result of the influence of the Model Penal Code,[136] most jurisdictions no longer recognize legal impossibility as a defense.[137] However, as discussed below,[138] some arguments exist for retaining the defense in some form.

[C] Factual Impossibility

[1] In General

"Factual impossibility" exists when a person's intended end constitutes a crime, but she fails to consummate the offense because of an attendant circumstance unknown to her or beyond her control.[139] Examples of factual impossibility are: (1) a pickpocket putting her hand in the victim's empty pocket;[140] (2) an abortionist beginning the surgical procedure on a nonpregnant woman;[141] (3) an impotent male trying to have nonconsensual sexual intercourse;[142] (4) an assailant shooting into an empty bed where the intended victim customarily sleeps;[143] or (5) an individual pulling the trigger of an unloaded gun aimed at a person who is present.[144]

In each of these examples the actor was mistaken regarding some fact relating to the actor, the victim, and/or the method of commission. More specifically, the target offense was not consummated because the actor chose the wrong victim (the

---

[135] American Law Institute, Comment to § 5.01, at 307–17; Williams, Note 1, *supra*, at §§ 206–07; Bandy v. State, 575 S.W.2d 278, 279–80 (Tenn. 1979); Masika v. Commonwealth, 757 S.E.2d 571, 573–74 (Va. Ct. App. 2014); United States v. Oviedo, 525 F.2d 881, 883 (5th Cir. 1976).

[136] *See* § 27.09[E][1], *infra.*

[137] United States v. Hsu, 155 F.3d 189, 199 (3d Cir. 1998) (stating that "the great majority of jurisdictions" have abolished the defense).

[138] *See* § 27.07[D][3][b], *infra.*

[139] United States v. Berrigan, 482 F.2d 171, 188 (3d Cir. 1973); *see* Robbins, Note 127, *supra*, at 380 n.13 (quoting similar definitions).

[140] *E.g.*, People v. Twiggs, 223 Cal. App. 2d 455 (Ct. App. 1963).

[141] *E.g.*, State v. Moretti, 244 A.2d 499 (N.J. 1968).

[142] *E.g.*, Waters v. State. 234 A.2d 147 (Md. Ct. Spec. App. 1967).

[143] *E.g.*, State v. Mitchell, 71 S.W. 175 (Mo. 1902).

[144] *E.g.*, State v. Damms, 100 N.W.2d 592 (Wis. 1960).

pickpocket and abortion cases), the victim was not present (the empty bed case), the actor was not physically capable of committing the offense (the impotency case), or inappropriate means were used to commit the crime (the unloaded gun case). Had the circumstances been as the actors believed them to be, or hoped that they were (*e.g.*, the pocket contained property; the woman was pregnant; the victim was in the bed; the actor was physically capable of having intercourse; the gun was loaded), the crimes would have been consummated.

It should not be surprising that lawmakers are unsympathetic to claims of factual impossibility. In the cases described above, the actor has demonstrated dangerousness (critical to subjectivists) and manifested criminality (important to objectivists). No good reason exists to recognize a defense merely because a person chooses her victim badly, does not use proper means to commit the crime, or for some other reason unrelated to her culpability does not successfully commit the offense.

[2] "Inherent" Factual Impossibility

Although factual impossibility is not a defense to a criminal attempt, "inherent impossibility" (or, more completely, "inherent *factual* impossibility") *may* be a defense. The doctrine of inherent impossibility has arisen primarily in scholarly literature and judicial dictum, but it is recognized as a statutory defense in at least one state.[145] To the extent that the defense is recognized, it applies if the method to accomplish the crime was one that "a reasonable person would view as completely inappropriate to the objectives sought."[146]

What is an example of an inherently impossible attempt? In one of the earliest cases to discuss the topic, an example was suggested: a " 'voodoo doctor' . . . [who] actually believed that his malediction would surely bring death to the person on whom he was invoking it."[147] However, this is a poor example, as an incantation is not a "completely inappropriate" means of killing another if the intended victim believes in voodoo and, as a consequence, could die of fright. A better example of the doctrine is attempting "to sink a battleship with a pop-gun."[148]

Should the law recognize an inherent-impossibility defense? For an objectivist, the answer is clear: If conduct is harmless and would appear so to a person of normal understanding, no societal apprehension will occur and, therefore, punishment is unjustified. For subjectivists, the defense is harder to support: The actor is no less morally blameworthy because she has chosen an inherently impossible way to consummate the offense; on the issue of dangerousness, one who is so far out of touch with reality that, for example, she believes that she can sink a battleship with a pop-gun, may later commit some other irrational and dangerous act, or such a person may come upon a more sensible way to accomplish her criminal task.

---

[145] Minn. Stat. Ann. § 609.17(2) (2015) (providing an impossibility defense, if "such impossibility would have been clearly evident to a person of normal understanding"). For the Model Penal Code approach, see § 27.09[F][2], *infra*.

[146] State v. Bird, 285 N.W.2d 481, 482 (Minn. 1979).

[147] Commonwealth v. Johnson, 167 A. 344, 348 (Pa. 1933) (Maxey, J., dissenting).

[148] State v. Logan, 656 P.2d 777, 779 (Kan. 1983).

[D] Legal Impossibility

[1] Introductory Comments

"Legal impossibility" is an unfortunate term, for two reasons. First, there are two different categories of attempts that have been identified by courts as implicating "legal impossibility." Those two versions will be termed here "pure" and "hybrid" legal impossibility. The failure of courts generally to distinguish between them creates considerable confusion.[149]

Second, neither version of legal impossibility should be identified as such. As is developed below, *hybrid* legal impossibility cannot be distinguished from factual impossibility in any principled manner, and may properly be merged with it. On the other hand, *pure* legal impossibility may as accurately be identified as an application of the general principle of legality.[150]

The overwhelming modern trend is to abolish legal impossibility (more accurately, "hybrid legal impossibility") as a defense.[151] However, "pure legal impossibility" presumably remains a basis for exculpation.

[2] Pure Legal Impossibility

"Pure legal impossibility" arises "when the law does not proscribe the goal that the defendant sought to achieve."[152] The simplest case of pure legal impossibility occurs when a person performs a lawful act with a guilty conscience, *i.e.*, she believes that she is committing a crime, but she is not. For example, as Jerome Hall has observed, "it is not a crime to throw even a Kansas steak into a garbage can."[153] If *D* commits this dastardly act, she is guilty of no offense. And, even if she believes that there is such an offense, she is not guilty of *attempting* to commit this fanciful crime. Just as a person may not ordinarily escape punishment on the ground that she is ignorant of a law's existence,[154] it is also true that "we cannot punish people under laws that are purely the figments of their guilty imaginations."[155] Similarly, *D* is not guilty of a criminal attempt if, unknown to her, the legislature has repealed a statute that *D* believes she is violating. For example, if *D* attempts to sell "bootleg" liquor after the repeal of the Prohibition laws, she is not guilty of an attempt even though she is unaware of their repeal.[156]

---

[149] *But see* People v. Thousand, 631 N.W.2d 694, 698–700 (Mich. 2001) (recognizing the distinction).

[150] *See* § 5.01, *supra.*

[151] *State v. Logan*, 656 P.2d at 779; United States v. Hsu, 155 F.3d 189, 199 (3d Cir. 1998).

[152] Robbins, Note 127, *supra*, at 389.

[153] Hall, Note 1, *supra*, at 595.

[154] *See* § 13.01[A], *supra.*

[155] Alexander, Note 127, *supra*, at 46.

[156] Thus, too, in the hypothetical described in the text at Note 134, *supra*, in which *D2* knew the age of the female with whom he had intercourse, but he mistakenly believed that his conduct constituted statutory rape, he would not be guilty of attempted statutory rape.

A more problematic situation occurs when an actor's conduct *is* prohibited, but cannot legally constitute the offense charged. *Wilson v. State*[157] is commonly treated as a "pure legal impossibility" case.[158] In *Wilson*, W was prosecuted for forgery because he added the number "1" to a check made out to him in the sum of "$2.50," so that he could receive "$12.50." Under state law, however, W's actions did not constitute forgery because he tampered with a legally "immaterial" part of the check.[159] Consequently, the trial judge informed the jury that it could not convict W of forgery, but he instructed that it could convict him of the lesser offense of attempted forgery, which it did.

W's conviction was reversed. Although W's actions may have constituted some offense,[160] they did *not* constitute the crime of forgery. Wisely or not, state lawmakers had excluded his conduct from the ambit of the crime of forgery. Therefore, W was not guilty of *attempted* forgery, even if it turned out that W thought he was committing forgery by his conduct. This is no different than if a male touches a woman on her breasts without consent, believing this constitutes rape or, even more crazily, forgery. What the male did is *not* rape or forgery, although it constitutes a battery; therefore, the male is not guilty of *attempted* rape or *attempted* forgery simply because he may believe he has "raped" or "forged" his victim.

Although courts may treat the *Wilson* facts, and the Kansas steak, bootleg-liquor, and breast-touching hypotheticals, as "legal impossibility" (more accurately, "pure legal impossibility") cases, the underlying basis for acquittal is the principle of legality. The legality principle provides that we should not punish people — no matter culpable or dangerous they are — for conduct that does not constitute the charged offense at the time of the action. Therefore, it is similarly wrong to convict a person of an *attempt* to violate a law that is not, in fact, encompassed by the defendant's conduct.

[3] Hybrid Legal Impossibility

[a]   In General

Hybrid legal impossibility (or what courts typically call, simply, "legal impossibility") exists if the actor's goal is illegal, but commission of the offense is impossible due to a *factual* mistake (and not simply a misunderstanding of the law) regarding the *legal* status of some attendant circumstance that constitutes an element of the charged offense.[161] As the preceding definition implies and as is clarified immediately below, this is a hybrid version of impossibility: The actor's impossibility claim includes both factual and legal aspects to it.

---

[157] 38 So. 46 (Miss. 1904).

[158] *E.g.*, Robbins, Note 127, *supra*, at 390–91.

[159] Under state forgery law at the time, when a discrepancy exists between the written words and the figures on a check, the words take precedence. As a result, W's alteration of the numbers without changing the words constituted an immaterial change.

[160] W may have been guilty of attempted receiving property by false pretenses.

[161] *See* Robbins, Note 127, *supra*, at 389–90.

Courts have recognized a defense of legal impossibility or have stated that it would exist if *D*: (1) receives *un*stolen property believing that it was stolen;[162] (2) tries to pick the pocket of a stone image of a human;[163] (3) offers a bribe to a "juror" who is not a juror;[164] (4) tries to hunt deer out of season by shooting a stuffed animal;[165] (5) shoots a corpse believing that it is alive;[166] (6) shoots at a tree stump believing that it is a human;[167] or (7) in a prosecution for distribution of obscene literature to a minor, sends pornography to an adult, believing that she is a minor.[168]

Notice that in each of the preceding examples of hybrid legal impossibility, *D* was mistaken about a fact: whether the property had been stolen; whether a person was a juror; whether the victims were living human beings; whether the victim was an animal; or whether the victim was a minor. What distinguishes these cases from simple "factual impossibility," however, is that these factual mistakes relate to the *legal* status of the defendant's conduct, *i.e.*, the fact is an "attendant circumstance" legal element of the offense in question. A person is not guilty (and *cannot* be guilty) of "receiving stolen property with knowledge that it is stolen" unless the property is "stolen" in character. Likewise, one cannot legally bribe a juror unless the person bribed is a juror. The status of a victim as a "human being" — rather than as a corpse, tree stump, or statue — legally is a necessary element of the crime of murder or to "take and carry away the personal property *of another*." Putting a bullet into a stuffed deer cannot legally constitute the crime of killing a deer out of season. And, it cannot constitute the crime of distribution of obscene materials to a minor if the person to whom the materials are sent is not a minor.[169]

Ultimately, hybrid legal impossibility cases may reasonably be characterized as factual impossibility.[170] That is, by skillful lawyerly characterization, one can describe virtually any case of hybrid legal impossibility, which is a common law defense, as an example of factual impossibility, which is *not* a defense. For example, if *D* shoots a corpse, believing that it is a human being, *D* would describe this as one of legal impossibility: "As a matter of law, shooting a corpse is not, and never can, constitute murder, because the offense of criminal homicide, by

---

[162] *E.g.*, People v. Jaffe, 78 N.E. 169 (N.Y. 1906); Booth v. State, 398 P.2d 863 (Okla Crim. App. 1964).

[163] Trent v. Commonwealth, 156 S.E. 567, 569 (Va. 1931) (dictum).

[164] *E.g.*, State v. Taylor, 133 S.W.2d 336 (Mo. 1939).

[165] *E.g.*, State v. Guffey, 262 S.W.2d 152 (Mo. Ct. App. 1953).

[166] State v. Taylor, 133 S.W.2d 336 (Mo. 1939) (dictum).

[167] See the citations at Note 130, *supra.*

[168] People v. Thousand, 631 N.W.2d 694 (Mich. 2001).

[169] The latter case is similar in principle to the hypothetical set out at Note 133, *supra*, in which *D1* had intercourse with a female old enough to consent, although he believed that she was underage. This example involves hybrid legal impossibility: *D1* was mistaken about a fact (the girl's age); but the attendant circumstance of her age is of legal significance in that sexual intercourse with a 17-year-old female (her true age) does not constitute statutory rape.

[170] *People v. Thousand*, 631 N.W.2d at 699 (quoting this text). The converse of the statement in the text is not necessarily true. For example, there is no realistic issue of legal impossibility when *D* fires an unloaded gun or puts her hand in an empty pocket in order to pick it.

definition, only applies to the killing of human beings." The prosecutor, however, would couch the claim in factual impossibility terms: "If the factual circumstances had been as *D* believed them to be — that the 'victim' had been alive when *D* shot him — he would be guilty of murder."

Something is amiss when semantics alone, and not underlying policy, determines whether a defense will be recognized.

[b]   Modern Approach: Abolition of the Defense

Most states have abolished the defense of hybrid legal impossibility on the subjectivist ground that an actor's dangerousness is "plainly manifested"[171] in such cases. In most jurisdictions, therefore, lawyers and courts no longer have to distinguish between hybrid legal impossibility and factual impossibility.

Is abolition a good idea? Two objectivist objections to the modern trend deserve attention. First, some cases of hybrid legal impossibility involve objectively innocuous conduct. For example, putting one's hands near the "pocket" of a statue, shooting a tree stump, or receiving unstolen property are innocuous acts. These acts, by themselves, do not manifest criminality of any kind, so they should not induce societal apprehension of impending crime. What converts these harmless actions into crimes are the actors' criminal thoughts. For objectivists, punishment based essentially on criminal thoughts is objectionable, and represents a troubling feature of the "impossibility defense" abolitionist movement.

Second, when conduct is objectively innocent, there exists "a significant risk of enforcement error or abuse."[172] That is, a conviction may be obtained of an entirely innocent person (one who does not even have a criminal thought) or one whose "guilt" constitutes little more than a passing guilty thought (thus, someone who is not even dangerous in subjectivist terms). Although abolitionists contend that the risk of punishment of such a person "is more theoretical than practical,"[173] prosecutions of this sort *do* occasionally occur.

For example, in *Anderton v. Ryan*,[174] *R* purchased a video recorder at a deep discount. Because of its price, *R* believed that it had been stolen and, therefore, she believed that she was guilty of the offense of "handling stolen property." Later, her house was burglarized. When the police routinely questioned her about the lost goods, including the video recorder, *R* told the officers that she had purchased what she believed at the time was a stolen recorder. Based on her admission, *R* was prosecuted for *attempted* handling of stolen property.[175] She was convicted, based exclusively on her guilt feelings expressed to police officers.[176]

---

[171] American Law Institute, Comment to § 5.01, at 309.

[172] Hasnas, Note 127, *supra*, at 60.

[173] American Law Institute, Comment to § 5.01, at 319–20.

[174] [1985] 2 All E.R. 355 (House of Lords).

[175] Because the recorder was never retrieved, no effort was made at trial to prove that it actually was stolen property when *R* purchased it. The court assumed, therefore, she had purchased *un*stolen property.

[176] In this case, the House of Lords ruled that *R* was not guilty of the offense, although it had to

As one scholar has observed, what the defendant in *Anderton* did is hardly unusual: "Almost all of us jump at the chance to purchase an item we want at a bargain price, often from non-retail sources."[177] Few of us, however, fear prosecution if the bargain turns out to be just that — a lawful bargain. So, why was *R* prosecuted in *Anderton*? Perhaps overzealousness or prosecutorial abuse explains her case. But, more often, those who will be prosecuted in the absence of an impossibility defense will be people with a "bad" background: "How secure can those of us with criminal records or other associations or characteristics that reduce our credibility with a jury be if a prosecutor can obtain a conviction for [attempted] receiving stolen property merely by convincing a jury that we believed the property to be stolen?"[178]

§ 27.08 DEFENSE: ABANDONMENT[179]

Once a person crosses the line from preparation to perpetration of an offense, *i.e.*, once a criminal attempt has commenced, may the actor avoid conviction for the attempt if she abandons her criminal conduct before consummation of the target offense? For example, in *People v. McNeal*,[180] *M*, with the intention of raping *V*, grabbed *V* from a bus stop, took her at knifepoint to his home, pushed her onto a couch, and then began to fondle *V*. In an effort to prevent her rape, *V* begged *M* to let her go, explaining that she was trying to finish her education and that she was on the way to school to take two examinations. After *V* promised not to report him if he let her go, *M* apologized, took her to the bathroom so that she could fix her hair, and then walked her back to the bus stop. Clearly, *M*'s acts satisfied any reasonable test of attempted rape, but should he be entitled to defend his actions on the ground that he abandoned the rape before consummation?

Although there is disagreement on the matter, most scholars believe that abandonment was not a common law defense to attempt,[181] and many courts today continue to decline to recognize the defense.[182] To the extent that a defense of

---

provide a very strained interpretation of a statute that appeared to abolish the defense of legal impossibility. Subsequently, the House of Lords overruled *Anderton*. Regina v. Shivpuri, [1986] 2 All E.R. 334. The defendant in *Shivpuri* was convicted on the basis of an admission to customs officers that the suitcase he was attempting to bring into the country contained prohibited drugs, when in fact the substance in the suitcase turned out to be harmless vegetable matter. His conviction was upheld.

[177] Hasnas, Note 127, *supra*, at 60.

[178] *Id.*

[179] *See generally* Paul R. Hoeber, *The Abandonment Defense to Criminal Attempt and Other Problems of Temporal Individuation*, 74 Cal. L. Rev. 377 (1986); Daniel G. Moriarty, *Extending the Defense of Renunciation*, 62 Temp. L. Rev. 1 (1989); Yaffe, Note 88, *supra*.

[180] 393 N.W.2d 907 (Mich. Ct. App. 1986) (affirming a conviction for attempted criminal sexual conduct).

[181] Hoeber, Note 179, *supra*, at 381; Williams, Note 1, *supra*, at § 199; United States v. Smauley, 39 M.J. 853, 855 (N.M.C.M.R. 1994) (citing numerous treatises); *but see* American Law Institute, Comment to § 5.01, at 356–57 (stating that there is uncertainty on the matter, but suggesting that the prevailing rule favored a limited defense).

[182] *E.g.*, United States v. Shelton, 30 F.3d 702, 706 (6th Cir. 1994). Even when abandonment is not recognized as a defense, however, a court may still find a defendant's abandonment relevant in an attempt prosecution. For example, in Commonwealth v. McCloskey, 341 A.2d 500 (Pa. Super. Ct. 1975),

abandonment is recognized today, however, it applies only if the defendant *voluntarily* and *completely* renounces her criminal purpose. Abandonment by the defendant is voluntary when it is the result of repentance or a genuine change of heart.[183] Abandonment is not voluntary if the actor is motivated by unexpected resistance, the absence of an instrumentality essential to the completion of the crime, or some other circumstance that increases the likelihood of arrest or unsuccessful consummation of the offense.[184] And, the abandonment is not complete if the actor merely postpones the criminal endeavor until a better opportunity presents itself.[185]

There is also support for the proposition that a person may not claim abandonment as a defense, even if the actor's desistance is motivated by genuine remorse and is complete, once she has performed the last act necessary to commit the offense, or has already caused serious harm to the victim. For example, in one case,[186] S stabbed V, his uncle, became remorseful, and rushed V to a hospital. In an ensuing attempted murder prosecution, the court held that S's abandonment could not be claimed in these circumstances.

The common law no-defense rule is motivated by objectivist principles, namely, that once the social harm of an attempt has occurred, a person should no more be able to avoid conviction for the harm caused than if a thief were to repent for her actions and return the property after the crime has transpired. Although abandonment of an attempt, like voluntary restitution by a thief, may be relevant in sentencing, renunciation of a criminal purpose cannot undo the harm already inflicted.

Jurisdictions that recognize the defense do so on subjectivist grounds. First, the defense encourages desistance by the attempter. Second, by voluntarily and completely abandoning an offense, an actor demonstrates that she possesses a less dangerous character than an ordinary attempter or person who quits the offense out of fear of arrest.[187]

M, a prison inmate, scaled the fence leading to the prison recreation yard, but he then returned because he did not want to shame his family by escaping. *M* was convicted of attempted prison escape, but his conviction was overturned on the questionable ground that *M*'s actions demonstrated that he was still only contemplating an escape, but had not yet begun attempting the act.

[183] Pyle v. State, 476 N.E.2d 124, 126 (Ind. 1985) (permitting a defense on the basis of repentance or "rising revulsion for the harm intended").

[184] People v. Cross, 466 N.W.2d 368, 369–70 (Mich. Ct. App. 1991); State v. Mahoney, 870 P.2d 65, 71 (Mont. 1994).

[185] American Law Institute, Comment to § 5.01, at 356.

[186] State v. Smith, 409 N.E.2d 1199, 1202 (Ind. Ct. App. 1980); *accord State v. Mahoney*, 870 P.2d at 71.

[187] Sheckles v. State, 501 N.E.2d 1053, 1056 (Ind. 1986); People v. Taylor, 598 N.E.2d 693, 699 (N.Y. 1992)

§ 27.09 MODEL PENAL CODE[188]

[A] Introductory Comments

According to the Commentary to Section 5.01 of the Model Penal Code, which is the Code provision on criminal attempts:

> The literature and the decisions dealing with the definition of a criminal attempt reflect ambivalence as to how far the governing criterion should focus on the dangerousness of the actor's conduct, measured by objective standards, and how far it should focus on the dangerousness of the actor, as a person manifesting a firm disposition to commit a crime.[189]

That is, the law has struggled with the competing principles of objectivism and subjectivism. The drafters of the Code, however, are not ambivalent: "[T]he proper focus of attention is the actor's disposition. The Model Code provisions are accordingly drafted with this in mind."[190]

The Model Code's approach to criminal attempts — indeed, to all of the inchoate offenses — is subjectivist nearly throughout. It defines a criminal attempt in a manner that "make[s] amenable to the corrective process those persons who have manifested a propensity to engage in dangerous criminal activity."[191] Its treatment of defenses to criminal attempts (it abolishes the defense of hybrid legal impossibility, but recognizes the defense of abandonment), and the punishment it imposes for inchoate offenses (in general, it grades an inchoate crime at the same level as the completed offense), are similarly motivated by subjectivist goals.

Section 5.01 has had significant impact on American attempt law. Most of the federal courts apply its doctrines, although Congress has not enacted the provision; and a large number of states have adopted the Code provision in its entirety or in part.[192]

[B] Criminal Attempt: In General

[1] Elements of the Offense

Generally speaking, a criminal attempt under the Code contains two elements: (1) the purpose to commit the target offense; and (2) conduct constituting a "substantial step" toward the commission of the target offense. These elements are explained more fully in subsections [C] and [D] below.

---

[188] *See generally* Wechsler et al., Note 88, *supra.*

[189] American Law Institute, Comment to § 5.01, at 298 (footnote omitted).

[190] *Id.* (footnote omitted).

[191] United States v. Dworken, 855 F.2d 12, 16 (1st Cir. 1988).

[192] By the author's own research, at least 25 states have codified the Model Penal Code's "substantial step" standard, discussed in subsection [D], *infra.* As noted earlier, *see* § 27.07[B], *supra*, the overwhelming trend is to abolish the legal impossibility defense, as the Code provides. At least 22 states statutorily recognize a Model Penal Code's renunciation (abandonment) defense.

[2]   Explaining Subsection (1)

Section 5.01, subsection (1), which defines a criminal attempt, is a complicated provision. It reads:

> A person is guilty of an attempt to commit a crime if, acting with the kind of culpability otherwise required for commission of the crime, he:
>
> (a) purposely engages in conduct that would constitute the crime if the attendant circumstances were as he believes them to be; or
>
> (b) when causing a particular result is an element of the crime, does or omits to do anything with the purpose of causing or with the belief that it will cause such result without further conduct on his part; or
>
> (c) purposely does or omits to do anything that, under the circumstances as he believes them to be, is an act or omission constituting a substantial step in a course of conduct planned to culminate in his commission of the crime.

To analyze an attempt issue under subsection (1), it is necessary to ask and answer one or two questions. First, does the case involve a complete or incomplete attempt? Second, if the case involves a complete attempt, is the target offense a "result" crime (*e.g.*, murder) or a "conduct" crime (*e.g.*, driving an automobile under the influence of alcohol)?

Subsections (1)(a) and (1)(b) pertain to *completed* attempts. Specifically, subsection (1)(a) should be considered when the target offense of the completed attempt involves conduct; subsection (1)(b) applies to results. If the prosecution involves an *incomplete* attempt, subsection (1)(c) is used. However, this subsection must be read in conjunction with subsection (2), which elaborates on the meaning of "substantial step."

[C] *Mens Rea*

In general, a person is not guilty of a criminal attempt unless it was her purpose, *i.e.*, her conscious objective, to engage in the conduct or to cause the result that would constitute the substantive offense.

There are two exceptions to the requirement of purpose. First, subsection (1)(b) expressly and subsection (1)(c) implicitly[193] provide that a person is guilty of an attempt to cause a criminal result if she *believes* that the result will occur, even if it was not her conscious object to cause it. For example, if *D* plants a bomb on an airplane in order to kill *V*, her husband, and the bomb fails to go off or is defused, she is guilty of attempted murder of *V*, because it was *D*'s conscious objective to take *V*'s life; but she would also be guilty of attempted murder of the other passengers in the airplane if she believed that they would die in the bombing.[194] The common law outcome in this case is uncertain.[195]

---

[193] American Law Institute, Comment to § 5.01, at 305 n.17.

[194] *Id.* at 304–05.

[195] *See* Note 65, *supra*.

Second, the Commentary to Section 5.01 explains that the prefatory phrase in subsection (1) — "acting with the kind of culpability otherwise required for the commission of the crime" — means that the *mens rea* of "purpose" or "belief" does not necessarily encompass the attendant circumstances of the crime.[196] For "attendant circumstance" elements, it is sufficient that the actor possessed the degree of culpability required to commit the target offense. For example, if *D* would be guilty of statutory rape on proof that he was reckless as to the girl's age (the attendant circumstance), then he may be convicted of *attempted* statutory rape if he was reckless, but not if he was negligent or innocent, as to the girl's age. If the material element of the girl's age is one of strict liability, *i.e.*, *D* may be convicted of statutory rape although he reasonably believed that she was old enough to consent, then he may also be convicted of *attempted* statutory rape although he lacked a culpable mental state as to this attendant circumstance. The common law rule on this matter is uncertain.[197]

[D] *Actus Reus*

[1] In General

In a significant departure from the common law, the Model Penal Code shifts the focus of attempt law from what remains to be done, *i.e.*, the actor's proximity to consummation of the offense, to what the actor has already done.[198] In incomplete attempt cases, subsection (1)(c) provides that, to be guilty of an offense, an actor must have done or omitted to do something that constitutes a "substantial step in a course of conduct planned to culminate in his commission of the crime." The premise of the Code is that one who engages in such purposive conduct is sufficiently dangerous to justify state intervention, even if she is not yet close to consummation of the offense. The "substantial step" standard is intended to "broaden the scope of attempt liability."[199]

Section 5.01(2) provides further content to the imprecise term "substantial step." First, it indicates that conduct is not a substantial step unless it strongly corroborates the defendant's criminal purpose. This language is meant to reduce the risk of conviction of innocent persons. It incorporates some aspects of the common law unequivocality test of attempt,[200] without including its potential stringencies. Specifically, this subsection does not require that the defendant's conduct *by itself* manifest criminality, as objectivists favor. Rather, the key words in the provision are "strongly corroborative": The actor's conduct, considered in light of all the circumstances, must add significantly to other proof of her criminal intent,

---

[196] American Law Institute, Comment to § 5.01, at 301–03.

[197] *See* § 27.05[D], *supra*.

[198] American Law Institute, Comment to § 5.01, at 329; United States v. Irving, 665 F.3d 1184, 1196 (10th Cir. 2011) ("The fact that further, major steps remain 'before the crime can be completed does not preclude a finding that the steps already undertaken are substantial'.") (quoting United States v. Savaiano, 843 F.2d 1280, 1297 (10th Cir. 1988)).

[199] *Id.*

[200] *See* § 27.06[B][7], *supra*.

such as a confession or other incriminating evidence.[201]

Second, subsection (2) provides a list of recurrent factual circumstances in which an actor's conduct, *if strongly corroborative of her criminal purpose,* "shall not be held insufficient as a matter of law." In other words, if any of the enumerated instances are established, and if the judge determines that a jury could (not necessarily would) find beyond a reasonable doubt that the defendant's conduct is strongly corroborative of her criminal purpose, then the case must go to the jury. The circumstances set out in subsection (2), drawn primarily from common law decisions in the field, include: lying in wait; searching for or following the contemplated victim of the crime; reconnoitering the contemplated scene of the crime; unlawful entry into a structure or building in which the crime will be committed; and possession of the materials to commit the offense, if they are specially designed for a criminal purpose.[202]

[2] Attempt to Aid

Suppose that *D1* furnishes a gun to *X1* so that *X1* can kill *V1*. If *X1* attempts to kill *V1*, *X1* is guilty of attempted murder, and *D1* is also guilty of attempted murder, as an accomplice.[203]

Compare the preceding example with the following: *D2* furnishes a gun to *X2* so that *X2* can kill *V2*. *X2*, however, does *not* attempt to commit the offense. In this example, *X2* is not guilty of attempted murder. *D2*, in turn, is not guilty of aiding and abetting an attempted murder, since *X2* committed no such offense. Is *D2* guilty of *any* offense?

Conceptually, *D1* aided and abetted an attempt; *D2* attempted to aid and abet. Although *D1*'s liability for attempted murder is clear at common law, *D2* is guilty of no common law offense.[204] The Model Penal Code, however, takes a different approach: Under Section 5.01(3), a person may be convicted of a criminal attempt, *although no crime was committed or attempted by another,* if: (1) the purpose of her conduct is to aid another in the commission of the offense; and (2) such assistance *would* have made her an accomplice in the commission of the crime under the Code's complicity statute[205] if the offense had been committed or attempted.

In the hypothetical above, *D2* would be guilty under the Code of attempted murder (conceptually, she is guilty of attempted aiding and abetting a murder), although *X2* did not attempt to commit the murder. *D2* is guilty because, if *X2 had* attempted the crime, *D2 would have been* an accomplice in the attempt, by furnishing the gun for the purpose of the homicide.

---

[201] American Law Institute, Comment to § 5.01, at 331.

[202] This list is used exclusively by the judge. The jury does not receive the list. If the case goes to the jury, the jury is informed that, to convict, there must be proof of a substantial step (not otherwise defined) in a course of conduct planned to culminate in commission of the crime, and that the substantial step must strongly corroborate her criminal purpose.

[203] *See generally* Chapter 30, *infra.*

[204] *See* § 30.02[A][2], *infra.*

[205] Model Penal Code § 2.06. *See* § 30.09, *infra.*

The rationale of the rule is straightforward: A person who attempts to aid in the commission of an offense is as dangerous as one who successfully aids in its commission or attempted commission.[206] Therefore, under subjectivist principles, her conduct justifies punishment.

[E] Defenses

[1] Impossibility

[a] Hybrid Legal Impossibility

Section 5.01(1), reprinted in subsection [B] above, is designed to abolish the defense of hybrid legal impossibility. This outcome may be seen by considering three examples. First, assume that *D1* receives unstolen property, believing that it was stolen, and is prosecuted for attempting to receive stolen property. As this case involves a completed attempt, and the offense charged is a conduct crime, subsection (1)(a) applies. Based on the language of subsection (1)(a), *D1* is guilty if she purposely engaged in conduct (receiving the property) that would constitute a crime *"if the attendant circumstances were as [s]he believes them to be."* In this case, the attendant circumstance is the stolen nature of the property. *D1* believed that the property was stolen. Had the circumstance been as she believed it to be, she *would* have been guilty of the offense of receiving stolen property. Therefore, she is guilty of *attempting* to receive stolen property.

Second, suppose that *D2* shoots to kill *V*, unaware that *V* is already dead. Although this might constitute hybrid legal impossibility, and a defense at common law,[207] *D2* is guilty of attempted murder under the Model Penal Code.[208] Because this involves a completed attempt, and criminal homicide is result crime, subsection (1)(b) applies. Here, *D2* performed an act — firing a gun at *V* — "with the purpose of causing or with the belief that it [would] cause such result [*V*'s death] without further conduct on [*D2*'s] part." The fact that *V* was a corpse rather than a human being does not exculpate *D2*.

Finally, suppose that in either of these examples, the defendant is arrested prior to completion of the last act, but after commission of a substantial step. For example, suppose that *D1* prepares to receive the unstolen property but is arrested immediately before she takes possession; or, suppose that *D2* is arrested with the gun aimed at the corpse. Because further actions were intended in these cases, subsection (1)(c), rather than (1)(a) or (1)(b), applies. Still, *D1* and *D2* will be convicted because they performed acts that, "under the circumstances as [they] believe[d] them to be" — the property was stolen, *V* was alive — constituted "a substantial step in a course of conduct planned to culminate in . . . commission of the crime[s]."

The abrogation of the impossibility defense conforms with subjectivist

---

[206] American Law Institute, Comment to § 5.01, at 356.

[207] *See* § 27.07[D][3][a], *supra.*

[208] People v. Dlugash, 363 N.E.2d 1155 (N.Y. 1977).

principles. One who intends to commit a crime, but who fails to consummate it because of a circumstance of which the person is unaware, is as dangerous (and culpable) as one who successfully commits the crime or who does not commit it because of police intervention.

One aspect of the Code's treatment of impossibility cases deserves special attention. Observe that only in subsection (1)(c) cases, *i.e.*, in cases of *incomplete* attempts, does the Code require that the actor's conduct be strongly corroborative of her criminal purpose. The typical impossibility case, however, involves a *completed* attempt, in which event subsection (1)(a) or (1)(b) applies. In the usual impossibility case, therefore, corroboration of the actor's criminal purpose is *not* required under the Code.

This feature of the Code is objectionable to advocates of objectivism. As discussed earlier,[209] some impossibility cases involve objectively innocuous conduct. Thus, if *D* buys unstolen electronic equipment on the street believing that it is stolen, her conduct objectively is innocent. Nonetheless, she may be convicted under the Code of an attempt to receive stolen property, although the radio was not stolen, on the basis of circumstantial evidence of criminal purpose. The danger of conviction of an innocent person, therefore, is unmitigated.[210]

[b]   Pure Legal Impossibility

Although the Code does not expressly so provide, the American Law Institute did not intend to abolish the defense of pure legal impossibility. The Commentary states that "it is of course necessary [pursuant to the principle of legality] that the result desired or intended by the actor constitute a crime."[211]

[2] Renunciation (Abandonment)

The Code recognizes an affirmative defense of "renunciation of criminal purpose" in incomplete attempts and completed attempts of result crimes if: (1) she abandons her effort to commit the crime or prevents it from being committed; and (2) her conduct manifests a complete and voluntary renunciation of her criminal purpose.[212] Thus, *assuming the second requirement is satisfied*, *D* is not guilty of attempted rape, even if his incomplete actions constitutes a "substantial step in a course of conduct planned to culminate in . . . commission of the crime," if he feels remorse and desists from completing the rape.[213] Similarly, if bomber *D* lights a fuse to blow up a building for the purpose of killing *V* and, thus, has completed her last act in the planned murder, she will be acquitted of attempted murder if she

---

[209] *See* § 27.07[D][3][b], *supra.*

[210] The Commentary's response to this criticism is that it is "unlikely . . . that persons will be prosecuted on the basis of admissions alone." American Law Institute, Comment to § 5.01, at 319–20. However, as discussed earlier, prosecutions of this sort do occur on occasion.

[211] American Law Institute, Comment to § 5.01, at 318.

[212] Model Penal Code § 5.01(4).

[213] The facts in *People v. McNeal*, discussed in the text at Note 180, *supra*, would be such a case under the Model Penal Code.

prevents the crime from occurring by, for example, defusing the bomb.[214] But, she would not be able to claim the defense if she shoots at *V* and misses. Here the "actor has put in motion forces that he is powerless to stop," unlike in the lit fuse example, and therefore the offense cannot be abandoned.[215]

Under this provision, renunciation is not complete if it is wholly or partially motivated "by a decision to postpone the criminal conduct until a more advantageous time or to transfer the criminal effort to another but similar objective or victim." For example, *D* is guilty of attempted bank robbery, if she arrives at the bank, but leaves without committing the offense because she determines that it is too risky to go ahead until she secures the assistance of an accomplice.[216] *D* would also be guilty of an attempt if, after taking a substantial step toward robbing Bank A, she shifted her efforts to Bank B.[217]

Renunciation is not voluntary if it is partially or wholly motivated by "circumstances, not present or apparent at the inception of the actor's course of conduct, that increase the probability of detection or apprehension or that make more difficult the accomplishment of the criminal purpose." Under this provision, an actor is not entitled to the defense if she desists from a theft because she is aware that she is being observed by a police officer. Similarly, a person is guilty of attempted rape if he desists due to the victim's resistance.

[F]   Grading of Criminal Attempts and Other Inchoate Crimes

[1]   In General

In a significant departure from common law tradition, the Code provides that, with one exception, the crimes of attempt, solicitation, and conspiracy are offenses of the same grade and degree — *i.e.*, subject to the same punishment — as the offense attempted, solicited, or that is the object of the conspiracy.[218] This is consistent with the Code's subjectivist view of inchoate crimes.

The only exception to this grading system relates to "felonies of the first degree,"[219] which are crimes that carry a maximum penalty of life imprisonment.[220] An attempt (or solicitation or conspiracy) to commit a felony of the first degree

---

[214] American Law Institute, Comment to § 5.01, at 360.

[215] *Id.*

[216] *E.g.*, United States v. Jackson, 560 F.2d 112 (2d Cir. 1977).

[217] If *D* proceeded to rob Bank B, she would be guilty of attempted robbery of Bank A *and* of robbery of Bank B of Bank B. If she were arrested before completing the Bank B robbery, *D* would be guilty of two counts of attempted robbery.

[218] Model Penal Code § 5.05(1).

[219] Model Penal Code § 6.01(1)(a).

[220] Model Penal Code § 6.06(1). Felonies of the first degree are expressly designated as such by the Code. Murder (§ 210.2), kidnapping (§ 212.1), rape (§ 213.1(1)), and robbery (§ 222.1) are felonies of the first degree.

constitutes a felony of the *second* degree,[221] the maximum penalty of which currently is 10 years.[222]

[2] Special Mitigation

The Model Penal Code grants a trial judge the authority to dismiss a prosecution of an inchoate offense, or to impose a sentence for a crime of a lower degree than is otherwise allowed, if the actor's conduct was so inherently unlikely to result in a crime that neither she nor her conduct represents a danger to society justifying her conviction and punishment at ordinary levels.[223] This provision provides flexibility to a judge in the rare case of an inherently impossible attempt, *e.g.*, when *D* attempts to sink a battleship with a pop-gun.[224]

---

[221] Model Penal Code § 5.05(1).

[222] Model Penal Code § 6.06(2).

[223] Model Penal Code § 5.05(2).

[224] *See* § 27.07[C][2], *supra*.

Chapter 28

SOLICITATION

§ 28.01 GENERAL PRINCIPLES[1]

[A] Definition

[1] In General

Subject to clarification below, a common law "solicitation" occurs when a person invites, requests, commands, hires, or encourages another to engage in conduct constituting any felony, or a misdemeanor relating to obstruction of justice or a breach of the peace. Solicitation is a common law misdemeanor, regardless of the grade of the offense solicited.

Until the adoption of the Model Penal Code, most state penal codes did not contain a general criminal solicitation statute.[2] Instead, solicitations to commit specific offenses, such as murder and prostitution, were prohibited. As a result of the Code's influence, many states now have a general solicitation statute that covers all crimes or, at least, all felonies. However, many of these states have followed the common law approach of treating solicitation as a lesser offense than the crime solicited.[3]

[2] *Mens Rea*

Common law solicitation is a specific-intent crime. A person is not guilty of solicitation unless he intentionally commits the social harm of the inchoate offense — he intentionally invites, requests, commands, hires, or encourages another to commit a crime — with the specific intent that the other person consummate the solicited crime. For example, *D1* is not guilty of solicitation if he jokingly suggests to *X1* that *X1* steal *V1*'s television set, even if *X1* takes the suggestion seriously and commits the crime.

Or, suppose that pickpocket *D2* encourages *X2* to pick *V2*'s pocket. *D2* knows that *V2*'s pocket is empty, but *X2* is unaware of this. If *X2* follows *D2*'s suggestion and puts his hand in *V2*'s empty pocket, *X2* is guilty of attempted larceny, as the factual

---

[1] *See generally* Glanville Williams, Criminal Law: The General Part §§ 193–95 (2d ed. 1961); Larry Alexander & Kimberly D. Kessler, *Mens Rea and Inchoate Crimes*, 87 J. Crim. L. & Criminology 1138 (1997).

[2] American Law Institute, Comment to § 5.02, at 367.

[3] Commonwealth v. Barsell, 678 N.E.2d 143, 145 (Mass. 1997) (summarizing statutory law).

impossibility of committing the larceny does not serve as a defense to $X2$'s conduct.[4] $D2$, however, should *not* be guilty of common law solicitation, because he knew that $X2$ could not succeed in the larceny; therefore, $D2$ lacked the specific intent required for solicitation.[5]

In contrast to the last example, suppose that $D2$, like $X2$, is *unaware* of the fact that $V2$'s pockets are empty when he encourages $X2$ to pick $V2$'s pocket. Under these changed circumstances, $D2$ *is* guilty of solicitation, because he *believed* that the crime (larceny) could be committed.

[3] *Actus Reus*

The *actus reus* component of a solicitation takes place when one person invites, requests, commands, hires, or encourages[6] another to commit a particular offense. For a solicitation to occur, neither the solicitor nor the solicited party needs to perform any act in furtherance of the target offense.[7] The solicitation is complete the instant the actor communicates the solicitation to the other person.[8] Thus, a solicitation occurs if D asks X to commit a crime but X refuses, or even if X agrees but does not intend to commit the crime (*e.g.*, if X is an undercover police officer feigning intent).

In the absence of clarifying statutory language, courts have struggled to determine how to deal with uncommunicated solicitations. For example, in *State v. Cotton*,[9] C, a jail inmate, wrote letters to X, his wife, in which he solicited criminal activities on her part. Although C attempted to mail or forward the letters to X, there was no evidence that they actually reached her. The court held that, on this evidence, C could not be convicted of solicitation,[10] although it suggested that a charge of *attempted* solicitation might have been allowed.[11]

---

[4] *See* § 27.07[C][1], *supra*.

[5] Williams, Note 1, *supra* at 611. Conceptually, $D2$ has solicited an *attempted* larceny, but the common law apparently did not recognize such an offense.

[6] The idea of the offense need not originate with the solicitor; it is enough that he encourages another to commit an offense, even if the other person already planned to commit the crime. In light of the *mens rea* requirement, however, a person is not guilty of solicitation if his comments are not uttered for the purpose of encouraging the commission of the crime. American Law Institute, Comment to § 5.02, at 371.

[7] People v. Cheathem, 658 N.Y.S.2d 84, 85 (1997).

[8] People v. Ruppenthal, 771 N.E.2d 1002, 1008 (Ill. App. Ct. 2002).

[9] 790 P.2d 1050 (N.M. Ct. App. 1990).

[10] The same analysis would apply if a solicitor sends a message in a language that the other party does not understand, or if the solicitor communicates the message orally, but the solicitee does not hear the words.

[11] *State v. Cotton*, 790 P.2d at 1054; Laughner v. State, 769 N.E.2d 1147 (Ind. Ct. App. 2002) (recognizing the offense of attempted solicitation of a child to engage in sexual intercourse); American Law Institute, Comment to § 5.02, at 380–81 (recognizing such an approach at common law).

[B]   Relationship of the Solicitor to the Solicited Party

[1]   In General

A typical solicitation occurs when D importunes X to perpetrate the substantive offense. In common law terms,[12] D intends for X to be the "principal in the first degree" — the perpetrator — of the solicited crime; D wishes to be the "principal in the second degree" or "accessory before the fact." Put less technically, "the essence of criminal solicitation is an attempt [by the solicitor] to *induce another to commit a criminal offense*";[13] the solicitor intends to be in the background — to "hide behind his hireling(s)"[14] — as an accomplice in the commission of the crime. Although there is relatively little case law on point, it also appears that a "solicitation of a solicitation" is itself a common law solicitation, *e.g.*, if D importunes X to procure *another* person to kill V.[15]

No common law solicitation occurs if the solicitor intends to commit the substantive offense himself, but requests assistance by another. For example, if D requests X to kill V, D has solicited a murder. However, if D asks X to supply a gun so that he (D) can kill V, a common law solicitation has *not* transpired.

[2]   Use of an Innocent Instrumentality

A person may sometimes use another as his "innocent instrumentality"[16] in the commission of an offense. It is critical to appreciate the difference between solicitation of another to commit an offense, on the one hand, and use of an innocent instrumentality, on the other hand.

For example, if $D1$ suggests to $X1$ that the latter steal $V1$'s television set, $D1$ is guilty of solicitation of the theft. This fits the solicitation paradigm: If $X1$ does as requested, $X1$ is the perpetrator of the offense; $D1$ is an accomplice. In contrast, suppose that $D2$ *fraudulently* says to $X2$: "My television set is at $V2$'s house. He asked me to pick it up. Would you do me a favor and get it for me?" In this example, $D2$ is *not* guilty of solicitation to commit larceny, because $D2$ is not requesting $X2$ to engage in conduct that would constitute a crime *by $X2$*. Instead, $D2$ is attempting to perpetrate the offense himself, by using $X2$ as his dupe. $X2$ is $D2$'s "innocent instrumentality" because, if $X2$ believes $D2$'s representations and takes $V2$'s property, $X2$ is not guilty of larceny since he lacks the specific intent to steal.

---

[12] *See* § 30.03[A], *infra*.

[13] People v. Herman, 97 Cal. App. 4th 1369, 1381 (Ct. App. 2002).

[14] People v. Kauten, 755 N.E.2d 1016, 1019 (Ill. App. Ct. 2001).

[15] Ganesan v. State, 45 S.W.3d 197, 201 (Tex. App. 2001); *see also* People v. Bloom, 133 N.Y.S. 708 (1912) (B attempted to bribe X to solicit Y to commit perjury at B's trial).

[16] *See* § 30.03[A][2][b], *infra*.

[C] Relationship of a Solicitation to the Target Offense

Solicitation is not only an inchoate offense — the crime of solicitation — but is also a basis for accomplice liability. That is, one who intentionally assists in an offense is, by way of accomplice law, guilty of the offense in which he assisted. Solicitation of a substantive offense is one way of assisting in an offense and, therefore, of being held accountable for the other's criminal acts.[17]

To see how this works, assume that *D* solicits *X* to murder *V.* In Scenario 1, *X* kills *V* because of the request. *D* is guilty of murder via his solicitation. However, *D* will not be punished for the *crime* of solicitation, *as the latter offense merges with the murder.*[18]

In Scenario 2, *X* attempts to murder *V* at *D*'s request, but *X* fails in the effort. *D* is now guilty, along with *X*, of attempted murder. *D* is not guilty of solicitation, *as this offense again merges with the attempt.*

In Scenario 3, *D* solicits *X* to murder *V*, and *X* agrees but takes no action in furtherance of their agreement. Here, as a result of the agreement, *D* is guilty with *X* of conspiracy to murder *V.*[19] As before, *the solicitation merges with the conspiracy.*

Finally, in Scenario 4, *X* refuses to commit the crime solicited. *X* is guilty of no offense; *D* is guilty of solicitation.

[D] Policy Considerations

Solicitation is a controversial offense. Some commentators believe that solicitations should not be punished because the offense suppresses conduct at too early a stage.[20] Indeed, no common law crime (except an *attempted* solicitation) punishes conduct more preparatory to a substantive offense than the crime of solicitation. According to Glanville Williams, the purpose of the offense is to enable police to "nip criminal tendencies in the bud."[21] In fact, however, his metaphor would be more accurate if he had stated that its purpose is to nip criminal tendencies at the stem.

The extremely inchoate nature of the crime of solicitation is evident if one carefully analyzes the offense. Essentially, solicitation is an attempted conspiracy.[22] That is, when *D* solicits *X* to commit an offense, he wants *X* to agree to commit the offense solicited; if *X* agrees, they have formed a conspiracy. In turn, a conspiracy can exist long before a crime is attempted. Thus, solicitation is an attempt to conspire to commit an offense — a *double* inchoate crime. (And, thus, an *attempted*

---

[17] *See* § 30.04, *infra.*

[18] Lewis v. State, 404 A.2d 1073, 1083 (Md. 1979).

[19] *See* § 29.01[A], *infra.*

[20] Solicitation statutes, unless carefully drafted and applied circumspectly, may also raise First Amendment free speech concerns. *See generally* Kent Greenawalt, *Speech and Crime*, 1980 Am. B. Found. Res. J. 645.

[21] Williams, Note 1, *supra*, at 609.

[22] State v. Jensen, 195 P.3d 512, 517 (Wash. 2008).

solicitation would be a *triple* inchoate offense!)

The contrasting view is that solicitations are dangerous precisely because they *are* attempted conspiracies. As discussed more fully elsewhere,[23] one rationale for punishing conspiracies is that there is more danger in two or more persons agreeing to commit a crime than in one person planning to commit the same offense. Therefore, when a solicitor attempts to create such a dangerous grouping, his conduct represents a threat that advocates of the offense believe society has a legitimate interest in deterring. Moreover, it has been argued that "solicitation poses special dangers not inherent in conspiracy, one of which is that the instigator will be a sophisticated operator, such as a gang leader, who will hide behind his hireling(s),"[24] therefore arguably justifying more severe penalties for a solicitation than for a conspiracy or a criminal attempt.[25]

§ 28.02 COMPARISON OF SOLICITATION TO OTHER INCHOATE OFFENSES

[A] Conspiracy

A conspiracy is an agreement between two or more persons to commit an unlawful act or series of unlawful acts.[26] As noted in the preceding subsection, a solicitation conceptually is an attempted conspiracy. However, it is possible to have a conspiracy without a prior solicitation. For example, suppose that A, intending to kill V, requests B's assistance in the crime. If B agrees to help, they have formed a conspiracy; however, as A did not request B to perpetrate the offense, no common law solicitation has occurred.[27]

Or, suppose that C informs D that he (C) intends to kill V. D tells C that, he, too, wishes V dead, so he offers to join C in the crime. As a consequence of their common goal, they form a pact to kill V. The latter agreement would constitute a conspiracy, although C never solicited the offense.[28]

[B] Criminal Attempt[29]

An issue that has perplexed courts is whether or when a solicitation can constitute an attempt to commit the crime solicited. That is, if D solicits X to rob V, under what circumstances, if any, may D be convicted of attempted robbery, rather than of solicitation? The matter is of considerable significance in jurisdictions in which a criminal attempt is punished more severely than a solicitation.

---

[23] *See* § 29.02[B], *infra.*

[24] People v. Kauten, 755 N.E.2d 1016, 1019 (Ill. App. Ct. 2001).

[25] *Id.* 1018–20.

[26] *See* § 29.01[A], *infra.*

[27] *See* § 28.01[B][1], *supra.*

[28] *See* People v. Stroner, 449 N.E.2d 1326, 1328 (Ill. 1983); Monoker v. State, 582 A.2d 525, 528 (Md. 1990) (dictum).

[29] *See* Williams, Note 1, *supra*, at § 198.

Courts have taken various approaches to this issue.[30] First, a substantial majority of courts state that the act of solicitation cannot, *by itself*, constitute an attempt to commit the offense solicited.[31] A minority of courts, however, provide that a solicitation can constitute an attempt, subject to ordinary attempt doctrines.[32] On this basis, a solicitation that is proximate to the target offense may constitute an attempt to commit it. For example, if *D* solicits unarmed *X* to murder *V* when *V* returns to town in a week, *D*'s conduct would not constitute an attempt because the crime is too remote. On the other hand, if *D* solicits *X*, who is armed and in *V*'s presence, to commit the offense immediately, *D*'s solicitation could constitute an attempt.[33]

Second, some courts hold that solicitation coupled with a "slight act" in furtherance of it *by the solicitor* is an attempt.[34] For example, in jurisdictions that follow this rule, if *D* solicits *X* to sell him an illegal drug, and then displays or proffers the money, the solicitation has matured into an attempt.[35] Likewise, if *D* pays *X* money to murder *V*, or furnishes *X* with a weapon to commit the offense, *D* is guilty of an attempt even if *X* does nothing further, and even if *X* is an undercover police officer who would never have committed the crime.[36]

Third, some courts hold that a solicitation is not an attempt unless the solicitor's overt acts would constitute an attempt if he had intended to commit the crime himself. For example, if *D* pays *X* money to commit a crime or furnishes him with an instrumentality to commit a future offense, *D* is *not* guilty of attempt. However, if *D* solicits *X* to burglarize *V*'s home, and then opens a window at *V*'s house for *X*'s later entry, *D* would be guilty of attempted burglary, even if *X* never arrives at the scene.

Finally, other courts hold that "no matter what acts the solicitor commits, he cannot be guilty of an attempt because it is not his purpose to commit the offense personally."[37]

All of these situations must be distinguished from the case in which a person seeks to use another as his innocent instrumentality to commit an offense. Suppose, as hypothesized earlier,[38] *D* fraudulently says to *X*: "My television set is at *V*'s house. He asked me to pick it up. Would you do me a favor and pick it up for me?" In this circumstance, *D* is *not* guilty of solicitation because he is not

---

[30] American Law Institute, Comment to § 5.02, at 368–69 (and citations therein).

[31] *E.g.*, State v. O'Neil, 782 A.2d 209, 216 (Conn. App. Ct. 2001); State v. Disanto, 688 N.W.2d 201, 213 (S.D. 2004).

[32] State v. Sunzar, 751 A.2d 627, 632 (N.J. Super. Law. Div. 1999) (adopting the "minority" position that "mere solicitation, even when unaccompanied by any other act in furtherance, can constitute an attempt").

[33] *See* Mettler v. State, 697 N.E.2d 502, 503 (Ind. Ct. App. 1998) (a solicitation does not constitute an attempt unless the solicitation urges *immediate* commission of a crime).

[34] People v. Decker, 157 P.3d 1017, 1022 (Cal. 2007); Stokes v. State, 46 So. 627, 629 (Miss. 1908).

[35] People v. York, 60 Cal. App. 4th 1499, 1506 (Ct. App. 1998).

[36] *E.g.*, People v. Decker, 157 P.3d 1017 (Cal. 2007).

[37] American Law Institute, Comment to § 5.02, at 369.

[38] *See* § 28.01[B][2], *supra*.

requesting *X* to commit larceny, but instead is trying to commit the offense himself through an innocent instrumentality, *X*. Although *D*'s request is not a solicitation, it plausibly constitutes an *attempt* by *D* to commit the offense solicited. *D* has committed the last act in his power to cause the property to be taken. Moreover, his conduct is more proximate to the theft than a solicitation, because *X* is more apt to agree to take the property when he believes that he is acting lawfully than when he is asked to knowingly commit a criminal act.

§ 28.03 MODEL PENAL CODE[39]

[A] In General

The Model Penal Code provides that a person is guilty of solicitation to commit a crime if: (1) the actor's purpose is to promote or facilitate the commission of a substantive offense; and (2) with such purpose, he commands, encourages, or requests another person to engage in conduct that would constitute the crime, an attempt to commit it, or would establish the other person's complicity in its commission or attempted commission.[40] The Code grades nearly all inchoate crimes, including solicitation, at the same level as the target offense.[41]

The Code definition of solicitation is broader than the original common law version in four key respects. First, it applies to the solicitation of all crimes and not simply of felonies and serious misdemeanors.

Second, reconsider the case discussed earlier,[42] in which *D* solicits *X* to put his hand in what *D* knows is an empty pocket of *V*. If *X* does as requested, *X* is guilty of attempted larceny; *D* would be guilty of no common law offense, however, because he did not intend for *X* to commit larceny (as there was no property to steal, as *D* knew). Under the Code, however, *D* would be guilty of solicitation of an *attempted* larceny. In the language of Section 5.02, *D* solicited *X* to "engage in specific conduct [picking *V*'s empty pocket] that would constitute . . . an attempt to commit such crime [of larceny]."

Third, the relationship of the solicitor to the solicited party need not be that of accomplice to perpetrator. Suppose that *D* asks *X* to provide him with a weapon so that *D* may kill *V*. At common law, *D* has not solicited a murder, because he has not requested *X* to perpetrate the offense. Under the Code, *D* is guilty of solicitation because, applying the Code, *D* has requested *X* to "engage in specific conduct [provide a weapon] that would . . . establish [*X*'s] complicity [as an accomplice] in its commission or attempted commission."[43]

---

[39] *See generally* Herbert Wechsler, et al., *The Treatment of Inchoate Crimes in the Model Penal Code of the American Law Institute: Attempt, Solicitation, and Conspiracy (Pt. 1)*, 61 Colum. L. Rev. 571 (1961).

[40] Model Penal Code § 5.02(1).

[41] Model Penal Code § 5.05(1). See § 27.09[F][1], *supra*, for clarification.

[42] *See* § 28.01[A][2], *supra*.

[43] Model Penal Code § 5.02(1).

Finally, an uncommunicated solicitation, *i.e.*, perhaps no more than an attempted solicitation at common law, is itself a solicitation under the Code.[44]

[B] Defense: Renunciation

The Model Code establishes a defense to solicitation of "renunciation of criminal purpose." A person is not guilty of solicitation if he: (1) completely and voluntarily renounces his criminal intent; and (2) either persuades the solicited party not to commit the offense or otherwise prevents him from committing the crime.[45]

This defense is recognized for the same reason that it applies to the other inchoate offenses of attempt and conspiracy: A person who abandons his criminal purpose and thwarts the commission of the offense demonstrates thereby that he is no longer dangerous. Establishment of the defense also serves as an incentive to the solicitor to prevent commission of the crime.

---

[44] Model Penal Code § 5.02(2).

[45] Model Penal Code § 5.02(3).

Chapter 29

CONSPIRACY

"Conspiracy" is both an inchoate offense and a complicity doctrine (that is, a basis for holding a person accountable for the *consummated* offenses of another). The crime of conspiracy is the subject of this chapter. Complicity doctrine is considered in the next chapter.

§ 29.01 CONSPIRACY: IN GENERAL[1]

[A] Common Law

A common law conspiracy is an agreement, express or implied, between two or more persons to commit a criminal act or series of criminal acts, or to accomplish a legal act by unlawful means.[2] Formulated by the English Star Chamber in 1611,[3] conspiracy was a common law misdemeanor. As discussed below,[4] the offense is punished more severely today than it was at common law.

Conspiracy is a frequently prosecuted,[5] but extremely controversial, crime. A few courts and more scholars have called for its reform or abolition.[6] The nature of the controversies become evident in subsequent sections of this chapter. Three interrelated criticisms of the crime, however, may be emphasized here. First, it has

---

[1] *See generally* Note, *Developments in the Law — Criminal Conspiracy*, 72 Harv. L. Rev. 920 (1959); Abraham S. Goldstein, *Conspiracy to Defraud the United States*, 68 Yale L.J. 405 (1959); Phillip E. Johnson, *The Unnecessary Crime of Conspiracy*, 61 Cal. L. Rev. 1137 (1973); Neal Kumar Katyal, *Conspiracy Theory*, 112 Yale L.J. 1307 (2003); Paul Marcus, *Criminal Conspiracy Law: Time to Turn Back from an Ever Expanding, Even More Troubling Area*, 1 Wm. & Mary Bill Rts. J. 1 (1992); Herbert Wechsler et al., *The Treatment of Inchoate Crimes in the Model Penal Code of the American Law Institute: Attempt, Solicitation, and Conspiracy (Pt. 2)*, 61 Colum. L. Rev. 957 (1961).

[2] People v. Carter, 330 N.W.2d 314, 319 (Mich. 1982); Carroll v. State, 53 A.3d 1159, 1169 (Md. 2012); Commonwealth v. Nee, 935 N.E.2d 1276, 1282 (Mass. 2010); United States v. Jimenez Recio, 537 U.S. 270, 274 (2003) ("[T]he essence of a conspiracy is 'an agreement to commit an unlawful act.'") (quoting Iannelli v. United States, 420 U.S. 770, 777 (1975)).

[3] Poulterers' Case, 9 Co. Rep. 55b, 77 Eng. Rep. 813 (1611).

[4] *See* § 29.03[A], *infra.*

[5] United States v. Reynolds, 919 F.2d 435, 439 (7th Cir. 1990) (Easterbrook, J.) ("[P]rosecutors seem to have conspiracy on their word processors as Count I; rare is the case omitting such a charge."). Perhaps "more than one-quarter of all federal criminal prosecutions and a large number of state cases involve prosecutions for conspiracy." Katyal, Note 1, *supra*, at 1310 (and accompanying supporting citations).

[6] For an example of the abolitionist position, see Johnson, Note 1, *supra*; *see also* Katyal, Note 1, *supra*, at 1309 (noting that critiques of conspiracy law "[f]or more than 50 years . . . have [unfortunately, to the author] successfully permeated the criminal law").

been said that the "crime of conspiracy is so vague that it almost defies definition."[7] The formlessness of the crime of conspiracy has served as a powerful tool of prosecutors to suppress inchoate conduct that they consider potentially dangerous or morally undesirable. Indeed, Judge Learned Hand once described the offense as the "darling of the modern prosecutor's nursery."[8]

Second, some see the offense as undesirable because of the highly inchoate nature of the offense: A person may be convicted of the common law version of the offense before she commits any act in perpetration of a substantive crime. Third, and closely related to the last point, the crime "is always 'predominantly mental in composition' because it consists primarily of a meeting of minds and an intent."[9] Because of conspiracy law's emphasis on *mens rea*, and its consequent de-emphasis on conduct, critics maintain that there exists a greater than normal risk that "persons will be punished for what they say rather than for what they do, or [simply] for associating with others who are found culpable."[10] Historically, conspiracy laws have been used to suppress controversial activity, such as strikes by workers and public dissent against governmental policies.[11]

[B] Model Penal Code

Section 5.03, subsection (1), of the Model Penal Code defines "conspiracy" as follows:

A person is guilty of conspiracy with another person or persons to commit a crime if with the purpose of promoting or facilitating its commission he:

(a) agrees with such other person or persons that they or one or more of them will engage in conduct that constitutes such crime or an attempt or solicitation to commit such crime; or

(b) agrees to aid such other person or persons in the planning or commission of such crime or of an attempt or solicitation to commit such crime.

This definition and other features of the Code's treatment of criminal conspiracies are explored throughout this chapter.

---

[7] Krulewitch v. United States, 336 U.S. 440, 446 (1949) (Jackson, J., concurring). Justice Jackson also described the crime as "chameleon-like." *Id.* at 447. Another critic has compared the crime to Einstein's theory of relativity, stating that the concept is "so far removed from ordinary human experience or modes of thought . . . [that] it escapes just beyond the boundaries of the mind." Jessica Mitford, The Trial of Dr. Spock 61 (1969).

[8] Harrison v. United States, 7 F.2d 259, 263 (2d Cir. 1925). An additional reason why "conspiracy" is a "darling" of prosecutors is that they can use the threat of a conspiracy prosecution against a relative "small fry" in a criminal transaction as a means to induce the individual to provide information and testimony against others. *See* Katyal, Note 1, *supra*, at 1328 (noting that one federal study "found that flipping [*i.e.*, assisting the prosecution of a colleague in crime in exchange for a light sentence] helped the government obtain guilty pleas of co-defendants, prosecution of new defendants, additional convictions and arrests, recovery of assets, cooperation of known and new co-defendants, and deportations").

[9] *Krulewitch*, 336 U.S. at 447–48 (Jackson, J., concurring) (footnote omitted).

[10] Johnson, Note 1, *supra*, at 1139.

[11] *See* Mitford, Note 7 *supra*, at 61–72.

§ 29.02 PUNISHING CONSPIRACIES: WHY?

[A] "Conspiracy" as an Inchoate Offense: Preventive Law Enforcement

As with other inchoate offenses, criminal conspiracy laws provide law enforcement agents with a basis for arresting persons whom they believe intend to commit other criminal offenses in the future.

Conspiracy laws allow police intervention at a much earlier point than is permitted under attempt law. As is explained below,[12] a common law conspiracy is formed the moment two or more persons agree that one of them will later commit an unlawful act. At common law, no conduct in furtherance of the conspiracy is required. Even when an overt act in furtherance of the conspiracy is statutorily required, as is often the case now, the act may be trivial and wholly preparatory to the commission of the target offense. Consequently, advocates of conspiracy laws believe that the offense unfetters police and fills in the gaps in the "unrealistic" law of criminal attempts.

It is said that an agreement to commit a criminal act is concrete and unambiguous evidence of the actors' dangerousness and the firmness of their criminal intentions,[13] therefore justifying early intervention. However, the agreement that serves as "concrete" and "unambiguous" evidence of the defendants' dangerousness and culpability is often proved inferentially, increasing the risk of false positives. Moreover, even if an agreement is conclusively proved to exist, the potential temporal remoteness of the agreement to the target offense increases the likelihood that some conspirators who might later renounce their intentions will be punished.

[B] Special Dangers of Group Criminality

The combination that constitutes a conspiracy is said to represent a "distinct evil."[14] According to advocates of conspiracy laws, two people united to commit a crime are more dangerous than one person, or even two people independently, planning to commit the same offense: "[T]he strength, opportunities and resources of many is obviously more dangerous and more difficult to police than the efforts of a lone wrongdoer."[15]

The purported dangers inherent in collective criminal action are many. First, out of fear of co-conspirators, loyalty to them, or enhanced morale arising from the collective effort, a party to a conspiracy is less likely to abandon her criminal plans

---

[12] *See* § 29.04, *infra.*

[13] American Law Institute, Comment to § 5.03, at 387–88.

[14] United States v. Jimenez Recio, 537 U.S. 270, 274 (2003) (quoting Salinas v. United States, 522 U.S. 52, 65 (1997)).

[15] Krulewitch v. United States, 336 U.S. 440, 448–49 (1949) (Jackson, J., concurring) (footnote omitted).

than if she were acting alone.[16] Other special dangers are said to inhere in conspiracies: collectivism promotes efficiency through division of labor; group criminality makes the attainment of more elaborate crimes possible; and the "[c]ombination in crime makes more likely the commission of crimes unrelated to the original purpose for which the group was formed."[17]

A half century ago, Professor Abraham Goldstein questioned whether these "special danger" claims were empirically correct.[18] He reasoned that it was as plausible to argue that conspiracies will frustrate rather than promote crime: With more people involved, there is an enhanced risk that someone will leak information about the offense, turn against others, or try to convince colleagues to desist from their criminal endeavor. According to Professor Neal Katyal, however, there is psychological and economic research supporting many of the traditional claims of special dangers inherent in group behavior.[19]

§ 29.03 PUNISHING CONSPIRACIES: HOW MUCH?

[A] In General

[1] Common Law and Non-Model Penal Code Statutes

At common law, a conspiracy to commit a felony or a misdemeanor was a misdemeanor.[20] Modern conspiracy statutes vary widely among the states. However, typically, the sanction for conspiracy is graded in relationship to the contemplated crime. Most states punish conspiracies to commit felonies as felonies, and conspiracies to commit misdemeanors as misdemeanors.[21] As well, a conspiracy to commit a felony is usually punished less severely than the target felony itself.[22]

[2] Model Penal Code

As with other inchoate offenses, the Model Penal Code grades a conspiracy to commit any crime other than a felony of the first degree at the same level as the object of the conspiracy.[23] If a conspiracy has multiple objectives, e.g., to rape and

---

[16] *United States v. Jimenez Recio*, 537 U.S. at 275 (the combination "decreases the probability that the individuals involved will depart from their path of criminality") (quoting Callanan v. United States, 364 U.S. 587, 593–94 (1961)).

[17] Callanan v. United States, 364 U.S. 587, 593–94 (1961); *see generally* State v. Pond, 108 A.3d 1083, 1097 (Conn. 2015) ("Conspiracies may bolster the resolve of their members; they may benefit from the division of labor in the execution of criminal schemes; and they made lead to the commission of additional crimes beyond those initially envisioned."); *accord* United States v. Gore, 636 F.3d 728, 738 (5th Cir. 2011).

[18] Goldstein, Note 1, *supra*, at 414.

[19] For a review of the literature the author believes justifies the "special danger" claim, see Katyal, Note 1, *supra*, at 1315–28.

[20] Glanville Williams, Criminal Law: The General Part § 221 (2d ed. 1961).

[21] *E.g.*, Ga. Code Ann. § 16-4-8 (2015).

[22] *E.g.*, Mass. Gen. Laws Ann. ch. 274, § 7 (2015).

[23] Model Penal Code § 5.05(1). See § 27.09[F][1], *supra*.

to steal,[24] the conspiracy is graded on the basis of the more or most serious target offense. The Code takes the subjectivist view[25] that people who agree to commit crimes but are arrested before consummation are as dangerous as those who commit the target offenses.

[B]   Punishment When the Target Offense Is Committed

[1]   Common Law

Unlike the crimes of attempt and solicitation, the offense of conspiracy does *not* merge into the attempted or completed offense that was the object of the conspiracy.[26] For example, if *D1* and *D2* conspire to rob *V*, and later attempt to commit or successfully consummate the robbery, they may be convicted and punished for both the conspiracy and the robbery or its attempt.[27]

The non-merger doctrine is unsupportable if the main purpose of conspiracy law is to provide the police with an opportunity to prevent commission of the target offense. Once the object of the conspiracy is committed or attempted, this purpose of conspiracy law evaporates. Similarly, if the focus of the offense is on the dangerousness of the individual conspirator, her punishment should be calibrated to the crime that she threatened to commit; punishing her for both crimes is duplicative. The non-merger rule makes sense, however, if one focuses on the alternative rationale of conspiracy law, *i.e.*, to attack the special dangers thought to inhere in conspiratorial groupings.[28]

[2]   Model Penal Code

The Model Penal Code diverges from the common law. It provides that a person may not be convicted and punished for both conspiracy and the object of the conspiracy or its attempt, unless the prosecution proves that the conspiratorial agreement involved the commission of additional offenses not yet committed or attempted.[29]

For example, if *D1* and *D2* conspire to rob Bank *V* and then do so, they may be convicted and punished for robbery or conspiracy, but not for both offenses. In contrast, if *D1* and *D2* conspire to rob Banks *V1*, *V2*, and *V3*, and they are arrested after robbing Bank *V1* — thus, before their other criminal objectives were fully

---

[24] As is explained more fully at § 29.08, *infra*, an agreement to commit multiple crimes constitutes only one conspiracy.

[25] *See* § 27.03, *supra.*

[26] Callanan v. United States, 364 U.S. 587, 593–94 (1961).

[27] *E.g.*, People v. Jones, 601 N.E.2d 1080, 1088 (Ill. App. Ct. 1992) (upholding conviction of attempted armed robbery and conspiracy to commit armed robbery); United States v. Boykins, 966 F.2d 1240, 1245 (8th Cir. 1992) (upholding against constitutional attack, punishment for conspiracy to possess cocaine and attempted possession, based on the same incident).

[28] "That [conspiratorial] agreement is 'a distinct evil,' which 'may exist and be punished whether or not the substantive crime ensues.'" United States v. Jimenez Recio, 537 U.S. 270, 274 (2003) (quoting Salinas v. United States, 522 U.S. 52, 65 (1997)). The special dangers are discussed in § 29.02[B], *supra.*

[29] Model Penal Code § 1.07(1)(b). *See* American Law Institute, Comment to § 1.07, at 109.

satisfied — the conspiracy does *not* merge with the completed offense. The drafters of the Code believed that, in these circumstances, the special dangers inherent in collective action justify independent punishment of the conspiracy.

§ 29.04 CONSPIRACY: THE AGREEMENT

[A] In General

The gist — or "essence"[30] — of a conspiracy is the agreement to commit an unlawful act or series of such acts.[31] An express agreement, however, need not be proved.[32] Indeed, a physical act of communication of an agreement (*e.g.*, a nod of the head or some verbal exchange) is not required. Furthermore, an agreement can exist although not all of the parties to it have knowledge of every detail of the arrangement, as long as each party is aware of its essential nature.[33] Moreover, a "conspiracy may exist even if a conspirator does not agree to commit or facilitate each and every part of the substantive offense."[34] It is enough that each person agrees, at a minimum, to commit or facilitate some of the acts leading to the substantive crime.

Nonetheless — and this is the essence of the agreement — there must be present "on the part of each conspirator communion with a mind and will outside [herself]."[35] In this very limited sense, the conspiracy is externalized; that is, the agreement takes the law beyond the individual mental states of the parties, in which each person separately intends to participate in the commission of an unlawful act, to a shared intent and mutual goal, to a spoken or unspoken understanding by the parties that they will proceed in unity toward their shared goal.

How does a prosecutor prove the existence of this amorphous yet critical agreement? "Conspiracy is by nature a clandestine offense,"[36] one in which the agreement that constitutes the crime "is seldom born of 'open covenants openly arrived at.' "[37] Ironically, the difficulty in demonstrating an agreement has proven to be the prosecutor's greatest advantage because, "in their zeal to emphasize that the agreement need not be proved directly, the courts sometimes neglect to say

---

[30] United States v. Jimenez Recio, 537 U.S. 270, 274 (2003); People v. Homick, 289 P.3d 791, 835 (Cal. 2012) (the agreement is "the crux" of a criminal conspiracy); Carroll v. State, 53 A.3d 1159, 1169 (Md. 2012) (it is "the heart" of the conspiracy).

[31] Cuellar v. State, 13 S.W.3d 449, 453 (Tex. App. 2000).

[32] Carroll v. State, 53 A.3d at 1169 (the agreement "need not be formal or spoken" (quoting Townes v. State, 548 A.2d 832, 834 (Md. 1988))).

[33] Blumenthal v. United States, 332 U.S. 539, 557–58 (1947); People v. Mass, 628 N.W.2d 540, 549 n.19 (Mich. 2001).

[34] Salinas v. United States, 522 U.S. 52, 63 (1997).

[35] *Developments in the Law*, Note 1, *supra*, at 926.

[36] *Id.* at 933.

[37] Lacaze v. United States, 391 F.2d 516, 520 (5th Cir. 1968); Cuellar v. State, 13 S.W.3d 449, 453 (Tex. App. 2000) ("[C]onspirators' work is often done in secrecy and under cover.").

that it need be proved at all."[38]

A conspiratorial agreement may be established directly or through entirely circumstantial evidence of a mutual, implied understanding.[39] As one court has acknowledged, "because of the clandestine nature of a conspiracy and the foreseeable difficulty of the prosecution's burden of establishing the conspiracy by direct proof, the courts have permitted broad inferences to be drawn . . . from evidence of acts, conduct, and circumstances."[40]

A conspiracy "may be inferred from a 'development and a collocation of circumstances.' "[41] A crime committed as the result of a prior agreement is apt to look choreographed.[42] For example, in one case,[43] the prosecution proved the following: D1 was driving an automobile in which D2 and D3 were passengers; as the car drove by V, a pedestrian, D1 stopped the car; D2 called V over to the curb; D2 and D3 got out of the vehicle leaving their car doors open, and robbed V; D2 and D3 re-entered the car; and D1 drove away. Based on these facts, the court held that a jury could rationally find, beyond a reasonable doubt, that a conspiracy to rob V had been formed, and that D1, the driver of the vehicle, was a party to the agreement. Countless cases based on far less evidence than this have found conspiratorial agreements.[44]

When the choreography is missing, however, a court is somewhat less likely to find an agreement, absent more direct evidence. For example, in *Commonwealth v. Cook*,[45] D1 and D2, brothers, conversed with V, a female, on a street. When D1 said he was out of cigarettes, the three began walking toward a nearby convenience store. Along the way, V slipped and fell to the ground, at which moment D1 jumped on top of V in order to rape her. D1 handed his trouser belt to D2, who encouraged

---

[38] *Developments in the Law*, Note 1, *supra*, at 933 (footnote omitted).

[39] Commonwealth v. Nee, 935 N.E.2d 1276, 1282 (Mass. 2010) ("[A] conspiracy may, and typically is, proved by circumstantial evidence, because often there is no direct evidence that an 'agreement' was reached.").

[40] People v. Persinger, 363 N.E.2d 897, 901 (Ill. App. Ct. 1977); State v. Samuels, 914 A.2d 1250, 1255 (N.J. 2007) ("Because the conduct and words of co-conspirators is generally shrouded in 'silence, furtiveness and secrecy,' the conspiracy may be proven circumstantially.").

[41] Glasser v. United States, 315 U.S. 60, 80 (1942) (quoting United States v. Manton, 107 F.2d 834, 839 (2d Cir. 1938)); Commonwealth v. Murphy, 844 A.2d 1228, 1238 (Pa. 2004) ("the agreement is almost always proven through circumstantial evidence, such as by 'the relations, conduct or circumstances of the parties or overt acts on the part of the co-conspirators' ") (quoting Commonwealth v. Wayne, 720 A.2d 456, 464 (Pa. 1998)).

[42] Garner v. State, 6 P.3d 1013, 1020 (Nev. 2000) ("Evidence of a coordinated series of acts . . . is sufficient to infer the existence of an agreement."), *overruled on other grounds by* Sharma v. State, 56 P.3d 868 (Nev. 2002); People v. Maciel, 304 P.3d 983, 1012 (Cal. 2013) ("the existence of a conspiracy may be inferred from the conduct, relationships, interests, and activities of the alleged conspirators before and during the alleged conspiracy") (quoting People v. Rodrigues, 885 P.2d 1 (Cal. 1994)).

[43] Commonwealth v. Azim, 459 A.2d 1244 (Pa. Super. Ct. 1983).

[44] *E.g.*, People v. Persinger, 363 N.E.2d 897 (Ill. App. Ct. 1977) (O, an undercover officer, purchased barbiturates from D1 at the latter's residence; during the meeting, D1 turned to D2, her husband, and requested a pocket knife to scratch the prescription label off the container in which the pills were enclosed; D2 was also present at other illegal purchases; held: there was sufficient evidence of a D1-D2 conspiracy).

[45] 411 N.E.2d 1326 (Mass. App. Ct. 1980).

D1 in the rape. *D2*'s conduct — holding the belt and encouraging *D1* — constituted assistance in the rape. As such, he was properly charged as an accomplice to the rape. Based on this evidence, however, an appellate court concluded that *D2* was *not* properly convicted of the crime of conspiracy with *D1* to rape *V.*

The court's conclusion was sound. It was a chance meeting of the two men with the victim; the rape occurred in an apparently spontaneous, unplanned manner, *i.e.*, *V* slipped and *D1* suddenly attacked her. As the court reasoned, it is as likely that *D2* became involved as an accomplice (rather than a co-conspirator) after the rape had begun as it is "to infer that the minds of the parties had met in advance" as part of an agreement to commit the rape.

[B] Distinguishing the Agreement from the Group That Agrees

The term "conspiracy" describes the agreement that constitutes the offense for which the parties may be punished. However, a common but misleading use of the word "conspiracy" is as a description of *the group itself* that intends to commit the unlawful acts.

These two different uses of the term — "conspiracy" as the agreement, and "conspiracy" as the people who have formed the agreement — are often blurred by commentators and courts. Thus, one treatise states that "the gist of a conspiracy is the combination which is formed."[46] Some courts repeat the unfortunate characterization of a conspiracy as a "combination" of people.[47] Holmes, too, has described a conspiracy as "a partnership in criminal purposes."[48]

The crime of conspiracy should not be described in this fashion. One danger in failing to distinguish between the agreement and the group is that conspiracy convictions may improperly be affirmed. For example, suppose that *X* and *Y* agree (conspire) to commit a robbery. Suppose that *D*, a stranger to *X* and *Y*, unaware of the conspiracy, nonetheless assists in the robbery at the scene in some spur-of-the-moment way. On these facts, as explained in the next chapter, *D* may be convicted of the robbery as an *accomplice* of *X* and *Y.* In view of the fact *X* and *Y* were conspirators, however, may *D* also be convicted of the crime of conspiracy? If the *X-Y* group is treated as the conspiracy rather than their agreement, then it follows that when *D* aids *X* and *Y*, she aids the "conspiracy" (*i.e.*, the group). Therefore, pursuant to complicity law, *D* would be an accomplice of the (group) "conspiracy" and, consequently, guilty of the crime of conspiracy.

This analysis is wrong.[49] The essence of a conspiracy is the agreement itself, and not the group of conspirators. *D*'s last-moment participation in the underlying offense does not mean that she agreed with *X* and *Y* to rob the bank, *i.e.*, that there was a meeting of the minds among the three. To properly convict *D* of conspiracy,

---

[46] Rollin M. Perkins & Ronald N. Boyce, Criminal Law 682 (3d ed. 1982).

[47] *E.g., Commonwealth v. Cook*, 411 N.E.2d at 1328.

[48] United States v. Kissel, 218 U.S. 601, 608 (1910).

[49] *Developments in the Law*, Note 1, *supra*, at 934–35; American Law Institute, Comment to § 5.03, at 420–21.

it would be necessary to prove that she aided and abetted the conspiracy (the agreement) — that is, *D* intentionally aided in the *formation* of the agreement, such as by arranging the meeting at which *X* and *Y* formed the agreement. *D* did not aid in this manner and, therefore, ought not be convicted of conspiracy.

[C] Object of the Agreement

At common law, the object[50] of a conspiracy must be "to do either an unlawful act or a lawful act by criminal or unlawful means."[51] As this quote may suggest, the contemplated act that is the basis of the conspiratorial agreement need not constitute a crime; "it will be enough if the acts contemplated are corrupt, dishonest, fraudulent, or immoral."[52] Thus, at common law it is possible for *two* people to be guilty of the offense of conspiracy because they have agreed to perform an act that is not criminal if performed in the absence of agreement by *one* of them. For example, it is a common law conspiracy for two or more persons to agree to perform a civil wrong (*i.e.*, an act that would subject them to civil damages),[53] or to agree to perform an act that is not a civil wrong but is otherwise considered immoral or dangerous to the public health or safety.[54]

This feature of common law conspiracy, followed in many pre-Model Penal Code statutes,[55] has been strongly criticized by commentators as violative of the principle of legality.[56] People are entitled to fair notice that their planned conduct is subject to criminal sanction. In an age in which legislatures rather than courts define criminal conduct, people should be able to turn to a written code for reasonable guidance in the conduct of their lives. If the legislature has not made a specified act criminal it is unfair to surprise people by punishing the *agreement* to commit the *non*criminal act.

Fair notice is also a constitutional requirement. Although the Supreme Court has never ruled on the validity of this feature of conspiracy law, it once hinted that the breadth of the "unlawfulness" element violates due process.[57] State court rulings on the subject are mixed.[58]

---

[50] For purposes of clarity it is assumed here that the conspirators have a single objective. However, a single agreement may include multiple objectives. *See* § 29.08, *infra*.

[51] State v. Parker, 158 A. 797, 799 (Conn. 1932).

[52] *Id.*

[53] *E.g.*, State v. Loog, 179 A. 623 (N.J. 1935) (conspiracy to defame another).

[54] *E.g.*, Shaw v. Director of Public Prosecutions, [1962] A.C. 220 (H.L.) (affirming a conviction for conspiracy to corrupt public morals, based on the publication of a lawful "Ladies' Directory" that contained the names and telephone numbers of prostitutes); Commonwealth v. Donoghue, 63 S.W.2d 3 (Ky. Ct. App. 1933) (affirming a conviction for conspiracy to exact usurious rates of interest, although usury was not a crime).

[55] American Law Institute, Comment to § 5.03, at 395.

[56] Commonwealth v. Bessette, 217 N.E.2d 893, 896 n.5 (Mass. 1966) (noting the criticism).

[57] Musser v. Utah, 333 U.S. 95, 96–97 (1948).

[58] *E.g.*, *compare* State v. Bowling, 427 P.2d 928, 932 (Ariz. Ct. App. 1967) (unconstitutional) *with* People v. Sullivan, 248 P.2d 520, 526 (Cal. Ct. App. 1952) (constitutional).

Following the Model Penal Code,[59] most states have avoided the unfairness of the common law rule by limiting the offense of conspiracy to agreements to commit criminal acts.

[D] Overt Act

A common law conspiracy is complete upon formation of the unlawful agreement. No act in furtherance of the conspiracy need be proved.[60] Nonetheless, many statutes diverge from the common law and require an allegation in the indictment and proof at trial of the commission of an overt act in furtherance of the conspiracy.

In jurisdictions requiring an overt act, the act need not constitute an attempt to commit the target offense.[61] Any act, no matter how trivial, is sufficient, if performed in furtherance of the conspiracy.[62] Furthermore, the overt act need not be illegal.[63] For example, the act of writing a letter or making a telephone call pursuant to the unlawful agreement, or the lawful purchase of an instrumentality to commit the offense, or even attendance at a lawful meeting,[64] can qualify as the overt act.

In "overt act" jurisdictions, the allegation and proof of a single overt act by *any* party to a conspiracy is sufficient basis to prosecute *every* member of the conspiracy,[65] including those who may have joined in the agreement *after* the act was committed.[66]

To the extent that an overt act is an element of the offense of conspiracy,[67] it is said to serve "to make certain that society does not intervene prematurely."[68] The overt act requirement, "like the substantial-step component of the law of attempt, helps to separate truly dangerous agreements from banter and other exchanges

---

[59] *See* § 29.04[E][2], *infra.*

[60] Carroll v. State, 53 A.3d 1159, 1169 (Md. 2012); State v. Merrill, 530 S.E.2d 608, 611 (N.C. Ct. App. 2000) ("As soon as the union of wills for the unlawful purpose is perfected, the crime . . . is complete, . . . and no overt act is required.").

[61] State v. Heitman, 629 N.W.2d 542, 553 (Neb. 2001).

[62] Commonwealth v. Weimer, 977 A.2d 1103, 1106 (Pa. 2009).

[63] *State v. Heitman*, 629 N.W.2d at 553.

[64] Yates v. United States, 354 U.S. 298, 333–34 (1957), *overruled on other grounds in* Burks v. United States, 437 U.S. 1 (1978) (attendance at a meeting of the Communist Party may constitute the overt act in furtherance of a conspiracy to overthrow the government).

[65] Bannon v. United States, 156 U.S. 464, 469 (1895); People v. Smith, 337 P.3d 1159, 1168 (Cal. 2014).

[66] Kaplan v. United States, 7 F.2d 594, 596 (2d Cir. 1925).

[67] In some jurisdictions, an overt act, although required to convict, is not a formal element of the offense. Instead, the act "merely affords a *locus penitentice*, so that before the act done either one or all of the parties may abandon their design, and thus avoid the penalty prescribed by the statute." United States v. Britton, 108 U.S. 199, 205 (1883). In other words, the overt-act requirement in such jurisdictions gives a conspirator, before that act occurs, "an opportunity to repent." People v. Russo, 25 P.3d 641, 645 (Cal. 2001).

[68] People v. Mass, 628 N.W.2d 540, 559 (Mich. 2001) (Markman, J., concurring).

that pose less risk."[69] It shows "that a conspiracy has moved beyond the talk stage and is being carried out,"[70] that the conspiracy is "at work."[71]

[E]   Model Penal Code

[1]   In General

Section 5.03, subsection (1) — the Model Penal Code definition of conspiracy[72] — "rests on the primordial conception of agreement as the core of the conspiracy idea."[73] The American Law Institute rejected the misleading[74] conception of conspiracy as a "combination" or as a "partnership."

Four types of agreement fall within the definition of conspiracy. A person is guilty of conspiracy if she agrees to: (1) commit an offense (*i.e.*, "engage in conduct that constitutes such crime"); (2) attempt to commit an offense;[75] (3) solicit another to commit an offense;[76] or (4) aid another person in the planning or commission of the offense.[77]

[2]   Object of the Agreement

In a significant departure from the common law, the Model Penal Code provides that the object of the conspiratorial agreement must be a criminal offense. All but three state penal code revisions since the adoption of the final draft of the Code in 1962 have agreed with the American Law Institute in this regard.[78]

[3]   Overt Act

The Code provides that a person may not be convicted of conspiracy to commit a misdemeanor or a felony of the third degree[79] unless she or a fellow conspirator performed an overt act in furtherance of the conspiracy. With felonies of the first and second degree, however, no overt act is required.[80]

---

[69]   United States v. Sassi, 966 F.2d 283, 284 (7th Cir. 1992).

[70]   People v. Abedi, 595 N.Y.S.2d. 1011, 1020 (Sup. Ct. 1993).

[71]   *State v. Heitman*, 629 N.W.2d at 553 (quoting State v. Hansen, 562 N.W.2d 840, 849 (Neb. 1997)).

[72]   The definition is set out in full in § 29.01[B], *supra.*

[73]   American Law Institute, Comment to § 5.03, at 421.

[74]   *See* § 29.04[B], *supra.*

[75]   The purpose of this aspect of the definition is examined at § 29.09[A][2], *infra.*

[76]   *E.g.*, *D1* may be convicted of conspiracy if she agrees with *D2* that *D2* will solicit *X* to steal *V*'s painting.

[77]   *E.g.*, *D1* agrees to provide *D2* with a gun to be used to kill *V*. *D1* is guilty of conspiracy to commit murder, although she did not agree to commit the offense herself.

[78]   American Law Institute, Comment to § 5.03, at 397.

[79]   All felonies under the Model Penal Code are of the third degree unless another degree is specified. Model Penal Code § 6.01(1).

[80]   Model Penal Code § 5.03(5).

As a result of this feature of the Code, the overt-act requirement has gained wide acceptance among the states. Most penal code revisions, however, have gone beyond the Code and apply the overt-act rule to all crimes.[81]

§ 29.05 CONSPIRACY: *MENS REA*

[A] In General

Common law conspiracy is a specific-intent offense. A criminal conspiracy does not occur unless two or more persons: (1) intend to agree; *and* (2) intend that the object of their agreement be achieved.[82] Absence of either intent renders the defendants' conduct non-conspiratorial. Thus, if *O*, an undercover police officer, agrees with *D* to murder *V*, *O* has the requisite intent to form an agreement with *D* (the first intent noted above), but she lacks the specific intent that the murder be consummated. As a result, *O* is not guilty of conspiracy. And, as discussed more fully elsewhere,[83] since *O* is not guilty of conspiracy, *D* cannot be convicted, because there are not "*two* or more persons" with the requisite intent.

It follows from the specific-intent nature of conspiracy that the culpability required for conviction of conspiracy at times must be greater than is required for conviction of the object of the agreement. For example, suppose that *D1* and *D2* agree to set fire to an occupied structure in order to claim the insurance proceeds. If the resulting fire kills occupants, they may be convicted of murder on the ground that the deaths, although unintentional, were recklessly caused. They are *not* guilty of conspiracy to commit murder, however, because their objective was to destroy the building, rather than to kill someone. Put another away, as a matter of logic, one "cannot agree to accomplish a required specific result unintentionally."[84]

[B] Special Issues

[1] "Purpose" Versus "Knowledge": The Meaning of "Intent"

The specific intent of conspiracy is the "intent" that the object of the agreement be achieved. In most cases, the word "intent" suffices to describe the state of mind required. Sometimes, however, it does not.

---

[81] American Law Institute, Comment to § 5.03, at 455–56.

[82] People v. Cortez, 960 P.2d 537, 542 (Cal. 1998).

[83] *See* § 29.06[A], *infra.*

[84] State v. Beccia, 505 A.2d 683, 684 (Conn. 1986) (holding that conspiracy to commit reckless arson is not a cognizable offense); *see also* People v. Cortez, 960 P.2d 537, 538 (Cal. 1998) (holding that all conspiracies to commit murder are necessarily *first*-degree [premeditated] murders, and not *second*-degree [intentional, spur-of-the-moment] murders); State v. Donohue, 834 A.2d 253, 257 (N.H. 2003) (holding that a person may not be convicted of conspiracy to commit a reckless assault). Similarly, it seems impossible as a matter of law for two people to conspire to commit a *sudden* heat-of-passion intentional killing, which constitutes common law voluntary manslaughter (*see* § 31.07, *infra*), since the formation of an agreement to kill demonstrates premeditation, which is the antithesis of sudden, provoked homicide.

It will be remembered that the common law term "intent" encompasses two alternative mental states, namely, what the Model Penal Code describes as "purpose" and "knowledge."[85] That is, *D* "intends" a result to occur if it is her conscious object (*purpose*) to cause the result or, even if it is not her purpose, if she *knows* that it will almost certainly occur from her conduct. The question that lurks, therefore, is whether the specific mental state of conspiracy is proved if either form of "intent" exists, or whether conspiracy can be demonstrated only if each party has as her *purpose* that the conspiratorial objective be achieved.

Usually this issue arises in a narrow context: A person or business furnishes goods or services to another person or group *knowing* that the goods or services will be used for illegal purposes. For example, consider these cases: *F* sells sugar to persons whom she knows are producers of illicit whiskey;[86] *L*, the operator of a telephone answering service, provides telephone messages to known prostitutes;[87] and *D*, a drug wholesaler, sells large quantities of legal drugs to *X*, knowing that *X* is using them for unlawful purposes.[88] In each of these cases, the person furnishing goods or services is aware of the customer's criminal intentions, but may not care whether the crime is committed.

The argument for requiring proof of criminal purpose, rather than mere knowledge — and, thus, potentially letting the defendants in the preceding cases off the criminal hook — is that conspiracy laws should be reserved for those with criminal motivations, rather than "seek to sweep within the drag-net of conspiracy all those who have been associated in any degree whatever with the main offenders."[89] In particular, it is argued, the law should not be broadened to punish those whose primary motive is to conduct an otherwise lawful business. Indeed, in extending liability to merchants who *know* harm will occur from their activities, there is a risk that merchants who only suspect their customers' criminal intentions (thus, are merely *reckless* in regard to their customers' plans) will also be prosecuted, thereby seriously undermining lawful commerce.

The argument in favor of permitting conviction on the basis of knowledge is that society has a compelling interest in deterring people from furnishing their wares and skills to those whom they know are practically certain to use them unlawfully. Free enterprise should not immunize an actor from criminal responsibility in such circumstances; unmitigated desire for profits or simple moral indifference should not be rewarded at the expense of crime prevention.

Case law is divided on this purpose-versus-knowledge issue.[90] However, even in jurisdictions in which purpose is required, the line between "purpose" and "knowledge" is very thin, and purpose may often be inferred from a defendant's

---

[85] *See* § 10.04[A][1], *supra*.

[86] United States v. Falcone, 109 F.2d 579 (2d Cir.), *aff'd*, 311 U.S. 205 (1940).

[87] People v. Lauria, 251 Cal. App. 2d 471 (Ct. App. 1967).

[88] Direct Sales Co. v. United States, 319 U.S. 703 (1943).

[89] *United States v. Falcone*, 109 F.2d at 581.

[90] American Law Institute, Comment to § 5.03, at 404 (and cases cited therein).

knowledge of the customer's plans.[91] The requisite purpose may be inferred, for example, if the person furnishing the service or instrumentality promotes the venture and has a "stake in its outcome,"[92] such as when she furnishes the goods or services at a grossly inflated price. Similarly, purpose may be inferred from knowledge if a grossly disproportionate share of D's business is with criminal X,[93] or with separate customers whose planned conduct is illegal.[94] Finally, purpose may be inferred from knowledge if D provides goods or services for which there is no lawful use.

[2] *Mens Rea* Regarding Attendant Circumstances

The specific-intent element of conspiracy applies to the proscribed conduct or results of conduct that are the object of the agreement, but what mental state is required regarding "attendant circumstance" elements of an offense? For example, consider the essential facts of *United States v. Feola*:[95] $D1$ and $D2$, drug dealers, agreed to attack V, a federal officer disguised as a drug customer. Clearly, $D1$ and $D2$ intended the prohibited result (battery), but were they guilty of the more serious federal offense of conspiracy to assault a federal officer in the performance of his official duties? That is, does the specific-intent requirement of conspiracy apply to the attendant circumstance of V's status as a federal law enforcement officer?

As explained in *Feola*, the substantive offense of "assault upon a federal officer" requires no culpable state of mind regarding the attendant circumstance. That is, a person may be convicted of "assault upon a federal officer" as long as she has the requisite intent to commit the assaultive acts, even if she does not know or have reason to know that the intended victim is an officer engaged in official duties. In light of this, the prosecution in *Feola* argued for symmetry: The *mens rea* required for conviction of *conspiracy* to assault a federal officer should be the same — neither more nor less — as that which is required for conviction of the substantive offense itself. Thus, in this case, to convict $D1$ and $D2$ of conspiracy, no *mens rea* would be required as to V's status as a federal officer.

The *Feola* defendants argued instead that even if a person may be convicted of assault upon a federal officer without knowledge of the victim's federal status, one can hardly *conspire* to assault a federal officer without knowing the victim's identity. In support of this proposition they quoted the reasoning of Judge Learned Hand, who provided this example:

> While one may, for instance, be guilty of running past a traffic light of whose existence one is ignorant, one cannot be guilty of conspiring to run

---

[91] *See* Commonwealth v. Nee, 935 N.E.2d 1276, 1282 (Mass. 2010); *People v. Lauria*, 251 Cal. App. 2d at 477–81.

[92] *United States v. Falcone*, 109 F.2d at 581.

[93] *E.g.*, Direct Sales Co. v. United States, 319 U.S. 703 (1943) (*D*, a drug wholesaler, sold morphine sulfate to X, a physician, in quantities 300 times the amount required for lawful purposes).

[94] *E.g.*, Shaw v. Director of Public Prosecutions, [1962] A.C. 220 (H.L.) (*S* sold space in a telephone and address directory to prostitutes).

[95] 420 U.S. 671 (1975).

past such a light, for one cannot agree to run past a light unless one supposes that there is a light to run past.[96]

Although Judge Hand's "attractive, but perhaps seductive"[97] reasoning "seems difficult to overcome,"[98] the Supreme Court in *Feola* rejected his reasoning, and held that the federal conspiracy statute does not require any greater *mens rea* as to an attendant circumstance than is embodied in the substantive offense itself.

Was the Court correct in rejecting Hand's traffic light analogy? Arguably, the circumstances in *Feola were* distinguishable from it. First, Hand's traffic offense was a *malum prohibitum* strict-liability crime, whereas an assault requires a wrongful intent to injure another. A court might wish to be more protective of defendants when the underlying offense is of the *malum prohibitum* variety.

Second, the moral-wrong doctrine[99] supports the distinction. As the Supreme Court said in *Feola*:

> This interpretation [that no *mens rea* is required as to the victim's status as a law enforcement officer] poses no risk of unfairness to defendants. It is no snare for the unsuspecting. Although the perpetrator of a narcotics [offense], such as the one involved here, may be surprised to find that his intended victim is a federal officer in civilian apparel, he nonetheless knows from the very outset that his planned course of conduct is wrongful.

The same cannot be said in the case of Judge Hand's hypothetical traffic violator, who was not committing a wrongful act based on the facts as she reasonably believed them to be.

Third, in *Feola* the attendant circumstance was a so-called "jurisdictional" element of the crime. That is, the fact that a victim is a federal officer performing her official duties is not a material element of the offense: It is included in the definition of the crime solely to provide the federal courts with authority to prosecute assaults that would otherwise constitute a state crime only. According to *Feola*, Congress did not intend for this jurisdictional feature of the law to stand in the way of conspiracy prosecutions based on the federal assault statute. In Hand's traffic light example, however, the issue of federal jurisdiction was not implicated.

Feola is not a constitutionally based decision. As such, states are not required to follow the principles of that case in interpreting their own conspiracy statutes. Thus, it remains an open question, on a state-by-state, offense-by-offense, basis, whether the crime of conspiracy may require a higher level of culpability regarding an attendant circumstance than is embodied in the underlying offense.

---

[96] United States v. Crimmins, 123 F.2d 271, 273 (2d Cir. 1941).

[97] *Feola*, 420 U.S. at 689.

[98] American Law Institute, Comment to § 5.03, at 413.

[99] *See* § 12.03[D][2], *supra.*

[3] Corrupt-Motive Doctrine

Some jurisdictions have applied what has come to be known as the "corrupt-motive doctrine."[100] This doctrine states that in addition to the usual *mens rea* requirements of conspiracy (*i.e.*, intent to agree and intent to commit the substantive offense), the parties to a conspiracy must also have a corrupt or wrongful motive for their actions.[101]

When the objective of a conspiracy is a *malum in se* offense, *e.g.*, murder, rape, or larceny, the effect of this requirement is minimal, in that it only requires that the parties have sufficient knowledge of the relevant facts that they can appreciate that their conduct is wrongful. Thus, if we reconsider *Feola*,[102] in which *D1* and *D2* agreed to assault *V*, an undercover police officer, the parties had the requisite corrupt motive to commit a wrongful act (assault a human being), although they did not realize the degree of seriousness of their wrongful plan (*i.e.*, they did not know that *V* was a law enforcement officer).

When the criminal objective is a *malum prohibitum* offense, however, the corrupt-motive doctrine potentially serves as an exception to the usual rule that ignorance of the law is no excuse. Thus, in a jurisdiction that applies this doctrine, if *D1* and *D2* agree to do X, a morally innocent but illegal act, they cannot be convicted of conspiracy to commit X if they did not realize that X was illegal. In the absence of knowledge of the law, the parties lack a corrupt motive.[103]

Assuming the propriety of the ignorance-of-the-law-is-no-excuse rule, is *this* exception to it justifiable? The best argument for the exception is that, in light of the highly inchoate nature of the offense of conspiracy, "breathing space" should be given to those who lack a corrupt motive for their planned conduct. That is, we may reasonably predict that, unlike those animated by criminal intent, those who agree to commit actions that constitute a *malum prohibitum* offense would voluntarily abandon their efforts if they were aware of its illegality. On the other hand, if the *malum prohibitum* statute in question is strict liability in nature, as is often the case, there may be no justification for requiring more culpability for the conspiracy charge than for the target offense.

---

[100] At one time, the doctrine was said to have "won general acceptance." *Developments in the Law*, Note 1, *supra*, at 936. In part because the issue only rarely arises today, the current status of the doctrine in most jurisdictions is uncertain, but the trend is to reject the doctrine, especially in the federal courts. *E.g.*, United States v. Cohen, 260 F.3d 68 (2d Cir. 2001) (refusing to apply the corrupt motive doctrine).

[101] *E.g.*, Commonwealth v. Benesch, 194 N.E. 905, 910 (Mass. 1935); State v. Jacobson, 697 N.W.2d 610, 615 (Minn. 2005) (requiring proof that the parties possessed a "conscious and intentional purpose to break law"); People v. Powell, 63 N.Y. 88, 92 (1875).

[102] United States v. Feola, 420 U.S. 671 (1975). *See* § 29.05[B][2], *supra*.

[103] *E.g.*, Commonwealth v. Gormley, 77 Pa. Super. 298 (1921) (*D1* and *D2*, election officials, were not guilty of conspiracy to violate a *malum prohibitum* election law when they agreed to commit acts that violated the substantive offense, because they were unaware that their activities were encompassed by the statute); *State v. Jacobson*, 697 N.W.2d at 615 (holding that, in a conspiracy prosecution, a defendant's mistake of law, based on a lawyer's wrongful advice and/or an official misinterpretation of the law, is sufficient to prove a lack of requisite intent).

[C]   Model Penal Code

A person is not guilty of conspiracy under the Model Penal Code[104] unless the conspiratorial agreement was made "with the purpose of promoting or facilitating" the commission of the substantive offense. This means that a person is not guilty of conspiracy unless the object of the agreement was to bring about the prohibited result or to cause the prohibited conduct to occur, even if such purpose is not an element of the target offense. For example, suppose that *D1* and *D2* agree to burn down an occupied building for the insurance proceeds and, in the ensuing fire, an occupant dies. The defendants are very plausibly guilty of murder, based on their reckless indifference to the value of human life.[105] However, they are not guilty of conspiracy to commit murder, unless another object of their agreement was to take human life.[106] The express requirement of purpose also resolves a common law debate: A conspiracy does *not* exist if a provider of goods or services is aware of, but fails to share, another person's criminal purpose.[107]

The Model Penal Code does not recognize the corrupt-motive doctrine.[108] Section 2.04, subsection (3), of the Code specifies the circumstances in which ignorance of the law is a defense. The drafters of the Code did not believe that a special defense in the case of conspiracy was justified. They reasoned that the real purpose of the corrupt-motive doctrine was to "import fair mens rea requirements into [strict liability] statutes."[109] Although the drafters agreed with this goal, they favored promoting it directly through abandonment of strict liability offenses, rather than through conspiracy doctrine.

The Code does not determine what culpability, if any, regarding an attendant circumstance of a substantive offense is required to convict for the offense of conspiracy.[110] The Commentary states that this issue is "best left to judicial resolution."[111]

---

[104] For the full Code definition of "conspiracy," see § 29.01[B], *supra.*

[105] Model Penal Code § 210.2(1)(b).

[106] American Law Institute, Comment to § 5.03, at 407–08. However, *D1* and *D2* may be convicted of conspiracy to recklessly endanger the occupants of the building. Model Penal Code § 211.2. This result is possible because their *purpose*, in the language of § 5.03(1)(a), was to "engage in conduct [setting fire to the building] that constitutes such crime [placing another person in danger of death or serious bodily injury, the social harm of reckless endangerment]."

[107] *See generally* American Law Institute, Comment to § 5.03, at 403–04. The issue is raised in 29.05[B][1], *supra.*

[108] *See* § 29.05[B][3], *supra.*

[109] American Law Institute, Comment to § 5.03, at 417 (footnote omitted).

[110] This issue is raised in § 29.05[B][2], *supra.*

[111] *See* American Law Institute, Comment to § 5.03, at 413.

§ 29.06 "PLURALITY" REQUIREMENT

[A] Common Law

According to Justice Cardozo, "[i]t is impossible . . . for a man to conspire with himself."[112] This observation follows from the fact that a conspiracy is an agreement, and an agreement is a group act. Unless two or more people form an agreement, no one does. As a consequence, a prosecution of common law conspiracy must fail in the absence of proof that at least two persons possessed the requisite *mens rea* of a conspiracy, *i.e.*, the intent to agree and the specific intent that the object of their agreement be achieved.[113] This is the so-called "plurality" requirement.

As a result of the plurality principle, there can be no common law conspiracy if one of two parties to an agreement lacks the specific intent to commit the substantive offense. For example, no conspiracy conviction is possible — although, perhaps, an *attempted* conspiracy charge might lie[114] — if one of the two persons is an undercover agent feigning agreement,[115] or lacks the capacity to form the agreement due to mental illness.[116] Indeed, although the rule is fast breaking down, in a *joint trial* of the two defendants in an alleged two-person conspiracy, the acquittal of one alleged conspirator traditionally requires the discharge of the remaining defendant, regardless of the jury's reasons for acquittal of the first party.[117]

---

[112] Morrison v. California, 291 U.S. 82, 92 (1934).

[113] People v. Justice, 562 N.W.2d 652, 658 (Mich. 1997).

[114] Can one *attempt* to conspire? There is little case law on this issue, but most courts have rejected the concept. Ira P. Robbins, *Double Inchoate Crimes*, 26 Harv. J. on Legis. 1, 54–55 (1989); United States v. Yu-Leung, 51 F.3d 1116, 1122 n.3 (2d Cir. 1995) ("an attempted conspiracy — a creature unknown to federal criminal law"); *but see* State v. Eames, 365 So. 2d 1361, 1364 (La. 1978). *Contra* United States v. Riddle, 44 M.J. 282, 284–85 (C.A.A.F. 1996) (recognizing the offense); People v. Anderson, 509 N.W.2d 548 (Mich. Ct. App. 1993) (*A* convicted of attempted conspiracy to deliver cocaine).

Conceptually, there is no reason why a jurisdiction could not recognize such an offense. Some courts, however, may be troubled on policy grounds about recognizing such a highly inchoate offense: A conspiracy can occur far sooner than an attempt; an attempted conspiracy, therefore, takes the process to an even earlier stage. The difficulty with this argument is that most states have enacted general solicitation statutes, and a *solicitation, by definition, is an attempted conspiracy. See* § 28.02[A], *supra.* Thus, the reason for not recognizing the defense may simply be that the prosecutor has mischarged the defendant. It is noteworthy, for example, that one court, *United States v. Riddle, supra*, in upholding an attempted conspiracy charge, observed that no general solicitation statute existed in that jurisdiction.

Note: Although a solicitation is always an attempted conspiracy, an attempted conspiracy does not always constitute a solicitation. *See* § 28.02[A], *supra.*

[115] *E.g.*, State v. Pacheco, 882 P.2d 183, 186 (Wash. 1994); Palato v. State, 988 P.2d 512, 515–16 (Wyo. 1999); United States v. Escobar de Bright, 742 F.2d 1196, 1199–200 (9th Cir. 1984).

[116] *See* Regle v. State, 264 A.2d 119 (Md. Ct. Spec. App. 1970) (the prosecutor alleged a four-person conspiracy, but one party was a police informant, the second was a police officer, and the third was insane, leaving only one defendant with the requisite *mens rea*; held: conspiracy conviction could not stand!).

[117] State v. Valladares, 664 P.2d 508, 512–13 (Wash. 1983). As noted in the text, this rule is breaking down. For example, in Commonwealth v. Campbell, 651 A.2d 1096 (Pa. 1994), the Supreme Court of Pennsylvania rejected earlier law and ruled that "acquittal of the sole alleged co-conspirator does not per se preclude the conviction of the remaining defendant, even if the defendants are jointly tried." *Id.* at

The plurality rule does not require, however, that two persons be prosecuted and convicted of conspiracy. It is enough that the prosecutor proves beyond a reasonable doubt that two persons are guilty of conspiracy. Thus, the conviction of a conspirator is not in jeopardy simply because the other person involved in the arrangement is unapprehended, dead, or unknown, or cannot be prosecuted because he has been granted immunity.[118] And, although the rule used to be to the contrary,[119] the modern rule is that a convicted conspirator is not automatically entitled to relief because of the acquittal of the remaining conspirators in a *separate trial.*[120] As long as the evidence at the first trial was "sufficient unto itself to support its verdict"[121] — that is, the prosecutor proved that there was a conspiratorial agreement between two or more persons, one of whom was the defendant — the failure to convince the second jury of the conspiracy does not impair the validity of the first conviction, since the acquittal at the second trial may have been the result of a multitude of factors, such as the unexpected absence of a critical state witness.

The plurality requirement has been criticized. First, the rule undermines the law enforcement purpose of conspiracy laws. For example, if *O*, an undercover police officer, feigns willingness to assist *D* in the commission of a murder, the plurality rule supposedly prevents *O* from arresting *D* until the latter's conduct reaches the more dangerous stage of an attempt.[122] Second, one who fails to conspire because her "partner in crime" is an undercover officer feigning agreement is no less personally dangerous or culpable than one whose colleague in

---

1099. In *Campbell*, the prosecutor presented sufficient evidence that a jury could conclude beyond a reasonable doubt that: (a) a two-person conspiracy existed; and (b) *C* was one of the two conspirators. The jury acquitted *C*'s co-defendant, but the apparent reason for this acquittal was that the jury had a reasonable doubt that the acquitted individual was, in fact, *C*'s co-conspirator — the government may have arrested the wrong person. The *Campbell* court held that *C*'s conviction could stand under these circumstances.

The California Supreme Court, as well, has rejected the traditional rule. In People v. Palmer, 15 P.3d 234 (Cal. 2001), *D1* and *D2* were accused of attempted murder and conspiracy to commit murder. They were tried jointly but in front of separate juries. *D1* was convicted of all charges; the second jury convicted *D2* of attempted murder but acquitted him of conspiracy. *D1* argued that, as a result of *D2*'s conspiracy acquittal, his conviction for that offense had to be reversed. The state supreme court, while conceding that the verdicts were logically inconsistent and that a person cannot conspire with himself, ruled that *D1*'s conspiracy conviction should stand. It reasoned that a jury can acquit a defendant for any reason or for no reason at all. It speculated that the jury may have acquitted *D2* out of compassion for the fact that he was 15 years old, while *D1* was nearly twice his age. As there was substantial evidence supporting *D1*'s conspiracy conviction, the court determined he should not receive a windfall as a result of the second jury's compassionate (or simply legally mistaken) decision to acquit *D2* of conspiracy. *Accord* United States v. Tyson, 653 F.3d 192, 206–07 (3rd Cir. 2011).

[118] *See* Commonwealth v. Byrd, 417 A.2d 173, 176–77 (Pa. 1980).

[119] *E.g.*, Sherman v. State, 202 N.W. 413, 414 (Neb. 1925), *overruled by* Platt v. State, 8 N.W.2d 849, 855 (Neb. 1943); *Developments in the Law*, Note 1, *supra*, at 972–73.

[120] *E.g.*, State v. Colon, 778 A.2d 875, 883 (Conn. 2001); State v. Johnson, 788 A.2d 628, 632–33 (Md. 2002) (also stating that this rule "is well-accepted in most state jurisdictions").

[121] Gardner v. State, 408 A.2d 1317, 1322 (Md. 1979).

[122] This criticism is overstated. Even with the plurality doctrine, *D* may be guilty of solicitation. Furthermore, if a jurisdiction recognizes the offense of *attempted* conspiracy, *D* could be arrested for the latter offense. *See* Note 114, *supra.*

fact possesses the specific intent to go through with the criminal plan.[123]

On the other hand, the plurality doctrine is consistent with the "special dangers in group criminality" rationale of conspiracy.[124]

[B] Model Penal Code

The Model Penal Code departs significantly from the common law by establishing a unilateral approach to conspiracy liability. Unlike the common law definition of conspiracy, which is phrased in terms of "two or more persons," the Code "focuses inquiry on the culpability of the actor whose liability is in issue, rather than on that of the group of which [she] is alleged to be a part."[125] That is, although the gist of the offense, as at common law, is the agreement, "conspiracy" is defined in terms of the guilt of a single party. This is evident from the Code's definition of "conspiracy,"[126] which starts, "*A person* is guilty of conspiracy with another person" if "*he agrees* with such other person" to commit an offense.

The unilateral nature of the Code's conspiracy provision affects legal analysis in various ways, some of which are discussed later in this chapter.[127] Its effect regarding the plurality doctrine, however, is straightforward. Although the prosecution may not convict a person of conspiracy in the absence of proof of an agreement, it is no defense that the person with whom the actor agreed: (1) has not been or cannot be convicted; or (2) is acquitted in the same or subsequent trial on the ground that she did not have the intent to go forward with the criminal plan (*e.g.*, she feigned agreement in an effort to frustrate the endeavor,[128] or is insane[129]).

The unilateral approach has been adopted in all but a very few recent revisions of state penal codes.[130]

---

[123] Miller v. State, 955 P.2d 892, 897 (Wyo. 1998).

[124] *See* § 29.02[B], *supra*.

[125] American Law Institute, Comment to § 5.03, at 393; *see generally id.* at 398–402.

[126] See § 29.01[B], *supra*, for the full definition.

[127] *See* §§ 29.07[E], 29.09[D][2], *infra*.

[128] *E.g.*, State v. Heitman, 629 N.W.2d 542 (Neb. 2001) (*H* conversed on the Internet with a police officer posing as a 14-year-old; "the child" agreed to have sexual relations with *H*; held: *H* was guilty of conspiracy to commit sexual assault on a child).

[129] Model Penal Code § 5.04(1)(b) expressly provides that it is no defense that the person with whom the defendant conspired is "irresponsible or has an immunity to prosecution or conviction." However, this result is already implicit in the unilateral conception. American Law Institute, Comment to § 5.03, at 399–400.

[130] *Id.* at 398–99; *see* Miller v. State, 955 P.2d 892, 897 (Wyo. 1998) ("[T]he modern trend in state courts is to rule that a conspiracy count is viable even when one of the participants is a government agent or is feigning agreement.").

§ 29.07   PARTIES TO A CONSPIRACY

[A]   The Issue

Frequently, the facts surrounding an incident demonstrate that a conspiracy is afoot, but what is unclear is whether there is a single conspiracy involving many defendants, or multiple conspiracies involving fewer persons in each group. Four cases illustrate the issue. They will be discussed throughout this section.

[1]   *Kotteakos v. United States*[131]

Brown served as a broker for 31 persons in obtaining fraudulent loans from the government. He and the loan recipients were indicted on one count of conspiracy. The evidence at trial demonstrated that the loan recipients were part of eight or more independent groups, none of which had any connection with any other group except that each used Brown as its broker.

The issue in the case was whether the 32 defendants were parties to a single conspiracy (as the prosecutor contended), or whether there existed eight or more smaller conspiracies, each consisting of a different group of loan recipients and Brown (as the loan recipients asserted).

[2]   *Blumenthal v. United States*[132]

In *Blumenthal*, the unnamed owner of a liquor wholesale agency distributed whiskey through two men, Weiss and Goldsmith, who arranged with Feigenbaum and Blumenthal to sell the whiskey to local tavern owners at a price in violation of the law.

The prosecutor alleged one conspiracy, the parties being the unidentified owner, the two distributors, and the salesmen. The salesmen claimed, however, that they never dealt with the owner or knew his identity. If they participated in a conspiracy, they asserted, it was one with the distributors alone; in turn the distributors were in a separate conspiracy with the owner.

[3]   *United States v. Peoni*[133]

Peoni sold a small quantity of counterfeit money to Regno, who in turn sold the money to Dorsey, who passed the money in commerce to innocent persons. The prosecutor alleged that the three men were parties to a single conspiracy. Peoni contended that if he was a party to any conspiracy it was with Regno alone, who in turn conspired with Dorsey.

---

[131]   328 U.S. 750 (1946).

[132]   332 U.S. 539 (1947).

[133]   100 F.2d 401 (2d Cir. 1938).

[4] *United States v. Bruno*[134]

Bruno and 87 others were prosecuted for conspiracy to import, sell, and possess narcotics. The evidence showed that a group of persons whose object it was to smuggle narcotics into the country through the Port of New York, distributed the drugs through middlemen to retailers in New York and other retailers serving the Texas-Louisiana region. The retailers distributed the drugs to individual addicts.

No communication between the importers and any of the retailers or between the New York retailers and the Texas-Louisiana retailers was proved. The importers did know, however, that the middlemen dealt with retailers, and the retailers knew that the middlemen obtained their drugs from importers.

On appeal, the petitioners claimed that instead of a single conspiracy, there were at least three conspiracies — one between the importers and the middlemen; a second between the middlemen and the New York retailers; and a third between the middlemen and the Texas-Louisiana retailers.

[B] Why the Issue Matters

[1] Liability for Conspiracy

The most obvious reason why the structure of a conspiracy is important is that it will affect the number of counts of conspiracy for which a particular person may be prosecuted and convicted. For example, in *Kotteakos*, as the prosecutor conceived of the case, Brown was guilty of one count of conspiracy with 31 loan recipients; alternatively, Brown was potentially guilty of eight or more counts of conspiracy, each involving a smaller number of parties.

[2] Liability of Parties for Substantive Offenses

As is discussed more fully elsewhere,[135] a conspirator is guilty of every offense committed by every other conspirator in furtherance of the unlawful agreement. The structure of the conspiracy, therefore, may dramatically affect an individual conspirator's liability for the substantive crimes of others.

For example, if the prosecutor in *Kotteakos* was correct in treating the 32 defendants as parties to a single conspiracy, each party could be convicted of 31 separate counts of fraud (assuming that the fraudulent loans were obtained); if the loan recipients' theory was correct, however, each of them was guilty of only a few fraudulently obtained loans, namely those obtained by the group composing the smaller conspiracy.

Similarly, in *Bruno* the prosecutor's theory could result in New York retailers being held accountable for every drug sale on the Texas-Louisiana streets (and vice-versa); their liability would be considerably less if the defense theory of the structure of the conspiracy was correct.

---

[134] 105 F.2d 921 (2d Cir. 1939), *rev'd on other grounds*, 308 U.S. 287 (1939).

[135] *See* § 30.08, *infra.*

[3]   Use of Hearsay Evidence

"Hearsay evidence" is evidence of a statement made other than by a witness while testifying at the hearing, which is offered to prove the truth of the matter stated. Subject to many exceptions, hearsay testimony is inadmissible at trial. Thus, under this rule, W, a witness, may not testify that X told her that she (X) saw D commit an offense.[136]

The hearsay rule is subject to two exceptions relevant here. First, an out-of-court admission by a defendant, *e.g.*, an assertion by $D1$ that she killed V, may be introduced at $D1$'s trial through the hearsay testimony of W, someone to whom $D1$ made the statement or who overheard the remarks. Second, an out-of-court statement of a conspirator made while participating in the conspiracy may be introduced in evidence against any or all of her co-conspirators. Thus, a statement by $D1$ to W that she and $D2$ murdered V may be introduced against both $D1$ and $D2$ and any other co-conspirators.

The structure of the alleged conspiracy, therefore, is critical to determination of the admissibility of hearsay testimony. For example, under the prosecutor's theory of the conspiracy in *Bruno*, an out-of-court statement made by a New York retailer that "we and the Texans and Louisianans are getting a rotten deal from the importers and middlemen," could be used against the importers, middlemen, Texas and Louisiana retailers, and every other New York retailer. Applying the retailers' theory of the conspiracy, however, the New York retailer's remarks would be inadmissible against the Texas-Louisiana retailers, because they were not parties to the New York conspiracy.

[4]   Joint Trial

Generally speaking, prosecutors prefer to bring every member of an alleged conspiracy to trial in a single proceeding, rather than to prosecute the conspirators in separate trials. Joint trials are more efficient (*e.g.*, all of the evidence may be introduced once to a single jury). Perhaps equally importantly, a joint trial makes it more difficult for innocent or barely culpable defendants to separate themselves from guilty co-defendants. As Justice Jackson has observed:

> A co-defendant in a conspiracy trial occupies an uneasy seat. There generally will be evidence of wrongdoing by somebody. It is difficult for the individual to make his own case stand on its own merits in the minds of jurors who are ready to believe that birds of a feather are flocked together.[137]

Thus, in *Bruno*, the most culpable importers were joined with comparatively small-time street retailers. Even if some of the 88 persons charged with conspiracy were innocent of wrongdoing, they faced substantial difficulties of proof.

---

[136] Hearsay testimony is inadmissible because if it were allowed, a defendant would be denied her constitutional right to cross-examine her accuser (X in the example in the text), and because it would render the trial less reliable than if the accuser were required to testify directly.

[137] Krulewitch v. United States, 336 U.S. 440, 454 (1949) (concurring opinion).

[5] Overt-Act Requirement

The structure of a conspiracy is critical in jurisdictions recognizing an overt-act requirement.[138] In these jurisdictions, an act of one conspirator in furtherance of the agreement renders a prosecution permissible against every other party to the same agreement.

For example, in *Kotteakos* proof of a single overt act by one person, for example by Brown, pertaining to a single fraudulent loan, would be sufficient to bring the conspiracy prosecution against all 32 defendants. If the loan recipients' argument was correct, however, at least eight separate conspiracies were involved, and proof of an overt act in each of these cases would be required.

[6] Venue

In general, a trial may be held in any jurisdiction in which the crime was committed. With conspiracies, a trial may be brought not only where the agreement was formulated, but also in any jurisdiction in which any member of the conspiracy performed any act in its furtherance.

The effect of this venue rule is especially dramatic in federal cases. The larger the conspiracy alleged by the prosecutor, the greater are the number of federal districts in the country in which it is permissible to bring the prosecution. The prosecutor, therefore, has an incentive to shape the conspiracy in a manner that will allow her to bring the case in a sympathetic venue. It also permits her to compel a defendant in a conspiracy prosecution "to defend at a great distance from any place he ever did any act because some accused confederate did some trivial and by itself innocent act in the chosen district."[139]

[C] Structure of Conspiracies

In conspiracy prosecutions involving multiple layers of actors, it is useful for a lawyer to conceptualize the alleged conspiracy in diagrammatic fashion. Usually the diagraming will demonstrate that a conspiracy looks something like a wheel, a chain, or a combination of the two.

[1] Wheel Conspiracies

Some conspiracies look like wheels. In the center of the wheel (*the hub*) is one person or group who transacts illegal dealings with various other persons or groups (*the spokes*). As the prosecutor conceptualized it, *Kotteakos* was a wheel conspiracy. Brown was the hub. Each of the persons for whom he obtained loans or, at least, each of the eight groups of persons with whom he dealt, was a spoke.

However, for a wheel conspiracy to be complete, *i.e.*, for it to be fair to say that there exists a single conspiracy that includes the hub and all of the spokes, there must be a rim around the wheel. That is, one must be able to draw a line around the wheel connecting the spokes. If this cannot be done, then there is no wheel

---

[138] *See generally* § 29.04[D], *supra.*

[139] *Krulewitch v. United States*, 336 U.S. at 453 (Jackson, J., concurring).

conspiracy; rather, there exist as many chain conspiracies (see below) as there are spokes, with the membership of each conspiracy consisting of the person/group in the hub and the individual at the other end of the spoke. The process of how the spokes are connected together to create a genuine wheel conspiracy is considered in subsection [D].

[2] Chain Conspiracies

A chain conspiracy ordinarily involves "several layers of personnel dealing with a single subject matter, as opposed to a specific person."[140] These conspiracies most often occur in business-like criminal activities, in which each person or group in the conspiracy has specialized responsibilities that link together the various aspects of the unlawful conduct.

As the prosecutors alleged the facts, *Blumenthal* and *Peoni* were three-link chain conspiracies. In *Blumenthal* the unidentified owner of the wholesale agency was linked to Weiss and Goldsmith, the distributors, who in turn were linked to Feigenbaum and Blumenthal, who sold the whiskey to taverns. In *Peoni*, Peoni was linked to Regno who was linked to Dorsey.

The issue with chain conspiracies is how many people or groups may properly be linked together. The longer the chain, the more tenuous the relationship between the distant links.

[3] Chain-Wheel Conspiracies

It is not unusual to find that the structure of a very large conspiracy has features of both a wheel and a chain. *Bruno* potentially fits this description. Notice that it was basically a chain consisting of smugglers, middlemen, and retailers. However, there existed at least two geographically disparate groups of retailers. It is possible, therefore, to conceptualize the conspiracy either as two chain conspiracies (in which the importers, middlemen, and the separate state retailers are linked) or as a chain conspiracy with spokes at the end (thus, the importers are linked to the middlemen, at which point the various retail groups become spokes connected to the middlemen).[141]

[D] Common Law Analysis

[1] In General

There is no simple method for determining the proper structure of a conspiracy. Many factors, such as the nature of the criminal activity, the number of defendants, and the extent of contact between the parties, will affect the ultimate result. One matter is clear, however: To be regarded as a co-conspirator, a person does not need

---

[140] People v. Macklowitz, 514 N.Y.S.2d 883, 886 (Sup. Ct. 1987).

[141] Of course, the New York and Texas-Louisiana spokes consisted of many individual retailers no more likely to be connected to one another than one state group was connected to the retailers in the other region. Thus, if one were inclined to do so, one could break up the two spokes into many more individual spokes.

to know the identity, *or even the existence*, of every other member of the conspiracy, nor must she participate in every detail or event of the conspiracy.[142] It follows, therefore, that a prosecutor's theory of a conspiracy is not fatally flawed solely because one party to the alleged agreement never communicated with certain other members. However, to be a co-conspirator, a defendant must "have a general awareness of both the scope and the objective of the enterprise";[143] in general, there must be a "community of interest [among the parties] or reason to know of each other's existence."[144]

[2] Wheel Conspiracies

Hubs and spokes frequently perceive events differently. The hub views each spoke as part of a broader criminal enterprise; the spokes, however, often interpret the situation more narrowly. For example, in *Kotteakos*, Brown was in the business of obtaining fraudulent loans for his customers. He sought each customer — each spoke — as a part of a broader plan. The customers, however, were interested only in their own loans.

A rim does not exist — there is no wheel conspiracy — unless the prosecutor demonstrates that the spokes viewed their contacts with the hub as part of a plan broader than any individual spoke's relationship with the hub: "What is required is a *shared*, single criminal objective, not just similar or parallel objectives between similarly situated people."[145]

In *Kotteakos*, the appellate court concluded that the spokes lacked this shared objective. No community of interest existed among the spokes. Each loan recipient wanted a loan, received it, and moved on. Each loan was independent of the others. Each fraudulent application stood or fell on the basis of the false claims asserted in that particular application. Thus, the spokes were correct in concluding that, rather than one wheel conspiracy, there existed multiple chain conspiracies involving Brown and each spoke.

An example of a genuine wheel conspiracy is *Anderson v. Superior Court*:[146] *A*, an illegal abortionist, hired as many as 17 persons, to whom he paid "finder's fees," to refer pregnant women to him. The court upheld an indictment charging the 18 persons (*A*, the hub; and the 17 spokes) as parties to a single conspiracy. Here, unlike in *Kotteakos*, the spokes had an ongoing relationship with the hub. And, arguably, each of the spokes shared a common objective, since their continued employment depended on the success of the broader illegal venture.

---

[142] United States v. Sophie, 900 F.2d 1064, 1080–81 (7th Cir. 1990).

[143] United States v. Evans, 970 F.2d 663, 670 (10th Cir. 1992).

[144] Kilgore v. State, 305 S.E.2d 82, 90 (Ga. 1983).

[145] *United States v. Evans*, 970 F.2d at 670; United States v. Shorter, 54 F.3d 1248, 1254 (7th Cir. 1995) (there is a single conspiracy if there is a shared design; there are separate conspiracies "if there are distinct illegal ends and no overlapping interest between parties").

[146] 177 P.2d 315 (Cal. Ct. App. 1947), *overruled on other grounds by* People v. Weiss, 327 P.2d 527 (Cal. 1958).

[3]　Chain Conspiracies

Large chain conspiracies are easier to prove than wheel conspiracies. This follows from the fact that chain conspiracies ordinarily involve unlawful plans that cannot succeed unless each link successfully perform her responsibilities in the arrangement.

Thus, in *Blumenthal*, the Supreme Court found that the prosecutor properly charged a single conspiracy. Although the salesmen claimed that they did not know of the owner's existence (much less his identity), the Court pointed out that they knew that the persons with whom they dealt were not the true owners of the wholesale agency. Therefore, the "salesmen knew or must have known that others unknown to them were sharing in so large a project." Each salesman "by reason of [his] knowledge of the plan's general scope, if not its exact limits, sought a common end, to aid in disposing of the whiskey."

This does not mean that every chain is a single conspiracy. *Peoni*, for example, was not a single conspiracy. Here, Peoni apparently sold only a small number of counterfeit bills to Regno. Peoni did not care whether Regno passed the money himself or, as he did, sold it to another person to pass. Peoni had no common interest, therefore, with Dorsey. Instead, there were two independent conspiracies, one between Peoni and Regno and a second one between Regno and Dorsey. If larger numbers of bills had been involved — enough that Peoni needed Regno to obtain assistance in passing the money — a single conspiracy might have been proved.[147]

[4]　Chain-Wheel Conspiracies

Quite arguably, *Bruno* involved a chain-wheel conspiracy. The court ruled that the importers, middlemen, and geographically disparate retailers were all part of a single chain conspiracy. The retailers knew that smugglers existed (and vice-versa). More importantly, each link had a stake in the larger venture. The court failed to explain, however, why and how the retailers — the separate spokes — were drawn together. The court properly analyzed the chain feature of the conspiracy, but it ignored the wheel aspect.

[E]　Model Penal Code

[1]　Relevant Provisions

The Model Penal Code provides a complex but potentially fairer approach to the party dimension of a conspiracy. Two aspects of the Code are relevant. First, Section 5.03(1), as reprinted above,[148] and discussed earlier,[149] adopts the unilateral approach to conspiracy, and provides that a person is guilty of conspiracy if, with the purpose of promoting or facilitating the commission of a crime, she agrees with another to commit the offense.

---

[147] *E.g.*, United States v. La Vecchia, 513 F.2d 1210 (2d Cir. 1975).

[148] *See* § 29.01[B], *supra*.

[149] *See* §§ 29.04[E], 29.05[C], 29.06[B], *supra*.

Second, Section 5.03(2) provides additional guidance in determining when parties to separate agreements to commit the same crime may be linked together:

Scope of Conspiratorial Relationship. If a person guilty of conspiracy . . . knows that a person with whom he conspires to commit a crime has conspired with another person or persons to commit the same crime, he is guilty of conspiring with such other person or persons, whether or not he knows their identity, to commit such crime.

[2] Example of the Code Approach: *United States v. Bruno*[150]

The Commentary to the Code explains how some of the cases discussed earlier in this section would be analyzed under the Model Penal Code.[151] The most interesting questions arise regarding *Bruno*, in which the Code would require a different mode of analysis and, very likely, would reach a different outcome. In order to understand how the Code provisions are applied, we will simplify the *Bruno* facts by assuming the existence of a single importer, a single middleman, and one retailer each in New York and Texas-Louisiana; also, for sake of clarity, certain facts not clear in *Bruno* will be assumed.[152]

Here is the *Bruno*-inspired hypothetical scenario: Importer meets with Middleman and agrees that Importer will smuggle narcotics into the country, in violation of Statute X. In their meeting, they further agree that Middleman will find retailers to sell the narcotics in their states, which sales would violate Statute Y. Middleman proceeds to meet with New York Retailer and, on another date, with Texas-Louisiana Retailer, and agrees with each of them that the retailers will sell drugs in their respective states, in violation of Statute Y. Neither retailer knows that Middleman is dealing with another retailer, nor do the retailers know the details of the Importer-Middleman dealings.

Based on these facts a lawyer would start by applying Section 5.03(1), in order to identify each agreement to commit a crime that occurred. Doing this, the evidence supports the existence of four agreements: (1) Importer and Middleman, to violate Statute X; (2) Importer and Middleman, to violate Statute Y; (3) Middleman and New York Retailer, to violate Statute Y; (4) Middleman and Texas-Louisiana Retailer, to violate Statute Y.

Based on Section 5.03(1) alone, therefore, we have four two-person agreements. At this point, however, Section 5.03(2) may be applied to add additional links to the conspiracies. Importer knew that Middleman, with whom she had conspired to violate Statute Y, would also conspire with New York Retailer and Texas-Louisiana Retailer to commit the same offense. Consequently, Importer is guilty of conspiring with both retailers to violate Statute Y.

---

[150] 105 F.2d 921 (2d Cir. 1939), *rev'd on other grounds*, 308 U.S. 287 (1939). *See* § 27.07[A][4], *supra.*

[151] *See* American Law Institute, Comment to § 5.03, at 425–35.

[152] As a consequence of the different facts being assumed here, a precise comparison between *Bruno* and the Model Penal Code approach is not possible.

The retailers, however, did not know that Middleman, with whom they dealt, had conspired with Importer to violate Statute Y; therefore, in light of the Code's unilateral approach to conspiracy, the retailers are not guilty of conspiring with Importer to violate Statute Y (although, as just seen, Importer is guilty of conspiring *with them* to commit the same offense). Moreover, there is probably no basis for finding that the New York and Texas-Louisiana retailers had the requisite purpose of promoting or facilitating the commission of the sales in the other region, so neither retailer should be joined in any conspiracy relating to the violation of Statute Y outside their own area.

Thus, we reach this conclusion. Importer conspired with Middleman to violate Statute X; and she conspired with Middleman, New York Retailer, and Texas-Louisiana Retailer to violate Statute Y. The same result applies to Middleman. New York Retailer is guilty of conspiring with Middleman to violate Statute Y, but is guilty of no other offense. Similarly, Texas-Louisiana Retailer conspired with Middleman to violate Statute Y.

Notice the difference between this analysis and the common law. The *Bruno* court described the conspiracy broadly to be "to smuggle narcotics into the Port of New York and distribute them to addicts both in [New York] and Texas and Louisiana." That was a fair description of the situation from the viewpoint of Importer and Middleman, but it was not either retailer's perception. Given the bilateral nature of common law conspiracy, however, if it is concluded that Importer and Middleman conspired with the retailers to import and sell drugs, the retailers are necessarily guilty of conspiring with them to violate the same laws.

The result under the Code, however, more accurately represents the divergent culpabilities of the parties: Importer and Middleman, who were deeply involved in the events, are guilty of conspiring with everyone; the retailers, who cared little about anything other than the sales in their respective region, would be guilty of conspiracy with Middleman to sell drugs in their region, but no more.

§ 29.08   OBJECTIVES OF A CONSPIRACY

[A]   The Issue

Suppose that *D1* and *D2* rob *V1* on Day 1, rob *V2* on Day 2, and rob and rape *V3* on Day 3. Assuming that these crimes were committed as the result of a conspiratorial relationship between *D1* and *D2*, a critical question remains: How many conspiracies were there? That is, do we say that there were four conspiracies, one for each crime (to rob *V1*, to rob *V2*, to rob *V3*, and to rape *V3*)? Or were there three conspiracies, one for each victim? Are there two conspiracies based on the statutes violated (robbery and rape)? Or, is there just one conspiracy to commit all of the criminal acts?

[B] Common Law Analysis

Although various approaches to the issue have developed, the Supreme Court in *Braverman v. United States*[153] announced the following rule regarding federal conspiracy prosecutions:

> [T]he precise nature and extent of the conspiracy must be determined by reference to the agreement which embraces and defines its objects. Whether the object of a single agreement is to commit one or many crimes, it is in either case that agreement which constitutes the conspiracy which the statute punishes. The one agreement cannot be taken to be several agreements and hence several conspiracies because it envisages the violation of several statutes rather than one.

It follows in the case discussed above, therefore, that the fact that *D1* and *D2* planned to violate two criminal statutes, or to violate a particular statute multiple times, does not in itself convert a single conspiracy with multiple objectives into multiple conspiracies with a single objective each.

Ultimately, under *Braverman*, the issue is whether a single agreement or many distinct ones were formed. In the hypothetical, for example, it is possible that *D1* and *D2* got together once and agreed to commit each of the offenses, in which case there was one conspiracy. On the other hand, they may have met various times, each time reaching a new and independent agreement to rob, and the rape may have been a spur-of-the moment group decision, in which case *D1* and *D2* are guilty of four conspiracies. It is also possible that the co-conspirators originally agreed to conduct robberies together (without specifying the number or identity of the victims), and (as in the last scenario) the rape of *V3* was a last-moment joint decision. Under these circumstances, there were two conspiracies.

Because of inherent difficulties of proof, and in order not to "place a premium upon foresight in crime,"[154] many courts avoid careful inquiry into the events, and instead treat the initial agreement between the parties as one that implicitly incorporated the later objectives.

[C] Model Penal Code

The Model Penal Code provides that a person with multiple criminal objectives is guilty of only one conspiracy if the multiple objectives are: (1) part of the same agreement; or (2) part of a continuous conspiratorial relationship.[155] Thus, in the *D1-D2* example discussed in subsection [A], each person would be guilty of only one count of conspiracy if the crimes were part of a single agreement (the *Braverman* approach) or, even if the crimes resulted from multiple agreements, if the crimes were committed as a result of "a single and continuous association [by *D1* and *D2*] for criminal purposes."[156]

---

[153] 317 U.S. 49, 53 (1942).

[154] *Developments in the Law*, Note 1, *supra*, at 930.

[155] Model Penal Code § 5.03(3).

[156] American Law Institute, Comment to § 5.03, at 439.

§ 29.09 DEFENSES

[A] Impossibility

[1] Common Law

Issues of factual and legal impossibility, matters of considerable complexity in the realm of criminal attempts,[157] also arise in conspiracy prosecutions. For example, are *D1* and *D2* guilty of conspiracy if they agree to: (1) perform an abortion on a nonpregnant woman;[158] (2) kill or have unlawful sexual intercourse with a non-existent person;[159] (3) receive stolen property that was not actually stolen;[160] or (4) steal trade secrets that turn out not to be secrets.[161]

Case law on the subject is thin. Some courts affirm or reverse convictions in this area without expressly identifying the issue as one of "impossibility." When identification of the issue is made, the stated majority rule is that neither factual impossibility nor legal impossibility is a defense to a criminal conspiracy.[162] To the extent that there are special dangers inherent in group criminality,[163] the factual or legal impossibility of committing a particular offense arguably does not negate the dangerousness of the conspiratorial agreement.[164]

[2] Model Penal Code

The Model Penal Code does not recognize a defense of impossibility in conspiracy cases. The Code's definition of conspiracy states that a person is guilty of an offense if she agrees with another person that "they or one of them will engage in conduct that constitutes . . . *an attempt* . . . to commit such crime," or if she "agrees to aid such other person or persons in . . . *an attempt* . . . to commit such crime."[165]

Of course, people do not conspire to attempt crimes; they conspire to successfully commit them. This language is meant to take account of the impossibility

---

[157] *See* § 27.07, *supra.*

[158] *E.g.*, People v. Tinskey, 228 N.W.2d 782 (Mich. 1975) (impossibility defense is recognized); State v. Moretti, 244 A.2d 499 (N.J. 1968) (defense is not recognized).

[159] State v. Houchin, 765 P.2d 178 (Mont. 1988) ("factual impossibility" defense rejected in conspiracy to murder case); United States v. Roeseler, 55 M.J. 286, 291 (C.A.A.F. 2001) (same); State v. Heitman, 629 N.W.2d 542 (Neb. 2001) (see the facts in Note 128, *supra*; conviction affirmed).

[160] United States v. Petit, 841 F.2d 1546 (11th Cir. 1988) (defense not recognized).

[161] United States v. Yang, 281 F.3d 534 (6th Cir. 2002) (defense rejected); United States v. Hsu, 155 F.3d 189 (3d Cir. 1998) (legal impossibility is not a defense).

[162] *State v. Houchin*, 765 P.2d at 179–80 (stating the majority rule, but interpreting its own state's conspiracy statute as allowing for a legal impossibility defense); *United States v. Hsu*, 155 F.3d at 203 (no legal impossibility defense to conspiracy charge, although such a defense was previously recognized for criminal attempts).

[163] *See* § 29.02[B], *supra.*

[164] Katyal, Note 1, *supra*, at 1376–77.

[165] Model Penal Code § 5.03(1) (emphasis added).

situation.[166] Thus, as the Commentary suggests, if *D1* and *D2* agree to rob a bank that they incorrectly believe is federally insured, they may be convicted of conspiracy to rob a federally insured bank, although commission of such offense is impossible, because they would have been guilty of criminal attempt (based on the Code's abrogation of the impossibility defense in the criminal attempt realm[167]) had they proceeded with the plan.

[B] Abandonment (or "Withdrawal")

[1] Common Law

The crime of conspiracy is complete the moment the agreement is formed or, in some jurisdictions,[168] once an overt act is committed in furtherance of a criminal objective. Once the conspiracy offense is complete, abandonment of the criminal plan by a party to the conspiracy — her withdrawal from the plan — is not a defense to the conspiracy.[169] The reasoning is the same as with attempts: Once a crime has occurred, a person cannot undo that offense.[170]

An actor's abandonment of the conspiratorial objective, however, is not without relevance. If a person withdraws from a conspiracy, she may avoid liability for *subsequent* crimes committed in furtherance of the conspiracy by her former co-conspirators. Also, once a person withdraws, the statute of limitations for the conspiracy begins to run in her favor.[171]

Courts are strict in their requirement of proof of abandonment. Usually they require that the abandoning party communicate her withdrawal to *each* of her fellow co-conspirators.[172] Some courts go further and require her successfully to dissuade the others from pursuing their criminal objectives.[173]

[2] Model Penal Code

Unlike the common law, the Model Penal Code provides an affirmative defense to the crime of conspiracy if the conspirator renounces her criminal purpose, and thwarts the success of the conspiracy under circumstances demonstrating a complete and voluntary renunciation of her criminal intent.[174]

---

[166] American Law Institute, Comment to § 5.03, at 421.

[167] *See* § 27.09[E], *supra.*

[168] *See* § 29.04[D], *supra.*

[169] American Law Institute, Comment to § 5.03, at 457; Gray v. Commonwealth, 519 S.E.2d 825, 829 (Va. Ct. App. 1999).

[170] United States v. Rogers, 102 F.3d 641, 644 (1st Cir. 1996).

[171] *Id.*; *see also Gray v. Commonwealth*, 519 S.E.2d at 829 n.2 (hearsay statement of co-conspirator is inadmissible if it is made after withdrawal).

[172] People v. Sconce, 228 Cal. App. 3d 693, 701 (Ct. App. 1991).

[173] *See* Eldredge v. United States, 62 F.2d 449, 451–52 (10th Cir. 1932).

[174] Model Penal Code § 5.03(6).

The drafters of the Code rejected the no-defense rule on the same ground that it recognizes the abandonment defense to other inchoate offenses,[175] namely, that a voluntary renunciation of a criminal purpose negates the actor's dangerousness. On the other hand, in light of the special dangers inherent in conspiratorial groupings, it is insufficient for a conspirator merely to withdraw — she must also negate the danger of the group she joined.

[C]   Wharton's Rule

[1]   Common Law

[a]   In General

According to the common law, an agreement by two persons to commit an offense that *by definition* requires the voluntary concerted criminal participation of two persons, cannot be prosecuted as a conspiracy. This has come to be known as "Wharton's Rule."[176]

The offenses of adultery, bigamy, and incest classically fall within the scope of Wharton's Rule. These offenses *by definition* require the willing participation of two persons; there is no way that just one person can commit these offenses. Other examples of crimes for which Wharton's Rule applies are: dueling; sale of contraband;[177] and receipt of a bribe.[178] A person cannot duel with herself, sell contraband in the absence of a willing buyer, or receive a bribe without a briber.

On the other hand, Wharton's Rule does not bar a conspiracy prosecution for: (1) possession of a controlled substance with the intent to deliver;[179] (2) "bartering, exchanging, or offering" an illegal narcotic to another;[180] or (3) unlawfully "receiving or disposing" of another person's property.[181] In each of these cases it is *possible* for the offense, as defined, to be committed in the absence of an agreement.[182]

The rationale of Wharton's Rule is that if a substantive offense cannot be committed in the absence of an agreement, the added dangers inherent in group criminality are absent. This reasoning ignores the other rationale of conspiracy: the preventive-law-enforcement goal. That is, even if there is no increased danger

---

[175] *See* §§ 27.09[E][2], 28.03[B], *supra.*

[176] 2 Francis Wharton, Criminal Law § 1604 (12th ed. 1932); Iannelli v. United States, 420 U.S. 770, 773 n.5 (1975); *Developments in the Law*, Note 1, *supra*, at 954.

[177] People v. Urban, 553 N.E.2d 740, 741–42 (Ill. App. Ct. 1990).

[178] People v. Wettengel, 58 P.2d 279, 281 (Colo. 1935).

[179] Johnson v. State, 587 A.2d 444, 452–53 (Del. 1991).

[180] State v. Cavanaugh, 583 A.2d 1311, 1314 (Conn. App. Ct. 1990).

[181] Guyer v. State, 453 A.2d 462, 466 (Del. 1982).

[182] In (1), it takes only one person to *possess* a controlled substance, and actual delivery (as distinguished from the intent) is not an element of the crime. In (2), it requires two persons to *barter* or *exchange*, but it takes only one willing person to *offer* an illegal narcotic. As the offense is defined in the disjunctive, Wharton's Rule does not apply. In (3), a person can *receive* property by finding it on the street; likewise, she can *dispose* of property by throwing it away.

resulting from, for example, two persons agreeing to duel, application of Wharton's Rule prevents the police from arresting the would-be duelers until they reach the more dangerous stage of an attempt.

Because Wharton's Rule can frustrate law enforcement, many courts limit the applicability of the doctrine to cases in which the substantive offense has been consummated or attempted.[183] That is, in jurisdictions that limit Wharton's Rule in this way, if *D1* agrees to sell *D2* heroin, the conspirators may be arrested, convicted, and punished for conspiracy to sell heroin. However, if the offense is attempted or completed before arrest, *D1* and *D2* may not be convicted and punished for the conspiracy. Instead, contrary to the usual rule,[184] the conspiracy merges into the substantive offense, for which they may be charged.

Although Wharton's Rule was described in 1959 as "firmly entrenched"[185] in American common law jurisprudence, the Supreme Court in 1975 ruled that the doctrine in the federal courts "has current vitality only as a judicial presumption, to be applied in the absence of legislative intent to the contrary."[186] Many state courts, too, now treat the rule as no more than a presumption.

[b]   Exceptions to the Rule

Even when Wharton's Rule otherwise applies, two exceptions are recognized. First, the "third-party exception" provides that if more than the minimum number of persons necessary to commit an offense agree to commit the crime, Wharton's Rule is not triggered.[187] For example, if *D1*, *D2*, and *D3* agree on the sale of illegal narcotics, one person more than is statutorily necessary to perform a sale is involved in the conspiracy. Now, the added dangers of collective criminality return, so that all three persons may be convicted of conspiracy to sell narcotics.[188]

Second, Wharton's Rule does not apply if the two persons involved in the conspiracy are not the two people necessarily involved in committing the substantive offense. For example, if *D1* and *D2*, two males, conspire for *D2* to commit adultery with female *X*, a conviction of *D1* and *D2* for conspiracy to commit adultery is proper.[189]

---

[183] *See, e.g.*, State v. Miller, 929 P.2d 372, 378 (Wash. 1997); United States v. Kohne, 347 F. Supp. 1178, 1185–86 (W.D. Pa. 1972).

[184] *See* § 29.03[B][1], *supra.*

[185] *Developments in the Law*, Note 1, *supra*, at 955.

[186] Iannelli v. United States, 420 U.S. 770, 782 (1975).

[187] Gebardi v. United States, 287 U.S. 112, 122 n.6 (1932); Brown v. Commonwealth, 390 S.E.2d 386, 389 (Va. Ct. App. 1990).

[188] Wharton's Rule can combine with the plurality doctrine to cause anomalous results. For example, in the three-person drug-conspiracy example, if one of the three is acquitted because she was insane or for some other reason lacked the requisite specific intent, only two guilty persons remain in the conspiracy. In that case, Wharton's Rule re-emerges, and neither of the remaining drug-sale co-conspirators may be convicted of conspiracy!

[189] State v. Martin, 200 N.W. 213, 214 (Iowa 1925).

[2] Model Penal Code

Wharton's Rule is not recognized under the Code. The drafters believed that the doctrine improperly "overlooks the functions of conspiracy as an inchoate crime."[190] On the other hand, as described earlier in this chapter,[191] a conspirator may not ordinarily be convicted and punished for both a conspiracy to commit a crime and for its attempt or successful commission. Therefore, the absence of a "Wharton's Rule" defense does not result in additional punishment of a conspirator who implements her criminal objectives.

[D] Legislative-Exemption Rule

[1] Common Law

A person may not be convicted of conspiracy to violate an offense if her conviction would frustrate a legislative purpose to exempt her from prosecution for the underlying substantive crime.

A classic example of the application of the legislative-exemption rule is *Gebardi v. United States.*[192] *Gebardi* involved a prosecution under the so-called Mann Act, which made it an offense to "knowingly transport . . . any woman or girl [in interstate commerce] for the purpose of prostitution . . . or for any other immoral purpose."[193] Although violation of this law can involve the willing concurrence of the female in her transportation across interstate boundaries, the offense can also occur as the result of transportation of the female against her will. The Mann Act, therefore, does not come within the ambit of Wharton's Rule, discussed immediately above.[194]

This does not end the analysis, however. As *Gebardi* explained, the legislative purpose of the Mann Act was to protect females from sexual exploitation. Thus, a female who willingly or unwillingly crossed state lines for immoral purposes was perceived by the legislature to be the victim of the transporter's conduct. It would frustrate this purpose if a female were subject to prosecution as an accomplice in the Mann Act violation of her own rights, or if she were convicted of conspiracy in her own transportation. The legislative-exemption rule precludes such a prosecution.[195]

---

[190] American Law Institute, Comment to § 5.04, at 482–83.

[191] *See* § 29.03[B][2], *supra.*

[192] 287 U.S. 112 (1932).

[193] 18 U.S.C. § 2421 (2011) (as since amended to make it gender-neutral).

[194] *Gebardi*, 287 U.S. at 122–23.

[195] The same analysis should apply to statutory rape. This offense is meant to protect a very young person (traditionally, females) from her less-than-fully informed decision to have sexual contact with an older individual (traditionally, a male). It would frustrate legislative intent, therefore, if the underage party could be convicted as an accomplice in her own statutory rape, or if she were subject to prosecution for conspiracy in her own victimization. *See* Queen v. Tyrrell, [1894] 1 Q.B. 710 (holding that an underage female cannot be convicted as an accomplice in her own statutory rape).

The legislative-exemption rule can result in an anomaly when it is applied in conjunction with the plurality doctrine. In *Gebardi*, for example, one defendant (a male) conspired with a female for her to cross interstate boundaries for immoral purposes. The female was not subject to prosecution for conspiracy under the legislative-exemption rule. Therefore, the court treated the male as if he had conspired with himself, a logical impossibility. Because "two or more persons" were not involved in the offense, the plurality doctrine precluded conviction of the *non*-immunized male defendant.

[2]   Model Penal Code

Unless the legislature otherwise provides, a person may not be prosecuted for conspiracy to commit a crime under the Model Code if she would not be guilty of the consummated substantive offense: (1) under the law defining the crime; or (2) as an accomplice in its commission.[196] In turn, a person is not guilty as an accomplice in the commission of an offense if she was the victim of the prohibited conduct, or if her conduct was "inevitably incident to its commission."[197]

For example, in the absence of express legislative authority to the contrary, if a male and an underage female have sexual intercourse, the female may not be convicted as an accomplice in her own "victimization." Similarly, in the absence of contrary legislative intent, a pregnant woman may not be convicted as an accomplice in a criminal abortion of her own fetus, because her conduct is "inevitably incident" to the commission of the crime. And, because underage females and pregnant women cannot be convicted as *accomplices* in these offenses, they are also immune from prosecution for *conspiracy* to commit these offenses upon themselves.

However, because conspiracy is a unilateral offense under the Model Code, one who conspires with the immunized party remains subject to conviction for conspiracy.[198]

---

[196] Model Penal Code § 5.04(2).

[197] Model Penal Code § 2.06(6)(a)–(b).

[198] Model Penal Code § 5.04(1)(b).

Chapter 30

LIABILITY FOR THE ACTS OF OTHERS: COMPLICITY

§ 30.01 COMPLICITY: OVERVIEW TO ACCOMPLICE AND CONSPIRATORIAL LIABILITY[1]

This chapter considers multi-party criminal conduct or, more specifically, the circumstances under which a person who does not personally commit a proscribed harm may be held accountable for the conduct of another person with whom he has associated himself. Complicity doctrine is complex and frequently criticized.[2]

Two bases of complicity are considered here. First and foremost, a person may be held accountable for the conduct of another person if he assists[3] the other in committing an offense. Liability of this nature is called "accomplice" or "accessory" liability. Second, in the great majority of jurisdictions, a person who has conspired with another may be held accountable for the conduct of his co-conspirator who commits a crime in furtherance of their agreement. In the latter case, the mere existence of the conspiracy is sufficient to justify liability for the other's conduct; assistance in commission of the crime is not required.

The common law of complicity used special terms to distinguish between parties to offenses, as described in § 30.03. For purposes of clarity, however, two general terms will also be used in this chapter — the "primary party" (*P*, for short), and the "secondary party" (*S*). The "primary party" is the person who personally commits the physical acts that constitute an offense. For example, in a criminal homicide, *P* is the one whose conduct directly causes the death of *V*, *e.g.*, the person who shoots

---

[1] *See generally* George P. Fletcher, Rethinking Criminal Law §§ 8.5–8.8 (1978); Glanville Williams, Criminal Law: The General Part §§ 118–41 (2d ed. 1961); Joshua Dressler, *Reassessing the Theoretical Underpinnings of Accomplice Liability: New Solutions to an Old Problem*, 37 Hastings L.J. 91 (1985); Michael Heyman, *Losing All Sense of Just Proportion: The Peculiar Law of Accomplice Liability*, 87 St. John's L. Rev. 129 (2013); Douglas Husak, *Abetting a Crime*, 33 L. & Phil. 41 (2014); Sanford H. Kadish, *Complicity, Cause and Blame: A Study in the Interpretation of Doctrine*, 73 Cal. L. Rev. 323 (1985); Michael S. Moore, *Causing, Aiding, and the Superfluity of Accomplice Liability*, 156 U. Pa. L. Rev. 395 (2007); Robert Weisberg, *Reappraising Complicity*, 4 Buff. Crim. L. Rev. 217 (2000); Daniel Yeager, *Helping, Doing, and the Grammar of Complicity*, 15 Crim. Just. Ethics. (Winter/Spring 1996) at 25.

[2] *E.g.*, Joshua Dressler, *Reforming Complicity Law: Trivial Assistance as a Lesser Offense?*, 5 Ohio St. J. Crim. L. 427, 427 (2008) ("American accomplice law is a disgrace."); Heyman, Note 1, *supra*, at 129 ("[C]omplicity law seems to violate the fundamental precept of personal wrongdoing as a predicate for punishment. And, though it need not, in practice it has with terrible frequency."); G.R. Sullivan, *Doing Without Complicity*, 2012 J. Commonwealth Crim. L. 199, 199 (complicity law gives rise to "complexity, uncertainty, escessive litigation and, on occasion, injustice").

[3] The word "assists" is used here in a very general sense. For more specifics, see § 30.04, *infra*.

or poisons V.[4] Any person who is *not* the primary party, but who is associated with him in commission of the offense, is a "secondary party." Generally speaking, S is the person who assists P to commit the offense. S's liability for P's acts is the focus of this chapter.

§ 30.02   ACCOMPLICE LIABILITY: GENERAL PRINCIPLES

[A]   General Rules

[1]   Definition of an "Accomplice"

Subject to substantial clarification below, S ("secondary party") is an accomplice of P ("primary party") in the commission of an offense if he intentionally assists P to engage in the conduct that constitutes the crime, *i.e.*, if S intends to assist in the crime and, in fact, assists.[5] The term "assists" is used here as a general term to encompass many forms of conduct, including aiding, abetting, encouraging, soliciting, or advising the commission of the offense.

[2]   Criminal Responsibility of an Accomplice: Derivative Liability

Accomplice liability is conceptualized as derivative in nature.[6] That is, an accomplice is not guilty of an independent offense of "aiding and abetting";[7] instead, as the secondary party, he derives his liability from the primary party with whom he has associated himself. The primary party's acts become *his* acts. In general, the accomplice may be convicted of any offense committed by the primary party that is the result of the accomplice's intentional assistance.[8]

For example, if S intentionally assists P to rob V, S is liable for the robbery committed by P. If P fails in his effort to rob V, but is guilty of attempted robbery, S is guilty of attempted robbery, as well.[9] If P's conduct does not proceed sufficiently far to constitute any offense, S is guilty of no offense as an accomplice;[10]

---

[4] More than one person can be a primary actor, *e.g.*, if *P1* and *P2* each shoot V, who dies as the result of both wounds; or in a burglary prosecution, if *P1* breaks and *P2* enters the dwelling house. People v. Delgado, 297 P.3d 859, 865 (Cal. 2013).

[5] Commonwealth v. Murphy, 844 A.2d 1228, 1236 (Pa. 2004).

[6] Kadish, Note 1, *supra*, at 337; People v. Perez, 113 P.3d 100, 104 (Cal. 2005). According to one scholar, much of the confusion relating to complicity law is the result of treating the liability of an aider-and-abettor as derivative in nature. *See* Husak, Note 1, *supra*.

[7] Sanquenetti v. State, 727 N.E.2d 437, 441 (Ind. 2000); People v. Robinson, 715 N.W.2d 44, 47 (Mich. 2006).

[8] As described in § 30.05[B][5], *infra*, there is considerable authority for the view that S is *also* liable for any crime committed by P that was a natural and probable consequence of the criminal activity in which S intentionally assisted.

[9] *See* People v. Rehkopf, 370 N.W.2d 296, 298 n.3 (Mich. 1985).

[10] *E.g.*, People v. Genoa, 470 N.W.2d 447 (Mich. Ct. App. 1991) (S furnished money to X, an undercover police agent, so that X could purchase drugs for sale; X did not purchase or attempt to purchase the drugs; held: S cannot be convicted as an accomplice in a drug purchase, as the underlying crime was not

since P committed no substantive crime, there is no liability for S to derive from P.[11]

[B] Theoretical Foundations of Accomplice Liability

The doctrine of accomplice liability is loosely such an old and now accepted part of American criminal law jurisprudence that few observers focus on why a person who does not directly engage in conduct that constitutes an offense should be held accountable for the wrongful behavior of others.

At first glance, the premise that a person may be held criminally responsible for the conduct of another should prove surprising, if not also disturbing.[12] After all, the concept of personal, as distinguished from vicarious, responsibility is "deeply rooted" in criminal law jurisprudence.[13] Yet Anglo-American courts impute the acts of the primary party to the secondary actor. That is, once a person is deemed to be an accomplice of another, his personal identity is subsumed in that of the primary party.

There are at least two ways to defend accomplice liability. First, accomplice liability is loosely analogous to civil agency law. In civil law, a person may be held accountable for the actions of another if he "consent[s] to be bound by the actions of his agent, whom he vests with authority for this purpose."[14] In criminal law, it is argued, an accomplice is held accountable for the conduct of the primary party because, by intentionally assisting the primary party, the accomplice voluntarily identifies himself with the other. His intentional conduct, therefore, is "equivalent to manifesting consent to liability under the civil law."[15]

Second, accomplice liability may be perceived in terms of "forfeited personal identity."[16] That is, we may euphemistically describe accomplice liability in agency terms, but underlying this language is the belief that "she who chooses to aid in a crime forfeits her right to be treated as an individual."[17] In essence, the accomplice authorizes the primary party's conduct: The accomplice says, as it were, "your acts are my acts."[18] The law treats the accomplice, therefore, as if he were no more than an incorporeal shadow of the primary party.

---

committed or attempted by X); *see also People v. Perez*, 113 P.3d at 105 ("aiding and abetting liability cannot attach unless the substantive elements of a predicate offense [or its attempt] are met").

[11] McKnight v. State, 658 N.E.2d 559, 561 (Ind. 1995) ("Logic alone would . . . require that one cannot be convicted of assisting a [crime] if there is no [crime] to assist."). However, S and P may be guilty of the offense of conspiracy to commit robbery. *See* Chapter 29, *supra.*

[12] *See* Note 2, *supra.*

[13] Francis Bowes Sayre, *Criminal Responsibility for the Acts of Another*, 43 Harv. L. Rev. 689, 702 (1930).

[14] Kadish, Note 1, *supra*, at 354.

[15] *Id.* at 355.

[16] Dressler, Note 1, *supra*, at 111; People v. Prettyman, 926 P.2d 1013, 1018 (Cal. 1996) (quoting the text).

[17] Dressler, Note 1, *supra*, at 111.

[18] *See* State v. Curry, 636 S.E.2d 649, 653 (S.C. Ct. App. 2006) (upholding an instruction to the jury in a multi-party prosecution that "the hand of one is the hand of all").

§ 30.03 ACCOMPLICE LIABILITY: COMMON LAW TERMINOLOGY

[A] Parties to a Felony

[1] General Comments

Except for the offense of treason,[19] the common law created two categories of parties to crime — principals and accessories — each of which category was further divided into two subgroups, discussed below.

As discussed in subsection [B], the common law distinctions between the parties were of considerable practical significance. Today, virtually every state has legislatively repealed the common law distinctions, in whole or in part. Nonetheless, courts often persist in using common law language. Therefore, knowledge of the terminology remains valuable.

[2] Principal in the First Degree

[a]   In General

A "principal in the first degree" is the person who, with the requisite *mens rea*: (1) physically commits the acts that constitute the offense; or (2) as described in subsection [b] below, commits the offense by use of an "innocent instrumentality" or "innocent human agent."[20] The principal in the first degree is "the criminal actor"[21] or "perpetrator" of the offense. It is *his* conduct from which all secondary parties' liability derives.

In most cases, the principal in the first degree is the individual who personally commits the crime. He is the one who strangles *V1*, has sexual intercourse with *V2*, or takes and carries away the personal property of *V3*, *i.e.*, he is the person who performs the proscribed physical acts.

[b]   Innocent-Instrumentality Rule

[i]   In General

The innocent-instrumentality rule provides that a person is the principal in the first degree if, with the *mens rea* required for the commission of the offense, he uses a non-human agent or a non-culpable human agent to commit the crime.

For example, suppose that *D* trains his dog to pick up his neighbor's newspaper every morning from the front lawn and bring it to *D*, who keeps the newspaper as his own. *D* is guilty of petty larceny — he is the principal in the first degree of the theft. Because the dog is not a human being and, therefore, does not have the

---

[19] The common law treated all parties to treason as "principals."

[20] State v. Williams, 916 A.2d 294, 307 (Md. 2007) (quoting earlier decisions).

[21] State v. Burney, 82 P.3d 164, 166 (Or. Ct. App. 2003).

capacity to form a culpable mental state, the animal is *D*'s innocent instrumentality. We no more treat the dog as the perpetrator of the theft than we would say that a gun is the "perpetrator" of a murder and that the person pulling the trigger is the gun's "accomplice."

A human being may also be an innocent instrumentality. A person is the principal in the first degree of an offense if he uses or manipulates another person to commit an offense, such that the other person is not guilty of the offense due to lack of *mens rea* or because of the existence of an excusing condition. For example, suppose that *D* falsely informs *X* that *V*'s lawn mower belongs to *D*. Based on the false representation, *D* convinces *X* to "retrieve" the property from *V*'s front lawn. On these facts, *X* is not guilty of larceny because he lacked the specific intent to steal. Instead, *D* is guilty of the theft as the principal in the first degree. In this example, *X* is like the dog in the preceding hypothetical: He is a non-culpable agent being manipulated — like the strings on a marionette — by a culpable party to commit an offense.

Similarly, *D* is also the principal in the first degree if he causes *X*, an insane person[22] or a child,[23] to commit an offense, or if he coerces *X* to commit the crime.[24] In these circumstances, *X* is innocent of the offense as the result of an excuse (insanity, infancy, or duress), and accountability for the crime shifts to *D*.

[ii]   Difficulty in Application of the Rule: "Nonproxyable" Offenses

Occasionally, the innocent-instrumentality doctrine creates problems for courts when dealing with what has been characterized by one scholar as a "nonproxyable"[25] offense. A "nonproxyable" offense is one that, *by definition*, can only be perpetrated by a designated person or category of persons.

For example, as ordinarily defined, perjury can only be committed by one who intentionally falsely testifies under oath as a witness in an official proceeding. Suppose that *D*, by deception, causes *W*, a witness in a judicial proceeding, to unintentionally give false testimony as to certain material facts. In these circumstances, *W* is not guilty of perjury, due to lack of *mens rea*. Ordinarily, therefore, *D* would be guilty of perjury as a principal in the first degree through the innocent-instrumentality doctrine. But, can someone, never under oath in a judicial proceeding, be said to have perjured himself? Perjury appears to be a nonproxyable offense.

Or, consider a twist on the Biblical story: Adam gives Eve an apple to eat, which Adam alone knows is a forbidden act. Are we prepared to hold Adam guilty,

---

[22] 4 William Blackstone, Commentaries on the Laws of England *35 (1769) (a party is a principal if he kills another by "inciting a madman to commit murder").

[23] Queen v. Manley, 1 Cox Crim. Cas. 104 (1844) (by dictum, *M* is the principal in the first degree if he convinces a child to take money from his father).

[24] People v. Hack, 556 N.W.2d 187 (Mich. Ct. App. 1996) (*H* forced a 3-year-old to perform a sex act on a 1-year-old; held: *H* was guilty of criminal sexual conduct through the innocent-instrumentality doctrine).

[25] Kadish, Note 1, *supra*, at 374.

through his innocent instrumentality, of "eating the apple," which he did not do?[26]

More seriously, consider the offense of rape. As the offense is defined at common law, a husband cannot be convicted of raping his own wife, nor can a woman be convicted of raping another woman, although either can be convicted as accomplices in a rape.[27] In short, the prohibited action of "rape" (at common law) only applies to a designated class of persons — males who have sexual intercourse with females not their wives. What happens, then, if D coerces X to rape D's wife? To convict D through the innocent-instrumentality doctrine — thus making D the principal in the first degree — would mean that he is guilty of raping his own wife, a legal impossibility.

In such nonproxyable cases, some,[28] but by no means all,[29] courts refuse to convict a person as a principal in the first degree through the innocent-instrumentality doctrine. In such circumstances, a court must either stretch to interpret the facts in a manner that allows the defendant to be treated as a secondary party,[30] or it must permit the culpable party to escape punishment for the offense, an obvious injustice.

[3] Principal in the Second Degree

A "principal in the second degree" is one who is guilty of an offense by reason of having intentionally assisted in the commission of the crime in the presence, either actual or constructive, of the principal in the first degree.[31] A person is "constructively" present if he is situated in a position to assist the principal in the first degree

---

[26] *See* Glanville Williams, Textbook on Criminal Law 317 (1978) (finding it improbable that a court would convict Adam as the principal in the first degree).

[27] *E.g.*, Cody v. State, 361 P.2d 307, 319 (Okla. Crim. App. 1961), *aff'd*, 376 P.2d 625 (Okla. Crim. App. 1962) (a husband may be an accomplice in the rape of his wife); People v. Reilly, 381 N.Y.S.2d 732, 739 (County Ct. 1976), *disapproved on other grounds*, People v. Liberta, 474 N.E.2d 567, 577 (N.Y. 1984) (a woman may be convicted as an accessory in the rape of another woman). Another "nonproxyable" example: burglary is defined in terms of breaking and entering the dwelling *of another*, so that a home dweller cannot be guilty as a principal in the first degree of this offense, although he can be an accomplice. Spriggs v. United States, 52 A.3d 878, 882 (D.C. 2012).

[28] *E.g.*, People v. Enfeld, 518 N.Y.S.2d 536, 537–38 (Sup. Ct. 1987) (*E*, a private party, fraudulently induced *X*, a public servant, to issue a false certificate; due to lack of *mens rea*, *X* was acquitted of violating a statute that prohibited public servants from issuing false certificates; held: *E* could not be convicted of the offense); Dusenbery v. Commonwealth, 263 S.E.2d 392, 394 (Va. 1980) (*D* coerced *X* and *Y* to have sexual intercourse with each other; *D* was prosecuted for rape of the female (*Y*); the court overturned *D*'s conviction as a principal in the first degree of *Y*'s rape because prior state rulings "establish[ed] that one element of rape is the penetration of the female sexual organ by the sexual organ of the principal in the first degree").

[29] *E.g.*, People v. Hernandez, 18 Cal. App. 3d 651, 656 (Ct. App. 1971) (*H* compelled her husband to have sexual intercourse with a nonconsenting woman; held: *H*'s conviction for rape may be upheld either as an accomplice or as a principal in the first degree); Morrisey v. State, 620 A.2d 207, 210–11 (Del. 1993) (*M* forced a couple to engage in sexual intercourse; held: *M* was guilty of unlawful sexual intercourse through the "innocent intermediary" doctrine); *People v. Hack*, 556 N.W.2d at 189–90 (*see* Note 24); United States v. Walser, 3 F.3d 380, 387–88 (11th Cir. 1993) (by deception, *W* caused *X* to testify falsely at a trial; held: *W* may be convicted of perjury).

[30] See § 30.06[B][3][a], *infra*, for one example of such stretching.

[31] State v. Burney, 82 P.3d 164, 167 (Or. Ct. App. 2003).

during the commission of the crime, *e.g.*, if *S* serves as a "lookout" or "getaway" driver outside a bank that *P* robs.

[4] Accessory Before the Fact

An "accessory before the fact" does not differ appreciably from a principal in the second degree, except that he is *not* actually or constructively present when the crime is committed. An accessory before the fact often is the person who solicits, counsels, or commands (short of coercing[32]) the principal in the first degree to commit the offense.

[5] Accessory After the Fact

An "accessory after the fact" is one who, with knowledge of another's guilt, intentionally assists the felon to avoid arrest, trial, or conviction.[33] The line between a principal in the second degree, on the one hand, and accessory after the fact, on the other hand, can be factually thin: For purposes of accomplice liability, the commission of an offense continues — and, therefore, those who aid are principals in the second degree — until all of the acts constituting the crime have ceased. For example, in a bank robbery, the offense is not deemed complete for complicity purposes until the principal in the first degree takes possession of another's property and carries it to a place of temporary safety.[34] Therefore, the driver of the "getaway" car is a principal in the second degree rather than an accessory after the fact; once the property has reached a point of temporary safety, however, anyone who intentionally assists the robber to avoid prosecution is an accessory after the fact.[35]

At common law, an accessory after the fact was derivatively liable for the original felony, although he did not assist in its commission.[36] His knowing involvement after the fact "tainted him with guilt of that very offense."[37] Today, jurisdictions treat accessoryship after the fact as an offense *separate* from, and often *less* serious than, the felony committed by the principal in the first degree.[38] As a result, this chapter does not consider further the liability of accessories after the fact.

---

[32] If *D* coerces *X* to commit the offense, *D* is the principal in the first degree through an innocent instrumentality. *See* § 30.03[A][2][b], *supra.*

[33] State v. Ward, 396 A.2d 1041, 1047 (Md. 1978).

[34] People v. Cooper, 811 P.2d 742, 747–48 (Cal. 1991).

[35] People v. Montoya, 874 P.2d 903, 912–13 (Cal. 1994) (for purposes of accomplice liability, a burglary remains underway as long as the principal in the first degree remains inside the dwelling; therefore, one who joins the scene after the initial entry and intentionally aids at that time is an accomplice to burglary).

[36] State v. Allred, 995 P.2d 1210, 1213 (Or. Ct. App. 2000).

[37] Rollin M. Perkins, *Parties to Crime*, 89 U. Pa. L. Rev. 581, 589 (1941).

[38] *E.g.*, Ind. Code § 35-44-3-2 (2015) ("Assisting a criminal"); Or. Rev. Stat. § 162.325 (2015) ("Hindering prosecution"); Wash. Rev. Code § 9A.76.050 (2015) ("Rendering criminal assistance"); Model Penal Code § 242.3 ("Hindering Apprehension or Prosecution").

[B] Principals Versus Accessories: Procedural Significance[39]

[1] General Comments

Although the common law distinguished between principals in the first and second degree, no matter of procedural significance depended on this dichotomy. However, the line between principals and accessories was of profound significance, as discussed below.

Why did the distinctions develop? As with other areas of substantive criminal law, the specter of the death penalty distorted legal doctrine. At common law, all felons were subject to the death penalty. As the number of felonies expanded, courts invented devices for reducing the number of people subject to execution. According to Professor Perkins, "[w]ithout doubt, the principal-accessory distinction was one of those devices, and because of this it is not surprising to find the development along lines which tended to prevent conviction in spite of clear evidence of guilt."[40] In short, the procedural devices served to protect many accomplices from the fate suffered by principals.

[2] Jurisdiction

At common law, a principal was prosecuted in the jurisdiction in which the crime was perpetrated. An accessory had to be tried in the jurisdiction in which the accessorial acts occurred. If the prosecutor was unsure where the acts took place, he ran the risk of losing the conviction of the accessory. For example, assume that S solicited P to murder V. If the prosecutor believed that the solicitation and homicide both occurred in jurisdiction X — and, therefore, he brought S and P to trial in X — S's conviction could not stand, even though the murder occurred in X, if the evidence at trial showed that S solicited the crime while he and P were eating lunch in neighboring jurisdiction Y.

[3] Rules of Pleading

At common law, an indictment had to state correctly whether the party charged was a principal or an accessory. If the prosecutor alleged that X was the principal in the first degree and that Y was the principal in the second degree, but evidence at trial demonstrated that the roles of the parties were reversed, both defendants could still be convicted. On the other hand, if the evidence demonstrated that Y was not the principal in the second degree as alleged in the indictment, but instead was an accessory before the fact, his conviction could not stand. Likewise, if a person was indicted as an accessory, but it was proved at trial that he was a principal, acquittal was required.[41]

---

[39] *See generally* Perkins, Note 37, *supra*, at 607–14.

[40] *Id.* at 607.

[41] Today, a defendant may virtually always be convicted as an accessory although indicted as a principal (or vice versa), State v. Burney, 82 P.3d 164, 168–69 (Or. Ct. App. 2003), as long as the defendant was put on adequate notice before or during trial that the prosecution might pursue alternative theories of liability. Commonwealth v. Spotz, 716 A.2d 580, 588 (Pa. 1998).

[4] Timing of the Trial of Accessories

At common law, principals and accessories could be tried jointly (assuming that the court had jurisdiction over all of the parties) or separately. However, under no circumstances could the accessory be tried in advance of the principal's trial. Consequently, if the principal could not be brought to trial, for example, because he had died, fled the jurisdiction, or was immune from prosecution, the accessory could not be brought to justice.

[5] Effect of the Acquittal of a Principal

Closely related to the preceding point, an accessory could not be convicted of a crime unless and until the principal was convicted. If the principal was acquitted in a separate trial, the accessory could not be prosecuted; if they were prosecuted jointly, the accessory could not be convicted if the jury failed to convict the principal. This rule applied regardless of the reason for the principal's acquittal, even if it was based on a jury finding that, although the crime occurred and the accessory assisted in it, the principal was not guilty of the offense due to, for example, insanity or because another person committed the crime.

[6] Degree of Guilt of the Parties

The common law rule was that an accessory could not be convicted of a more serious offense, or higher degree of an offense, than his principal. For example, if *P* were convicted of assault, the accessory could not be convicted of the more serious offense of assault with intent to kill.

One exception to this rule existed: An accessory could be convicted of a higher degree of criminal homicide than the principal.[42] For example, an accessory could be convicted of murder, although the principal was guilty of the lesser offense of voluntary manslaughter. This outcome was possible if the principal killed in sudden heat of passion,[43] but the accomplice acted with malice aforethought, *i.e.*, he calmly and intentionally assisted the enraged principal to kill the victim.[44]

§ 30.04 ACCOMPLICE LIABILITY: ASSISTANCE

[A] Types of Assistance

[1] In General

An accomplice is a person who, with the requisite *mens rea*, assists the primary party in committing an offense. Generally speaking, there are three forms of assistance: (1) assistance by physical conduct; (2) assistance by psychological influence; and (3) assistance by omission (assuming that the omitter has a duty to act).

---

[42] Williams, Note 1, *supra*, at § 130; 1 Matthew Hale, History of the Pleas of the Crown *438 (1736).

[43] *See* § 31.07, *infra*.

[44] Parker v. Commonwealth, 201 S.W. 475, 478 (Ky. Ct. App. 1918).

[2] Physical Conduct

The most straightforward cases of assistance involve physical conduct. For example, S may assist P by furnishing him with an instrumentality to commit an offense,[45] or by providing the principal in the first degree with a service, such as "casing" the scene in advance,[46] locking the door to keep an assault victim from escaping,[47] or driving a "getaway" car from the scene of the crime.

[3] Psychological Influence

Assistance by psychological influence occurs when S incites, solicits, or encourages P to commit the crime. The most controversial cases involve assistance by *encouragement*, because juries and courts must often speculate as to whether the secondary party has psychologically influenced the primary party by his presence or words.

May mere presence at the scene of a crime constitute encouragement? It is frequently said that presence at a crime scene, even when coupled with undisclosed determination not to interfere[48] or passive acquiescence,[49] is insufficient to convict a person as an accomplice.[50] Even presence at the scene, coupled with the *hidden* intention to aid if necessary, is also insufficient.[51] Thus, it has been held that an indictment founded simply on the allegation that S accompanied P to the location of a crime and watched as the offense occurred, was insufficient to sustain an accomplice prosecution.[52]

While mere presence is insufficient to justify conviction as an accomplice, presence coupled with *very little else* can justify a finding of accomplice liability based on psychological encouragement. For example, encouragement may be found from the *expressed* assurance of a bystander that he will not interfere with the perpetrator's plans.[53] Likewise, as one court explained, "[i]t is sufficient encouragement that the accomplice is standing by at the scene ready to give some aid if needed, [if] . . . the principal [is] actually [aware] of the accomplice's intention." Proof of presence, *coupled with a prior agreement* to assist if necessary, will also

---

[45] *E.g.*, Hensel v. State, 604 P.2d 222, 239 (Alaska 1979) (furnishing fuses used to destroy a structure as part of a burglary).

[46] *E.g.*, State v. Arillo, 553 A.2d 281, 283 (N.H. 1988).

[47] *E.g.*, Commonwealth v. Hatchin, 709 A.2d 405, 410 (Pa. Super. Ct. 1998).

[48] *See* State v. Richardson, 923 S.W.2d 301, 317 (Mo. 1996).

[49] *E.g.*, Pace v. State, 224 N.E.2d 312, 313 (Ind. 1967); State v. Flint H., 544 A.2d 739, 741 (Me. 1988); State v. Vaillancourt, 453 A.2d 1327, 1328 (N.H. 1982).

[50] State v. V.T., 5 P.3d 1234, 1236 (Utah Ct. App. 2000) ("Passive behavior, such as mere presence — even continuous presence — absent evidence that the defendant affirmatively did something to instigate, incite, embolden, or help others in committing a crime is not enough to qualify as 'encouragement' as that term is commonly used.").

[51] State v. Noriega, 928 P.2d 706, 709 (Ariz. Ct. App. 1996); *see* Hicks v. United States, 150 U.S. 442, 450 (1893).

[52] State v. Vaillancourt, 453 A.2d 1327 (N.H. 1982).

[53] State v. Doody, 434 A.2d 523, 530 (Me. 1981).

support a claim of encouragement, even if such assistance is not rendered.[54] Thus, assistance-by-encouragement serves as a powerful, and yet highly speculative, basis for allowing accomplice liability.

[4] Assistance by Omission

In general, neither failure to inform police authorities of an impending crime, nor failure to attempt to stop the crime that is occurring, will establish accomplice liability.[55] The result is different, however, if the omitter has a legal duty to intervene. For example, a property owner may have a legal duty to prevent the commission of a crime on his property, *e.g.*, *S*'s knowing failure to prevent the commission of a drug offense on his property would justify a finding of assistance-by-omission.[56] Likewise, for example, a mother may be convicted as an accomplice in the commission of an offense committed by another person upon her child, if she fails to make efforts to prevent commission of the offense.[57] Similarly, the failure of a police officer to stop a crime, *if coupled with the requisite mens rea*, would support a conviction on the basis of accomplice liability.

[B] Amount of Assistance Required

[1] In General

A person is not an accomplice unless his conduct (or omission) in fact assists in the commission of the offense. Thus, *S* is not an accomplice in the commission of a robbery if he is present at the scene of the crime in order to aid *P* if necessary, but his assistance is not called upon, and assuming there are no additional facts to support a claim of assistance by encouragement.[58] Likewise, *S* is not an accomplice of *P* if he performs an act to assist *P*, but his conduct is wholly ineffectual. For example, *S* is not an accomplice if he utters words of encouragement to *P* who fails to hear them, or if *S* opens a window to allow *P* to enter a dwelling unlawfully, but *P* (unaware of the open window) enters through a door.[59]

Once it is determined that *S* has assisted *P*, however, the degree of aid or influence provided is immaterial.[60] Any aid, *no matter how trivial*, suffices.[61] For example, *S* may be deemed an accomplice of *P* if, acting with the requisite *mens rea*, he: (1) purchasing a ticket to attend a performance by a musician illegally in the

---

[54] State v. Anderson, 707 So. 2d 1223, 1225 (La. 1998); *accord Hicks v. United States*, 150 U.S. at 450 (presence, coupled with a prior agreement to assist if necessary, constitutes assistance by encouragement).

[55] Hutcheson v. State, 213 S.W.3d 25 (Ark. Ct. App. 2005).

[56] Porter v. State, 570 So. 2d 823, 826–27 (Ala. Crim. App. 1990).

[57] People v. Rolon, 160 Cal. App. 4th 1206, 1209 (Ct. App. 2008).

[58] *See* Hicks v. United States, 150 U.S. 442, 450 (1893).

[59] Kadish, Note 1, *supra*, at 358–59.

[60] Fuson v. Commonwealth, 251 S.W. 995, 997 (Ky. Ct. App. 1923).

[61] State v. Noriega, 928 P.2d 706, 709 n.2 (Ariz. Ct. App. 1996); Commonwealth v. Murphy, 844 A.2d 1228, 1234 (Pa. 2004) (amount of aid "need not be substantial").

country, in order to write a review for a magazine;[62] (2) holds *P*'s child while *P* commits the crime;[63] (3) prepares food for *P* to give *P* sustenance during the planning or commission of the crime;[64] or (4) provides moral support by asking *P* to bring home bananas from the grocery store that *P* plans to rob.[65]

[2] Accomplice Liability and the Doctrine of Causation[66]

[a]   The Law

Consider this remarkable fact: A secondary party is accountable for the conduct of the primary party *even if his assistance was causally unnecessary to the commission of the offense.* That is, *S* is guilty of an offense as an accomplice even if, but for his assistance, *P* would have committed the offense anyway.[67] Thus, it would be immaterial to *S*'s liability in each of the examples of trivial assistance noted in the preceding subsection, that *P* would have committed the crime when he did without *S*'s minor aid or encouragement. *S* must help (albeit trivially), but need not cause, the crime.

The absence of a causation requirement is premised on the underlying rationale of accomplice liability. It will be remembered that accomplice liability is derivative in nature:[68] *S* is not guilty of an independent, substantive offense of "aiding and abetting"; instead, *S*'s guilt is derived from that of *P.* Therefore, once it is determined that *S* assisted *P* with the requisite *mens rea* (*i.e.*, *S* is *P*'s accomplice), "proof that the *principal* [*P*] caused the [social harm] satisfies the requirement of establishing the causal relationship of the *accomplice.*"[69] Since *S* is an accomplice and, as such, forfeits his personal identity in the criminal transaction,[70] it is no longer relevant whether *S*'s assistance caused the harm. It is enough that he assisted someone else who caused the harm.

---

[62] Wilcox v. Jeffery, [1951] 1 All E.R. 464, 465. The court noted that *S*'s presence was not accidental, but was meant to encourage *P*; it opined that the result might have been different had *S* booed at the concert.

[63] State v. Duran, 526 P.2d 188 (N.M. Ct. App. 1974).

[64] Alexander v. State, 102 So. 597 (Ala. Ct. App. 1925).

[65] *See* State v. Helmenstein, 163 N.W.2d 85, 89 (N.D. 1968).

[66] *See generally* Dennis J. Baker, *Complicity, Proportionality, and the Serious Crime Act*, 14 New Crim. L. Rev. 403 (2011); Luis E. Chiesa, *Reassessing Professor Dressler's Plea for Complicity Reform: Lessons from Civil Law Jurisdictions*, 40 N. E. J. Crim. & Civ. Con. 1 (2014); Dressler, Notes 1 and 2, *supra*; Kadish, Note 1, *supra*; Moore, Note 1, *supra*; Weisberg, Note 1, *supra*; Yeager, Note 1, *supra*.

[67] State ex rel. Martin, Att'y Gen. v. Tally, 15 So. 722, 738–39 (Ala. 1893).

[68] *See* § 30.02[A][2], *supra.*

[69] Commonwealth v. Smith, 391 A.2d 1009, 1011 (Pa. 1978) (emphasis added).

[70] *See* § 30.02[B], *supra.*

[b]   Criticism of the Law

The requirement of a causal relationship between a person's conduct and the social harm for which he is being punished is a fundamental feature of criminal responsibility.[71] Its irrelevance to accomplice liability, therefore, is troubling.

Causality serves two important functions in the criminal law. First, it guarantees that criminal liability will be personal rather than vicarious. Second, causation is a tool used to calibrate the appropriate level of a wrongdoer's punishment.

The element of causation could serve the same valuable purposes in the field of accomplice law. First, as previously shown,[72] a person whose connection to a crime is exceedingly remote can be ensnared as an accomplice. If a causal connection between S's assistance and P's criminal conduct were required, however, the risk of highly attenuated liability would be reduced.

Second, accomplice law can result in disproportionate punishment. At common law and under modern statutes, accomplices are treated alike in terms of punishment: One whose participation in an offense is substantial and one whose conduct is trivial are subject to the same punishment. This approach, however, may be inconsistent with the retributive principle of just deserts. In this context, recall how the common law treats inchoate conduct: Although one who unsuccessfully attempts to commit a crime is as dangerous and morally culpable as one who commits the offense, the unsuccessful criminal is punished less severely than the successful one. One reason for this outcome is that the harm actually caused by the would-be murderer, robber, or rapist is less than the harm caused by the successful murderer, robber, or rapist.[73]

The same principle arguably ought to apply to accomplices. The accomplice whose assistance was a *sine qua non* factor in the harm caused by the primary party should be punished proportionally to the harm that he and the primary party intentionally caused. Thus, if S solicits P to commit an offense that P would not otherwise have committed, there should be no objection if S is punished at the same level as P. Similarly, if S provides essential assistance to P — aid but for which the crime would not have occurred when it did — S may fairly be punished as severely as P is punished. Non-causal accomplices, however, arguably should be punished less than causal accomplices and primary parties.[74] For example, if S provides encouragement to P, but P would have committed the crime when he did notwithstanding the psychological aid, S should be punished less than P.

---

[71] *See* § 14.01, *supra.*

[72] *See* § 30.04[B][1], *supra.*

[73] *See* § 27.04[B][3], *supra.*

[74] *See* United States v. Hansen, 256 F. Supp. 2d 65, 67 n.3 (D. Mass. 2003) (sentencing H more leniently because of his lesser contribution to the offense, and citing Dressler, Note 1, *supra*, which distinguishes between causal and non-causal assistance); *see also* Dressler, Note 2, *supra*, at 446–48 (suggesting alternative reform proposals, including a "substantial participant" standard).

§ 30.05   ACCOMPLICE LIABILITY: *MENS REA*

[A]   In General

Courts frequently state that a person is an accomplice in the commission of an offense if he intentionally aids the primary party to commit the offense charged.[75] This statement is sometimes broken down into "dual intents": (1) the intent to render the conduct that, in fact, assisted the primary party to commit the offense; and (2) the intent, by such assistance, that the primary party commit the[76] offense charged. Thus, in a robbery prosecution, in which S hands a gun to P, which the latter uses in a robbery, S would be an accomplice if he intentionally provided the gun to P (the first intent), and S did so with the intention that P commit the robbery (the second intent).[77]

This formulation usually is adequate, because most offenses are defined in terms of "intent." However, in some cases, primarily when a person is charged as an accomplice in the commission of an offense for which recklessness or negligence suffices for liability, it is necessary to be somewhat more precise about the mental state.[78] Therefore, although not all courts agree on the matter, it is more precisely correct to state that an accomplice must possess: (1) the intention to do the acts that constitute the assistance; and (2) whatever mental state is required for commission of the offense, as provided for in the definition of the substantive crime.[79]

---

[75] *E.g.*, Commonwealth v. Murphy, 844 A.2d 1228, 1234 (Pa. 2004); *see* Kadish, Note 1, *supra*, at 346 ("[H]e must act with the intention of influencing or assisting the primary party to engage in the conduct constituting the crime.").

[76] The key word here is "the" and not simply "a." That is, in order that a person may be considered an accomplice, his intention must be to assist in the commission of the offense charged, and not simply that he intended to assist in some other offense. State v. Bauer, 329 P.3d 67, 74 (Wash. 2014).

[77] Almost always, the second mental state may be inferred upon proof of the first; likewise, the *absence* of proof of the first mental state will demonstrate the *lack* of the second mental state. For example, suppose that S is a customer in a bank when P enters and announces that he is robbing it. S, startled, unthinkingly exclaims, "He'll never succeed because the guard is right behind him." Alerted by these words, P disarms the guard and successfully robs the bank. Based on these facts, S *in fact* assisted P in the robbery by providing a warning to P that facilitated him in the commission of the crime. Nonetheless, S is not an accomplice because he lacked both mental states required for accomplice liability. First, he did not intend for his words to assist P to engage in the robbery. At most, he was reckless in this regard. Second, and following almost inextricably from the first point, S did not want the bank robbed, *i.e.*, it was not his objective to have the bank deprived permanently of its property, the specific intent required for the offense. *See* People v. Tewksbury, 544 P.2d 1335, 1341 (Cal. 1976) ("Although it is undisputed that Mary aided appellant [in a robbery] by [intentionally] calling the restaurant, by [intentionally] supplying Sheila with pencil and paper, and by [intentionally] driving some of the principals to a point of rendezvous in the vicinity of the crimes, such actions do not confer upon her accomplice status unless she also acted with the requisite guilty intent [the second intent].").

[78] See § 30.05[B][3], *infra*, for further discussion.

[79] State v. Foster, 522 A.2d 277, 283–84 (Conn. 1987).

[B]   Significant *Mens Rea* Issues

[1]   The Feigning Accomplice

It is frequently said that, to be an accomplice, a person "must not only have the purpose that someone else engage in the conduct which constitutes the particular crime charged, but the accomplice must also *share in the same intent which is required for commission of the substantive offense.*"[80] It is almost always reasonable to infer that when a person intentionally assists another to engage in the conduct that constitutes an offense, he does so because he wants the other person to succeed in his endeavor, *i.e.*, he shares the criminal intent of the primary party. Sometimes, however, this inference is inaccurate. Matters of complexity arise, for example, when a police officer or private person joins a criminal endeavor as an "accomplice" and feigns a criminal intent in order to obtain incriminating evidence against the primary party or in order to ensnare the other in criminal activity.

Consider the classic case of *Wilson v. People*.[81] S and P, drinking partners, got into an argument over S's assertion that P had stolen his watch. A conversation followed in which the two men agreed to steal property from V's drugstore. In furtherance of the agreement, S assisted P to enter V's store. While P was inside, S called the police and then returned to the drugstore and took property handed to him by P. Before the parties could leave, the police arrived and arrested S and P for burglary and larceny.

S's conviction as an accomplice in the two offenses was overturned by the state supreme court. Some of its reasoning was unpersuasive. It analogized S's conduct to that of a detective who enters an existing criminal endeavor in order to "explode" it. S, however, hardly fit that characterization. He did not join a crime already in play; he helped devise the plan, apparently in order to set up P for arrest, in retaliation for the latter's alleged theft of S's watch.

So, was S properly acquitted as an accomplice in these crimes? S had the intent to assist P to engage in the conduct that (on P's part) constituted burglary and larceny; that is, he intended to assist P to enter V's store and to take property out of it. But, did S possess the second (and, ultimately, key) *mens rea* of an accomplice, namely, the mental states required for commission of the offenses of larceny and burglary?

Larceny requires a specific intent to deprive another person of his property permanently. Although P possessed this intent (and, therefore, was guilty of larceny as the perpetrator), S's act of calling the police demonstrated that he did not intend for V to be deprived of the property permanently. Consequently, S lacked the specific intent of larceny, and was properly acquitted as an accomplice of this offense.

The burglary charge is a more difficult issue. Plausibly, S should have been convicted of burglary as an accomplice. The argument would run as follows: S knew

---

[80]   State v. Williams, 718 A.2d 721, 723 (N.J. Super. Ct. Law Div. 1998) (emphasis added).

[81]   87 P.2d 5 (Colo. 1939).

that P intended to enter V's drugstore for the purpose of committing larceny (which made P guilty of burglary), and with that knowledge *and for the very purpose of securing P's conviction for burglary*, S assisted P to enter V's drugstore — the social harm of the burglary. Therefore, S *did* want a burglary (as distinguished from a larceny) to occur, and thus should be convicted for assisting in that offense.

But, there is a case for relieving S of responsibility for the burglary. The reason goes back to the *mens rea* requirement, as stated in subsection [A]: an accomplice must possess two states of mind: (1) the intent to assist the primary party to engage in the conduct that forms the basis of the offense; and (2) the mental state required for commission of the offense, as provided in the definition of the substantive crime. Here, S possessed the first intent: As noted in the preceding paragraph, he intended to assist P to engage in the conduct (entering the drugstore) that constituted the social harm of burglary. But, S did not possess the second mental state: Because S did not intend for a larceny to occur, he personally lacked the "specific intent" requirement of burglary. He did not share with P the felonious intent that constitutes the "specific intent" that converts a criminal trespass into a burglary.

The latter analysis does not provide a ready-made escape hatch for persons to join crimes in order to arrest or ensnare suspects. *Wilson* was an unusual case because both of the offenses charged are "inchoate offenses in disguise,"[82] and also required proof of specific states of mind that S lacked. However, if S had intentionally assisted P to kill V, S would be guilty of murder because he shared with P the intent for the latter to kill V. The fact that S's motive for wanting V dead was to set up P for arrest would not negate the requisite *mens rea*.

[2] "Purpose" Versus "Knowledge": The Meaning of "Intent"

The *mens rea* of accomplice liability is usually described in terms of "intention." As with the crime of conspiracy, however, there is considerable debate regarding whether a person may properly be characterized as an accomplice if he merely *knows* that his assistance will aid in a crime, but he lacks the *purpose* that the crime be committed. For example, suppose that S rents his house to P, the manager of an illegal gambling enterprise.[83] Is S an accomplice in P's illegal activities if he rented the property with knowledge of his tenant's intended activities, or must it be proved that he shared P's criminal purpose?

The policy arguments for and against imposing liability on the basis of knowledge, rather than purpose, have been summarized in the context of conspiracy law.[84] Apparently most courts hold that a person is not an accomplice in the commission of an offense unless he "share[s] the criminal intent of the principal; there must be a community of purpose in the unlawful undertaking."[85] In the oft-cited words of Judge Learned Hand, the complicity doctrine requires that the

---

[82] *See* § 27.02[F], *supra.*

[83] United States v. Giovannetti, 919 F.2d 1223, 1227 (7th Cir. 1990) (holding that a person may not be convicted as an accomplice unless he participates in something that he wishes to bring about).

[84] *See* § 29.05[B][1], *supra.*

[85] State v. Duran, 526 P.2d 188, 189 (N.M. Ct. App. 1974); *see* State v. Gladstone, 474 P.2d 274, 278

secondary party "in some sort associate himself with the venture, that he participate in it as in something that he wishes to bring about, that he seek by his action to make it succeed. All the words used — even the most colorless 'abet' — carry an implication of purposive attitude towards it."[86] Nonetheless, the law is mixed, and some courts permit conviction on the basis of knowledge.

As a sign of the lack of consistency in this area, consider the United States Supreme Court's recent venture into the debate in *Rosemond v. United States*.[87] On the one hand, Justice Kagan, writing for the majority, quoted Judge Hand's words, set out above, even describing them as "the canonical formulation of [the] needed state of mind" to be an accomplice. That seems to support the majority rule that purpose, rather than knowledge, is the requisite state of mind. But, in the very next paragraph, she stated that the Court had "previously found that intent requirement [described by Learned Hand] satisfied when a person actively participates in a criminal venture with full *knowledge* of the circumstances constituting the charged offense."[88] That suggests that knowledge is sufficient.

So, where does that leave the law under the federal criminal code?[89] Justice Alito, who concurred in part, and dissented in part in *Rosemond*, observed that, on the purpose-versus-knowledge issue, "[t]here is some tension in our cases on this point," citing cases that suggest purpose is required, and then citing cases for which knowledge apparently is sufficient. He observed, accurately, that the Court here "refers interchangeably to both of these tests and thus leaves our [federal] case law in the same, somewhat conflicted state that previously existed."[90] But, with a judicial shrug of the shoulders, Justice Alito stated that "because the difference between acting purposely . . . and acting knowingly is slight, this is not a matter of great concern."[91]

(Wash. 1970); Weisberg, Note 1, *supra*, at 239 (stating that "the majority of jurisdictions . . . require a showing of purpose").

[86] United States v. Peoni, 100 F.2d 401, 402 (2d Cir. 1938).

[87] 134 S. Ct. 1240 (2014); *see generally* Stephen P. Garvey, *Reading* Rosemond, 12 Ohio St. J. Crim. L. 233 (2014).

[88] *Rosemond*, 134 S. Ct. at 1248 (emphasis added).

[89] The Court was not applying constitutional law in *Rosemond*, so its discussion only applies to the enforcement of federal statutes. States are free to ignore *Rosemond* in applying their own accomplice liability laws.

[90] *Id.* at 1253.

[91] There is one additional intriguing footnote in *Rosemond* worthy of mention. Justice Kagan observed that the Court has never had to draw a distinction between one "who incidentally facilitate[s] a criminal venture rather than actively participate in it." As to the incidental facilitator — presumably she means a person whose assistance is trivial — "[w]e express no view about what sort of facts, *if any*, would suffice to show that such a third party has the intent necessary to be convicted of aiding and abetting." *Rosemond*, at 1249 n.8. (emphasis added). This suggests that one solution to the controversy raised earlier in the text (§ 30.04[B][2][b]) is to treat non-causal secondary parties guilty, *if at all*, only if they have a more culpable state on mind (purpose) than is required (knowledge) if the actor is a more active participant.

[3]   Liability for Crimes of Recklessness and Negligence[92]

Courts and statutes frequently express the culpability requirement for accomplice liability in terms of "intent," *e.g.*, the "intent to promote or facilitate the commission of the offense."[93] The implication of these words is that the secondary party must want the crime to be committed by the primary party (or, at least, know that it will take place). If so, it is logically impossible for a person to be an accomplice in the commission of a crime that prohibits a reckless or negligent result. For example, suppose that *S* encourages *P* to drive well above the legal speed limit on a public road near a school. While speeding, *P* loses control of his car and strikes and kills *V*, a child leaving school for the day. Assume for purposes of this hypothetical that *P* is guilty of manslaughter as the result of criminal negligence. Of what is *S* guilty? Based on an accomplice statute interpreted to require an intention to commit the substantive office, *S* cannot be convicted as an accomplice in the negligent manslaughter. If *S* must "intend that the offense be committed," then he must "intend that the offense [of negligent manslaughter] be committed." However, can one *intend* a *negligent* killing? Essentially, that would mean that *S* intended *V* to die in a negligent manner, which means that *S* intended *P* to cause *V*'s death. In that case, the offense should be murder, not negligent homicide.

In the past, some courts analyzed accomplice liability in this manner, and barred conviction of an accomplice for crimes of recklessness or negligence, [94] but the overwhelming majority rule now is that accomplice liability *is* allowed in such circumstances. Conviction of an accomplice in the commission of a crime of recklessness or negligence is permitted as long as the secondary party has the two mental states described in the second paragraph of subsection [A]: (1) the intent to assist the primary party to engage in the conduct that forms the basis of the offense; and (2) the mental state — intent, recklessness, or negligence, as the case may be — required for commission of the substantive offense.[95]

In the present hypothetical, *S* should be treated as an accomplice in the negligent death. First, he *intended* to encourage *P* to engage in the conduct that formed the basis of the offense, *i.e.*, he intended to encourage *P* to drive at a high rate of speed

---

[92] *See generally* Sanford H. Kadish, *Reckless Complicity*, 87 J. Crim. L. & Criminology 369 (1997).

[93] *E.g.*, Alaska Stat. § 11.16.110(2) (2015).

[94] *E.g.*, Echols v. State, 818 P.2d 691, 694–95 (Alaska Ct. App. 1991) (overturning accomplice conviction for reckless assault on the ground that such an offense does not exist), *overruled by*, Riley v. State, 60 P.3d 204 (Alaska Ct. App. 2002); State v. Etzweiler, 480 A.2d 870, 874–75 (N.H. 1984) (quashing an indictment of *S* as an accomplice of *P* in a negligent homicide), *superseded by statute as recognized in*, State v. Anthony, 861 A.2d 773, 775 (N.H. 2004).

[95] Young v. Commonwealth, 426 S.W.3d 577, 581 (Ky. 2014) ("the general rule . . . imposes accomplice liability on those persons who participate in conduct causing criminal results when such persons have the requisite state of mind with respect to those results"); *e.g.*, Ex parte Simmons, 649 So. 2d 1282, 1284–85 (Ala. 1994) (*S* may be convicted of reckless murder if he purposely aided or encouraged another to fire a weapon on a public street, recklessly resulting in the death of a child); State v. Garnica, 98 P.3d 207, 209 (Ariz. Ct. App. 2004) (affirming conviction of an accomplice for second-degree reckless murder on similar grounds); State v. Anthony, 861 A.2d 773, 776 (N.H. 2004) (affirming conviction of an accomplice to the crime of negligent cruelty to animals; held: conviction is permitted if the secondary party (1) intended to promote or facilitate the other person's dangerous *conduct*; and (2) acted with the culpable mental state regarding the *result* specified in the underlying statute).

on a public road near a school. Second, it is reasonable to conclude that S was at least criminally negligent in relation to V's death by encouraging P to drive in this manner.[96]

On the other hand, if P, while speeding at S's encouragement, had negligently turned the wrong way on a one-way street, thereby striking and killing V, S might not be an accomplice in *this* negligent homicide. It is quite arguable that the conduct that formed the basis of *this* homicide was the act of wrong-way driving, and not the conduct that S intentionally encouraged, *i.e.*, the speeding.

[4] Attendant Circumstances

Suppose that S intentionally assists P to have sexual intercourse with V, a nonconsenting female. P realizes that V is not consenting (and, therefore, is guilty of rape), but S negligently believes that V is consenting. Is S guilty of rape as P's accomplice? Notice the unusual situation: S intended to assist P in the conduct (sexual intercourse) that constituted the rape; however, S did not intend to assist in a *nonconsensual* act of intercourse, *i.e.*, he did not share P's knowledge of the attendant circumstance of V's lack of consent.

The issue here is what mental state *as to an attendant circumstance* must be proven to attach accomplice liability to an actor. This is a matter that courts have rarely considered. It is submitted that the appropriate rule is that, as long as the secondary party acts with the intent of assisting the principal in the *conduct* that constitutes the offense — and has the level of culpability required as to the prohibited *result*, if any, of the offense — he should be deemed an accomplice if his culpability as to the attendant circumstance would be sufficient to convict him as a principal. Put simply, the *mens rea* policy regarding the substantive offense should control the accomplice's situation. For example, in a jurisdiction in which the rape statute is interpreted to require proof of recklessness regarding the female's lack of consent, the secondary party should be held responsible for the rape if he acted with at least that level of culpability as to the attendant circumstance, but not if his culpability was less than that of recklessness.[97] Alternatively, in a prosecution for statutory rape, in which the age element is one of strict liability, a secondary party should be convicted even if he lacked any culpability as to the victim's age.[98]

[5] Natural-and-Probable-Consequences Doctrine

At common law, and today in most jurisdictions, "a person encouraging or facilitating the commission of a crime [may] be held criminally liable not only for that crime, but for any other offense that was a 'natural and probable consequence' of the crime aided and abetted."[99] That is, if S is an accomplice in the commission

---

[96] If S was reckless — and, thus, had a *more* culpable state of mind than P, S potentially may be convicted of a *greater* offense than P. See § 30.06[C], *infra*.

[97] Bowell v. State, 728 P.2d 1220, 1222–23 (Alaska Ct. App. 1986), *overruled on other grounds*, Echols v. State, 818 P.2d 691 (Alaska Ct. App. 1991).

[98] Commonwealth v. Harris, 904 N.E.2d 478, 485 (Mass. Ct. App. 2009).

[99] People v. Prettyman, 926 P.2d 1013, 1019 (Cal. 1996); State v. Henry, 752 A.2d 40, 44 (Conn. 2000). Apparently there are approximately 10 states that have rejected the natural-and-probable-consequences

of Crime A, he is also responsible for every other crime (*e.g.*, Crimes B and C) perpetrated by the primary party that was a natural and probable consequence of Crime A, the target offense.

As one court has explained, liability under this doctrine "is measured by whether a reasonable person in the [accomplice's] situation would have or should have known that the charged offense was a reasonably foreseeable consequence of the act aided and abetted."[100] Accordingly, an accomplice to Crime A is also an accomplice in Crime B, if Crime B was "within the normal range of outcomes that may be expected to occur if nothing unusual has intervened."[101]

To apply the natural-and-probable-consequences doctrine, one should ask four questions: (1) Did *P* commit target Crime A?; (2) If yes,[102] was *S* an accomplice in the commission of that offense?; (3) If yes, did *P* commit any other crimes?; and (4) If yes, were *those* crimes, although not contemplated or desired by *S*, reasonably foreseeable consequences of Crime A?[103]

For example, suppose that *S* intentionally aids *P* in the commission of an armed bank robbery, by driving *P* to the bank and serving as a lookout from that position. During the robbery, *P* forcibly moves bank teller *V* to a back room (kidnapping). On these facts, *P* is guilty of robbery; and *S* is guilty as an accomplice. *P* is also guilty of the offense of kidnapping. And, in a jurisdiction applying the natural-and-probable-consequences doctrine, *S* is *also* guilty of kidnapping, because it was a reasonably foreseeable consequence of the armed bank robbery in which *S* assisted. In contrast, if *P* had taken the opportunity of the bank robbery to sexually assault a customer in the bank, *S* should not be guilty of the latter offense, as this was not a reasonably foreseeable consequence of the bank robbery. The rape should be treated as separate and distinct from the robbery in which *S* assisted.[104]

The natural-and-probable-consequences doctrine has been subjected to substantial justifiable criticism.[105] Notice the effect of the rule: An accomplice may be convicted of a crime of intent (*e.g.*, kidnapping) although his culpability regarding its commission may be no greater than that of negligence. Thus, the effect of the rule is to permit conviction of an accomplice whose culpability as to the non-target

---

doctrine. Gonzales v. Duenas-Alvarez, 549 U.S. 183, 127 S. Ct. 815, 821 (2007) (citing the respondent's brief, and setting the cites to the minority position in Appendix B of the opinion).

[100] People v. Smith, 337 P.3d 1159, 1164–65 (Cal. 2014).

[101] Roy v. United States, 652 A.2d 1098, 1105 (D.C. 1995).

[102] *But see People v. Prettyman*, 926 P.2d at 1020 n.4 (raising, but leaving open, the issue "whether a defendant may be convicted under the 'natural and probable consequences' doctrine when the target criminal act was not committed").

[103] People v. Woods, 8 Cal. App. 4th 1570, 1586 (Ct. App. 1992).

[104] *See also* 4 *Blackstone*, Note 22, *supra*, at *37 ("But if A. commands B. to burn C.'s house and he, in so doing, commits a robbery; now A., though accessory to the burning, is not accessory to the robbery, for that is a thing of a distinct and unconsequential nature.").

[105] *E.g.*, American Law Institute, Comment to § 2.06, at 312 n.42 (characterizing the rule as "incongruous and unjust"); Heyman, Note 1, *supra*, at 132 (describing the doctrine as "mindless" and unjust); Audrey Rogers, *Accomplice Liability for Unintentional Crimes: Remaining Within the Constraints of Intent*, 31 Loy. L.A. L. Rev. 1351, 1361 (1998) (stating that "most commentators" are critical of the doctrine, and citing scholarly criticism of the rule).

offense is *less* than is required to prove the guilt of the primary party.[106] And yet, in view of the relative roles of the primary and secondary parties, one would assume that an accomplice should not be convicted of an offense unless he has the same or higher degree of culpability required to convict the perpetrator.[107]

§ 30.06 LIABILITY OF THE SECONDARY PARTY IN RELATION TO THE PRIMARY PARTY

[A] General Principles

At common law, an accessory could not be convicted of the crime in which he assisted until the principal was convicted and, with the limited exception of criminal homicide, could not be convicted of a more serious offense or degree of offense than that of which the principal was convicted.[108] Nearly all states have abrogated these rigid common law rules. It does not follow from this, however, that issues regarding the relationship between the primary party and secondary parties no longer arise, for they often do.

Accomplice liability is derivative in nature.[109] This means that for an accomplice to be liable for an offense, there must be a primary party: that is, logically, for an accomplice to be guilty of a crime, there must have been a crime committed by another person from whom the accomplice's liability originates.[110]

What does it mean, however, to say that the primary party "has committed a crime" for which the accomplice may be held accountable? Some cases are straightforward. For example, it is no longer a procedural bar to the conviction of a secondary party that the primary party was not prosecuted for the offense. The non-prosecution of the alleged perpetrator of an offense does not in itself suggest that a crime did not occur. His non-prosecution might be the result of any one of countless factors extraneous to his guilt (*e.g.*, death, flight from the jurisdiction, or immunity from prosecution).

Difficulties arise, however, when the primary party is acquitted of the offense. Does an acquittal imply that a crime was not committed? Not necessarily. For example, if *P* and *S* are charged with raping *V*, and *V* is unable to identify her attacker, but provides a clear identification of his accomplice, a jury could logically

---

[106] Sharma v. State, 56 P.3d 868, 872 (Nev. 2002) ("reevaluat[ing] the wisdom of the doctrine," the court rejects as "unsound" the use of the natural-and-probable-consequences doctrine in cases involving specific-intent offenses).

[107] American Law Institute, Comment to § 2.06, at 312 n.42. Recently, the California Supreme Court, while generally retaining the natural-and-probable-consequences doctrine, held that an aider and abettor may not be convicted of first-degree premeditated murder pursuant to the doctrine. Instead, "direct aiding and abetting principles" apply, *i.e.*, it must be shown that the accomplice premeditated the intentional killing, and not simply that it was a natural and probable consequence of another crime in which he aided. People v. Chiu, 325 P.3d 972, 979 (Cal. 2014).

[108] *See* § 30.03[B][5]–[6], *supra*.

[109] *See* § 30.02[A][2], *supra*.

[110] *See* McKnight v. State, 658 N.E.2d 559, 561 (Ind. 1995) ("Logic alone would seem to require that one cannot be convicted of assisting a criminal if there is no criminal to assist.").

acquit P and convict S. P's acquittal does not imply that a rape did not occur, only that the jury had a reasonable doubt that P, rather than some unidentified person, was the perpetrator of the crime.[111]

Some acquittals do suggest that a crime has not occurred. For example, if P is charged with stealing V's car, and he proves at trial that V consented to the taking, then no larceny occurred. Conceptually, P's acquittal precludes the conviction, at least at the same trial, of an accomplice to this *non*-offense.[112]

The next subsection deals with other acquittal-based circumstances in which it could be argued that a "crime" has not occurred in some sense, and yet S is convicted. An additional question, considered in subsection [C], is this: Under what circumstances, if any, may S derive *more* guilt than arises from P's conviction?

[B] Liability When the Primary Party Is Acquitted

[1] "Primary Party" as an Innocent Instrumentality

If D coerces X to commit a theft by threatening X's life, X will be acquitted of larceny on the basis of duress. Today, and according to common law principles, D may be convicted of larceny. X was D's innocent instrumentality. Therefore, D is the principal in the first degree of the offense.[113] Conceptually, as D and X "were enemies in an adversarial relationship"[114] and shared no common criminal intent, D's *guilt is not founded on accomplice liability principles*. Instead, D is *directly* liable for committing the crime through the instrumentality; D's guilt is *not* derived from another culpable person. X's acquittal, therefore, presents no bar to the conviction of the only culpable party.

[2] Acquittal on the Basis of a Defense

[a]   Justification Defenses

Suppose that V unlawfully threatens to immediately kill P. S assists P to kill V. P is acquitted of murder on the ground of self-defense. Is S guilty in the homicide? Although case law in this area is sparse, the proper result seems evident: As P was

---

[111] People v. Vaughn, 465 N.W.2d 365, 369 (Mich. Ct. App. 1990) (although there must be a principal for there to be an accomplice, the "evidence need not show that a specifically named individual was the guilty principal").

[112] Modern courts hesitate to disapprove of inconsistent jury verdicts — *e.g.*, conviction of the accomplice while acquitting the principal in the first degree — because it is often difficult or impossible to determine why the jury acquitted one defendant while convicting another. This hesitancy is particularly strong when the accomplice is convicted in a *separate* trial — in front of a *different* jury, potentially based on *different* evidence — after the acquittal of the principal. *E.g.*, State v. Cotto, 305 S.W.3d 420, 423 Tex. App. 2010) (permitting the conviction of an accomplice following the acquittal of the primary party). As the Supreme Court recently stated, although "symmetry of results may be intellectually satisfying, it is not required." Standefer v. United States, 447 U.S. 10, 25 (1980).

[113] *See* § 30.03[A][2][b], *supra*.

[114] Commonwealth v. Gaynor, 648 A.2d 295, 298 (Pa. 1994).

acquitted because his actions were justified, S should also be acquitted.[115] Although V was killed, recognition of the justification defense of self-defense implies that no crime has occurred, or even that a positive good has resulted. In the absence of wrongdoing by P, there is no crime to impute to S.[116]

[b]   Excuse Defenses

When the primary party is acquitted on the basis of an excuse (*e.g.*, insanity), his acquittal should not bar a successful prosecution of a secondary party to whom the excuse does not extend. An acquittal on the ground of an excuse means that the actions of the primary party *were* wrongful, but that he was not responsible for them because of a personal excusing condition.[117] If the primary party is guilty of all of the elements of the crime, and his conduct is otherwise wrongful, there is no policy reason why the secondary party should not be convicted of assisting in the wrongful conduct, assuming that the secondary party has no personal excuse of his own.[118]

For example, in *United States v. Lopez*,[119] S assisted P to escape from prison. P sought to show at her trial that she fled the prison because of unlawful threats on her life. The prosecution did not object to P seeking to defend her actions on this ground, but it did resist S's efforts to introduce evidence of the threats as a basis for acquittal of S in his prosecution as an accomplice.

The court held that S's right to introduce such evidence depended on whether P's defense claim was founded on necessity (justification) or duress (excuse).[120] As the court explained, and as considered in subsection [a], "[a] third party has the right to assist an actor in a justified act." Therefore, if P's claim was that she did the right thing by escaping, S was entitled to show that he assisted in this justified act. On the other hand, excuses "are always personal to the actor."[121] If P's claim was that she did the wrong thing by escaping, but that she was not to blame because she was coerced, this was *her* personal excusing condition. As S was not

---

[115] Some scholars would limit the statement in the text to cases in which S was aware of the justificatory condition when he assisted. This subject — whether justification defenses should be limited to persons who act for the right reason or, at least, act with knowledge of the justifying circumstance — has been the subject of rich debate. *See, e.g.,* Paul H. Robinson, *A Theory of Justification: Societal Harm as a Prerequisite for Criminal Liability*, 23 UCLA L. Rev. 266 (1975) (favoring the defense even when the actor lacks knowledge of the justifying condition); George P. Fletcher, *The Right Deed for the Wrong Reason: A Reply to Mr. Robinson*, 23 UCLA L. Rev. 293 (1975) (responding to Robinson).

[116] *See* State v. Montanez, 894 A.2d 928, 937–41 (Conn. 2006); *see also* United States v. Lopez, 662 F. Supp. 1083 (N.D. Cal. 1987) (discussed in subsection [b], *infra*).

[117] *See* §§ 16.04 and 17.03, *supra.*

[118] *See* Fletcher, Note 1, *supra*, at 664–67; Kadish, Note 1, *supra*, at 380–81.

[119] 662 F. Supp. 1083 (N.D. Cal. 1987).

[120] *See* § 23.05, *supra.*

[121] *Lopez*, 662 F. Supp. at 1086; *see also* Taylor v. Commonwealth, 521 S.E.2d 293, 297 (Va. Ct. App. 1999) (S was convicted as an accomplice of P, her fiancé, who abducted his son from his son's mother; held: whatever excuse P might claim did not apply to S); State v. Stokes, 718 S.E.2d 174, 178 (N.C. Ct. App. 2011) (observing that the recognition of an excuse by the primary party "did not transform those acts into non-criminal activity"; therefore, a secondary party may be convicted as an accomplice.).

personally coerced, he was *not* entitled to avoid conviction for assisting in an *unjustified* escape.[122]

[3]   Acquittal on the Basis of Lack of *Mens Rea*

[a]   In General

Suppose that a culpable secondary party assists a primary party to commit a wrongful act, but the primary actor is acquitted because he lacked the requisite *mens rea*. For example, consider *Regina v. Cogan and Leak*.[123] Leak convinced Cogan to have sexual intercourse with Leak's wife by falsely telling Cogan that she would agree to the intercourse. In fact, Leak had compelled his wife to submit to Cogan. Cogan was acquitted of rape on the basis of then-existing English precedent that his unreasonable mistake of fact regarding the wife's consent negated the *mens rea* of the offense.[124]

In light of Cogan's acquittal, was Leak guilty of rape? The court answered the question affirmatively, providing two alternative theories. First, since Leak caused Cogan to misunderstand the attendant circumstances, Cogan was Leak's innocent instrumentality. Thus, Leak was the principal in the first degree who used Cogan's "body as the instrument for the necessary physical act."[125] The difficulty with this analysis, however, is that it makes Leak guilty of raping his own wife, a conclusion that some courts are unwilling to reach, on the ground that rape is a "nonproxyable" offense.[126]

Second, the court opined that there was no reason why Leak should not be viewed as an accomplice of Cogan: "The fact that Cogan was innocent . . . does not affect the position that she was raped." It said further, "[n]o one outside a court of law would say that she had not been [raped]." In essence, the *actus reus* of rape was committed: The victim was forced to have sexual intercourse against her will. Therefore, a "crime" occurred. Cogan committed it. Leak encouraged it. Cogan's "crime" may be imputed to Leak, who had the requisite *mens rea*.

This latter analysis, however, also has serious conceptual difficulties. Can we truly say that the "crime" of rape occurred? According to Glanville Williams, "this will not do at all. [The court] uses popular . . . language, on the question whether the *fact* of 'rape' has occurred, instead of legal language, on the question whether the *crime* of rape has occurred."[127] Certainly, the most common legal understanding of the term "crime" is that it involves an *actus reus and a mens rea* — that is, after all, what the prosecutor must prove (beyond a reasonable doubt) against a perpetrator. Cogan did not commit "rape" in *that* sense, as he lacked the

---

[122] In *Lopez*, the court concluded that *P*'s defense more nearly resembled a justification claim; therefore, *S* was permitted to raise *P*'s defense.

[123] [1976] Q.B. 217.

[124] Regina v. Morgan, [1976] App.Cas. 182 (H.L.). *See* § 12.03[E], *supra*.

[125] *Cogan and Leak*, Q.B. at 223.

[126] *See* § 30.03[A][2][b][ii], *supra*.

[127] Williams, Note 26, *supra*, at 320 (emphasis added).

requisite *mens rea*. Therefore, this case is not like that of a party who commits the *actus reus* with the requisite *mens rea* (*i.e.*, commits all of the elements of a crime), but is acquitted on the ground of an excuse. Since Leak's liability must be derived from that of Cogan, and Cogan committed no "crime" on *this* understanding of the term, it is questionable whether Leak should have been convicted of rape as an accomplice.

Some scholars advocate the conviction of a secondary party as long he assists in the commission of the *actus reus* of an offense. For example, Professor Peter Alldridge, while disagreeing with the *Cogan and Leak* court's use of the innocent-instrumentality doctrine in that case,[128] sees no difficulty in treating Leak as an accomplice:

> The answer appropriate to the case . . . is to say that the norm laid down by the law relating to rape is that it is wrongful for a man to have intercourse with a woman who does not in fact consent. *That wrongful act is rape.* The excuse [lack of *mens rea* of Cogan] . . . is personal to [Cogan], and there is no reason why there should not be liability [of Leak] as an accessory.[129]

Thus, under this view, the "wrongful act" (as distinguished from a "crime") of the primary party is imputed to the secondary party, which when coupled with the secondary party's own *mens rea*, creates the "crime."

It is submitted that this analysis is misguided. It is one thing to impute a *crime* to the accomplice, and then measure the culpability of the respective parties on the basis of each person's *mens rea*;[130] it is quite another matter to derive criminal liability from a person *who has committed no offense*. It would be sensible, applying Alldridge's reasoning, to convict Leak *as a perpetrator, rather than an accomplice*, of a new crime, such as "causing or encouraging a wrongful act by another."[131] It is inaccurate, however, to say that there was a *crime* committed by *Cogan* that may be imputed to Leak.

[b]   Special Problem: The Feigning Primary Party

Earlier in this chapter we considered the liability of a putative accomplice to a crime whose purpose for participation was to ensnare the primary party in criminal activity.[132] Suppose that the converse occurs — the primary party tries to ensnare the accomplice. Consider the classic case of *State v. Hayes*.[133]

S proposed to *P* that *P* join *S* in the burglary of *V*'s store. *S* was unaware of the fact that *P* was a relative of *V*. With *V*'s approval, *P* agreed to the plan. *S* assisted

---

[128] He viewed rape as nonproxyable: "[T]o allege . . . that [Leak] had intercourse with his wife without her consent . . . is not what happened and, , had this been what had happened, it would not have constituted a crime." Peter Alldridge, *The Doctrine of Innocent Agency*, 2 Crim. L.F. 45, 52 (1990).

[129] *Id.* (emphasis added) (footnote omitted).

[130] This happens, particularly with criminal homicides. *See* § 30.06[C], *infra.*

[131] *See* Kadish, Note 1, *supra*, at 382.

[132] *See* § 30.05[B][1], *supra.*

[133] 16 S.W. 514 (Mo. 1891), *overruled on other grounds*, State v. Barton, 44 S.W. 239 (Mo. 1898).

P into the building, and took possession of property handed to him by P. Before they could leave the scene, S was arrested for burglary. S was convicted of the offense, but the state supreme court overturned the conviction.

At first glance the court's ruling seems incorrect: S intentionally assisted P; and S had the requisite felonious intent. On a closer look, however, the result is unexceptionable. P was the primary party: P committed the acts that arguably constituted the burglary. S's liability, therefore, had to derive from P. Yet, P was not guilty of burglary because he entered the building with the express approval of the owner, his father; therefore he lacked the specific intent to commit a felony (theft, which itself requires proof of a specific intent to *permanently* deprive the father of his property) therein.

Is there any way to justify S's burglary conviction? One possible theory would be to suggest that *he* was the primary party, who used P as his innocent instrumentality. The innocent-instrumentality doctrine, however, should not apply here because that rule is limited to circumstances in which the instrumentality is used or manipulated by another person. In this case P was not S's puppet; if anything, S was duped by P.

Alternatively, we could say that P committed the *actus reus* of burglary. Therefore, a crime occurred for which S may be held accountable. This argument, however, is subject to the criticism noted in subsection [a], namely that it is inappropriate to say that a burglary has occurred when a person commits the *actus reus* of an offense without the requisite *mens rea*. This criticism is especially compelling here since P not only lacked the requisite *mens rea* of burglary, but he had an antagonistic mental state, *i.e.*, the intent to cause S's arrest, hardly the type of situation that ordinarily suggests a principal-accomplice relationship.

[C] Liability of an Accomplice When the Primary Party Is Convicted

At common law and today, there is no bar to convicting an accessory before the fact or a principal in the second degree of a *lesser* offense or degree of offense than is proven against the primary party/perpetrator, if the secondary party's culpability is less than that of the primary actor. For example, even if P is guilty of first-degree premeditated murder, S is properly convicted of second-degree murder if he did not premeditate or if he lacked the specific intent to kill, required elements of first-degree murder.[134] Or, suppose that S and P walk into S's house and discover S's spouse in an act of adultery with V. If S, in sudden heat of passion, provides a gun to P, who calmly kills V, S may be guilty of voluntary manslaughter,[135] although P is guilty of murder.

---

[134] State v. O'Brien, 857 S.W.2d 212, 217–18 (Mo. 1993) (the element of deliberation or premeditation cannot be imputed from the principal to the accomplice); Commonwealth v. Huffman, 638 A.2d 961, 962 (Pa. 1994) (stating the general principle that an accomplice's liability must be found on his own mental state and "cannot depend upon proof of the intent to kill only in the principal").

[135] *See* § 31.07[B][2] (provocation), *infra.*

The more difficult issue is whether a secondary party may be convicted of a *more serious* offense or degree of offense than the primary party. At common law, the general rule was that an accessory (as distinguished from a principal in the second degree) could *not* be so convicted. The one apparent exception to this rule was in criminal homicide prosecutions. Now that the distinctions between principals and accessories have largely been abandoned, most commentators have concluded that there should be no conceptual obstacle to convicting *any* secondary party of a more serious offense than is proved against the primary party. The reasoning is that once it is agreed that a crime has occurred, each person's level of guilt should be assessed according to his own *mens rea*.[136]

In homicide prosecutions, where this issue most commonly arises, an accomplice may be convicted of first-degree murder, even though the primary party is convicted of second-degree murder or of manslaughter.[137] This outcome follows, for example, if the secondary party premeditates and calmly assists in a homicide, while the primary party kills without premeditation or in provocation. Likewise, it is possible for a primary party negligently to kill another (and, thus, be guilty of involuntary manslaughter), while the secondary party is guilty of murder, because he encouraged the primary actor's negligent conduct with the intent that it result in the victim's death.

This approach makes sense as long as we view "criminal homicide" as a single offense — that of causing the death of another with a culpable mental state — involving multiple levels of blameworthiness. It is fair to say, then, that when P commits the "offense" of criminal homicide, this "crime" is imputed to S, whose own liability for the homicide should be predicated on his own level of *mens rea*, whether it is greater or less than that of the primary party.

It does not necessarily follow that this analysis should be applied in every non-homicide circumstances.[138] Consider, for example, the English case of *Regina v. Richards*:[139] S procured two men — we will call them, together, P — to severely beat up her husband, V. In American terms, S solicited an aggravated battery. However, P did not do as procured, but instead committed the lesser offense of "unlawful wounding" (in American terms, a simple misdemeanor battery). Of what is S guilty? Is it "unlawful wounding" (the crime committed by P) or, as the jury concluded, the more serious offense of "unlawful wounding with the intent to commit grievous bodily harm"? The *Richards* court held that S could be convicted only of the lesser offense of which P was convicted, although she concededly had a more culpable state of mind than P.

---

[136] Jaiman v. State, 55 A.3d 224, 235 (R.I. 2012) (quoting this text); People v. McCoy, 24 P.3d 1210, 1214, 1215 (Cal. 2001) (quoting this text, and observing that the accomplice's "mental state is her own; she is liable for her mens rea, not the other person's").

[137] *McCoy*, 24 P.3d at 1215 (holding that even if the primary party is convicted of voluntary manslaughter, the secondary party may be convicted of murder).

[138] *Id.* at 1217 n.3 (in a homicide prosecution, holding that a secondary party may be convicted of a greater offense than the primary party, but concluding that "[b]ecause we cannot anticipate all possible non-homicide crimes or circumstances, we express no view on whether or how these principles apply outside the homicide context").

[139] [1974] Q.B. 776.

Richards has been the subject of both ardent criticism and support by commentators.[140] Ultimately, it was overruled.[141] At first glance, the problem in *Richards* seems indistinguishable from the homicide cases. Although the crimes of "wounding" and "wounding with the intent to cause grievous bodily harm" were separate offenses, they could easily have been treated as different degrees of the same offense, much as criminal homicide is divided into degrees and/or separate offenses severable only in terms of *mens rea*. Therefore, we can say that *P* committed the crime — not just the *actus reus* of the offense — of wounding, and we can then convict *S* and *P* of different degrees of this offense, based on their respective levels of culpability. So interpreted, *Richards* was properly overruled.

But, notice this: The issue here is not so much the respective mental states of *S* and *P*. What *S* wanted *P* to do was to commit a *different and greater* social harm than *P* actually perpetrated. What *S* wanted — what she solicited — was a battery resulting in grievous bodily harm. If *P* had done as solicited, *S* would uncontroversially have been guilty of that offense. But here a *different, lesser social harm* (essentially a simple battery) occurred. Thus, this is *not* precisely like a homicide case, in which the secondary party wants precisely what has occurred — the wrongful death of another — and in which the only difference between the parties is their degree of culpability *as to the harm that has been inflicted*.

As already seen, a person cannot be an accomplice to a crime that never occurred, as there is no crime from which to derive liability. In *Richards*, if we permit conviction of *S* for the greater offense, are we not effectively convicting her for a crime that did not transpire? The crime that occurred was a simple battery. What *S* wanted to occur, but did not, was an aggravated battery. At least in a legal system in which attempts are punished less severely than completed offenses because less harm has occurred, it is submitted that a person who assists in a "mini-crime" (unlawful wounding), with the intent that it result in a "maxi-crime" (aggravated battery), should *not* be convicted of the greater offense simply because she desired its commission. Thus, following this reasoning, *S* should be guilty as an accomplice of the crime that occurred (unlawful wounding) and not an offense that did not occur (unlawful wounding with the intent to cause grievous bodily harm).

§ 30.07 LIMITS TO ACCOMPLICE LIABILITY

[A] Legislative-Exemption Rule

A person may not be prosecuted as an accomplice in the commission of a crime if he is a member of the class of persons for whom the statute prohibiting the conduct was enacted to protect. For example, statutory rape laws were enacted to protect young females from immature decisions to have sexual intercourse; legislatures considers her to be the victim of the offense. It would conflict with

---

[140] *Compare* Williams, Note 26, *supra*, at 322–23, and J.C. Smith & Brian Hogan, Criminal Law 132–36 (5th ed. 1983) (criticizing the decision), *with* Kadish, Note 1, *supra*, at 388–91, and Fletcher, Note 1, *supra*, at 672–73 (providing support for the court's analysis).

[141] Regina v. Howe, [1987] App. Cas. 417 (H.L.).

legislative intent, therefore, if she could be prosecuted as a secondary party to her own statutory rape.[142]

[B] Abandonment

As with the law of conspiracy,[143] many courts hold that a person who provides assistance to another for the purpose of promoting or facilitating the offense, but who subsequently abandons the criminal endeavor, can avoid accountability for the subsequent criminal acts of the primary party.

A spontaneous and unannounced withdrawal will not do.[144] Instead, the accomplice must communicate his withdrawal to the principal and make bona fide efforts to neutralize the effect of his prior assistance. For example, one who provides an instrumentality for use in the crime must regain possession of it or otherwise neutralize its effect. Thus, a person who provides a fuse for dynamiting a building, must remove the fuse; and, "if [it] has been set, he must step on the fuse."[145] On other hand, one who has offered nothing more than mild encouragement may be able to neutralize his effect by communicating his objection to the crime, unless he provides it at the point at which the event is virtually unstoppable.

§ 30.08   CONSPIRATORIAL LIABILITY: THE *PINKERTON* DOCTRINE[146]

[A] "Accomplice" Versus "Conspiratorial" Liability

Courts and lawyers frequently fail to distinguish between *accomplice* liability, the subject of the preceding sections of this chapter, and *conspiracy* liability — complicity based *solely* on a *conspiratorial* relationship — which is the topic of this chapter section. This is because the two concepts "normally go hand-in-hand."[147] However, it is sometimes necessary to distinguish between the two forms of complicity liability, particularly because, as will be seen, conspiratorial liability is potentially a broader form of liability than accomplice doctrine.

---

[142] *In re* Meagan R., 42 Cal. App. 4th 17 (Ct. App. 1996) (*R* cannot legally be an accomplice in her own statutory rape; therefore, she is also not guilty of burglary based on the intent to commit the felony of statutory rape). The legislative-exemption rule is discussed more fully at § 29.09[D], *supra*.

[143] *See* § 29.09[B], *supra*.

[144] State v. Thomas, 356 A.2d 433, 442 (N.J. Super. Ct. App. Div. 1976), *rev'd on other grounds*, 387 A.2d 1187 (N.J. 1978).

[145] *See* Eldredge v. United States, 62 F.2d 449, 451 (10th Cir. 1932) (discussing withdrawal from a conspiracy).

[146] Alex Kreit, *Vicarious Criminal Liability and the Constitutional Dimensions of Pinkerton*, 57 Am. U.L. Rev. 585 (2008); Mark Noferi, *Towards Attenuation: A (New Due Process Limit on Pinkerton Conspiracy Liability*, 33 Am. J. Crim. L. 91 (2006); Jens David Ohlin, *Group Think: The Law of Conspiracy and Collective Reason*, 98 J. Crim. L. & Criminology 147 (2007).

[147] Rollin M. Perkins & Ronald N. Boyce, Criminal Law 703 (3d ed. 1982).

The distinction between the two forms of accountability is this: An agreement between two or more persons to participate in the commission of a crime is the key to a conspiracy and, therefore, to conspiratorial liability. *Actual assistance in committing the crime that is the object of the conspiracy is not required.* In contrast, accomplice liability requires proof that an actor at least indirectly participated (assisted) in the crime; an agreement to do so is not needed.[148]

In most circumstances, an accomplice is also a conspirator with the primary party in the commission of the crime. For example, if S drives P to a bank, which P robs with S's weapon, and S drives P away from the bank, it is reasonable to infer a prior conspiratorial agreement between S and P. And, looking at the matter from the other direction, the sheer act of agreeing may serve as encouragement to the primary party, and thereby render the conspirator an accomplice in the commission of the crime.

Nonetheless, one can be a conspirator without being an accomplice. For example, in *Pinkerton v. United States*,[149] S and P conspired to violate certain provisions of the Internal Revenue Code. Thereafter, P violated the Revenue Code provisions. However, he did so while S was incarcerated for unrelated reasons. The prosecutor did not claim that S assisted P in the planning or commission of the substantive offenses. And, S's presence in prison negated any reasonable inference that his earlier act of agreeing encouraged P when he committed the crimes. S's responsibility in P's conduct, therefore, was not based on accomplice principles, and had to find its source exclusively in conspiracy law.

Accomplice liability in the absence of a conspiracy is also possible. For example: P enters a bank to rob it; S, a customer, observes P's actions and silently assists in the crime by disabling a bank security camera. Here, P and S never agreed to commit the robbery together. But, S is P's accomplice in light of his assistance.[150]

Thus, in most cases an accomplice is a co-conspirator, and vice-versa. Sometimes, however, only one theory of complicity will apply.

[B]   Rule of Conspiratorial Liability

According to the Supreme Court in *Pinkerton v. United States*,[151] co-conspirators are "partners in crime"; therefore, "the overt act of one partner in crime is attributable to all." And, "we fail to see why the same or other acts in furtherance of the conspiracy are likewise not attributable to the others for the purpose of holding them responsible for the substantive offense."[152] There are

---

[148] Chisler v. State, 553 So.2d 654, 664 (Ala. Crim. App. 1989); Manlove v. State, 901 A.2d 1284, 1288 (Del. 2006); State v. Roldan, 714 A.2d 351, 360 (N.J. Super. Ct. App. Div. 1998).

[149] 328 U.S. 640 (1946).

[150] *See also* State ex rel. Martin, Att'y Gen. v. Tally, 15 So. 722 (Ala. 1894) (*S*, aware that *P1* and *P2* have set out to kill *V*, independently prevents a warning from reaching *V*; *S* may be an accomplice in the subsequent homicide even though he did not conspire with the others). For another excellent example of accomplice liability in the absence of a conspiracy, see Commonwealth v. Cook, 411 N.E.2d 1326 (Mass. App. Ct. 1980), discussed at § 29.04[A], *supra.*

[151] 328 U.S. 640 (1946).

[152] *Id.* at 647.

limits to this so-called "*Pinkerton* doctrine":

> A different case would arise if the substantive offense committed by one of
> the conspirators was not in fact done in furtherance of the conspiracy, did
> not fall within the scope of the unlawful project, or was merely a part of the
> ramifications of the plan which could not be reasonably foreseen as a
> necessary and natural consequence of the unlawful agreement.[153]

As one court has summarized the *Pinkerton* rule, "[e]ach member of the conspiracy
is liable for the acts of any of the others in carrying out the common purpose, *i.e.*,
all acts within the reasonable and probable consequence of the common unlawful
design."[154]

It has been said that the *Pinkerton* rule, adopted in the federal courts, is the
majority rule in states that have considered the issue.[155] However, one should be
cautious in measuring the strength of the *Pinkerton* rule: Many courts that have
approved of the rule have done so in cases in which the result would have been the
same had traditional accomplice rules been invoked.[156]

[C]   Comparison of Liability

Accomplice and conspiracy liability often overlap completely. For example,
suppose that S and P agree to commit an armed robbery and work together in its
planning stages. P commits the offense. On these facts, S will be held accountable
for the robbery under either theory of liability: He intentionally assisted P to rob
the bank; and, as the robbery was the object of the conspiracy, he is liable for it
under conspiracy rules. And, if P kills bank teller V during the same robbery, S is
likely accountable for the death under either theory: The killing was likely a
natural and probable consequence of the crime in which S intentionally assisted;
and the homicide was a foreseeable consequence of the conspiracy to commit the
robbery.

The rules potentially diverge in dramatic ways, however, when the conspiracy is
broad or open-ended. To see the difference, suppose that D1 and D2 conspire to
run a prostitution ring and live off the earnings of the female prostitutes they
hire.[157] Depending on circumstances, the individual prostitutes may properly be
considered fellow conspirators.[158] If so, D1 and D2 are guilty under *Pinkerton*, and
very likely under doctrines of accomplice liability, of every act of prostitution
committed by every prostitute they hired.

But, consider the prostitutes' position in this far-flung conspiracy. It is unlikely
that any prostitute assisted in the acts of prostitution by others. Under accomplice
liability doctrine, therefore, a prostitute would not be guilty of any substantive

---

[153] *Id.* at 647–48.

[154] People v. Maciel, 304 P.3d 983, 1012 (Cal. 2013) (quoting *In re* Hardy, 163 P.3d 853 (Cal. 2007)).

[155] State v. Walton, 630 A.2d 990, 998 (Conn. 1993).

[156] *Developments in the Law — Criminal Conspiracy*, 72 Harv. L. Rev. 920, 993–95 (1959).

[157] People v. Luciano, 14 N.E.2d 433 (N.Y. 1938).

[158] *See* § 29.07, *supra.*

offenses except her own prostitution acts. Pursuant to *Pinkerton*, however, once it is determined that a prostitute was a party to an open-ended broad conspiracy to commit prostitution, she would be liable for every act of prostitution performed by every other co-conspiring prostitute *and of every other reasonably foreseeable offense committed by D1, D2 and any other prostitute committed in furtherance of the common unlawful design.* Rigid application of the *Pinkerton* rule, therefore, may result in extensive liability of comparatively minor parties to a criminal agreement.

Critics of the *Pinkerton* doctrine assert that the law "lose[s] all sense of just proportion if simply because of the conspiracy itself each [conspirator is] held accountable for thousands of additional offenses of which he was completely unaware and which he did not influence at all."[159] Defenders of the rule state that "such harshness may be considered as an occupational hazard confronting those who might be tempted to engage in a criminal conspiracy within a jurisdiction that adheres to the so-called *Pinkerton* rule."[160]

§ 30.09   MODEL PENAL CODE

[A]   Forms of Liability

[1]   In General

Under the Model Penal Code a person is guilty of an offense if he commits it "by his own conduct or by the conduct of another person for which he is legally accountable, or both."[161] In other words, a person can be convicted of an offense if he personally commits the crime, or if his relationship to the person who commits it is one for which he is legally accountable. Three forms of accountability for the acts of others are recognized by the Code and are described below.

[2]   Accountability Through an Innocent Instrumentality

The Code adopts the accepted principle that one is guilty of the commission of a crime if he uses an innocent instrumentality to commit the crime. A person (*D*) is legally accountable for the conduct of "an innocent or irresponsible person" (*X*) if he (*D*): (1) has the mental state sufficient for commission of the offense; and (2) causes the innocent or irresponsible person to engage in the criminal conduct.[162]

It should be observed that the Code is explicit where the common law is implicit: The innocent-instrumentality doctrine applies only if *D causes X* to engage in the conduct in question. Thus, this section does not apply merely because *X* is insane or otherwise "innocent or irresponsible." *D* must have done something to manipulate or otherwise use *X*, so that it may fairly be said that, but for *D*'s conduct, *X* would

---

[159] American Law Institute, Comment to § 2.06, at 307; *see* State v. Nevarez, 130 P.3d 1154, 1158 (Idaho Ct. App. 2005).

[160] State v. Barton, 424 A.2d 1033, 1038 (R.I. 1981).

[161] Model Penal Code § 2.06(1).

[162] Model Penal Code § 2.06(2)(a).

not have engaged in the conduct for which D is being held accountable.

If D causes X, an innocent or irresponsible person, to engage in criminal conduct, D is responsible for X's conduct if, but only if, D possessed the mental state sufficient for the commission of the crime. For example, if D coerces X to have nonconsensual sexual intercourse with V, D is guilty of rape because he possessed the mental state required for that offense.[163] Or, suppose that D provides his car to X, an insane person with a known "penchant for mad driving."[164] If X proceeds to drive D's car in a dangerous manner, D may be convicted of reckless endangerment, on the basis of D's recklessness in providing the car to a known mad driver. However, if D is unaware of X's dangerous tendencies, D would not be guilty of reckless endangerment: He has caused X to engage in the conduct, but he does not possess the mental state (recklessness) sufficient for commission of the offense.

[3] Miscellaneous Accountability

A person may be held accountable for another person's conduct if the law defining an offense so provides.[165] This provision is not of broad importance, but it does recognize that a legislature may wish to enact special laws of accomplice liability, as, for example, when it prohibits aiding and abetting a suicide attempt,[166] or knowingly causing or facilitating a prison escape.[167]

[4] Accomplice Accountability

A person is legally accountable for the conduct of another person if he is an accomplice of the other in the commission of the criminal offense.[168]

Two features of accomplice liability should initially be observed. First, it is a form of liability independent of the innocent-or-irresponsible-person doctrine described in subsection [2], *i.e.*, the rules of accomplice liability described below have *no bearing* on the situation in which a person uses an innocent instrumentality.

Second, accomplice liability is dependent on the relationship of the parties in the commission of a *specific offense.* In other words, if S is prosecuted for robbery because he allegedly served as P's accomplice, the issue that must be resolved is whether S was P's accomplice *in that robbery*, and not whether S was P's accomplice in the commission of some other crime or of crimes in general.

---

[163] Morrisey v. State, 620 A.2d 207, 211 (Del. 1993).

[164] American Law Institute, Comment to § 2.06, at 302.

[165] Model Penal Code § 2.06(2)(b).

[166] Model Penal Code § 210.5(2).

[167] Model Penal Code § 242.6.

[168] Model Penal Code § 2.06(2)(c).

[5] Rejection of Conspiratorial Liability

The Model Code does not apply the *Pinkerton*[169] doctrine of conspiratorial liability. That is, under the Code, a person is not accountable for the conduct of another solely because he conspired with that person to commit an offense. The liability of one who does not personally commit an offense must be based on one of the preceding forms of accountability. The drafters of the Code rejected the *Pinkerton* doctrine because they believed there was "no better way to confine within reasonable limits the scope of liability to which conspiracy may theoretically give rise."[170]

[B] Nature of an "Accomplice"

[1] Conduct

[a]   In General

S is an accomplice of *P* in the commission of an offense if, with the requisite *mens rea*, he: (1) solicits *P* to commit the offense; (2) aids, agrees to aid, or attempts to aid *P* in the planning or commission of the offense; or (3) has a legal duty to prevent the commission of the offense, but makes no effort to do so.[171]

[b]   Accomplice Liability by Solicitation

S is an accomplice of *P* in the commission of an offense if he solicits *P* to commit the crime. The complicity section does not define the term "solicits." Rather, accomplice liability exists if *S*'s conduct would constitute criminal solicitation, as that offense is defined elsewhere in the Code.[172]

[c]   Accomplice Liability by Aiding

The Code dispenses with the many common law and statutory terms used to describe the conduct that may constitute assistance in the commission of an offense, and replaces them with the single word "aids." It should be observed, however, that in the Model Code, "soliciting" a crime is *not* a form of "aiding"; it is an independent basis for accomplice liability. This distinction can prove significant, as discussed in the next two subsections.

[d]   Accomplice Liability by Agreeing to Aid

S is an accomplice of *P* if he agrees to aid *P* in the planning or commission of an offense. This requirement is met, for example, if *S* tells *P* that he will help to plan the commission of the offense, or if he agrees to provide *P* with an instrumentality for the commission of the crime, *even if S does not fulfill his promise.* However,

---

[169] Pinkerton v. United States, 328 U.S. 640 (1946). *See* § 30.08, *supra.*

[170] American Law Institute, Comment to § 2.06, at 307.

[171] Model Penal Code § 2.06(3)(a).

[172] Model Penal Code § 5.02. *See generally* § 28.03, *supra.*

because this form of accomplice liability is based on "aiding," rather than "soliciting," *S* is *not* an accomplice of *P* merely because he agrees to solicit the commission of an offense but fails to do so.

This feature of the Code differs at least in form from the common law. In most cases, *S*'s agreement to aid in the commission of an offense serves as encouragement to *P* and, therefore, functions as a basis for common law accomplice liability. The Code does not require proof of such encouragement, as such; it is enough that *S* manifested his participation in the offense by agreeing to aid.

On the other hand, "agreeing to aid" is *not* equivalent to conspiring to commit an offense. That is, this is not the *Pinkerton* doctrine in disguise. One can conspire to commit an offense (and, therefore, be guilty of conspiracy) and yet not "agree to aid" another person in a particular offense (and, therefore, not be an accomplice of a co-conspirator in the commission of that crime). For example, suppose that *S* agrees to aid *P* to rob Bank A. In furtherance of their conspiracy, *P* steals a "getaway" car. Under *Pinkerton* doctrine, *S* is guilty of the theft, as that offense was committed in furtherance of their conspiracy to rob Bank A. However, under the Code, *S* is *not* guilty of the car theft, as he did not agree to aid (or, for that matter, solicit, aid, or attempt to aid) *P* in the commission of *that* offense.

[e] Accomplice Liability by Attempting to Aid

[i] In General

In a significant departure from the common law,[173] the Code provides that *S* may be held accountable as an accomplice of *P* in the commission of an offense if he attempts to aid in the planning or commission of the crime, even though his aid proves ineffectual. For example, if *S* opens a window so that *P* may enter to commit a felony inside the building, *S* is an accomplice in the burglary, even if *P* enters by the door. In such circumstances, *S* has "attempted" to aid *P*, *i.e.*, he has taken a substantial step in a course of conduct intended to culminate in assistance in the commission of an offense.

[ii] The Relationship of § 2.06 (Complicity) to § 5.01 (Criminal Attempt)

It is useful to see how Section 2.06, the Model Code's complicity provision, relates to Section 5.01, which prohibits criminal attempts. In particular, Section 5.01(3), discussed elsewhere in this text,[174] should be considered here.

Suppose that *S* provides *P* a gun in order to assist *P* in the commission of a robbery. If *P* performs the robbery, *S* is guilty as an accomplice of *P* in its commission. Similarly, if *P*, in the midst of the robbery, is arrested before he can complete it, *P* is guilty of *attempted* robbery under the Code's criminal attempt

---

[173] *See* § 30.04[B][1], *supra.*

[174] *See* § 27.09[D][2], *supra.*

provision. In turn, S would be guilty of the attempt under the Code's complicity statute.

However, suppose that P is arrested *before* he takes a substantial step in a course of conduct intended to result in the robbery. Under these circumstances, P is not guilty of attempted robbery.[175] In this case, S is not accountable under the complicity statute, because the person from whom he would derive his liability committed no crime. Nonetheless, S is guilty of a criminal attempt by *his own conduct* (*i.e., not* through the doctrine of complicity), by application of Model Penal Code Section 5.01(3), which provides that a person who engages in conduct designed to aid[176] in the commission of an offense "that would establish complicity under Section 2.06 if the crime were committed by such other person, is guilty of an attempt . . . although the crime is not committed or attempted by such other person."[177]

Notice the irony in this result: S is guilty of attempted robbery; P, the primary participant, is not guilty of attempt.

[f]   Accomplice Liability by Omission

Ordinarily, one cannot be an accomplice in the commission of an offense by failing to act. The rule is to the contrary, however, if the omitter has a duty to prevent the commission of the offense, for example, if he is a police officer standing by while a crime is committed in his presence.

It should be remembered, however, that the omitter must possess the mental state required of an accomplice, *i.e.*, he must have failed to act with the purpose of promoting or facilitating the commission of the offense. An omission that is the result of fright or ignorance, rather than dereliction of duty, would not result in accomplice liability.

[2]   Mental State

[a]   In General

A person is an accomplice if he assists "with the purpose of promoting or facilitating the commission of the offense."[178] This provision conforms with common law precedent. For example, if S drives P to a liquor store where P commits a

---

[175] He may be guilty of another offense, *e.g.*, conspiracy to commit robbery.

[176] Notice that Section 5.01(3) uses the word "aid" in relationship to the complicity statute; and further notice that Section 2.06(3) of the complicity statute itself distinguishes "solicits" from "aids, agrees [to aid] or attempts to aid"; thus, seemingly, upon a careful reading of Section 5.01(3), this provision does not apply if S *solicits* another to commit an offense that is neither committed nor attempted.

[177] This provision also comes into play when a person, with criminal purpose, provides aid to one whom he believes will commit an offense, but who actually is an undercover officer who does not attempt to commit the offense. *E.g.*, United States v. Washington, 106 F.3d 983 (D.C. Cir. 1997) (based on the MPC, W was convicted of attempted possession of cocaine with intent to distribute, when he "assisted" an undercover officer whom he believed to be a drug dealer to possess what he believed was cocaine).

[178] Model Penal Code § 2.06(3)(a).

robbery, S is guilty of robbery if his act of assistance (driving the automobile) was committed with the purpose of facilitating the robbery; however, he is not guilty if he did not know what P intended to do in the store.

After considerable debate, the American Law Institute rejected the argument that complicity liability should apply to one who knowingly, but not purposely, facilitates the commission of an offense.[179] For example, if S, a merchant, sells dynamite to P, with knowledge that P intends to use the explosives to blow open a safe, S is not an accomplice in the subsequent crime, unless it was his conscious object to facilitate the commission of the offense.

[b]   Liability for Crimes of Recklessness and Negligence

The requirement of purposeful conduct set out in Section 2.06 triggers the same question that confronts courts interpreting the common law and pre-Model Code statutes: Under what circumstances, if any, is a person an accomplice in the commission of a crime of recklessness or negligence?

The Code expressly deals with this issue. Section 2.06(4) provides that, when causing a particular result is an element of a crime, a person is an accomplice in the commission of the offense if: (1) he was an accomplice in the *conduct* that caused the *result*; and (2) he acted with the culpability, if any, regarding the *result* that is sufficient for commission of the offense.[180]

Reconsider an earlier hypothetical:[181] S encourages P to speed on a public road near a school. P loses control of the car and strikes and negligently kills V, a child. Under the Code, S and P would be prosecuted for negligent homicide. On these facts, S may be held accountable for the death caused by P.

To see this, one must go through a three-step process. First, determine P's potential responsibility. For sake of discussion, assume that P is guilty of negligent homicide. Second, ask whether S was an accomplice in the *conduct* that caused the *result* (rather than asking the ordinary question of whether S was an accomplice in the commission of the charged offense). The answer is that S was an accomplice in the *conduct*: He assisted by encouraging the conduct (speeding) that caused the result (the death); and he uttered the words of encouragement with the purpose of promoting or facilitating the conduct (the speeding). Third, now ask whether S acted with the culpability in regard to the *result* (the death) that is sufficient for commission of the offense. In this case, S quite arguably acted with the requisite culpability (negligence) as to the death.

This provision has special significance in states that recognize the common law

---

[179] *See* American Law Institute, Comment to § 2.06, at 314–19.

[180] *See* Commonwealth v. Roebuck, 32 A.3d 613, 618–21 (Pa. 2011) (stating that under the MPC, on which the state's complicity statute is based, it is not logically impossible for one to be an accomplice in an unintentional result; for crime to which the principal actor need not intend the result, "it is also not necessary for the accomplice to do so").

[181] *See* § 30.05[B][3], *supra.*

doctrines of felony-murder and misdemeanor-manslaughter.[182] These common law rules allow the primary party in a homicide to be convicted if the death occurs accidentally while he is committing a felony or misdemeanor. The effect of Section 2.06(4) is to make the accomplice in the *conduct* (the underlying felony or misdemeanor) that causes the result strictly liable for the ensuing death, on the ground that he possessed the level of culpability in regard to the *result* that is sufficient for commission of the offense, *i.e.*, no culpability.

[c]   Attendant Circumstances

Reconsider an earlier case:[183] S purposely assists P to have sexual intercourse with V, a nonconsenting female. P realizes that V is not consenting (and, therefore, is guilty of rape), but S unreasonably believes that V is consenting. Is S guilty of rape as P's accomplice?

The Code does not address this question. The Commentary states that "[t]here is deliberate ambiguity"[184] in this regard. Thus, a court might determine that the requirement of purpose extends to the attendant circumstances, in which case S is not guilty of the rape. Alternatively, the policy of the substantive offense might control, *i.e.*, S would be guilty of the offense if he has the culpable state of mind regarding the victim's nonconsent that is sufficient to convict the perpetrator of that offense.

[d]   Natural-and-Probable-Consequences Doctrine

The Code does not apply the common law natural-and-probable-consequences rule.[185] The liability of an accomplice does not extend beyond the purposes that he shares. For example, suppose that S aids P in the commission of a bank robbery by furnishing P with the details of the bank's security system. Later, P steals an automobile, which he uses as his "getaway" vehicle in the robbery. Although S is an accomplice of P in the commission of the robbery (he aided P with the purpose of promoting that offense), he is *not* an accomplice in the commission of the theft: Although the theft may have been a foreseeable consequence of the offense in which he was an accomplice, he did not purposely aid in the car theft.

[C] Liability of the Accomplice in Relation to the Perpetrator

The Model Code provides that an accomplice in the commission of an offense may be convicted of a crime, upon proof of its commission by another person, regardless of whether the other person is convicted, acquitted, or not prosecuted.

---

[182] *See* §§ 31.06 and 31.09, *infra*. Although the Code rejects these doctrines, a state could adopt Section 2.06(4) and yet retain one or both of these homicide rules.

[183] *See* § 30.05[B][4], *supra*.

[184] American Law Institute, Comment to § 2.06 at 311 n.37.

[185] *E.g.*, State v. Lopez-Minjares, 260 P.3d 439, 443 (Or. 2011) (the common law "natural and probable consequences" doctrine is not recognized by the state's complicity statute, which is modeled on the MPC).

Furthermore, an accomplice may be convicted of a different offense or different degree of offense than the primary party is convicted.[186] Thus, the fact that P is acquitted of an offense does not preclude the conviction of S for that offense, as long as the prosecutor shows that *someone* committed the crime in question, and that S aided that person.[187] It is also possible to convict S of assault with intent to kill, and P of simple assault, if S has a more culpable frame of mind regarding the attack.

The Code also expressly provides that a person who is legally incapable of committing an offense personally may be held accountable for the crime if it is committed by another person for whom he is legally accountable.[188] For example, although a husband cannot legally rape his own wife at common law or under the Model Penal Code,[189] he may be convicted as an accomplice in her rape.

[D] Limits to Accomplice Liability

Section 2.06(6) states that, unless the Code expressly provides to the contrary, a person is not an accomplice in the commission of an offense if any one of three circumstances exist. First, S may not be convicted as an accomplice if he is the victim of the offense. For example, the parent of a kidnapped child who pays a ransom may not be convicted as an accomplice in the kidnapping of his own child.

Second, S is not an accomplice of P if S's conduct is "inevitably incident" to the commission of the offense. For example, a purchaser of narcotics is not an accomplice in the commission of the sale or delivery of the controlled substance to himself.[190]

Third, the Code establishes a defense of abandonment. A person is not an accomplice in the commission of a crime if he terminates his participation before the crime is committed, and if he: (1) neutralizes his assistance; (2) gives timely warning to the police of the impending offense; or (3) in some other manner attempts to prevent the commission of the crime.[191]

---

[186] Model Penal Code § 2.06(7).

[187] Although the acquittal of the perpetrator is not a bar to conviction of an accomplice, as noted, the Code *does* require proof of "the commission of the offense." The Code does not indicate, however, what it means by the word "offense" in this context. Thus, the Code does not expressly resolve the issues raised in § 30.06[B][2]–[3], *supra*.

[188] Model Penal Code § 2.06(5).

[189] Model Penal Code § 213.1.

[190] State v. Celestine, 671 So. 2d 896 (La. 1996); Robinson v. State, 815 S.W.2d 361 (Tex. App. 1991).

[191] See § 30.07[B] for general discussion of how the defense is applied.

Chapter 31

CRIMINAL HOMICIDE

§ 31.01 HOMICIDE[1]

[A] Definition of "Homicide"

At very early common law, "homicide" was defined as "the killing of a human being by a human being."[2] This definition includes suicide within its compass. However, the later common law definition of "homicide," followed in modern statutes, is "the killing of a human being by *another* human being." Suicide, therefore, is no longer a form of homicide.[3]

"Homicide" is a legally neutral term. That is, a homicide may be innocent or criminal. The duly authorized execution of a convicted felon, for example, is no less a homicide than the most "cold-blooded" murder.

[B] Definition of "Human Being"

[1] The Beginning of Human Life[4]

At common law, a fetus must be born alive to constitute a "human being" within the meaning of that term in criminal homicide law.[5]

This rule is anomalous. Following the common law approach, a homicide occurs when one causes the death of a being that is *not* considered human at the time of the death-producing act, as long as it is "human" when it dies. Thus, if *D* strikes *V*, a pregnant woman, in the abdomen causing lethal injury to the fetus, a homicide occurs if the fetus is expelled from the womb alive and dies from the pre-birth blow

---

[1] *See generally* Homicide Law in Comparative Perspective (Jeremy Horder ed., 2007); Herbert Wechsler & Jerome Michael, *A Rationale of the Law of Homicide* (Pts. I & II), 37 Colum. L. Rev. 701 (1937), 37 Colum. L. Rev. 1261 (1937).

[2] Royal Commission on Capital Punishment Report, (Cmd. 8932) ¶ 72 (1953).

[3] Attempted suicide was a common law misdemeanor. Today, a person who assists another to commit suicide may be charged with aiding and abetting a suicide, an independent statutory offense in many jurisdictions. *E.g.*, Model Penal Code § 210.5.

[4] *See generally* Clarke D. Forsythe, *Homicide of the Unborn Child: The Born Alive Rule and Other Legal Anachronisms*, 21 Val. U. L. Rev. 563 (1987); Alan S. Wasserstrom, Annotation, *Homicide Based on Killing of Unborn Child*, 64 A.L.R.5th 671 (1998).

[5] *See* Meadows v. State, 722 S.W.2d 584, 585 (Ark. 1987); Keeler v. Superior Court, 470 P.2d 617, 622 (Cal. 1970); State v. Beale, 376 S.E.2d 1, 3 (N.C. 1989); Commonwealth v. Booth, 766 A.2d 843, 844 (Pa. 2001).

seconds after birth.[6] Yet, if the same act is more efficient, in that it causes immediate death of the fetus in the womb, a homicide has not occurred.

Critics of the common law rule consider it outdated. One stated basis of the "born alive" rule was that a live birth was needed to prove that the "unborn child" was alive at the time of the accused's actions, and that these acts were the cause of its subsequent death.[7] In light of advances in modern medical technology, it is now possible to determine whether a fetus is alive in the mother's womb, to determine with much greater likelihood of accuracy its chances of being born alive, and to identify the cause of its death if it is born dead. Therefore, it is reasoned, the definition of "human being" should include unborn fetuses.

According to one recent survey, 38 states have abandoned the "born alive" rule, some holding that criminal homicide liability attaches, despite the absence of a live birth, at the point of conception, others using quickening, and still others focusing on viability.[8]

[2]   The End of Human Life[9]

When does a person cease to be a "human being" for purposes of homicide law, *i.e.*, what constitutes the legal death of a human being? The traditional rule, based on then-prevailing medical standards, recognized a cardiopulmonary definition of "death": A human being was dead when there was a complete and permanent stoppage of the circulation of the blood and the "cessation of the animal and vital functions consequent thereon, such as respiration, pulsation, etc."[10]

Since the development of life-support devices and procedures, this definition has proven unsatisfactory. It is now possible artificially to maintain the heart and lung activities of persons who have lost the spontaneous capacity to perform these "animal and vital functions." As one court put it, "human bodies can be made to breathe and blood to circulate even in the utter absence of brain function."[11] The effect of the machinery, therefore, is to keep some people legally "alive" long after their capacity for independent life has ceased. Furthermore, in an era of sophisticated organ transplant technology, the traditional definition prevents medical personnel from "harvesting" healthy organs from "artificially alive" persons, resulting in the death of patients in desperate need of healthy organs.

---

[6] *E.g.*, State v. Cotton, 5 P.3d 918 (Ariz. Ct. App. 2000); State v. Courchesne, 998 A.2d 1 (Conn. 2010).

[7] Commonwealth v. Cass, 467 N.E.2d 1324, 1328 (Mass. 1984); Hughes v. State, 868 P.2d 730, 732 (Okla. Crim. App. 1994); *cf. Keeler v. Superior Court*, 470 P.2d at 633 (Burke, Acting C.J., dissenting) ("The common law reluctance to characterize the killing of a quickened fetus as a homicide was based solely upon a presumption that the fetus would have been born dead.").

[8] http://www.ncsl.org/research/health/fetal-homicide-state-laws.aspx (National Conference of State Legislatures, viewed May 13, 2015); *see also* State v. Lamy, 969 A.2d 451, 457 (N.H. 2009) (providing statutory and case law citations).

[9] *See generally* Alexander Morgan Capron & Leon R. Kass, *A Statutory Definition of the Standards for Determining Human Death: An Appraisal and a Proposal*, 121 U. Pa. L. Rev. 87 (1972).

[10] Smith v. Smith, 317 S.W.2d 275, 279 (Ark. 1958) (quoting Black's Law Dictionary 488 (4th ed. 1951)).

[11] *In re T.A.C.P.*, 609 So. 2d 588, 591 (Fla. 1992).

In 1968, an influential Harvard Medical School committee reported that the medical conception of death was changing.[12] It concluded that cessation of brain function is a more suitable measure of death, especially when a patient's respiration and circulation are being supported artificially. The committee set forth a multi-step test designed to identify "brain death syndrome."

As is now understood, the brain anatomically is divided into three parts. The cerebrum (the "higher brain") controls cognitive functions, including consciousness. The cerebellum ("middle brain") controls motor coordination. And the brain stem ("lower brain") provides the "animal functions," *i.e.*, reflexive and spontaneous activities such as breathing and swallowing.[13] "Brain death" exists when the whole brain — all three portions — irreversibly cease to function. The fact that respiration and pulsation are artificially induced by machinery does not affect the conclusion.

In 1970, the Kansas legislature enacted the first statute recognizing termination of brain functions as a basis for determining legal death. The statute provided that death occurs when, according to accepted medical standards, the individual experiences an irreversible cessation of breathing and heartbeat (the common law definition) *or* there is an absence of spontaneous brain activity.[14] "Brain death," or more precisely, "whole brain death," is now commonly incorporated by statute or judicial decision[15] in the definition of human "death."

[C] Year-and-a-Day Rule[16]

The common law provides that a defendant may not be prosecuted for criminal homicide unless the victim dies within a year and a day of the act inflicting the fatal injury.[17] That is, if *D* shoots *V* on January 1, 2015, and *V* dies on or before January 1, 2016, a homicide has resulted; but, if *V* dies on or after January 2, 2016, a criminal homicide prosecution is barred, although a non-homicide prosecution, such as for assault with a deadly weapon,[18] is permitted.

---

[12] Report of the Ad Hoc Committee of the Harvard Medical School to Examine the Definition of Brain Death, *A Definition of Irreversible Coma*, 205 J.A.M.A. 337 (1968).

[13] People v. Eulo, 472 N.E.2d 286, 291–92 (N.Y. 1984).

[14] Kan. Stat. Ann. § 77-202 (repealed in 1984). Kansas law now provides: "An individual who has sustained either (1) irreversible cessation of circulatory and respiratory functions, or (2) irreversible cessation of all functions of the entire brain, including the brain stem, is dead." Kan. Stat. Ann. § 77-205 (2015).

[15] *E.g.*, State v. Guess, 715 A.2d 643, 651–52 (Conn. 1998); *People v. Eulo*, 472 N.E.2d at 288–89.

[16] *See generally* D.E.C. Yale, *A Year and a Day in Homicide*, 48 Cambridge L.J. 202 (1989).

[17] 4 William Blackstone, Commentaries on the Laws of England *197 (1769) ("In order . . . to make the killing murder, it is requisite that the party die within a year and a day after the stroke received, or cause of death administered.").

[18] *E.g.*, Commonwealth v. Pinnick, 234 N.E.2d 756 (Mass. 1968), *overruled on other grounds by* Commonwealth v. Lewis, 409 N.E.2d 771 (Mass. 1980).

The year-and-a-day rule dates back to 1278,[19] and is "well established"[20] in Anglo-American common law. The rule apparently "reflects the judgment that proof of causation for murder 'should not be unduly speculative.' "[21] In light of the inexactitude of medical science at the time the rule originated, there was virtually no way to ensure that a death after an extended passage of time was attributable to human rather than to natural causes. Consequently, the arbitrary time limitation was devised.

The year-and-a-day-rule is now considered "an outdated relic of the common law."[22] As a result of advances in medical technology, an assault victim can be kept alive indefinitely, well past the year-and-a-day line. And, medical science can now determine the cause of death with considerable precision, even if the person suffers a lingering death. As a consequence, the overwhelming trend is to abrogate the rule or apply a longer time limitation.[23]

§ 31.02 CRIMINAL HOMICIDE: GENERAL PRINCIPLES

[A] "Murder" and "Manslaughter": Common Law Definitions

A criminal homicide is one committed without justification or excuse. In very early English legal history, "criminal homicide" was a single offense, punishable by death; later, it was divided by statute into "murder" and the lesser non-capital offense of "manslaughter." These two offenses are part of the American common law.

The common law definition of "murder" is "the killing of a human being by another human being with malice aforethought."[24] Manslaughter is "an unlawful killing of a human being by another human being *without* malice aforethought."[25] Thus, as Blackstone has put it, "malice aforethought" is the "grand criterion which

---

[19] Statutes of Gloucester, 6 Edward 1, ch. 9 (1278).

[20] People v. Stevenson, 331 N.W.2d 143, 145 (Mich. 1982); *see* State v. Picotte, 661 N.W.2d 381, 385 (Wis. 2003).

[21] United States v. Jackson, 528 A.2d 1211, 1216 (D.C. 1987) (quoting State v. Young, 390 A.2d 556, 562 (N.J. 1978)).

[22] Rogers v. Tennessee, 532 U.S. 451, 462 (2001).

[23] *Id.* at 463 (stating that the rule "has been legislatively or judicially abolished in the vast majority of jurisdictions recently to have addressed the issue"); *see also, e.g.,* Cal. Penal Code § 194 (2015) (creating a rebuttable presumption that a killing after three years and a day is not criminal); *contra,* Ex parte Kay, 890 So. 2d 1056, 1060 (Ala. 2003) (state legislature's silence regarding the year-and-a-day rule when it enacted the modern penal code means that the lawmakers did not intend to abolish the rule).

[24] United States v. Wharton, 433 F.2d 451, 454 (D.C. Cir. 1970); American Law Institute, Comment to § 210.2, at 13–14. Coke defined murder as follows: "When a man of sound memory and of the age of discretion unlawfully kills any reasonable creature in being, and under the King's peace, with malice aforethought, either express or implied by the law, the death taking place within a year and a day." Quoted in *id.* at 14 n.1.

[25] 4 Blackstone, Note 17, *supra,* at *191 (emphasis added).

now distinguishes murder from other killing."[26]

At common law, there were no degrees of murder or manslaughter. However, for purpose of clarity, judges often distinguished between "voluntary" (really, "intentional") and "involuntary" ("unintentional") manslaughter. These terms have largely persisted to this day. Originally, the punishment for the two forms of manslaughter was the same;[27] today, voluntary manslaughter is a statutorily more serious crime than involuntary manslaughter.[28]

[B] Murder: Definition of "Malice Aforethought"

[1] "Aforethought"

In very early English history, the word "aforethought" probably required that a person think about, or premeditate, the homicide long before the time of the killing.[29] It gradually lost this meaning, so that the term "aforethought" is now superfluous in English homicide law.[30]

The word "aforethought" has always been superfluous to the definition of murder in American law. Therefore, unless a statute modifies the common law by requiring proof of premeditation,[31] a spur-of-the-moment killing may constitute murder.[32]

[2] "Malice"

"Malice" is a legal term of art with little connection to its non-legal meaning. As the term has developed, a person who kills another acts with "malice" if she possesses any one of four states of mind: (1) the intention to kill a human being; (2) the intention to inflict grievous bodily injury on another; (3) so-called "depraved heart" murder; or (4) the intention to commit a felony during the commission or attempted commission of which a death results (so-called "felony murder"). These four mental states are discussed in detail in subsequent sections of this chapter.

These disparate mental states have one feature in common: In the absence of justification (e.g., self-defense), excuse (e.g., insanity), or mitigating circumstance (e.g., adequate provocation), each mental state manifests the actor's extreme indifference to the value of human life. In the first case — intent-to-kill murder — the malice is said to be "express"; the other forms involve so-called "implied" malice.

---

[26] *Id.* at *198–99; *see* People v. Mendoza, 664 N.W.2d 685, 692 (Mich. 2003) ("[T]he only element distinguishing murder from manslaughter is malice.").

[27] Rollin M. Perkins & Ronald N. Boyce, Criminal Law 83 (3d ed. 1982).

[28] *See* § 31.02[D][1], *infra.*

[29] Perkins & Boyce, Note 27, *supra*, at 57.

[30] Royal Commission, Note 2, *supra*, at ¶ 74.

[31] Frequently, such a requirement exists. *See generally* § 31.03[C], *infra.*

[32] State v. Heidelberg, 45 So. 256, 258 (La. 1907).

[C]   Manslaughter: Types of "Unlawful Killings"

Manslaughter is an unlawful killing that does *not* involve malice aforethought or, as the Commentary to the Model Penal Code puts it, it is a "homicide without malice aforethought on the one hand and without justification or excuse on the other."[33]

Traditionally, three types of unlawful killings constitute manslaughter, described more fully in subsequent sections of this chapter. First, an intentional killing committed in "sudden heat of passion" as the result of "adequate provocation" is voluntary manslaughter.

Second, an unintentional killing that is the result of "an act, lawful in itself, but [done] in an unlawful manner, and without due caution and circumspection"[34] is involuntary manslaughter. In modern terminology, this is a homicide committed in a criminally negligent manner.

Third, an unintentional killing that occurs during the commission or attempted commission of an unlawful act may constitute involuntary manslaughter. If the killing occurs during the commission of an unlawful act amounting to a felony, the homicide is murder, "but if no more was intended than a mere trespass [*i.e.*, a non-felony], [the homicide] will amount only to manslaughter."[35] This type of manslaughter is sometimes dubbed "unlawful-act manslaughter" or "misdemeanor-manslaughter."

[D] Statutory Reformulation of Criminal Homicide Law

[1] In General

At common law, murder was a capital offense. Over time, a judicial and legislative consensus developed that not every homicide committed with malice aforethought merited the death penalty. Therefore, criminal homicide law — murder law, in particular — underwent statutory change.

American reform of homicide law began in Pennsylvania in 1794, when that State's legislature passed a statute dividing murder into two degrees: murder in the first degree, for which the death penalty remained intact; and murder in the second degree, for which a lesser sentence was imposed. Pennsylvania did not materially change the nature of manslaughter law, although it formally divided the offense into "voluntary" and "involuntary" components; and, whereas the common law graded both forms of manslaughter equally, Pennsylvania imposed a more severe penalty for voluntary manslaughter than for involuntary manslaughter. By 1953, 37 states and the District of Columbia had divided murder into degrees, with most of them adopting verbatim the "Pennsylvania Model" of murder and manslaughter.[36]

---

[33] American Law Institute, Comment to § 210.3, at 44.

[34] 4 Blackstone, Note 17, *supra*, at *192.

[35] *Id.* at *193.

[36] Smith v. State, 398 A.2d 426, 434 (Md. Ct. Spec. App. 1979).

In more recent years, reform of the common law has taken three separate paths. Many states continue to follow the Pennsylvania approach, discussed immediately below. A few states have modified the Pennsylvania Model by dividing murder into *three* degrees.[37] And, some states have followed the path of the Model Penal Code, discussed later in this chapter,[38] which rejects the degrees-of-murder approach, divides criminal homicide into three crimes (murder, manslaughter, and negligent homicide), and significantly reformulates these offenses.

[2] The Division of Murder into Degrees ("Pennsylvania Model")

The common law of murder remains relevant in the 21st century, particularly in states that apply the Pennsylvania Model of murder. This is because such statutes either do not expressly define "murder" (in which case the common law definition is assumed to apply) or they define "murder" in common law terms. The murder statute's role is to divide common law murder into statutory degrees of the offense.

To apply a murder statute modeled on the Pennsylvania system, a lawyer must first determine whether a murder (as distinguished from a lesser offense or no offense) has occurred. That is, a lawyer cannot logically determine what statutory *degree* of murder is implicated until she determines, in the first place, that the killing is properly characterized as "murder." Ultimately, this means that a lawyer must decide whether the homicide was committed with any one of the four mental states that constitutes common law "malice aforethought."[39]

Assuming that a murder has occurred, three types of murder fall within the first-degree category in the Pennsylvania model. First, murders that are committed in a statutorily specified manner are considered sufficiently morally heinous to merit the stiffest penalty. In the original Pennsylvania statute, there were two such means: killing by means of poison; or by lying in wait. Second, a "wilful, deliberate, and premeditated" killing constitutes first-degree murder.[40] Third, a homicide that occurs during the perpetration or attempted perpetration of a statutorily enumer-

---

[37] In fact, Pennsylvania now divides murder into three degrees. 18 Pa. Cons. Stat. § 2502 (2015).

[38] *See generally* § 31.10, *infra.*

[39] Collman v. State, 7 P.3d 426, 444 (Nev. 2000) ("It must be emphasized . . . that a *killing* . . . is not murder of the first degree unless it is first established that it is *murder.* If the killing was not murder, it cannot be first degree murder, and a killing cannot become murder in the absence of malice aforethought.") (quoting People v. Mattison, 481 P.2d 193, 196 (Cal. 1971)).

[40] The original Pennsylvania statute read: "All murder, which shall be perpetrated by means of poison, or by lying in wait, or *by any other kind of wilful, deliberate and premeditated killing* . . . ." On the face of it, poisoning and lying-in-wait are examples of a "wilful, deliberate, premeditated" killing, and do not constitute an independent form of first-degree murder. Nonetheless, courts have typically interpreted this language to mean that any murder that occurs by means of poison or lying in wait (or in any other manner specified in the homicide statute) is first-degree murder, *even if the actor did not intend to kill the victim.* For example, one who lies in wait in order to inflict serious bodily injury, but who inadvertently kills the victim, is guilty of first-degree murder according to the following reasoning: (1) the defendant's *mens rea* (intent to inflict serious bodily injury) constitutes one of the four common law forms of "malice"; (2) as a consequence, the killing constitutes "murder"; and (3) since the murder occurred by lying-in-wait, it is first-degree murder. *E.g., see* People v. Laws, 12 Cal. App. 4th 786 (Ct. App. 1993) (holding *L* guilty of first-degree murder for a "depraved heart" lying-in-wait homicide).

ated felony (in the original Pennsylvania statute: arson, rape, robbery, and burglary) is murder in the first degree.

All other forms of murder constitute second-degree murder. That is, within the class of homicides that constitute murder under common law principles, any killing that is *not* specifically covered by the first-degree murder statute necessarily constitutes the lesser form of murder. In general, this means that the following murders would constitute second-degree murder: intentional killings that are *not* premeditated and deliberate; intent-to-inflict-grievous-bodily-injury killings; "depraved heart" killings; and deaths that occur during the commission of any felony *not* listed in the first-degree section of the murder statute.

§ 31.03   MURDER: INTENT TO KILL

[A]   In General

One who intentionally kills another human being without justification (*e.g.*, self-defense), excuse (*e.g.*, insanity), or mitigating circumstance (*e.g.*, sudden heat of passion) is guilty of killing with "malice aforethought" — "express malice" — and, therefore, is guilty of common law murder.[41] Typically, a murder involving the specific intent to kill is first-degree murder in jurisdictions that grade the offense by degrees if the homicide was also "deliberate" and "premeditated," as these terms are defined in subsection [C].

[B]   Proving the Intent to Kill

[1]   In General

[a]   Natural-and-Probable-Consequences Rule

An intentional killing involves subjective fault. That is, the prosecutor must prove beyond a reasonable doubt that the defendant formed the actual intent to kill another person, rather than , simply, that a reasonable person would have known that the conduct would result in death.

How is this subjective fault proved? Absent a properly obtained confession, how does the fact finder "get into the head" of the accused? Often "intent to kill" is proved by means of a syllogism: (1) ordinary people intend the natural and probable (or "foreseeable") consequences of their actions; (2) the defendant is an ordinary person; and (3) therefore, she intended the natural and probable consequences of her actions.

When the probable consequence of a defendant's conduct is that another person will die, the preceding syllogism invites the jury to infer the requisite specific intent. For example, if *D* savagely beats *V* over the head with a baseball bat, which actions cause *V*'s death, the prosecution may seek to prove that *D* intended to kill *V* by demonstrating to the jury (and emphasizing in closing arguments) that the

---

[41] 4 Blackstone, Note 17, *supra*, at *199.

probable consequence of such a beating was *V*'s death; therefore, in the absence of evidence that *D* was not an ordinary person, the jury may infer that *D* intended the natural and probable consequence of her conduct, *i.e.*, *V*'s death.

[b]   Deadly-Weapon Rule

When a person kills another with a deadly weapon, proof of intent-to-kill is buttressed further. The more general proposition that a person intends the natural and probable consequences of her actions is supported by the somewhat more specific proposition that when she intentionally uses a deadly weapon[42] or, more precisely, intentionally uses a deadly weapon directed at a vital part of the human anatomy, an intention to kill may properly be inferred.[43] This is sometimes called the "deadly-weapon rule."

[2]   Constitutional Limitation

In the past, judges instructed juries on the rules described above, by stating that, in essence, "the law *presumes* that a person intends the natural and probable consequences of her voluntary acts," or that "the law *presumes* that a person intends to kill another if she intentionally uses a deadly weapon on another."

Although it is permissible, even desirable, for jurors to draw common sense *inferences* from objective circumstances, a jury instruction of the sort just described violates the Due Process Clause of the United States Constitution. It is violative because the instruction requires or might cause a reasonable juror to shift the burden of persuasion regarding an element of the offense — here, intent — to the defendant, notwithstanding the constitutional rule that the prosecutor must prove every element of the crime beyond a reasonable doubt.[44]

[C]   "Wilful, Deliberate, Premeditated" Killings[45]

[1]   Overview of the Issue

Nearly all states that grade murder by degrees provide that a "wilful, deliberate, premeditated" killing is murder in the first degree. Unfortunately, courts do not agree on the meaning of this phrase. One matter, however, is fairly clear: Although

---

[42] A "deadly weapon" is variously defined as anything "designed, made, or adapted for the purpose of inflicting death or serious physical injury," Ala. Code § 13A-1-2(7) (2015), or that is "likely to produce," People v. Rodriquez, 50 Cal. App. 3d 389, 396 (Ct. App. 1975), or is "under the circumstances in which it is used . . . capable of causing," Alaska Stat. § 11.81.900(b)(15) (2015), such harm. The Model Penal Code defines it broadly as an animate or inanimate substance that, as used or intended, is capable of causing death or serious physical injury. Model Penal Code § 210.0(4).

[43] Glenn v. State, 511 A.2d 1110, 1126–28 (Md. Ct. Spec. App. 1986); Commonwealth v. O'Searo, 352 A.2d 30, 35–37 (Pa. 1976).

[44] Sandstrom v. Montana, 442 U.S. 510, 524 (1979). See § 8.02, *supra*, for further details.

[45] *See generally* David Crump, *"Murder, Pennsylvania Style": Comparing Traditional American Homicide Law to the Statutes of Model Penal Code Jurisdictions*, 109 W. Va. L. Rev. 257 (2007); Joshua Dressler, *Rethinking Criminal Homicide Statutes: Giving Juries More Discretion*, 47 Tex. Tech L. Rev. 89 (2014); Kimberly Kessler Ferzan, *Plotting Premeditation's Demise*, 75 Law & Contemp. Prob. 83

the term "wilful" has various definitions in the criminal law,[46] in this context it means, simply, "a specific intent to kill."[47]

But, what do the other two words — "deliberate" and "premeditated" — add to this, if anything? Presumably they should add *something*, or else why are these terms included in the murder statute? There are discredited judicial opinions in which both terms are expressly treated as superfluous, *i.e.*, the phrase "wilful, deliberate, and premeditated" is understood to constitute, simply, the intent to kill.[48] There are also courts that "consolidate the elements of premeditation and deliberation into a single element of 'premeditation,' "[49] or otherwise de-emphasize the "deliberation" element.[50] If that were not enough, as is explained more fully in subsection [3], courts disagree on how much time must elapse in order for it to be said that a person has "premeditated."

Properly understood, the legislative division of murder into degrees — wherein an intentional, deliberate, and premeditated killing is first degree, but one that is merely intentional is second degree — is meant to separate the most heinous forms of murder, which deserve the most severe penalties, from "those which, although 'intentional' in some sense, lack the gravity associated with first degree murders."[51] To the extent that these three elements — intent-to-kill, deliberation, and premeditation — are not treated as separate, significant elements, the legislative line between first- and second-degree murder is lost.[52]

Some judicial opinions treat the terms "wilful," "deliberate," and "premeditated" as genuinely independent elements of first-degree murder.[53] In these states, a significant line is drawn between, on the one hand, a spur-of-the-moment, albeit intentional, killing, and what lay people might describe as a "cold-blooded" killing, *i.e.*, a homicide committed after calm and careful reflection by the wrongdoer, on the other hand. The view of these jurisdictions is that one who acts "cold-bloodedly" is

---

(2012); Mordechai Kremnitzer, *On Premeditation*, 1 Buff. Crim. L. Rev. 627 (1998); Michael J. Zydney Mannheimer, *Not the Crime but the Cover-up: A Deterrence-Based Rationale for the Premeditation-Deliberation Formula*, 86 Ind. L.J. 879 (2011); Suzanne Mounts, *Premeditation and Deliberation in California: Returning to a Distinction Without a Difference*, 36 U.S.F. L. Rev. 261 (2002); Matthew A. Pauley, *Murder by Premeditation*, 36 Am. Crim. L. Rev. 145 (1999).

[46] *See* § 10.04[C], *supra.*

[47] Byford v. State, 994 P.2d 700, 713 (Nev. 2000).

[48] *E.g.*, Smith v. State, 398 A.2d 426, 443 (Md. Ct. Spec. App. 1979) ("This is not a series of distinct mental states but a repetitive stressing of the same mental state — the requirement that the killing itself and not merely the murder-producing act, be intentional"), *abrogated by* Lipinski v. State, 636 A.2d 994, 996–97 (Md. Ct. App. 1994).

[49] State v. Ros, 973 A.2d 1148, 1168 (R.I. 2009).

[50] *E.g.*, *Byford v. State*, 994 P.2d at 713 (conceding that it had previously insufficiently emphasized the element of deliberation, and abandoning this previous line of authority).

[51] State v. Garcia, 837 P.2d 862, 865 (N.M. 1992).

[52] State v. Brown, 836 S.W.2d 530, 540 (Tenn. 1992) (conceding that the line between first- and second-degree murder had been "substantially blurred," and seeking to remedy that failing); State v. Guthrie, 461 S.E.2d 163, 181 (W. Va. 1995) (conceding that prior definitions of "premeditation" and "deliberation" had been "confusing, if not meaningless" in that they "completely eliminate[d] the distinction between the two degrees of murder," and seeking to remedy that failing).

[53] *E.g.*, People v. Morrin, 187 N.W.2d 434, 436 (Mich. Ct. App. 1971).

"more dangerous, more culpable[,] or less capable of reformation than one who kills on . . . impulse."[54]

But, *is* it true that a person who intentionally kills upon careful reflection is more dangerous or more culpable than one who acts impulsively? Premeditation and deliberation might only reflect "the uncertainties of a tortured conscience rather than exceptional depravity."[55] Compare, for example, a person who impulsively pushes a child sitting on a bridge into the river to a loving child who kills her terminally ill parent after long and careful consideration in order to end the parent's suffering.[56] Under current law, if "premeditation" means anything, the impulsive killer is guilty of second-degree murder, and the mercy killer might be guilty of first-degree murder. Yet, as a function of depravity or dangerousness, most people would reverse the results. Therefore, some commentators believe that the current dividing lines between degrees of murder should be abandoned in favor of another line.[57] Others advocate returning to the common law no-degree approach.[58]

[2] "Deliberate"

Some courts treat "deliberate" as a synonym for "intentional," as when the statement "I *deliberately* did X" means "I *intentionally* did X."[59] Other courts, as noted above, submerge the concept into the element of premeditation.

If the term is to have independent meaning, as it should, the best view is that "deliberate" — as in "to deliberate" — means "to measure and evaluate the major facets of a choice or problem."[60] It is "the process of determining upon a course of action to kill as a result of thought, including weighing the reasons for and against the action and considering the consequences of the action."[61] As such, deliberation presupposes a *"cool* purpose."[62] This state of mind is "free from the influence of

---

[54] Bullock v. United States, 122 F.2d 213, 214 (D.C. Cir. 1941).

[55] American Law Institute, Comment to § 210.6, at 127–28.

[56] *See* 3 James Fitzjames Stephen, A History of the Criminal Law in England 94 (1883) (positing the drowning child example); State v. Forrest, 362 S.E.2d 252 (N.C. 1987) (upholding a conviction for first-degree murder in a "mercy killing" by a son of his father).

[57] *E.g.*, Tom Stacy, *Changing Paradigms in the Law of Homicide*, 62 Ohio St. L.J. 1007 (2001) (proposing a draft statute containing aggravating and mitigating circumstances that a jury would weigh in determining whether a criminal homicide constitutes first-degree murder, second-degree murder, or voluntary manslaughter).

[58] *E.g.*, Crump, Note 45, *supra*, at 349 (characterizing the deliberation-premeditation formula as "a dysfunctional method of separating the most serious homicides from lesser ones," and advocating a single degree of murder); Mounts, Note 45, *supra*, at 332 ("[A] persuasive argument could be made that the degrees of murder no longer play any essential role in the larger homicide scheme."). This is the position of the Model Penal Code. *See* § 31.10, *infra.*

[59] *E.g.*, Commonwealth v. Carroll, 194 A.2d 911, 917 (Pa. 1963) (in which the state supreme court found adequate evidence that the killing was wilful, deliberate, and premeditated from the fact that *C* testified that he "remembered the gun, *deliberately* took it down, and *deliberately* fired two shots into the head of his sleeping wife") (emphasis added).

[60] People v. Morrin, 187 N.W.2d 434, 449 (Mich. Ct. App. 1971).

[61] Byford v. State, 994 P.2d 700, 714 (Nev. 2000).

[62] State v. Brown, 836 S.W.2d 530, 538 (Tenn. 1992) (emphasis added).

excitement, or passion."[63] It is the term "deliberation" that brings to first-degree murder the idea that the most heinous killings are those that are "cold-blooded."

Properly understood, it takes time to deliberate.[64] Therefore, it should be considered impossible for a person to deliberate unless she premeditates.[65] Nonetheless, it is possible to premeditate (as that concept is explained below) without possessing the frame of mind characteristic of the concept of "deliberation." Whereas "premeditation" involves the *quantity* of time that a person put into formulating her design, "deliberation" speaks — or, at least, *ought* to speak — to the *quality* of the thought processes.

Thus, one who kills in a sudden rage may be guilty of manslaughter if her anger is the result of adequate provocation.[66] But, even if her anger does not mitigate the homicide to manslaughter, it may reduce the degree of murder because the killing is "hot-blooded," rather than "cold-blooded." Similarly, a severely intoxicated person might not be able to act with sufficient depth of reflection to be guilty of first-degree murder, no matter how long she premeditates.[67]

[3] "Premeditated"

To "premeditate" means "to think about beforehand."[68] The law is sharply divided, however, on how much prior thought must go into a homicide before it is considered premeditated. At one extreme is a line of cases that finds its origins in an 1868 court opinion that stated that "if sufficient time be afforded to enable the mind fully to frame the design to kill, and to select the instrument, or to frame the plan . . ., it is premeditated."[69] Specifically, "*no* time is too short for a wicked man to frame in his mind the scheme of murder."[70]

Courts following this line of reasoning state that the time required to premeditate is not "days or hours, or even minutes."[71] It may be no more than "a brief moment of thought."[72] Indeed, according to this view, "[a]ny interval of time between the forming of the intent to kill and the execution of that intent, which is of sufficient duration for the accused to be fully conscious of what he intended" is

---

[63] Clarke v. State, 402 S.W.2d 863, 868 (Tenn. 1966) (quoting Lewis v. State, 40 Tenn. 127, 148 (1859)).

[64] State v. Ros, 973 A.2d 1148, 1168 (R.I. 2009).

[65] Smith v. State, 398 A.2d 426, 444 (Md. Ct. Spec. App. 1979).

[66] *See* § 31.07, *infra.*

[67] This might explain the outcome in *Midgett v. State*, 729 S.W.2d 410, 413 (Ark. 1987), in which *M*, while disciplining his child, beat the youth to death. *M* was convicted of first-degree murder. The state supreme court overturned the conviction. It stated that even if *M* intended to kill his child in the "overheated" and "drunken disciplinary beating . . . , there [was] still . . . no evidence whatever of a premeditated and deliberate killing." What presumably was missing was the calm (not "overheated" or "drunken") reflection implicit in the concept of "deliberation."

[68] People v. Morrin, 187 N.W.2d 434, 449 (Mich. Ct. App. 1971).

[69] Commonwealth v. Drum, 58 Pa. 9, 16 (1868).

[70] *Id.*

[71] Bostic v. United States, 94 F.2d 636, 639 (D.C. Cir. 1937).

[72] Government of Virgin Islands v. Lake, 362 F.2d 770, 776 (3d Cir. 1966); Watson v. United States, 501 A.2d 791, 793 (D.C. 1985) ("as brief as a few seconds").

sufficient.[73] Premeditation "may be as instantaneous as successive thoughts of the mind."[74]

In jurisdictions that follow this approach, "premeditation" loses its independent status. It undermines the legislative division of murder into degrees. As one court has stated, "if the only difference between first and second degree murder is the mere passage of time, and that length of time can be 'as instantaneous as successive thoughts of the mind,' then there is no meaningful distinction between first and second degree murder."[75]

In order to ensure that the elements of premeditation and deliberation retain independent significance, some courts provide that it takes "some appreciable time" to premeditate.[76] No specific period of time is required, but the essence of the term is preserved by requiring proof that the killer had time not only to form the intent, but also to turn the matter over in her mind and to give the matter at least a second thought.[77] Obviously, the greater the substance of the deliberation requirement, the longer the period of premeditation must be. It is not possible to conduct unhurried, careful, thorough, and cool calculation and consideration of effects and consequences — the essence of the deliberative process — in a matter of a split second.

§ 31.04   MURDER: INTENT TO INFLICT GRIEVOUS BODILY INJURY

Malice aforethought is implied if a person intends to cause grievous bodily injury to another, but death results.[78] In states that grade murder by degree, this form of malice nearly always constitutes second-degree murder.

The term "grievous bodily injury" (or, equivalently, "great bodily harm," or "serious bodily injury") is often undefined in the murder context, but the term is often explained in case law or statutes in relation to other offenses, such as "assault with intent to commit grievous bodily harm," and these definitions typically are carried over to "implied malice" murder prosecutions.

"Grievous bodily injury" is sometimes judicially defined, e.g., "such injury as is grave and not trivial, and gives rise to apprehension of danger to life, health, or

---

[73] State v. Guthrie, 461 S.E.2d 163, 182–83 (W. Va. 1995); see also Standard Jury Inst. In Crim. Cases, 137 So. 3d 995, 997 (Fla. 2014) ("The decision must be present in the mind at the time the act was committed. The law does not fix the exact period of time that must pass between the formation of the premeditated intent to kill and the act. *The period of time must be long enough to allow reflection by the defendant.*") (emphasis added).

[74] Kazalyn v. State, 825 P.2d 578, 583 (Nev. 1992); see also State v. Lloyd, 325 P.3d 1122, 1133 (Kan. 2014) ("Premeditation does not necessarily mean an act is planned, contrived, or schemed beforehand; rather, it indicates a time of reflection or deliberation.").

[75] State v. Thompson, 65 P.3d 420, 427 (Ariz. 2003); see also People v. Plummer, 581 N.W.2d 753, 757 (Mich. Ct. App. 1998) ("To speak of premeditation and deliberation being instantaneous . . . destroys the statutory distinction between first- and second-degree murder.").

[76] State v. Moore, 481 N.W.2d 355, 361 (Minn. 1992).

[77] People v. Morrin, 187 N.W.2d 434, 449 (Mich. Ct. App. 1971).

[78] 3 James Stephen, A History of the Criminal Law in England 80–81 (1883).

limb."[79] Some jurisdictions define the term by statute. For example, the District of Columbia defines "serious bodily injury" as bodily injury that "involves a substantial risk of death, unconsciousness, extreme physical pain, protracted and obvious disfigurement, or protracted loss or impairment of a function of a bodily member, organ or mental faculty."[80] Depending on state law, a person who experiences a broken rib, a black eye, and a two-and-a-half-inch cut in the back of her head requiring stitches,[81] is likely to have experienced serious bodily injury. It follows, therefore, that a person who unjustifiably and inexcusably *intends* to cause injuries of this level of severity is guilty of murder if the victim dies as a result of the attack.

Serious issues regarding this form of malice rarely arise. If the defendant intentionally used a deadly weapon on the victim, it is likely that the jury will find express malice, *i.e.*, intent to kill, unless the injuries or wounds were directed at a non-vital part of the body, in which case implied malice is easily proven. Also, virtually any time a person intends to imperil life (but does not intend to kill) she acts with a "depraved heart," still another version of malice, discussed immediately below.

§ 31.05   MURDER: "DEPRAVED HEART" ("EXTREME RECKLESSNESS") MURDER[82]

[A]   In General

[1]   Terminology

Malice aforethought is implied if a person's conduct manifests an extreme indifference to the value of human life. In states that separate murder into degrees, this type of murder almost always constitutes second-degree murder.

At common law, this state of mind is often described colorfully — or, as one court put it, "more visceral[ly] than intellectual[ly]"[83] — as conduct demonstrating "an abandoned heart,"[84] "an abandoned and malignant heart,"[85] a "depraved heart,"[86] or (to change bodily organs) "a depravity of mind."[87] Some courts have characterized this form of malice in terms of both the heart and the mind: "wickedness of disposition, hardness of heart, cruelty, recklessness of consequences, and a mind

---

[79]   State v. Bogenreif, 465 N.W.2d 777, 780 (S.D. 1991).

[80]   D.C. Code § 22-3001(7) (2015).

[81]   State v. Perry, 426 P.2d 415, 418 (Ariz. Ct. App. 1967).

[82]   *See generally* Pillsbury, Note 45, *supra*, at 161–88; Hannah B. Schieber, Comment, *Utter Confusion: Why "Utter Disregard for Human Life" Should Be Replaced with an Objective Analysis of the Defendant's Activity*, 2011 Wis. L. Rev. 691.

[83]   People v. Love, 111 Cal. App. 3d 98, 105 (Ct. App. 1980). Some judges find this "visceral" concept downright silly.

[84]   4 Blackstone, Note 17, *supra*, at *200.

[85]   Cal. Penal Code § 188 (2011).

[86]   Windham v. State, 602 So. 2d 798, 800 (Miss. 1992).

[87]   People v. Register, 457 N.E.2d 704, 706 (N.Y. 1983).

regardless of social duty."[88] For current purposes, it will be described as "depraved heart" murder, probably the most common label attached to this form of common law murder.

The meaning of this common law concept — or, at least, examples of it — are discussed below. Although some scholars and courts find "depraved heart" a useful description,[89] others do not.[90] Those that attempt to provide a more precise and modern meaning to the concept often describe a depraved-heart murder as a "reckless" or "extremely reckless" homicide. The addition of the adverb "extremely" is useful because many court opinions antedating the Model Penal Code used the word "recklessness" as a synonym for "criminal negligence," the mental state required for a form of involuntary manslaughter summarized in Section 31.08 below. If "recklessness" (as in, today, "criminal negligence") is required for manslaughter, it follows that "extreme recklessness" is the form of risk-taking that constitutes murder.

[2] Facts Supporting a Finding of "Depraved Heart" Murder

With depraved-heart murder, the accused does not intend to kill her victim, but malice is implied because the defendant's conduct is "so wanton, so deficient in a moral sense of concern, so devoid of regard of the life or lives of others, and so blameworthy as to warrant the same criminal liability as that which the law imposes upon a person who intentionally causes the death of another."[91] A depraved-heart killer evinces a "don't give a damn attitude, in total disregard of the public safety."[92]

Cases falling within this category of murder "are not stereotyped";[93] each case is determined on the basis of the specific circumstances of the homicide. However, it is sometimes said that a depraved heart homicide involves risk-taking serious enough that "it might be fairly said that the actor 'as good as' intended to kill his victim and displayed . . . unwillingness to prefer the life of another person to his own objectives."[94] Thus, under this view, a depraved-heart homicide is one in which the actor's conduct manifested extreme recklessness, *i.e.*, risk-taking that evinces an extreme indifference to the value of one or more human lives.[95]

---

[88] Commonwealth v. Malone, 47 A.2d 445, 447 (Pa. 1946) (quoting Commonwealth v. Drum, 58 Pa. 9, 17 (1868)).

[89] *E.g.*, Dressler, Note 45, *supra*, at 56.

[90] *E.g.*, *Windham*, 602 So. 2d at 808 (Miss. 1992) (Robertson, J., concurring) (describing "depraved heart" as a "meaningless metaphor," and observing that "I doubt it would mean much to a cardiologist").

[91] People v. Suarez, 844 N.E.2d 721, 728 (N.Y. 2005) (quoting earlier N.Y. cases).

[92] King v. State, 505 So. 2d 403, 408 (Ala. Crim. App. 1987).

[93] People v. Love, 111 Cal. App. 3d 98, 105 (Ct. App. 1980).

[94] Lloyd Weinreb & Dan M. Kahan, *Homicide: Legal Aspects, in* 2 Encyclopedia of Crime and Justice 790 (Joshua Dressler ed., 2d ed. 2002).

[95] Some jurisdictions appear to take the view that this form of homicide, "except in rare an extraordinary circumstances," does *not* apply to a person's reckless attack on one person, but rather is intended to apply to cases in which the conduct threatens the life of more than one person. *E.g.*, People v. Jones, 100 A.D.3d 1362, 1362–65 (N.Y. App. Div. 2012).

For example, a jury may find implied malice if a person, without intending to kill or seriously injure another: (1) intentionally shoots a firearm into an occupied room, killing a person;[96] (2) drives her car at a high rate of speed in inclement weather and while intoxicated, killing a pedestrian or car occupant;[97] (3) purchases Rottweiler dogs, fosters their aggression through improper training, and places them in an unsecured yard, resulting in the mauling death of a child;[98] or (4) plays "Russian roulette" by loading a gun with one "live" and four "dummy" shells, spinning the revolver, and intentionally firing it at another person, killing her.[99] Malice may also be manifested by a lethal omission, such as when a parent, out of indifference, fails to feed her infant for two weeks.[100]

[B] Distinguishing Murder from Manslaughter

There is no common law bright line between "negligence" and "recklessness," complicated by the fact there is no universally accepted common law definition of "recklessness." Consequently, the line between unjustified risk-taking that constitutes involuntary manslaughter (based on criminal negligence) and that which constitutes depraved-heart, so-called reckless, murder cannot be drawn with clarity.

In general, however, most present-day courts provide that implied malice is proven if the actor's conduct involves "the deliberate perpetration of a *knowingly* dangerous act with . . . unconcern and indifference as to whether anyone is harmed or not,"[101] or "where the killing was proximately caused by an act, the natural consequences of which are dangerous to [human] life, which act was deliberately performed by a person who *knows* that his conduct endangers the life of another and who acts with *conscious* disregard for life."[102]

In more precise terms, a person kills "recklessly" if she *consciously* disregards a *substantial* and *unjustifiable* risk to human life. When such recklessness is extreme — when the risk of death to one or more persons is great and especially if the justification for taking the risk is weak or non-existent — the actor is probably guilty of murder.[103]

In contrast, when a person *should be*, but is not, aware that her conduct is very risky (and unjustifiably so) — the risk-taking is inadvertent — her behavior may justify the modern appellation of "criminal negligence," but the callousness that

---

[96] *E.g.*, People v. Jernatowski, 144 N.E. 497 (N.Y. 1924).

[97] *E.g.*, Davis v. State, 593 So. 2d 145 (Ala. Crim. App. 1991); *see also* State v. Fuller, 531 S.E.2d 861 (N.C. Ct. App. 2000) (*F*, with high blood-alcohol content, led police on a 17-mile chase, driving at speeds in excess of 90 miles per hour, driving through stop signs and stop lights).

[98] *E.g.*, State v. Davidson, 987 P.2d 335 (Kan. 1999).

[99] *E.g.*, People v. Roe, 542 N.E.2d 610 (N.Y. 1989).

[100] People v. Burden, 72 Cal. App. 3d 603 (Ct. App. 1977).

[101] De Bettencourt v. State, 428 A.2d 479, 484 (Md. Ct. Spec. App. 1981) (emphasis added).

[102] People v. Knoller, 158 P.3d 731, 742 (Cal. 2007) (quoting People v. Phillips, 414 P.2d 353 (Cal. 1966)) (internal quotations omitted) (emphasis added).

[103] This is *not* to suggest that the risk of death must be more like than not to occur. The risk of death may be well below 50%, especially if there is no meaningful justification for taking the risk.

connotes "implied malice" is lacking. In these less culpable circumstances, a killing constitutes involuntary manslaughter.

§ 31.06   MURDER: FELONY-MURDER RULE[104]

[A]   The Rule

"The classic formulation of the felony-murder doctrine declares that one is guilty of murder if a death results from conduct during the commission or attempted commission of any felony."[105] This so-called "felony-murder rule" was abolished by statute in England in 1957.[106] It never existed in France or Germany. The rule is richly criticized in this country.[107] Nonetheless, the rule, at least in limited form, "still thrives"[108] in the United States, and is retained in some manner in nearly every state.[109]

Most modern murder statutes provide that a death that results from the commission of a specifically listed felony (such as arson, rape, robbery, or burglary) constitutes first-degree murder for which the maximum penalty is death or life imprisonment. If a death results from the commission of an unspecified felony, it is second-degree murder.

The felony-murder rule facially applies whether a felon kills the victim intentionally, recklessly, negligently, or accidentally and unforeseeably. Thus, the felony-murder rule potentially authorizes strict liability for a death that results

---

[104] *See generally* Guyora Binder, *Making the Best of Felony Murder*, 91 B.U. L. Rev. 403 (2011); Guyora Binder, *The Culpability of Felony Murder*, 83 Notre Dame L. Rev. 965 (2008); David Crump, *Reconsidering the Felony Murder Rule in Light of Modern Criticisms: Doesn't the Conclusion Depend upon the Particular Rule at Issue?*, 32 Harv. J.L. & Pub. Pol'y 1155 (2009); David Crump & Susan Waite Crump, *In Defense of the Felony Murder Doctrine*, 8 Harv. J.L. & Pub. Pol'y 359 (1985); George P. Fletcher, *Reflections on Felony-Murder*, 12 Sw. U. L. Rev. 413 (1981); Nelson E. Roth & Scott E. Sundby, *The Felony-Murder Rule: A Doctrine at Constitutional Crossroads*, 70 Cornell L. Rev. 446 (1985); James J. Tomkovicz, *The Endurance of the Felony-Murder Rule: A Study of the Forces That Shape Our Criminal Law*, 51 Wash. & Lee L. Rev. 1429 (1994).

[105] American Law Institute, Comment to § 210.2, at 30; *see* 4 Blackstone, Note 17, *supra*, at *200–01 ("And if one intends to do another felony, and undesignedly kills a man, this is also murder."); State v. Williams, 24 S.W.3d 101, 110 (Mo. Ct. App. 2000). Professor Guyora Binder has recently asserted that this classical formulation is false. According to Binder, historical research indicates that "the harsh 'common law' felony murder rule [is] a myth," and, specifically, that "the draconian doctrine of strict liability for all deaths resulting from all felonies was never enacted into English law or received into American law." Guyora Binder, *The Origins of American Felony Murder Rules*, 57 Stan. L. Rev. 59, 63 (2004).

[106] Homicide Act, 1957, 5 & 6 Eliz. 2, ch. 11 § 1.

[107] People v. Howard, 104 P.3d 107, 111 (Cal. 2005) ("legal scholars have criticized the rule for incorporating an artificial concept of strict criminal liability that erodes the relationship between criminal liability and moral culpability") (internal quotes omitted).

[108] State v. Maldonado, 645 A.2d 1165, 1171 (N.J. 1994).

[109] The rule is not recognized by statute in Hawaii, *see* Haw. Rev. Stat. §§ 707-701, 707-701.5 (2015); Kentucky, *see* Ky. Rev. Stat. Ann. § 507.020 (2015); and Michigan, *see* People v. Aaron, 299 N.W.2d 304, 321 (Mich. 1980) (interpretation of a statute). In New Mexico, the state supreme court imposed a *mens rea* requirement for felony-murder. State v. Ortega, 817 P.2d 1196, 1204 (N.M. 1991).

from commission of a felony.[110] Although some courts have candidly suggested that the felony-murder rule dispenses with the requirement of malice,[111] the more usual explanation is that the intent to commit the felony — itself frequently a dangerous, life-threatening act — constitutes the implied malice required for common law murder.

In light of the potential strict-liability nature of the rule, *D1*, a robber, is guilty of murder if *V1* dies from fright caused by the robbery.[112] Similarly, *D2* is guilty of felony-murder if she accidentally shoots *V2* in the chest during the commission of a felony, and *V2* dies years later from a heart attack during a backyard basketball game, as the result of permanent damage to the heart produced by the original wound.[113] And, since the rule in its classically-stated form applies to a homicide that occurs during the commission of *any* felony, in the absence of any special limitation[114] *D3* is guilty of murder if she attempts to steal *V3*'s watch from *V3*'s purse and a gun concealed in it discharges, killing *V3*. Furthermore, the felony-murder rule extends implicitly (and often expressly by statute) to accomplices in the commission of felonies. Therefore, if *S* were an accomplice in any of the hypothesized felonies, she would be guilty of murder, without regard to her own state of mind relating to the death.

[B] Rationale of the Rule

[1] Initial Observations

Consider these observations: (1) "[p]rincipled argument in favor of the felony-murder doctrine is hard to find";[115] (2) the "ancient rule . . . has been bombarded by intense criticism and constitutional attack";[116] and (3) "[c]riticism of the rule constitutes a lexicon of everything that scholars and jurists can find wrong with a legal doctrine."[117] What follows are the most common arguments in defense of the much condemned rule.

---

[110] Lomax v. State, 233 S.W.3d 302, 306–07 (Tex. Crim. App. 2007) ("[T]he very nature of the felony-murder rule is that there is no culpable mental state 'for the act of murder.' ").

[111] *E.g.*, People v. Howard, 104 P.3d 107, 110–11 (Cal. 2005).

[112] People v. Stamp, 2 Cal. App. 3d 203 (Ct. App. 1969) (*S* ordered *V* and others to lie down on the floor during a robbery; *V*, who had heart disease, died from fright); *see* State v. Dixon, 387 N.W. 2d 682 (Neb. 1986) (*D* broke into *V*'s house; *V* suffered cardiac arrhythmia and died from the emotional trauma of the burglary).

[113] *See* People v. Harding, 506 N.W.2d 482 (Mich. 1993) (in actual case, original shooting was not accidental).

[114] Many courts have placed limits on the felony-murder rule. *See* § 31.06[C], *infra.*

[115] American Law Institute, Comment to § 210.2, at 37.

[116] State v. Maldonado, 645 A.2d 1165, 1171 (N.J. 1994).

[117] Roth & Sundby, Note 104, *supra*, at 446.

[2] Deterrence

The most common defense of the felony-murder rule is that it is intended to deter negligent and accidental killings during the commission of felonies.[118] As Holmes explained this theory, the law ought to throw on the felon the peril that if a death results, even an unforeseeable one, she will be punished as a murderer.[119] This enhanced risk, the argument proceeds, will cause a felon to be more careful, *i.e.*, she may commit the felony,[120] but she will do so in a manner less likely to result in death.

Critics of the felony-murder rule reject the deterrence argument. They ask, "[q]uite simply, how does one deter an unintended act?"[121] Of course, the act of committing the felony *is* intended, but the *result* of the death is unintended, and may even be unforeseeable to the most rational and far-sighted felon.

Advocates of the felony-murder rule cannot provide empirical evidence to support the deterrence thesis. Although there is little recent data on point, homicides during the commission of most felonies seemingly are rare. According to old data, for example, only one-half of one percent of all robberies result in a homicide.[122] Even this figure overstates the case because it does not differentiate between homicides intentionally or recklessly caused during the commission of robberies (cases in which murder convictions would be possible without the need for the felony-murder rule) and ones that accidentally or negligently occur. In short, it is hard to make the case for the need for the felony-murder rule on deterrence grounds.

[3] Reaffirming the Sanctity of Human Life

Two commentators[123] defend the felony-murder rule on the ground that it reaffirms the sanctity of human life. The rule reflects society's judgment that the commission of a felony resulting in death is more serious — and, therefore, deserves greater punishment — than the commission of a felony *not* resulting in death. If a criminal is required to "pay her debt" to society, the felony-murderer has a greater debt to pay than the felon who does not take a life.

This argument arguably proves too much. Even if a felony that results in a death should be punished more severely than one that does not result in a homicide, it hardly follows that a felon who accidentally takes a life should be subject to the severe penalties, including death or life imprisonment, reserved for murderers. Moreover, in order to properly calculate a wrongdoer's debt to society, and thus to

---

[118] People v. Washington, 402 P.2d 130, 133 (Cal. 1965).

[119] Oliver Wendell Holmes, The Common Law 59 (1881).

[120] It is important to observe that the felony-murder rule cannot easily be successfully defended on the ground that it deters *the underlying felony*. The rational way to deter *that* offense is to increase the penalty for the felony (or, better still, increase the arrest rate for the felony), and not to increase the penalty for the unintended, and potentially unforeseeable, byproduct of it, the homicide.

[121] Roth & Sundby, Note 104, *supra*, at 451.

[122] Enmund v. Florida, 458 U.S. 782, 799–800 nn. 23–24 (1982) (reporting the data).

[123] Crump & Crump, Note 104, *supra*, at 361–69.

set an appropriate punishment for an offense, legislators must also consider the actor's culpability, and not simply the harm that she has caused.[124] In the context of felony-murder, it must be kept in mind that the offense involves two different social harms: the felony and the homicide. The actor's culpability should be analyzed separately for each. The penalty for the felony serves to punish for the intentional social harm of *that* crime. The real issue, therefore, is whether it is fair to increase the felon's punishment for the social harm of a death that may have been caused unintentionally, non-recklessly, and non-negligently.

Consider two pickpockets, *P1* and *P2*. *P1* puts her hand in *V1*'s pocket and finds a wallet containing two hundred dollars. *P2* puts her hand in *V2*'s pocket and discovers a wallet with the same amount of money, but *V2* dies of shock from the experience. The property harm caused is the same — the loss of two hundred dollars. And, the culpability of *P1* and *P2* as to the thefts is identical. Therefore, as to the larcenies, they should be punished alike.

As for the social harm of the death, *P2* is no more culpable than *P1*, as the death was unforeseeable. It is true, of course, that *P2* caused a death, but in terms of *mens rea*, her culpability (as that of *P1*) is that of an intentional thief, and no more. Even if it were concluded that *P2* should pay *some* debt for the unforeseeable death, it surely violates ordinary concepts of just deserts, and proportional punishment, to treat the unlucky pickpocket as deserving of punishment equal to that of an intentional, premeditated killer.[125]

[4] Transferred Intent

The felony-murder rule is sometimes defended on the basis of the transferred-intent doctrine. The argument is that the felon's intent to commit a felony is transferred to the homicide.[126] Thus, the offense is not one of strict liability but one of intent.

This is a misuse of the transferred intent doctrine. That doctrine provides that an actor's intention to commit a particular social harm (call it Social Harm X) relating to a particular victim (call her Victim *A*) may be transferred to a different, unintended victim (Victim *B*) of the same social harm (Social Harm X).[127] Ordinarily, however, the law does not recognize a transference of intent to cause one social harm (Social Harm X) to a different and greater harm (Social Harm Y), involving the same victim. Thus, when *D* intends to steal rum on a boat (Social Harm X), and in the process accidentally sets fire to the boat (Social Harm Y), she is not guilty of intentionally burning the boat.[128] Yet, this is precisely what occurs with felony-murder: The felon's intent to commit a felony (Social Harm X) is transferred

---

[124] *See* § 6.03, *supra.*

[125] *See* People v. Dillon, 668 P.2d 697, 719 (Cal. 1983) (holding that, on the specific facts of this case involving a 17-year-old defendant, a sentence of life imprisonment under the felony-murder rule, based on the underlying felony of attempted robbery of a marijuana crop, violated the state's prohibition on cruel and unusual punishment).

[126] State v. O'Blasney, 297 N.W.2d 797, 798 (S.D. 1980).

[127] *See* § 10.04[A][3], *supra.*

[128] Regina v. Faulkner, 13 Cox Crim. Cas. 550 (1877).

to the different, and more serious, social harm of a homicide (Social Harm Y).

[5]　Easing the Prosecutor's Burden of Proof

Many felony-murder convictions do not involve non-culpable homicides. For example, a robber may intentionally shoot the victim or a police officer during commission of the crime. In such a case, one may infer that the felon intended to kill or, at least, seriously injure the victim. Thus, malice aforethought can be proven independently of the felony. The felony-murder rule is unnecessary. Even when a felon does not intend to kill or seriously injure another person, her felonious conduct will often manifest a depraved heart, *i.e.*, extreme recklessness. For example, an arsonist may burn down a house knowing that the building is probably occupied, or a rapist may wound the victim in order to overcome her resistance.

However,, even in felony cases involving one of these alternative forms of malice, prosecutors often charge the defendant on the basis of felony-murder. The effect of the doctrine, if not its explicit rationale, is to ease the prosecutor's burden of proof regarding malice aforethought, by dispensing with the requirement that she show that the felon intended to kill or injure the victim grievously or that the felon was aware that her conduct was highly dangerous to human life.[129] All that the prosecutor must do is prove that the defendant committed the felony and that the death occurred during its commission.

[C]　Limits on the Rule

Many courts have engrafted limitations on the felony-murder rule, the most common of which are considered below.

[1]　Inherently-Dangerous-Felony Limitation

In order to avoid the potential harshness of the felony-murder rule, many states limit the rule to homicides that occurred during the commission of a felony dangerous to human life.

What is an "inherently dangerous" felony? There are two approaches. First, some courts consider felonies in the abstract. That is, to determine whether a felony is inherently dangerous, a court will ignore the facts of the specific case and, instead, consider only the elements of the offense in the abstract, *i.e.*, look at the offense as it is defined by statute. The test in such circumstances is whether the crime, "by its very nature, . . . cannot be committed without creating a substantial risk that someone will be killed."[130] Or, it has been stated that an offense "carrying

---

[129] One other prosecutorial benefit: Most homicide statutes will permit a prosecutor to charge a defendant with first-degree murder (for example, if the underlying felony is robbery) based on the felony-murder rule in a circumstance in which, absent the rule, the homicide would constitute the lesser offense of second-degree murder (based on depraved-heart).

[130] People v. Burroughs, 678 P.2d 894, 900 (Cal. 1984), *overruled in part on other grounds*, People v. Blakeley, 999 P.2d 675 (Cal. 2000); *see also* Fisher v. State, 786 A.2d 706, 727 (Md. 2001) (stating that the dangerous-in-the-abstract test "is satisfied only when the elements of the crime, considered in the abstract, do not admit any state of facts under which the crime could be committed without danger to life").

'a high probability' that death will result" or "poses special danger" is an inherently dangerous felony.[131]

Applying the in-the-abstract rule, one state court has held that theft is not an inherently dangerous felony, even though the felon in the particular case caused the death of a cancer-ridden child by falsely claiming that he had a cure for the disease, which assurances induced the parents to forego traditional medical care.[132] Similarly, the offense of false imprisonment (statutorily defined as imprisonment "effected by violence, menace, fraud, *or* deceit") is not dangerous in the abstract, because the offense can be committed in nonviolent fashion (by fraud or deceit).[133] The fact that the felon in the actual case used *force* to imprison the victim was immaterial to the analysis "in the abstract." Likewise, the felony offense of "driving with a willful or wanton disregard for the safety of persons *or property* while fleeing from a pursuing police officer" — an offense that further defined the required wantonness to include any driving-while-fleeing that results in three or more traffic violations of any kind or that causes any damage to property — is excluded from the felony-murder rule because the offense as defined "include[s] conduct that ordinarily would not be considered particularly dangerous."[134] And, the offense of "being a felon in possession of a firearm" is not inherently dangerous, whereas *use* of a firearm by a former felon *is* inherently dangerous.[135]

Apparently a majority of states hold that inthe dangerousness of a felony is determined by the nature of the crime in the abstract *or* by the manner in which was perpetrated on the particular occasion.[136]

Advocates of the in-the-abstract test favor it because, if "a court were to examine the particular facts of the case prior to establishing whether the underlying felony is inherently dangerous, the court might well be led to conclude the rule applicable despite any unfairness which might redound to the defendant by so broad an application."[137] Advocates of using the facts-of-the-case test argue that "the abstract approach undermines one of the primary purposes of the modern felony murder rule," namely, "to deter dangerous conduct by punishing as murder a homicide resulting from dangerous conduct in the perpetration of a felony. . . . If the felonious conduct, under all of the circumstances, made death a foreseeable consequence, it is reasonable for the law to infer . . . the malice that qualifies the homicide as murder."[138]

---

[131] People v. Patterson, 778 P.2d 549, 558 (Cal. 1989) ("high probability"); State v. Anderson, 666 N.W.2d 696, 701 (Minn. 2003) ("special danger").

[132] People v. Phillips, 414 P.2d 353 (Cal. 1966), *overruled on other grounds*, People v. Flood, 957 P.2d 869 (Cal. 1998).

[133] *See* People v. Henderson, 560 P.2d 1180, 1183–84 (Cal. 1977), *overruled on other grounds*, People v. Flood, 957 P.2d 869 (Cal. 1998).

[134] People v. Howard, 104 P.3d 107, 113 (Cal. 2005).

[135] State v. Anderson, 666 N.W.2d 696, 701 (Minn. 2003).

[136] *Fisher*, 786 A.2d at 733.

[137] *People v. Burroughs*, 678 P.2d at 897–98.

[138] *Fisher*, 786 A.2d at 732.

Either version of the inherently-dangerous-felony limitation brings felony-murder very close to the depraved-heart or extreme-recklessness concept of malice. A felony the commission of which is likely to result in death is a crime the commission of which is apt to demonstrate the "wickedness of disposition, hardness of heart, cruelty, recklessness of consequences and . . . mind regardless of social duty" that constitutes depraved-heart murder. The reason there is not a perfect overlap is that the depraved-heart form of murder usually requires conscious risk-taking; it is theoretically possible (although rarely the case) that a felon will be unaware of the dangerousness of her actions.

[2] Independent Felony (or Merger) Limitation[139]

Most states recognize an "independent felony" limitation on the felony-murder rule.[140] That is, the felony-murder rule only applies if the predicate (underlying) felony is independent of, or collateral to, the homicide. If the felony is *not* independent, then the felony is said to "merge" with the homicide and cannot serve as the basis for a felony-murder conviction. Although courts do not all apply this limitation similarly,[141] perhaps the most common approach is to provide that assaultive-type felonies, but no others, merge with the homicide and render the felony-murder doctrine inapplicable.[142]

One reason for this felony-murder limitation is easy to appreciate upon reflection. Suppose *D* negligently kills *V.* A criminally negligent homicide constitutes involuntary manslaughter. Involuntary manslaughter is a felony. Because a death occurred during *D*'s commission of a felony (involuntary manslaughter), *D* would be guilty of murder under the felony-murder rule if there were no merger doctrine! That is, without *some* felony-murder limitation of the sort described here, all assaultive conduct resulting in death "would be bootstrapped up to . . . murder."[143] The offense of involuntary manslaughter would effectively evaporate. Surely legislatures did not intend for that result.

Or, consider this situation: *D* arrives home and discovers her husband in bed with *V.* In sudden heat of passion, she shoots and kills *V.* Under normal principles, *D* is guilty of voluntary manslaughter, a felony. Just as with involuntary manslaughter, the felony of voluntary manslaughter should not serve as the basis for a felony-murder prosecution, or else the offense of voluntary manslaughter would, as a practical matter, disappear despite the legislature's intention to recognize such an offense.

---

[139] *See generally* Claire Finkelstein, *Merger and Felony Murder* in Defining Crimes: Essays on the Special Part of the Criminal Law 218 (R.A. Duff & Stuart P. Green, eds. 2005); and Kimberly Kessler Ferzan, *Murder After the Merger: A Commentary on Finkelstein,* 9 Buff. Crim. L. R. 561 (2006).

[140] A few states do not apply this limitation. *E.g.,* State v. Grove, 259 P.3d 629, 641 (Idaho Ct. App. 2011); Barnett v. State, 263 P.3d 959, 964–66 (Okla. Crim. App. 2011) (abandoning the merger doctrine that the state has employed for more than a century).

[141] *See generally* State v. Campos, 921 P.2d 1266, 1269–71 (N.M. 1996) (summarizing various versions of the "independent felony" limitation in different jurisdictions).

[142] *E.g.,* People v. Chun, 203 P.3d 425 (Cal. 2009) (looking at the statutory elements of the crime, the felony offense of shooting at an occupied vehicle, an assaultive offense, is not an independent felony).

[143] Lewis v. State, 34 So. 3d 183, 184–85 (Fla. Dist. Ct. App. 2010).

May the prosecutor, however, take this latter case one step back to avoid this outcome? May she say that the predicate felony is not voluntary manslaughter, but is the felony of "assault with a deadly weapon"? May *that* felony be used to raise D's offense to murder? Unless a jurisdiction applies an assaultive-based "independent felony" limitation, the offense of felonious assault could be used, as well, to take what was, in effect, a case of voluntary manslaughter and convert it to murder.

There is another justification for recognizing the "independent felony" limitation. If one assumes that the rationale of felony-murder is to reduce the likelihood of accidental deaths occurring during the commission of felonies,[144] the felony-murder rule can only serve this deterrent function if the wrongdoer has a felonious purpose independent of the assault. That is, if D's felonious purpose is, simply, to physically attack V, there is no way that the felony-murder doctrine can serve its function — there is no way to convince D to achieve her felonious purpose (attack V) in a safer manner. On the other hand, if D's purpose, for example, is to take V's property — a felonious intent independent of any assaultive conduct — she can seek to obtain the property violently (robbery) or nonviolently (larceny). If the felony-murder rule has a deterrent effect, operation of the rule here warns D that if she chooses to go ahead with her felonious plan to take another person's property, she should do so in a comparatively non-dangerous manner. If she fails to heed this message, and she takes the property forcibly and a person accidentally dies during the robbery, she is properly chargeable with felony murder.

All of the above requires a proviso. Many state homicide statutes provide that if a death occurs during commission of a specifically listed felony, then the death constitutes *first*-degree felony-murder, whereas a death resulting during the commission of any other felony — a felony not specifically enumerated — constitutes *second*-degree murder.[145] Some states that have this type of felony-murder arrangement provide that "where the felonies that are predicate crimes for the felony murder rule are specifically enumerated by statute . . . the merger rule is not appropriate."[146]

For example, aggravated child abuse is specifically listed in Florida's first-degree felony-murder statute. Therefore, although the abuse involves assaultive conduct, the merger rule does not apply to this offense in Florida.[147] Likewise, when a person breaks and enters a home unlawfully in order to assault or kill someone inside — thereby committing burglary — the merger rule does not apply if burglary is listed as an applicable felony in the felony-murder statute.[148] Jurisdictions that refuse to apply the independent felony limitation in these circumstances do so because "the power to define crimes lies exclusively with the Legislature";[149] therefore, if a legislature specifies a felony in its felony-murder statute, the assumption is that it

---

[144] *See* § 31.06[B][2], *supra.*

[145] *E.g.*, Cal. Penal Code § 189 (2015).

[146] *Lewis v. State*, 34 So. 3d at 185; People v. Farley, 210 P.3d 361, 406–09 (Cal. 2009).

[147] *Lewis*, 34 So. 3d at 185.

[148] People v. Farley, 210 P.3d 361 (Cal. 2009); State v. Contreras, 46 P.3d 661 (Nev. 2002); Finke v. State, 468 A.2d 353 (Md. Ct. Spec. App. 1983).

[149] *People v. Farley*, 210 P.3d at 409.

intends for the felony to serve as a predicate even if it is not independent of the homicide.

[3]   The *Res Gestae* Requirement

[a]   Overview

The common law felony-murder rule applies when a killing occurs "*during* the commission or attempted commission" of a felony. Taken literally, this would seemingly suggest that the felony-murder rule has a temporal requirement. That is, it would seem that the felony-murder rule applies if the killing occurs *while* the felony is being committed, even if there is no causal relationship between the felony and the death, and it would also seem that the rule does *not* apply if the killing occurs *before* the felony is attempted or *after* it has been completed, *i.e.*, when all of the elements of the felony offense have been committed.

Notwithstanding these appearances, courts commonly state that, in order for the felony-murder rule to operate, the homicide must occur "within the res gestae of [things done to commit] the felony."[150] This "*res gestae*" requirement has time, distance, and causal components,[151] as discussed below. As will be seen, the *res gestae* doctrine potentially serves both as a limitation and an extension of the felony-murder rule.

[b]   Time and Distance Requirements

In general, in order for the felony-murder rule to apply, there must be relatively close proximity in terms of time and distance between the felony and the homicide.[152] The *res gestae* period typically begins when the actor has reached the point at which she could be prosecuted for an attempt to commit the felony,[153] but it does *not* necessarily end the moment all of the statutory elements of the offense are complete.[154] For purposes of felony-murder, most courts provide that the *res gestae* of a felony continues, *even after commission of the crime*, as long as the felony and the homicidal act can be interpreted as part of "one continuous transaction."[155] Thus, the felony-murder rule applies while the felon flees the scene until she reaches a place of temporary safety.[156] Pursuant to this principle, an armed robber who flees across urban roofs during the night, may be convicted of felony-murder if a police officer, in hot pursuit, falls into an air shaft on a roof and

---

[150] State v. Leech, 790 P.2d 160, 163 (Wash. 1990).

[151] State v. Griffin, 112 P.3d 862, 870 (Kan. 2005); People v. Gillis, 712 N.W.2d 419, 432–33 (Mich. 2006).

[152] State v. Dudrey, 635 P.2d 750, 752 (Wash. Ct. App. 1981).

[153] Payne v. State, 406 P.2d 922, 924 (Nev. 1965).

[154] Sanchez-Dominguez v. State, 318 P.3d 1068, 1074 (Nev. 2014).

[155] People v. Cavitt, 91 P.3d 222, 227 (Cal. 2004); Woodard v. Commonwealth, 739 S.E.2d 220, 222 (Va. 2013).

[156] People v. Salas, 500 P.2d 7, 15 (Cal. 1972). Some states reach substantially the same conclusion by statute. *E.g.*, Kan. Stat. Ann. § 21-3401(b) (2015) ("Murder in the first degree is the killing of a human being committed . . . in the commission of, attempt to commit, or *flight from* . . . [a] felony.") (emphasis added).

dies.[157] Likewise, a felon who commits a robbery in a building, leaves, and is confronted outside by a victim of the crime, is guilty of felony-murder if she kills the resisting victim on the street,[158] and she may be convicted if, 10 minutes after committing a crime, and 10 miles away, a police car encounters her and, in an ensuing high-speed chase, she collides with another car killing its driver.[159]

In terms of the "time" component, however, the critical issue — causation questions aside, which are considered immediately below — is when the *killing* conduct occurred and not when the *death* itself ensued. For example, if a felon snatches a purse from an elderly person, who succumbs days later from a heart attack brought on by the crime, the felony-murder rule is operative.[160]

[c] Causation Requirement

Suppose a bank robber spots a lifelong enemy in the teller line and chooses to kill him during the robbery.[161] The killing occurred at the scene of the crime and during the robbery. Therefore, does the felony-murder rule apply? If so, her co-felon, in the getaway car, is also guilty of the murder. The *res gestae* requirement, however, includes more than a coincidental connection in time and place between the felony and the homicidal act. Sometimes a court will say that there must be a "logical nexus" between the homicidal act and the felony.[162] Another way of putting it is that there must be a causal — actual and proximate — relationship between the felony and the homicide.[163]

The causal connection is often easy to satisfy. For example, if *V* suffers a fatal heart attack brought on by *D*'s felonious conduct, the connection is satisfied, even if the heart failure occurs two hours after the crime and is the result of other causal factors, as well.[164] On the other hand, consider *King v. Commonwealth*:[165] *K*, accompanied by accomplice *X*, piloted an airplane containing marijuana through a thick fog. A crash ensued, in which *X* died. The court held that the felony-murder rule did not apply. Here, the relationship between the felony and the death was

---

[157] People v. Matos, 634 N.E.2d 157 (N.Y. 1994).

[158] Payne v. State, 406 P.2d 922 (Nev. 1965); *see also* People v. Bodely, 32 Cal. App. 4th 311 (Ct. App. 1995) (*B* took $75 from supermarket cash register, fled, began to drive away in parking lot, and struck and accidentally killed a supermarket employee who was attempting to stop *B*).

[159] People v. Gillis, 712 N.W.2d 419, 435–36 (Mich. 2006). But, the felony-murder rule does *not* apply if the felon was 62 miles away from the scene of the offense and has been driving at a lawful speed for more than an hour after the crime was committed. People v. Wilkins, 295 P.3d 903, 912 (Cal. 2013).

[160] Matter of Anthony M., 471 N.E.2d 447 (N.Y. 1984); *see also* State v. Griffin, 112 P.3d 862 (Kan. 2005) (*G* and a co-felon unlawfully entered an apartment, pushed over a stove causing a gas pipe to break; after their flight from the burglary, gas continued to escape, resulting in an explosion and deaths almost three hours later; held: felony-murder rule applies).

[161] *See* Morris, *The Felon's Responsibility for the Lethal Acts of Others*, 105 U. Pa. L. Rev. 50, 73 (1956).

[162] People v. Cavitt, 91 P.3d 222, 230 (Cal. 2004).

[163] State v. Adams, 98 S.W.2d 632, 637 (Mo. 1936).

[164] Stewart v. State, 500 A.2d 676 (Md. Ct. Spec. App. 1985); Matter of Anthony M., 471 N.E.2d 447 (N.Y. 1984) (see the text to Note 160, *supra*).

[165] 368 S.E.2d 704 (Va. Ct. App. 1988).

coincidental: K was not flying unduly low to avoid radar sighting because of the felonious cargo, nor was he flying in a reckless manner in order to avoid capture; the accident was, simply, the result of bad weather.

[4] Killing by a Non-Felon

[a] The Issue

Suppose that $F1$ and $F2$ enter a liquor store in order to rob it. $F1$ points a gun at X, a store employee, and threatens to kill her unless she hands over the money in the cash register. To prove her point, $F1$ fires warning shots over X's head. In response, X justifiably fires a weapon at $F1$ to prevent the robbery and in self-defense. Two people — $F1$ and V, a customer in the store — are struck and killed by the bullets from X's weapon. May $F2$ be convicted of felony-murder of $F1$ and V?

Notice the problem raised by these facts — the fatal shots were fired by X, rather than by one of the felons. In a literal sense, the killings occurred "*during* the commission or attempted commission of the felony," but they did not occur in *furtherance* of it. The question for consideration, therefore, is whether the felony-murder rule should apply in these circumstances.

[b] The "Agency" Approach

A majority of states that have considered the issue apply the "agency" theory of felony-murder,[166] which provides that the felony-murder rule "does not extend to a killing, although growing out of the commission of the felony, if directly attributable to the act of one other than the defendant or those associated with him in the unlawful enterprise."[167] In short, the felony-murder rule does not apply if an adversary to the crime, rather than a felon, personally commits the homicidal act. Therefore, in the hypothetical described in subsection [a], $F2$ may not be convicted of felony-murder for the deaths of $F1$ and V at the hands of non-felon X. The same result would apply if the shooter were a bystander or police officer, rather than the direct victim of the felony.

Why should a felon escape punishment as a murderer when the shooter is not a felon? Conceptually, the explanation is this: Generally speaking, a person is criminally responsible for her own acts, but not for the actions of others. Therefore, applying this general principle, a felon who does not shoot anyone ($F2$ in the hypothetical) is not responsible for the actions of a non-felon shooter (X).

There is an exception, however, to the latter principle. A person *is* responsible for the acts of another if the actor-shooter is functioning as an agent of the non-shooter. This agency relationship exists when the secondary party is an accomplice

---

[166] State v. Sophophone, 19 P.3d 70, 74–76 (Kan. 2001) (citing the text, and applying the agency theory); State v. Canola, 374 A.2d 20, 29–30 (N.J. 1977) (applying the agency rule, and citing other cases in support of this approach; Davis v. Fox, 735 S.E.2d 259, 262 (W. Va. 2012) (characterizing the agency rule as the majority position)); State v. Oimen, 516 N.W.2d 399, 407–08 (Wis. 1994) (rejecting the agency approach, but stating that it is the position of the "vast majority of state courts that have addressed this issue").

[167] *State v. Canola*, 374 A.2d at 23.

of the primary party.[168] Under such circumstances, the primary party's acts are properly imputed to the secondary party. Therefore, in the ordinary felony-murder situation, when a felon kills an innocent person, all co-felons are also responsible for the shooting — the shooting felon acts as an agent of the non-shooting co-felons. (It is as if the non-shooting co-felons said to the shooting felon in advance, "We are in this together, so your acts are our acts.") In the present hypothetical, however, the shooter (X) was *not* an accomplice of the felons: X was acting antagonistically to their interests, *not* as their agent. Therefore, non-agent X's actions (killing *F1* and *V*) cannot be imputed to *F2*.

The agency approach is supported by two additional arguments. First, the killing cannot truly be said to be within the *res gestae* of the offense, since the killing was not in furtherance of the crime, but in resistance to it. Second, the felony-murder rule can have little or no deterrent effect when the shooter is a non-felon, since the felon has no control over the actions of the innocent person.

[c]   The "Proximate Causation" Approach

[i]   In General

A minority of courts apply the "proximate causation" theory of felony-murder.[169] Following this approach, a felon is liable for any death that is the proximate result of the felony, even if the shooter is not one of the felons. This rule is justified on the ground that "when a felon's attempt to commit a forcible felony sets in motion a chain of events which were or should have been within his contemplation when the motion was initiated, he should be held responsible for any death which by direct and almost inevitable sequence results from the initial criminal act."[170]

As with any other proximate-causation issue, the result will depend on the particular facts of the case, and the matter ultimately is one for the jury to decide. For example, in the hypothetical under discussion, *F1* pointed a gun at X, threatened her life, and fired warning shots. This conduct could be viewed as the proximate cause of X's reasonable and foreseeable response. If the circumstances were so viewed, *F2* could be convicted of the death of her colleague, *F1*, and of *V*, the innocent bystander. In contrast, the felony-murder rule might not apply if a pickpocket took money and fled, and the crime victim unforeseeably pulled a gun and fired it at the felon, killing a bystander.

[ii]   Limited Version

Should a court that permits the operation of the felony-murder rule when the shooter is a non-felon take into consideration *who was shot*? In the hypothetical under discussion, for example, should a proximate-causation jurisdiction distinguish between the deaths of *V* (the innocent bystander) and *F1*, for purposes

---

[168] *See* § 30.02[B], *supra.*

[169] *E.g.,* People v. Hudson, 856 N.E.2d 1078 (Ill. 2006); Palmer v. State, 704 N.E.2d 124 (Ind. 1999); People v. Hernandez, 624 N.E.2d 661 (N.Y. 1993); State v. Oimen, 516 N.W.2d 399 (Wis. 1994).

[170] People v. Lowery, 687 N.E.2d 973, 976 (Ill. 1997).

of *F2*'s felony-murder responsibility? Pennsylvania once drew such a distinction: The rule was that a felon (*F2*) could be convicted of murder in a bystander's (*V*'s) death, but not as to the death of a co-felon (*F1*).[171] Even today, there is apparent limited support for this distinction.[172]

This differentiation is presumably based on the principle that when a non-felon kills a felon this homicide is *justifiable*, whereas the death of a bystander accidentally shot by a non-felon is *excusable* homicide. As these italicized words are explained elsewhere in this text,[173] a justifiable homicide is a proper or permissible killing; an excusable homicide involves a wrongful result for which the actor is not morally accountable. A court that draws this distinction presumably believes that a felon should not be convicted of a justifiable homicide, because it would be as if she were being punished for causing a good result (*i.e.*, the death of a co-felon). This reasoning is hardly self-evident, however, since the felon who would otherwise be convicted wrongfully assisted in creating the condition that made her co-felon's death justifiable.

[d]   Distinguishing Felony-Murder from Other Theories (The "Provocative Act" Doctrine)

Even in an agency jurisdiction, a felon may be held responsible for the death of another at the hands of a third party if the basis for the charge is *not* felony-murder, but instead is founded on what is sometimes termed the "provocative act" doctrine, which is simply a form of reckless (depraved-heart) homicide.

For example, in the hypothetical in subsection [a], *F1*'s conduct — pointing a loaded gun at *X*, threatening *X*'s life, and shooting over *X*'s head — arguably manifested an extreme indifference to the value of human life. Consequently, if *F1* had unintentionally killed *X* by her provocative actions, *F1* would have been guilty of murder, not simply on felony-murder grounds, but also on the basis of depraved-heart murder. And, *F2* would have been guilty of that murder as well, under traditional complicity principles, since *F1*'s reckless acts would have been imputed to her.

Suppose, however, that *F1*'s reckless and provocative behavior had caused *X* to fire a gun in self-defense, and further suppose that a bullet from *X*'s weapon had accidentally struck and killed bystander *V* instead. Now the provocative-act

---

[171] *See* Commonwealth v. Almeida, 68 A.2d 595 (Pa. 1949) (police officer killed another police officer; held: felony-murder rule applies); Commonwealth v. Redline, 137 A.2d 472, 483 (Pa. 1958) (police officer killed co-felon; held: felony-murder does *not* apply); Commonwealth ex rel. Smith v. Myers, 261 A.2d 550 (Pa. 1970) (overruling *Almeida*, and adopting agency theory).

[172] For example, compare two Michigan cases: People v. Podolski, 52 N.W.2d 201, 204 (Mich. 1952) (Felon is guilty of felony-murder in excusable death of Police Officer 1, who was accidentally shot by Police Officer 2); and People v. Austin, 120 N.W.2d 766, 774–75 (Mich. 1963) (Victim justifiably kills Felon 1; co-felons are *not* guilty under felony-murder). New Mexico, as well, seems to draw the distinction. State v. Harrison, 564 P.2d 1321, 1324 n.1 (N.M. 1977) (in dictum, the court stated that the felony-murder rule would apply if a police officer were to kill an innocent bystander while shooting at a felon); Jackson v. State, 589 P.2d 1052, 1053 (N.M. 1979) (Victim killed Felon 1; held: felony-murder charge is properly dismissed against co-felon).

[173] *See* §§ 16.03–.04, *supra*.

doctrine applies: On these facts, since *F1* recklessly caused *X* to fire the weapon that killed *V*, *F1* would be guilty of depraved-heart, reckless murder — her provocative acts proximately caused the result — and *F2* would be held responsible for *V*'s death, since *F1*'s reckless conduct may be imputed to *F2*, her accomplice.[174]

On the other hand, suppose that *X*'s aim had been better, and that she had shot and killed *F1*, as intended, in self-defense. Now, *F2* may *not* be convicted of *F1*'s death at *X*'s hands, because *F1*'s malicious (reckless) conduct did *not* result in the unlawful killing of *another* human being, but rather in her own justifiable homicide. Therefore, in the case of *F1*'s death, there is no criminal homicide to impute to *F2*![175]

§ 31.07 MANSLAUGHTER: PROVOCATION ("SUDDEN HEAT OF PASSION")[176]

[A] In General

At common law, an intentional homicide committed in "sudden heat of passion" as the result of "adequate provocation" mitigates the offense to voluntary manslaughter.[177] Although the issue rarely arises, the "provocation defense" may also negate other forms of malice aforethought, *e.g.*, cases in which the actor is provoked to inflict grievous bodily injury upon another or to act in an extremely reckless manner, in which death unintentionally results.[178]

The common law defense contains four elements, discussed in the next subsection: (1) the actor must have acted in heat of passion; (2) the passion must have been the result of adequate provocation; (3) the actor must not have had a reasonable opportunity to cool off; and (4) there must be a causal link between the provocation, the passion, and the homicide.[179]

---

[174] People v. Washington, 402 P.2d 130, 133 (Cal. 1965).

[175] *See* People v. Antick, 539 P.2d 43, 50 (Cal. 1975), *overruled on other grounds*, People v. McCoy, 24 P.3d 1210 (Cal. 2001).

[176] *See generally* Kate Zitz Gibbon, Homicide Law Reform, Gender and the Provocation Defence: A Comparative Perspective (2014); Jeremy Horder, Provocation and Responsibility (1992); Joshua Dressler, *Why Keep the Provocation Defense?: Some Reflections on a Difficult Subject*, 86 Minn. L. Rev. 959 (2002); Joshua Dressler, *Provocation: Partial Justification or Partial Excuse?*, 51 Mod. L. Rev. 467 (1988); Joshua Dressler, *Rethinking Heat of Passion: A Defense in Search of a Rationale*, 73 J. Crim. L. & Criminology 421 (1982); Aya Gruber, *Murder, Minority Victims, and Mercy*, 85 U. Colo. L. Rev. 129 (2014); Aya Gruber, *A Provocative Defense*, 103 Calif. L. Rev. 273 (2015); Victoria Nourse, *Passion's Progress: Modern Law Reform and the Provocation Defense*, 106 Yale L.J. 1331 (1997).

[177] Comber v. United States, 584 A.2d 26, 42 (D.C. 1990).

[178] People v. Lasko, 999 P.2d 666, 668 (Cal. 2000); State v. Blish, 776 A.2d 380, 386 (Vt. 2001).

[179] Girouard v. State, 583 A.2d 718, 721 (Md. 1991); State v. Mauricio, 568 A.2d 879, 883 (N.J. 1990).

[B] Elements of the Defense

[1] State of Passion

The provocation defense does not apply unless the defendant is in a state of passion at the moment of the homicide.[180] Although anger may be the emotion most often claimed in heat-of-passion cases, the defense is not so limited. "Passion" includes any "[v]iolent, intense, high-wrought, or enthusiastic emotion."[181] This term is "sufficiently broad to encompass a range of emotions[,] including fear,"[182] jealousy,[183] "furious resentment,"[184] and "wild desperation."[185]

[2] Adequate Provocation

[a]   Early Common Law Categories

Early English case law defined "adequate provocation" as "an amount of provocation as would be excited by the circumstances in the mind of a reasonable man."[186] Common law courts developed a small and fixed list of categories that met this standard. These "paradigms of misbehavior"[187] were: (1) an aggravated assault or battery;[188] (2) mutual combat;[189] (3) commission of a serious crime against a close relative of the defendant;[190] (4) illegal arrest;[191] and (5) observation of spousal adultery.[192]

Among the provocative acts that were *not* considered adequate were: (1) a trivial

---

[180] State v. Johnson, 23 N.C. 354, 362 (1840) ("[P]rovocation furnishes no extenuation, unless it produces passion.").

[181] People v. Borchers, 325 P.2d 97, 102 (Cal. 1958) (quoting Webster's New International Dictionary (2d ed. 1950)); State v. Ruffner, 911 A.2d 680, 687 (R.I. 2006) (citing the text).

[182] LaPierre v. State, 734 P.2d 997, 1001 (Alaska Ct. App. 1987).

[183] People v. Berry, 556 P.2d 777, 781 (Cal. 1976).

[184] State v. Ritchey, 573 P.2d 973, 975 (Kan. 1977).

[185] *People v. Borchers*, 325 P.2d at 102.

[186] Regina v. Welsh, 11 Cox Crim. Cas. 336, 338 (1869).

[187] Brown v. United States, 584 A.2d 537, 540 (D.C. 1990).

[188] Stewart v. State, 78 Ala. 436, 440 (1885) (a blow to the face, intentionally inflicted, is adequate provocation to reduce homicide to manslaughter). The line between provocation and self-defense is subtle. If *V* unjustifiably strikes *D* with the intent to kill her, *D* is justified in killing *V* in self-defense, assuming that she reasonably believes that the attack will continue and that deadly force is necessary. If *V* commences a *non*deadly attack, *D* may justifiably use *non*deadly force to protect herself, and if an accidental death ensues she will not be guilty of any homicide offense. If *V* starts a *non*deadly assault and *D*, enraged, *intentionally* kills *V*, her disproportionate response undermines her claim of self-defense, but the provocation defense comes into play.

[189] Mutual combat is "a fight or struggle which both parties enter willingly or in which two persons, upon a sudden quarrel, and in hot blood, mutually fight upon equal terms and death results from the combat." People v. Neal, 446 N.E.2d 270, 274 (Ill. App. Ct. 1983).

[190] *E.g.*, State v. Cooper, 36 So. 350 (La. 1904) (rape of a close relative).

[191] John Bad Elk v. United States, 177 U.S. 529, 534 (1900).

[192] Dennis v. State, 661 A.2d 175, 179 (Md. Ct. Spec. App. 1995).

battery;[193] (2) learning about (but not observing) adultery;[194] (3) observation of the sexual unfaithfulness of a fiancé or other unmarried sexual partner;[195] and (4) words, no matter how insulting or offensive.[196]

[b]   Modern Law

[i]   In General

The rigid common law categories of "adequate provocation" described above have given way to the view that the issue of what constitutes adequate provocation should be left to the jury to decide. As one court explained, "[w]hat is sufficient provocation . . . must vary with the myriad shifting circumstances of men's temper and quarrels."[197] No court can "catalogue all the various facts and combinations of facts which shall be held [sufficient]."[198]

Jurors are variously instructed on the meaning of "adequate provocation." For example, provocation is sufficient ("adequate") to mitigate an intentional killing to manslaughter if the unlawful[199] provocation: "would render any ordinarily prudent person for the time being incapable of that cool reflection that otherwise makes it murder";[200] "might render ordinary men, of fair average disposition, liable to act rashly or without due deliberation or reflection, and from passion, rather than judgment";[201] is "sufficient to cause an ordinary man to lose control of his actions and his reason";[202] "is so gross as to cause the ordinary reasonable man to lose his self-control and to use violence";[203] or is " 'calculated to inflame the passion of a reasonable [person] and tend to cause [that person] to act for the moment from passion rather than reason.' "[204]

Although the clear trend is away from recognizing only a limited number of

---

[193] Commonwealth v. Webb, 97 A. 189, 191 (Pa. 1916).

[194] *See* Holmes v. Director of Public Prosecutions, [1946] 2 All E.R. 124, 127. Observation of "sexual intimacy" or "significant sexual contact" short of intercourse apparently is also insufficient at common law. *See Dennis v. State*, 661 A.2d at 179–80.

[195] *See* Rex v. Greening, 3 K.B. 846, 23 Cox Crim. Cas. 601 (1913).

[196] Perkins & Boyce, Note 27, *supra*, at 93.

[197] Commonwealth v. Paese, 69 A. 891, 892 (Pa. 1908).

[198] Maher v. People, 10 Mich. 212, 222–23 (1862).

[199] Provocation at common law, even in its expanded version, is limited to *unlawful* — illegal or, at least, wrongful — provocative conduct. Dandova v. State, 72 P.3d 325, 339 (Alaska Ct. App. 2003).

[200] Addington v. United States, 165 U.S. 184, 186 (1897) (jury instruction apparently approved).

[201] *Maher v. People*, 10 Mich. at 220 (emphasis omitted); *accord* People v. Beltran, 301 P.3d 1120, 1125 (Cal. 2013) ("the reason of the accused was obscured or disturbed by passion to such an extent as would cause the ordinarily reasonable person of average disposition to act rashly and without deliberation and reflection, and from such passion rather than from judgment") (citing People v. Barton, 906 P.2d 531 (Cal. 1995)).

[202] State v. Guebara, 696 P.2d 381, 385 (Kan. 1985).

[203] State v. Ruffner, 911 A.2d 680, 686 (R.I. 2006) (internal quotation marks omitted) (quoting prior cases).

[204] Dennis v. State, 661 A.2d 175, 179 (Md. Ct. Spec. App. 1995) (emphasis omitted) (alterations in original) (quoting Girouard v. State, 583 A.2d 718 (Md. 1991)).

categories of "adequate provocation,"[205] one common law rule that has persisted in most non-Model Penal Code jurisdictions is that "words alone" do not constitute adequate provocation.[206] This can prove to be a harsh rule. For example, in one incident, *G*, an African-American, killed *V*, his white neighbor, in a rage after *V* informed *G* that he had purposely shot *G*'s dog a few weeks earlier, and that he had done so because "it was bad enough living around niggers, much less dogs."[207] Thus, two types of words were involved in this situation: informational words (words informing the listener of an incident — killing a dog — that might have constituted adequate provocation had it been observed contemporaneously); and highly insulting words. In such circumstances, the words-alone rule bars an instruction to the jury on manslaughter, even though this "ignores the fact that sometimes words may be even more inflammatory than aggressive actions."[208]

This rule is slowly breaking down. A few courts openly allow or suggest that they would permit the defense to be raised, particularly in the context of informational words.[209] Also, one jurisdiction has suggested that there are very special words that constitute adequate provocation: "words that disclose the adulterous conduct of a spouse are not *just* words, at least to the extent that they cause the accused to genuinely and reasonably believe that his spouse has been unfaithful."[210] Also, the "words alone" rule does not apply in jurisdictions following the Model Penal Code.[211]

Another common law rule that persists in most jurisdictions involves the "misdirected retaliation" rule, which provides that the defense may only be

---

[205] However, running against this trend, the American Bar Association adopted a resolution on August 12, 2013 recommending that states specify, as a matter of law, that "neither a non-violent sexual advance, nor the discovery of a person's sex or gender identity, constitutes legally adequate provocation." (Resolution 113A.) The California legislature has passed legislation in conformity with this recommendation. Cal. Pen. Code § 192(f) (2015). For debate on the wisdom of such legislation, see Joshua Dressler, *When "Heterosexual" Men Kill "Homosexual" Men: Reflections on Provocation Law, Sexual Advances, and the "Reasonable Man" Standard*, 85 J. Crim. L. & Criminology 726 (1995); Robert B. Mison, *Homophobia in Manslaughter: The Homosexual Advance as Insufficient Provocation*, 80 Calif. L. Rev. 133 (1992);

[206] State v. Horn, 91 P.3d 517, 529 (Kan. 2004); Girouard v. State, 583 A.2d 718, 722 (Md. 1991) (describing this as the "overwhelming" rule).

[207] People v. Green, 519 N.W.2d 853, 856 (Mich. 1994).

[208] State v. Shane, 590 N.E.2d 272, 277 (Ohio 1992).

[209] *E.g.*, People v. Valentine, 169 P.2d 1 (Cal. 1946) (rule fully abolished); People v. Pouncey, 471 N.W.2d 346, 351 (Mich. 1991) (informational words may constitute adequate provocation, and "we decline to issue a rule that insulting words per se are never adequate provocation"); State v. Coyle, 574 A.2d 951 (N.J. 1990) (informational words may constitute adequate provocation); *State v. Shane*, 590 N.E.2d at 278 (stating that words will rarely be sufficient, but ruling that, in *any* words-alone case, the "trial judge must determine whether evidence of reasonably sufficient provocation occasioned by the victim has been presented to warrant a voluntary manslaughter instruction"); Commonwealth v. Berry, 336 A.2d 262, 264 (Pa. 1975) (informational words qualify); Commonwealth v. Benjamin, 722 N.E.2d 953, 959 (Mass. 2000) (stating that "in certain circumstances, words may convey information constituting adequate provocation," but warning that "this is a very limited exception," one that only applies "where the statements constitute a 'peculiarly immediate and intense offense to [one's] sensitivities' ") (alteration in original) (quoting Commonwealth v. Bermudez, 348 N.E.2d 802 (Mass. 1976)).

[210] Lynn v. State, 765 S.E.2d 322, 324 (Ga. 2014).

[211] *See* § 31.10[C][3][b], *infra*.

asserted if the defendant attempts to kill the person who performed the provocative act rather than an innocent bystander.[212]

[ii]   The Nature of the "Reasonable Person"[213]

Who is the "reasonable person" to whom the provoked defendant is compared, in order to determine what constitutes "adequate provocation"? First, it should be observed that the word "reasonable" is an odd term to apply in this context, since the "reasonable man" is sometimes considered to be "the public embodiment of rational behavior,"[214] which is hardly an apt description of a provoked killer. It is perhaps more accurate, therefore, to describe the objective character in this context — as some courts do — as an "ordinary" (or, at least, "ordinarily reasonable") person, one who sometimes, unfortunately, acts out of uncontrolled emotion rather than reason.

Second, to the extent that one seeks to determine the nature of the "reasonable/ordinary person" on the basis of traditional Anglo-American case law, we learn that such a person is: of average disposition,[215] *i.e.*, not exceptionally belligerent;[216] sober at the time of the provocation;[217] and of normal mental capacity.[218]

As in other areas of the criminal law,[219] however, there is a movement to subjectivize the standard, *i.e.*, to include at least some of the defendant's personal characteristics and life experiences in the "ordinary/reasonable person" standard.[220] Due to the influence of the Model Penal Code,[221] juries are increasingly instructed to test the defendant's reaction to a provocation by the standard of the ordinary person "in the actor's situation." Left ambiguous is what "the actor's situation" might include.

In this regard it is useful to consider two possible ways a defendant's personal characteristics — "the actor's situation" — *might* be legally relevant: (1) in measuring the *gravity* of the provocation to the reasonable/ordinary person; and

---

[212] Mackool v. State, 213 S.W.3d 618, 623 (Ark. 2005); Commonwealth v. LeClair, 840 N.E.2d 510, 515–17 (Mass. 2006).

[213] *See generally* B. Sharon Byrd, *On Getting the Reasonable Person Out of the Courtroom*, 2 Ohio St. J. Crim. L. 571 (2005); Dressler, Note 205, *supra*; Kevin Jon Heller, *Beyond the Reasonable Man? A Sympathetic but Critical Assessment of the Use of Subjective Standards of Reasonableness in Self-Defense and Provocation Cases*, 26 Am. J. Crim. L. 1 (1998); William I. Torry, *The Doctrine of Provocation and the Reasonable Person Test: An Essay on Culture Theory and the Criminal Law*, 29 Int'l J. Soc. L. 1 (2001). *See also* §§ 10.04[D][2][d] and 18.05[A], *supra*, and the cites therein.

[214] Ronald K.L. Collins, *Language, History and the Legal Process: A Profile of the "Reasonable Man*," 8 Rutgers-Cam. L.J. 311, 315 (1977).

[215] Maher v. People, 10 Mich. 212, 220 (1862).

[216] Mancini v. Director of Public Prosecutions, [1941] 3 All E.R. 272, 277.

[217] Regina v. McCarthy, [1954] 2 All E.R. 262, 265.

[218] Rex v. Lesbini, [1914] 11 Crim. App. 7.

[219] *See especially* § 18.05[A]–[B], *supra*.

[220] State v. Thunberg, 492 N.W.2d 534, 536 (Minn. 1992) (noting the trend).

[221] *See* § 31.10[C][3][a], *infra*.

(2) in assessing the *level of self-control* to be expected of a reasonable/ordinary person.

In regard to the gravity of the provocation, American courts are struggling with this question. In England, however, the door is seemingly wide open: The House of Lords has held that the "reasonable man referred to [in the law] . . . share[s] such of the accused characteristics as [the jury] think[s] would affect the gravity of the provocation to him."[222] Thus, under this standard, a defendant's height, weight, sex, religion, race, culture, or virtually any other personal factor is incorporated into the "reasonable person," if the jury believes that the factor in question would affect the gravity of the provocation.

To appreciate the significance of the English approach, consider two American cases. In the first case,[223] the defendant observed two women in lesbian lovemaking. Inflamed, he killed one of the women and wounded the other. He sought to reduce the homicide to manslaughter by introducing psychiatric testimony that, while growing up, he had been rejected by his mother, whom he long suspected had been involved in a lesbian relationship. In effect, the defendant sought to be measured by the standard of a "reasonable/ordinary man who, because of family trauma, has pathological animus towards lesbians." Although the proffered testimony might arguably support a valid diminished capacity claim,[224] it is submitted that subjectivization of the sort sought here is out of place in a provocation case, which focuses on the type of provocation that would cause an ordinary person, with *ordinary* human frailties, to become so inflamed as to lose self-control.[225]

In a second case,[226] the defendant, who had come to the United States from China a year earlier, brutally killed his wife because she refused to have sex with him and admitted that she had been seeing other men. The defense proffered expert testimony of an anthropologist, who asserted that the accused's reaction "would not be unusual at all . . . for a normal Chinese [person] in that situation." The defense went on to state that, in part because of the shame or humiliation such a person would feel in the close-knit Chinese community, "one could expect a Chinese to react in a much more volatile, violent way to those circumstances that

---

[222] Director of Public Prosecutions v. Camplin, [1978] 2 All E.R. 168, 175. Under recent legislation, a defendant is entitled to a partial defense if a "person of D's sex and age, with a normal degree of tolerance and self-restraint and in the circumstances of D, might have reacted in the same or similar way of D." And "the circumstances of D" is a "reference to all of D's circumstances other than those whose only relevance to D's conduct is that they bear on D's general capacity for tolerance or self-restraint." Coroners and Justice Act 2009, §§ 54(1)(c), 54(3).

[223] Commonwealth v. Carr, 580 A.2d 1362 (Pa. Super. Ct. 1990).

[224] *See* § 26.03, *supra.*

[225] The trial court did not allow the psychiatric testimony. The appellate court affirmed, observing that "[t]he sight of naked women engaged in lesbian lovemaking is not . . . an event which is sufficient to cause a reasonable person to become so impassioned as to be incapable of cool reflection. A reasonable person would simply have discontinued his observation and left the scene." *Commonwealth v. Carr,* 580 A.2d at 1364.

[226] People v. Dong Lu Chen, No. 87-7774 (N.Y. Sup. Ct. Dec. 2, 1988) (discussed in Leti Volpp, *(Mis)identifying Culture: Asian Women and the "Cultural Defense,"* 17 Harv. Women's L.J. 57, 64–77 (1994)).

someone from our own society." Even assuming arguendo the accuracy of this testimony, does this mean that the gravity of the provocation should be measured by the standards of an "ordinary/reasonable man brought up in a Chinese culture"? The trial judge apparently thought so,[227] but decisions of this sort bring the law dangerously close to the proverbial slippery slope. In an understandable, even commendable, effort to take cognizance of cultural disparities in our multicultural society, and thus to be fair to persons who are not fully integrated into the dominant culture, the law runs the risk of trivializing the normative anti-killing message of the criminal law by permitting juries to evaluate provoked killers on the basis of values generally considered abhorrent in American society.

However the issues raised above are ultimately resolved in this country in regard to the gravity of a particular provocation, it is submitted that the standard for determining the level of self-control that should be expected of the reasonable/ordinary person should remain purely objective, *i.e.*, the standard of a person of "average" or "ordinary" temperament. To subjectivize *this* standard could mean, for example, we would have to apply a "reasonable drunk person" or "reasonable short-tempered person" standard if a defendant could show she is an alcoholic or otherwise short-tempered.

[3] Cooling off Time

The defense of provocation involves *sudden* heat of passion. The defense is unavailable if a reasonable person would have cooled off in the time that elapsed between the provocation and the fatal act.[228]

Historically, this element was strictly applied. The homicidal act had to occur "in the first transport of passion."[229] As a result, the defense was unavailable to a person subjected, over an extended period of time, to multiple minor provocative acts that cumulatively caused the individual to boil over; likewise, the provocation defense could not successfully be asserted by one who brooded over the provocation before acting. In one famous case,[230] *V* sodomized *G* while the latter was unconscious. For three weeks, *V* ridiculed *G*, by informing others of what had taken place. Finally, *G* could take no more of it, and he killed *V* in a rage. The appellate court held that *G* was not entitled to claim provocation, as too much time had elapsed between the original provocative act and the homicide.

As with the issue of adequate provocation, the "cooling off" element of the provocation defense, which used to be resolved by the judge, is typically left to the jury today.

---

[227] The judge found the defendant guilty of manslaughter, based in considerable part on evidence of the defendant's culture.

[228] American Law Institute, Comment to § 210.3, at 59. In England today, "it does not matter whether or not the loss of control was sudden." Coroners and Justice Act 2009, § 54(2).

[229] State v. Yanz, 50 A. 37, 38 (Conn. 1901).

[230] State v. Gounagias, 153 P. 9 (Wash. 1915).

[4] Causal Connection

Even if a person is adequately provoked, the provocation defense is unavailable to a defendant whose motivation for the homicide is causally unrelated to the provocation. For example, suppose that Alice calmly plans to kill Barbara, her business rival. Alice arrives at Barbara's home, gun in hand, with a fully formed intention to kill Barbara. Coincidentally, Alice discovers Barbara committing adultery with Alice's husband. Enraged, Alice kills Barbara. Under these circumstances, Alice is not entitled to claim heat-of-passion. Although observation of adultery is adequate provocation, and Alice was in a state of high emotion at the time of the offense, the provocation did not cause Alice to kill Barbara: Alice intended to kill her enemy regardless of the adultery; the preconceived design to kill, and not the provocation, was the impetus for the homicide.

[C] Rationale of the Defense

[1] Partial Justification or Partial Excuse?: Initial Inquiry[231]

The provocation doctrine was developed in order to mitigate the harshness of the death penalty, which originally applied to all unjustifiable homicides.[232] This rationale, however, fails to explain the doctrine's continued vitality in England, which no longer has capital punishment, and in the United States, in which there are no more mandatory death penalty laws.

Why should people who become angry enough to kill when provoked be given a defense (partial as it is) when they intentionally take a human life, and why does the defense apply to some provocations and not to others? The common law sheds little light on the subject. Indeed, as English courts and commentators have observed, the doctrine developed "largely [for] reasons of the heart and of common sense, not [for] reasons of pure juristic logic."[233] Put simply, the doctrine has lacked a clear and consistent rationale.

In an effort to identify a sensible rationale for the doctrine, it is useful to focus initially on the role of the provocative act in stirring the defendant's homicidal conduct. What is the relevance of the provocation? One philosopher has phrased the issue this way:

> Is [the provoker] partially responsible [for the homicide] because he roused a violent impulse or passion in me so that it wasn't truly or merely me "acting of my own accord"? Or is it rather that, he having done me such injury, I was entitled to retaliate?[234]

---

[231] *See generally* the Dressler citations in Note 176, *supra*; Mitchell N. Berman & Ian P. Farrell, 52 Wm. & Mary L. Rev. 1027 (2011); Reid Griffith Fontaine, *Adequate (Non)Provocation and Heat of Passion as Excuse Not Justification*, 43 U. Mich. J.L. Reform 27 (2009); Susan D. Rozelle, *Controlling Passion: Adultery and the Provocation Defense*, 37 Rutgers L.J. 197 (2005).

[232] Royal Commission on Capital Punishment Report, (Cmd. 8932) ¶ 144 (1953).

[233] Director of Public Prosecutions v. Camplin, [1978] 2 All E.R. 168, 180.

[234] J. Austin, *A Plea for Excuses*, "The Presidential Address to the Aristotelian Society, 1956,"

In essence, the issue comes down to this: Does provocation serve as a partial justification or, instead, a partial excuse for a homicide, or is it a combination of both concepts?[235] In partial-justification terms, do we say that a heat-of-passion killing is a less serious offense than an ordinary homicide, because the decedent (partially) deserved to die because of the provocation? Or, instead, do we partially *excuse* the killer because — although the killing is fully unjustified — we believe that the passion she experienced at the moment of the fatal act makes her less responsible — less to blame — for her conduct? Or is it reduced because the homicide is less wrong than the ordinary homicide *and* because the killer is less to blame than the ordinary killer, and that it requires both of these elements?

[2] Justification or Excuse: A Deeper Look

[a]   The Argument for Provocation as a Partial Justification

Various features of the defense, most notably, the original categories of "adequate provocation,"[236] suggest that a provoked killing is partially justified. For example, upon a husband witnessing his wife in an act of adultery, "if the husband shall stab the adulterer, or knock out his brains, that is bare manslaughter,"[237] but it is murder if a man kills after discovering his fiancé in such a tryst. The common law explanation for this dichotomy was that "adultery is the highest invasion of property,"[238] whereas a man "has no such control" over his faithless lover.[239] In short, a husband is justified in protecting his "property" from a "trespasser"; the fiancé has no such right!

The other categories of "adequate provocation," as well, involve affronts that, in an earlier era, "men of honour" were expected to respond to by "inflict[ing] proportional . . . retaliation . . . on the perpetrator of the injustice."[240] In other words, provokers deserved to be harmed, but homicide was an over-response; therefore, the provoked actor was only partially justified in his actions.

Another justificatory feature of the defense is the "misdirected retaliation" rule.[241] For example, in *Rex v. Scriva*,[242] S observed P, a reckless driver, strike X, S's young child. Provoked, S attempted to attack P with a knife. V, a bystander, intervened. S intentionally killed V. The court held that the issue of provocation was properly withdrawn from the jury. Although S was adequately provoked, the

---

reprinted in Ordinary Language 43 (V. Chappell ed., 1964).

[235] For definitions of "justification defense" and "excuse defense," see §§ 16.03–.04, *supra*; for consideration of the importance of distinguishing between the two types of defenses, see § 17.05, *supra*.

[236] *See* § 31.07[B][2][a], *supra*.

[237] Regina v. Mawdridge, [1707] Kel. J. 119, 137, 84 Eng. Rep. 1107, 1115.

[238] *Id.*

[239] Rex v. Greening, 3 K.B. 846, 849, 23 Cox. Crim. Cas. 601, 603 (1913).

[240] Horder, Note 176, at 51.

[241] See the text to Note 212, *supra*.

[242] [1951] Vict. L.R. 298.

provoker — the person who (partially) deserved to die — was *P*, and not *V*.[243]

[b] The Argument for Provocation as a Partial Excuse

Various arguments, and language from court opinions, support the proposition that the provocation defense should be understood as a partial excuse, and not a partial justification. It is essential at the outset, however, to distinguish between the *anger* (or other passion) that the provoked party experiences and the *homicidal act* arising from it. A person may be justified in becoming enraged when she is provoked — for example, if she is physically or nonconseusally sexually touched or otherwise mistreated in some deeply provocative way — but this does not mean that the homicidal reaction to the provocation — which, after all, is what serves as the basis for prosecution — is justified, even partially.

Instead, as most modern courts have come to realize, the heat-of-passion defense is "the legal system's recognition of the weaknesses or infirmity of human nature and that those who kill [in sudden heat of passion] . . . are less morally blameworthy than those who kill in the absence of such influence."[244] In short, the anger or other emotion of a provoked defendant is justifiable or, at least, excusable; the homicide itself is wholly unjustifiable, but partially excusable.

Under this reasoning, why are adequately provoked killers less blameworthy? The provocation doctrine is controversial,[245] but two explanations may be offered in its defense. First, there is a character-based explanation: A person who kills in such circumstances does not act from a "bad or corrupt heart, but rather from the infirmity of passion to which even good men are subject."[246] The more serious the provocation, the more likely it is that the bad act can be explained by "the extraordinary character of the situation . . . rather than [by] any extraordinary deficiency in . . . [human] character."[247]

A more common and preferable way to explain the defense is in terms of voluntariness. The defense is a "concession to human weakness,"[248] in that the law recognizes that a person disturbed or obscured by passion is less able to control her actions than one who is in a normal state of mind. Therefore, assuming that the provocation is of a nature that would cause a similar reaction in an ordinary (or, ordinarily reasonable) person, the provoked actor is not fully to blame for her homicidal act. In essence, she lacks sufficient free choice to be held fully

---

[243] *See also* Thibodeaux v. State, 733 S.W.2d 668 (Tex. App. 1987) (*X* told *T*, her common law husband, that he was not the father of *V*, a 2-month-old baby; devastated by the news, *T* killed *V*; held: *T* was not entitled to an instruction on manslaughter because, by statute, the provocation that incites the homicide must come from "the individual killed or another acting with the person killed").

[244] Simpson v. United States, 632 A.2d 374, 377 n.8 (D.C. 1993).

[245] *See* § 31.07[C][3], *infra.*

[246] Collins v. State, 102 So. 880, 882 (Fla. 1925).

[247] Wechsler & Michael, Note 1, *supra*, at 1281.

[248] Holmes v. Director of Public Prosecutions, [1946] 2 All E.R. 124, 128; American Law Institute, Comment to § 210.3, at 55.

accountable for her actions, but possesses sufficient free choice to be partially blamed.

[3]   Criticism of the Provocation Doctrine[249]

The provocation defense is controversial. Some criticisms will be summarized here. First, there is utilitarian criticism. The argument is that the defense is counter-utilitarian in that it diminishes the incentive of persons to learn self-control in provocative circumstances. Moreover, those who lose self-control as a result of provocation are arguably as dangerous as persons who kill without provocation. A man who kills his wife because she has been sexually unfaithful may be as dangerous as one who calmly kills for money. "One need not believe that all [provoked] killers are likely to repeat their offenses or that all [such] killers find emotional reassurance in the provocation defense, to believe that some do."[250]

Second, some critics claim that the voluntariness excuse argument is unsatisfactory. If persons truly lose their *capacity* for self-control as the result of adequate provocation — if they are truly acting in a "blind rage" — it would seem that a *full* defense would be necessary. The only way to justify the *partial* defense is to say that provoked persons maintain the capacity for self-control, but that they simply find it harder to control themselves because of the anger. But, if they have the capacity to control themselves, why not fully blame the killer for failing to exercise self-control, at least for failing to direct the anger in a non-homicidal direction?

Abolitionist arguments today also are made by some feminist critics of the provocation doctrine. One opponent of the defense has asserted that "provocation operates as a deeply sexed excuse for murder."[251] The defense disadvantages women because "men are by far the most frequent victimizers [killers], and women the most frequent victims."[252] One need only skim the case law and consider the types of provocation generally considered adequate, to see that the doctrine is mostly a "male defense."[253]

Some feminists would narrow, rather than abolish, the defense. For example, Professor Victoria Nourse argues that a defendant who seeks to have a homicide reduced to manslaughter "asks for our compassion." But, she argues, "[t]o merit the reduction of verdict . . ., the defendant's claim to our compassion must put him in a position of normative equality vis-à-vis his victim. A strong measure of that equality can be found by asking whether the emotion reflects a wrong that the law

---

[249] *See generally* Gruber, *A Provocative Defense*, Note 176, *supra* (favoring the defense); Horder, Note 176, *supra*, at 156–97 (favoring abolition of the doctrine); Dressler, *Why Keep the Provocation Defense*, Note 176, *supra* (favoring retention of the doctrine); Nourse, Note 176, *supra* (favoring narrowing of the doctrine).

[250] Nourse, Note 176, *supra*, at 1374.

[251] Adrian Howe, *More Folk Provoke Their Own Demise (Homophobic Violence and Sexed Excuses) — Rejoining the Provocation Law Debate, Courtesy of the Homosexual Advance Defence*, 19 Sydney L. Rev. 336, 337 (1997).

[252] Nourse, Note 176, *supra*, at 1335 (summarizing the author's study of American provocation cases).

[253] Not always. The provocation defense is frequently the only (or best) ground available to a battered woman who kills her abuser in non-confrontational corcumstances, *i.e.*, when the plea self-defense is unavailable.

would independently punish."[254] In other words, unless the provocation is itself punishable, the impassioned homicide should not be mitigated. Thus, for example, as long as the law does not punish adultery, the defense would be unavailable to an enraged person who kills due to infidelity; it would be available as a defense if adultery were punished.

§ 31.08   MANSLAUGHTER: CRIMINAL NEGLIGENCE[255]

According to Blackstone, a homicide is manslaughter when "a person does an act, lawful in itself, but in an unlawful manner *and without due caution and circumspection.*"[256] Although common law courts have used many terms to explain the italicized language — including "gross negligence," "culpable negligence," and "recklessness" — the best modern term is "criminal negligence." In states that distinguish between forms of manslaughter, a criminally negligent homicide is "involuntary" manslaughter, a lesser offense than "voluntary" ("sudden heat of passion") manslaughter.

As "criminal negligence" is generally defined,[257] involuntary manslaughter involves a gross deviation from the standard of care that reasonable people would exercise in the same situation.[258] It is "something more than the slight degree of negligence" sufficient to justify tort liability; it must be "so gross as to be deserving of punishment."[259]

On the other end of spectrum, the line most commonly drawn between criminal negligence and the sort of risk-taking that justifies a finding of malice aforethought (and consequent murder) is one founded on the consciousness of the actor's risk-taking. One who is aware that she is taking a substantial and unjustifiable risk to human life, but proceeds anyway, manifests an indifference to the value of human life that constitutes malice aforethought; one who should be aware of the risk, but is not, is negligent.

For example, one who playfully fires a gun that she knows has bullets in it, in the direction of another person, may be convicted of murder;[260] if the same person performs the same act incorrectly convinced that the gun is unloaded, she is guilty of manslaughter.[261] Or, if a parent knowingly ignores her child's need for food or medical care to survive, the ensuing death may constitute murder.[262] If the parent

---

[254] *Id.* at 1396.

[255] *See generally* Stephen P. Garvey, *What's Wrong with Involuntary Manslaughter?*, 85 Tex. L. Rev. 333 (2006); A.P. Simester, *Can Negligence Be Culpable?*, in Oxford Essays in Jurisprudence (4th Series 2000), at 85.

[256] 4 Blackstone, Note 17, *supra*, at *192 (emphasis added).

[257] *See* § 10.04[D][2], *supra.*

[258] State v. Hernandez, 815 S.W.2d 67, 70 (Mo. Ct. App. 1991).

[259] Hazelwood v. State, 912 P.2d 1266, 1279 n.16 (Alaska Ct. App. 1996).

[260] *See* § 31.05[A][2], *supra.*

[261] *In re* Dennis M., 450 P.2d 296, 298 (Cal. 1969).

[262] *E.g.*, People v. Burden, 72 Cal. App. 3d 603 (Ct. App. 1977).

is unaware of the peril, but should be, the offense is manslaughter.[263]

§ 31.09　MANSLAUGHTER: UNLAWFUL-ACT (MISDEMEANOR-MANSLAUGHTER) DOCTRINE

An accidental homicide that occurs during the commission of an unlawful act not amounting to a felony (or, at least, not amounting to felony that would trigger the felony-murder rule) constitutes common law involuntary manslaughter.[264] This is the analogue to the felony-murder rule and, as such, is often termed the "misdemeanor-manslaughter" rule. More accurately, it is characterized as "unlawful-act manslaughter."

The scope of the doctrine varies widely by jurisdiction. Some states permit a prosecution for involuntary manslaughter for all offenses, even when the predicate offense is a minor misdemeanor traffic offense.[265] In such jurisdictions, a driver who fails to stop at a stop sign, in violation of the law, may be convicted of manslaughter if she non-negligently causes the death of a pedestrian.[266] In contrast, some courts limit the doctrine to inherently dangerous misdemeanors.[267] Limited this way, the offense will often overlap involuntary (criminally negligent) manslaughter.[268] Other courts distinguish between misdemeanors *mala in se* and *mala prohibita*, limiting the homicide rule to offenses of the former variety.[269]

As an historical matter, the unlawful-act doctrine has not always been limited to misdemeanor conduct. In jurisdictions that do not apply the felony-murder rule to some felonies (*e.g.*, non-dangerous felonies), a killing that occurs during the commission of an excluded felony may constitute manslaughter. On the other end of the spectrum, there is limited historical precedent, seemingly not followed today, for the view that morally wrongful, but not criminal, conduct may serve as the predicate for a manslaughter conviction: thus, if a person attempts to commit suicide (an immoral act), she could be convicted of manslaughter if a bystander dies successfully preventing the suicide.[270]

---

[263] *E.g.*, State v. Williams, 484 P.2d 1167 (Wash. Ct. App. 1971).

[264] *See* 4 Blackstone, Note 17, *supra*, at *192–93; Comber v. United States, 584 A.2d 26, 49 (D.C. 1990).

[265] *E.g.*, State v. Weitbrecht, 715 N.E.2d 167 (Ohio 1999) (upholding conviction for involuntary manslaughter, and finding no constitutional violation in the maximum penalty of five years' imprisonment, based on deaths resulting from minor misdemeanor traffic offenses).

[266] *E.g.*, State v. Hupf, 101 A.2d 355 (Del. 1953).

[267] *E.g.*, *Comber v. United States*, 584 A.2d at 51 ("if the manner of its commission entails a reasonably foreseeable risk of appreciable physical injury").

[268] *See also* State v. Yarborough, 930 P.2d 131, 136, 138 (N.M. 1996) (observing that a majority of jurisdictions now require that the predicate offense in misdemeanor-manslaughter prosecutions involve criminal negligence or recklessness, and holding that criminal negligence is required to convict of involuntary manslaughter in New Mexico).

[269] *E.g.*, Mills v. State, 282 A.2d 147 (Md. Ct. Spec. App. 1971).

[270] Commonwealth v. Mink, 123 Mass. 422 (1877), *overruled in part*, Commonwealth v. Catalina, 556 N.E.2d 973 (Mass. 1990) (limiting the offense to deaths arising from batteries).

§ 31.10   CRIMINAL HOMICIDE: MODEL PENAL CODE[271]

[A]   In General

A person is guilty of criminal homicide under the Model Code if she unjustifiably and inexcusably takes the life of another human being[272] purposely knowingly, recklessly, or negligently.[273] Unlike the common law, the death need not occur within a year and a day of the homicidal act.[274] The Code recognizes three forms of criminal homicide: murder, manslaughter, and (unlike the common law) negligent homicide.

[B]   Murder

A criminal homicide constitutes murder when the actor unjustifiably, inexcusably, and in the absence of a mitigating circumstance, kills another: (1) purposely or knowingly; or (2) recklessly, under circumstances manifesting extreme indifference to the value of human life.[275] Thus, if one applies common law terminology, a homicide is murder (defenses aside) if the actor intentionally takes a life, or if she acts with extreme recklessness (*i.e.*, essentially depraved-heart murder).

There are no degrees of murder under the Code. However, the offense of murder is graded as a felony of the first degree,[276] which originally meant under the Code that the offense carried a minimum sentence of from 1 to 10 years' imprisonment, and a maximum sentence of death[277] or life imprisonment.[278]

The Model Penal Code definition of murder abandons the common law element of malice aforethought. As such, the common law mental state of "intent to commit grievous bodily injury" — one form of malice — has no independent significance under the Code. Any case involving this state of mind could constitute extreme recklessness (*i.e.*, murder) or a lesser form of unintentional homicide (*i.e.*, reckless manslaughter or negligent homicide).[279]

---

[271] Franklin E. Zimring & Gordon Hawkins, *Murder, the Model Code, and the Multiple Agendas of Reform*, 19 Rutgers L.J. 773 (1988).

[272] The Code applies the common law born-alive definition of "human being." Model Penal Code § 210.0(1). *See* § 31.01[B][1], *supra*. The Code does not define legal death. *See* § 31.01[B][2], *supra*.

[273] Model Penal Code § 210.1(1).

[274] American Law Institute, Comment to § 210.1, at 9. The common law rule is discussed at § 31.01[C], *supra*.

[275] Model Penal Code § 210.2(1)(a)–(b).

[276] Model Penal Code § 210.2(2).

[277] Although the Reporters of the Model Penal Code favored abolition of the death penalty, *see* American Law Institute, Comment to § 210.6, at 111–17, the American Law Institute took no position on the issue. In order to accommodate pro-death penalty legislatures, procedures for implementing the death penalty for murder were adopted. Model Penal Code § 210.6. In 2009, the ALI withdrew its death penalty provision.

[278] Model Penal Code § 6.06(1).

[279] American Law Institute, Comment to § 210.2, at 28–29.

The Code's approach to felony-murder is more complicated. The drafters of the Code were opposed in principle to the rule, but they considered it politically unfeasible to abolish it. Therefore, the Code provides that extreme recklessness (and, thus, murder) is non-conclusively presumed if the homicide occurs while the actor is engaged in, or is an accomplice in, the commission or attempted commission of, or flight from, one of the dangerous felonies specified in the statute.[280] For example, under this provision, if *D* unintentionally kills *V* during the commission of a robbery, the jury should be instructed that it may, but need not, infer extreme recklessness from commission of the crime.[281] If the felony was not committed in a manner that manifested an extreme indifference to the value of human life, the felon is not guilty of murder for the resulting homicide.

[C]   Manslaughter

[1]   In General

A person is guilty of manslaughter if she: (1) recklessly kills another; or (2) kills another person under circumstances that would ordinarily constitute murder, but which homicide is committed as the result of "extreme mental or emotional disturbance" for which there is a "reasonable explanation or excuse."[282] These forms of manslaughter are discussed below. The Code does not recognize any form of criminal homicide based on the unlawful-act (misdemeanor-manslaughter) rule.

Manslaughter is a felony of the second degree. It carries a minimum punishment of imprisonment from one to three years and a maximum sentence of 10 years.[283]

[2]   Reckless Homicide

A person who kills another recklessly is guilty of manslaughter. It should be observed, however, that a homicide committed recklessly may also constitute murder under the Model Penal Code. The difference between the two offenses is that, in the case of murder, the recklessness must manifest extreme indifference to the value of human life. This feature is not included in the definition of manslaughter.

Reckless manslaughter is a necessarily-included lesser offense of reckless murder.[284] That is, in any case in which a defendant is prosecuted for reckless murder, she is entitled to a jury instruction regarding reckless manslaughter, and may be convicted of the lesser offense if the jury determines that her conscious risk-taking, although unjustifiable and substantial, was not extreme enough to merit treatment as murder.

In a sharp departure from the common law, liability for manslaughter under the Code cannot be founded on criminal negligence. The drafters of the Code believed

---

[280] Model Penal Code § 210.2(1)(b).

[281] *See* American Law Institute, Comment to § 210.2, at 30.

[282] Model Penal Code § 210.3(1)(a)–(b).

[283] Model Penal Code § 6.06(2).

[284] American Law Institute, Comment to § 210.3, at 53.

that no person should be convicted of an offense as serious as manslaughter in the absence of subjective fault, *e.g., conscious* disregard of a substantial and unjustifiable risk.

[3]   Extreme Mental or Emotional Disturbance[285]

[a]   In General

A person who would be guilty of murder because she purposely or knowingly took a human life, or because she killed a person recklessly under circumstances manifesting an extreme indifference to the value of human life, is guilty of the lesser offense of manslaughter if she killed the victim while suffering from an "extreme mental or emotional disturbance" (EMED) for which there is "reasonable explanation or excuse." The reasonableness of the explanation or excuse regarding the EMED is "determined from the viewpoint of a person in the actor's situation under the circumstances as he believes them to be."

The Model Penal Code provides that the defendant has the burden of producing evidence regarding this affirmative defense, after which the prosecution must disprove the defense beyond a reasonable doubt.[286] However, most states that have adopted this provision of the Code require the defendant to prove the affirmative defense by a preponderance of the evidence.[287]

The concept of EMED is intended to incorporate two common law doctrines: (1) sudden heat of passion (but in a much expanded form); and (2) partial responsibility (diminished capacity). The latter form of manslaughter is discussed elsewhere in the text.[288]

This manslaughter provision has two components, one subjective and the other objective. The subjective component is the EMED — the "extreme[289] mental or emotional disturbance." This condition need not involve "a state of mind so far from the norm as to be characteristic of a mental illness."[290] Instead, it is enough that the defendant experienced intense feelings, sufficient to cause loss of self-control, at the time of the homicide.[291]

Second, there must be a "reasonable explanation or excuse" for the EMED, which is the objective portion of the defense. It is critical to observe that this standard relates to the mental or emotional condition, and not to the homicide, *i.e.,*

---

[285] *See generally* Nourse, Note 176, *supra*; Richard Singer, *The Resurgence of Mens Rea: I — Provocation, Emotional Disturbance, and the Model Penal Code*, 27 B.C. L. Rev. 243 (1986).

[286] Model Penal Code § 1.12(2).

[287] 1 Paul H. Robinson, Criminal Law Defenses 483 (1984); American Law Institute, Comment to § 210.3, at 63.

[288] *See* § 26.03[A][3], *supra.*

[289] The term "extreme" refers to "the greatest degree of intensity away from the normal for that individual." State v. Elliott, 411 A.2d 3, 8 (Conn. 1979).

[290] State v. Ott, 686 P.2d 1001, 1011 (Or. 1984) (interpreting state statute based on the Model Penal Code).

[291] *Id.*; State v. Dumlao, 715 P.2d 822, 828 (Haw. 1986); Smith v. Perez, 722 F. Supp. 2d 356, 369 (W.D.N.Y. 2010) (applying New York state law).

the defense is *not* based on the ground that there is a reasonable explanation or excuse for the homicide, but rather that there is a reasonable explanation or excuse for the EMED that caused the actor to kill.[292] In turn, this objective standard is partially subjective, in that the reasonableness of the explanation is considered from the viewpoint of a person "in the actor's situation under the circumstances as he believes them to be."

The Commentary states that the phrase "the actor's situation" is intended to incorporate the accused's personal handicaps and other relevant external characteristics; however, in order to preserve the normative message of the criminal law, the "idiosyncratic moral values" of the defendant must be excluded. For example, if *V* touches *D* on the shoulder and makes a homosexual proposition, *D* presumably may not claim EMED manslaughter on the ground that his rage was brought on by his "moral" view that gay people who make advances deserve to be killed. The drafters took no position regarding less extreme personal characteristics, *e.g.*, abnormal sensitivity to verbal attacks or "an abnormally fearful temperament." These factors are left to judicial interpretation.[293]

Although the Commentary is not specific in this regard, at least two jurisdiction have held that, upon a finding of EMED, the defendant is always entitled to a jury instruction regarding manslaughter, *i.e.*, the objective element of the defense must be left to the trier of fact to consider.[294]

[b]   Comparison of Model Code to Common Law "Heat-of-Passion"

The EMED manslaughter provision is much broader than the common law provocation defense. First, a specific provocative act is not required to trigger the EMED defense.[295] All that must be proven is that the homicide occurred as the result of an EMED for which there is a reasonable explanation of excuse. For example, if a psychiatrist testifies that *D* killed *V*, his brother, under the influence of EMED, brought on by a combination of factors, including "child custody problems, the inability to maintain a recently purchased home and an overwhelming fear of his brother,"[296] a jury instruction on manslaughter is warranted, although *V* did nothing to provoke the incident.[297]

Second, even if there is provocation, it need not involve "an injury, affront, or other provocative act perpetrated upon [the defendant] by the decedent."[298]

---

[292] People v. Casassa, 404 N.E.2d 1310, 1316 n.2 (N.Y. 1980).

[293] American Law Institute, Comment to § 210.3, at 62–63.

[294] State v. Sawyer, 966 P.2d 637, 645–46 (Haw. 1998); *People v. Casassa*, 404 N.E.2d at 1317.

[295] State v. Elliott, 411 A.2d 3, 7 (Conn. 1979); *but see* Foster v. Commonwealth, 827 S.W.2d 670, 678 (Ky. 1991) (a triggering event is required; EMED "based on a gradual victimization from his or her environment" is insufficient "unless the additional proof of a triggering event is . . . shown").

[296] *State v. Elliott*, 411 A.2d at 5.

[297] *See* People v. Tabarez, 497 N.Y.S.2d 80 (App. Div. 1985), *aff'd*, 503 N.E.2d 1369 (1986) (*D* shot at *V* while experiencing EMED brought on by depression, prolonged unemployment, a very fragile personality, and an I.Q. of 66).

[298] American Law Institute, Comment to § 210.3, at 61.

Therefore, the person may successfully claim the defense if she simply believes, although incorrectly, that the decedent was responsible for the affront, or if there was a provocation and the defendant "strikes out in a blinding rage and kills an innocent bystander."[299]

Third, even if the decedent provoked the incident, it need not fall within any fixed category of provocations; and, contrary to the common law, words alone *can* warrant a manslaughter instruction. For example, if D kills V as a result of EMED, a jury instruction on manslaughter is warranted (although, of course, a *verdict* of manslaughter is not required) if the basis for the EMED was that: (1) V derided D because he was unable to have an erection when he attempted to have intercourse with her;[300] (2) V took D's reserved parking space in an apartment building;[301] or (3) in a restaurant, V demanded money owed to him by D from an earlier drug transaction, a verbal argument ensued, and V placed his hand on D's plate.[302]

Fourth, there is no rigid cooling-off rule. The suddenness requirement of the common law is absent here.[303]

[D] Negligent Homicide

A criminally negligent homicide — involuntary manslaughter at common law — constitutes the lesser offense of negligent homicide under the Code.[304] The offense is graded as a felony of the third degree, which carries a minimum sentence of one to two years' incarceration, and a maximum sentence of five years.[305]

---

[299] *Id.*

[300] People v. Moye, 489 N.E.2d 736 (N.Y. 1985) (based on the facts set out in the text, murder conviction reversed on ground that evidence was sufficient to warrant manslaughter instruction).

[301] State v. Raguseo, 622 A.2d 519 (Conn. 1993) (EMED instruction given; D was convicted of murder; conviction upheld on sufficiency-of-evidence grounds).

[302] People v. Walker, 473 N.Y.S.2d 460 (App. Div.), *aff'd in memorandum*, 475 N.E.2d 445 (N.Y. 1984) (murder conviction affirmed; no jury instruction on EMED given; this ruling was upheld on ground that there was no evidence that D suffered from EMED; had he experienced EMED, instruction would presumably have been required).

[303] State v. Elliott, 411 A.2d 3, 7 (Conn. 1979).

[304] Model Penal Code § 210.4.

[305] Model Penal Code § 6.06(3).

Chapter 32

THEFT

§ 32.01 THEFT: HISTORICAL OVERVIEW[1]

This chapter considers three traditional[2] theft[3] offenses: larceny, embezzlement, and false pretenses. As is explained below, larceny is a common law felony; the other offenses find their origins in English misdemeanor statutes.

In very early English history, only *forcible* appropriation of property, *i.e.*, robbery, was punished.[4] By the middle ages, however, jurists expanded the scope of the criminal law to prohibit nonviolent, albeit nonconsensual, dispossessions of personal property, *i.e.*, larceny.

The law of larceny did not develop simply or smoothly. Various economic conditions, originating as early as the 15th century, placed pressure on the English courts to expand the scope of theft law in order to deter new forms of dishonest conduct. To a significant extent the courts cooperated with the economic interests of the time. Rather than create new theft offenses, however, the judges manipulated the elements of larceny to encompass the new conduct. The outcome was a law riddled with technicalities and intricacies.

At the same time, judicial displeasure with capital punishment, the penalty for all but the most petty larcenies, deterred English courts from broadening the law to the extent that economic conditions might have justified. Consequently, various lacunae in the law of larceny developed. The "cure" for the gaps was the enactment of statutory "gap-fillers," most importantly the misdemeanor offenses of false pretenses and embezzlement.

In recent years, many legislatures have consolidated the three crimes discussed in this chapter into a single offense, often denominated, simply, as "theft." These

---

[1] *See generally* Jerome Hall, Theft, Law and Society (2d ed. 1952); Kathleen F. Brickey, *The Jurisprudence of Larceny: An Historical Inquiry and Interest Analysis*, 33 Vand. L. Rev. 1101 (1980); George P. Fletcher, *The Metamorphosis of Larceny*, 89 Harv. L. Rev. 469 (1976); Lloyd L. Weinreb, *Manifest Criminality, Criminal Intent, and the "Metamorphosis of Larceny,"* 90 Yale L.J. 294 (1980).

[2] Legislators have enacted other theft crimes to fill in holes in the traditional offenses, particularly with the advent of computer crime and identity theft. These new statutory crimes, themselves founded on the traditional offenses, are not the subject of this chapter.

[3] The word "theft" is used in this chapter to signify the involuntary and unlawful transfer of property. Unless otherwise noted, the term is not used to describe any particular common law or statutory offense.

[4] Robbery is essentially an aggravated larceny, *i.e.*, larceny from the person by use or threatened use of force. People v. Tufunga, 987 P.2d 168, 174 (Cal. 1999).

efforts at consolidation are briefly noted later.[5] Notwithstanding the reform movement, lawyers cannot confidently ignore the centuries of theft law that preceded consolidation. "History has its own logic."[6] Many of the substantive doctrines discussed below remain relevant today.

§ 32.02 LARCENY: GENERAL PRINCIPLES

[A] Definition

Common law larceny is the trespassory taking and carrying away of the personal property of another with the intent to permanently deprive the possessor of the property.[7]

It is useful to break this definition down into its components and to become familiar with the different ways that each element is described by judges and commentators. The social harm of larceny is the "trespassory taking and carrying away of the personal property of another." It should be observed that larceny is a "conduct," rather than a "result," crime. That is, it prohibits the conduct of taking and carrying away personal property; the offense is complete when those acts occur. It is not necessary that the property taken be damaged, destroyed, or converted to the personal use of the wrongful taker. Instead, if the offender has the requisite *mens rea*, it is assumed that injury to the property or to the victim's interest in it will occur (if it has not already occurred). In this limited sense, larceny may be viewed as an inchoate offense.

The most complicated legal aspect of the *actus reus* of larceny is the requirement that there be a "trespassory taking." More specifically, the trespassory taking involves the nonconsensual taking *of possession* of the property in question.[8] A person who by trespass obtains title — ownership — to the property of another is guilty, if anything, of obtaining property by false pretenses, a different offense. The element of "taking" is frequently described in the case law as the *caption* of the property.

The element of "carrying away" is frequently described as the *asportation* of the property. Legal issues regarding this element rarely arise.

Larceny prohibits only the trespassory caption and asportation of another person's *personal* property. Real property is not the subject of larceny law.[9] Moreover, only tangible forms of personal property are encompassed in the common law offense.

---

[5] *See* § 32.11, *infra.*

[6] American Law Institute, Comment to § 223.1, at 130.

[7] *See* Lee v. State, 474 A.2d 537, 539 (Md. Ct. Spec. App. 1984); United States v. Waronek, 582 F.2d 1158, 1161 (7th Cir. 1978); 4 William Blackstone, Commentaries on the Laws of England *230 (1769) ("the felonious taking, and carrying away, of the personal goods of another").

[8] *See* Bell v. United States, 462 U.S. 356, 358 (1983) (noting that the original purpose of larceny law was to prevent breaches of the peace, and the concern of the courts was that violence was more apt to occur when property was taken from the possession of another).

[9] People v. Sanders, 67 Cal. App. 4th 1403, 1415 (Ct. App. 1998).

Larceny is a specific-intent crime. The actor who takes and carries away the personal property of another must do so with the specific intent to deprive the other of the property on a permanent basis. Sometimes this *mens rea* is described in shorthand, simply, as "the intent to steal," "felonious intent," or by the Latin words, "*animus furandi.*" The wrongdoer must possess this intent at the time of the trespassory caption and asportation.

[B]   Grading of the Offense

The common law distinguished between grand and petit (now "petty") larceny. Grand larceny involved the stealing of goods above the value[10] of 12 pence.[11] This amount, now worth well less than 10 American cents, equaled the value of a sheep.[12]

Although grand and petty larceny were felonies at common law, the death penalty applied only to grand larceny. In this country, grand larceny is a felony, and petty larceny is a misdemeanor.[13]

§ 32.03   LARCENY: TRESPASS

The act of taking and carrying away the personal property of another is not, in itself, an offense. The beginning point is that "[t]here can be no larceny without a trespass, and there can be no trespass unless the property was in the possession of the one from whom it is charged to have been stolen."[14]

The term "trespass" as used here is not related to the tort or crime of trespass to land. Rather, the origin of the term is the ancient writ of *trespass be bonis asportatis* (trespass for goods carried away), which was the basis for the tort of trespass to chattel. In the larceny context, a "trespass" occurs if one takes possession of the victim's personal property — he dispossesses the other of the property — without consent, or in the absence of a justification for the nonconsen-

---

[10] The value of property for the purpose of determining whether the offense is "grand" or "petty" is ordinarily based on the stolen item's current market value, or "the price at which the minds of a willing buyer and a willing seller would meet." United States v. Di Gilio, 538 F.2d 972, 979 (3d Cir. 1976). Although case law on the point is scant, apparently the thief's belief regarding the value of the property is irrelevant at common law. American Law Institute, Comment to § 223.1, at 145–46. Thus, a thief who steals a Picasso painting, believing it is a nearly valueless copy, is guilty of grand larceny; he is guilty of petty larceny if he takes the nearly worthless copy, believing it is the original.

The Model Penal Code departs from the common law in this regard. Under Section 223.1(2), the value of property is determined on the basis of the "highest value, by any reasonable standard, of the property . . . the actor stole *or attempted to steal.*" Thus, the thief who tries to steal a Picasso, but whose plan is frustrated by the police who substitute a copy, can be convicted of grand larceny. For fuller discussion of this situation, see American Law Institute, Comment to § 223.1, at 144–47.

[11] 4 Blackstone, Note 7, *supra*, at *229.

[12] Rollin M. Perkins & Ronald N. Boyce, Criminal Law 290 (3d ed. 1982).

[13] The Model Penal Code treats theft as a felony if the value of the property exceeds $500 or is a specified type of property (*e.g.*, a firearm or automobile). Below that figure, it is a misdemeanor or (if the amount involved is less than $50) a petty misdemeanor. Model Penal Code § 223.1(2)(a)–(b).

[14] People v. Hoban, 88 N.E. 806, 807 (Ill. 1909).

sual dispossession.[15]

The concept of trespass originally was limited to acts of stealth. The doctrine of *caveat emptor* ("let the buyer beware") prevailed: One who obtained possession of another person's property by fraud was viewed as a clever person, rather than as a criminal deserving of the death penalty. Gradually this *laissez faire* attitude changed. In 1757, the Parliament enacted the misdemeanor offense of "obtaining property by false pretenses."[16] This offense, however, prohibited the use of deception to obtain *title* to another's property; mere dispossession of personal property by fraud was not covered by the statute.

Fraud became a part of larceny law in 1779 with *Pear's Case*.[17] In *Pear*, *P* rented *V*'s horse for a day with the fraudulent intent to take it and sell it immediately, which he did. Because stealth was not involved, the delivery of the horse to *P* by *V* was outwardly consensual. Nonetheless, a majority of judges in the case concluded that *P* was guilty of larceny or, as it is often identified by statute, "larceny by trick."

The reasoning of *Pear* is disputed.[18] Nonetheless, it is clear that obtaining possession of property by fraud constitutes a trespassory taking that may result in conviction for larceny.

§ 32.04 LARCENY: TAKING (CAPTION)

[A] The Significance of "Possession"

Larceny involves the trespassory taking of personal property from the *possession* of another. Ownership is not the key.[19]

"Possession" is a term of art in larceny law. As a result of competing pressures on the common law courts — the need to broaden the scope of larceny law to meet the economic needs of the time, and yet the desire of judges to avoid undue use of the death penalty — various legal fictions developed in the law of possession.

In order to understand larceny law, therefore, one must distinguish between the doctrines of "possession" and "custody." It is also important to focus on the relationship of the parties involved in the transfer of property, *e.g.*, whether there is a "master-servant" (employer-employee) or bailor-bailee relationship.

---

[15] *E.g.*, no trespass occurs if a law enforcement officer takes property pursuant to a court order.

[16] *See* § 32.10, *infra.*

[17] King v. Pear, 1 Leach 212, 168 Eng. Rep. 208 (1779).

[18] *See* § 32.04[B][5], *infra.*

[19] 2 Frederick Pollock & Frederic William Maitland, History of English Law 498 (2d ed. 1898) ("[T]he crime involves a violation of possession; it is an offence against a possessor and therefore can never be committed by a possessor."); People v. Sanders, 67 Cal. App. 4th 1403, 1415 (Ct. App. 1998); People v. Sheldon, 527 N.W.2d 76, 77–78 (Mich. Ct. App. 1995).

[B] "Custody" Versus "Possession"

[1] In General

A person has *possession* of property when he has sufficient control over it to use it in a reasonably unrestricted manner. Possession can be actual or constructive. It is *actual* if the person is in physical control of it; it is *constructive* if he is not in physical control of it but nobody else has actual possession of it, either because the property was lost or mislaid or because another person has mere "custody" of it (as that term is defined immediately below). *All non-abandoned property is in the actual or constructive possession of some party at all times.*

A person has mere "custody" of property if he has physical control over it, but his right to use it is substantially restricted by the person in constructive possession of the property.

Unfortunately, the terms "possession" and "custody" largely represent legal conclusions regarding the comparative rights of the parties; there is no bright-line point at which the degree of control over property shifts from custody to possession.

Whenever a court must ascertain whether larceny has occurred, it must determine who initially had possession of the property that allegedly was stolen, and then it must decide whether, when, and to whom "possession" (as distinguished from "custody") transferred. If the person charged with larceny *did* obtain possession from another, the issue will then be whether such possession occurred trespassorily or lawfully.

As a starting point, a person in physical control of property ordinarily is in *possession* of it. However, a person in physical control of property has mere *custody* of the property if he: (1) has temporary and extremely limited authorization to use the property; (2) received the property from his employer for use in the employment relation; (3) is a bailee of goods enclosed in a container; or (4) obtained the property by fraud. These examples of "custody" are considered immediately below.

[2] Temporary and Limited Use of Property

A person with temporary and extremely limited authority to use a piece of property has mere custody of it.[20] Thus, *D*, a dinner guest, has only custody of the cutlery used at *V*'s dining room table.[21] Similarly, if *V*, a jewelry merchant, hands a ring to *D*, a customer, for inspection, *D* has custody of the item; *V* retains constructive possession.[22]

The line between custody and possession can be fuzzy. A critical factor, however, is whether *D* uses the property in *V*'s presence. Thus, if *D* test-drives an automobile, *D*'s control over it largely depends on whether *V*, the car dealer, is in the vehicle during the drive. If he is, *D* has *custody* of the car. If he is allowed to drive the car alone, *possession* of the car shifts from *V* to *D* when *D* leaves the lot.

---

[20] United States v. Mafnas, 701 F.2d 83, 84 (9th Cir. 1983).

[21] 1 Matthew Hale, History of the Pleas of the Crown *506 (1736).

[22] Chisser's Case, 83 Eng. Rep. 142 (1678).

Why does it matter whether D has "custody" or "possession"? Reconsider the test-drive hypothetical. Suppose that D test-drives the car in V's presence (*i.e.*, D has custody). When they return to the lot, V gets out of the car, at which time D speeds away in the vehicle. At the instant of this act, D has dispossessed V of the car; D no longer has mere custody of the automobile, because he is using the property in a manner far in excess of his limited right to test-drive it in V's presence. Consequently, D's act would represent a "taking" of the property, *i.e.*, he has "taken possession" of the vehicle from V. As the taking was nonconsensual, it was "trespassory." Therefore, D would be guilty of larceny if D intended to steal the car when he drove away.

On the other hand, suppose that D was permitted to test-drive the car alone. As he is driving the car, D decides he likes it so much that he is not going to return it, so he drives it out of town. In this case, there is *no* common law larceny. Here, D took possession of the car from V when he left the lot by himself for the test-drive. This taking was nontrespassory because it was consensual. When he later decided to steal the car and drive it away, no trespassory taking occurred because he already had lawful possession of the property. Although not guilty of larceny, D could be guilty of the statutory offense of embezzlement, which generally prohibits the misappropriation of property by one who obtains possession of it in a nontrespassory manner.[23]

[3]   Employers and Employees

[a]   Employer to Employee

By necessity employers must frequently furnish their personal property to employees in furtherance of the employment relation. In such circumstances, the employer consensually transfers the property to his employee.

In order to make sure that dishonest employees could be convicted of larceny of property furnished to them by their employers, the common law adopted the fiction that when a master furnishes property to his servant for use by the servant in the master-servant relationship, the master retains *constructive possession* of the property, and the servant has mere *custody* of it.[24]

For example, if V, the owner of a pizza-delivery franchise, furnishes D, his employee, with a car in order to deliver pizzas, D has mere custody of the automobile. If D does not return with the car, he violates V's possessory right to the property and, consequently, trespassorily takes possession of it. If the taking was felonious, *i.e.*, with the intent to steal the car, D is guilty of larceny.

[b]   Third Person to the Employee for the Employer

The rule described in subsection [a] applies when an employer furnishes property to his employee. The premise that the employee has limited control over the property because of the employment relation does not apply when an employee

---

[23] *See* § 32.09, *infra*.

[24] 2 East, Pleas of the Crown 564–65 (1803); *United States v. Mafnas*, 701 F.2d at 84.

receives property from a person who has no special authority over him, but who wants the property delivered to the employee's employer. Ordinarily, therefore, an employee who obtains property from a third person for delivery to the employee's employer takes lawful *possession* upon delivery. Therefore, in the absence of some other legal fiction, the servant cannot be convicted of larceny of the property if he carries it away.

Notice how this situation can play out in a banking situation. In the famous *Bazeley* case,[25] *B*, a teller of Bank *X*, apparently took customer *V*'s deposit and immediately pocketed it. *B* was prosecuted for larceny. Essentially, this is what occurred: *V* had possession of the money when he entered the bank; *B* took actual possession of the property from *V* when it was delivered to him for the purpose of transferring it to *B*'s employer, Bank *X*;[26] as this taking was consensual, it was not trespassory; therefore, no larceny occurred when *B* absconded with the money.[27] Consequently, shortly after *Bazeley* was decided, the Parliament enacted an embezzlement statute encompassing *B*'s conduct.[28]

A slight change in the facts in *Bazeley*, however, would have changed the outcome. For example, assume that *B*, having no dishonest intention, places *V*'s deposit in Bank *X*'s bank drawer, as is proper. At the end of the day, however, *B* decides to abscond with the cash, which he does. Now, *B* *is* guilty of common law larceny.[29] In these circumstances, possession of the money moved nontrespassorily from *V* to *B* to Bank *X* (when it was placed in the drawer for the day). Then, when *B* removed the money from the drawer at the end of the day, possession shifted from Bank *X* to *B*. The latter act, however, constituted a trespassory taking. The victim of the larceny, however, was Bank *X*, rather than *V*.

[4]　Bailors and Bailees

The 15th century marked a period of economic chaos in England as that country was transformed from a feudal, agricultural society into one in which manufacturing sprung up in every town, and international commercial ties developed.[30] As a result of these changes, members of the European mercantile class were forced to entrust their property to carriers who would transport their goods long distances. Unfortunately for the merchants, with the new industry came a new form of criminal conduct committed by many carriers. Their *modus operandi* was to take containers, wrongfully open them, remove some or all of the contents so that they could be sold for personal profit, close the containers, and then deliver them.

In terms of larceny law, this presented a problem. The merchant consensually entrusted the goods to the carrier, so there appeared to be a non-trespassory

---

[25] King v. Bazeley, 2 Leach 835, 168 Eng. Rep. 517 (1799).

[26] *See* 1 Hale, Note 21, *supra*, at *667.

[27] *See* Commonwealth v. Ryan, 30 N.E. 364 (Mass. 1892) (Customer gives $4 to *R*, a bartender, for liquor; *R* who places the money in a business drawer and shortly thereafter retrieves and pockets it; held: this is embezzlement, not larceny.).

[28] *See* § 32.09[A], *infra*.

[29] Nolan v. State, 131 A.2d 851 (Md. 1957).

[30] Hall, Note 1, *supra*, at 21.

transfer of possession. Beginning with the *Carrier's Case*,[31] therefore, the King's Council of the Star Chamber developed a new legal fiction, the "breaking bulk" doctrine, which expanded larceny law.

The precise reasoning of *Carrier's Case* is a matter of some dispute. The most common interpretation of the case, however, is that when a person is entrusted with a container for delivery in unopened condition, the bailee receives possession of the container but mere custody of its contents. When the bailee wrongfully opens the container and removes the contents, *i.e.*, when he "breaks bulk," a trespassory taking of possession of the contents results.[32]

The significance of the breaking-bulk doctrine is that the timing and means used by the carrier to steal goods determines whether larceny has occurred. For example, suppose that *C*, a carrier, receives property belonging to the bailor, *B*, for delivery to *A*, but he improperly sells the unopened container to *X* (*i.e.*, he does not break bulk). In this case, there is no larceny,[33] because *C* had lawful possession of the container and he never had legal possession of the contents. On the other hand, if *C* opens the container prior to delivery and sells the contents to *X*, *C* has committed larceny. Similarly, if *C* delivers the container whole to *A*, and then nonconsensually takes it from *A*, larceny has occurred, although the victim now is *A*, who was dispossessed, rather than *B*.[34]

[5] Fraud

Pear's Case[35] involves another legal fiction that developed regarding the nature of possession of property. In *Pear*, *P* rented a horse from *V* with the intent to sell it, which he did immediately. Eleven of 12 judges to whom the case was referred concluded that *P*'s fraudulent conduct constituted a trespass and that, therefore, the taking constituted larceny (or "larceny by trick").

The apparent reasoning of the judges was that, in light of *P*'s fraud, "the parting with the property had not changed the nature of the possession, but that it remained unaltered in the prosecutor [*V*] at the time of the conversion." In other words, because of *P*'s fraud, constructive possession of the horse remained with *V*; *P* received only custody of the steed. When he sold the horse in violation of the arrangement, therefore, *P* trespassorily took possession of the animal.[36]

---

[31] Anon. v. The Sheriff of London (The *Carrier's Case*), Year Book 13 Edw. IV pl. 5 (1473), *reprinted in* 64 Selden Soc'y 30 (1945). The case is discussed in great detail in Hall, Note 1, *supra*, at 3–33.

[32] Another interpretation of the case is that the bailee receives possession of *everything*, but that when he opens the container, constructive possession springs back to the bailor, so that the subsequent act of taking the contents out of the container is a trespassory taking.

[33] Edward Coke, Third Institute *107 (1644).

[34] 4 Blackstone, Note 7, *supra*, at *230.

[35] King v. Pear, 1 Leach 212, 168 Eng. Rep. 208 (1779).

[36] There is another interpretation of this case: that *P* took possession of the horse when he rented it with the fraudulent intent; since this taking was deceitful, it was trespassory. Perkins & Boyce, Note 12, *supra*, at 305. If this interpretation is right, *P* was guilty of larceny the moment he rode away, although it would have been next to impossible to prove *P*'s felonious intent at that time. According to the reading of the case expressed in the text, however, larceny did not occur until *P* acted in violation of the rental agreement.

Notice the prosecutor's quandary in light of *Pear*: If *D* receives property from *V* based on a false promise to return it, he receives only custody of the property, and is guilty of larceny if he appropriates it. On the other hand, if *D* has an honest intention when he receives the property (and, thus, no fraud is involved), *D* receives *possession* of the property, and any subsequent misappropriation constitutes embezzlement, rather than larceny, or no offense.

In these latter two hypotheticals, the objective, external circumstances are the same. The difference — which will determine whether the offense is larceny or embezzlement (if anything) — is a function of when *D* formed the felonious intent. Even if we put aside the fact that *D*'s moral culpability is the same in either case,[37] the critical fact is one likely to be known only by the defendant. Yet, under common law procedural rules, an error by the prosecutor in charging the defendant with the wrong offense could result in acquittal or reversal of the conviction of an obviously dishonest person.[38]

§ 32.05 LARCENY: CARRYING AWAY (ASPORTATION)

A person is not guilty of larceny unless he carries away the personal property that he took trespassorily from another.[39] However, virtually any movement of the property — even a "hair's breadth"[40] — away from the point of caption is sufficient.[41] Thus, common law larceny, rather than attempted larceny, occurs if a shoplifter is caught with the merchant's property in his possession while walking to the exit,[42] or if a person pulls an earring from the victim's ear, and moves it only a few inches before it gets snagged in her hair.[43]

The asportation requirement is not satisfied, however, unless the movement of the property constitutes a "carrying away" motion. For example, if *D* moves a box from the floor to a table in order to open it and steal the contents, this change of position of the property does not meet the asportation requirement; instead, it is an act in furtherance of the process of taking possession of the contents of the container; it was not a "carrying away" motion. Therefore, if *D* were arrested at this

---

If Perkins and Boyce are right, there are other interesting implications. First, if *P* abandoned his felonious intent after renting the horse (but before he sold it) he would still be guilty of larceny, although it would be much harder to prove the felonious intent. Second, if *P* loaned the horse for one day to *X* before selling it, *X* would be guilty of receiving stolen property, assuming he knew of *P*'s intentions! Under the holding of the case described in the text, neither of these results would follow.

[37] Yet, at common law, embezzlement was a misdemeanor; larceny was a capital felony.

[38] This problem is considered in greater detail in § 32.11, *infra*.

[39] People v. Sanders, 67 Cal. App. 4th 1403, 1415 (Ct. App. 1998).

[40] Hall, Note 1, *supra*, at 259.

[41] American Law Institute, Comment to § 223.2, at 164.

[42] People v. Olivo, 420 N.E.2d 40, 44 (N.Y. 1981).

[43] Rex v. Lapier, 1 Leach 320, 168 Eng. Rep. 263 (1784); *see* Harrison v. People, 50 N.Y. 518 (1872) (pickpocket moved a wallet in victim's pocket a few inches before he was caught). Today, the earring example could constitute robbery rather than larceny, as the act of pulling the earring from the victim's ear would constitute a *forcible* taking.

moment, he would be guilty of *attempted* larceny.[44]

In view of the nearly trivial nature of the "carrying away" requirement, one scholar has observed that "it is frequently difficult to see where taking ends and asportation begins."[45] As a consequence, the Model Penal Code does not require proof of asportation.[46] This feature of the Code has been followed by most states that have revised their theft laws.[47]

§ 32.06 LARCENY: PERSONAL PROPERTY OF ANOTHER

[A] Personal Property

[1] Land and Attachments Thereto

The common law of larceny does not protect land.[48] By its nature, land is immovable; a wrongdoer cannot carry it away and thereafter damage, destroy, or lose it. The underlying purpose of larceny law, therefore, does not apply to real estate. Moreover, land can only be "taken" in the sense that a person may come onto it and evict the rightful possessor, or obtain title to unoccupied land by adverse possession. These injuries can be righted adequately by civil action.

Items attached to the land, such as trees, crops, and inanimate objects affixed in the earth,[49] also fall outside the scope of the offense. Once they are severed from the land, however, they become personal property and subject to larceny law.

Certain fictions were developed by the courts to deal with the taking and carrying away of trees and crops recently severed from the land. For example, suppose *D* wrongfully enters *V*'s land and chops down a tree. Once the tree is severed from the land, its legal nature changes from real to personal property. Because *D* is the first person to control the timber after it has become personal property, he is in possession of it. Because *V* never had possession of the severed tree *as personal property*, *D* did not take possession of it trespassorily (or otherwise) from *V*. Even though the severed tree lies on *V*'s land, *D* retains possession of it as long as he remains near it. If he takes the tree from *V*'s land immediately, therefore, he has committed no larceny, although he is liable in tort for trespass to the land.

On the other hand, suppose that *D* leaves the land with the intention of returning the next day to retrieve the timber he severed. As soon as he leaves, *D* loses

---

[44] *See* Cherry's Case, 168 Eng. Rep. 221 (1781) (defendant picked up a package containing cloth in order to remove the cloth; held: no larceny).

[45] Hall, Note 1, *supra*, at 259.

[46] *E.g.*, Model Penal Code § 223.2(1) (providing that theft occurs if a person "unlawfully takes" another's property).

[47] American Law Institute, Comment to § 223.2, at 165.

[48] 4 Blackstone, Note 7, *supra*, at *232.

[49] *E.g.*, Parker v. State, 352 So. 2d 1386 (Ala. Crim. App. 1977) (wires attached to poles embedded in the earth are real property).

possession of the timber. Because it sits on *V*'s land in *D*'s absence, possession of the personal property immediately shifts to *V.* When *D* enters the land the next day and carries away the timber with the intent of depriving *V* of it permanently, *D* is guilty of larceny.[50]

The Model Penal Code and many modern statutes dispense with these rules. The Model Penal Code's theft laws cover all property ("anything of value"[51]), including "immovable" property, such as real estate, and "movable" property, "including things growing on, or found in land."[52]

[2]   Animals

At common law, animals in the state of nature or *ferae naturae* (*e.g.,* wild deer, wild birds, fish in an open river) were not "property" within the meaning of larceny law. However, once an animal was confined by a person on his land or killed, it became his personal property, subject to the law's protection.[53]

Domesticated animals of a "base nature" also fell outside the scope of the common law definition of larceny. Horses and cattle were subject to larceny laws; dogs were "base."[54] Such distinctions were primarily based on economic factors, but today all domesticated animals and birds are protected by theft statutes.

[3]   Stolen Property and Contraband

It is larceny for a person to take and carry away the property of another, even if the "victim" also had no right to possess the property in question. Thus, it is larceny to steal stolen property from a thief, or to steal contraband, *e.g.,* illegal narcotics, that no person has a lawful right to possess.[55]

It is easy to rationalize a contrary result. It might plausibly be argued that thieves, persons who are not bona-fide purchasers of stolen goods, and possessors of contraband, should be deemed to have no possessory interest in wrongfully secured property. However, theft laws are applicable in order to deter the free-for-all that might ensue if criminals could steal from each other with impunity.[56]

---

[50] *See* 2 East, Pleas of the Crown 587 (1803).

[51] Model Penal Code § 223.0(6).

[52] Model Penal Code § 223.0(4). *See* American Law Institute, Comment to § 223.2, at 166–68.

[53] 4 Blackstone, Note 7, *supra,* at *235.

[54] *See* 2 East, Note 50, *supra,* at 614.

[55] *See* People v. Otis, 139 N.E. 562, 562–63 (N.Y. 1923) (involving theft of bootleg liquor during prohibition); *see also* Model Penal Code § 223.0(7) (defining property "of another" broadly to include persons who would be precluded from civil recovery of the property because it was used in an unlawful transaction or was contraband).

[56] Commonwealth v. Crow, 154 A. 283, 286 (Pa. 1931) ("To establish the rule that the owner of liquor, illegally held, had no property right therein, would lead to a condition of terror and bloodshed among rival bootleggers far worse than we have known.").

[4] Intangible Personal Property

Because common law larceny involves the wrongful taking and carrying away of personal property, property without a corporeal existence, i.e., intangible property, is excluded from its coverage.[57] For example, labor or services are not the subject of traditional theft laws.[58] Thus, if a college student wrongfully takes a computer print-out that lists the computer-access account numbers of other students, and then uses the numbers to obtain computer services to which he is not entitled, he is not guilty of common law larceny of the computer services, although he is technically guilty of theft of the sheet of paper on which the account numbers were found.[59]

Today the vast majority of larceny statutes follow the Model Penal Code's lead and prohibit the unlawful transfer of intangible personal property rights.[60]

[B] Of Another

It is not common law larceny, of course, to take and carry away one's own personal property. However, because larceny involves the trespassory taking of *possession* of another person's property, a person may be convicted of larceny of property he owns. For example, if *D*, landlord of an apartment building and owner of the furnishings therein, enters an apartment unit leased to *V*, and takes and carries away the furniture in violation of the lease agreement, *D* has taken the personal property "of another" for purposes of larceny law.

The Model Penal Code defines "property of another" broadly to include "property in which any person other than the actor has an interest."[61] This definition includes a possessory or ownership interest. It is also broad enough to make it a crime for a partner to steal partnership funds in which he shares an interest,[62] contrary to the common law rule.[63]

---

[57] 4 Blackstone, Note 7, *supra*, at *234.

[58] United States v. Delano, 55 F.3d 720, 727 (2d Cir. 1995).

[59] *See* Lund v. Commonwealth, 232 S.E.2d 745 (Va. 1977), *superseded by statute, as recognized in* Evans v. Commonwealth, 308 S.E.2d 126 (Va. 1983); People v. Tansey, 593 N.Y.S.2d 426 (Sup. Ct. 1992) (in prosecution for possession of stolen goods, *T* is not guilty if the "stolen" property is an intangible telephone authorization code).

[60] Model Penal Code § 223.2(2).

[61] Model Penal Code § 223.0(7).

[62] American Law Institute, Comment to § 223.2, at 169.

[63] *E.g.*, People v. Zinke, 555 N.E.2d 263 (N.Y. 1990).

§ 32.07   LARCENY: INTENT TO STEAL (*ANIMUS FURANDI*)

[A]   Nature of the Felonious Intent

[1]   In General

Courts commonly state that a person is not guilty of larceny unless he takes and carries away the personal property of another with the "specific intent to steal" the property. In this context, "intent to steal" is a shorthand way of describing the felonious intent of larceny, which is the intent to deprive another person permanently of the property.[64] Thus, *D* is guilty of larceny if he trespassorily drives away in *V*'s automobile, with the intent of keeping the car. However, he is not guilty of larceny (although he may be guilty of a statutory offense of "joyriding"), if he intends to keep the vehicle temporarily and then return it.[65]

It should be observed that the felonious intent of larceny is *animus furandi* (intent to deprive), not *lucri causa* (for the sake of gain). That is, it is neither necessary nor sufficient that the thief intended to obtain personal benefit from the taking.[66] For example, if *D* takes and carries away *V*'s valuable vase with the intention of destroying it, he has committed larceny although he may gain nothing (except some nonpecuniary pleasure) from the act. On the other hand, if *D* takes *V*'s framed college diploma off the wall and carries it away with the purpose of using it temporarily to fraudulently obtain money from another, *D* is not guilty of larceny of the diploma although he has taken it for personal gain.

It follows from this, as well, that the *nature* of the property taken can be relevant in determining whether a person has acted with the requisite felonious intent. If property is perishable, for example, cut flowers from a florist shop, an intent to deprive the victim of the property long enough to "appropriate a major portion of its economic value"[67] constitutes the requisite "permanent" deprivation.[68]

[2]   Recklessly Depriving Another of Property Permanently

Courts will frequently uphold a conviction for larceny in circumstances in which the most accurate characterization of the defendant's mental state is that he knew that his conduct would create a substantial risk of permanent loss, *i.e.*, that the actor was guilty of recklessly exposing the property to permanent loss. Although

---

[64]   People v. Brown, 38 P. 518, 519 (Cal. 1894).

[65]   Impson v. State, 58 P.2d 523 (Ariz. 1936); *see* People v. Kunkin, 507 P.2d 1392 (Cal. 1973) (*A*, an employee of the state attorney general, unlawfully took a confidential state document to *B* and *C*, journalists, for their inspection, with the intention of returning the document; held: since *A* lacked the intent to steal the document, he did not commit theft; therefore, *B* and *C* were not guilty of possession of *stolen* property).

[66]   *See* Jupiter v. State, 616 A.2d 412, 416 (Md. 1992); State v. Gordon, 321 A.2d 352, 356 (Me. 1974).

[67]   American Law Institute, Comment to § 223.3, at 175 (defining the word "deprive" in the statutory provision).

[68]   People v. Avery, 38 P.3d 1, 2 (Cal. 2002) (holding that the intent to take property only temporarily nonetheless constitutes the intent to steal if the actor's intention is to take property "for so extended a period of time as to deprive the owner of a major portion of [the property's] value or enjoyment").

this is a different *mens rea* than "intent to steal," many courts treat these two states of mind alike or, at least, infer the felonious intent from the actor's recklessness.[69]

For example, *D1* is guilty of the larceny of a car if he trespassorily takes *V*'s vehicle in City X, with the intention of driving it to City Y and abandoning it there.[70] Although *D1* may hope that the abandoned car will eventually be returned to *V*, he knows there is a very high likelihood that it will be re-stolen or its component parts taken before it can be recovered. *D1*'s recklessness in this regard is enough to justify a larceny conviction. Similarly, the intent to steal may be inferred if *D2* takes property which does not belong to him with the intention of "selling" the property back to its owner or returning it only if he is paid a reward.[71]

[B]   Concurrence of *Mens Rea* and *Actus Reus*

[1]   In General

A larceny does not occur unless the actor possesses the intent to steal the property at the time of commission of the *actus reus* of larceny. For example, if *D* takes and drives away *V*'s car, intending to steal it, *D* has committed larceny. On the other hand, if *D* obtains permission to use *V*'s automobile for the day and, hours later, decides to abscond with it, he is *not* guilty of larceny, because he did not have the felonious intent at the moment he took possession of the car.

[2]   Continuing-Trespass Doctrine

Suppose that *D* nonconsensually takes *V*'s car with the intention of keeping it for the day and then returning it. Hours later, *D* decides to keep the automobile permanently and drives out of town with it. Is *D* guilty of larceny? On its face, it would seem not. *D* initially took the car without permission, *i.e.*, a trespassory taking occurred. At the time of the trespassory taking, *D* had a wrongful intent (intent to keep the car without permission for one day), but he did not have the intent to steal. The felonious intent was an afterthought. Consequently, it would seem that the requisite concurrence of *mens rea* and *actus reus* is missing.

Courts developed the legal fiction of "continuing trespass" to deal with such cases. According to this doctrine, when a person takes possession of another person's property by trespass, *every moment that he retains possession of it constitutes a new trespassory taking that continues until he terminates possession of the property*.[72] Therefore, in the preceding hypothetical, because *D*'s nonconsen-

---

[69] *See State v. Gordon*, 321 A.2d at 357–58. The Model Penal Code is in accord: although a person is not guilty of theft unless he acts with the "purpose to deprive" the other of the property (§ 223.2(1)), the word "deprive" is defined broadly in Section 223.0(1) to include disposal of property "so as to make it unlikely that the owner will recover it."

[70] United States v. Sheffield, 161 F. Supp. 387, 390 (D. Md. 1958) (*S* is guilty of larceny, even if he intended to abandon the vehicle six blocks from the site of the original taking).

[71] People v. Davis, 965 P.2d 1165, 1169 (Cal. 1998); State v. Hauptmann, 180 A. 809, 819 (N.J. 1935) ("intent to return should be unconditional; and where there is an element of coercion, or of reward, as a condition of return, larceny is inferable"); *see* American Law Institute, Comment to § 223.2, at 174.

[72] State v. Somerville, 21 Me. 14, 19 (1842).

sual taking of the vehicle was trespassory, every moment he retained the car he was committing the *actus reus* of larceny anew. Consequently, when he decided hours later to deprive V of the automobile permanently, this intent to steal concurred with the "new" trespassory taking, and D is guilty of larceny.

[C]   Claim of Right

[1]   In General

A person is not guilty of larceny if he takes property belonging to another person based on a good faith belief that he has a right to possess the property.[73] The actor's belief negates the specific intent to steal.[74] After all, one cannot intend to trespassorily deprive another of property that one believes one has a right to possess.

For example, suppose that D, a landlord, believes that V, a tenant, has failed to pay his rent. In fact, the rent was paid, but D inadvertently failed to credit V's account. As a result, D enters V's premises and mistakenly impounds V's furniture pursuant to a default clause in the lease that authorizes D to seize a tenant's property and sell it to recover unpaid rent. Under these circumstances, D is not guilty of larceny. Even if his mistake of fact was unreasonable, the mistake negates the intent to steal.

The same analysis would apply in the landlord-tenant hypothetical if D's mistake related to a matter of law, rather than fact. For example, suppose that V, in fact, had defaulted on the rent. If D entered the premises and seized V's property based on an *incorrect* reading of the lease, D would not be guilty of larceny: Whether his mistake of law was reasonable or not, he believed that he had a right to take the property; therefore, he did not have the intent to permanently deprive V of his furniture.[75]

Most claim-of-right cases involve nonviolent action of the sort described above. However, the traditional rule is that the specific intent to steal is negated even if a person uses force to retrieve the specific property to which he claims a good-faith right of possession. For example, if D believes he is entitled to a car in V's possession, and seeks to obtain it at gunpoint, D is not guilty of robbery (*i.e.*, larceny by force),[76] although he may be guilty of aggravated assault inasmuch as the latter offense does not require the intent to steal.[77] The modern trend, however, is to

---

[73] State v. Varszegi, 635 A.2d 816, 818 (Conn. App. Ct. 1993); *accord* Model Penal Code § 223.1(3)(b). The Code's more expansive "claim of right" defense is discussed at American Law Institute, Comment to § 223.1, at 151–59.

[74] People v. Tufunga, 987 P.2d 168, 174 (Cal. 1999).

[75] *See State v. Varszegi*, 635 A.2d at 819.

[76] *See* State v. Smith, 86 A.3d 498, 520–21 (Conn. App. Ct. 2014); *People v. Tufunga*, 987 P.2d at 177. The Model Penal Code is in accord with this rule. Model Penal Code § 222.1 defines "robbery" as the infliction of serious bodily injury or a threat thereof upon another "in the course of committing a theft." As no theft occurs if there is a claim of right, there can be no robbery in such circumstances. For criticism of the prevailing rule, see State v. Schaefer, 790 P.2d 281 (Ariz. Ct. App. 1990).

[77] Butts v. Commonwealth, 133 S.E. 764, 768 (Va. 1926).

reject the claim-of-right defense when force is used.[78]

[2] Forced Sale

Suppose that *D* takes *V*'s property with the intention of paying *V* fair market value for the item. In this circumstance, *D* intends to deprive *V* permanently of the specific property in question, but he does not intend to deprive *V* of its value. May *D* assert a claim-of-right defense on the ground that he believed that he had a right to take the property as long as he paid for it?

If the property *D* takes was *not* for sale, *D* should be convicted of larceny, even if he intends to pay fair market value for the item.[79] Nonetheless, the law on the subject is sparse and inconsistent. The case for conviction is strongest, however, if *D* has reason to know that *V* would refuse to accept payment in lieu of the return of the item.

Suppose, however, a good *is* for sale, but the merchant does not want to sell it to *D*. For example, suppose that *D* attempts to purchase a beer from bartender *V*, who refuses to serve *D* because *D* is intoxicated. If *D* takes the beer, and throws down change to pay for the drink, is *D* guilty of larceny? Blackstone suggested this would not be an offense;[80] and this appears to be the prevailing, although non-unanimous,[81] American view.[82]

§ 32.08   LARCENY: LOST AND MISLAID PROPERTY

The law is confronted with competing policy concerns when a person loses or misplaces his property. On the one hand, there is the interest of the owner in regaining his property; on the other hand, society has an interest in promoting the relatively unrestricted use or transfer of property. As a result, courts developed rules that seek to balance these competing interests.

The common law rights of a finder of lost property depend on two factors: (1) the possessory interest of the owner at the time the property is discovered; and (2) the finder's state of mind when he retrieves the lost property.

Regarding the first factor, an owner of property retains constructive possession of his lost property if there exists a reasonable clue to ownership of it when it is discovered. A reasonable clue to ownership exists if the finder: (1) knows to whom the lost property belongs; or (2) "has reasonable ground to believe, from the nature of the property, or the circumstances under which it is found, that if he . . . deals

---

[78] State v. Miller, 622 N.W.2d 782, 785 (Iowa Ct. App. 2000) (reaching this conclusion based on an "examination of other states' cases"); *People v. Tufunga*, 987 P.2d at 177 (noting that a majority of recent cases refuse to permit use of force in such circumstances).

[79] *See* Perkins & Boyce, Note 12, *supra*, at 345 (stating that it is robbery to require a person at gunpoint to "sell" property that is not for sale).

[80] 4 Blackstone, Note 7, *supra*, at *242 ("it is doubted, whether the forcing [of a merchant] . . . to sell his wares, and giving him the full value of them, amounts to so heinous a crime as robbery").

[81] *See* Jupiter v. State, 616 A.2d 412, 414 (Md. 1992) (noting and citing support for the contrary view, and taking no position on the matter).

[82] American Law Institute, Comment to § 223.1, at 158; Perkins & Boyce, Note 12, *supra*, at 345.

honestly with it, the owner will appear or be ascertained."[83] Thus, a court is more apt to rule that there exists a reasonable clue to ownership of an expensive piece of jewelry found on the floor of a grocery store than a dollar bill aimlessly blowing down the street.

If there is *no* reasonable clue to ownership of the lost property, the finder may use the property as he wishes; the act of picking up the property and using or disposing of it is not a "taking" (trespassory or otherwise). However, if there is a reasonable clue to ownership of the property, the finder's state of mind upon discovery is critical. When *D*, the finder, picks up the lost (reasonable-clue-to-ownership) property, he takes possession of it from *V*, the owner. If *D* takes possession with the intent to steal the property, he is guilty of larceny.[84] If *D* picks up the article with the intent to find the owner, the taking is not trespassory; if *D* subsequently absconds with the property, he is not guilty of larceny since the original taking was lawful. Moreover, because *V* did not entrust the property to *D*, *D*'s actions may fall outside the scope of a typical embezzlement statute.[85]

Mislaid property is treated somewhat differently than lost property.[86] An object is "mislaid" if "it is intentionally put in a certain place for a temporary purpose and then inadvertently left there when the owner goes away."[87] Supposedly, there is *always* a clue to ownership of mislaid property: Because it was misplaced, rather than lost, the owner knows where it is, and is likely to return to pick it up once he notices that he has left it behind.[88] Therefore, the lawfulness of the finder's actions depends entirely on his state of mind when he takes possession of the property from the owner. If he takes it with the intent to steal it, he is guilty of larceny;[89] if he picks it up with honest intentions, he is not guilty of any theft offense.

§ 32.09 EMBEZZLEMENT

[A] Historical Background

Embezzlement is not a common law offense. The offense is the result of 18th century legislative efforts to compensate for gaps in the law of larceny. As described earlier, common law jurists were willing to punish new forms of dishonest conduct by manipulating the meaning of the term "trespassory taking" to expand the scope of larceny law. But, there were limits to their willingness to stretch the law. In particular, they were not prepared to treat dishonest employees,

---

[83] Brooks v. State, 35 Ohio St. 46, 50 (1878).

[84] *Id.*

[85] *See* § 32.09[B], *infra.*

[86] The Model Penal Code treats lost and mislaid property similarly. *See* Model Penal Code § 223.5 ("Theft of Property Lost, Mislaid, or Delivered by Mistake").

[87] Perkins & Boyce, Note 12, *supra*, at 310.

[88] *Id.* at 310–11.

[89] If the finder genuinely believes that the item was abandoned by its owner, he lacks the specific intent to steal it. *See* Model Penal Code § 223.1(3)(a); American Law Institute, Comment to § 223.5, at 227–28.

who appropriated property lawfully entrusted to them by third persons for delivery to employers, as capital felons.

In 1799, shortly after the acquittal of a dishonest bank employee in the *Bazeley* case,[90] Parliament enacted the first general embezzlement statute.[91] The statute provided in pertinent part:

> [I]f any servant or clerk, or any person employed . . . by virtue of such employment receive or take into his possession any money, goods, bond, bill, note, banker's draft, or other valuable security, or effects, for or in the name or on the account of his master or masters, or employer or employers, and shall fraudulently embezzle, secrete, or make away with the same, or any part thereof . . . [he] shall be deemed to have feloniously stolen the same.[92]

Subsequent embezzlement statutes were enacted to deal with other persons not encompassed by this law.

Under English law, embezzlement was a misdemeanor. In the United States today, embezzlement is a felony or misdemeanor, depending on the value of the property embezzled.

[B]   Elements of the Offense

Because of the statutory nature of the offense, and the piecemeal manner in which embezzlement laws were enacted, no single definition of the crime exists. At a minimum, however, embezzlement involves two basic ingredients: (1) *D* came into possession of the personal property of another in a *lawful* manner; and (2) *D* thereafter fraudulently converted the property (*i.e.*, *D* performed some act that demonstrated his intent to deprive another of the property permanently). Most embezzlement statutes include a third element: (3) *D* came into possession of the property as the result of entrustment by or for the owner of the property.

[C]   Distinguishing Larceny from Embezzlement

The most significant distinction between larceny and embezzlement is that "[i]n embezzlement, the property comes lawfully into possession of the taker and is fraudulently or unlawfully appropriated by him; in larceny, there is a trespass in the unlawful taking of the property."[93] It is useful to summarize here some of the subtle differences between the two offenses, as developed in earlier sections of this chapter.

First, a person who fraudulently secures property from another obtains mere *custody* of the property. Consequently, the subsequent appropriation of the property, which constitutes a trespassory taking of possession thereof, renders the

---

[90]   King v. Bazeley, 2 Leach 835, 168 Eng. Rep. 517 (1799). *See* § 32.04[B][3][b], *supra.*

[91]   Previously, it had enacted statutes prohibiting embezzlement by officers and servants of the Bank of England, South Sea Company, and the post office. Hall, Note 1, *supra*, at 39.

[92]   39 Geo. III, c. 85 (1799).

[93]   State v. Smith, 98 P.2d 647, 648 (Wash. 1939), *overruled in part*, 798 P.2d 1146 (Wash. 1990).

fraudulent actor guilty of larceny (by trick).[94]

Second, an employee who receives property from his employer for use in the employment relationship ordinarily obtains mere *custody* of the property. Therefore, if the employee takes and carries away the employer's property with the concurrent intent to steal it, he is guilty of larceny, rather than embezzlement.[95]

Third, an employee who receives property *for* his employer from a third person ordinarily receives *possession* of the property. Therefore, if he later decides to convert the property, he is potentially guilty of embezzlement.[96]

Fourth, a bailee entrusted with property ordinarily obtains possession of it, except that if the property is enclosed in a container he obtains possession of the container but only custody of its contents.[97] Therefore, if the bailee subsequently decides to sell or otherwise convert the entrusted property in the condition in which it was received (*e.g.*, in its original container if there was one), he is guilty of embezzlement. In contrast, if the bailee wrongfully opens the container and converts the contents, he is guilty of larceny of the contents. If he is responsible for delivering the container to a third party, and he does so without opening it, and thereafter decides to steal the property, he is guilty of larceny.

Finally, in jurisdictions in which entrustment is an element of the offense of embezzlement, a person who finds lost or mislaid property, takes it with the intent to find the true owner, and then changes his mind and converts the property to his own use, is guilty of no offense. It is larceny, however, if he had a wrongful intent when he found the property.[98]

§ 32.10 FALSE PRETENSES

[A] In General

The offense of "obtaining property by false pretenses" or, simply, "false pretenses," is statutory in nature. Originally, it was a misdemeanor in England. In the United States, it is now a felony or misdemeanor, depending on the value of the property obtained.

The original false pretenses statute was enacted in England in 1757.[99] According to that statute, any person who "knowingly and designedly" by false pretenses obtains title to "money, goods, wares or merchandizes" from another person "with the intent to cheat or defraud" the other person is guilty of false pretenses. A "false pretense" is a false representation of an existing fact.[100]

---

[94] *See* § 32.04[B][5], *supra*.

[95] *See* § 32.04[B][3][a], *supra*.

[96] *See* § 32.04[B][3][b], *supra*.

[97] *See* § 32.04[B][4], *supra*.

[98] *See* § 32.08, *supra*.

[99] 30 Geo. II, c. 24 § 1 (1757).

[100] *See* Lund v. Commonwealth, 232 S.E.2d 745, 748 (Va. 1977); American Law Institute, Comment to § 223.3, at 184.

[B] Distinguishing False Pretenses from Larceny and Embezzlement

Larceny, embezzlement, and false pretenses may occur as the result of fraud. False pretenses and larceny-by-trick are alike in one critical way: Fraud is used to *obtain* the property. In contrast, an embezzler obtains property lawfully, but thereafter fraudulently *converts* it to his own use. The primary difference between larceny and false pretenses is that a thief who uses trickery to secure *title*, and not simply possession, of property, is guilty of false pretenses; one who merely secures possession through fraud is guilty of larceny-by-trick.[101]

The line between larceny-by-trick and false pretenses is sometimes clear. For example, in *Pear's Case*,[102] P fraudulently rented a horse from V, intending from the outset to steal the animal. Clearly, this was not false pretenses: The existence of the rental arrangement demonstrates that title to the horse did not pass with possession.

Often the line between the two offenses is very thin. Frequently, a court will rule that, although the thief obtained *possession* of property through fraud, *title* to it did not transfer because some condition had not yet been satisfied. For example, in one case,[103] H drove his car to V's gas station and asked the operator to fill his tank. H did not intend to pay for the gasoline. After the tank was filled, H drove away without paying. The court determined that H committed larceny-by-trick rather than false pretenses because V did not intend title to the gas to pass until payment was made. In contrast, if H had paid for the gasoline with counterfeit money, title would have passed, and the offense would have been false pretenses.

One who provides money to another for a special purpose does not transfer title to it until that purpose is met. For example, in *Graham v. United States*,[104] G, a lawyer, obtained money from V, his client, for the stated purpose of bribing X, a police officer, for V's benefit. Instead, G converted the cash to his own use. The court held that G was guilty of larceny, not false pretenses: V did not intend to part with title to the money until it was delivered to X as a bribe.

[C] Elements of the Offense

[1] False Representation

False pretenses requires a false representation. The representation itself may be in writing, orally presented, or in the form of misleading conduct.[105] Usually, *nondisclosure* of a material fact does *not* constitute false pretenses, even if the omitter of the information knows that the other party is acting under a false

---

[101] Bell v. United States, 462 U.S. 356, 359 (1983).

[102] King v. Pear, 1 Leach 212, 168 Eng. Rep. 208 (1779).

[103] Hufstetler v. State, 63 So. 2d 730 (Ala. Ct. App. 1953).

[104] 187 F.2d 87 (D.C. Cir. 1950).

[105] In one famous case, B obtained property from V by giving the false impression that he was an Oxford student by wearing a cap and gown identified with the college. Rex v. Barnard, 173 Eng. Rep. 342 (1837).

impression.[106] However, nondisclosure constitutes misrepresentation if the omitter has a duty of disclosure, such as when he has a fiduciary relationship to the victim.

The representation, of course, must be false. A person is not guilty of false pretenses if he obtains title to property by making a "false" claim that turns out to be true. For example, if *D*, a scam artist, sells a book purporting to be the diary of Hitler, he cannot be convicted of false pretenses if the diary turns out to be genuine, although *D* believed that it was forged. Instead, *D* would be guilty of *attempted* false pretenses.

[2] Existing Fact

[a]   Fact Versus Opinion

Expression of an opinion, uttered with the intent to defraud another, does not constitute false pretenses.[107] For example, "seller's talk" or "puffing" (*e.g.*, "this is the best product that has ever been manufactured") is not actionable. The justification for this rule is that such statements cannot be taken literally as fact, but must be considered to be the seller's opinion. As such, a listener should not rely on the utterance.

The fact/opinion distinction may also preclude conviction of persons not involved in puffing. For example, a statement by a seller regarding the value of his property is traditionally treated as a non-actionable representation of opinion.[108] This is because the value of property is the price agreed upon by a willing buyer and seller. A representation regarding value, therefore, is no more than an expression of opinion by the speaker of the price he thinks the property would bear in the market.

As the fact/opinion distinction might suggest, the ethic of *caveat emptor* was strong while the law of false pretenses developed. It is commonly acknowledged today, however, that if this distinction is inflexibly followed it will result in "the clever [person] . . . be[ing] able to steal with impunity."[109] Consequently, many states have expanded the scope of false pretenses. For example, Model Penal Code Section 223.3 provides that a person is guilty of "theft by deception," the Code's equivalent offense, if he creates or reinforces a false impression regarding the value of property. However, puffing is not prohibited unless the statement would deceive an ordinary listener.

[b]   Fact versus Promise of Future Conduct

Suppose that *D* purchases an automobile with a three-year loan from the dealer,[110] and later fails to make payments. May *D* be convicted of false pretenses if it can be shown he had no intention of paying his debt when he entered into the

---

[106] People v. Johnson, 150 N.Y.S. 331 (Sup. Ct. 1914).

[107] Regina v. Bryan, 7 Cox. Crim. Cas. 312, 317 (1857).

[108] *E.g.*, Commonwealth v. Quinn, 111 N.E. 405, 407 (Mass. 1916).

[109] American Law Institute, Comment to § 223.3, at 192.

[110] Although title technically is retained by the vendor of property until full payment is received on

agreement?

Conceptually, a promise to make payment in the future is an assertion of the present fact of the speaker's intention to perform a future act. Nonetheless, common law courts were reluctant to treat a debtor's breach of contract as the basis for criminal prosecution for false pretenses. The traditional explanation is that "the act complained of . . . is as consonant with ordinary commercial default as with criminal conduct . . . . Business affairs would be materially encumbered by the ever present threat that a debtor might be subjected to criminal penalties . . . ."[111] The majority rule, therefore, is that the offense of false pretenses does not apply to misrepresentations regarding future conduct.

In recent years, many states have redrafted their theft laws to encompass false promises. The Model Penal Code is typical of this trend. It prohibits deception regarding a person's "intention or other state of mind." The Code expressly provides, however, that deception regarding the intention to fulfill a promise cannot be inferred solely from the fact that the promisor did not perform as guaranteed.[112]

[3] *Mens Rea*

The original false pretenses statute and others modeled on it require proof not only that the actor uttered a false representation of an existing fact, but that it was uttered "knowingly and designedly" and with "the intent to defraud."

The phrase "knowingly and designedly" means only that the actor made the representation knowing that it was false. The phrase "intent to defraud" constitutes the specific intent of false pretenses; it approximates the meaning of "intent to steal" required in larceny prosecutions. Thus, D is not guilty of false pretenses if he knowingly utters a false statement in order to obtain property to which he believes he is entitled. In such circumstances, D lacks the intent to defraud another.[113]

§ 32.11 CONSOLIDATION OF THEFT OFFENSES

As the preceding chapter sections demonstrate, many legal fictions complicate the law of larceny, embezzlement, and false pretenses, and the lines between the offenses are often exceedingly thin. And, the view of legal reformers has been that there is no meaningful difference between the offenses in terms of the culpability of the actors, their dangerousness, or the seriousness of the harm caused.

Making matters worse, the key distinctions between the offenses often depend on the hidden intentions of the parties. The line between larceny and embezzlement, for example, depends on whether the defendant formed the wrongful mental state prior to, or after, the property was delivered to him. The line between larceny-by-

---

an installment contract, the equitable interest obtained by the purchaser is sufficiently great that the offense of false pretenses applies. Whitmore v. State, 298 N.W. 194, 195 (Wis. 1941).

[111] Chaplin v. United States, 157 F.2d 697, 698–99 (D.C. Cir. 1946).

[112] Model Penal Code § 223.3(1).

[113] People v. Thomas, 3 Hill 169 (N.Y. Sup. Ct. 1842).

trick and false pretenses, on the other hand, depends on whether title passed in a property transaction; yet this critical fact depends largely on the victim's intent at the time of transfer.

These distinctions served as encumbrances in the prosecution of wrongdoers. At one time, a prosecutor of a theft offense was required to prove commission of the form of theft alleged in the indictment. Thus, if the indictment charged larceny, the prosecutor could not obtain a conviction for embezzlement or false pretenses. Even when a prosecutor was allowed to allege alternative offenses in an indictment, this was only a slight benefit: He still had to convince all of the jurors as to which crime was committed. As a result, thieves sometimes escaped punishment because the prosecutor was unable to prove beyond a reasonable doubt whether the wrongdoer had a felonious intent at the time he took possession of property (larceny) or later (embezzlement), or whether the wrongdoer's admitted fraud resulted in transfer of title (false pretenses) or only possession (larceny).

As the result of difficulties of proof, most states have sought to ease the prosecutor's burden by consolidating the three theft crimes (and other property crimes, such as extortion, blackmail, and receiving stolen property) into a single theft offense. However, lawyers in jurisdictions that have reformed the law in this manner have needed to be wary of what consolidation does and does not do. Specifically, unless a theft statute provides to the contrary, the consolidation may do nothing more than bring the various theft crimes under a single statutory umbrella. The umbrella may actually not eliminate the prosecutor's responsibility to prove the elements of the specific type of theft alleged.[114]

To avoid continued problems of pleading and proof, some states have followed the lead of the Model Penal Code. The Code sets out separate forms of theft — *e.g.*, theft by unlawful taking, theft by deception, theft by extortion — but the offenses are consolidated in the sense that the prosecutor may prove a different form of theft than was specified in the indictment, as long as the defendant's right to a fair trial is ensured.[115] Another approach is to allow the prosecutor to allege simply that the defendant "stole" the property in question, and to support the allegation at trial with evidence of any form of theft.[116]

---

[114] People v. Sanders, 67 Cal. App. 4th 1403, 1416–17 (Ct. App. 1998).

[115] Model Penal Code § 223.1(1).

[116] Mass. Gen. Laws ch. 277, § 41 (2015).

Chapter 33

RAPE (SEXUAL ASSAULT)

§ 33.01 RAPE: GENERAL PRINCIPLES[1]

[A] Definition: Common Law

Blackstone defined *rape* as "carnal knowledge[2] of a woman forcibly and against her will."[3] At common law, however, a husband who forced his wife to engage in sexual intercourse with him was not guilty of rape.[4] Common law rape is a general-intent offense.

An ancient English felony statute prohibited sexual intercourse by a male with a "woman child" under the age of 10 years with or without her consent.[5] This offense has come to be known today as "statutory rape," although it is a feature of the common law of the United States.[6]

As will be seen in this chapter, modern rape law looks very different than the common law in many regards. (Indeed, in some jurisdictions, the offense has been renamed to emphasize the changes that have occurred.) But, it is a starting point to understanding 21st Century sexual offense law.

---

[1] *See generally* Susan Brownmiller, Against Our Will (1975); Susan Estrich, Real Rape (1987); Stephen J. Schulhofer, Unwanted Sex: The Culture of Intimidation and the Failure of Law (1998); David P. Bryden, *Redefining Rape*, 3 Buff. Crim. L. Rev. 317 (2000); Anne M. Coughlin, *Sex and Guilt*, 84 Va. L. Rev. 1 (1998); Joshua Dressler, *Where We Have Been, and Where We Might Be Going: Some Cautionary Reflections on Rape Law Reform*, 46 Clev. St. L. Rev. 409 (1998); Susan Estrich, *Rape*, 95 Yale L.J. 1087 (1986). For a searing account of one woman's rape, and an eloquent description of her "road to recovery," see Nancy Venable Raine, After Silence: Rape and My Journey Back (1998).

[2] "Carnal knowledge" is sexual intercourse, *i.e.*, genital copulation. (Anal and oral penetration fall outside the scope of common law rape, but constitute the offense of sodomy.) Sexual penetration by the penis of the vulva is necessary to constitute rape; sexual emission is neither sufficient nor necessary. 1 Matthew Hale, History of the Pleas of the Crown *628 (1736).

[3] 4 William Blackstone, Commentaries on the Laws of England *210 (1769).

[4] 1 Hale, Note 2, *supra*, at *628–29.

[5] 18 Eliz. ch. 7, § 4; *see* 4 Blackstone, Note 3, *supra*, at *212.

[6] Regarding statutory rape, *see generally* Catherine L. Carpenter, *On Statutory Rape, Strict Liability, and the Public Welfare Offense Model*, 53 Am. U. L. Rev. 313 (2003); Michelle Oberman, *Regulating Consensual Sex with Minors: Defining a Role for Statutory Rape*, 48 Buff. L. Rev. 703 (2000); Michelle Oberman, *Turning Girls into Women: Re-Evaluating Modern Statutory Rape Law*, 85 J. Crim. L. & Criminology 15 (1994); Frances Olsen, *Statutory Rape: A Feminist Critique of Rights Analysis*, 63 Tex. L. Rev. 387 (1984).

[B] Statutes: Traditional and Reform

Modern American rape statutes vary considerably. In recent years many legislatures have redrafted their rape statutes, often in recognition of, and agreement with, feminist critiques of the common law and early statutory definitions of rape.[7] The Model Penal Code, which was largely drafted in the 1950s and adopted by the American Law Institute in 1962 — well before modern scholarly and public criticism of rape law fully developed — has had little impact on rape law reform. Given modern sensibilities, the Code's sexual offense provisions are seen today by many as relics that "should be pulled and replaced."[8] And, indeed, the American Law Institute is currently in the process of redrafting the Sexual Offenses section of the MPC.[9]

Traditional (non-reformed) statutes focus on forcible rape, or sexual intercourse achieved "forcibly," "against the will" of the female, and "without her consent." As is considered below,[10] these terms — sometimes all contained in a single statute[11] — are not necessarily synonymous. Traditional rape statutes, as is the common law, are also gender-specific: Only males are legally capable of perpetrating the offense,[12] and only females can be victims of the crime.

Most states now prohibit *non*forcible forms of nonconsensual sexual intercourse. For example, sexual intercourse by a male with an unconscious or intoxicated female,[13] and sexual intercourse procured by "fraud-in-the factum,"[14] will constitute rape. And, increasingly, states have redefined the offense in gender-neutral terms in regard to both the perpetrator and the victim.[15] In the most reformed versions of the law, the offense has been broadened to include all forms of sexual penetration (including nonconsensual oral and anal penetration); the name of the crime has been changed (*e.g.*, "criminal sexual conduct" or "sexual assault"); the offense is divided into degrees; and the marital immunity rule — the common law rule that a husband could not legally rape his wife — has been narrowed or abolished.[16] Some states now also criminalize nonconsensual sexual contact short of penetration.[17]

---

[7] *E.g.*, State in the Interest of M.T.S., 609 A.2d 1266, 1274–75 (N.J. 1992) (summarizing that state's rape reform, formulated by a coalition of feminist organizations).

[8] Deborah W. Denno, *Why the Model Penal Code's Sexual Offense Provisions Should Be Pulled and Replaced*, 1 Ohio St. J. Crim. L. 207 (2003).

[9] For the MPC approach, see § 33.08, *infra*.

[10] *See* § 33.04, *infra*.

[11] *E.g.*, Md. Ann. Code of 1957 art. 27, § 463(a)(1) ("[b]y force or threat of force against the will and without the consent of the other person") (since repealed).

[12] However, a female may be convicted of rape as an accomplice of a male.

[13] *E.g.*, 18 Pa. Cons. Stat. § 3121(3)–(4) (2015); *see generally* Christine Chambers Goodman, *Protecting the Party Girl: A New Approach for Evaluating Intoxicated Consent*, 2009 BYU L. Rev. 57.

[14] Cal. Penal Code § 261(a)(4)(C) (2015)("fraud in fact"). *See* § 33.04[C], *infra*.

[15] *E.g.*, Mich. Comp. Laws §§ 750.520a–750.520l (2015); N.J. Stat. Ann. § 2C:14–2 (2015).

[16] Bryden, Note 1, *supra*, at 321 (and citing statutes). The marital exemption rule is considered in § 33.06, *infra*.

[17] *E.g.*, Ind. Crim. Code § 35-42-4-8 (2015).

Today, "statutory rape" remains an offense. Not uncommonly, states apply a two-level approach to this offense: Sexual intercourse with a very young girl remains punishable at the level of forcible rape; intercourse with an older girl (especially if the male is older than the female by a specified number of years) is a felony of a lesser degree.[18]

[C] Grading of the Offense

Under Saxon law, rape was a felony punishable by death. For a short time in the 13th century, it was treated as only a trespass punishable by two years' imprisonment and a fine. Subsequently, the offense was treated again as a capital crime.[19]

In the United States, as late as the mid-1920s, 18 states, the District of Columbia, and the federal government authorized capital punishment for rape. However, "the death penalty [was] reserved overwhelmingly for black defendants, especially those convicted of raping white women."[20] In 1977 and 2008, the Supreme Court ruled that the penalty of death is unconstitutionally disproportionate to the crime of rape.[21]

Today, rape is typically treated as a very serious — often the most serious — non-homicide felony. Penalties vary, but most states set the maximum penalty at life imprisonment[22] or a substantial terms of years.[23]

§ 33.02 STATISTICS REGARDING RAPE

Accurate figures on the commission of rape are almost impossible to find.[24] Indeed, the two primary national sources for all United States crime statistics — the Uniform Crime Report and National Crime Victimization Survey (NCVS) — have shown "markedly different [rape] trends."[25] What *is* known is that rape is and has been an under-reported crime.[26] Complicating efforts to determine numbers

---

[18] *E.g.*, N.J. Stat. Ann. § 2C:14-2(a)(1) & (c)(4) (2015) (if the victim is less than 13 years of age, the offense is first-degree sexual assault; where the victim is at least 13 years old but less than 16, and the actor is at least four years older, the offense is second-degree sexual assault).

[19] 4 Blackstone, Note 3, *supra*, at *211–12.

[20] James R. Acker, *Social Science in Supreme Court Death Penalty Cases: Citation Practices and Their Implications*, 8 Just. Q. 421, 431 (1991).

[21] Coker v. Georgia, 433 U.S. 584 (1977) (rape of an adult woman); Kennedy v. Louisiana, 554 U.S. 407 (2008) (rape of a child). *See* § 6.05[B], *supra.*

[22] *E.g.*, Mich. Comp. Laws § 750.520b (2015).

[23] *E.g.*, N.Y. Penal Law § 130.35 (2015) (defining rape in the first degree as a Class B felony) and § 70.02(3)(a) (2015) (authorizing imprisonment of from 5 to 25 years for Class B felonies).

[24] For discussion of some of the problems in this regard, see Helen M. Eigenberg, *The National Crime Survey and Rape: The Case of the Missing Question*, 7 Just. Q. 655 (1990).

[25] David P. Bryden & Sonja Lengnick, *Rape in the Criminal Justice System*, 87 J. Crim. L. & Criminology 1194, 1218 (1997).

[26] According to a late 20th century NCVS estimate, only 32% of all rapes and lesser forms of sexual assault were reported to law enforcement agencies. "The most common reason given by victims of rape/sexual assault for reporting the crime . . . was to prevent further crimes by the offender against

and trends is that the definition of "rape" for purposes of data collection by the Federal Bureau of Investigation has undergone substantial change. Prior to 2012, the FBI used Blackstone's definition of rape.[27] As such, it excluded nonforcible (but still nonconsensual) forms of rape, rape within the marital relationship, nonconsensual sexual penetration other than intercourse, and same-sex sexual attacks.[28] As of 2012, "rape" data include all of these forms of sexual attack.

According to NCVS figures, about 270,000 females experienced rape, attempted rape, or other forms of unwanted sexual contact in 2010. Females under the age of 34, those living in lower-income homes, and women who lived in rural areas, suffered the highest rates of sexual victimization. Most sexual attacks occurred at or near the victim's home. Approximately 75% of the victims knew their offender. About 10% of the cases involved a weapon used by the perpetrator.[29]

Based on 2009 data, persons characterized by the U.S. Department of Justice as "black" were three times more likely per capita to be victims of rape or sexual assault than "whites"; Hispanics and non-Hispanics were equally likely to be victims.[30]

§ 33.03 SOCIAL ATTITUDES REGARDING RAPE[31]

[A] Social Harm of Rape

[1] The Original Perspective

The law of rape is rooted in ancient male concepts of property.[32] A virgin daughter was a valuable commodity owned by her father; a wife was a chattel of her husband. As a consequence, rape was a property offense. For example, according to one Biblical passage, the punishment for rape of a virgin daughter was 50 shekels,

---

them. The most common reason cited by the victim for not reporting the crime . . . was that it was considered a personal matter." U.S. Department of Justice, Bureau of Justice Statistics, Sex Offenses and Offenders (NCJ-163392, Feb. 1997).

[27] *See* § 33.01[A], *supra.*

[28] On the latter issue, see Bennett Capers, *Real Rape Too*, 99 Calif. L. Rev. 1259 (2011).

[29] U.S. Dept. of Justice, Bureau of Justice Statistics, Female Victims of Sexual Violence, 1994–2010 (NCJ 240655, Mar. 2013).

[30] U.S. Department of Justice, Bureau of Justice Statistics, Criminal Victimization, 2009, (NCJ 231327, Oct. 2010) (by Bonnie S. Fisher, et al.), at 5 (Table 5).

[31] *See generally* Michal Buchhandler-Raphael, *The Failure of Consent: Re-Conceptualizing Rape as Sexual Abuse of Power*, 18 Mich. J. Gender & L. 147 (2011); Michael Davis, *Setting Penalties: What Does Rape Deserve?*, 3 Law & Phil. 61 (1984); Aya Gruber, *Rape, Feminism, and the War on Crime*, 84 Wash. L. Rev. 581 (2009); Aya Gruber, *A "Neo-Feminist" Assessment of Rape and Domestic Violence Law Reform*, 15 J. Gender Race & Just. 583 (2012); Catherine A. MacKinnon, *Feminism, Marxism, Method, and the State: Toward Feminist Jurisprudence*, 8 Signs: J. Women Culture & Soc'y 635 (1983); Stephen J. Schulhofer, *Taking Sexual Autonomy Seriously: Rape Law and Beyond*, 11 Law & Phil. 35 (1992); David Subotnik, *"Hands Off": Sex, Feminism, Affirmative Consent, and the Law of Foreplay*, 16 S. Cal. Rev. L. & Social Justice 249 (2007). See also the cites in Note 1, *supra.*

[32] Brownmiller, Note 1, *supra*, at 376; *see generally id.* at 16–30.

to be paid to her "owner" (the father), and forced marriage to the victim.[33]

The marital exemption, *i.e.*, the doctrine that a husband is legally incapable of raping his wife, is a manifestation of the view that the husband "owned" sexual rights over his wife. According to this view, the husband had the right to sexual relations with his wife whenever he chose, regardless of her wishes.

[2] Modern Perspective

Lawmakers and feminist scholars have sought to provide a modern explanation of the loss suffered by rape victims. Generally speaking, rape is viewed today as a crime of violence, but also as a privacy/autonomy offense.

The conception of rape as a crime of violence is easy to understand. Any rape involves, at a minimum, a battery of the victim. When it is committed forcibly, it has all the earmarks of an aggravated battery. According to this view, the social harm of rape is not the sex act itself, but the way in which it is executed: violently. One scholar has gone so far as to claim that rape should be treated "as a variety of ordinary (simple or aggravated) battery because that is what rape is."[34]

However, this is an inadequate view of the offense. Rape surely involves more than bruises or breaks to the body. Rape is a sexual invasion of the victim's body, in which her "private, personal inner space" is violated without her consent.[35] It is an internal assault, an assault on her psyche, and a severe violation of the privacy of the victim. The act of rape denies the victim's autonomy[36] by abridging her right to determine when, with whom, and how she will have sexual intimacy.[37] Perhaps as significantly, rape is a hostile, humiliating, degrading act of sexual domination by

---

[33] *Deuteronomy* 22:28–29.

[34] Davis, Note 31, *supra*, at 62–63.

[35] Brownmiller, Note 1, *supra*, at 376.

[36] Professor Anne Coughlin believes that none of the conventional explanations of rape law, including the autonomy concept, fully explains the offense as it is traditionally defined. She argues that rape laws were developed at a time when "sexuality was [decreed to be] a force so dangerous that it could not safely be left to self-regulation, but rather should be closely confined, by state law, within marital relationships." Coughlin, Note 1, *supra*, at 6. That is, sexual autonomy — by either sex — was *discouraged*, rather than *valued*. Coughlin contends that rape laws arose in a culture that also criminalized adultery and fornication; as she sees it, traditional rape law can be understood if one considers the efforts of that earlier society to regulate all forms of heterosexual intercourse outside the marital union. Because sexual autonomy now *is* valued, Coughlin reasons, rape law should be reshaped accordingly.

[37] One victim of rape — a harrowing three-hour sexual assault in her home — powerfully described her loss of autonomy this way:

> The rapist had violated my most basic human need — my bodyright. By destroying my ability to control my own body, he made my body an object. I lost a sense of it as the boundary of self, the fundamental and most scared of all borders. A self without boundaries is like a weak country that has been overrun by a stronger one.

Raine, Note 1, *supra*, at 163. She also wrote, at 206–07, that "[t]he most personal part of being raped had less to do with what happened to my body for three hours . . . , than with what happened to my spirit." She said she lost "faith that there is order and continuity in life . . . . To lose faith in life was, for me, the loss of connection with the intangible world — with soul, spirit, anima, essence, vital force, or what one chooses to call it."

the perpetrator of the victim.[38]

[B] Perceptions of the Seriousness of the Offense

[1] In General

Although rape is considered a serious offense in all states, in terms of public perceptions, there is empirical evidence that not all rapes are considered equally serious. Indeed, even if the force used in a sexual assault remains constant, the perceived character and background of the victim of the rape, and her relationship, if any, to the rapist, impacts attitudes regarding the severity of the crime.

[2] Blaming the Victim

Historically, both men and women have tended to attribute some blame for a rape to the victim, even when the circumstances of the assault do not suggest any causal responsibility on her part. To some extent, victim-blaming occurs with *all* offenses. One explanation for this phenomenon is that people psychically need to believe that the world is just. This belief is cast in doubt when innocent people are victims of crime. Therefore, when a person is victimized, the observer — and even the victim herself — wants to believe that the victim was partially responsible for her own fate, and thus the rest of us can avoid becoming a crime victim by our own proper conduct.[39]

This phenomenon is exacerbated in rape cases, however. Various not-entirely-recent studies suggest that males and females, but especially males, consider the character and behavior of the female victim highly relevant in determining the seriousness of the offense.[40] For example, in one study,[41] college students were provided descriptions of two rapes. In each, the victim was forcibly attacked by a stranger, late at night, as she walked across campus following an evening college class. In one rape, however, the victim was described as a divorced, topless dancer, out of jail awaiting trial on a drug charge. The other victim was a married social worker.

The study demonstrated that the respectability of the victim — her supposed character — affected male perceptions of responsibility for the crime. Males placed more blame for the crime on a victim's "low" character (the topless dancer) than did

---

[38] Brownmiller, Note 1, *supra*, at 376–78; *see* State v. Smith, 372 A.2d 386, 389–90 (N.J. Super. Ct. Law Div.1977), *rev'd*, 426 A.2d 38 (N.J. 1981) ("Rape is necessarily and essentially an act of male self-aggrandizement . . . Rape subjugates and humiliates the woman."). One commentator has described rape as an "act of terrorism" that keeps women dependent on men. Susan Griffin, *Rape: The All-American Crime, in* Rape Victimology 36 (L. Schultz ed. 1975).

[39] *See generally* Melvin J. Lerner, *The Desire for Justice and Reactions to Victims, in* Altruism and Helping Behavior (J. Macaulay & L. Berkowitz eds., 1970).

[40] *E.g.*, L.G. Calhoun et al., *The Effect of Victim Physical Attractiveness and Sex of Respondent on Social Reactions to the Victims of Rape*, 17 Brit. J. Soc. & Clinical Psychol. 191 (1978); James Luginbuhl & Courtney Mullin, *Rape and Responsibility: How and How Much Is the Victim Blamed?*, 7 Sex Roles 547 (1981); James W. Selby et al., *Sex Difference in the Social Perception of Rape Victims*, 3 Personality & Soc. Psychol. Bull. 412 (1977).

[41] Luginbuhl & Mullin, Note 40, *supra.*

women. Females also placed some responsibility for the incident on the victim, but they were more likely than males to attribute responsibility to the victim's behavior, *e.g.*, walking home late at night, as well as to explain the case as a matter of chance (simply being in the wrong place at the wrong time).

As might be expected from these findings, when the students were asked to assign a penalty to the rapists, men and women responded differently. The females assigned penalties virtually alike in the two cases (as the victim's behavior was the same in both cases). Male respondents, however, were harsher than females in the case of the rape of the social worker. They were substantially more lenient than were females in setting the penalty for the rape of the topless dancer.

How do we explain the male view that the rape of a social worker is far more serious (based on assigned penalties) than the rape of a topless dancer? It is submitted that male respondents may believe that there is greater social harm in raping a female of "high" sexual character than raping one of "low" character. That is, at least at the time of the study, males persisted in the traditional view that a female who is chaste is a more "valuable prize" than one thought to be promiscuous.[42] In contrast, female respondents focused on the victims' right to physical integrity and sexual autonomy, which interests are not impaired by the woman's sexual history.

[3]　Victim's Relationship to Rapist

Other factors affect attitudes regarding rape. For example, in one now-dated study of public attitudes, rape of a stranger was considered a significantly more serious offense than rape of an acquaintance.[43] Respondents treated the forcible rape of a stranger in a park as an extremely serious crime, even more serious than the assassination of a public official. On the other hand, the forcible rape of a neighbor, although still a serious offense, was considered less egregious. Both of these cases, however, were perceived as significantly more serious than the forcible rape of a former wife, the latter offense of which was considered only slightly more serious than "driving while drunk" and "practicing medicine without a license."[44]

This attitude is also seen in the original Model Penal Code rape provision, adopted in 1962, which treat rape as a lesser offense if the victim was a "voluntary social companion" of the perpetrator, who "previously permitted him sexual

---

[42] *See* Comment, *Forcible and Statutory Rape: An Exploration of the Operation and Objectives of the Consent Standard*, 62 Yale L.J. 55, 72 (1952) (suggesting that there exists "a masculine pride in the exclusive possession of a sexual object. The consent [of the female] . . . awards the man a privilege of bodily access, a personal 'prize' whose value is enhanced by sole ownership.") (footnotes deleted); United States v. Wiley, 492 F.2d 547, 555 (D.C. Cir. 1973) (Bazelon, J., concurring) (criticizing the view that penalties for rape "are high because a 'good' woman is a valued possession of a man").

[43] Peter H. Rossi et al., *The Seriousness of Crimes: Normative Structure and Individual Differences*, 39 Am. Soc. Rev. 224, 228–29 (1974).

[44] *Id.* An attitudinal study of college students, beginning law students, and students who had taken a course in criminal law, found that the victim's relationship to the rapist was much less important than in the study reported in the text. *See* Joshua Dressler et al., *Effect of Legal Education upon Perceptions of Crime Seriousness: A Response to* Rummel v. Estelle, 28 Wayne L. Rev. 1247 (1982). Students who had had a course in criminal law were least likely to consider this factor relevant.

liberties."[45] Modern social attitudes doubtlessly are undergoing change, however, as so-called "acquaintance rape" is increasingly condemned as a serious violation of the victim's trust.

§ 33.04 RAPE: *ACTUS REUS*

[A] In General

Generally speaking, sexual intercourse by a male, with a female not his wife, constitutes rape if it is committed: (1) forcibly; (2) by means of certain forms of deception; (3) while the female is asleep or unconscious; or (4) upon a female incompetent to give consent (*e.g.*, she is drugged, mentally disabled, or too young). The first two criteria are discussed below.

As previously noted,[46] rape law is undergoing dramatic change. To summarize the law is to shoot at a moving target or, perhaps, at 50 state moving targets. It is useful, therefore, to distinguish between what might be characterized as traditional rape law and the more expansive definitions of forcible rape developing in some jurisdictions.

[B] Forcible Rape

[1] Traditional Law

[a] Overview

The traditional rule is that a successful prosecution for forcible rape requires proof that the female did not consent to the intercourse *and* that the sexual intercourse was secured by force. That is, where there is lack of consent, but no showing of force, a forcible rape conviction is inappropriate.[47]

As explained more fully below, the traditional position is that nonconsensual intercourse is "forcible" only if the male uses or threatens to use force likely to cause serious bodily harm to the female (or, possibly, to a third person[48]), or if the male uses sufficient force to overcome the female's physical resistance to his actions.

Intercourse secured by a *non*-physical threat does not ordinarily constitute forcible rape. Thus, under traditional law, it is not "forcible rape" for an adult guardian to threaten to recommit a 14-year-old girl to a juvenile detention facility if she does not submit to his advances,[49] or for a high school principal to threaten

---

[45] Model Penal Code § 213.1(1).

[46] *See* § 33.01[B], *supra*.

[47] Commonwealth v. Berkowitz, 641 A.2d 1161, 1164 (Pa. 1994); State v. Alston, 312 S.E.2d 470 (N.C. 1984).

[48] Fitzpatrick v. State, 558 P.2d 630, 631 (Nev. 1977).

[49] Commonwealth v. Mlinarich, 542 A.2d 1335 (Pa. 1988) (evenly divided opinion).

not to allow a senior to graduate unless she has sex with him.[50]

[b]   Lack of Consent: Issues to Consider

Typically, the elements of nonconsent and force merge in a forcible rape prosecution. The male's use (or threatened use) of grave force proves both elements.[51] Nonetheless, the two concepts are distinct. A female may not want sexual intercourse — it is nonconsensual — but she may passively acquiesce to an act of penetration performed without undue force. If so, this does not constitute common law rape.

"Consent" (or "nonconsent") is a concept of considerable complexity.[52] "Consent" may be understood as an attitudinal, or internal (subjective), state of mind. For example, a female may, in her mind, want intercourse (thus, intercourse was "consensual" in this sense) or not want it ("nonconsensual"), but fail to manifest her wishes outwardly. Alternatively, "consent" may be an expressive (objective), or external, concept: It exists when permission is given verbally or by some other external act by the party (a literal or figurative "yes"); under this view, "consent" is absent when permission is actively refused (a "no" or physical resistance). Unfortunately, courts and legislatures rarely clarify which version of "consent" renders intercourse lawful.[53] And, even if "consent" is regarded as an expressive concept, there remains the issue of how the law should deal with silence. Should the legal onus be placed on the person who seeks intercourse to obtain affirmative permission, or on the other person to deny it? Inevitably, this is a policy question for legislative or judicial consideration.

Three other "consent" issues may be noted here. First, the attitudinal version of "consent" necessarily can result in miscalculation by the other party: He may honestly believe she wants intercourse when she does not, thereby raising *mens rea* issues.[54] The expressive form of consent is less ambiguous, but even here one cannot entirely avoid the questions of whether "no" always means "no"[55] and, if it does, how long the "no" applies.

---

[50] State v. Thompson, 792 P.2d 1103 (Mont. 1990), *overruled on other grounds*, State v. Spreadbury, 257 P.3d 392 (Mont. 2011).

[51] *See* People v. Denbo, 868 N.E.2d 347, 356 (Ill. App. Ct. 2007) ("By proving force, the State necessarily proves nonconsent.").

[52] *See especially* Peter Westen, *Some Common Confusions About Consent in Rape Cases*, 2 Ohio St. J. Crim. L. 333 (2004).

[53] *But see* State in the Interest of M.T.S., 609 A.2d 1266, 1277 (N.J. 1992) (interpreting "consent" to require proof of "affirmative and freely-given *permission* of the victim to the specific act of penetration") (emphasis added); Vt. Stat. Ann. tit. 13 § 3251(3) (2011) (defining "consent" as "words or actions by a person indicating a voluntary agreement to engage in a sexual act").

[54] *See* § 33.05, *infra.*

[55] *See* Charlene L. Muehlenhard & Lisa C. Hollabaugh, *Do Women Sometimes Say No When They Mean Yes? The Prevalence and Correlates of Women's Token Resistance to Sex*, 74 J. Personality & Soc. Psychol. 872 (1988) (finding that 39% of female respondents admitted putting up mild resistance although they intended to engage in intercourse); George C. Thomas III & David Edelman, *Consent to Have Sex: Empirical Evidence About "No,"* 61 U. Pitt. L. Rev. 579, 616 (2000) (concluding from 1992 and 1997 data that "remnants [] of the old view that women want sex more than they acknowledge" persists).

Second, "yes" may not always mean "yes" because consent, to be legally valid, must be voluntary; even if externalized, permission must be given freely. Unfortunately, the concept of voluntariness, or its antithesis of duress,[56] is largely a normative concept. In some sense all choices people make in life are "voluntary" (the woman who agrees to intercourse rather than be injured has in one sense rationally "chosen" intercourse), and likewise are "involuntary" (even in a loving relationship, the women may feel psychological pressure from the circumstances to have intercourse), so the line between consensual and nonconsensual intercourse at the outer edges can be little more than a normative line drawn to distinguish between pressures a person should, and should not, be expected to resist.

Third, even if voluntary consent is granted, it may be withdrawn. If the female withdraws consent before intercourse occurs — *mens rea* issues aside — the male is guilty of rape if he proceeds forcibly to have sexual intercourse. But, what if the female withdraws consent *after* penetration but while sexual intercourse is still underway? The traditional rule, apparently still adhered to in most jurisdictions,[57] is that post-penetration withdrawal of consent does not convert lawful intercourse into rape, even if the male uses force or threats of force after consent is withdrawn.[58] In such states, continued intercourse, although not rape, may constitute a lesser offense, such as a battery.

[c]   Force and Resistance

Traditionally, courts rarely needed to define the term "force" in rape prosecutions. If the perpetrator used or threatened to use extreme force — force likely to cause serious injury or death — the element of "force" was (and is) uncontroversially satisfied.

Moreover, if a male exerted only moderate force, the traditional rule was that a rape conviction would not stand unless it was proven at trial that the female resisted the male's unwanted overtures "and her resistance was overcome by force or . . . she was prevented from resisting by threats to her safety."[59] Thus, even if a sexual encounter did not begin forcibly, or began with only moderate use of force, the traditional resistance requirement imposed on the female the obligation to physically respond in a manner that demonstrated her lack of consent and caused the perpetrator, if he intended to persist, to use violence (or its threat) in order to overcome her will. It was the latter act by the perpetrator that satisfied the force

---

[56] *See* § 23.02[B], *supra.*

[57] *See generally* Michelle Oberman, *Two Truths and a Lie:* In re John Z. *and Other Stories at the Juncture of Teen Sex and the Law,* 38 Law & Soc. Inquiry 364 (2013); Matthew R. Lyon, Comment, *No Means No?: Withdrawal of Consent During Intercourse and the Continuing Evolution of the Definition of Rape,* 95 J. Crim. L. & Criminology 277, 291 (2004).

[58] This rule is breaking down. *E.g.,* People v. John Z., 60 P.3d 183 (Cal. 2003) (post-penetration withdrawal of consent nullifies earlier consent and subjects the male to forcible rape charges if he forcibly persists in what has become nonconsensual intercourse); State v. Siering, 644 A.2d 958 (Conn. App. Ct. 1994) (same); State v. Bunyard, 133 P.3d 14 (Kan. 2006) (same); State v. Robinson, 496 A.2d 1067 (Me. 1985) (same).

[59] Hazel v. State, 157 A.2d 922, 925 (Md. 1960).

element, if not already proven.[60]

The resistance requirement has been expressed in different ways. In the distant past, courts sometimes required the victim to resist "to the utmost." In its most extreme version, courts would state that the female must "follow the natural instinct of every proud female"[61] to resist the sexual attacker "until exhausted or overpowered,"[62] or to resist "the attack in every way possible and continue[] such resistance until she [is] overcome by force, [is] insensible through fright, or cease[s] resistance from exhaustion, fear of death or great bodily harm."[63] As discussed later in this chapter section, however, the resistance rule has been sharply criticized and does not hold sway to the extent that it once did.

[d] Threat of Force Versus Fear of Force

Forcible rape prosecutions may be based on a threat of serious force rather than its infliction. The threat may be manifested verbally or nonverbally (*e.g.*, waving a knife at the victim),[64] or reasonably implied from the circumstances.[65]

In order for a forcible rape charge to be upheld on the basis of "threat of force," it is not ordinarily enough for the prosecution to show, simply, that the female *feared* serious bodily injury if she resisted. *Fear* is a subjective emotion — a feeling in the mind of the victim — whereas a *threat* is an objective act emanating from another person. In general, both components — the female's subjective apprehension of serious harm, and some conduct by the male that places her in *reasonable* apprehension for her safety — are required.[66] Thus, no forcible rape occurs if a female accedes to intercourse with a male simply "because he is bigger than she is and she is afraid of him."[67] Some courts go further, however, and provide that a forcible rape prosecution is appropriate, even if the female's fears are unreasonable, if the male "*knowingly* takes advantage of that fear in order to accomplish sexual intercourse."[68]

---

[60] It follows that, traditionally, "the force inherent to all sexual penetration" is insufficient to constitute forcible rape. People v. Denbo, 868 N.E.2d 347, 355 (Ill. App. Ct. 2007). But see § 33.04[B][2][b], *infra*, to see how the definition of "force" is changing.

[61] State v. Rusk, 424 A.2d 720, 733 (Md. 1981) (Cole, J., dissenting).

[62] People v. Dohring, 59 N.Y. 374, 386 (1874).

[63] King v. State, 357 S.W.2d 42, 45 (Tenn. 1962).

[64] People v. Barnes, 721 P.2d 110, 122 (Cal. 1986).

[65] *E.g.*, if the perpetrator says, "I wouldn't resist if I were you."

[66] *See* People v. Iniguez, 872 P.2d 1183, 1188 (Cal. 1994).

[67] People v. Kinney, 691 N.E.2d 867, 870 (Ill. App. Ct. 1998) (dictum); Farrar v. United States, 275 F.2d 868, 876 (D.C. Cir. 1959) ("[F]ear, to be sufficient [to constitute rape], must be based upon something of substance . . . She must have a reasonable apprehension, as I understand the law, of something real; her fear must be not fanciful but substantial.") (Prettyman, C.J., concurring in denial of rehearing en banc).

[68] *People v. Barnes*, 721 P.2d at 122 n.20 (emphasis added); *see also* K.S.A. § 21-3502(1)(a) (2015) (defining rape as nonconsensual sexual intercourse, obtained by "force or *fear*") (emphasis added).

[e]   Cases Applying the Traditional Doctrine

The strictness of the traditional definition of forcible rape is evident by considering three cases.

State v. Alston[69] provides a classic example of pre-reform rape law: *A* and *V* had participated in an abusive relationship, in which *V* sometimes had sexual relations with *A* "just to accommodate" his violent demands. On those occasions, *V* "would stand still and remain entirely passive while [*A*] undressed her and had intercourse with her."

At the time of the incident, *V* was living with her mother because she wanted out of the relationship. *A* telephoned her and demanded that *V* return to him. The next day, *A* grabbed *V* in a parking lot, and warned that he would "fix" her face "so that her mother could see he was not playing." *A* escorted *V* to a friend's house where they had had sexual relations in the past. Inside, *A* asked her if she was "ready." *V* said that she did not want to have sex with him, but when *A* told her to lie down on a bed, she complied, after which *A* pushed apart her legs and had intercourse. *A* was convicted of forcible rape.

The appellate court overturned the conviction. It held that there was sufficient evidence that *V* had not consented to the intercourse, but there was no evidence that *A* "used force or threats to overcome the will of the victim *to resist the sexual intercourse.*" That is, in a remarkable "example of narrow time-framing and psychological naivete,"[70] the court discounted *V*'s reasonable fear of *A* that was based on his prior use of violence, and even ignored his specific threat to "fix" her face because it was not linked directly to a demand for sexual intercourse on the present occasion.

Consider now *Rusk v. State.*[71] *V* agreed to give *R*, a man she met at a bar,[72] a drive home. When they arrived, *R* invited *V* upstairs. When she refused, *R* took the keys from the ignition and asked, "Now will you come up?" *V* agreed: It was late at night; and, as she was in an unfamiliar neighborhood, she feared for her safety. Inside, *R* pulled her on the bed and began to remove her blouse. She took off the rest of her clothing when he asked her to do so. Throughout the process, *V* begged to be allowed to leave, and at one point, as he put his hands lightly on her throat, she asked *R*, "If I do what you want, will you let me go?" *R* said "yes," after which *V* "proceeded to do what he wanted me to do." *R* was convicted of forcible rape.

The Court of Special Appeals reversed *R*'s conviction. It applied traditional analysis to conclude that no forcible rape occurred: *V* did not physically resist *R*; nor did the evidence support the claim that she reasonably feared that, had she resisted, *R* would have seriously harmed her. This judgment was reversed, however, *i.e.*, the conviction was ultimately upheld, by the Court of Appeals, which

---

[69] 312 S.E.2d 470 (N.C. 1984).

[70] Dressler, Note 1, *supra*, at 418.

[71] 406 A.2d 624 (Md. Ct. Spec. App. 1979), *rev'd*, 424 A.2d 720 (Md. 1981).

[72] The Maryland Court of Special Appeals stated *V* was "bar hopping." *Rusk*, 406 A.2d at 625. As Judge Wilner in dissent suggested, the court may have intended by this language to suggest that *V* was "on the make." *Id.* at 633.

more sensibly — and somewhat less traditionally — held that the "reasonableness of [*V*'s] apprehension of fear [and, thus, her justification for not physically resisting] was plainly a question of fact for the jury to determine."

Finally, consider *Commonwealth v. Berkowitz*,[73] a case involving sexual intercourse between two college students in the defendant's (*B*'s) dormitory room. *V*, a friend of *B*'s roommate, came by to talk to the roommate, but he was not there. After some conversation between *V* and *B*, *B* asked *V* to give him a back rub. She refused. While *V* was sitting on the floor, *B* came over and "kind of pushed" *V* down. She described it as a "leaning-type of thing." On the floor, *B* straddled *V*, lifted up her shirt and bra, and began fondling *V*. At various times, *V* objected. *B* unsuccessfully attempted to put his penis in *V*'s mouth. Although *V* did not physically resist, she continued to say "no." *B* got off, locked the door (although it could be opened freely from the inside), and then put *V* on the bed ("kind of like a push"), straddled her, and had intercourse. *V* did not physically resist or cry out. *B* was convicted of forcible rape.

B's conviction was overturned. As in *Alston*, there was no consent, but "[i]n regard to the critical issue of forcible compulsion, [*V*'s] testimony [was] devoid of any statement which clearly or adequately describes the use of force or the threat of force against her."[74] As for *V*'s repeated "no's," the state supreme court stated that "while such an allegation of fact would be relevant to the issue of consent, it is not relevant to the issue of force."

These three cases provide the following lessons regarding the traditional rule in forcible rape cases. First, nonconsent and force are separate elements, each of which must be proved by the government. Second, in order to prove force, the female must physically resist the male (a verbal "no" will not do), who then overcomes her resistance, or the male must use or threaten force on the present occasion to an extent that would cause a reasonable female to fear grievous injury if she were to resist the sexual intercourse.

[2]　The Law in Transition[75]

[a]　　Resistance Requirement

As explained above,[76] the common law developed a resistance requirement in forcible rape cases. This resistance requirement has been sharply criticized by some modern courts and many scholars. First, "studies have demonstrated that

---

[73] 609 A.2d 1338 (Pa. Super. Ct. 1992), *aff'd*, 641 A.2d 1161 (Pa. 1994).

[74] *Berkowitz*, 641 A.2d at 1164.

[75] *See generally* Schulhofer, Unwanted Sex, Note 1, *supra*; Michelle J. Anderson, *Reviving Resistance in Rape Law*, 1998 U. Ill. L. Rev. 953; Vivian Berger, *Rape Law Reform at the Millennium: Remarks on Professor Bryden's Non-Millennial Approach*, 3 Buff. Crim. L. Rev. 513 (2000); Bryden, Note 1, *supra*; Dressler, Note 1, *supra*; Donald A. Dripps, *Beyond Rape: An Essay on the Difference Between the Presence of Force and the Absence of Consent*, 92 Colum. L. Rev. 1780 (1992); Lois Pineau, *Date Rape: A Feminist Analysis*, 8 Law & Phil. 217 (1989); Subotnik, Note 31, *supra*; Robin L. West, *Legitimating the Illegitimate: A Comment on Beyond Rape*, 93 Colum. L. Rev. 1442 (1993).

[76] *See* § 33.04[B][1][c], *supra*.

while some women respond to sexual assault with active resistance, others 'freeze'" and "become helpless from panic and numbing fear."[77] Indeed, some women 'do what they were taught to do as girls — to remain passive in the face of a rapist."[78] Therefore, whether out of fear or training, many females do not resist and, as a consequence, cannot have their attackers successfully prosecuted for forcible rape in jurisdictions strictly enforcing the resistance rule.

Second, resisting a rapist can prove dangerous. Although a female who resists a sexual assault may in some cases be less likely to be raped than one who takes no self-protective measures, substantial resistance increases the risk of aggravated injury to the female confronting a determined rapist. The would-be victim should not be compelled to enhance the risk to her safety in order to enhance the chances of a successful criminal prosecution of her attacker.

It is difficult to measure the extent to which the resistance rule is eroding. It has been written that "[t]he legal requirement that a woman strongly resist a man's sexual advances to prove that she was raped has largely disappeared from the statute books."[79] And, "[i]n recent decades, statutory reforms nominally have eroded the resistance requirement."[80] But, notice the careful words selected in the preceding quotations: The rule that a female "strongly resist" (what about lesser resistance?) has "largely disappeared" (but not entirely?) from "the statute books" (what about case law?); and legislative reform has "nominally eroded" the resistance rule.

A few jurisdictions by statute[81] or common law interpretation[82] have abolished the resistance requirement. Although many states seemingly retain the resistance requirement, the trend is to reduce the significance of the rule by lowering the barrier. Today, states seemingly no longer require a female to physically resist her attacker "to the utmost," but instead require only "earnest" resistance, or resistance sufficient "to establish that an act of sexual intercourse was without consent and by force,"[83] or resistance that is "reasonable" under the circumstances.[84] And, some courts, while retaining a resistance requirement, now state that verbal resistance — "no" or its equivalent — is sufficient.[85]

Even as courts and legislatures explicitly abolish or, more often, soften the resistance rule, a female's resistance — or lack thereof — remains relevant in rape

---

[77] People v. Barnes, 721 P.2d 110, 119 (Cal. 1986).

[78] Anderson, Note 75, *supra*, at 958.

[79] *Id.* at 953 (emphasis deleted) (syllabus to the article).

[80] Bryden, Note 1, *supra*, at 357.

[81] *E.g.*, Mich. Comp. Laws § 750.520i (2015) ("A victim need not resist the actor in prosecution [for rape].").

[82] *E.g.*, *People v. Barnes*, 721 P.2d at 121 ("This court therefore concludes that the Legislature's purposes in amending [the rape statute] were (1) to relieve the state of the need to establish resistance as a prerequisite to a rape conviction, and (2) to release rape complainants from the potentially dangerous burden of resisting an assailant in order to substantiate allegations of forcible rape.").

[83] Anderson, Note 75, *supra*, at 964.

[84] *See generally id.* at 962–68.

[85] *E.g.*, State v. Jones, 299 P.3d 219, 227 (Idaho 2013).

prosecutions. Consider a Pennsylvania statute that provides: "The alleged victim need not resist the actor in prosecutions under this chapter [on sexual offenses]: Provided, however, That nothing in this section shall be construed to prohibit a defendant from introducing evidence that the alleged victim consented to the conduct in question."[86] That is, although substantial resistance may no longer be an essential element in a rape prosecution, resistance retains evidentiary significance: Proof of the female's resistance may be critical in proving beyond a reasonable doubt that a rape has occurred (*i.e.*, that the intercourse was forcible and nonconsensual), and/or that the defendant was on reasonable notice of the female's lack of consent (*i.e.*, he possessed the requisite *mens rea*).

[b]   "Force": Changing Its Definition (or Abolishing the Requirement)

Consider the following judicial observation:

> [T]he fundamental wrong at which the law of rape is aimed is not the application of physical force that causes physical harm. Rather, the law of rape primarily guards the integrity of a woman's will and the privacy of her sexuality from an act of intercourse undertaken without her consent. Because the fundamental wrong is the violation of a woman's will and sexuality, the law of rape does not require that "force" cause physical harm. Rather, . . . "force" plays merely a supporting evidentiary role, as necessary only to insure an act of intercourse has been undertaken against a victim's will.[87]

This statement expresses the reformist position that a definition of rape that requires proof of force *and* lack of consent should be abandoned. If the social harm of a sexual assault is, primarily, the loss of a person's sexual and bodily autonomy, the only real issue should be whether the complainant (be that person a female or, modernly, male) desired intercourse. According to this view, just as resistance should no longer be an element of the offense — it should only be an evidentiary factor that helps determine whether there was lack of consent — so, too, a perpetrator's use of force should simply be one way of proving that the person did not consent.

Of course, legislatures can amend their rape statutes, as some have done, to define various forms of nonforcible intercourse as rape. Once they start down this path, the critical issues become: (a) Should all forms of nonconsensual intercourse be criminalized?; (b) How should "non-consent" be proved without re-instituting *sub silentio* the requirements of force and resistance?; and (c) Should some or all nonforcible forms of prohibited nonconsensual intercourse be graded as a lower degree of rape than the forcible variety?

In states that maintain the requirement of force, interpretive issues have arisen.

---

[86] 18 Pa. Cons. Stat. § 3107 (2015).

[87] People v. Cicero, 157 Cal. App. 3d 465, 475 (Ct. App. 1984); *see also* Regina v. Park, [1995] 2 S.C.R. 836, 839 ("The primary concern animating and underlying the present offence of sexual assault is the belief that women have an inherent right to exercise full control over their own bodies, and to engage only in sexual activity that they wish to engage in.").

At common law, "force" was largely defined in terms of the female's resistance, so definitions rarely were offered. As courts abolish or soften the "resistance" rule, it becomes necessary to define or redefine "force." Some courts have interpreted the term broadly to include minor physical acts[88] and/or *non*-physical forms of coercion.[89] Still other courts have left the term undefined and invited juries to resolve the issue of force without judicial assistance, or have defined "force" in a manner that essentially reads the element out of the statute, leaving only the requirement of nonconsent.

For example, in *People v. Griffin*,[90] the California Supreme Court stated that there is nothing "in the common usage definitions of the term 'force,' or in the express statutory language . . . that suggests force . . . actually means force '*substantially* different from or *substantially* greater than' the physical force normally inherent in an act of consensual sexual intercourse." As "force" has "a common usage meaning," *Griffin* holds, "there is no sua sponte duty to specially instruct the jury in a rape case on the definition of that term." Thus, in California, "the prosecution need only show the defendant used physical force of a degree sufficient to support a finding that the act of sexual intercourse was against the will of the [victim]."[91]

California arguably requires somewhat more force — just not *substantially* more force — than is inherent in the sexual act itself. But, the New Jersey Supreme Court ruled in *State in the Interest of M.T.S.*[92] that a person is guilty of "forcible" sexual assault if he commits an act of sexual penetration of another person in the absence of "affirmative" and "freely-given" permission, either express or implied, for the specific act of penetration. In short, without such permission, *any* force used, *even the force inherent in the sexual act itself*, justifies a forcible sexual assault prosecution. This means that, under *M.T.S.*, the complainant is not required to say "no" or physically resist in order that lawful sexual intercourse is legally converted into forcible rape. Indeed, a defendant cannot avoid conviction by seeking to show that the other person may have concurred in mind and spirit with having intercourse. "Consent" here must be manifested objectively — externally — in the form of freely given "permission." In short, a person commits forcible rape under *M.T.S.* if he (or she) has intercourse without securing a voluntary "yes" in words or action from the other person before proceeding with the specific act of penetra-

---

[88] *E.g.*, State v. Brown, 420 S.E.2d 147, 152 (N.C. 1992) (in a hospital setting, the court held that *B*'s "actions in pulling back the bedclothing, pulling up the victim's gown, and pulling her panties aside amounted to actual physical 'force' as that term is to be applied in sexual offense cases").

[89] *E.g.*, Commonwealth v. Rhodes, 510 A.2d 1217, 1226 (Pa. 1986) (interpreting the statutory term "forcible compulsion" to include "not only physical force or violence but also moral, psychological or intellectual force used to compel a person to engage in sexual intercourse against that person's will").; Dasher v. State, 636 S.E.2d 83 (Ga. Ct. App. 2006) (*D* impersonated a police officer and, by intimidation, coerced intercourse; held: *D*'s acts constituted "force"); Ex Parte Williford, 931 So. 2d 10 (Ala. 2005) (suggesting "force" is a relative term; the force required to constitute rape when the victim is a 14-year-old girl is less than with an adult).

[90] 94 P.3d 1089, 1094 (Cal. 2004).

[91] *Id.* (quoting People v. Young, 190 Cal. App. 3d 248, 257–58 (Ct. App. 1987)).

[92] 609 A.2d 1266 (N.J. 1992).

tion.[93]

M.T.S. is questionable as a matter of statutory construction,[94] but it is consistent with the underlying principle set out at the beginning of this subsection, namely, that the core purpose of modern rape law is to protect sexual autonomy. The underlying reasoning of *M.T.S.* seems to be this: If a person is not required to say "no" when a thief takes her property (a thief cannot successfully claim, "I had the right to take *V*'s unlocked car because she did not object when I entered her car and drove away"), then a person should not be required to object, even verbally, to another's sexual advances in order to render a subsequent sexual act of penetration criminally punishable.

As might be expected, *M.T.S.* has adherents and critics.[95] But, if the approach of *M.T.S.* is followed, a number of issues remain to be resolved. First, what conduct short of an express "yes" is sufficient to prove permission? In *M.T.S.*, two teenagers were involved in consensual "kissing and heavy petting," but the female did not give permission for the *specific* act of sexual penetration, and it was *this* failure that rendered the teenage boy's actions criminal. So, again, what *will* suffice short of express permission to have sexual intercourse? Presumably, physical acts that demonstrate a willingness to proceed (*e.g.*, moving into position for sexual penetration[96]) should satisfy a jury, but what else?

Second, as permission must be given freely, courts must determine what conduct renders permission tainted. For example, if a female consents to intercourse with her male employer in order to avoid a wrongful reduction in her salary, is this freely-given consent? Does it matter whether the salary reduction is substantial or trivial? Suppose that a female gives permission because he offers her a salary *raise* to which she would not otherwise be entitled? Various possible rules come to mind. First, the rule could be that permission is invalid if it is secured as the result of *any* illegal or tortious act by the male, regardless of whether it had a coercive effect on the other person. Second, the standard could be that permission is not "freely given" if it is the result of a *threat* or *offer* that would cause a person of reasonable firmness to grant permission. Third, the latter standard could apply but be limited to threats. As Professor Stephen Schulhofer has observed, *M.T.S.* does not ultimately resolve the problem of "identifying the boundary between autonomy and compulsion, between free choice and coerced consent. The innovative New Jersey test, though seemingly straightforward, obscures the problem rather than addressing it."[97]

---

[93] *Accord* State v. Sedia, 614 So. 2d 533, 535 (Fla. Dist. Ct. App. 1993).

[94] The statute requires proof of "force or coercion"; "lack of consent" is not an express element. The practical effect of the case, however, is to delete "force or coercion" from the statute, and to replace it with an "affirmative permission" requirement.

[95] *E.g.*, Schulhofer, Unwanted Sex, Note 1, *supra*, at 94–98 (stating it offers clear benefits, but with reservations); Dressler, Note 1, *supra*, at 422–30 (somewhat critical).

[96] Notice, however, that such evidence may prove highly embarrassing to the complainant, which may make some rape victims unwilling to proceed to trial, thereby undermining one of the goals of rape reform legislation.

[97] Schulhofer, Unwanted Sex, Note 1, *supra*, at 97–98.

[C] Fraud[98]

At common law, a seducer is not a rapist.[99] That is, a male may use any nonforcible "sales technique," no matter how deceptive, to obtain the consent of a female to have sexual intercourse, and escape criminal punishment as a rapist.[100] It would not constitute common law rape, for example, for a George Clooney look-alike, to induce star-struck *V* to have sexual intercourse with him by claiming to be the actor. Likewise, it is not common law rape for *D* to pay for intercourse with a prostitute with counterfeit money, or for a doctor to induce a woman to have intercourse with him by falsely claiming that it will cure her of an illness.[101] Each of these examples have one fact in common — the victim knew that she was consenting to sexual intercourse. The fraud was in the *inducement* to have intercourse. Because fraud-in-the-inducement does not vitiate consent under the common law, the law treats the intercourse as consensual.

In contrast, a female's consent to engage in sexual intercourse is invalid if, as a result of fraud, she is unaware that she has consented to the act of sexual intercourse itself. This is "fraud in the factum," as distinguished from "fraud in the inducement." For example, *D*, a physician, is guilty of rape if he obtains permission from *V*, his patient, to "insert an instrument" in her vagina while she is under anaesthesia, if the "instrument" used is his penis.[102]

Courts have struggled with the question of how to deal with one particular fact pattern — a male who engages in sexual intercourse by deceiving the female into believing that he is her husband. For example, is it rape if *D* enters *V*'s bed at night in the dark and knowingly exploits the fact that *V* believes that he is her husband. Some early English cases treated this as fraud-in-the-inducement (and, thus, not rape), since the victim knew that she was consenting to sexual intercourse.[103] Other courts have treated this deception as fraud-in-the-factum (and, therefore, rape), on the ground that the attendant circumstance that the male was not the female's husband is a fundamental aspect of the sexual act itself.[104]

---

[98] *See generally* Patricia J. Falk, *Rape by Fraud and Rape by Coercion*, 64 Brook. L. Rev. 39 (1998).

[99] People v. Evans, 379 N.Y.S.2d 912, 919 (App. Div. 1975).

[100] Obtaining sexual intercourse by fraudulent inducement may constitute an offense less serious than rape. *E.g.*, Cal. Penal Code § 266 (2015) (procuring female for illicit intercourse by false pretenses; punishable by incarceration not exceeding one year).

[101] *See* Boro v. Superior Court, 163 Cal. App. 3d 1224 (Ct. App. 1985) (*B* falsely claimed to *V* that he was a doctor, that she had contracted a dangerous, perhaps fatal, disease, and that the only way to treat the disease was through surgery or sexual intercourse with an anonymous donor injected with a serum; *V* agreed to the latter "cure"; *B* had sexual intercourse with *V*; held: rape conviction overturned).

[102] *See* Pomeroy v. State, 94 Ind. 96 (1883).

[103] *E.g.*, Regina v. Barrow, 11 Cox Crim. Cas. 191 (1868).

[104] Regina v. Dee, 15 Cox Crim. Cas. 579 (1884). Arguably the same rule should apply if the defendant impersonates an intimate sexual partner, even if they are not married. Schulhofer, Unwanted Sex, Note 1, *supra*, at 284; R. v. Elbekkay, [1995] Crim. L. R. 163 (impersonation of *V*'s boyfriend to secure intercourse constitutes rape). Not all courts agree. Suliveres v. Commonwealth, 865 N.E.2d 1086 (Mass. 2007) (*D* entered *V*'s bedroom at night and impersonated her long-time boyfriend, *D*'s brother; held: this was fraud in the inducement and, therefore, not rape).

If the law of rape is meant to protect a woman's sexual autonomy, should fraud-in-the-inducement vitiate consent? The question poses difficult matters of line-drawing and policy. For example, if fraud converts every induced act of sexual intercourse into rape, a male could be subject to prosecution if he falsely claimed love or promised marriage in order to secure the female's consent to intercourse. Prosecutions in such circumstances would result in problems of proof and could expend finite judicial resources to deal with failed relationships. Quite arguably, the law should not require a person who ends a relationship to bear the risk of a felony rape prosecution in such circumstances.

On the other hand, what if a man fraudulently claims that he is sterile,[105] or what if he fails to disclose that he has a communicable disease,[106] in order to secure consent to intercourse? Some argue that cases of this sort should be resolved, as they now are, in tort actions; and, when the physical harm resulting from fraud is substantial, a prosecution for aggravated battery, reckless endangerment, or even attempted murder, might be provable. The contrary claim is that these prosecutions do not directly redress the victim's interest in sexual autonomy. If fraud in a business context can result in a theft prosecution, the argument proceeds, fraud in this context should result in a sexual assault prosecution.

§ 33.05 RAPE: *MENS REA*[107]

Rape is ordinarily denominated as a general-intent offense in non-Model Penal Code jurisdictions.[108] As such, a defendant need not possess an intention that sexual intercourse be nonconsensual.[109] It is enough that he possessed a morally blame-worthy state of mind regarding the female's lack of consent. Therefore, the general rule is that a person is not guilty of rape if he entertained a genuine *and reasonable* belief that the female voluntarily consented to intercourse with him.[110] This rule

---

[105] *E.g.*, Barbara A. v. John G., 145 Cal. App. 3d 369 (Ct. App. 1983) (battery and deceit action, in tort, resulting from pregnancy based on the defendant's claim of sterility).

[106] Kathleen K. v. Robert B., 150 Cal. App. 3d 992 (Ct. App. 1984) (civil suit, based on defendant's false claim that he did not have a venereal disease); R. v. Cuerrier, [1998] 162 D.L.R.4th 513 (Can.) (Canadian Supreme Court: *C* may be prosecuted for aggravated assault for having unprotected sexual relations, knowing he was HIV-positive, and without disclosing this fact to *V*).

[107] *See generally* I. Bennett Capers, *The Unintentional Rapist*, 87 Wash. U. L. Rev. 1345 (2010); Rosanna Cavallaro, *A Big Mistake: Eroding the Defense of Mistake of Fact About Consent in Rape*, 86 J. Crim. L. & Criminology 815 (1996); Robin Charlow, *Bad Acts in Search of a Mens Rea: Anatomy of a Rape*, 71 Fordham L. Rev. 263 (2002); R.A. Duff, *Recklessness and Rape*, 3 Liverpool L. Rev. 49 (1981); Douglas N. Husak & George C. Thomas III, *Date Rape, Social Convention, and Reasonable Mistakes*, 11 Law & Phil. 95 (1992).

[108] State v. Ayer, 612 A.2d 923, 925 (N.H. 1992) ("[r]ape . . . is held by the overwhelming weight of authority to be a general intent, rather than a specific intent, crime"); *e.g.*, Steve v. State, 875 P.2d 110, 115 (Alaska Ct. App. 1994); State v. Cantrell, 673 P.2d 1147, 1154 (Kan. 1983).

[109] Commonwealth v. Grant, 464 N.E.2d 33, 36 (Mass. 1984).

[110] *E.g.*, People v. Hall, 174 Cal. App. 4th 1367, 1380 (Ct. App. 2009); State v. Smith, 554 A.2d 713, 717 (Conn. 1989); State in the Interest of M.T.S., 609 A.2d 1266, 1279 (N.J. 1992) ("[T]he State must demonstrate either that defendant did not actually believe that affirmative permission had been freely-given or that such a belief was unreasonable under all of the circumstances"); United States v. Everett, 41 M.J. 847, 852 (A.F.C.M.R. 1994).

conforms with ordinary common law mistake-of-fact principles relating to general-intent offenses.[111]

In recent years, some American jurisdictions have ruled that even a defendant's *reasonable* mistake of fact regarding the female's lack of consent is *not* a 'defense."[112] In contrast, in England, the defendant's honest but *unreasonable* mistake of fact *does* exculpate if he was not reckless in his belief.[113]

It is submitted that the American trend is disquieting. In traditional forcible rape cases, the issue of *mens rea* rarely arises. A male of normal intelligence who uses or threatens force likely to cause serious bodily injury will almost always know that the female is not consenting, so his culpability is obvious. Furthermore, if the female resists her assailant, her lack of consent is even more clearly demonstrated. But, with the expansion of rape law to include intercourse secured in the absence of grave force or resistance — indeed, in some jurisdictions, on the basis of only such force as is inherent in the act of penetration[114] — the issue of *mens rea* becomes more critical. If a male *genuinely and reasonably* believes that the female is consenting, then he is acting without moral culpability. The effect of dispensing with the reasonable-mistake-of-fact doctrine is, effectively, to convert rape, a felony carrying very severe penalties, into a strict liability offense.[115]

Even in states that permit a reasonable-mistake-of-fact "defense," some courts are increasingly hesitant to authorize jury instructions in this regard. The California Supreme Court, for example, has ruled that a "reasonable mistake" instruction should not be given in a criminal case unless there is "substantial evidence of equivocal conduct [on the female's part] that would have led a defendant to reasonably and in good faith believe consent existed where it did not."[116] According to this rule, where there is an evidentiary chasm — the defendant says she consented, whereas the female claims a forcible rape occurred, and no evidence is introduced of equivocal conduct by the female that the defendant could have mistaken for consent — a mistake-of-fact instruction is inappropriate.

---

[111] *See* § 12.03[D], *supra.*

[112] Commonwealth v. Lopez, 745 N.E.2d 961 (Mass. 2001); Clifton v. Commonwealth, 468 S.E.2d 155, 158 (Va. Ct. App. 1996); *see* Commonwealth v. Williams, 439 A.2d 765, 769 (Pa. Super. Ct. 1980); *see* Charlow, Note 107, *supra*, at 281 n.68 (providing further citations). At least under traditional rape law, nonconsent is an element of the offense, rather than that consent is an affirmative defense.

[113] Regina v. Morgan, [1976] A.C. 182; *see* Sexual Offenses (Amendment) Act of 1976 (permitting conviction on the basis of knowledge or recklessness as to the victim's lack of consent). *See* § 12.03[D][4], *supra.*

[114] *See* § 33.04[B][2][b], *supra.*

[115] One court has defended the no-defense rule by arguing that "proof of rape requires proof of intent, . . . [namely,] proof that the accused knowingly and intentionally committed the acts constituting the elements of rape." *Clifton v. Commonwealth*, 468 S.E.2d at 158. But, of course, the act in question — sexual intercourse — is not a wrongful act in itself, nor is knowingly and intentionally having intercourse in itself the crime of rape. The "act" that is wrongful is the *nonconsensual* act of intercourse. When the defendant reasonably believes that the other person consented, he is not committing the "act" of rape knowingly and intelligently.

[116] People v. Williams, 841 P.2d 961, 966 (Cal. 1992); *see also* R. v. Park, [1995] 2 S.C.R. 836 (there must be an "air of reality" to the mistake claim).

§ 33.06   MARITAL IMMUNITY RULE[117]

[A]   The Immunity and Its Rationales

[1]   Rule

In 1736, Sir Matthew Hale stated that a "husband cannot be guilty of rape committed by himself upon his lawful wife."[118] He cited no authority for this proposition as, indeed, there was none.[119] Nonetheless, the so-called marital immunity rule became a part of Anglo-American common law, and was adopted by most American legislatures as part of the original definition of rape.

[2]   Rationales

[a]   Consent/Property Rationale

According to Hale, "by their matrimonial consent and contract the wife hath given up herself in this kind unto her husband, which she cannot retract."[120] However, the concept of irrevocable consent by the wife makes no sense in modern times, if it ever did. The general understanding of marital partners today is that each person consents generally to have sexual intercourse with the other, subject to the right of either to refuse on particular occasions. Moreover, if a husband uses force to secure intercourse with his wife, he is subject to prosecution for assault or battery; the principle of consent does not carry over to *these* offenses, so there is no reason why consent should be assumed in the rape context.

The more accurate explanation of the common law marital immunity rule is that the wife was the virtual property of the husband.[121] She was "incorporated and consolidated into that of the husband."[122] Therefore, the husband possessed an unlimited right of sexual access to her. As this archaic reasoning is just that — archaic — it cannot sustain the marital immunity rule today.

[b]   Protection of the Marriage

Defenders of the marital immunity rule sometimes argue that it is needed to protect "against governmental intrusion into marital privacy," and to promote "reconciliation of the spouses."[123]

---

[117] *See generally* Michelle J. Anderson, *Marital Immunity, Intimate Relationships, and Improper Inferences: A New Law on Sexual Offenses by Intimates*, 54 Hastings L.J. 1465 (2003); Jill Elaine Hasday, *Contest and Consent: A Legal History of Marital Rape*, 88 Cal. L. Rev. 1373 (2000).

[118] 1 Hale, Note 2, *supra*, at *629.

[119] Regina v. R., [1991] 4 All E.R. 481, 483 ("There is no similar statement in the works of any earlier English commentator.").

[120] 1 Hale, Note 2, *supra*, at *629.

[121] American Law Institute, Comment to § 213.1, at 343.

[122] 4 Blackstone, Note 3, *supra*, at *430.

[123] People v. Liberta, 474 N.E.2d 567, 574 (N.Y. 1984) (rejecting the argument).

This argument vastly overstates the case for the immunity. If a husband's use of force to have intercourse with his wife is an isolated act in an otherwise salvageable marriage, it is unlikely that the wife would seek a rape prosecution of her husband. On the other hand, if the husband is guilty of ongoing physical or sexual abuse, the marriage presumably is not worth saving; at the least, it should be the woman's decision whether to try to preserve it or, instead, seek prosecution. Beyond this, the interest in protecting the safety of the woman certainly outweighs the privacy concern.

[c] Protection of the Husband in Divorce Proceedings

Some advocates of the marital exemption rule assert that if a husband could be prosecuted for rape of his wife, she might use this threat as leverage in property settlement negotiations in divorce proceedings.

This argument is unpersuasive. There is no reason to believe that a woman's ability to take unfair advantage of her husband would be significantly heightened by the repeal of the marital immunity rule. Even in jurisdictions that apply the exemption, a husband may be prosecuted for assault or battery if he uses force to secure intercourse; therefore, a wife could always use the threat of prosecution for these offenses as leverage. Beyond this, it is odd at best for the law to take sides with a wrongdoer against his victim on the unproven assumption that the victims, as a group, will behave improperly in civil proceedings.

[d] Less Serious Harm

Some advocates of the marital immunity doctrine contend that the existence of the marital relationship "is not irrelevant to the concerns of the law of rape."[124] They reason that an important aspect of the harm of rape is the degradation of the woman that results from forcing her to have sexual intimacy with someone with whom she does not wish such a relationship. Although a female's sexual autonomy, as a male's, should include the right to refuse sexual relations on any given occasion, the marital relationship arguably implies a *general* willingness — indeed, desire — by the parties to have intercourse with each other. When intercourse is coerced on a given occasion in the marital relationship, the argument proceeds, the wife's autonomy is less seriously violated than if the perpetrator were a stranger or someone with whom the victim had not indicated a general willingness to have sexual relations.

This argument has the aroma of plausibility in the case of nonforcible rape. Nonetheless, there are important reasons for treating nonconsensual sexual intercourse in the marital bedroom as a form of rape. Even in the marriage context, rape causes harm not protected by the laws of assault and battery. Spousal rape impairs the wife's sexual autonomy; and, particularly if the husband's conduct is ongoing, the sex act by the husband becomes a means of subordinating the wife within the marital relationship. Spousal rape is also a violation of the trust and mutual respect implicit in the marital union. These special violations should be

---

[124] American Law Institute, Comment to § 213.1, at 344.

denounced by the law, and the offense of rape is better suited to do this than the laws of assault and battery.

[B] Breakdown of the Rule

The marital immunity rule was judicially abolished in England in 1991.[125]

The law in the United States is in transition. According to one fairly recent survey,[126] 24 states (and the District of Columbia) abolished the rule for all sexual offenses. Among the remaining states, some jurisdictions have abolished marital immunity for the specific offense of forcible rape, while retaining immunity for other sexual offenses, such as intercourse with a mentally or physically helpless spouse, as well as with lesser forms of nonconsensual sexual contact. Often, however, when there is a marital immunity rule, it does not apply if the parties are legally separated or living apart at the time of the rape.[127]

§ 33.07 PROVING RAPE AT TRIAL

[A] Corroboration Rule and Cautionary Jury Instructions[128]

At common law, the testimony of the complainant — the alleged rape victim — was sufficient to uphold a conviction for rape; her testimony did not need to be corroborated.[129] However, a minority of states, by statute or case law, instituted a corroboration requirement. This rule provided that a defendant could not be convicted of rape (or, often, of any other sexual offense) upon the uncorroborated testimony of the alleged victim. The prosecution had to produce corroborative evidence, such as the complainant's bruises, broken bones, or torn clothing, or an eyewitness to the sexual assault.

The corroboration requirement was the result of "legitimate concerns, out-dated beliefs, and deep-seated prejudices."[130] Defenders of the rule believed that there is a higher risk of conviction of an innocent person in the prosecution of a sex offense than in the prosecution of other crimes. Lord Hale asserted that rape "is an accusation easily to be made and hard to be proved, and harder to be defended by the party accused, though never so innocent."[131] Indeed, these words or a paraphrase of them formed the basis of a cautionary jury instruction at one time in over half of the states.[132]

---

[125] Regina v. R., [1991] 4 All E.R. 481.

[126] Anderson, Note 117, *supra*, at 1468–73, 1486–89 (and citations therein).

[127] *Id.* at 1494–95.

[128] *See generally* Denise R. Johnson, *Prior False Allegations of Rape: Falso in Uno, Falsus in Omnibus?*, 7 Yale J.L. & Feminism 243 (1995); Note, *The Rape Corroboration Requirement: Repeal Not Reform*, 81 Yale L.J. 1365 (1972).

[129] American Law Institute, Comment to § 213.6, at 422; State v. Matlock, 660 P.2d 945, 946 (Kan. 1983).

[130] United States v. Wiley, 492 F.2d 547, 552 (D.C. Cir. 1973) (Bazelon, J., concurring).

[131] 1 Hale, Note 2, *supra*, at *635.

[132] A. Thomas Morris, Note, *The Empirical, Historical and Legal Case Against the Cautionary*

Why would some lawmakers have believed that conviction of an innocent person is more likely in a rape case than, for example, a robbery? One reason given was a particularly bizarre one: The testimony of women in rape prosecutions was particularly suspect because, it was said, some women fantasize being raped and, therefore, genuinely come to believe that they were raped, when in fact the sexual contact was consensual.[133]

Other advocates of the corroboration rule asserted that women have a strong motive to "cry rape" falsely. Traditionally, females were expected to avoid sexual relations until marriage; those who violated this moral code were subject to embarrassment, stigmatization, and even ostracism. Therefore, an unmarried female who had sexual intercourse or, more significantly, became pregnant, had an incentive to allege that she was raped, rather than to admit that she had consented to sexual intimacy.

There was also a legitimate concern for the accused founded on the realities of societal racism.[134] Historically, society disapproved of interracial sexual relations. A racist stereotype was that black men were prone to rape white women. A white woman who was known or suspected to have had sexual relations with an African-American male, therefore, was under substantial social pressure to falsely claim that she was raped. The corroboration requirement reduced the risk of racist-motivated convictions.

Opponents of the corroboration rule point out that Lord Hale's "comment does not reflect contemporary thought or experience."[135] The premise that women commonly fantasize rape is unfounded, and the other concerns are overstated or are outdated. For example, today's society is tolerant of premarital sexual activity, so that women have less reason to falsely claim rape. Finally, in light of the stigma attached to the crime of rape, and embarrassment that rape victims often suffer in the legal system, there is little reason to believe that false claims of rape occur often enough to justify a special corroboration requirement.

Opponents of the corroboration rule have won the day. Only two states retain the rule in rape prosecutions, and even then only in exceedingly limited circumstances.[136] And, only eight states require a cautionary jury instruction, and then only if there was no corroboration of the alleged sexual assault.[137]

Instruction: A Call for Legislative Reform, 1988 Duke L.J. 154, 156.

[133] American Law Institute, Comment to § 213.6, at 426–27; *see* Brownmiller, Note 1, *supra*, 319–33 (describing this attitude); Comment, *Forcible and Statutory Rape: An Exploration of the Operation and Objectives of the Consent Standard*, 62 Yale L.J. 55, 66 (1952) ("Many women . . . require as a part of preliminary 'love play' aggressive overtures by the man. . . . [T]heir erotic pleasure . . . depend[s] upon an accompanying physical struggle."). A more accurate psychological view is that men fantasize that women fantasize being raped.

[134] *See generally* Capers, Note 107, *supra*.

[135] State v. Bashaw, 672 P.2d 48, 49 (Or. 1983).

[136] N.Y. Penal Law § 130.16 (2013) (only requiring corroboration when non-consent is exclusively based on the complainant's mental incapacity to consent);. Tex. C.C.P. art. 38.07(a) (2015) (corroboration is only required if the complainant failed to inform another of the alleged rape within one year of its alleged occurrence).

[137] Michelle J. Anderson, *The Legacy of the Prompt Complaint Requirement, Corroboration*

[B] Rape-Shield Statutes[138]

In a criminal trial, two basic principles determine the admissibility of proffered evidence. First, no evidence is admissible unless it is relevant. Second, subject to limited exceptions, relevant evidence is admissible. Evidence is relevant if it has the tendency to prove or disprove any disputed fact at issue, including the credibility of a witness. However, a judge has discretion to exclude relevant evidence if its probative value — its relevance — is outweighed by the risk that it will cause undue prejudice to an opposing party.

In rape trials, defense attorneys have traditionally sought to introduce evidence relating to the alleged rape victim's sexual history and moral character. Specifically, three classes of evidence regarding the complainant have been proffered: (1) her prior consensual sexual acts with the accused; (2) her prior consensual sexual acts with persons other than the accused; and (3) her reputation for lack of chastity.

The first category of evidence has always been admissible if the defendant contends that the female consented to sexual intercourse with him on the present occasion. Thus, if *V* claims that she was raped by *D* on January 15, it is relevant to the issue of guilt that she consented to sexual relations with *D* on prior dates. Of course, the fact that she consented on one day does not necessarily mean that she consented on another day; nonetheless, the evidence is of some relevance in determining whether *V* consented on the day in dispute, and it is relevant in determining *D*'s *mens rea* as to *V*'s alleged consent. Therefore, the jury is entitled to consider the fact of their prior consensual sexual relations, and to give the evidence as much (or little) weight as it believes is justified. This remains the rule today.

The other two categories of evidence have always been problematic. In the past, however, many states permitted testimony regarding the complainant's prior sexual history with other men and/or her reputation for lack of chastity as substantive evidence relevant to the issue of her consent to intercourse with the accused. The traditional justification for this rule was that "no court can overrule the law of human nature, which declares that one who has already started on the road of [sexual unchastity], would be less reluctant to pursue her way, than another who yet remains at her home of innocence, and looks upon such a [pursuit] . . . with horror."[139] Such evidence was also admissible in the past to impeach the female's credibility, apparently on the peculiar ground that there is a connection between "sexual immorality" and lack of veracity. The practical effect of these rules of evidence was to put the complaining witness on trial along with the defendant.

Requirement, and Cautionary Instructions on Campus Sexual Assault, 84 B.U. L. Rev. 945, 950 (2004).

[138] *See generally* Ann Althouse, *Thelma and Louise and the Law: Do Rape Shield Rules Matter?*, 25 Loy. L.A. L. Rev. 757 (1992); I. Bennett Capers, *Real Women, Real Rape*, 60 UCLA L. Rev. 826 (2013); Elizabeth J. Kramer, *When Men Are Victims: Applying Rape Shield Laws to Male Same-Sex Rape*, 73 N.Y.U. L. Rev. 293 (1998); Cassia Spohn & Julie Horney, *"The Law's the Law, but Fair Is Fair:" Rape Shield Laws and Officials' Assessments of Sexual History Evidence*, 29 Criminology 137 (1991).

[139] People v. Abbot, 19 Wend. 192, 196 (N.Y. 1838).

In the past few decades, however, "rape-shield" laws have been enacted throughout the United States. Although the statutes vary, these laws generally deny a defendant in a rape case the opportunity, absent good cause to the contrary, to cross-examine the complainant, or to offer extrinsic evidence, concerning her prior sexual conduct with persons other than the defendant, or her reputation for chastity. Rape-shield laws are founded on the view that "[c]onsent to engage in sexual activity with one person does not, without more, give rise to a reasonable claim that consent is more likely with another,"[140] and that such sexual activity provides no reason to believe that the woman is less truthful than a "chaste" female. Rape-shield laws also make it more difficult for a defense lawyer to humiliate the accuser in the courtroom, with the resulting hope that such statutes will increase the likelihood that rapes will be reported to the police.

Although rape-shield laws reduce the risk of prejudice to rape victims, they also increase the risk that an accused person might be denied the opportunity to introduce evidence that would demonstrate his innocence. In an extreme case, enforcement of a rape-shield law may conflict with the Constitution. Specifically, the Sixth Amendment provides that a defendant is entitled to confront and cross-examine his accuser (in this case, the alleged victim of the rape), as well as to present evidence in his own behalf. However, these constitutional rights are not absolute, and courts have resorted to a balancing test, in which the weighty interests of a rape-shield law are balanced against the defendant's need to introduce the "shielded" evidence in the specific case.

For example, in *State v. Colbath*,[141] C and V were in a tavern. V directed "sexually provocative statements" toward C as well as other customers. While in the bar, V also allowed C to feel her breasts and buttocks, and she rubbed C's penis. Later, the two left the bar together and went to C's trailer, where they had sexual intercourse. When C's live-in companion unexpectedly arrived, she assaulted V. V sought to explain the situation on the ground that C had raped her. In support of C's claim that the sexual acts were consensual, C unsuccessfully sought at trial to introduce evidence of V's public sexual behavior with other men in the tavern on the day of the incident, including the fact that she had left the bar with other men in the hours immediately preceding her actions with C.

The court held that the rape-shield law had to give way in this case to the defendant's constitutional rights to confront the witnesses against him and to present his own exculpatory evidence. The court emphasized that the evidence involved public acts by V: "[E]vidence of public displays of general interest in sexual activity can be taken to indicate a contemporaneous receptiveness to sexual advances that cannot be inferred from evidence of private behavior with chosen sex partners." The court stated that the evidence C sought to introduce was more than "merely . . . relevant." Instead, it strongly supported C's claim that V had made a false accusation, in light of the "undignified predicament" in which she found herself when she was discovered by C's live-in companion.

---

[140] United States v. Lauture, 46 M.J. 794, 800 (A. Ct. Crim. App. 1997).

[141] 540 A.2d 1212 (N.H. 1988).

Although *Colbath* does not stand alone,[142] rulings of this sort are uncommon absent special facts.[143] In general, courts have ruled that "the probativeness of the [defendant's proffered] evidence is so minuscule when weighed against the potential prejudice to the complaining witness that . . . the sixth amendment rights must bend to protect the innocent victims."[144]

§ 33.08 MODEL PENAL CODE

[A] Sex Offenses, In General

Article 213 of the Model Penal Code sets out the sexual offenses recognized under the Code: rape; gross sexual imposition; deviate sexual intercourse; corruption of minors; sexual assault; and indecent exposure. Only rape, deviate sexual intercourse, and some forms of corruption of minors constitute felony offenses. Consensual sexual conduct between adults is not prohibited.

The offenses of rape and gross sexual imposition are summarized here. However, because the provisions are outdated in view of modern attitudes, the Code's approach to these offenses has been followed in whole or in part by only a few states.[145] As a result, the American Law Institute is working to redraft new provisions, which are discussed briefly in subsection [E] below.

[B] Rape

[1] In General

Under the MPC, as adopted in 1962, a male is guilty of rape if, acting purposely, knowingly, or recklessly regarding each of the material elements of the offense, he has sexual intercourse with a female under any of the following circumstances: (1)

---

[142] *E.g.*, State v. Perez, 995 P.2d 372 (Kan. Ct. App. 1999) (holding that *P* was permitted to introduce evidence that *V* had engaged in sexual intercourse with two other men in full view of *P* and others at a party hours earlier); Gagne v. Booker, 596 F.3d 335 (6th Cir. 2010) (in a prosecution of two men for allegedly raping the accuser, the court ruled, 2-1, that the judge could not constitutionally bar the defendant's proffered evidence that the accuser had had consensual "threesome" sex with others before).

[143] In a case somewhat similar to *Colbath*, the rape-shield law prevailed. In People v. Wilhelm, 476 N.W.2d 753 (Mich. Ct. App. 1991), *W* and *V* were at a bar, although not together. *W* wished to introduce evidence at the trial that he saw *V* expose her breasts to two men sitting at her table, and that she permitted one of them to fondle her breasts. Another witness also observed the activity. However, the court upheld the trial court's exclusion of this evidence. It stated that "we fail to see how a woman's consensual sexual conduct with another in public indicates to third parties that the woman would engage in similar behavior with them." *Id.* at 759. The court distinguished *Colbath* on the ground that the woman in that case had left the bar with various men during the afternoon in question, and that the beating she received from *C*'s girlfriend provided a motive for fabrication.

See also State v. Thompson, 884 P.2d 574 (Or. Ct. App. 1994) (*T* claimed he had consensual intercourse with *V* in exchange for drugs; held: evidence that *V* had previously offered other men sex in exchange for drugs was inadmissible under the rape-shield statute).

[144] State v. Herndon, 426 N.W.2d 347, 361 (Wis. Ct. App. 1988), *overruled on other grounds*, State v. Pulizzano, 456 N.W.2d 325 (Wis. 1990).

[145] American Law Institute, Comment to § 213.1, at 299.

the female is less than 10 years of age;[146] (2) the female is unconscious; (3) he compels the female to submit by force or by threatening her or another person with imminent death, grievous bodily harm, extreme pain or kidnapping; or (4) he administers or employs drugs or intoxicants in a manner that substantially impairs the female's ability to appraise or control her conduct.[147] The Code recognizes a partial marital exemption: The preceding conduct does *not* constitute rape if the female is his spouse, unless the parties are living apart under a formal decree of separation. Moreover, the immunity extends to persons "living as man and wife," although they are not formally married.[148]

Rape is characterized as a felony of the first degree (and, thus, graded as seriously as murder) in either of two circumstances: (1) the defendant inflicted serious bodily injury upon the female or another in the course of the rape; or (2) the female was *not* a "voluntary social companion" who had "previously permitted him sexual liberties." In all other circumstances, the offense is a felony of the second degree.

[2] Comparison to Common Law

The Code's treatment of rape is quite traditional in various regards. First, it is gender-specific, *i.e.*, legally only males can commit the offense, and only females are victims. Second, the Code affirms the general principle that nonconsensual intercourse with a spouse is not rape.

The Code differs from the common law in various respects. First, the term "sexual intercourse" is defined broadly to include genital, oral, and anal sexual penetration by the male of the female.[149]

Second, rape is defined in terms of the male's acts of aggression or overreaching, rather than in the negative terms of the female's lack of consent. The drafters favored this approach because "[t]he deceptively simple notion of consent may obscure a tangled mesh of psychological complexity, ambiguous communication, and unconscious restructuring of the event by the participants."[150] By shifting the focus to the male's conduct, the drafters of the Code sought to avoid the common law's emphasis on objective proof of the victim's lack of consent. In particular, the Code does *not* require proof of resistance by the victim, although the Commentary recognizes that evidence of resistance may sometimes be required to convince the jury that the sexual act was compelled.[151]

Third, the definition of rape is broader than the common law in certain respects: The offense is committed if the female submits as the result of violence directed at

---

[146] In an exception to general Code principles, it is no defense that the male did not know the girl was under the age of 10, nor is it a defense that he reasonably believed that she was over the age of 10. Model Penal Code § 213.6(1).

[147] Model Penal Code § 213.1(1).

[148] Model Penal Code § 213.6(2).

[149] Model Penal Code § 213.0(2).

[150] American Law Institute, Comment to § 213.1, at 303.

[151] *Id.* at 305.

a third party; and it is rape if the victim submits as a result of a threat to kidnap her or another. On the other hand, as with the common law, sexual intercourse obtained by fraud-in-the-*factum* does not constitute the offense of rape, but it does make constitute the offense of gross sexual imposition, as discussed below.

[C] Gross Sexual Imposition

Subject to the exemptions discussed above relating to spouses and persons living together "as husband and wife," a male is guilty of gross sexual imposition, a felony of the third degree, if he has sexual intercourse with a female in any one of three circumstances. First, he is guilty if the female submits as the result of a "threat that would prevent resistance by a woman of ordinary resolution."[152] Thus, a man who obtains intercourse by threatening a woman with loss of employment would be guilty of gross sexual imposition, assuming the factfinder determines that such a threat meets the objective standard defined in the law.

The objective standard — "a woman of ordinary resolution" — is "not a staple of the law,"[153] but the drafters believed it was sufficiently clear to permit the jury to distinguish between serious threats (*e.g.*, loss of a job) and trivial ones (*e.g.*, a threat by a police officer to give the victim a parking ticket). It should also be noted that *offers* do not fall within the scope of the offense; for example, a man is not guilty of gross sexual imposition if he offers a poverty-stricken woman a high-paying job if she submits to intercourse.

Second, gross sexual imposition is committed if a male has sexual relations with a female with knowledge that, as the result of mental illness or defect, she is unable to appraise the nature of her conduct.[154]

Finally, a male is guilty of this offense if "he knows that [the woman] is unaware that a sexual act is being committed upon her or that she submits because she mistakenly supposes that he is her husband."[155] Essentially, this incorporates the common law approach to fraudulent rape.[156]

[D] Proving a Sexual Offense

The Model Penal Code adheres to the highly questionable corroboration requirement.[157] It also requires that juries be instructed to treat a complainant's testimony "with special care in view of the emotional involvement of the witness and the difficulty of determining the truth with respect to alleged sexual activities carried out in private."[158]

---

[152] Model Penal Code § 213.1(2)(a).

[153] American Law Institute, Comment to § 213.1, at 313.

[154] Model Penal Code § 213.1(2)(b).

[155] Model Penal Code § 213.1(2)(c).

[156] *See* § 33.04[C], *supra.*

[157] Model Penal Code § 213.6(5). The corroboration requirement is discussed at § 33.07[A], *supra.*

[158] Model Penal Code § 213.6(5).

The Code also includes a dubious prompt-complaint rule. A prosecution is barred if an adult complainant fails to bring the offense to the attention of a law enforcement agency within three months of its occurrence.[159]

The Code is silent regarding the admissibility of evidence of the complainant's sexual history or reputation for chastity.[160]

[E] MPC Sexual Offense Laws in Transition?

The sexual offense provisions of the Model Penal Code were considered progressive at the time of their adoption in 1962. Attitudes regarding sex have changed so dramatically in the intervening half-century that the Code, which is intended as a forward-looking document, is now backward-looking in this area. Therefore, in 2012, the American Law Institute (ALI) launched a review of the provisions in Article 213 (Sexual Offenses), with the intention that they be modernized and, again, forward-looking.

At the date this Text is being sent to the publisher (June 2015), the ALI review of Article 213 is still underway. On April 28, 2015, the members of the ALI responsible for redrafting the sexual offense provisions submitted "Discussion Draft #2" to its members, which in turn was discussed at the ALI's annual meeting on May 19, 2015. That discussion demonstrated that the April 28 draft will undergo significant additional changes before the members of the ALI will vote on a new version of Article 213. That said, here is a brief review of some of the provisions that were under consideration at the 2015 meeting. They provide a sense of the probable direction the drafters are moving.

First, the proposed version (PV) would criminalize far more sexual acts than does the 1962 version. The PV includes the offenses of: Aggravated Forcible Rape; Forcible Rape; Sexual Penetration Against the Will; Sexual Penetration Without Consent; Rape of a Vulnerable Person; Sexual Penetration of a Vulnerable Person; Sexual Penetration by Coercion; Sexual Penetration by Exploitation; Rape of a Child; Incest; Sexual Penetration of a Minor; Sexual Exploitation of a Minor; Aggravated Criminal Sexual Contact; Forcible Criminal Sexual Contact; Criminal Sexual Contact Without Consent; Aggravated Felonious Sexual Contact with a Child; Incestuous Sexual Contact with a Child; Felonious Sexual Contact with a Child; Sexual Contact with a Child; and Commercial Sex Acts.[161]

Second, all of the offenses are gender-neutral.

---

[159] Model Penal Code § 213.6(4).

[160] Rape-shield laws, which generally prohibit the introduction of such evidence, are considered in § 33.07[B], *supra.*

[161] In some sense, some of these offenses can be seen as different degrees of the same crime. For example, Forcible Rape, as defined, is a felony of the second degree, whereas Aggravated Forcible Rape, which consists of the same elements and certain aggravating factors (*e.g.*, use of a deadly weapon), is a felony of the first degree.

Notice, as well, that some offenses as denominated as "rape" (higher level felonies) and others as "sexual penetration" (lower-level felonies or misdemeanors).

Third, the offenses do not use the term "intercourse" — historically understood to mean penile penetration of the vagina. Rather, the key element of each such offense would be "sexual penetration," a term defined as "any act involving penetration, however slight, of the anus or vulva by any object or body part, unless done for bona fide medical, hygienic, or law-enforcement purposes" or "direct contact between the mouth or tongue of one person and the anus, penis, or vulva of another person."[162]

Fourth, the Code would also prohibit "sexual contact" short of penetration. This term is defined in the Discussion Draft as "any touching of any body part of another person, whether clothed or unclothed, by any body part, body fluid, or object," as well as "any undressing that reveals the breast, genitals, or buttocks of another person," when "the touching or undressing is for the purpose of sexual gratification, sexual humiliation, sexual degradation, or sexual arousal."[163]

Fifth, the Discussion Draft defines "consent" as a "person's positive agreement, communicated by either words or actions, to engage in a specific act of sexual penetration or sexual contact."[164]

---

[162] Proposed MPC § 213.0(6) (Discussion Draft No. 2, April 28, 2015).

[163] Proposed MPC § 213.0(5) (Discussion Draft No. 2, April 28, 2015).

[164] Proposed MPC § 213.0(3) (Discussion Draft No. 2, April 28, 2015).

TABLE OF CASES

[References are to pages]

[References are to pages]

C

[References are to pages]

[References are to pages]

[References are to pages]

H

I

[References are to pages]

[References are to pages]

[References are to pages]

[References are to pages]

[References are to pages]

[References are to pages]

T

[References are to pages]

[References are to pages]

TABLE OF STATUTES

[References are to pages]

[References are to pages]

[References are to pages]

INDEX

[References are to sections.]

[References are to sections.]

[References are to sections.]

[References are to sections.]

[References are to sections.]

[References are to sections.]

[References are to sections.]

[References are to sections.]